STATISTICAL METHODS *for*

DIGITAL COMPUTERS

VOLUME III

Edited by

KURT ENSLEIN
Genesee Computer Center
Rochester, New York

ANTHONY RALSTON, Ph.D.
Professor of Mathematics and Director of Computer Center
State University of New York at Buffalo

HERBERT S. WILF, Ph.D.
Professor of Mathematics
The University of Pennsylvania

A Wiley-Interscience Publication
New York · London · Sydney · Toronto   John Wiley & Sons, Inc.

STATISTICAL METHODS

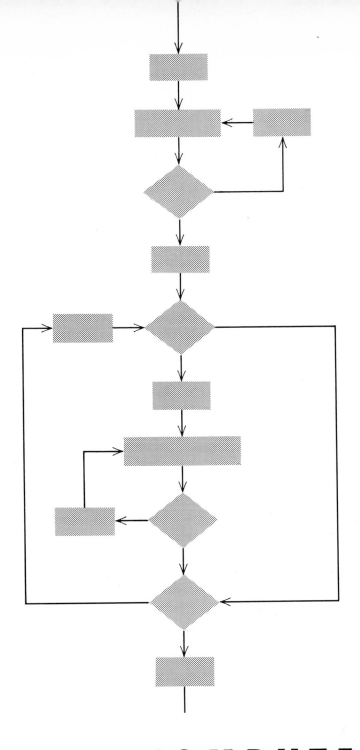

for

DIGITAL COMPUTERS

VOLUME III

of MATHEMATICAL METHODS FOR DIGITAL COMPUTERS

To the Memory of

HARRY HARMAN and LOUIS POTSDAMER

Library of Congress Cataloging in Publication Data (Revised)

Ralston, Anthony, ed.
  Mathematical methods for digital computers.

  Vol. 3 also has special title: Statistical
methods for digital computers.
  Vol. 3: Edited by K. Enslein, A. Ralston, and
H. S. Wilf.
  Includes bibliographies.
  1. Mathematics—Data processing. I. Wilf,
Herbert S., 1931–   joint ed. II. Enslein, Kurt,
joint ed. III. Title. IV. Title: Statistical
methods for digital computers.

QA39.R26   519.5'3   60-6509
ISBN 0-471-70690-6 (v. 3)

Printed in the United States of America

10 9 8 7 6 5 4 3 2 1

PREFACE

Statistical computations account for a major portion of the jobs at any scientifically oriented computing facility. Volume I of this series did have four articles on statistical computation, but these are obsolete or very unsophisticated by current standards, and Volume II contained no articles in this area. The original editors (AR and HSW) felt, therefore, that it was surely time to devote a complete book to this most important area. The third editor (KE), who is an expert in the area of statistical computation with broad practical experience in this area, was invited to join in the production of this volume.

Our philosophy has been to include articles on as many of the most important and widely used techniques of statistical computation as possible in a book of approximately the same size as the previous two. We have tried to retain the main strengths of the previous volumes, in particular, by including essentially the same topics in each article and by keeping the format of each article as consistent as possible.

As in Volume II, we have included actual programs when the length of relevant programs is not excessively long. All such programs are in Fortran, still the language of statistical computation in an overwhelming majority of cases. Chapter 1 contains a guide to programs for all topics covered in the book.

To obtain full value from each chapter the reader should have at least some experience with elementary statistics, as well as a fair level of mathematical maturity. Others, however, will still benefit from using this book as a compendium of calculation procedures, flow charts, programs, and references.

Our contributors are outstanding research workers who have made important discoveries in the fields they discuss, and they have fully availed themselves of their opportunities for depth of discussion. We express our appreciation to them here, as well as the hope that the interested reader will benefit from their expertise, as we did.

KURT ENSLEIN
ANTHONY RALSTON
HERBERT S. WILF

Rochester, New York
Buffalo, New York
Philadelphia, Pennsylvania
April 1976

v

CONTENTS

PART I   **INTRODUCTION**   **1**

1. A Guided Tour Through the Statistical Computing
   Garden
   K. Enslein   3

2. Solution of Statistical Distribution Problems
   by Monte Carlo Methods
   H. O. Hartley   16

PART II   **REGRESSION AND DISCRIMINANT ANALYSIS**   **35**

Editorial Preface to Part II   37

3. Selection of the Best Subset of Regression
   Variables
   R. R. Hocking   39

4. Stepwise Regression
   R. I. Jennrich   58

5. Stepwise Discriminant Analysis
   R. I. Jennrich   76

6. A Method of Coalitions in Statistical Discriminant
   Analysis
   H. S. Wilf   96

PART III   **PRINCIPAL COMPONENTS AND FACTOR ANALYSIS**   **121**

Editorial Preface to Part III   123

7. Factor Analysis by Least-Squares and Maximum-Likelihood Methods
   K. G. Jöreskog   125

8. Minres Method of Factor Analysis
   H. J. Harman   154

9. Principles and Procedures for Unique Rotation in Factor Analysis
   R. B. Cattell & Dev Khanna   166

10. Multivariate Analysis of Variance and Covariance
    J. Finn   203

PART IV   CLUSTER ANALYSIS AND PATTERN RECOGNITION   **265**

Editorial Introduction to Part IV   267

11. Hierarchical Classificatory Methods
    W. T. Williams & G. N. Lance   269

12. Multidimensional Scaling and Other Methods for Discovering Structure
    J. B. Kruskal   296

13. The ISODATA Method
    Computation for the Relative Perception of Similariteis and Differences in Complex and Real Data
    D. J. Hall & Dev Khanna   340

PART V   TIME SERIES   **375**

14. The Fast Fourier Transform and Its Application To Time Series Analysis
    J. W. Cooley, P. A. W. Lewis & P. D. Welch   377

15. Time Series Forecasting
    D. W. Bacon & L. H. Broekhoven   424

Appendix   440

Author Index   445

Subject Index   449

PART **I**

Introduction

1. PURPOSE

In Volume 1 of *Mathematical Methods for Digital Computers* there were four chapters on statistical computation—Multiple Regression Analysis, Factor Analysis, Autocorrelation, and Spectral Analysis and Analysis of Variance. In 1960, when Volume 1 was published, that was a fairly representative coverage of the field of statistical computation. The last 15 years, however, have witnessed major growth in this area, and many new and valuable techniques of statistical computation are now in standard use. The 15 chapters of this volume are a sampling of the most important and most useful of these, but only a sampling, since no one volume could hope to be comprehensive because of the great scope of statistical computation today. Some areas of importance not covered by this volume are, however, mentioned briefly in Chapter 1.

2. FORMAT OF THE CHAPTERS

As in the previous two volumes of this series, the editors have tried to make the format as consistent as possible in as many chapters as possible. In this volume Chapter 1 does not follow the standard format because of its survey character and neither does Chapter 2 because its content does not lend itself well to the standard format. Chapters 3 through 15, however, all contain, with minor exceptions, the following materials:

Function

What is the function of the method that is about to be described? The contributor has endeavored to give a concise and accurate formulation of the particular problem which is considered in his chapter, sometimes in the context of prior art.

Mathematical Discussion

Insofar as the scope of the chapter extends, the contributor has tried to give a complete mathematical description of the problem which is to be solved and the method or methods by which he proposes to solve it. Here one may find relevant mathematical theorems with proofs or references to proofs, an error analysis if applicable and available including a discussion of the circumstances under which the technique may be expected to perform well or poorly, comparisons with other available techniques, and citations of the relevant literature.

Summary of the Calculation Procedure

All too often when a statistical discussion is interlaced with the derivation of a method the reader may finish quite unaware of what precise sequence of steps are required to carry out the solution of the problem. In this section, therefore, the reader will find the method previously derived stated in "recipe" form; that is, first do this, then this, and so on.

Flowchart

The flowcharts are as detailed as the generality of the material covered and the limitations of space allow.

The boxes in the flowcharts have been restricted to what is considered a bare minimum of different types. Flowcharts begin with a box labeled START and end with a box labeled STOP. The other types of boxes used are:

1. The assertion box. This box asserts that the operations contained within it are executed at this time.

$$\boxed{a + b \rightarrow c}$$

2. The test box.

$$N > 9 \longleftarrow \langle N : 9 \rangle \longrightarrow N < 9$$
$$N = 9$$

This box has one input line and three possible output lines. When three output terminals are used one is chosen for greater than, less than, or equality output. When only two output terminals are used these indicate whether the answer to the question con-

tained in the box is affirmative or negative.

3. The remote connector

This circle indicates that logical control is transferred to the point where another such circle appears with the same number in it.

Description of the Flowchart

A box-by-box description of the flowchart is given to aid the reader in following it.

Program and Subroutines

Due to space limitations, only crucial Fortran IV subroutines are provided. In any case, standard subroutines that would be required by a program are listed. Chapter 1 also provides the name of organizations from which the programs can be obtained.

Sample Problem

A representative sample problem is worked through to give the reader a feeling for the behavior of the process in practice.

References

The references cited in the text are listed. References are indicated in the text by numbers enclosed in square brackets.

A Guided Tour Through the Statistical Computing Garden

I

Kurt Enslein
Genesee Computer Center

1. INTRODUCTION

Whereas the previous two volumes in this series have dealt mainly with *mathematical* methods for digital computers, and only occasionally with *statistical* methods for digital computers, this volume deals almost exclusively with the latter. The great variety of statistical computing means that any work such as this cannot be totally comprehensive. The editors were, therefore, faced with difficult choices as to which methods to include and which to exclude. Those methods included are the ones we felt were of outstanding significance both because of their importance as statistical techniques and because of their widespread use on computers.

In this chapter we review the present state of the art of statistical computing, and more particularly *multivariate* statistical computing with particular relevance to the chapters in this volume. For an excellent review of recent trends of development in multivariate analysis we refer the reader to the comprehensive article by C. R. Rao [1].

The present author considered providing descriptive text elaborating on each of the techniques covered in this volume as well as descriptions of some that are not covered. However, after much deliberation he decided that presenting this chapter from a problem-solving viewpoint and, as much as possible, in an organized tabular form would be of more use to the reader. Consequently, this chapter is short on words and relatively long on tables.

2. TECHNIQUES RELATED TO PROBLEM SOLVING

In the determination as to which statistical analytical methods are to be used for the solution of a given problem it is not so much the statistical problem which determines the technique but rather how the *use* of a given technique is viewed by the problem solver. In other words, it all depends on what the problem solver is trying to accomplish. In Table 1 we show an oversimplified structure of the uses of multivariate analytic methods. Since this table is

3

Table 1. LIMITATIONS AND CHARACTERISTICS OF STATISTICAL COMPUTER TECHNIQUES

Chapter Characteristic	3 Subset Selection	4 Stepwise Regression	5 Stepwise Discriminant Analysis	6 Coalitions	7 Factor Analysis Joreskog	8 Factor Analysis Minres
Central memory size						
Low (20K wds)	V	20V	V × G = 80	V × G = 50	V × F = 80	V × F = 100
Medium (60K wds)		100V	V × G = 200	V × G = 100	V × F = 200	V × F = 300
Large (≥ 100K wds)		400V	V × G = 600	V × G = 400	V × F = 600	V × F = 800
Word size, bits						
32	P	P	P	P?	P	P
36	P?	P	P	P?	P	P
48–60				P?	P–	
Computational speed, arithmetic						
Floating add < 1 μsec	70V					
≥ 1 μsec	30V	50V	V × G = 200	V × G = 150	V × F = 300	V × F = 400
Logical						V × F = 100
Output graphics	No	Yes	Yes	Yes	No	No
"Cost" Proportional to	V		V × G × N	V × G × N	V × F	V × F
Solution Uniqueness	No	No	No	No	No	Yes
Optimality	Yes	No	No	Yes	Yes	Yes
Auxiliary storage		Needed	Needed	Needed		

Chapter	9	10	11	12	13	14	15
Characteristic	Unique Rotation	Mancova	Hierarchical Classification	Multidimensional Scaling	ISODATA Clustering	FFT	Forecasting
Central memory size							
Low (20K wds)	V	N × V × F = 200	40N	N × F = 40	N × V = 2,000	100I	100I
Medium (60K wds)		N × V × F = 600	100N	N × F = 100	N × V = 50,000	500I	500I
Large (≥ 100K wds)		N × V × F = 1,000	400N	N × F = 400	N × V = 200,000	2000I	2000I
Word size, bits							
32	P	P		P	P	P	P
36	P	P?		P?		P?	P?
48–60	P?						
Computational speed, arithmetic							
Floating add < 1 μsec	50V	N × V × F = 200		N × F = 100			
≥ 1 μsec							
Logical			N		N		
Output graphics	Yes	No	Yes?	Yes?	No	Yes	Yes
"Cost"	V × F	N × V × F	N	N × F	N	I	I
Proportional to							
Solution Uniqueness	No	?	No	No	No	No	No
Optimality	Yes?	Yes	No	Yes?	Yes?	Yes?	Yes?
Auxiliary storage		Needed	Helpful		Helpful		

F = Factors
G = Groups
I = Intervals
N = Cases
NU = Nonuniqueness of solution
O = Optimality of solution
P = Precision
V = Variables
? = Indicates uncertain importance

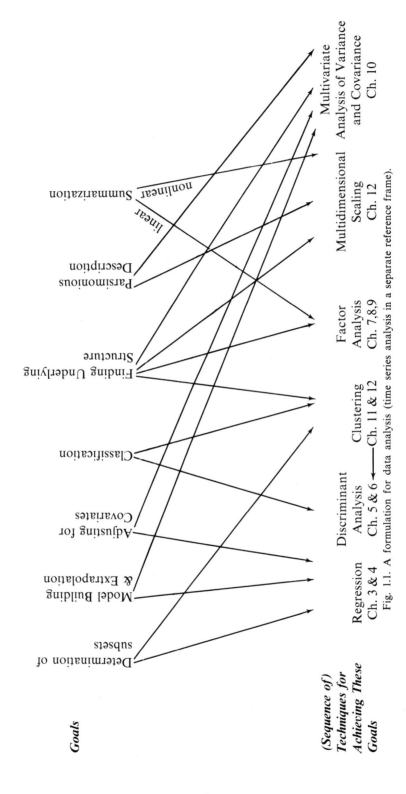

Goals

Determination of subsets

Model Building & Extrapolation

Adjusting for Covariates

Classification

Finding Underlying Structure

Parsimonious Description

linear Summarization nonlinear

(Sequence of)
Techniques for
Achieving These
Goals

Regression
Ch. 3 & 4

Discriminant
Analysis
Ch. 5 & 6

Clustering
Ch. 11 & 12

Factor
Analysis
Ch. 7,8,9

Multidimensional
Scaling
Ch. 12

Multivariate
Analysis of Variance
and Covariance
Ch. 10

Fig. 1.1. A formulation for data analysis (time series analysis in a separate reference frame).

6

not a sufficient description of the relationship between methods and goals we have given in Fig. 1.1 a somewhat different viewpoint in which we describe the use of a *sequence* of techniques as contrasted to a single technique for a single task.

A definition of terms used in Fig. 1.1 may be of some aid to the reader:

1. *Model building and extrapolation*: The derivation of an equation or set of equations that explains the variance (variability) in a criterion variable. For example, one observes age at death of a population and wishes to explain the variation in terms of observed parameters such as life habits, attitudes, and genetic background [2].

2. *Adjusting for covariates*: This situation is much more common than is usually appreciated. The aim is to normalize the variables, preferably the dependent variables, in such a way that the effect of disturbing factors that were thought to be controlled but were in fact not controlled, are removed. For example, in the study of a psychotropic drug on which observations were made by a variety of physicians, ranging in specialties from surgeons to psychiatrists, one would find that, if each of these physicians were asked to rate the degree of anxiety of the patient, surgeons would tend to rate the anxiety lower than psychiatrists, with general practitioners and internists falling somewhere in between. In this case, the purpose of covariance adjustment is then to adjust the anxiety judgements of each of the observers in such a way that they become comparable across observers. For this purpose the physician's characteristics, such as his specialty and the size of his practice, are taken into account [3].

3. *Classification* is the assignment of objects to groups. We discuss the topic more thoroughly in the Editorial Preface to the Clustering and Pattern Recognition chapters. However, let it be said now that we call classification using previously established references *learning with a teacher* and using previously unestablished references *learning without a teacher*.

Clustering can be thought of as "learning without a teacher." *Discriminant analysis* in which the groups are preestablished and one wishes to find the separating hypersurfaces between the groups, is "classification with a teacher."

4. *Finding underlying structure*: Given an ensemble of variables or observations, the question is whether the dimensionality of the data is really as large as the number of variables or objects. Is there a subset and, more particularly, a weighted subset of the variables or objects which is able to explain the entire complex within a preset degree of error? The classical approach to this problem has been factor analysis. Multidimensional scaling has come into use in recent years as a nonlinear factor analytic approach. Structure might also imply components of variance and for this reason, of course, multivariate analysis of variance and covariance are often used.

The classical underlying structure problem is found in the use of factor analysis of personality traits, and we would refer the reader to the many works in this area particularly Harman [4] and Chapter 8, and Cattell (Chapter 9) in this volume.

5. *Parsimonious description*: This bears some relation to the finding of underlying structure except that the requirement is to minimize the number of variables used to explain the entire data complex. For example, while all sorts of symptoms may be observed in a biological process, in fact most of the symptoms can be explained by relating them to a very few underlying traits. Here again there is a clear relationship to simple structure.

6. *Summarization*: By summarization we mean something akin to parsimonious description, but extended over multiple populations, for example, the description of personality characteristics in terms of a factor structure or some other multidimensional representation, be it linear or nonlinear.

The last three categories are not very easily separable, yet, in terms of problem solving, they represent clear entities. For this reason, we have chosen to maintain their identity in this chapter.

3. REGRESSION AND DISCRIMINANT ANALYSIS

a. State of the Theoretical and Algorithmic Art

Since the work of Fisher [5] only modest theoretical development has in fact taken place. For regression, most workers have addressed themselves to the problem of selecting the "best" subset of variables. This trend was engendered by the flourishing of numerous, often nonorthogonal variables in many studies. The need, therefore, arose to select those subsets of variables that would best "explain" the variance of the dependent variables in multiple regression, and "best" separate the preidentified groups in multiple discriminant analysis. The methods are generally separable into step-up (or aggregation) and step-down (or backward elimination) procedures. By step-up procedures we mean those in which variables are added to the regression equation one at a time under some criterion, such as: Add that variable which explains the maximum amount of residual variance in the dependent variable, or that which increases the multiple correlation coefficient maximally, and so on. Step-down procedures start with all the variables in the equation and those variables are removed which, for example, will reduce the multiple correlation coefficient the least, either one at a time or several at a time.

There exists presently a lively controversy as to which stepwise methods produce the most robust results. While the most commonly used algorithms aggregate variables [6] (see Chapters 4 and 5) several workers, notably Mantel [7], argue with a great deal of conviction that step-down procedures produce more robust equations. A con-

tender on the scene which might settle the argument is ridge or damped regression [8]. This technique has been used for many years by engineers in nonlinear optimization problems. By the addition of a small damping factor to the diagonal of the correlation or covariance matrix, it is possible to orthogonalize interrelated variables, and by an extension of the technique to treat the over-determined problem that is, the case in which there are more variables than observations. Ridge regression can then be used as a step-down method and in fact lends further support to Mantel's arguments in favor of step-down procedures.

In discriminant analysis, particularly stepwise discriminant analysis, the original theoretical formulation assumed equal covariance matrices for the separate groups. Recently, Wilf developed the necessary theory and algorithm to permit the treatment of groups with unequal covariance matrices. This method is represented in this book in Chapter 6. This is a distinct advance in the state of the art and in some respects can be equated with the *piecewise linear* discriminant analysis techniques embodied by, for example, ISODATA (Chapter 13), as well as with those which combine the use of linear and piecewise linear techniques in a discrimination problem.

b. Computational Art

ROBUSTNESS

The problem of robustness has also been attacked through the methods for which Tukey coined the term "jackknifing." In multiple regression or discriminant analysis this involves computing estimates of coefficients by removing subsets of the objects or variables with replacement and later calculating an overall estimate of the averaged coefficients. Among the main references in this area, the work of Arvesen and Salsburg [11], Gray and Schucany [12], and the highly readable paper by Mosteller [13] are typical.

MULTIPLE REGRESSION

The most widely used program is that included in the BMD series from the University of California at Los Angeles [14]. For many years a version called BMD02R was used. In the more recent past, the version BMDP02R was introduced. This includes additional variable selection algorithms as well as more comprehensive plots of residuals. BMDP02R is most emphatically a step-up procedure. It is in many ways a further implementation of the Efroymson algorithm [6]. A major expanded implementation of the step-up procedure is also available under the name of STEPREG. This method is described in this book in Chapter 4 by Jennrich.

Step-down procedures are not commonly available. Most have been implemented as special in-house programs and have not been generally released.

RIDGE REGRESSION

A number of private implementations exist. The only known publicly available procedure is RIDGE [15]. This incorporates automatic deletion of "poor" variables, and, in this form, is a step-down procedure.

STEPWISE DISCRIMINANT ANALYSIS

The history of this procedure is quite similar to that of stepwise regression. The most commonly available program is in the BMD series of UCLA, BMD07M. This is a step-up procedure. It is described in this book in Chapter 5.

OTHER SUBSET SELECTION PROCEDURES

LaMotte and Hocking have developed a procedure called SELECT. Through a relatively simple branch and bound algorithm, this procedure computes the multiple correlation coefficient for the best subsets of $2, 3, 4, \ldots, n$ variables and is an approximation to the obvious procedure of examining all possible combinations of variables and picking that combination which has the highest multiple correlation coefficient and which "makes most sense." This procedure is described in Chapter 3.

4. PRINCIPAL COMPONENTS AND FACTOR ANALYSIS

a. State of the Theoretical and Algorithmic Art

Historically, the methods of *principal components* and *factor analysis* were mostly developed to fill the needs of psychometricians, long before the advent of high-speed digital computers. Although methods of finding principal components were early formalized by Hotelling [16], there has been a substantial difference of opinion as to methods of rotation of the principal component vectors. The problem has been that of deciding on the definition of optimum rotation. From the earliest methods which rotated the principal component vectors to the so-called Varimax position, that position which reduced the sum of squares of the residuals of the covariance matrix to a minimum while maintaining orthogonality of the factors, the art has progressed to so-called oblique solutions in which the factors are not necessarily orthogonal, but some other criterion, such as minimum number of variables on which there are significant loadings, is optimized. One of the foremost expounders of the pros and cons of different criteria for rotation has been Cattell, whose work is represented in this book in Chapter 9.

Generalized analysis of variance and covariance were formulated by Bock [9] and implemented by various authors. This problem is now at the stage where one of the few remaining aspects to be solved is that of dealing with missing observations. While a number of solutions, all makeshift in one way or another (see for example Enslein [17]), are presently in use, no truly satisfactory and theoretically sound solution to this problem currently exists. One might speculate that no such solution is in fact possible.

b. State of the Computational Art

Since the appearance of high-speed large memory digital computers, factor analysis and multivariate analysis of variance and covariance have come into profuse usage. For factor analysis the formulations are still changing and the work of Joreskog represented in this volume in Chapter 7 is a good example of how a careful rethinking of the underlying mathematics and the resulting algorithms results in a much cleaner and more efficient procedure.

Multivariate analysis of variance and covariance has been reformulated and programmed by a number of authors. Notable among these are Dean Clyde [10] and Jeremy Finn (Chapter 10). Finn's latest formulation permits empty cells and a symbolic representation of contrast vectors. These desirable characteristics are achieved with substantially less ease in other implementations. It should also be appreciated that multivariate analysis of variance and covariance are strongly related to the methods of regression and discriminant analysis of Section 2. In fact, one could consider regression and discriminant analysis to be special cases of the analysis of variance. However, in this volume we have chosen to treat the two topics as though they were not so strongly linked because the flexibility one wishes to have in regression and discriminant analysis programs is difficult to achieve in the generalized analysis of variance framework. This flexibility has not as yet been implemented and remains as a task for someone who wishes to tackle that very difficult computational task.

5. CLUSTER ANALYSIS AND PATTERN RECOGNITION

a. State of the Theoretical and Algorithmic Art

The best-known formal start for clustering and particularly hierarchical clustering is the volume on *Numerical Taxonomy* published by Sokal and Sneath in 1957 [18]. The techniques used in those early days were limited to what one might term common-sense methods. The methods used in this more modern period still tend to be classi-

fied as numerical taxonomy. The methods were nearest neighbor, furthest neighbor, and similar algorithms from which dendograms (family trees) were developed. In this field there appeared early the question as to how different features contributing to "similarity" between objects were to be weighted. Should they be weighted equally, in proportion to their variance, to their contribution to the grand mean, etc.? At the present the consensus appears to be that unless there is a priori information available that would favor weighting one variable over another, equal, that is, unit, weights should be used.

A distinction needs to be made as to the distance functions used in different clustering and pattern recognition methods. Generally speaking, hierarchical methods represented in this volume by the work of Lance and Williams (Chapter 11) use similarity coefficients, whereas methods based on finding subsets of observations which are most nearly hyperspherical of necessity use Euclidean distance or sometimes Mahalabonis distances. One could of course consider the latter two measures to be really a subset of a more general class of similarity measures. In fact Euclidean distance measures are used in many hierarchical procedures though the identity of variables is lost once pairwise distances have been calculated. This is not the case for methods such as ISODATA represented in this volume in Chapter 13. In ISODATA the identity of the variables is preserved.

As mentioned in an earlier section of this discussion, we also need to separate methods for the clustering and pattern recognition problems into those that allow learning without a teacher and those that require a teacher. All the clustering methods described in this volume are of the learning-without-a-teacher type. In other words they attempt to find underlying structure without the specification of a model or typical observation. In this regard they can be related to a more general system of pattern recognition termed the Perceptron [19, 20, 21]. This method has also been implemented by the author [22] and can be viewed, as can ISO-DATA, as a method for piecewise linear classification.

A common way of using both the hierarchical classification as well as the ISO-DATA methods is to let them define the groups of observations and then, by parametric methods such as discriminant analysis (Chapters 5 and 6), find the best discriminant functions that separate the newly found groups. In the classification process one usually finds multivariate outliers, that is, observations that simply do not fit the ensemble of the remaining observations. These often show up as clusters with very few members.

We mentioned earlier that the problem of differential scaling of features or variables has not been solved. Techniques such as ISODATA, however, do *implicitly* assign different weights to different variables. In the case of ISODATA more weight is given to those variables with the largest normalized standard deviations. Clearly, this cannot be the case for the hierarchical clustering methods since the variable identity is lost in these.

Multidimensional scaling, represented in this volume in Chapter 12, while generally viewed as a pattern recognition approach, in fact is more nearly a method of finding structure related to variables. Now it should be mentioned that any of these clustering methods can be used interchangeably to find either patterns of observations or variables, simply by rotating the data matrix by 90°, and the same thing of course obtains for multidimensional scaling. The reader might justifiably wonder why we did not include this method in the section on principal components and factor analysis. We believe we are more nearly following common practice by including it in the section on Cluster Analysis and Pattern Recognition (Part IV) even though multidimensional scaling and related methods are more nearly nonlinear methods for discovering structure

or, as previously mentioned, methods akin to nonlinear factor analysis.

b. State of the Computational Art

Many implementations of hierarchical clustering methods exist. Most data analysts at one time or another will have written at the very least a nearest neighbor routine. For this volume we have chosen Lance and Williams' generalized formulation of hierarchical classification since by means of their "flexible" algorithm it is possible to organize the process to produce either looser or tighter clusters, more or less separated in space. The ISODATA program was chosen partly because it was one of the earliest of the formulations that attempted to break up a population into subgroups that would be most nearly multivariate normal. The version published in this book has been greatly modified from earlier interactive versions. A parallel effort has for some time been carried out by Wolfe [23], although in that instance the problem has been more specifically addressed to finding multivariate normal subsets in mixed populations. Another similar endeavor has been that labeled AID [24] and originates from the University of Michigan. This method is to some degree different in that it is really based on regression as contrasted to true learning without a teacher. The implementation of multidimensional scaling described in this volume is by one of the originators of the technique and again represents only part of a larger class more effectively covered in the references. Rather than describing the varieties at length in this section, we refer the reader to Chapter 12 for a more detailed and comprehensive explanation of the different methods.

6. TIME SERIES

In this section we shall combine the discussion of the theoretical and algorithmic art with that of the computational art since the two are so closely interwoven.

Time-series analysis in terms of serial auto- and cross-correlation has, of course, been practiced for many years particularly with applications to econometrics, but surprisingly few applications to biology [25]. More complex analyses, usually involving transformation to the frequency and/or phase plane, for example Fourier transforms, until relatively recently were very expensive to carry out on digital computers and instead were performed on analog devices using banks of filters and the like. The reinvention of the Fast Fourier Transform (FFT), which in this book is covered in Chapter 14, has totally changed the picture in this regard. The advent of the FFT has meant a reduction in computational requirements of some two orders of magnitude. In fact, the reduction has been so great that it has become possible to construct economical special-purpose computers for the implementation of the various transforms. We thus see the paradoxical situation wherein both special-purpose and general purpose computers can carry out the transformations efficiently and where the choice is dictated more by convenience than by some other considerations. In fact, hybrid computers would seem to be an even better solution to the problem with the advent of the FFT. This too is a return to prior art in that the integration functions of the Fourier transform, for example, were usually carried out on analog equipment, this analog equipment being coupled to digital equipment both at the input and output (hybrid computers).

The question of time-series forecasting, that is, predicting the behavior of variables in the future from their behavior in the past was restricted for many years to univariate series. The advent of hybrid computers and the FFT again has permitted the extension of these principles to multivariate time series [26]. It is interesting to note that in different fields multivariate time series analysis and forecasting are called by different names. For example, in electrical engineering they

have long been called transient analysis. In the environmental field the techniques are called intervention analysis, that is, intervention being the promulgation of a new law, the shutting down of a polluting source, and so on. In biology the terms "seasonal," "diurnal," or "circadian" are often used. Other examples could be found, but the lesson to be learned is that all these techniques really deal with the same underlying phenomenon, namely, the fluctuation of parameters with time whether the time be measured on a micro or macro scale.

We leave a more detailed discussion of the pros and cons of time series forecasting to Chapter 15 by Bacon and Broekhoven since a discussion at this point would be mostly redundant.

Thus the impact of high-speed digital computers on the facility of carrying out time-series analysis of various sorts has been enormous. Its character parallels the development of the use of regression and discriminant analysis techniques, though lagging by perhaps a decade. The true potential of time-series analysis remains yet to be realized, but the pace of change in recent years has been so great that we expect progress in the next few years to be substantial.

7. LIMITATIONS AND CHARACTERISTICS OF TECHNIQUES

In Table 1 we have attempted to portray the limitations and salient characteristics of the statistical computer techniques described in this volume. Like all attempts at categorization this one also leaves much to be desired. The entries in the table are intended as a guide not as dogma.

A note about the item labeled "cost": By this parameter, we attempt to portray both what affects costs and what limits the technique in terms of costliness, with the emphasis on the latter. In the single case for which this item has not been filled in, that is, for stepwise regression, our opinion is that while "cost" *is* affected by the number of

Table 2. PROGRAM AVAILABILITY TABLE

Chapter No.	3	4	5	6	7	8	9	10	11	12	13	14	15
	Subset Selection	Stepwise Regression	Stepwise Discriminant Analysis	Coalitions	Factor Analysis Joreskog	Factor Analysis Minres	Unique Rotation	Manova	Hierarchical Classification	Multidimensional Scaling	ISODATA Clustering	FFT	Forecasting
Author	X	X	X	X	X	X	X		X	X	X		X
BMD		X	X										
SPSS		X	X										
Omnitab		X	X										
Universities		X	X					X					
Genesee	X	X	X	X	X	X	X	X	X	X	X		X
Bell Telephone Labs										X			
Cybernet		X	X										
Multiple Access		X	X									X	
IBM		X	X									X	
UNIVAC		X	X										
Xerox		X	X										
Educational Test Serv.					X	X							
CSIRO									X				
Notes	1				5			2			3		

Notes:

1. The method covered in this volume is due to LaMotte and Hocking. A method reportedly more efficient has been developed at Yale Forestry Laboratories by Furneval. A copy of his program is available from that source.

2. The MULTIVARIANCE program Version 5 is available from National Educational Resources, Inc., 215 Kenwood Avenue, Ann Arbor, Michigan 48103. The program is no longer available from the author (Jeremy Finn). However a version updated and maintained by Genesee is believed to be the most up-to-date version emphasizing features to enhance economy of computation.

3. The original interactive version of ISODATA available from the author is specific to particular hardware: the Genesee version operates on Control Data Corporation 6600 computers using a remote batch system.

4. Many other sources for time-series forecasting programs exist. The particular formulation used by the authors in this volume is believed to be nearly optimal.

5. The program called EFAP is available from International Educational Services. P.O. Box A3650, Chicago, Ill. 60690. (Note added in proof.)

Table 2a. PROGRAM AVAILABILITY TABLE AND SOURCES

BMD	BMD Program Librarian Health Sciences Computing Facility University of California Los Angeles, California 90024
SPSS	National Opinion Research Center University of Chicago Chicago, Illinois
OMNITAB	National Bureau of Standards Handbook 101 Superintendent of Documents U.S. Government Printing Office Washington, D. C. 20402
GENESEE	Genesee Computer Center, Inc. 20 University Avenue Rochester, New York 14605
Bell	Mrs. Jih Jie Chang Bell Telephone Laboratories Murray Hill, New Jersey 07971
Cybernet	Minneapolis/St. Paul Midwest Cybernet Center 4550 West 77th Street Minneapolis, Minnesota 55435
Multiple Access	Multiple Access Toronto Data Centre 885 Don Mills Road Don Mills 403 Ontario
IBM	IBM Thomas J. Watson Research Center P. O. Box 218 Yorktown Heights, New York 10598
ETS	Educational Testing Service Princeton, New Jersey 08540
P-STAT	Princeton Computer Center Princeton University Princeton, New Jersey 08540
CSIRO	Pastoral Research Laboratory Division of Tropical Pastures Private Bag Townsville, Qld 4810 University Road Australia
XEROX	Xerox Corporation 701 South Aviation Boulevard El Segundo, California 90245

variables and the number of cases, this dependency generally is not a *limitation*.

One can also infer from this table that large word-size machines have few precision problems. Note particularly that for 60-bit words, precision has not been a problem at the present state of the art.

8. PROGRAM AVAILABILITY

In Tables 2 and 2a we show sources that make available the programs covered in this volume. No attempt has been made to cover all the possible sources but only the most common. Inasmuch as all the programs covered in this volume are written in Fortran, we have not attempted to categorize their availability by machine types, or source language.

9. REFERENCES

1. C. R. Rao, "Recent Trends of Research Work in Multivariate Analysis," *Biometrics*, **28**, 3–22 (1972).

2. K. Enslein, "Computer-Based Data Analysis in Longevity Research," *Comput. Biomed. Res.*, **3**, 289–329 (1970).

3. K. Enslein, "Adjustment for Physician Variability and Placebo in Drug Evaluation" (in press).

4. H. H. Harman, *Modern Factor Analysis*, Univ. of Chicago Press, 1960 and 1971.

5. R. A. Fisher, *Statistical Methods for Research Workers*, Hafner Publishing Co., New York, 1958.

6. M. A. Efroymson, "Multiple Regression Analysis," in *Mathematical Methods for Digital Computers*, Vol. I, A. Ralston and H. Wilf (eds.), Wiley, New York, 1964.

7. N. Mantel, "Why Stepdown Procedures vs. Variable Selection," *Technometrics*, **12**, 621–5 (1970). "More on Variable Selection and an Alternative Approach," **13**, 455–7 (1971).

8. A. E. Hoerl and R. W. Kennard, "Ridge Regression: Biased Estimation for Nonorthogonal Problems," *Technometrics*, **12**, 55–67 (1970).

9. R. D. Bock, "Programming Univariate and Multivariate Analysis of Variance," *Technometrics*, **5**, 95–117 (1963).

10. D. J. Clyde, E. M. Crammer, R. J. Sherin, *Multivariate Statistical Programs*, Biometric Lab., University of Miami, Coral Gables, Fla. 33124, 1966.

11. J. Arvesen and D. Salsburg, *Approximate Tests and Confidence Intervals using the Jackknife*, Mimeograph series #267, Purdue University Statistics Dept., 1971.

12. D. Gray and Schucany, *The Generalized Jackknife Statistic*, Marcel Dekker, New York, 1972.

13. F. Mosteller, "The Jackknife," *Rev., Inter. Stat, Institute*, **39**, 363 (1971).

14. W. J. Dixon (Ed.), *BMD Biomedical Computer Programs*, University of California Press, Berkeley, California, 1960 and 1970.

15. Genesee Computer Center, Rochester, New York, 1973.

16. H. Hotelling, "Analysis of a Complex of Statistical Variables into Principal Components," *J. Educat. Psychol.*, **26**, 139–42 (1935).

17. K. Enslein, *A Novel Method for the Resolution of the Missing Observations Problem*, Spring Meeting of ENAR, Chapel Hill, N.C., 1969.

18. R. R. Sokal and P. A. H. Speath, *Principles of Numerical Taxonomy*, W. H. Freeman and Co., San Francisco, Cal., 1963 and 1973.

19. F. Rosenblatt, *Principles of Neurodynamics*, Spartan Books, Washington, D. C., 1962.

20. H. D. Block, B. W. Knight Jr., and F. Rosenblatt, "Analysis of A Four-Layer Series-Coupled Perceptron, II," *Rev. Mod. Phys.*, **34**, 135–43 (1962).

21. M. Minsky and S. Papert, *Perceptrons, An Introduction to Computational Geometry*, MIT-The Science Press, Cambridge, Mass., 1969.

22. K. Enslein, "A General-Purpose Perceptron Simulator," *Comput. Biomed. Res.*, **1**, 187–214 (1967).

23. J. H. Wolfe, "Pattern Clustering by Multivariate Mixture Analysis," *Multivariate Behav. Res.*, **5**, 329–50 (1970).

24. J. A. Sonquist, *Searching for Structures (Alias Aid-III)*, Institute for Social Research, University of Michigan, Ann Arbor, Michigan, 1971.

25. J. S. Bendat, A. G. Piersol, *Measurement and Analysis of Random Data*, Wiley, New York, 1966.

Solution of Statistical Distribution Problems by Monte Carlo Methods

2

H. O. Hartley
Texas A & M University

INTRODUCTION

Monte Carlo methods may be briefly described as follows: Given a mathematical formula that cannot be easily evaluated by analytic reduction and the standard procedures of numerical analysis, it is often possible to find a stochastic process generating statistical variables whose frequency distributions can be shown to be simply related to the mathematical formula. The Monte Carlo method then actually generates a large number of the variables, determines their empirical frequency distributions, and employs them in a numerical evaluation of the formula.

An excellent and comprehensive account of these methods is given in a book edited by Meyer [20] and a research memorandum by Kahn [16], as well as in numerous articles a small fraction of which are cited in the References.

In view of the rapidly growing literature on these techniques, this chapter must be confined mainly to a very special area of their application, namely, the numerical solution of statistical distribution problems; moreover, our definitions of statistical distributions do not aim at any generality in terms of measure theory but are, for purposes of simplicity, confined to distribution density functions which are all integrable in the classical Riemann sense. The concepts are explained in terms of statistics depending on independent univariate samples, but examples of multivariate distributions are used to indicate that there is no inherent problem in multivariate generalizations.

Sections 7–12 are concerned with the considerable increase in efficiency effected by the use of the stratified Monte Carlo method.

1. THE ROLE OF MONTE CARLO METHODS IN SOLVING STATISTICAL DISTRIBUTION PROBLEMS

In the special case when Monte Carlo methods are used for the solution of statistical distribution problems, the "mathematical formula" to be evaluated is the frequency distribution of what is known as "a statistic,"

$$h = h(x_1 x_2 \cdots x_n) \qquad (1)$$

that is a mathematical function (say, a piecewise continuous function) of a random sample of n independent variate values, x_i, drawn from a "parental" distribution with ordinate frequency $f(x)$, and cumulative distribution function (c.d.f.)

$$F(x) = \int_{-\infty}^{x} f(v) \, dv \qquad (2)$$

In this particular case the "mathematical formula" to be evaluated is the n-dimensional integral

$$\Pr\{h \leqslant H\} = \int \cdots$$

$$\cdots \int \left(\prod_{i=1}^{n} f(x_i) \right) \Pi \, dx_i \qquad (3)$$

where the range of the n-dimensional integration in (3) is defined by

$$h(x_1 x_2 \cdots x_n) \leqslant H \qquad (4)$$

An "analytic solution" of the distribution problem (3) would consist in a simplification of the formula (3) to make it "amenable" to numerical evaluation, a concept not clearly defined since it depends on the tabular and mechanical aids available for evaluation. A solution of (3) by Monte Carlo methods would consist of generating a large number of samples, $x_1, x_2, \ldots, x_n$, of computing (1) for each sample and using the proportion of statistics $h \leqslant H$ as an approximation to (3). With statistical distribution problems the "stochastic process" mentioned in the Introduction is therefore trivially available by the definition of the problem. In fact it is the process of generating variables x_i from the parental distribution.

To illustrate the above concepts by a simple example for which an analytic solution for (3) is well known, consider a random sample of independent values from the Gaussian $N(0, 1)$ so that

$$f(x) = (2\pi)^{-1/2} \exp\{-\tfrac{1}{2}x^2\} \qquad (5)$$

and consider the χ^2-statistic

$$h(x_1 \cdots x_n) \equiv \chi^2 = \sum_{i=1}^{n} x_i^2 \qquad (6)$$

then

$$\Pr\{h \leqslant H\} = \Gamma^{-1}(\tfrac{1}{2}n) \int_{0}^{H} \exp\{-\tfrac{1}{2}h\}$$

$$\times \left(\tfrac{1}{2}h\right)^{1/2n-1} d\left(\tfrac{1}{2}h\right) \qquad (7)$$

which will be recognized as the incomplete gamma function extensively tabulated by statisticians under the name of the probability integral of χ^2 (see, e.g., [23]). While in the preceding example an analytic reduction of (3) to a simple form (7) (which can be expanded in a Poisson series for even n) enabled its numerical evaluation, there are numerous instances when no exact analytic reduction is possible but the approximations of numerical analysis such as the Euler–MacLaurin formula of numerical integration can be used effectively. For example, if with a random normal sample (drawn from (5)) we consider as a statistic the sample range

$$h(x_1 \cdots x_n) = R = x_{\max} - x_{\min} \qquad (8)$$

then we have from (3) for the "probability integral of range"

$$\Pr\{h \leqslant H\} = n \int_{-\infty}^{+\infty} f(x)\{F(x + H)$$

$$- F(x)\}^{n-1} dx \qquad (9)$$

With $f(x)$ and $F(x)$ available in tabular form or as computer routines, the integral (9) can be readily evaluated by numerical integration as has been done, for example, for the "normal range" [22, 9]. Indeed the only well-known distributions for which the integration in (9) can be performed analytically are the exponential distribution

$$f(y) = \alpha e^{-\alpha y} \qquad y \geqslant 0 \qquad (10)$$

and the uniform distribution

$$f(u) = 1 \qquad \text{for } 0 \leqslant u \leqslant 1 \qquad (11)$$

There has been of late a tendency to ignore the approximations provided by classical numerical analysis and to resort unnecessarily to the novel Monte Carlo methods whenever a complete analytic reduction fails.

2. MONTE CARLO PROCEDURES FOR EVALUATING STATISTICAL DISTRIBUTIONS

It is clear from the description of Monte Carlo procedures given in (1), that the principal steps of computing estimates of frequency distributions for statistics $h(x_1 \cdots x_n)$ are as follows:

2.1. The generation of random samples $x_1 \cdots x_n$ drawn from the parent population with ordinate frequency $f(x)$.

2.2. The computation of the statistic h for each sample and computation of a frequency distribution (3) for varying H from the grouped frequencies of the individual statistics h.

The standard procedure in 2.1 is first to generate sets of random numbers or digits and interpret these as the decimal digits of a uniform variate u_i following the distribution (11). One of the early methods of generating the u_i is known under the name of "the power residue method." It consists of the following algorithms:

Choose a k-digit integer U_0 and define further k-digit integers U_i ($i = 1, 2, \ldots$) by the recurrence

$$U_i = \text{integer consisting of last } k$$
$$\text{digits of } (CU_{i-1}) \qquad (12)$$

where C is a specially chosen constant k-digit integer. The u_i are then defined by

$$u_i = 10^{-k}U_i \qquad (13)$$

in which the kth decimal is usually omitted, since it may have non-random features.

For a description of this method, including rules for the choice of C, U_0, and k see [14].

More recently certain shortcomings with this method have been identified and numerous alternatives have been developed of which we mention here R. C. Tausworthe [26] and W. J. Westlake [29]. Fortran implementations of these two programs written by C. E. Gates and E. L. Butler of Texas A & M University are given below:

FORTRAN IMPLEMENTATION OF THE TAUSWORTHE (1965) RANDOM NUMBER GENERATOR (FOR SYSTEMS WITH EØR)

```
      FUNCTION RAND(IX)
      REAL FACTOR/.4656613E-9/,KU1,KU2
      EQUIVALENCE (KU2,KU3),(KU1,LU1)
      DATA KU1,KC,N2TM,N2TCM/Z40000003,Z7FFFFFFF,Z00002000,Z00040000/
C     KU1      ENTERS WITH U(I) UNIFORM RANDOM VARIABLE
C     KU2      LEAVES WITH U(I + 1) UNIFORM RANDOM VARIABLE
C     KCU1     COMPLEMENT OF KU1
C     KCU2     COMPLEMENT OF KU2
C     KC       COMPLEMENTING CONSTANT
C     LXXX     LOGICAL EQUIVALENCES OF ABOVE KXXX
C     N2TM     2**M WHERE M IS SHIFTING FACTOR
```

```
C      N2TCM  2**P-M WHERE P IS WORD SIZE
C      FACTOR FLOAT VALUE OF 2**P
C      EOR IS THE EXCLUSIVE OR OPERATOR
       KU1 = EOR(KU1,LU1/N2TM)
       KU2 = EOR(KU1,AND(LU1*N2TCM,KC))
       RAND = FLOAT(KU3)*FACTOR
       KU1 = KU2
       RETURN
       END
```

FORTRAN IMPLEMENTATION OF THE WESTLAKE (1967) RANDOM NUMBER GENERATOR

```
       SUBROUTINE RANDC (IX,JX,YFL)
       DATA IX,JX/Z7B83C4D3,Z7C235FF5/
C      IX,JX ARE EACH PSEUDO-RANDOM INTEGERS ON THE INTERVAL
C      (0,2**31 − 1)
C      YFL IS THE REAL EQUIVALENT OF THE PSEUDO-RANDOM COMPOSITE
C      GENERATOR
C      65539 = 2**16 + 3
C      262147 = 2**18 + 3
       IX = IX*65539
       JX = JX*262147
       YFL =.4656613E-9*FLOAT(IABS(IX + JX))
       RETURN
       END
```

In order to compute (from the uniform variates u_i) random variates x_i following a given distribution $f(x)$ it is customary to employ the inverse F^{-1} to the probability integral $F(x)$ given by (2), and compute the random variates x_i from

$$x_i = F^{-1}(u_i) \qquad (14)$$

using either a table of $F^{-1}(u)$ or a computer routine for this purpose.

The evaluation of $F^{-1}(u)$ is sometimes easy, as for example when $f(x) = \alpha e^{-\alpha x}$ or $1 - F(x) = e^{-\alpha x}$ so that (14) becomes

$$x_i = -\frac{1}{\alpha} \log_e(1 - u_i) \qquad (15)$$

but is often more complex for example when $f(x)$ is the normal ordinate (5). Although good computer routines are available for the inverse of the normal integral (see, e.g., [13]), the so-called "normal deviate

function," normal variates have often been approximated by the sum of k uniform variables

$$x_i \doteq \left(\frac{12}{k} \right)^{1/2} \left(\sum_{i=1}^{k} u_i - \tfrac{1}{2}k \right) \qquad (16)$$

or indeed as the components of a χ^2 variable for two degrees of freedom [3] from

$$x_i = \sqrt{-2 \log_e u_i} \ \cos 2\pi u_{i+1}$$

$$x_{i+1} = \sqrt{-2 \log_e u_i} \ \sin 2\pi u_{i+1} \qquad (17)$$

It will be seen that (17) generates two normal variates, x_i and x_{i+1}, from two uniform variates u_i and u_{i+1}, using a log, cosine, and square-root routine. Since n random variables x_i are involved in the computation of just one statistic $h(x_1 \cdots x_n)$ and a large number (say N) of h values are required for the empirical estimation of (3) (see Section

5), the number of parental variables x_i (which is $N \cdot n$) will usually have to be a very large number. Particular attention must therefore be paid to the computational economy of the generation of the $h(x_1 \cdots x_n)$. The example given in Section 4 shows that considerable gains can sometimes be made here by a suitable stochastic redefinition of the statistic $h(x_1 \cdots x_n)$.

3. GENERATION OF ORDERED SAMPLES (ORDER-STATISTICS)

A special case frequently encountered arises when the arguments $x_1, \ldots, x_n$ of the statistics $h(x_1, \ldots, x_n)$ refer to the n sample values x_i arranged in ascending order of magnitude so that

$$x_1 \leqslant x_2 \leqslant \cdots \leqslant x_n \qquad (18)$$

Such a sample of n order statistics x_i could, of course, be computed by first generating the uniform variables u_i, then the x_i from (14) and finally by "sorting" the x_i into ascending order of magnitude. However, such an operation may require a considerable computing effort particularly for large n. A number of alternatives have, therefore, been used of which two are described by Lurie and Hartley [17].* The first method generates the uniform order statistics u_i sequentially: Since the c.d.f. of u_1 is given by

$$\Pr\{u_1 \leqslant U_1\} = 1 - (1 - U_1)^n$$

$$0 \leqslant U_1 \leqslant 1 \quad (19)$$

then (using (14) and the fact that $1 - v$ is a uniform variable if v is) u_1 can be computed from a random uniform variable v_1 through

$$u_1 = 1 - v_1^{1/n} \qquad (20)$$

*Although the authors of this paper believe to have provided the first published account of these, it is apparent that such methods have been used by computing agencies for some time.

Next the conditional c.d.f. of u_{i+1} given u_i is given by

$$\Pr\{u_{i+1} \leqslant U_{i+1}\} = 1 - \left\{ \frac{1 - U_{i+1}}{1 - u_i} \right\}^{n-i}$$

$$(21)$$

so that u_{i+1} can be computed from

$$u_{i+1} = 1 - (1 - u_i)v_{i+1}^{1/(n-i)} \qquad (22)$$

where v_{i+1} is a random uniform variable. Finally the x_i are computed from the u_i by (14).

Equations (19)–(21) and (14) may be implemented by the following (remarkably simple) Fortran program

```
DIMENSION X(N)
TEMP = 0.0
DO 10 I = 1,N
V = RANDOM(0, 1)
U = 1.0-(1.0-TEMP)*V**(1.0/(N-I + 1))
X(I) = FINV(U)
10 TEMP = U
RETURN
END                                    (23)
```

In the preceding program RANDOM(0, 1) is the output of a random number generator and FINV(U) is the output of a function subroutine giving the inverse (14) of the c.d.f. of the parental distribution of the x variables. It should be noted that the above method, although attractive through its simplicity, is often slower than alternative methods. Therefore, when N is large it will be preferable to avoid the functional routines V** and FINV and replace them by the extremely fast "content addressing" order into pre-stored arrays of these functions (possibly followed by 2-point Lagrangian interpolation). The second method (which is usually faster) employs the fact that the ith uniform order statistics u_i can be computed from the cumulative sums S_j of j exponential variables. For details see [17].

4. AN EXAMPLE OF A STOCHASTIC REDEFINITION OF THE STATISTIC h (GENERATION OF SAMPLE VARIANCES AND COVARIANCES IN NORMAL CORRELATION PROBLEMS)

There are numerous problems in the distribution theory of statistics computed from bivariate normal samples which cannot be solved analytically. A solution by Monte Carlo requires the generation of sample variances and covariances in paired samples x_i, y_i from a bivariate normal distribution. Notable among these are the distribution of "heritability" and "genetic correlation" estimates computed from an analysis of variance and covariance of two correlated traits x and y, when the data are classified according to the parentage of the observed individuals.

To fix the idea, consider n random pairs of observations x_i, y_i for $i = 1, 2, \ldots, n$, following a standardized bivariate normal distribution with frequency ordinate

$$Z(x, y) = \left(2\pi\sqrt{1 - \rho^2}\right)^{-1}$$
$$\times \exp\left\{-\tfrac{1}{2}(1 - \rho^2)^{-1}\right.$$
$$\left.\times (x^2 + y^2 - 2\rho xy)\right\} \quad (24)$$

where ρ is the correlation coefficient. It is now required to generate random triplets of

$$S_{xx} = \sum_{i=1}^{n} (x_i - \bar{x})^2$$

$$S_{xy} = \sum_{i=1}^{n} (x_i - \bar{x})(y_i - \bar{y}) \quad (25)$$

$$S_{yy} = \sum_{i=1}^{n} (y_i - \bar{y})^2$$

where $\bar{x}$ and $\bar{y}$ are the sample means. The genetical statistics, h, for which Monte Carlo distributions are required are then simple functions of S_{xx}, S_{xy}, and S_{yy} not here given.

The customary method of obtaining the preceding statistics is to generate $2n$ independent standardized normal variates x_i for $i = 1, 2, \ldots, 2n$, to define

$$y_i = \sqrt{1 - \rho^2}\, x_{n+i} + \rho x_i$$
$$\text{for } i = 1, 2, \ldots, n \quad (26)$$

and then compute S_{xx}, S_{xy} and S_{yy} from (25). It can now be shown that these three statistics can be generated by *three* normal variates instead of using $2n$ normal variates. With n (often) in the neighborhood of several hundred the work reduction may be considerable. For details we refer to Hartley and Harris [12]. We give here the relevant formulas only: It can be shown from the standard "analysis of variance" for the regression coefficient of y on x that (see, e.g., [12, 21, 25]).

$$S_{xy} = \sqrt{S_{xx}(1 - \rho^2)}\, X_1 + S_{xx}\rho \quad (27)$$

$$S_{yy} = (1 - \rho^2)\{X_1^2 + \chi_{n-2}^2\}$$
$$+ 2\rho S_{xy} - \rho^2 S_{xx} \quad (28)$$

where X_1 is a standardized normal variate and χ_{n-2}^2 an independent χ^2 statistic for $n - 1$ degrees of freedom. The three *dependent* statistics S_{xx}, S_{xy}, and S_{yy} can be therefore generated from the three independent statistics S_{xx}, χ_{n-2}^2, and X_1. Although the χ^2 variables could be computed from uniform variables u_2 and u_3 by using a machine-stored table of the inverse to the incomplete gamma function (7), they can be more easily obtained from normal variates X_2 and X_3 using for example the so-called Wilson–Hilferty [23] formula

$$\chi_\nu^2 = \nu\left\{1 - \frac{2}{9\nu} + X_i\sqrt{\frac{2}{9\nu}}\right\}^3 \quad (29)$$

where the degrees of freedom ν are $n - 1$ and $n - 2$, respectively. Generalizations to computing sums of squares and products in

p-variate normal samples (random Wishart matrices) have been given by Odell and Feiveson [21] and Smith and Hocking [25].

5. AN EXAMPLE OF A DISTRIBUTION PROBLEM SOLVED BY MONTE CARLO

Special redefinitions of h as described in (4) will not in general be available and the standard generation of h must be used. As an illustrative example we use here the distribution of Spearman's rank correlation r_s for dependent rankings [6], a problem virtually intractable by mathematical analysis: Consider a sample of n paired observations x_i, y_i from the bivariate normal distribution (24) with correlation coefficient ρ. Assume that the x_i are arranged in order of ascending magnitude and denote by

$$j(i) = \text{rank number of the } y_i \text{ paired with } x_i$$

$$(30)$$

so that the $j(i)$ represent a permutation of the n integers. Spearman's rank correlation

is then defined as the product-moment correlation of the paired rankings i and $j(i)$ and can be reduced to the formula

$$r_s = 1 - 6 \sum \frac{d_i^2}{(n^3 - n)}$$

$$\text{where } d_i = i - j(i) \quad (31)$$

Although for independent rankings ($\rho = 0$), the exact distribution of r_s can be worked by combinatorial evaluation of the complete range of values of $\sum d_i^2$, no such results are available for dependent rankings generated as the subscripts of the order statistics of paired samples form a bivariate normal distribution.

A moderate sequence of $N = 500$ sets of $n = 30$ paired x_i, y_i and a sequence of $N = 833$ sets of $n = 30$ paired x_i, y_i were generated to examine the z-transform

$$z_s = \tanh^{-1} r_s \quad (32)$$

for normality and variance stability. The results are shown in the following table.

STANDARD DEVIATIONS OF THE MONTE CARLO DISTRIBUTIONS OF z_s									
$\rho =$	.1	.2	.3	.4	.5	.6	.7	.8	.9
$n = 30$	.191	.194	.201	.193	.202	.197	.195	.202	.216
$n = 50$	.143	.155	.154	.150	.152	.157	.146	.151	.153

It will be noted that the standard deviations are virtually independent of ρ and are well approximated by the empirical formula $1.03/\sqrt{n - 3}$. Associated tests on the normality of z_s confirm the merit of the simple approximation

$$z_s = N\left(\phi(\rho), \frac{(1.03)^2}{n - 3}\right) \quad (33)$$

where $\phi(\rho)$ depends on ρ only but not on n. The implications of these results on test "comparisons" or rank correlations are discussed in Fieller, Hartley, and Pearson [6]. Corresponding results for Kendall's and

Fisher's rank correlations have recently been published by Fieller and Pearson [7].

6. METHODS OF REDUCING "SAMPLE SIZES"

As is well known, a very large number N of random values of the statistic $h(x_1 \cdots x_n)$ is required so that the empirical frequencies of the N values of h provide even moderately accurate estimates of its cumulative probability distribution. An idea of the magnitude of N can be obtained by probability distribution. An idea of the magnitude of N can be obtained by applying the well-known Kolmogorov–

Smirnov criterion of goodness of fit. This criterion measures the maximum discrepancy D_N between the true cumulative distribution $\Pr\{h \leqslant H\}$ and its empirical approximation by the proportion of h values below H. It can be shown (see, e.g., [19]) that approximately

$$\Pr\left\{ D_N \leqslant \frac{1.63}{\sqrt{N}} \right\} \doteq 0.99 \qquad (34)$$

This formula shows that the error in our Monte Carlo estimates decreases with $1/\sqrt{N}$. To give an example suppose it is desired to compute a Monte Carlo distribution which, with 99% confidence, has 3 accurate decimals, then

$$\frac{1.63}{\sqrt{N}} = 5 \times 10^{-4} \text{ or } N = 1.06 \cdot 10^{7} \quad (35)$$

It is not surprising, therefore, that considerable efforts were made by the "Monte-Carlists" to modify their method to reduce the number N of sample sequences required to obtain estimates of adequate precision. An excellent account of these methods is given by Meyer [20] and by Kahn [16] as well as in numerous journal articles dealing with such methods. Of these we may mention here

Importance or Correction Sampling	(Kahn and Marshall) [15]
Multistage Sampling	(Marshall) [18]
Conditional Sampling	(Tukey and Trotter) [28]
Antithetic Variables	(Hammersley and Morton) [8]
Control Variables	(Fieller and Hartley) [5]
Stratified Sampling	(Cochran) [4]

Of these the last one is described in Section 7. It can be regarded as a special case of the method of "Control Variables." For details of the remaining methods the reader is referred to the papers in question (see References). May it suffice here to say that with all these methods sampling can be reduced considerably at no loss of precision and that the relative merits of these methods depend on the circumstances of the sampling problem and on the gadgetry of the high-speed computer that is available. It is of interest that most of the preceding methods are closely related to devices which sample surveyors use when sampling life populations, that is, stratification, regression estimates, optimum allocations, and the like. Designers of sample surveys have always been concerned with reducing the variance of estimates at constant cost or sample size. We may in the future look forward to further blending of efforts between the sample surveyor and the mathematical "Monte-Carlist."

7. STRATIFIED MONTE CARLO

The method of stratified sampling (see, e.g., Cochran [4]) is closely related to that of using "Control Variables" [5]. In the present case of estimating the c.d.f. of a statistic $h(x_i)$ we may describe (without much loss of generality) stratified sampling as follows: Divide the variate range of x into k *equal probability* ranges R_t $(t = 1, \ldots, k)$. Thus, if ξ_t (the tth k-tile) is defined by

$$\xi_t = F^{-1}\left(\frac{t}{k} \right) \qquad t = 1, \ldots, k-1 \quad (36)$$

then the tth variate range R_t is given by

$$R_t : \xi_{t-1} \leqslant x \leqslant \xi_t \qquad (37)$$

with $\xi_0 = -\infty$ and $\xi_k = \infty$. Denote by n_t the number of units of a random sample of size n which fall into R_t. The n_t represent a partition of n indexed by $s = \{n_t\}$ and the total number of partitions, S, is given by

$$S = \binom{n + k - 1}{k - 1} \qquad (38)$$

The probability that a particular partition will occur in the random sample is given by the multinomial distribution

$$p_s = \frac{n!}{\Pi n_t! k^n} \qquad (39)$$

and the conditional probability that $h \geqslant H$, given a partition $s = \{n_t\}$, is denoted by $\Pr\{h \geqslant H | s\}$. Clearly we have that

$$\Pr\{h \geqslant H\} = \sum_{s=1}^{S} p_s \cdot \Pr\{h \geqslant H | s\} \qquad (40)$$

where the p_s are the known strata (partition) probabilities and the $\Pr\{h \geqslant H | s\}$ will now be estimated by stratified sampling as follows: Allocate N_s samples to partition stratum s. Proportional allocation

$$N_s = Cp_s, \quad \sum_s N_s = N \qquad (41)$$

is recommended. For a given partition $s = \{n_t\}$ a random sample of size n_t is drawn from the variate range R_t. This is achieved by computing

$$x_{ti} = \xi_{t-1} + F_t^{-1}(u_{ti}) \qquad \begin{array}{l} t = 1, \ldots, k \\ i = 1, \ldots, n_t \end{array} \qquad (42)$$

where the u_{ti} are uniform $(0, 1)$ variates and where $F_t(x)$ is the c.d.f. for R_t given by

$$F_t(x) = k\{F(x) - F(\xi_{t-1})\} \qquad (43)$$

An unbiased estimate of $\Pr\{h \geqslant H | s\}$ is then given by

$$\hat{\Pr}\{h \geqslant H | s\} = N_s^{-1}\{\# \ h(x_{ti}) \geqslant H\} \qquad (44)$$

so that an unbiased estimate of $\Pr\{h \geqslant H\}$

can be computed from

$$\hat{\Pr}\{h \geqslant H\} = \sum_s p_s \hat{\Pr}\{h \geqslant H | s\} \qquad (45)$$

With this procedure the number of u_{ti} and x_{ti} in (42) and the number of evaluations of $h(x_{ti})$ in (44) is $n \cdot N$. However, it is possible to reduce the number of evaluations of the u_{ti} and x_{ti} to the considerably smaller number $n \cdot k$ by the following device: A random sample of n variables x_{ti} is computed from *each* of the k ranges $t = 1, \ldots, k$, and to compute the N_s values of $h(x_{ti})$ for stratum s the n_t values of x_{ti} required from range R_t are randomly subsampled from the sample of n values of x_{ti}. This procedure makes the N_s values of $h(x_{ti})$ in (44) dependent. However, introducing the indicator variables

$$v_{ti} = \begin{cases} 1 & \text{if } h(x_{ti}) \geqslant H \\ 0 & \text{if not} \end{cases} \qquad (46)$$

it is evident that $Ev_{ti} = \Pr\{h \geqslant H | s\}$ so that (45) remains an unbiased estimator of $\Pr\{h \geqslant H\}$ although the $\Pr\{h \geqslant H | s\}$ are then no longer binomial variables. It should further be noted that, if $\Pr\{h \geqslant H\}$ is required for a dense grid of H values, again the $n \cdot k$ sample values are all that is needed to obtain an unbiased estimate of the c.d.f. of $h(x_i)$ for all H values by merely repeating (44) for the various values of H. The fact that the unbiased estimate (45) will have a small variance can be seen from the fact that in (40) most of the $\Pr\{h \geqslant H | s\}$ will be zero or one so that their binomial variances will be zero. Should the proportional allocation (41) yield fractional $N_s \ll 1$, one would pool strata and implement a single sample from the pooled strata choosing the partition $\{n_t\}$ with probabilities proportional to the p_s in the pool. Apart from this, rounding to the integral values nearest to the $p_s N$ will be acceptable, resulting in minor modifications in the original total number of samples N. The method is extremely effective for computing the c.d.f. of statistics $h(x_i)$ depending on small sample sizes n. Experience has indicated reductions in variance of from $\frac{1}{4}$ to $\frac{1}{20}$ compared with random Monte Carlo.

Finally we should point out the relation between stratified Monte Carlo as described previously and the evaluation of the multiple integral (3) by numerical integration: If we replace all values of x_{ti} sampled in the range R_t by the median η_t of the variate range R_t, that is, by

$$\eta_t = \xi_{t+1} - F_t^{-1}\left(\tfrac{1}{2}\right) \qquad (47)$$

and compute in place of (44)

$$\tilde{\mathrm{pr}}\{h \geqslant H | s\} = N_s^{-1}\{h(\eta_t) \geqslant H\} \qquad (48)$$

then the estimate corresponding to (45) would be given by

$$\tilde{\mathrm{pr}}\{h \geqslant H\} = \sum_s p_s \,\tilde{\mathrm{pr}}\{h \geqslant H | s\} \qquad (49)$$

as an estimate of $\Pr\{h \geqslant H\}$ will have no variance but will be biased. Now (49) is identical with a "midpoint formula" of numerical integration applied to (3) if the variates $u_i = F(x_i)$ are used as variables of integration. It follows that the bias in (49) is simply given by the truncation error of the numerical integration formula.

To summarize, therefore, stratified Monte Carlo comprises simple Monte Carlo as the special case $k = 1$ and numerical integration as its asymptotic form for $k \to \infty$.

8. GAIN IN PRECISION THROUGH STRATIFIED SAMPLING

In this section we consider questions of the design of a stratified sample in relation to the attained variance reduction of the Monte Carlo estimates and illustrate the results with two examples. The discussion is confined to the case where the n_t values of

$h(x_{ti})$ are all independent sample values so that the v_{ti} are independent binomial variables.

We may then use standard formulas for stratified sampling (see, e.g., Cochran [4], pp. 100–107). Denoting $\hat{\Pr}\{h \geqslant H\}$ by $\hat{p}_H$ and omitting the "finite population correction" (since our population is infinite) we obtain

$$\mathrm{Var}\,\hat{p}_H = \sum_s p_s^2 N_s^{-1} p_{H,s}(1 - p_{H,s}) \qquad (50)$$

where $p_{H,s} = \Pr\{h \geqslant H | s\}$. For the special case of proportional allocation (41), that is, using a sample allocation $N_s = Cp_s$, we denote our estimator $\hat{\Pr}\{h \geqslant H\}$ by $\tilde{p}_H$ and find that (50) reduces to

$$\mathrm{Var}\,\tilde{p}_H = N^{-1}\sum_s p_s\, p_{H,s}(1 - p_{H,s}) \qquad (51)$$

The corresponding formula for the estimator $\bar{p}_H$ computed from completely random sample of size N is given by

$$\mathrm{Var}(\bar{p}_H) = N^{-1} p_H(1 - p_H) \qquad (52)$$

where $p_H = \Pr\{h \geqslant H\}$. Accordingly, the reduction in variance can be computed from

$$\mathrm{Var}(\bar{p}_h) - \mathrm{Var}(\tilde{p}_H)$$
$$= N^{-1}\sum_s p_s(p_{H,s} - p_H)^2 \qquad (53)$$

Hence the gain in precision is given by the familiar "between strata mean square" of the v_{ti} and will depend on the value of H for which an estimate of p_H is required.

If the interest centers on a particular range of H, "optimum allocation" may be employed. Such an allocation (see, e.g., Cochran [4], pp. 95–96) minimizes the variance of $\hat{\Pr}\{h \geqslant H\}$ subject to a constant sample size N. The optimum allocation is given by

$$N_{s,\,\mathrm{opt}} = \frac{p_s\{p_{H,s}(1 - p_{H,s})\}^{1/2} N}{\sum_s p_s\{p_{h,s}(1 - p_{H,s})\}^{1/2}} \qquad (54)$$

and the variance of the stratified estimates (say p_{op}) based on the optimum allocation is given by

$$\text{Var}(p_{op})$$
$$= N^{-1}\left\{\sum_s p_s[p_{H,s}(1-p_{H,s})]^{1/2}\right\}^2$$

(55)

Accordingly, the variance reduction compared with proportional allocation can be computed as the ratio

$$\frac{\text{Var}(p_{op})}{\text{Var}(\tilde{p})} = \frac{\left\{\sum_s p_s[p_{H,s}(1-p_{H,s})]^{1/2}\right\}^2}{\sum_s p_s p_{H,s}(1-p_{H,s})}$$

(56)

The usefulness of optimal allocation (54) is limited by the fact that it depends on the knowledge of the parameters $p_{H,s}$ for which only rough estimates will be known. Even if prior estimates of $p_{H,s}$ are available it must be remembered that Monte Carlo estimations must usually be planned to estimate p_H for a *range* of H values from the *same* sample allocation so that formula (54) cannot be used since it depends on H. In such situations the dilemma may be overcome by setting upper bounds V_H for the variances var $\hat{p}_h$ (given by (50)) and minimizing $N = \sum_s N_s$ as a function of the N_s subject to Var $\hat{p}_h \leqslant V_h$ by convex programming. The utility of this approach is limited by the necessity of obtaining rough advance estimates of the $p_{H,s}$. Although the N_s are known to be integers the complication of using convex integer programming is not warranted.

We now illustrate the above concepts by two examples. As a first example, samples of size 3 were drawn from a uniform distribution (11). By using $k = 3$ and 5, the stratified Monte Carlo estimate of the distributions of the sample mean and the sample range are obtained. Comparison of the values $\hat{\text{Pr}}\{h \leqslant H\}$ for $k = 3$ and $k = 5$ and the exact values $\text{Pr}\{h \leqslant H\}$ are given in

Tables 1 and 2. Tables 3 and 4 show the variances of the estimators for the sample mean and the sample range, respectively, and the relative precision of the stratified procedure over the random Monte Carlo procedures.

As a second example, we consider the so-called Bartlett statistic. A useful test for heterogeneity of variance among normally distributed observations was given by Bartlett [1]. The problem may be defined as follows: Let us denote by s_i^2, $i = 1, 2, \ldots, n$ mean square estimates of variance with v_i degrees of freedom, respectively. The s_i^2 are distributed independently as $\chi^2\sigma_i^2/v_i$, and we wish to test the hypothesis that the σ_i^2's have a common but unknown value, σ^2. The criterion used here is

$$M = K \ln\left(K^{-1}\sum_{i=1}^{n} v_i s_i^2\right) - \sum_{i=1}^{n} v_i \ln s_i^2$$

(57)

where $K = \sum_{i=1}^{n} v_i$.

If none of the degrees of freedom v_i is small, M is distributed approximately as χ^2 with $n - 1$ degrees of freedom, provided that $\sigma_i^2 = \sigma^2$. Hartley [10] gives a slightly better approximation of M which permits the v_i to be as low as 2. Tables based on the Hartley approximation are given in *Biometrika Tables for Statisticians*, Vol. I, edited by Pearson and Hartley [23].

Table 1. COMPARISON OF STRATIFIED SAMPLING ESTIMATE AND EXACT DISTRIBUTION OF SAMPLE MEAN OF THREE OBSERVATIONS FROM (11)

H	Estimate		Exact
	$k = 3$	$k = 5$	
1/4	.07109	.07050	.07031
1/3	.16533	.16660	.16667
1/2	.50391	.49810	.50000
2/3	.83282	.83100	.83333
3/4	.93045	.92780	.92969

Table 2. Comparison of stratified sampling estimate and exact distribution of sample range of three observations from (11)

H	Estimate		Exact
	k = 3	k = 5	
1/4	.15772	.15330	.15625
1/3	.26667	.26090	.25926
1/2	.49846	.50360	.50000
2/3	.74372	.74210	.74074
3/4	.84815	.84250	.84375

Table 3. Variances for estimate $\hat{\Pr}\{h \geqslant H\}$, distribution of sample mean of three observations from (11)

H	Stratified	Random	Rel. Prec.
	k = 3, N = 9720		
1/4	2.786×10^{-6}	6.725×10^{-6}	2.41
1/3	4.763	14.289	3.00
1/2	7.601	25.720	3.38
2/3	4.763	14.289	3.00
3/4	2.786	6.725	2.41
	k = 5, N = 10,000		
1/4	1.579×10^{-6}	6.537×10^{-6}	4.14
1/3	2.778	13.889	5.00
1/2	4.387	25.000	5.70
2/3	2.778	13.889	5.00
3/4	1.579	6.537	4.14

Table 4. Variances for estimate of p_H, distribution of sample range of three observations from (11)

H	Stratified	Random	Rel. Prec.
	k = 3, N = 9720		
1/4	7.003×10^{-6}	13.563×10^{-6}	1.93
1/3	10.161	19.756	1.94
1/2	10.955	25.720	2.35
2/3	10.796	19.756	1.83
3/4	10.198	13.563	1.33
	k = 5, N = 10,000		
1/4	5.193×10^{-6}	13.184×10^{-6}	2.54
1/3	5.480	19.204	3.50
1/2	6.433	25.000	3.89
2/3	6.304	19.204	3.05
3/4	4.591	13.184	2.87

As an example of the application of the stratified Monte Carlo procedure the evaluation of the approximate distribution of the statistic M, when $\nu_i = 1$ and $\nu_i = 2$ is given. (For a definition of M, see, e.g., Hartley [10, 11] and the above discussion.)

To evaluate the accuracy of the approximation, we made use of the fortunate fact that the exact solution for the probability integral of M is known in the special case when $n = 2$. In this case, we can express M in terms of the known values of $F = s_1^2/s_2^2$. For $n = 2$, we can write (57) as

$$
\begin{aligned}
M &= (\nu_1 + \nu_2) \ln\left[(\nu_1 + \nu_2)^{-1}(\nu_1 s_1^2 + \nu_2 s_2^2)\right] \\
&\quad - \nu_1 \ln s_1^2 - \nu_2 \ln s_2^2 \\
&= -(\nu_1 + \nu_2) \ln(\nu_1 + \nu_2) \\
&\quad + (\nu_1 + \nu_2) \ln\left(\nu_1 \frac{s_1^2}{s_2^2} + \nu_2\right) \\
&\quad + (\nu_1 + \nu_2) \ln s_2^2 - \nu_1 \ln s_1^2 - \nu_2 \ln s_2^2 \\
&= -(\nu_1 + \nu_2) \ln(\nu_1 + \nu_2) \\
&\quad + (\nu_1 + \nu_2) \ln(\nu_1 F + \nu_2) - \nu_1 \ln F
\end{aligned}
$$

(58)

It can now be verified that the upper tail of the M distribution for which $M \geqslant M_\alpha$, will correspond to the two tails in the F distribution, $F \geqslant F_{\alpha_1}$ and $F \leqslant F_{\alpha_2}$. In particular, when $\nu_1 = \nu_2 = \nu$, that is, when $F_{\alpha_1} = 1/F_{\alpha_2}$, the M test will correspond to the F test with equal tails, $\alpha/2$. For this particular case, we can write (58) as

$$
M_\alpha = -2\nu \ln 2\nu + 2\nu \ln \nu(1 + F_{\alpha/2})
$$

$$
- \nu \ln F_{\alpha/2} \quad (59)
$$

By using the values of $F_{\alpha/2}$ as the upper percentage points for $\nu = 1$ and $\nu = 2$, we obtain, for various α values, the values M_α shown in Table 5.

Samples of size 2 of s_i^2's were generated by using the stratified Monte Carlo procedure with $k = 10$ and $N = 2000$, for $\nu = 1$

Table 5. PERCENTAGE POINTS OF M

α	$\nu = 1$	$\nu = 2$
.01	8.3072	7.8341
.05	5.0905	4.6558
.10	3.7099	3.3215
.20	2.3485	2.0433
.50	0.6932	0.5754

and $\nu = 2$. Then the statistic M was computed for each sample by using equation (57), and the proportion for which $M \geqslant M_\alpha$ was obtained. Table 6 shows a very close approximation of $\Pr(M \geqslant M_\alpha)$ with the exact values α. As a comparison, for the usual Bartlett statistic, M/c, which in this case would be approximately χ_1^2, the $P(\chi_1^2 \geqslant M_\alpha/c)$ is shown, where χ_1^2 is a chi-square variate with 1 degree of freedom and c is Bartlett's correction factor given by

$$c = 1 + \frac{1}{3(n-1)} \left[\sum_{i=1}^{n} \frac{1}{\nu_i} - \left[\frac{1}{\sum_{i=1}^{n} \nu_i} \right] \right].$$

(60)

Table 6. APPROXIMATION OF $\Pr(M \geqslant M_\alpha)$ FOR $\nu = 1$ AND $\nu = 2$ BY USING THE STRATIFIED MONTE CARLO PROCEDURE WITH $n = 2$, $k = 1$, AND $N = 2000$, AS COMPARED WITH THE EXACT VALUES AND THE χ^2 APPROXIMATION

	$\Pr(M \geqslant M_\alpha)$		$\Pr(\chi_1^2 \geqslant M_\alpha/c)$	
α	$\nu = 1$	$\nu = 2$	$\nu = 1$	$\nu = 2$
.01	.010	.012	.019	.013
.05	.049	.050	.065	.054
.10	.100	.099	.116	.103
.20	.200	.199	.212	.202
.50	.500	.499	.497	.497

It is obvious that stratified Monte Carlo gives considerably better approximations to the true α then Bartlett's χ^2 approximation.

9. APPLICATIONS TO PROBLEMS IN SYSTEMS RELIABILITY

We shall confine ourselves to "systems" whose "reliability" can be identified with the probability

$$P = \Pr\{h_t \geqslant H_t\}, \qquad t = 1, \ldots, T \quad (61)$$

that a set of critical "performance measures" h_t of the system are all above their respective "lower tolerance values" H_t. Each of the performance measures h_t are assumed to be deterministic functions

$$h_t = h_t(x_1, \ldots, x_i, \ldots, x_m) \equiv h_t(x) \quad (62)$$

of the "performances" x_i of a set of m "system components." These component performance measures may be measurements (continuous variables) such as "tensile strength" and "capacitance" and "resistance," or may be discrete variables such as $x_i = 1$ for "component effective" or $x_i = 0$ for "component ineffective" as in life testing situations. If we denote by $f(x_1, \ldots, x_m)$ the joint probability density function for the m values of x_i then the system's reliability P is given by the multiple integral

$$P = \Pr\{h_t \geqslant H_t\}$$

$$= \int \cdots \int_R f(x_1, \ldots, x_m)\Pi \, dx_i \quad (63)$$

where the space of integration R is given by

$$x \text{ in } R \text{ iff } h_t(x) \geqslant H_t, \qquad t = 1, \ldots, T$$

(64)

Compared with the distribution problem for a statistic h (see Sections 1–4 above) the reliability problem is more involved mainly because the "components" x_i are not a random sample from the same population as the x_i will now refer to the performance distribution of *different* components. However, simplifications arise in the important special case when there is only one performance measure h (i.e., $k = 1$) and when the component performances x_i are independently distributed so that

$$f(x_1, \ldots, x_n) = \Pi f_i(x_i) \qquad (65)$$

where the $f_i(x_i)$ and their c.d.f.'s

$$P(x_i) = \int_0^{x_i} f_i(v_i) \, dv_i \qquad (66)$$

are usually available as mathematical graduations of the empirical distributions of extensive performance records for each of the components. Such results are usually available from a quality control or reliability assurance program associated with the production of the components. However, if the performance range of each of the components, x_i, is split into k_i subranges the total number of strata will now be Πk_i (in place of $S = \binom{n}{k}$ as in Section 7). The k_i must, therefore, be kept small (usually $k_i = 2$). This technique has recently been applied (Tremelling, Smith, Ringer, and Oglesby [27]) to a reliability study of an electronic assembly (television set) involving $m = 16$ "components" (13 circuit characteristics and 3 factors affecting components), $k = 9$ performance characteristics obtained as the solution of 9 simultaneous linear equations with coefficients depending on the x_i. In order to reduce the number of strata, which would be 2^{16} if each $k_i = 2$, we choose $k_i = 1$ for six of the components based on an initial study of the differentials $\partial h_i / \partial x_i$ leaving $2^{10} = 1024$ strata and hence Monte Carlo samples (see Section 10).

10. AN ELECTRONICS EXAMPLE

a. Technical Background

The problem to be considered in this section is concerned with the reliability of a television amplifier circuit. For more details of the technical background, we must refer the reader to Bosinoff and Jacobs [2]. In terms of our notation of Section 9, there are $m = 16$ system components or "input variables" $x_1 \cdots x_{16}$, 13 of which $(R_1 \cdots R_{11}, r_{b1} r_{b2})$ are circuit resistances and the remaining 3 $(\beta_1 \beta_2 \beta_3)$ are factors affecting certain of the components. Table 7 shows mean values (μ), standard deviations (σ), and anticipated lower and upper limits for the uniform or truncated normal distributions of these component characteristics. There are $k = 9$ "output variables" or performance characteristics, h_t, of the amplifier (all voltages and currents) for which mean values from our Monte Carlo computations are shown in Table 13. The functional relations (62) (here called the transfer functions) between inputs and outputs are given in Bosinov and Jacobs [2] and are not reproduced here. It is sufficient to state that the h_t are the solutions of a system of linear equations whose coefficient matrix and right-hand sides depend on the x_i. Finally, since in [2] there is no specification of the tolerance levels H_t for the output variables, this example will be concerned with the estimation of the *complete* distribution of the h_t, or more specifically with the marginal distribution of each of the h_t by stratified Monte Carlo and represents a report on a study by Tremelling, Smith, Ringer, and Oglesby [27]. The findings of this study (described in Section 10b) provides information on items such as the following:

1. The Monte Carlo samples provide the probability with which a specific output variate remains in an acceptable control range. These acceptable boundary conditions must be met for proper operation of the circuit.

2. The reliability of the entire circuit can be found as a result of the probabilities calculated as in 1.

3. The expected output, and variation, of any output variate can be estimated. Thus the sensitivity and potential output of the circuit is also established.

4. Possible changes in the circuit may be examined. This can be done by changing

one or more of the input variables (e.g., a resistor's value). The ease of changing these variables when simulating makes this a very advantageous aspect of the Monte Carlo technique.

In place of evaluating estimates of reliability $\hat{Pr}\{h_t \geqslant H_t\}$, this study (because of the absence of specified tolerance limits H_t) evaluated the roots $\hat{H}_t(p)$ of $\hat{Pr}\{h_t \geqslant \hat{H}_t(p)\} = p$ for the five levels $p = .01, .10, .50, .90, .99$.

b. Simulation Results

Two separate cases are presented, the only difference being the number of subranges in each variate. The first simulation is described as follows: Input variables R_1, R_3, r_{b1}, r_{b2}, β_1, and β_2 were not partitioned since their description suggested that their effect on the output variables was smaller. All the other variables were partitioned into two subranges each with equal probability. Therefore, there were $2^{10} = 1024$ possible strata. Each possible stratum was sampled once. Simple random sampling took place in the six variates not partitioned, and in each subrange of the given stratum. Each time the 16 observations were drawn from the variates, an estimate of the 9 parameters was calculated using the transfer functions (62). These estimates were arranged in frequency arrays to form estimated cumulative distribution functions. Thus we used $k_i = 2$ for $i = 2, 4, \ldots, 11, 16, n_s = 1$, and $N = 1024$.

Table 7. PROPERTIES OF THE INPUT VARIABLES

Variate	μ	σ	Lower Limit	Upper Limit
R_1	1,000	29	950	1,050
R_2	10,000	290	9,500	10,500
R_3	220	6	209	231
R_4	5,600	162	5,320	5,880
R_5	1,500	43	1,425	1,575
R_6	1,500	43	1,425	1,575
R_7	2,200	64	2,090	2,310
R_8	22,000	640	20,900	23,100
R_9	470	14	446	493
R_{10}	330	10	313	346
R_{11}	100,000	2887	95,000	105,000
β_1	20	4	10	38
β_2	20	4	10	38
r_{b1}	10,000	2887	5,000	15,000
r_{b2}	10,000	2887	5,000	15,000
β_3	75	26	30	120

Note: All distributions are uniform except β_1 and β_2 which are truncated normal distributions.

Now, the entire experiment above was repeated ten times. A measure of the precision of $\hat{H}_t$ is given by the variation among the ten estimates. For five of the performance characteristics, h_t, selected, Tables 8 through 13 present these variances for each of the five values of $\hat{H}_t$. Also presented are the means of the ten repetitions for the five values of $\hat{H}_t$. In order to compare the precision of these estimates to those of simple Monte Carlo simulation, the relative

Table 8. ELECTRONICS PROBLEM SIMULATION (V_{C3})
CASE 1

Prob. Level	$\hat{H}$ Standard Monte Carlo		$\hat{H}$ Stratified Monte Carlo		Rel. Eff.
p_H	Mean	Est. Var.	Mean	Est. Var.	
.01	$.116107 \times 10^2$	$.222756 \times 10^{-4}$	$.116090 \times 10^2$	$.778711 \times 10^{-5}$	2.86
.10	.116405	.019138	.116401	.266622	0.72
.50	.116822	.010840	.116825	.071600	1.51
.90	.117205	.036557	.117208	.156889	2.33
.99	.117461	.033432	.117445	.285122	1.17

efficiency of the two is also given in the tables. The variances of the estimates under simple Monte Carlo are divided by the variances of the estimates under stratified Monte Carlo. That is,

$$\text{Rel. Eff.} = \frac{V_{\text{simple M.C.}}}{V_{\text{strat. M.C.}}} \qquad (67)$$

Of course, the relative efficiency must be greater than one for the estimates of the stratified Monte Carlo technique to be considered more precise than those of simple Monte Carlo.

An examination of the structure of the h_t $(x_1 \cdots x_m)$ revealed that three of the important performance characteristics h_t

Table 9. ELECTRONICS PROBLEM SIMULATION (V_{E3})
CASE 1

Prob. Level	$\hat{H}$ Standard Monte Carlo		$\hat{H}$ Stratified Monte Carlo		Rel. Eff.
p_H	Mean	Est. Var.	Mean	Est. Var.	
.01	.381742	$.517067 \times 10^{-5}$	.381389	$.398820 \times 10^{-5}$	1.30
.10	.411175	.459186	.410665	.289403	1.59
.50	.462427	.135016	.462366	.137394	0.98
.90	.516090	.855973	.516282	.331403	2.58
.99	.549877	.637205	.550947	.369709	1.00

Table 10. ELECTRONICS PROBLEM SIMULATION (I_{C3})
CASE 1

Prob. Level	$\hat{H}$ Standard Monte Carlo		$\hat{H}$ Stratified Monte Carlo		Rel. Eff.
p_H	Mean	Est. Var.	Mean	Est. Var.	
.01	$.786625 \times 10^{-3}$	$.282933 \times 10^{-10}$	$.786782 \times 10^{-3}$	$.115702 \times 10^{-10}$	2.45
.10	.856450	.256597	.857189	.153871	1.67
.50	.969355	.051767	.969939	.041193	1.26
.90	1.093970	.197664	1.092440	.173798	1.14
.99	1.175990	.893328	1.179175	.325035	2.75

Table 11. ELECTRONICS PROBLEM SIMULATION (V_{C2})
CASE 1

Prob. Level	$\hat{H}$ Standard Monte Carlo		$\hat{H}$ Stratified Monte Carlo		Rel. Eff.
p_H	Mean	Est. Var.	Mean	Est. Var.	
.01	$.856440 \times 10^{1}$	$.259819 \times 10^{-1}$	$.852126 \times 10^{1}$	$.116855 \times 10^{-1}$	2.22
.10	.979099	.049765	.980027	.062278	0.80
.50	1.168578	.047606	1.169089	.033915	1.40
.90	1.297381	.013208	1.298896	.010302	1.28
.99	1.374930	.081555	1.375080	.025597	3.19

Table 12. ELECTRONICS PROBLEM SIMULATION (I_{C2})
CASE 1

Prob. Level	$\hat{H}$ Standard Monte Carlo		$\hat{H}$ Stratified Monte Carlo		Rel. Eff.
p_H	Mean	Est. Var.	Mean	Est. Var.	
.01	$.536282 \times 10^{-2}$	$.261677 \times 10^{-8}$	$.535357 \times 10^{-2}$	$.368939 \times 10^{-8}$	0.71
.10	.593239	.085200	.593956	.089589	0.95
.50	.696824	.153290	.695981	.143572	1.07
.90	.851900	.345381	.851611	.324374	1.06
.99	.943925	.810209	.946719	.532489	1.52

Table 13. MEAN VALUES OF THE ELECTRONICS PROBLEM OUTPUT
VARIATES, CASE 1, STRATIFIED MONTE CARLO

V_{C3}	V_{E3}	I_{C3}	V_{C1}
$.116792 \times 10^2$	.461915	$.970100 \times 10^{-3}$	$.116924 \times 10^2$

V_{C2}	V_{E1}	V_{E2}	I_{C1}
$.114914 \times 10^2$	.648594	$.110924 \times 10^2$	$.901027 \times 10^{-3}$

I_{C2}
$.707002 \times 10^{-2}$

(namely V_{C3}, V_{E3}, and I_{C3}) depended only on five of the x_i (namely R_7, R_8, R_9, R_{10}, and β_3). It was, therefore, decided to partition these variables R_7, R_8, R_9, R_{10}, and β_3 into four equiprobable subranges, and to use simple random sampling for all other input variables. It can be seen that although the precision of V_{C3}, V_{E3}, and I_{C3} will increase, the precision of the other six variates' estimates will not increase. The total number of strata is $4^5 = 1024$. Each stratum is sampled once. The values of p remain the same, as does the number of repetitions of the partitioning of the ranges

Table 14. ELECTRONICS PROBLEM SIMULATION (V_{C3})
CASE 2

Prob. Level	$\hat{H}$ Standard Monte Carlo		$\hat{H}$ Stratified Monte Carlo		Rel. Eff.
p	Mean	Est. Var.	Mean	Est. Var.	
.01	$.116107 \times 10^2$	$.222756 \times 10^{-4}$	$.116094 \times 10^2$	$.461511 \times 10^{-5}$	4.83
.10	.116405	.019138	.116404	.104278	1.84
.50	.116822	.010840	.116824	.036989	2.93
.90	.117205	.036567	.117210	.117778	3.10
.99	.117461	.033432	.117448	.354322	0.94

Table 15. ELECTRONICS PROBLEM SIMULATION (V_{E3})
CASE 2

Prob. Level	$\hat{H}$ Standard Monte Carlo		$\hat{H}$ Stratified Monte Carlo		Rel. Eff.
p	Mean	Est. Var.	Mean	Est. Var.	
.01	.381742	$.517067 \times 10^{-5}$	.382661	$.753775 \times 10^{-5}$	0.69
.10	.411175	.459186	.410682	.171080	2.68
.50	.462427	.135016	.462381	.096589	1.40
.90	.516090	.855973	.516092	.104406	8.20
.99	.549877	.637205	.549905	.221565	2.88

Table 16. ELECTRONICS PROBLEM SIMULATION (I_{C3})
CASE 2

Prob. Level	$\hat{H}$ Standard Monte Carlo		$\hat{H}$ Stratified Monte Carlo		Rel. Eff.
p	Mean	Est. Var.	Mean	Est. Var.	
.01	$.786625 \times 10^{-3}$	$.282933 \times 10^{-10}$	$.790302 \times 10^{-3}$	$.129681 \times 10^{-10}$	2.18
.10	.856450	.256597	.855414	.095030	2.70
.50	.969355	.051767	.971124	.033381	1.55
.90	1.093967	.197664	1.090862	.091537	2.16
.99	1.175988	.893328	1.175332	.268644	3.32

of the sixteen input variables. Estimates similar to these for Case 1 are presented in Tables 14–16. Estimates of the other six output variates are not given, as they are, in fact, found by simple random sampling.

Of course, the number of subranges and variates partitioned was somewhat arbitrary. Other possible combinations, and a larger number of subranges, are expected to produce even better results than these.

c. Discussion

The relative efficiencies in the tables above indicate the degree to which stratification has improved the estimated variance. The parameters were estimated ten times. In the limiting case, the relative efficiency of stratified Monte Carlo to simple Monte Carlo can never be less than one. However, with only ten repetitions, random variation causes the relative efficiency to be less than one in a few cases. In most cases, the stratified Monte Carlo technique produced a significant reduction in variance. Also, Case 2 produced estimates that were again more precise than Case 1.

11. REFERENCES

1. M. S. Bartlett, "Properties of Sufficiency and Statistical Tests," *Proc. Roy. Statist. Soc., London Ser. A*, **160**, 268–282 (1937).

2. I. Bosinoff and R. Jacobs, *Using Transfer Function in Reliability Predictions*, 9th National Symposium on Reliability and Quality Control, Institute of Radio Engineering, Inc., New York, 1963.

3. G. E. P. Box and M. E. Muller, "A Note on the Generation of Random Normal Variables," *Annals Math. Statist.*, **29**, 601–611 (1958).

4. W. G. Cochran, *Sampling Techniques*, Wiley, New York, 1963.

5. E. C. Fieller and H. O. Hartley, "Sampling with Control Variables," *Biometrika*, **41**, 494–501 (1954).

6. E. C. Fieller, H. O. Hartley, and E. S. Pearson, "Tests for Rank Correlation Coefficients, I," *Biometrika*, **44**, 470–481 (1957).

7. E. C. Fieller and E. W. Pearson, "Tests for Rank Correlation Coefficients, II," *Biometrika*, **48**, 29–40 (1961).

8. J. M. Hammersley and K. W. Morton, "On Counters with Random Dead Time I," *Proc. Cambridge Philosoph. Soc.*, **49**, 623–637 (1955).

9. H. L. Harter, *Order Statistics and Their Use in Testing and Estimation*, Vol. 2, Aerospace Research Laboratories, Office of Aerospace Research, U.S. Air Force, 1964.

10. H. O. Hartley, "Testing the Homogeneity of a Set of Variances," *Biometrika*, **31**, 249–255 (1940).

11. H. O. Hartley, "Tables for Testing the Homogeneity of a Set of Estimated Variances," *Biometrika*, **33**, 296–304 (1946).

12. H. O. Hartley and D. Harris, "Monte Carlo Computations in Normal Correlation Problems," *J. Assoc. Comput. Mach.*, **10**, 302–306 (1963).

13. C. Hastings, T. Hayward, Jr., and J. P. Wong, Jr., *Approximations for Digital Computers*, Princeton Univ. Press, London, 1955.

14. IBM Reference Manual 20-8011 (1959). *Random Number Generation and Testing*.

15. H. Kahn and A. W. Marshall, "Methods of Reducing Sample Size in Monte Carlo Computations," *J. Operat. Res. Soc. Amer. I*, 263–278 (1953).

16. H. Kahn, *Applications of Monte Carlo*, Rand Corporation Research Memorandum AUCU-3259, prepared under Contract with U.S. Atomic Energy Commission No. AT(11-1)-135, 1954.

17. D. Lurie and H. O. Hartley, "Machine Generation of Order Statistics for Monte Carlo Computations," *Amer. Statistician*, **26**, 26–27 (1972).

18. A. W. Marshall, "The Use of Multi-stage Sampling Schemes in Monte Carlo Computations," in *Symposium on Monte Carlo Methods* (H. A. Meyer, ed.), Wiley, New York, 123–144, 1954.

19. F. J. Massey, "The Kolmogorov–Smirnov Test for Goodness of Fit," *J. Amer. Statist. Assoc.*, **46**, 68–78 (1951).

20. H. Meyer (ed.), *Symposium on Monte Carlo Methods*, Wiley, New York, 1954.

21. P. L. Odell and A. H. Feiveson, "A Generalization of the Gauss-Markov Theorem," *J. Amer. Statist. Assoc.*, **61**, 1063–1082 (1966).

22. E. S. Pearson and H. O. Hartley, "The Probability Integral of the Range in Samples of *n* Observations from a Normal Population," *Biometrika*, **32**, 302–310 (1945).

23. E. S. Pearson and H. O. Hartley, *Biometrika Tables for Statisticians*, Vol. I, Cambridge University Press, 1954.

24. E. S. Pearson and H. O. Hartley, *Biometrika Tables for Statisticians*, Vol. I, Cambridge University Press (3rd edit.), 1966.

25. W. B. Smith and R. R. Hocking, *J. Roy. Statist. Soc. Ser. C*, **21**, 341–345 (1972).

26. R. C. Tausworthe, "Random Number Generated by Linear Recurrence Modulo Two," *Math. Computat.*, **19**, 201–209 (1965).

27. R. N. Tremelling, W. B. Smith, L. J. Ringer, and J. L. Oglesby, *Statistical Simulation Procedures*, Technical Report No. 4, NASA Grant NGR 44-001-095, Institute of Statistics, Texas A & M University, 1970.

28. J. W. Tukey and H. F. Trotter, "Conditional Monte Carlo for Normal Samples," in *Symposium on Monte Carlo Methods*, H. A. Meyer (ed.), Wiley, New York, 64–88, 1954.

29. W. J. Westlake, "A Uniform Random Number Generator Based on the Combination of Two Congruential Generators," *J. Assoc. Comput. Mach.*, **14**, 337–340 (1967).

30. E. B. Wilson and M. M. Hilferty, "The Distribution of Chi-Squares," *Proc. Nat. Acad. Sci. U.S.A.*, **17**, 684–688 (1931).

PART II | REGRESSION AND DISCRIMINANT ANALYISIS

Editorial Preface to Part II

The methods in Chapters 3–6 represent the present state of the art in regression and discriminant analysis. Chapter 3 treats the general problem of selecting a best subset of regression variables under a variety of constraints. The methodological problem in selecting a subset of variables in multiple regression is that one would like to examine all possible subsets with respect to a certain criterion function, say the multiple correlation coefficient with the dependent variable. When the number of variables is moderately large, the number of subsets becomes too great for practical computation. One solution to this problem is embodied in Chapter 3 by R. R. Hocking.

Hocking's method of subset selection becomes inordinately expensive of computer time beyond some 30–50 variables. Consequently, the stepwise aggregation method described by R. I. Jennrich in Chapter 4 is a frequently used alternative. In fact, this method, which was described in this series by M. A. Efroymson (*Mathematical Methods for Digital Computers* Vol. 1, Ralston and Wilf, Eds., Wiley 1964), has probably been the most commonly used technique in stepwise regression analysis. Its essence is to select that subset of the variables which explains the largest fraction of the variance of the dependent variable.

It should be noted, however, that there are problems with the stepwise aggregation method. Mantel (*Technometrics*, **12**, 621–5, 1970 and **13**, 455–7, 1971) has pointed out that the step-up method of selecting variables leaves much to be desired, and that it is possible to miss the more important variables. He suggested instead (but was not the first to use) step-down procedures wherein all variables are initially used and those which explain the smallest amount of variance are removed, one by one.

Another method that has come into use in recent years is ridge or damped regression, first formally described by A. E. Hoerl and R. W. Kennard in "Ridge regression: biased estimation for nonorthogonal problems," *Technometrics*, **12**, 55–67, 1970. In this method damping factors are added to the diagonal of the correlation matrix prior to inversion. This tends to orthogonalize interrelated variables, and, by the study of the robustness of the regression coefficients with changes in the damping factors (ridge trace), one determines variables that should be removed. This method also permits one to deal with the overdetermined case, that is, when there are more variables than observations. It may also be noted that stepwise regression may produce larger R^2 than optimum regression, in the *sample* correlation matrix case, as contrasted to the *population* matrix case.*

The discriminant analysis methods of

*Note added in proof: R. R. Hocking has recently published an excellent summary and comparison of the various subset selection methods which must be consulted by the reader concerned with this topic. *Biometrics*, **32**, 1–49 (1976).

Chapters 5 and 6 can be distinguished from one another in that Jennrich's stepwise method of Chapter 5 assumes a common covariance matrix for the variables, whereas that of H. S. Wilf in Chapter 6 permits unequal covariance matrices. Furthermore, the stepwise discriminant analysis method of Chapter 5 is a step-up method similar to that of stepwise regression in Chapter 4, whereas the method of coalitions of Chapter 6 uses all the variables rather than a subset of them.

The editors considered unifying the notation in these four chapters but decided that each author's notation had sufficient internal logic so as to make this undesirable. For this reason, hereafter is a list of terms and the corresponding symbols which are used in the four chapters. When definitions were absolutely unique or a symbol was not used in more than one chapter, that particular symbol does not appear in this chart.

	Chapter 3	Chapter 4	Chapter 5	Chapter 6
Total number of variables			m	N
Total number of observations (cases)	n, t		n	k
Number of groups			g, N	M
Index for observations	t, s			
Index for variables in regression	k			
Number of coalitions				N_c
Number of variables eligible for deletion which are retained		s		
Number of variables deleted		q		
Set of predictor variables	S			
Total number of predictor variables used, excluding constant term	p	t	p	
Total variables eligible for deletion		k		
Total variables in the regression including constant term and all variables forced in		p		
Covariance matrix	A	X		
Total sum of squares			T	
Total cross-products matrix			$T(\mathbf{x})$	
Within cross-products matrix			$W(\mathbf{x})$	
"Tolerance" on variable k	t_k			
Multiple correlation coefficient	R	R^2		
Regression or discriminant function coefficient	b	p	b	
An approximation to Wilk's Λ			F	

Selection of the Best Subset of Regression Variables

3

R. R. Hocking
Mississippi State University

1. FUNCTION

The classical multiple linear regression problem is that of estimating the coefficients, β_i, $i = 0, 1, \ldots t$, in the linear model,

$$\hat{y} = \beta_0 + \sum_{i=1}^{t} \beta_i x_i + e \qquad (1)$$

based on a set of n responses, y, to various values of the input variables, x_i, in the presence of errors, e. In many cases a subset of size s of the original t input or predictor variables x_i will be adequate to describe the data. If the size of the desired subset, s, is specified, then it only remains to select that subset of size s which is best in some sense. If the principle of least squares is adopted, a natural definition of the "best" subset of size s is that one with smallest residual sum of squares. This definition will be used throughout this chapter. In most instances the value of s is not specified in advance, and, hence, the investigator attempts to determine, based on the existing data, both the number of variables defined in the subset regression and the best subset of that size.

If the residual sum of squares is evaluated for all 2^t possible subset regressions, the problem of determining the best subset of any size would be resolved and the only remaining problem would be to determine the appropriate value of s. If t is large, the evaluation of all possible subset regressions is computationally infeasible. We thus identify the two main problems in selecting subset regressions: The first is that of deciding upon criteria for determination of the value of s, and the second, the computational problem of computing the residual sums of squares for all subsets.

The purpose of this chapter is to provide a solution to the second of these problems. Numerous authors, such as Garside [7], Schatzoff et al. [17], and Furnival [5], have proposed efficient methods for evaluating all possible regressions, but the exponential increase in the amount of computation with increasing t clearly restricts such methods to moderate values of t. Using a monotonicity relation between the values of the residual sum of squares, a number of authors such as Beale et al. [2], Hocking and Leslie [11], and LaMotte and Hocking [14] have proposed "branch and bound" type algorithms which enable the determination of the best subset of any size s, without requiring the evaluation of all of the $\binom{t}{s}$ subsets of that size. In this chapter, we describe and illustrate the method developed by LaMotte and Hocking which represents an extension of the earlier method by Hocking and Leslie. (For brevity we refer to these two methods as L-H and H-L, respectively.)

The problem of determining the size of the subset to be used is less easily solved; and indeed, it is quite likely that a single criterion does not exist that is uniformly applicable. No attempt will be made here to resolve this question, but it does seem appropriate to provide a summary of a few of the concepts used by practicing statisticians so that the user may have some guidance.

The simplest idea is to plot the value of the residual sum of squares for the best subset of each size against the size of the subset. As s is decreased the values are monotonically increasing, very slowly at first, as unimportant variables are eliminated, and then quite rapidly, as important variables are excluded. The value of s for which the plot turns abruptly upward is then recommended.

There are many shortcomings of such a procedure: (i) The value of s may not be clearly defined due to a gradually increasing plot in the region of interest, (ii) even if s is precisely determined, the resulting best subset may be unacceptable for other reasons, such as the availability and cost of data for future predictions, and (iii) there is not unanimous agreement that the residual sum of squares plot focuses on the proper range of values for s.

In view of reasons (i) and (iii) various simple functions of the residual sum of squares have been recommended which will hopefully define the proper range of s and

ideally focus more sharply on the value of s. In the case of (ii) it is desirable to have not only the best subset of size s, but also a number of nearly best subsets to provide the user with reasonable alternatives.

In practice, several different functions are used to identify a number of candidate subsets; then technical and economic reasons are applied to select the final subset. In addition to the residual sum of squares, functions commonly used are

1. the multiple correlation coefficient, R^2
2. the residual mean square, RMS
3. the adjusted multiple correlation coefficient,

$$R_a^2 = \left(1 - (n-1)\frac{(1-R^2)}{(n-p)}\right),$$
$$p = s + 1$$

4. $J_p = (n+p)RMS, \qquad p = s+1$
5. $C_p = (n-p)\left(\frac{RMS}{\sigma^2} - 1\right) + p$
$$p = s + 1$$

The multiple R^2 plot provides the same information as the residual sum of squares. The residual mean square and adjusted R^2 are not necessarily monotonic. The statistic J_p arises by considering the average prediction variance over the observed data (see Hocking [10]). The statistic C_p, proposed by Mallows [15], considers the total mean squared error of prediction over the observed data in an attempt to identify bias as well as total error. The use of this latter criterion is also described in Gorman and Toman [8] and Daniel and Wood [3]. (For a relation between C_p and R_a^2 see Kennard [12].) These concepts will be illustrated by example in Section 7.

There are other measures of a subset regression which are not simple functions of the residual mean square, such as the concept of "ridge regression" introduced by Hoerl and Kennard [9], and the notion of the prediction sum of squares proposed by

Allen [1]. These ideas are not considered in this chapter.

Finally, we mention the well-known "stepwise" techniques as summarized by Draper and Smith [4]. These techniques will identify a subset regression without regard to any well-defined optimality criterion, and also fail to provide the user with the opportunity to select from several contending subsets.

2. MATHEMATICAL DISCUSSION

a. Symbols Used

t	Total number of predictor variables used, not including the constant term
k	Total number of variables eligible for deletion, $k \leqslant t + 1$
s	Number of variables, eligible for deletion, which are retained, $1 \leqslant s \leqslant k$
r	Number of variables deleted, $r = k - s$
p	Total number of variables in the regression including the constant term and all variables forced in, $1 \leqslant p \leqslant t + 1$
S	A subset of s indices corresponding to variables in the subset
R	A subset of r indices corresponding to variables deleted from the subset
RSS	Residual sum of squares
$RSS(R)$	RSS if the subset R is deleted

b. Description of the Algorithm

In this section we describe a procedure that will yield, for each value of s, $1 \leqslant s \leqslant k$, the subset of size s which has minimum residual sum of squares. This is accomplished by a technique which, in general, will not require the evaluation of all 2^k subsets, and experience indicates that only a very small fraction of these subsets need be evaluated.

FUNDAMENTAL OPTIMALITY PRINCIPLE

In order that we may determine that we have the subset of size s with smallest residual sum of squares without evaluating all subsets, it is necessary to have a means of comparing two subsets without actually doing the computations. The very simple but fundamental idea is as follows: Let S_1 and S_2 be two subsets selected from the indices $(1, \ldots, k)$; then if RSS_1 and RSS_2 are the residual sums of squares obtained by fitting these submodels it is easily shown that

$$S_1 \subseteq S_2 \Rightarrow RSS_1 \geqslant RSS_2 \qquad (2)$$

That is, if we add variables to an existing set of variables, the residual sum of squares cannot increase.

It is somewhat easier to describe the algorithm in terms of the variables to be deleted rather than those to be retained; hence, we restate the fundamental principle (2) as follows: Let R_1 and R_2 denote the two subsets of indices selected from the set $(1, \ldots, k)$ which are deleted to form the subsets S_1 and S_2. Then

$$S_1 \subseteq S_2 \Leftrightarrow R_1 \supseteq R_2 \qquad (3)$$

hence,

$$R_1 \supseteq R_2 \Rightarrow RSS(R_1) \geqslant RSS(R_2) \qquad (4)$$

RELABELING OF VARIABLES

The first step of the procedure is to compute the full regression, that is, to fit the model with all k predictors. We then fit each of the k models in which one of the variables has been deleted. The residual sum of squares for the model in which variable i has been deleted is denoted by $RSS(i)$. It is assumed that the variables are indexed according to the order on $RSS(i)$, that is,

$$RSS(1) \leqslant RSS(2) \leqslant \cdots \leqslant RSS(k) \qquad (5)$$

Thus the subset of size $k - 1$ with minimum residual sum of squares is obtained by deleting variable 1.

DETERMINATION OF BEST SUBSET OF SIZE s (HOCKING–LESLIE)

For ease of understanding, we describe first the determination of the best subset of size s as described by Hocking and Leslie [11]. This procedure is a special case of the LaMotte–Hocking method and will illustrate the fundamental ideas and provide for easier understanding of the more complex extensions.

As mentioned previously, it is convenient to think in terms of deleting variables, hence we let $r = k - s$ denote the number of variables deleted. It is clear that there are $\binom{k}{s}$ subsets of size s to be considered, or equivalently, that there are $\binom{k}{r}$ subsets of size r which are candidates for deletion. These $\binom{k}{r}$ subsets are divided into $s + 1$ groups, the qth group containing a total of $\binom{r + q - 2}{q - 1}$ subsets of size r, consisting of the index $r + q - 1$ and $r - 1$ smaller indices. That is, all subsets of the form $(i_1, i_2, \ldots, i_{r-1}, r + q - 1)$ where $1 \leqslant i_1 < i_2 < \cdots < i_{r-1} < r + q - 1$. For brevity, we shall refer to subsets of size r as "r-subsets." The following example will illustrate the concept.

EXAMPLE 1: With $k = 6$ and $r = 4$ we have $s + 1 = 3$ groups as follows:

Group 1	Group 2		Group 3	
(1, 2, 3, 4)	(1, 2, 4, 5)	(1, 2, 5, 6)	(1, 4, 5, 6)	
	(2, 3, 4, 5)	(2, 3, 5, 6)	(1, 2, 4, 6)	
	(1, 3, 4, 5)	(1, 3, 5, 6)	(2, 3, 4, 6)	
	(1, 2, 3, 5)	(3, 4, 5, 6)	(1, 3, 4, 6)	
		(2, 4, 5, 6)	(1, 2, 3, 6)	

The procedure is to inspect the groups, sequentially, in the hope that by employing the optimality principle (4), we may identify the subset with minimum residual sum of squares without evaluating the subsets in all $s + 1$ groups.

The procedure is as follows: At Stage 1, RSS is computed for those subsets obtained by deleting the r-subsets in Group 1. This consists of the single subset with indices $(1, 2, \ldots, r)$ and will be denoted by R_1, indicating that it is the best r-subset in Stage 1. The associated RSS is denoted by $RSS(R_1)$. If $RSS(R_1) \leqslant RSS(r + 1)$, then the complementary subset S_1 has the smallest RSS among all subsets of size s, and the search is terminated. To see this, note that any other r-subset of deleted variables will contain an index $r + 1$ or greater; hence by (4), the associated RSS will exceed $RSS(r + 1)$, and hence, $RSS(R_1)$. If $RSS(R_1) > RSS(r + 1)$ then the search must continue to Stage 2. It is of interest to note, however, that if $RSS(R_1) \leqslant RSS(v)$ for $v > r + 1$, then, using the same argument, we are assured that we will not have to evaluate the subsets in Groups $v + 1 - r$ through $s + 1$, for again, all such subsets would have RSS greater than $RSS(v)$, and hence, greater than $RSS(R_1)$.

At Stage 2, the RSS associated with each of the r-subsets in Group 2 are evaluated. Group 2 consists of r-subsets with index $r + 1$, and $r - 1$ lower indices. Let R_2 (with complement S_2) be the subset from Stages 1 and 2 with smallest RSS denoted by $RSS(R_2)$. If $RSS(R_2) \leqslant RSS(r + 2)$, then the subset S_2 has minimum RSS among all subsets of size s, and the search is terminated; if not, we continue to Stage 3, and so on.

In general, the procedure may be summarized as follows: At Stage q, the RSS associated with each deleted set in Groups $1, 2, \ldots, q$ has been evaluated. Let R_q denote the subset yielding the minimum RSS, say $RSS(R_q)$. If $RSS(R_q) \leqslant RSS(r + q)$ the search is terminated, and S_q is optimal. If not, continue to Stage $q + 1$ and continue until the termination criterion is satisfied or all $s + 1$ groups have been evaluated.

DETERMINATION OF BEST SUBSET OF SIZE s (LaMOTTE–HOCKING)

The procedure described in the preceding paragraph becomes computationally inefficient for moderately large k ($k > 15$). There are two primary sources for the inefficiency. First, as r increases, the termination criterion based on comparison with $RSS(i)$ becomes less sensitive, frequently requiring the evaluation of all $s + 1$ groups to determine the best subset of size s. Second, as q increases, the number of subsets in Group q increases. In the following development, the optimality principle (4) is applied in two ways to yield a vastly improved algorithm.

Generalization of H-L Method. The first extension consists of basing the termination criterion on the residual sum of squares for subsets of size $k - m$ rather than $k - 1$ as in the previous method. Typically $m = 1, 2, 3, 4$.

Again, assume that the variables have been relabeled as in (5). The next step is to evaluate RSS for each of the $\binom{k}{m}$ subsets of size $k - m$. Again, for convenience, we shall identify the subsets by the m variables that have been deleted. We adopt the convention that a subset will be denoted by the m indices written in increasing order. Thus, an m-subset will be denoted by $(i_1, i_2, i_3, \ldots, i_m)$ with $1 \leqslant i_j \leqslant k$, and $i_1 < i_2 < \cdots < i_m$. The associated residual sums of squares will be denoted by $RSS(i_1, i_2, \ldots, i_m)$. These m-subsets are now ordered in increasing order of magnitude and will serve to define groups for inspecting the r-subsets.

The r-subsets are now divided into $\binom{k - r + m}{m}$ groups. The r-subsets in any group are defined by an m-subset and consist of those indices in that m-subset and $r - m$ indices which are smaller than the first index in the m-subset. The groups are numbered according to the magnitude of the RSS associated with the m-subset defining the group. Thus, Group 1 consists of those r-subsets defined by the m-subset associated with the smallest RSS. Note that for a given value of r, only m-subsets with

first index $r - m + 1$ or greater can be used to define a group.

We observe in passing that although this description is more complex, it reduces to the H-L definition of groups with $m = 1$ and is a natural generalization of the principle used by H-L.

The following example will illustrate the concept.

EXAMPLE 2: With $k = 6$, $r = 4$, and $m = 2$ the only 2-subsets which define groups are, (3, 4), (3, 5), (3, 6), (4, 5), (4, 6), and (5, 6). The 2-subset (2, 6) for example, does not define a group since there are not $r - m = 2$ indices less than the first index. The groups, labeled by their defining subset are as follows:

Group (3, 4)	Group (3, 5)	Group (3, 6)
(1, 2, 3, 4)	(1, 2, 3, 5)	(1, 2, 3, 6)

Group (4, 5)	Group (4, 6)	Group (5, 6)
(1, 2, 4, 5)	(1, 2, 4, 6)	(1, 2, 5, 6)
(1, 3, 4, 5)	(1, 3, 4, 6)	(1, 3, 5, 6)
(2, 3, 4, 5)	(2, 3, 4, 6)	(1, 4, 5, 6)
		(3, 4, 5, 6)
		(2, 4, 5, 6)
		(2, 3, 5, 6)

(Note that the ordering on the groups will depend on the magnitude of RSS associated with the defining 2-subset hence will, in general, differ from that used in this example.)

The procedure for identifying the subset of size s with minimum RSS is the direct generalization of that used in the H-L method. Again the groups are inspected sequentially. At each stage, the smallest RSS obtained is compared with the RSS for the m-subset defining the next stage. Thus, in Stage 1, the RSS associated with the r-subsets in Group 1 are computed. Denote the minimum by $RSS(R_1)$ corresponding to the deletion of the r-subset, R_1. If $RSS(R_1)$

is less than the *RSS* obtained by the deletion of the *m*-subset defining Stage 2, the search is terminated and the complementary subset is optimal. If not, continue to Stage 2.

In general, at the *q*th stage, we consider the minimum *RSS* from Groups 1, 2, . . . , *q*, say, $RSS(R_q)$, and ask if it is less than the *RSS* associated with the *m*-subset defining Stage *q* + 1. If so, we terminate, having identified the subset S_q with minimum *RSS*; if not, we proceed to Stage *q* + 1 and continue until termination or until all groups have been evaluated.

The verification of the optimality of the procedure is exactly the same as that in the H-L algorithm employing the principle (4).

The use of the *m*-subsets for *m* > 1 clearly requires more initial computation to set up the algorithm, as all $\binom{k}{m}$, *m*-subsets must be evaluated. However, this is more than offset by the decrease in the number of *r*-subsets that must be evaluated.

Reduction of Computations within a Stage. As observed earlier in the H-L algorithm, the number of subsets in Group *q* increases as *q* increases. This is again the case with the generalized method. Indeed, if the group is defined by the *m*-subset $(i_1, \ldots, i_m)$ then a total of $\binom{i_1 - 1}{r - m}$ subsets must be evaluated. To check for optimality, we do not need to evaluate all of these subsets, but rather, we are interested only in the one yielding the smallest *RSS*, and in practice, a few others with nearly minimum *RSS*. The problem of determining the best subset within a group is exactly analogous to the overall problem of determining the best subset.

To see this, suppose we are using subsets of size m_1 in the application of the generalized algorithm described above. This is hereafter referred to as Level 1 of the application of the optimality principle. Suppose further, that we are required to evaluate Stage *q* which is defined by the

m_1-subset $(i_1, i_2, \ldots, i_{m_1})$. Rather than evaluate all of the subsets in Group *q*, we now apply the optimality principle within Stage *q* as follows: Since m_1 of the variables, namely $i_1, \ldots, i_{m_1}$, are common to all subsets in Group *q*, we note that we are thus seeking that $(r - m_1)$ subset of the variables 1, 2, . . . , $(i_1 - 1)$ such that the *RSS* for the resulting $s = (k - r)$-subset is minimum.

To illustrate, in Example 2 with $m_1 = 2$ and *r* = 4, consider the group defined by the m_1-subset, (5, 6). We are seeking the subset of two indices selected from (1, 2, 3, 4) such that the *RSS* obtained by deleting those two variables from the *k* − 2 variable model (5 and 6 deleted) will have minimum *RSS*.

To apply the optimality principle within Stage *q*, we proceed as usual with the $k - m_1$ variable model. Thus, the first step is to evaluate $RSS(i)$ for *i* = 1, 2, . . . , $(i_1 - 1)$, where $RSS(i)$ is the *RSS* obtained by deleting variable *i* from the $k - m_1$ variable model, or equivalently, variable *i* and the variables in the m_1-subset from the *k*-variable model. The variables 1, . . . , $(i_1 - 1)$ are now relabeled so that the $RSS(i)$ are in increasing order as in (5). Denote the relabeled variables as $1', 2', \ldots, (i_1 - 1)'$. Suppose we choose to base the comparisons for termination within Stage *q* on the *RSS* associated with the deletion of subsets of size m_2. We must then compute *RSS* corresponding to the deletion of all m_2-subsets that can be formed from the variables $1', 2', \ldots, (i_1 - 1)'$. The *RSS* associated with these m_2-subsets are again ordered, and the m_2-subsets are used to define groups consisting of $(r - m_1)$-subsets as before. Thus, the m_2-subset $(j'_1, j'_2, \ldots, j'_{m_2})$ defines a group of $(r - m_1)$ subsets which consist of those subsets containing the indices $(j'_1, j'_2, \ldots, j'_{m_2})$ and $r - m_1 - m_2$ indices selected from $(1', 2', \ldots, (j'_1 - 1))$.

Having defined and ordered the groups, the search within Stage *q* proceeds as usual. Thus, at Stage *l*, within Stage *q*, we ask if the minimum *RSS* obtained in Stages 1 through l is less than the *RSS* associated with the m_2-subset defining Stage $l + 1$. If so, we terminate; if not, continue.

We refer to the application of the optimality principle within a stage of Level 1 as a Level 2 application. Note that it is comparable to a Level 1 search with $i_1 - 1$ variables; hence, the amount of computation should be considerably less.

It should also be noted that, in many cases, after setting up to consider Level 2 in Stage q, it may be possible to eliminate all subsets of Stage q without further computation. This follows since the *RSS* associated with the best r-subset in Stage q will be at least as big as the smallest *RSS* obtained by deleting the m_2-subsets. This *RSS* may already exceed the minimum *RSS* from Stages 1 through $q - 1$; hence, we may immediately terminate Stage q.

Once the concept of a Level 2 application within Stage q of Level 1 is clear, it is natural to continue with this idea. Thus, we might consider a Level 3 application within Stage l of Level 2 within Stage q of Level 1 using, say, m_3-subsets to define the termination criterion.

These two extensions suggest a number of questions:

1. How many levels should be considered?
2. What determines when a new level should be defined in a stage?
3. What values of m_i should be used in the different levels?

Answers to these questions depend, to a certain extent, on the number of subsets the investigator might like to have to inspect in addition to the best one. This number is greatly decreased as m_i and the number of levels is increased, a fact which is critical in terms of analyzing problems with many independent variables. Clearly, no firm rules can be established to answer these questions; hence, the decisions are based on such considerations as the programming complexity introduced and experience gained with sample problems. In the program described in Section 6, the number of levels is set at four, the value of m_i increases with r up to a maximum of $m_i = 4$, $i = 1, 2, 3, 4$. The decision to define a level within a stage is based on the number of subset evaluations which would be required in that stage. In particular, if this number exceeds 100, a new level is defined.

FORCING CERTAIN VARIABLES INTO THE REGRESSION

In Section 1, it was implied that only the t predictor variables would be eligible for deletion, since it is natural to assume that the constant term would be desirable in the final equation. In other situations, the investigator may wish to force certain other variables into the regression; hence, the number of variables, k, eligible for deletion is less than t. Also, but more rarely, the constant term may be eligible for deletion. Conceptually, there is no difficulty involved since one would just apply the method described here to those variables eligible for deletion. Operationally, this would appear to complicate the computer program whose input is essentially the matrix and right-hand side vector of the normal equations. However, the solution is quite simple.

To illustrate, suppose the linear model, in the familiar matrix form, is given by

$$Y = X\beta + e \tag{6}$$

where $X = (X_1, X_2)$, $\beta' = (\beta_1', \beta_2')$. Assume that the variables corresponding to the columns of X_1 are to be forced into the subset and those in X_2 are eligible for deletion. It is easily shown, by writing the equation in partitioned form, that the least-squares estimate of β_2 in the model (6) can be determined by solving the 'adjusted' normal equations.

$$X_2'(I - X_1(X_1'X_1)^{-1}X_1')X_2\hat{\beta}_2$$
$$= X_2'(I - X_1(X_1'X_1)^{-1}X_1')Y \tag{7}$$

The estimates of β_1 are then given by,

$$\hat{\beta}_1 = (X_1'X_1)^{-1}[X_1'Y - X_1'X_2\hat{\beta}_2] \quad (8)$$

For example, in the simplest case where only the constant term is to be forced in, X_1 is just a column vector of ones, and the observations are simply adjusted for the mean.

The simple solution to forcing the variables in X_1 into the model is to input the quantities from (7) as if these were the normal equations and all variables were eligible for deletion.

c. Computational Considerations

Although the method described in Section b has proved to be quite efficient, in the sense that best subsets can be determined by evaluating only a small fraction of the total number of subsets, the computations that must be performed are such that some consideration must be given to computational efficiencies.

For each subset evaluation, the *RSS* must be determined, and this can be obtained by inverting a matrix of dimension $a = \min(r, s)$. Such an inversion normally requires of the order of $a^3/3$ operations. For a given value of r, it is possible to order the subsets, within the order prescribed by the algorithm, in such a way that only one variable changes from one subset to the next. This enables the use of a "product-form" of inverse described by Hocking and Leslie [11] which requires on the order of $2a^2$ operations. This form of the inverse, commonly used in linear programming computations, has also proven to be effective in controlling round-off errors, but occasional re-inversions are used if the string of computations is very long. There are a number of ways of ordering the subsets as described above, one of which is given by LaMotte and Hocking [14].

If the subset evaluation is accomplished by actually inverting the required matrix, then the regression coefficients for the best subset may also be evaluated. Depending on the ultimate use of the regression equation (see, e.g., Draper and Smith [4]), the investigator may be interested in the values of certain regression coefficients when these variables are used in combinations with others. Since only *RSS* is needed for the selection process it may be more efficient to use only a forward solution of the normal equations. In a recent paper, Furnival [6] describes three such algorithms and then applies this idea along with the basic principles of the L-H method to develop a program that may be computationally faster than the one described in Section 6, at the expense of providing slightly less information. The Furnival program evaluates the subsets in a different order, from that used in L-H, which may increase the speed, but also increases the storage requirements.

3. SUMMARY OF CALCULATION PROCEDURE

A computer program implementing the L-H method has been written by L. R. LaMotte of the University of Kentucky [13]. This program, called SELECT, is written to be attached as a subroutine, if desired, to the user's existing regression program. To avoid requiring that the user understand the method in detail, many of the desirable computational options of SELECT have been automated. Thus the user has no control over the values of m_i, $i = 1, \ldots, 4$ used at the four levels available. The values of m_i are preset, based on our experience, to gradually increase with r until for $r = 17$, $m_i = 4$, $i = 1, \ldots, 4$. Neither can the user specify when an additional level is defined. Currently the program defines a new level whenever the stage under consideration will require the evaluation of 100 or more subsets. Also, the possibly desirable feature of suboptimal termination for each value of r is not available. This is a point worth considering since, usually, the best subset is identified early in the process but several additional groups may have to be inspected to prove optimality. A bound on the possible decrease in *RSS*, if a better subset is found in one of these groups, is obtained by comparing the current best *RSS* with the *RSS* for the defining *m*-subsets. Hence we can assess the consequences of early termination. On the other hand, evaluation of these groups may well reveal some "nearly best" subsets of interest.

With these simplifications, the input required for SELECT is minimal. The necessary input quantities are described below. The output of SELECT is also described. This output does not include plots or values, apart from R^2, of any of the criteria described in Section 1; however, these could easily be adjoined if desired.

a. Input Quantities

The call to SELECT is,
CALL SELECT (K,IPL,IPU,XPX,XPY, ISCALE,SCALE)
The arguments are defined below.

K — The total number of predictor variables from which the best subset is to be selected. For the current program $K \leqslant 50$.

IPL — The smallest size of subset desired, $1 \leqslant IPL \leqslant IPU$.

IPU — The largest size of subset desired, $IPL \leqslant IPU \leqslant K - 1$. (Best subsets of all sizes *IPL*, $IPL + 1, \ldots, IPU$ will be determined.)

XPX — From the $K \times K$ matrix of "adjusted" sums of squares and products,

$$X_2'\big(I - X_1(X_1'X_1)^{-1}X_1'\big)X_2$$

XPX is determined by factoring the square-root of each diagonal element from its corresponding row and column. (Recall $X = (X_1, X_2)$ where X_1 denotes those variables forced into the model.)

XPY — From the K-dimensional vector

$$X_2'\big(I - X_1(X_1'X_1)^{-1}X_1'\big)Y$$

XPY is determined by dividing each element by the square-root of the corresponding diagonal element of $X_2'(I - X_1(X_1'X_1)^{-1}X_1')X_2$ and also by the square-root of

$$Y'\big(I - X_1(X_1'X_1)^{-1}X_1'\big)Y$$

Note 1: In the most common situation, the constant term is to be forced in and all other variables are eligible for deletion. In this case *XPX* is the matrix of simple correlations between the predictor variables and *XPY*, their correlation with the dependent variable *Y*.

ISCALE: If *SCALE* is defined *ISCALE* = 1; otherwise *ISCALE* = 0.

SCALE: A vector of dimension $K + 1$ containing the diagonal elements of $X_2'(I - X_1(X_1'X_1)^{-1}X_1')X_2$ and the quantity $Y'(I - X_1(X_1'X_1)^{-1}X_1')Y$ must be defined if *ISCALE* = 1.

Note 2: In the situation described in Note 1, the first K elements of *SCALE* are $\sum_{j=1}^{n} (x_{ij} - \bar{x}_i)^2$, $i = 1, \ldots, K$ and the $(K + 1)st$ element is $\sum_{j=1}^{n} (y_j - \bar{y})^2$.

b. Output from SELECT

Note 3: The computations in SELECT are done in terms of *XPX* and *XPY*, thus, the regression is actually computed in terms of these normalized variables. The output includes the regression coefficients for these variables (unrescaled) as well as the corrected (rescaled) coefficients obtained by introducing the SCALE vector.

The output includes:

1. The results of the regression on all K variables including the value of R^2 and the values of the regression coefficients, β_2, for those variables eligible for deletion, both rescaled, labelled as $B(i)$, and unrescaled, labelled as $G(i)$, $i = 1, \ldots, K$.

2. For each value of s, $IPL \leqslant s \leqslant IPU$, the output includes the value of R^2 and the corresponding regression coefficients for the best subset and the next nine best subsets computed, or all others computed if less than nine. (It should be emphasized that these are the next nine best observed but there is no guarantee for example, that the second best subset is included.) The indexing on the regression coefficients corresponds to the indexing of the variables in XPX. That is, the relabeling accomplished internally for the purpose of the algorithm is undone prior to the output.

3. Finally, the output records the total number of regressions evaluated prior to identification of the best subset. This is primarily, of academic interest, but might guide the user in consideration of alternate choices of m_i, especially in large problems.

4. FLOW CHART

The flow chart is given on pp. 48–49.

5. DESCRIPTION OF THE FLOW CHART

Box 1: Provide input data for SELECT as described in Section 3.

Box 2: Solve the "adjusted" normal equations for the full k-variate model. Compute $RSS(i)$, the residual sum of squares for all subsets of size $k - 1$. Relabel the variables.

Box 3: Output regression data for k-variable model. Output best 10 subsets of size $k - 1$. Set $r = K - IPU$.

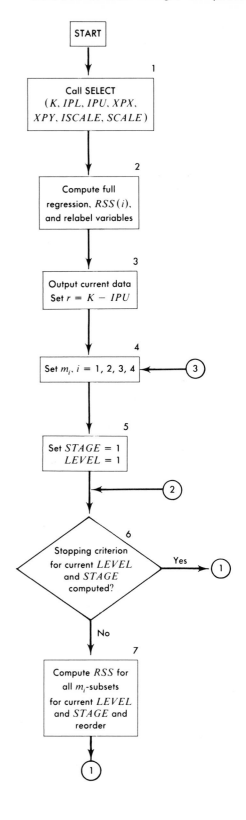

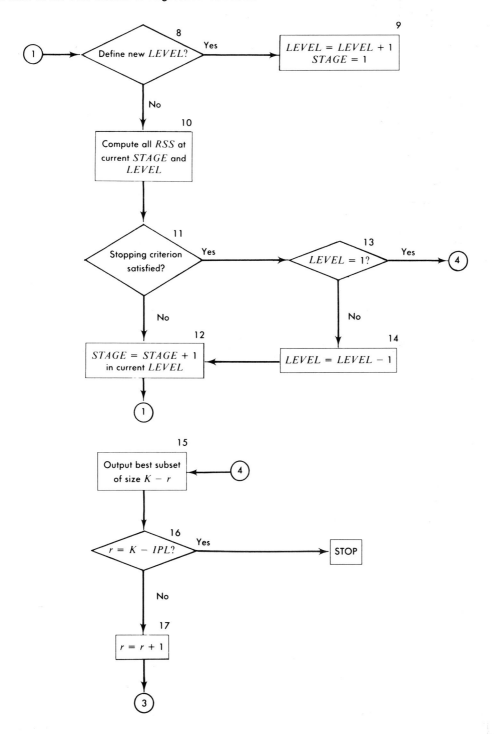

Box 4: Set the values for the number of variables m_i used in the stopping criterion for the four levels for the current value of r.

Box 5: Initialize the stage and level counters.

Box 6: If the stopping criterion (RSS) has been computed for the current level and stage, go to Box 8; otherwise, go to Box 7.

Box 7: Compute RSS for all m_i-subsets for current level and stage and reorder them by magnitude.

Box 8: The decision to define a new level is based on the number of subsets to be evaluated in the current stage at the current level. If greater than 100, go to Box 9; if not, go to Box 10.

Box 9: Increment level counter, initiate new stage counter, and return to Box 6.

Box 10: Compute RSS for all subsets in current stage of current level.

Box 11: If the stopping criterion is satisfied in the current level, go to Box 13; if not, go to Box 12.

Box 12: Increment the current stage counter and return to Box 8.

Box 13: If the level is one, go to Box 15, if not go to Box 14.

Box 14: Decrement the level counter and return to Box 12 where the stage counter at this new level is incremented.

Box 15: If the level is one in Box 13, the best subset has been identified. Output corresponding data for it and the next best subsets observed up to a maximum of nine.

Box 16: If $r = K - IPL$, best subsets have been determined for all sizes specified; hence, stop. If not go, to Box 17.

Box 17: Increment r and return to Box 4.

6. PROGRAM

The program SELECT and its associated subroutines are written in Fortran IV and require two standard subroutines as described in the IBM Applications Program, 1130 Scientific Subroutine Package, Programmers Manual, Program Number 1130-CM-02X. The routines are (1) ARRAY as found on page 86 of the manual and (2) DINV which is a double precision version of MINV found on page 61.

7. SAMPLE PROGRAM

To illustrate the concepts described in Section 2, we present an example with $k = 10$ using the data described in Gorman and Toman [8].

Since we want to force the constant term into the final subset and are only concerned with the variables selected and the relative magnitudes of the RSS, it is sufficient to work with the correlation matrix. Thus, the RSS have not been rescaled but are relative to a total sum of squares of unity. The RSS for fitting all 10 variables is $RSS(0) = .1024$. In Table 1 we show the $RSS(i)$ for each of the subsets of size 9 obtained by deleting variable i. Note that the variables have been relabeled according to the magnitude of $RSS(i)$. The alphabetic labeling used by Gorman and Toman is shown for reference with that paper.

Reference to Table 1 shows that the best subset of size 9 is obtained by deleting variable 1, or variable k in the Gorman–Toman labeling.

Table 1. RELABELING AND RESIDUAL SUMS OF SQUARES FOR $s = 9$

Variable Deleted	Gorman–Toman Label	$RSS(i)$
1	k	.1089
2	d	.1090
3	j	.1101
4	a	.1141
5	b	.1279
6	g	.1310
7	e	.1389
8	c	.1562
9	h	.1645
10	f	.1721

To illustrate the H-L procedure let us consider the determination of the best subset of size $s = 6$ or equivalently the best $r = 4$ variables to be deleted. The $s + 1 = 7$

groups are defined by the indices 4, . . . , 10, where in each group, the defining index is combined with 3 lower indices to define the *r*-subsets. Thus Group 1 consists of the single *r*-subset $R_1 = (1, 2, 3, 4)$. The associated residual sum of squares, that is, the residual sum of squares for the model consisting of variables $S_1 = (5, 6, 7, 8, 9, 10)$, is given by $RSS(R_1) = .1391$. Comparing this with $RSS(r + 1) = RSS(5) = .1279$ from Table 1, we see that the search cannot be terminated. Further inspection shows that $RSS(R_1) < RSS(8)$; hence, we are assured that we will not have to evaluate Stage 5 or higher. It is, of course, possible that further information would preclude the necessity of evaluating Stage 4, but such will not be the case here. Indeed, the subset (1, 2, 3, 4) will be seen to be optimal.

Reference to Table 2 under Stage 2 shows that the subset (1, 2, 3, 4) has minimum *RSS* among subsets in the first two groups; hence, $R_2 = (1, 2, 3, 4)$ and $RSS(R_2) = .1391$. Comparing this with $RSS(r + 2) = RSS(6) = .1310$, we again see that the search cannot be terminated. Continuing through Stages 3 and 4, we see that the subset (1, 2, 3, 4) remains optimal; hence, $R_3 = R_4 = (1, 2, 3, 4)$. Termination is not possible at the end of Stage 3, since $RSS(R_3) > RSS(7) = .1389$, but we do terminate after Stage 4, with the identification of the best set of size 6 variables being $S = (5, 6, 7, 8, 9, 10)$.

Table 2. H-L METHOD, $r = 4$, $s = 6$.

Stage 1		Stage 2		Stage 3		Stage 4	
Variables Deleted	*RSS*	Variables Deleted	*RSS*	Variables Deleted	*RSS*	Variables Deleted	*RSS*
1234	.1391	1245	.1849	1256	.1861	1267	.1709
		2345	.1539	2356	.1485	2367	.1846
		1345	.1883	1356	.1934	1367	.1956
		1235	.1682	3456	.1680	3467	.1964
				2456	.1587	2467	.1663
				1456	.2044	1467	.1754
				1246	.1760	4567	.1752
				2346	.1594	3567	.1904
				1346	.1866	2567	.1644
				1236	.1716	1567	.1961
						1257	.1918
						2357	.1908
						1357	.2138
						3457	.2059
						2457	.1770
						1457	.2037
						1247	.1627
						2347	.1931
						1347	.1895
						1237	.1843
$R_1 = (1234)$		$R_2 = (1234)$		$R_3 = (1234)$		$R_4 = (1234)$	

We thus see that to identify the best subset of size 6, we had to evaluate *RSS* for 35 of the 210 possible subsets. In Table 5, we show the required computation if the algorithm is applied for $r = 2$ through 9. It should also be noted that the six subsets evaluated for $r = 2$ are, in fact, the best six subsets. For $r = 3$ we actually had to evaluate the four best subsets, and for $r = 4$ we evaluated twelve of the best thirteen. Thus an added bonus of the method is that in addition to obtaining the best subset, we also obtain a number of nearly best subsets of each size. For $r = 6, 7, 8, 9$, all subsets had to be evaluated before the optimum was identified.

Further investigation of Table 2 indicates two possibilities. The relatively large amount of computation required in Stages 3 and 4 just to verify the optimal subset suggests a need for reducing the computation in these stages, which is the second improvement described on pp. 44–45. Alternately, we might have decided to eliminate Stages 3 and 4 completely at the risk of missing the optimal subset. Based on the relative magnitudes of $RSS(R_2)$ and $RSS(6)$ and $RSS(7)$ the chance of this is slight and an evaluation might be made as to whether the additional computation is warranted.

The two extensions of the H-L procedure which were incorporated to yield the L-H procedure may now be described in terms of the above example. For clarity, these two ideas will be illustrated separately, but both are applied in the L-H algorithm.

The first extension, described on pp. 43–44 consists of basing the termination on the RSS for subsets of size $k - m$ rather than $k - 1$. We will illustrate with $m = 2$, but the concept will be clear for higher values of m.

Assuming that the variables have been relabeled as in Table 1, the first step is to compute the residual sum of squares for all subsets of size $k - 2$. These subsets are ordered according to the magnitude of the residual sum of squares. As before, it is convenient to identify a subset by the variables which have been deleted rather than those that are retained. A partial list of these subsets and their associated RSS are shown in Table 3. Note that 2-subsets whose first index is one are not shown since they cannot define r-subsets for $r > 2$. For $r = 3$ the groups are defined by 2-subsets with first index 2 or greater and for $r = 4$ the first

index must be at least 3. The group indices for $r = 3$ and 4 are shown in Table 3.

Table 3. RESIDUAL SUMS OF SQUARES FOR ORDERED TWO-SUBSETS

Variables Deleted	$RSS(ij)$	Group Index for $r = 3$	Group Index for $r = 4$
2, 3	.1147	1	
2, 4	.1224	2	
3, 4	.1236	3	1
2, 5	.1293	4	
3, 5	.1327	5	2
2, 6	.1338	6	
5, 6	.1396	7	3
3, 6	.1416	8	4

To determine the best subset of size $s = 6$, that is, $r = 4$, the 4-subsets are now divided into $\binom{8}{2}$ groups, each group being defined by a 2-subset and two additional indices less than the first index in the 2-subset. Note that for $r = 4$, only those subsets in Table 3 with first index greater than 2 need be considered. These groups are numbered according to the ordering on the subsets in Table 3. Thus the pair (3, 4) defines Group 1, the pair (3, 5) defines Group 2, and so on.

The algorithm now proceeds in the same way as the H-L algorithm and is summarized in Table 4. Thus at Stage 1 we first evaluate the RSS associated with all subsets in Group 1. In this case this consists of the single subset $R_1 = (1, 2, 3, 4)$ with $RSS(R_1) = .1391$. This is compared with the RSS associated with the pair defining Group 2, namely the pair (3, 5) with $RSS(3, 5) = .1327$. Since $RSS(R_1) > RSS(3, 5)$ the search cannot be terminated. Further inspection shows that $RSS(R_1) < RSS(5, 6) = .1396$; and hence, the search is guaranteed to stop prior to the stage defined by the pair (5, 6), in this case Stage 3. We must, however, continue with Stage 2 and evaluate the subsets defined by the pair (3, 5). This group consists of the single subset (1, 2, 3, 5) with associated $RSS = .1682$. Thus, at Stage 2 the subset (1, 2, 3, 4) still yields the minimum RSS; hence $R_2 =$ (1, 2, 3, 4) with $RSS(R_2) = .1391$. As we observed above, $RSS(R_2) < RSS(5, 6)$; hence the search is terminated; and as in the H-L procedure, the subset $S = (5, 6, 7, 8, 9, 10)$ is best. Since both Stages 1 and 2 contained only one subset, and hence, did not illustrate the general procedure for generating subsets in a stage, the subset in Stages 3

and 4 are shown in Table 4, even though they were not used in the computation.

Thus of the possible 210 contending subsets, the best subset was identified after evaluating only two of them. On the other hand, although this extension required considerably less computation than the H-L method, we are penalized by seeing only one additional subset, (1, 2, 3, 5), and it is

Table 4. L-H METHOD, FIRST EXTENSION
$r = 4, s = 6, m_1 = 2$

Defining Subset	Stage 1 (3, 4)		Stage 2 (3, 5)		Stage 3 (5, 6)	Stage 4 (3, 6)
	Variables Deleted	RSS	Variables Deleted	RSS	Variables Deleted	Variables Deleted
	1234	.1391	1235	.1682	1256	1236
					1356	
					1456	
					3456	
					2456	
					2356	
	$R_1 = (1234)$		$R_2 = (1234)$			

not the second best as seen from Table 5. In Table 5, we show, for $r = 2, 3, \ldots, 9$ the required subset evaluations using this first modification.

Table 5. COMPARISON OF NUMBER OF SUBSET EVALUATIONS FOR H-L AND FIRST EXTENSION OF L-H METHOD, $m_1 = 2$

r	Total Possible Subsets	H-L Required	Extension 1 Required
2	45	6	45
3	120	4	2
4	210	35	2
5	252	126	32
6	210	210	60
7	120	120	64
8	45	45	45
9	10	10	10

The second extension to be illustrated is that of reducing the amount of computation within a stage. Referring again to the original example, we see, in Table 2, that a

considerable amount of computation is required in Stages 3 and 4 if we apply the H-L algorithm, (or equivalently, the L-H modification with $m_1 = 1$). Looking first at the subsets in Group 3 as defined by the m_1-subset consisting of the single variable 6, we now proceed to define a new level, Level 2, for application of the optimality principle. The first step is to evaluate the RSS associated with the subsets obtained by eliminating the variables in the defining m_1-subset and each of the variables with index less than the smallest index in this m_1-subset. In this case we consider the elimination of the variable 6 with each of the variables 1 through 5. These five variables are relabeled 1' through 5' according to the magnitude of these RSS, as shown in Table 6.

Again for simplicity, we base the comparisons at Level 2 on the RSS associated with subsets of size $m_2 = 1$. The investigation of Stage 3 is now carried out in the

Table 6. L-H Method, second extension, level two applied to stages 3 and 4, $r = 4$, $s = 6$, $m_1 = m_2 = 1$

			Stage 3, Level 2			
Relabeling of Variables			Stage 1		Stage 2	
New	Old	$RSS(i', 6)$	Variables Deleted	RSS	Variables Deleted	RSS
1'	2	.1338	1'2'3'6	.1485	1'2'4'6	.1587
2'	5	.1396			2'3'4'6	.1680
3'	3	.1416			1'3'4'6	.1594
4'	4	.1447				
5'	1	.1538				
			$R_1 = (1'2'3'6) = (2356)$		$R_2 = (1'2'3'6) = (2356)$	

			Stage 4, Level 2					
Relabeling of Variables			Stage 1		Stage 2		Stage 3	
New	Old	$RSS(i', 7)$	Variables Deleted	RSS	Variables Deleted	RSS	Variables Deleted	RSS
1'	1	.1429	1'2'3'7	.1627	1'2'4'7	.1709	1'2'5'7	.1918
2'	2	.1460			2'3'4'7	.1663	2'3'5'7	.1770
3'	4	.1468			1'3'4'7	.1754	1'3'5'7	.2037
4'	6	.1493					3'4'5'7	.1752
5'	5	.1607					1'4'5'7	.1961
6'	3	.1728					2'4'5'7	.1644
			$R_1 = (1'2'3'7) = (1247)$		$R_2 = (1'2'3'7) = (1247)$		$R_3 = (1'2'3'7) = (1247)$	

usual way. That is, since $r = 4$, we must determine the subsets of three variables selected from variables 1' through 5' such that this subset, along with variable 6, if eliminated, yields minimum *RSS*. Specifically, we see that there are three groups defined in the usual way by the variables 3', 4', and 5'. In Stage 1 we consider the single subset (1', 2', 3'). The *RSS* due to the 4-subset (1', 2', 3', 6) is .1485 which exceeds *RSS* (4', 6) = .1447; hence Stage 2 must be considered. In Stage 2 of Level 2, we consider the additional subsets (1', 2', 4'), (1', 3', 4'), and (2', 3', 4') in conjunction with variable 6. The minimum *RSS* is still that associated with the subset (1', 2', 3', 6). This is now less than *RSS* (5', 6) = .1538; hence the search is terminated. Thus only four of the ten subsets

in Stage 3 of Level 1 had to be evaluated to identify the best subset in that stage. Further investigation shows that these are the best four subsets in Stage 3 of Level 1.

In Stage 4, we may again go to Level 2. The computations are illustrated in Table 6 using $m_2 = 1$ as in Stage 3. Proceeding, we find that after completing three stages of Level 2 requiring the evaluation of ten of the twenty possible subsets, the subset (1', 2', 3', 7) with *RSS* = .1627 is identified as best.

Again, the best subset in Stage 4, as just determined, is still not as good as the subset (1, 2, 3, 4) previously identified; hence (1, 2, 3, 4) is still best, and as observed in Table 2, is, in fact, optimal.

We thus observe that the application of Level 2 within a stage may substantially reduce the number of subsets to be evaluated. It may also be observed that the effort per subset is reduced, since the inversion of $r \times r$ matrices (if $s > r$) is replaced by the inversion of one $m_1 \times m_1$ matrix, and the the inversion of $(r - m_1) \times (r - m_1)$ matrices.

There is a further savings in effort which may be far more significant. To illustrate, consider the Level 2 application in Stage 3 as shown in Table 6. We note that, after setting up Level 2, $RSS(3', 6) = .1416$. The best subset in Stage 3 of Level 1 is thus assured to have an RSS in excess of this, and since the subset (1, 2, 3, 4) has already been observed to have $RSS = .1391$, we are assured that no subset in Stage 3 of Level 1 can beat the current best subset; hence, no further computations are necessary. Similarly in Stage 4 of Level 1, we note, after setting up for Level 2, that $RSS(3', 7) = .1468$; hence again, no subset in Stage 4 can beat the current contender (1, 2, 3, 4); thus, no further computations are required in Stage 4.

We see that the application of the second extension of the H-L method requires the investigation of only the five subsets in the first two stages to determine the optimum.

There is, of course, the additional effort required to define Level 2, but is is considerably less than would be required without the extension.

In larger problems, we may actually have to carry out the Level 2 computations as indicated. A given stage in Level 2 may then require excessive computations; hence, we may again apply the optimality principle at Level 3, and so on.

The combination of these two extensions of the H-L algorithm, that is, (i) using m_i-subsets for $m_i > 1$ to provide the termination criterion, and (ii) reapplication of the optimality principle at various levels within a stage has greatly improved the efficiency of the method. As a result, the size of k, which may be considered, is increased substantially.

The best subsets of each size for $p = s + 1 = 2, \ldots, 11$ for this example are shown in Table 7. As indicated in Section 1, the problem at this point is to determine the value of p and, as suggested earlier, possibly consider suboptimal sets when external factors enter into the consideration. Four of the criteria discussed in Section 1 have been evaluated for the best subsets in the example data and are shown in Table 7. In Fig.

Table 7. VALUES OF VARIOUS CRITERIA FOR BEST SUBSETS

p	Best Subset	RSS	$RMS(\times 10^2)$	J_p	C_p
11	(1–10)	.1024	.4096	.1925	11.
10	(2–10)	.1080	.4153	.1910	10.36
9	(1, 4–10)	.1138	.4214	.1896	9.78
8	(4–10)	.1221	.4360	.1918	9.80
7	(5–10)	.1391	.4797	.2063	11.96
6	(1, 7–10)	.1691	.5636	.2367	17.28
5	(1, 7, 9, 10)	.2007	.6474	.2654	23.00
4	(1, 9, 10)	.2437	.7615	.3060	31.49
3	(4, 8)	.2781	.8427	.3287	37.88
2	(10)	.3374	.9923	.3771	50.38

3.1, these values are plotted as a function of p to provide a graphical means of determining p. The slope of the RSS plot is so gradual that it is of little help. The RMS plot is, in this case, monotone, but does turn up rather sharply for $p = 8$. The J_p plot has a minimum at $p = 9$, but $p = 7$ or 8 would seem just as reasonable. C_p also has a

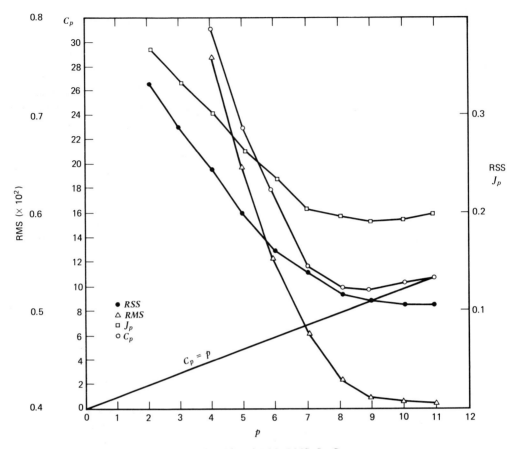

Fig. 3.1. Plot of *RSS, RMS, J_p, C_p*.

minimum for $p = 8$, but the distance above the line $C_p = p$ indicates a bias which might suggest $p = 9$. In this case, we see that there is general agreement as to the size of the best subset, and the decision of the investigator on the ultimate subset would be quite easy. Unfortunately, there are many instances when this is not the case, suggesting a need for better criteria, or at least better understanding of the existing ones.

8. ESTIMATION OF RUNNING TIME

The time required to determine the best subset of size s, $1 \leqslant s \leqslant k$ will depend on (i) the magnitude of k, since this determines the total number of possible subsets, and (ii) the correlation structure, as this influences

the sensitivity of the stopping criterion. An indication of the efficiency of the algorithm is given by noting the fraction of the total number of subsets that must actually be evaluated, as indicated in Table 5 for the Gorman–Toman data. The behavior on larger problems has been quite favorable. For example, SELECT was applied to the data presented by McDonald and Schwing [16]. In this case with $k = 15$, a total of 1465 subsets out of a possible $2^{15} = 32,768$ had to be evaluated in order to determine the best subset for $1 \leqslant s \leqslant 15$. Using the 26-variable data of LaMotte and Hocking [14] on the current version of SELECT, a total of 3545 subsets out of a possible $2^{26} = 67,108,864$ had to be evaluated to determine the best subset for $1 \leqslant s \leqslant 96$.

Of prime interest to the user is the cost of obtaining such information. Using the program in Section 6 on the UNIVAC 1108 at the University of Houston, the McDonald–Schwing data was analyzed in 16.6 seconds (CPU time) and the LaMotte–Hocking data required 3 minutes, 22.8 seconds (CPU time). Many problems of the order of $k = 10$ have been run in under 10 seconds. For example, the Gorman–Toman data required less than 7 seconds.

The exponential increase in computing time with k is readily apparent. For k much greater than 30, some careful preliminary analysis of the potential predictor variables is suggested. Also, it often happens that the size of the optimal subset is much greater than one; hence best subsets for small values of s could be suppressed.

9. REFERENCES

1. D. M. Allen, *The Prediction Sum of Squares as a Criterion for Selecting Prediction Variables*, Dept. of Statistics, Univ. of Kentucky, T. R. No. 23, 1971.

2. E. M. L. Beale, M. B. Kendall, and D. W. Mann, "The Discarding of Variables in Multivariate Analysis," *Biometrika*, **54**, 357–365 (1968).

3. C. Daniel and F. S. Wood, *Fitting Equations to Data*, Wiley, New York, 1971.

4. N. R. Draper, and H. Smith, *Applied Regression Analysis*, Wiley, New York, 1966.

5. G. M. Furnival, "All Possible Regressions with Less Computation," *Technometrics*, **13**, 403–408 (1971).

6. G. M. Furnival, *Regression by Leaps and Bounds*, Yale Forestry School, 1970.

7. M. J. Garside, "The Best Subset in Multiple Regression Analysis," *J. Roy. Statist. Soc., Ser. C*, **14**, 196–200 (1965).

8. J. W. Gorman and R. J. Toman, "Selection of Variables for Fitting Equations to Data," *Technometrics*, **8**, 27–51 (1966).

9. A. E. Hoerl and R. W. Kennard, "Ridge Regression: Biased Estimation for Non-Orthogonal Problems," *Technometrics*, **12**, 69–92 (1970).

10. R. R. Hocking, "Criteria for Selection of a Subset Regression: Which One Should Be Used," *Technometrics*, **14**, 967–970 (1972).

11. R. R. Hocking, and R. N. Leslie, "Selection of the Best Subset in Regression Analysis," *Technometrics*, **9**, 531–540 (1967).

12. R. W. Kennard, "A Note on the C_p-Statistic," *Technometrics*, **13**, 899 (1971).

13. L. R. LaMotte, "The SELECT Routines: A Program for Identifying Best Subset Regressions," *J. Roy. Statist. Soc., Ser. C*, **21**, 92–93 (1972).

14. L. R. LaMotte, and R. R. Hocking, "Computational Efficiency in the Selection of Regression Variables," *Technometrics*, **12**, 89–93 (1970).

15. C. L. Mallows, *Choosing a Subset Regression*, Presented at Joint Statistical Meetings, Los Angeles, California, 1966.

16. G. C. McDonald and R. C. Schwing, *Instabilities of Regression Estimates Relating Air Pollution to Mortality*, General Motors Corporation, Research Publication, GMR-1124, 1971.

17. M. Schatzoff, S. Feinberg, and R. Tsao, "Efficient Calculation of All Possible Regressions," *Technometrics*, **10**, 768–779 (1968).

Stepwise Regression

Robert I. Jennrich*

University of California (Los Angeles)

1. FUNCTION

Linear regression analysis is concerned with finding an approximate linear relation between a dependent variable y and one or more predictors, $x_1, \ldots, x_p$. This relation, called a regression function, has the form:

$$\hat{y} = b_0 + b_1 x_1 + \cdots + b_p x_p. \quad (1)$$

The regression coefficients $b_0, \ldots, b_p$ are chosen so that the residual $y - \hat{y}$ is as small as possible in the least squares sense (Chapter 3, Section 1). The computer and readily available regression programs have made it possible to consider many such approximate functional relations. Since early regression programs did little more than compute regression coefficients corresponding to a given dependent variable y and a preselected set of predictors $x_1, \ldots, x_p$, curiosity about the effect of adding or deleting predictors to the preselected set led to multiple executions of the programs in an attempt to add variables to improve prediction or remove variables to simplify the regression function. Stepwise regression pro-

vides a partial automation of this procedure. It is based on a technique which in the process of computing an ordinary multiple regression on p predictors, obtains, at essentially no additional expense, p intermediate regressions which may provide useful insights about functional relations between y and selected subsets of the total set of predictors. In the simplest case, the procedure moves step by step from one regression to the next, adding a predictor at each step. This produces a sequence of regression functions:

$$\hat{y} = b_0$$
$$\hat{y} = b_0 + b_1 x_1$$
$$\hat{y} = b_0 + b_1 x_1 + b_2 x_2 \quad (2)$$
$$\vdots$$
$$\hat{y} = b_0 + b_1 x_1 + \cdots + b_p x_p.$$

Rather than adding predictors in order, it is possible to steer the additions by statistically meaningful criteria. For example:

1. Add the predictor whose partial correlation with y, given the previously selected predictors, is maximum.

*This work was supported by the National Institutes of Health Grant RR-3.

2. Add the predictor that produces the greatest increase in the multiple correlation between y and the selected predictors.

3. Add the predictor that makes the greatest decrease in the residual sum of squares.

4. Add the predictor whose F-to-enter statistic has the largest value.

The F-to-enter statistic for a predictor is the F-statistic for testing the significance of the regression coefficient the predictor would have if it were added. All four of these criteria are mathematically equivalent and may be used interchangeably.

What has been described thus far is called forward stepping. Backward stepping produces a sequence of regression functions by starting with a complete regression on p predictors and removing one predictor at a time. Removal may be steered by criteria analogous to the four enumerated previously. Forward and backward stepping generally produce different intermediate regressions. It is helpful to understand why this is so.

One way it may happen is illustrated in Fig. 4.1. The figure displays a dependent variable y which is above the plane spanned by the predictors x_1 and x_3 but is not highly correlated with either. In particular, y has highest correlation with x_2 which is slightly below the plane. Forward stepping will enter x_2 first and then enter x_1 and x_3 in some order. Backward stepping, however, will re-move x_2 first because this will produce the smallest decrease in the multiple correlation of y with the remaining predictors and then remove x_1 and x_3 in some order. Thus the one and two variable regression functions contain x_2 when stepping forward but not when stepping backward. The situation illustrated in Fig. 4.1 may occur in practice when the dependent variable is an approximate linear function of the difference of two predictors each of which have modest correlation with the dependent variable.

In addition to pure forward and pure backward stepping, numerous modifications and hybrids exist ([5], Chapter 6). Step-inhibiting rules are often introduced. For example:

1. Do not remove a predictor if its F-to-remove value exceeds a specified threshold.

2. Do not enter a predictor if its F-to-enter value is below a specified threshold.

3. Do not enter a predictor if its tolerance value is below a specified threshold.

The F-to-remove value of an entered predictor is simply the value of the F-statistic used to test the significance of its regression coefficient. The tolerance of a non-entered predictor is one minus the square of the multiple correlation between the predictor and those predictors presently in the regression function. The tolerance threshold is intended to prevent the entry of highly correlated predictors and to avoid rounding error in the computations.

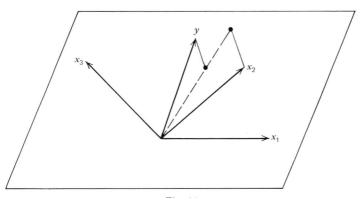

Fig. 4.1

The most common hybrid scheme, and the scheme presented here, proceeds as follows. Each step corresponds to the removal or entry of a predictor:

I. Remove the predictor that makes the least increase in the residual sum of squares from among all predictors whose removal is not inhibited by the F-to-remove inhibiting rule.

II. Enter the predictor that produces the greatest decrease in the residual sum of squares from among all predictors whose entry is not inhibited by the F-to-enter or tolerance inhibiting rules.

Rule II is executed only when it is not possible to execute Rule I. If neither can be executed, the stepping is complete.

2. MATHEMATICAL DISCUSSION

a. The Sweep Operator

It is a pleasant fact that many parameters in a great variety of statistical computations can be obtained by the application of a surprisingly simple operator called the *sweep operator* [1], [3, p. 62]. This is a special type of exchange operator similar to those used in linear programming, matrix inversion, and elsewhere. Let $\mathbf{A} = (a_{ij})$ be a square matrix whose kth diagonal element $a_{kk} \neq 0$. The result of sweeping $\mathbf{A}$ on its kth diagonal element is a new matrix $\tilde{\mathbf{A}} = (\tilde{a}_{ij})$ of the same size given by:

$$\tilde{a}_{kk} = -\frac{1}{a_{kk}}$$

$$\tilde{a}_{ik} = \frac{a_{ik}}{a_{kk}}$$

$$\tilde{a}_{kj} = \frac{a_{kj}}{a_{kk}} \qquad (3)$$

$$\tilde{a}_{ij} = a_{ij} - \frac{a_{ik}a_{kj}}{a_{kk}}$$

for $i \neq k$ and $j \neq k$. It is easy to see that a

sweep operation may be undone by means of an inverse sweep defined as follows:

$$\tilde{a}_{kk} = -\frac{1}{a_{kk}}$$

$$\tilde{a}_{ik} = -\frac{a_{ik}}{a_{kk}}$$

$$\hat{a}_{kj} = -\frac{a_{kj}}{a_{kk}} \qquad (4)$$

$$\tilde{a}_{ij} = a_{ij} - \frac{a_{ik}a_{kj}}{a_{kk}}$$

for $i \neq k$ and $j \neq k$.

In his account in Volume 1 of this series, Efroymson [2] used an exchange operator that differs from (3) in that it assigns the opposite sign to the right-hand members of the first and third equations. The advantage of the sweep operator is that it transforms symmetric matrices into symmetric matrices. This leads to savings in computation and storage.

It is useful to characterize the sweep operator as an exchange as follows:

THEOREM 1: *Let $\mathbf{U}$ and $\mathbf{V}$ be matrices of the same size and let $\mathbf{A}$ be a square matrix such that*

$$\mathbf{V} = \mathbf{U}\mathbf{A}$$

Let $\tilde{\mathbf{U}}$ be obtained from $\mathbf{U}$ by replacing its kth column by the kth column of $\mathbf{V}$ and let $\tilde{\mathbf{V}}$ be obtained from $\mathbf{V}$ by replacing its kth column by minus the kth column of $\mathbf{U}$. If the kth diagonal element of $\mathbf{A}$ is nonzero and $\tilde{\mathbf{A}}$ is the result of sweeping $\mathbf{A}$ on its kth diagonal element, then

$$\tilde{\mathbf{V}} = \tilde{\mathbf{U}}\tilde{\mathbf{A}}.$$

Proof: Let $u_1, \ldots, u_k$ and $v_1, \ldots, v_k$ denote the columns of U and V respectively. Then for all j,

$$v_j = \sum_i a_{ij}u_i.$$

Thus

$$\tilde{v}_k = -u_k = -a_{kk}^{-1}\left(v_k - \sum_{i \neq k} a_{ik}u_i\right)$$

$$= \tilde{a}_{kk}\tilde{u}_k + \sum_{i \neq k} \tilde{a}_{ik}\tilde{u}_i = \sum_i \tilde{a}_{ik}\tilde{u}_i.$$

Similarly for all $j \neq k$,

$$\tilde{v}_j = v_j = \sum_{i \neq k} a_{ij}u_i + a_{kj}a_{kk}^{-1}\left(v_k - \sum_{i \neq k} a_{ik}u_i\right)$$

$$= \sum_{i \neq k} \tilde{a}_{ij}\tilde{u}_i + \tilde{a}_{kj}\tilde{u}_k = \sum_i \tilde{a}_{ij}\tilde{u}_i.$$

Thus $\tilde{v}_j = \sum_i \tilde{a}_{ij}\tilde{u}_i$ for all j, which is the vector form of the assertion $\tilde{\mathbf{V}} = \tilde{\mathbf{U}}\tilde{\mathbf{A}}$. This completes the proof.

In tabloid form the characterization of a sweep on the first diagonal element of (a_{ij}) becomes:

$$
\begin{array}{c|ccc}
 & v_1 & \cdots & v_r \\
\hline
u_1 & a_{11} & \cdots & a_{1r} \\
\vdots & \vdots & & \vdots \\
u_r & a_{r1} & \cdots & a_{rr}
\end{array}
\longrightarrow
\begin{array}{c|ccc}
 & -u_1 & \cdots & v_r \\
\hline
v_1 & \tilde{a}_{11} & \cdots & \tilde{a}_{1r} \\
\vdots & \vdots & & \vdots \\
u_r & \tilde{a}_{r1} & \cdots & \tilde{a}_{rr}
\end{array}
$$

The coefficients in the body of the tables are used to express the vectors across the top as linear combinations of the vectors down the side. A sweep on a_{11} corresponds to changing the sign of u_1 and interchanging it with v_1. This characterization shows, incidentally, that the inverse of a sweep operator is equal to the cube of the operator.

The following theorem summarizes the consequences of a sequence of sweep operations.

Theorem 2: *If it is possible to sweep the partitioned matrix on the left below on each diagonal element of the square submatrix $\mathbf{A}_{11}$ in some order, i.e., if the required nonzero elements are encountered, then $\mathbf{A}_{11}$ is nonsin-* gular and the result of the sweeping is displayed on the right:

$$
\begin{pmatrix}
\mathbf{A}_{11} & \mathbf{A}_{12} \\
\mathbf{A}_{21} & \mathbf{A}_{22}
\end{pmatrix}
$$

$$
\longrightarrow
\begin{pmatrix}
-\mathbf{A}_{11}^{-1} & \mathbf{A}_{11}^{-1}\mathbf{A}_{12} \\
\mathbf{A}_{21}\mathbf{A}_{11}^{-1} & \mathbf{A}_{22} - \mathbf{A}_{21}\mathbf{A}_{11}^{-1}\mathbf{A}_{12}
\end{pmatrix}
\quad (5)
$$

Proof: Let $\mathbf{A}$ be the entire partitioned matrix and let $\mathbf{I}$ be an identity matrix of the same size. The trivial equality, $\mathbf{A} = \mathbf{IA}$, can be written in partitioned form as

$$
\begin{pmatrix}
\mathbf{A}_{11} & \mathbf{A}_{12} \\
\mathbf{A}_{21} & \mathbf{A}_{22}
\end{pmatrix}
=
\begin{pmatrix}
\mathbf{I}_{11} & \mathbf{O} \\
\mathbf{O} & \mathbf{I}_{22}
\end{pmatrix}
\begin{pmatrix}
\mathbf{A}_{11} & \mathbf{A}_{12} \\
\mathbf{A}_{21} & \mathbf{A}_{22}
\end{pmatrix}
$$

Let $\tilde{\mathbf{A}}$ be the result of the sweeping. Using the same partitioning as before, the characterization in Theorem 1 gives

$$
\begin{bmatrix}
-\mathbf{I}_{11} & \mathbf{A}_{12} \\
\mathbf{O} & \mathbf{A}_{22}
\end{bmatrix}
=
\begin{bmatrix}
\mathbf{A}_{11} & \mathbf{O} \\
\mathbf{A}_{21} & \mathbf{I}_{22}
\end{bmatrix}
\begin{bmatrix}
\tilde{\mathbf{A}}_{11} & \tilde{\mathbf{A}}_{12} \\
\tilde{\mathbf{A}}_{21} & \tilde{\mathbf{A}}_{22}
\end{bmatrix}
$$

which implies that

$$-\mathbf{I}_{11} = \mathbf{A}_{11}\tilde{\mathbf{A}}_{11} \qquad \mathbf{A}_{12} = \mathbf{A}_{11}\tilde{\mathbf{A}}_{12}$$

$$\mathbf{O} = \mathbf{A}_{21}\tilde{\mathbf{A}}_{11} + \tilde{\mathbf{A}}_{21} \quad \mathbf{A}_{22} = \mathbf{A}_{21}\tilde{\mathbf{A}}_{12} + \tilde{\mathbf{A}}_{22}.$$

It follows easily that

$$\tilde{\mathbf{A}}_{11} = -\mathbf{A}_{11}^{-1} \qquad \tilde{\mathbf{A}}_{12} = \mathbf{A}_{11}^{-1}\mathbf{A}_{12}$$

$$\tilde{\mathbf{A}}_{21} = \mathbf{A}_{21}\mathbf{A}_{11}^{-1} \qquad \tilde{\mathbf{A}}_{22} = \mathbf{A}_{22} - \mathbf{A}_{21}\mathbf{A}_{11}^{-1}\mathbf{A}_{12}$$

which proves the theorem.

The similarity between Theorem 2 and definition (3) should be noted. In effect the theorem asserts that one can carry out a sequence of sweeps simultaneously by a single application of (3) to the appropriate submatrices.

Theorem 2 also implies that if it is possible to sweep on a set of diagonal elements of a matrix $\mathbf{A}$ in more than one order, the result of the sweeping is independent of the order used. The following theorem will be used to guarantee that required sweep operations are defined.

THEOREM 3: *If $\mathbf{A}$ is a positive definite matrix, then its diagonal elements are nonzero and remain nonzero after any sequence of sweeps.*

Proof: The result of a sequence of sweeps is displayed on the right in (5). Since the entire partitioned matrix $\mathbf{A} = (\mathbf{A}_{ij})$ is positive definite, $\mathbf{A}_{11}^{-1}$ and $\mathbf{A}_{22} - \mathbf{A}_{21}\mathbf{A}_{11}^{-1}\mathbf{A}_{12}$ are positive definite also ([7], p. 137), and consequently, these two matrices and $\mathbf{A}$ have nonzero diagonal elements.

Theorem 3 guarantees that the required sweeps in Theorem 2 are defined, regardless of order, whenever $\mathbf{A}_{11}$ is positive definite. Conversely, if the entire partitioned matrix $(\mathbf{A}_{ij})$ is nonnegative definite and the required sweeps can be carried out, then $\mathbf{A}_{11}$ is positive definite. Moreover, $\mathbf{A}_{22} - \mathbf{A}_{21}\mathbf{A}_{11}^{-1}\mathbf{A}_{12}$ will be nonnegative definite ([7], p. 137). As a consequence, if $(\mathbf{A}_{ij})$ is nonnegative definite, a diagonal element of the matrix on the right in (5) will be negative, if and only if, a diagonal element in the same position has been used to define one of the sweeps.

b. Stepwise Regression

We turn now to using the sweep operator to carry out regression computations. Let x_{ti} denote the tth observation of variable x_i for $i = 1, \ldots, m$ and $t = 1, \ldots, n$. Let

$$\bar{x}_i = \frac{1}{n} \sum_{t=1}^{n} x_{ti}$$

denote the mean of variable x_i and let

$$a_{ij} = \sum_{t=1}^{n} \left(x_{ti} - \bar{x}_i \right)\left(x_{tj} - \bar{x}_j \right) \qquad (6)$$

denote the corrected sum of cross-products for x_i and x_j.

The matrix $\mathbf{A} = (a_{ij})$ is positive semidefinite and we will consider the result of sweeping $\mathbf{A}$ on diagonal elements with indices in a set S. Let $\tilde{\mathbf{A}} = (\tilde{a}_{ij})$ denote the result of the sweeping. We wish to interpret the components of $\tilde{\mathbf{A}}$ as statistical parameters. For simplicity of exposition assume that $S = \{1, \ldots, p\}$. The variables $x_1, \ldots, x_p$ will be viewed as independent variables that are in the regression function and the remainder, $x_{p+1}, \ldots, x_m$, as dependent variables. If $\mathbf{A}$ is partitioned as on the left in (10) below in such a way that $\mathbf{A}_{11}$ is p by p, then $\mathbf{A}_{11}$ is the corrected sum of cross-products matrix for the independent variables, $\mathbf{A}_{22}$ is the corrected sum of cross-products matrix for the dependent variables, $\mathbf{A}_{21}$ is the corrected sum of cross-products matrix for the independent variables with the dependent variables and $\mathbf{A}_{21}$ is the transpose of $\mathbf{A}_{12}$. When divided by $(n - 1)$ these matrices become the corresponding sample covariance matrices. The standard formulas of regression theory (e.g., [6, p. 108]) tell us that the matrix $\mathbf{B}$ of regression coefficients for the least squares regression $\hat{\mathbf{X}}_2 = \mathbf{X}_1\mathbf{B}$ of the dependent variables $\mathbf{X}_2 = [x_{p+1}, \ldots, x_m]$ on the independent variables $\mathbf{X}_1 = [x_1, \ldots, x_p]$ is given by

$$\mathbf{B} = \mathbf{A}_{11}^{-1}\mathbf{A}_{12}. \qquad (7)$$

Moreover, the matrix for the residual sums of cross-products for the dependent variables after regression on the independent variables is

$$\mathbf{A}_{22.1} = \mathbf{A}_{22} - \mathbf{A}_{21}\mathbf{A}_{11}^{-1}\mathbf{A}_{12}. \qquad (8)$$

If it is assumed that the observations on the kth dependent variable are statistically uncorrelated and have equal variance σ_k^2, then the p by p matrix of sampling variances for the p regression coefficients in the kth column b_k of B is

$$\mathrm{cov}(b_k) = \sigma_k^2 \mathbf{A}_{11}^{-1}. \qquad (9)$$

Now it follows from (7), (8), and Theorem 2 that when the matrix $\mathbf{A}$ is swept on the diagonal elements of $\mathbf{A}_{11}$ it becomes the matrix on the right below

$$
\begin{pmatrix} \mathbf{A}_{11} & \mathbf{A}_{12} \\ \mathbf{A}_{21} & \mathbf{A}_{22} \end{pmatrix} \rightarrow \begin{pmatrix} -\mathbf{A}_{11}^{-1} & \mathbf{B} \\ \mathbf{B} & \mathbf{A}_{22.1} \end{pmatrix}. \quad (10)
$$

That is, it consists of the regression coefficients $\mathbf{B}$ for the regression of all the dependent variables on all the independent variables, the residual cross-products $\mathbf{A}_{22.1}$ for the dependent variables after regression and, to within a scale factor which is a function of the dependent variable considered, the negative of the matrix $\mathbf{A}_{11}^{-1}$ of sampling variances and covariances for the regression coefficients corresponding to an arbitrary dependent variable. Thus the sweep operator, which takes 11 Fortran statements to program, computes essentially all of the building blocks of a standard regression analysis. Moreover, the whole procedure is automatically stepwise. A sweep of $\tilde{\mathbf{A}}$ on $\tilde{a}_{kk}$, $k \notin S$, will change the status of x_k from that of a dependent variable to that of a predictor. Similarly an inverse sweep of $\tilde{\mathbf{A}}$ on $\tilde{a}_{kk}$, $k \in S$, has the opposite effect.

We turn now to the problem of steering the stepping. One variable, say x_d, is the real dependent variable y. The computation proceeds by updating the matrix $\tilde{\mathbf{A}}$ which we will call the status matrix. The variables with indices in S are said to be in the regression function at a particular step. They correspond to the negative diagonal elements of $\tilde{\mathbf{A}}$. For a forward step, one seeks to add that variable x_k, $k \notin S$, which has a tolerance value at least as great as a specified tolerance threshold and which produces the greatest reduction in the residual sum of squares for x_d. Since this residual sum of squares is simply the current value of $\tilde{a}_{dd}$, the reduction (see (3)) that would result from entering x_k, that is, from sweeping $\tilde{\mathbf{A}}$

on $\tilde{a}_{kk}$, is

$$
V_k = \frac{\tilde{a}_{kd}^2}{\tilde{a}_{kk}}. \quad (11)
$$

Since the tolerance for the variable x_k is one minus its squared multiple correlation with the previously entered variables, it may be computed as the ratio of the residual sum of squares for x_k after fitting the entered variables to the original corrected sum of squares for x_k before any variables were entered, that is, as the ratio

$$
t_k = \frac{\tilde{a}_{kk}}{a_{kk}}. \quad (12)
$$

Using (11) and (12) it is a simple matter to locate the appropriate variable for entry. The variable is not entered, however, if its F-to-enter value

$$
F_k = \frac{(n - p - 2)V_k}{\tilde{a}_{dd} - V_k} \quad (13)
$$

is below the specified F-to-enter threshold. The aim of a backward step is to remove that variable x_k, $k \in S$, which makes the smallest increase

$$
-V_k = \frac{-\tilde{a}_{kd}^2}{\tilde{a}_{kk}} \quad (14)
$$

in the residual sum of squares. The variable is not removed if its F-to-remove value

$$
F_k = \frac{-(n - p - 1)V_k}{\tilde{a}_{dd}} \quad (15)
$$

is greater than the specified F-to-remove threshold.

c. Sums of Cross-Products

Like the regression itself, the sums of cross-products matrix may be computed stepwise. In this instance the stepping is case by case rather than variable by variable. The term case refers to a set of m corresponding observations $(x_{t1}, \ldots, x_{tm})$, that is, a row of the data matrix (x_{ti}). Case-by-case stepping provides a simple numerically accurate one-pass algorithm referred to as the method of provisional means. Let

$$\bar{x}_i^{(t)} = \frac{1}{t} \sum_{s=1}^{t} x_{si}$$

$$a_{ij}^{(t)} = \sum_{s=1}^{t} \left(x_{si} - \bar{x}_i^{(t)} \right)\left(x_{sj} - \bar{x}_j^{(t)} \right)$$

denote means and sums of cross-products computed from the first t cases. It is easy to verify that $\bar{x}_i^{(t)}$ and $a_{ij}^{(t)}$ may be stepped as follows:

$$\bar{x}_i^{(t+1)} = \frac{t\bar{x}_i^{(t)} + x_{t+1, i}}{t + 1}$$

$$a_{ij}^{(t+1)} = a_{ij}^{(t)} + \left(x_{t+1, i} - \bar{x}_i^{(t)} \right) \qquad (16)$$

$$\times \left(x_{t+1, i} - \bar{x}_j^{(t+1)} \right)$$

The stepping begins with $\bar{x}_i^{(0)} = a_{ij}^{(0)} = 0$ and ends with the means and sums of cross-products $\bar{x}_i^{(n)} = \bar{x}_i$ and $a_{ij}^{(n)} = a_{ij}$ for all n cases.

3. SUMMARY OF CALCULATION PROCEDURE

a. Symbols Used

m = Total number of variables

n = Number of cases

x_i = ith variable

x_{ti} = tth value of the ith variable

$\bar{x}_i$ = Mean of the ith variable

a_{ij} = Corrected sum of cross-products for variables x_i and x_j

$\tilde{a}_{ij}$ = Current status matrix value for variables x_i and x_j

d = Index of the dependent variable

$\tilde{a}_{dd}$ = Current value of the residual sum of squares for x_d

V_k = Decrease in $\tilde{a}_{dd}$ resulting from a sweep or inverse sweep on the kth diagonal element of $(\tilde{a}_{ij})$

p = Current number of variables in the regression function

b. Sums of Cross-Products

Reading the data one case at a time, the method of provisional means (Section 2c) is used to compute means $\bar{x}_i$ and sums of cross-products a_{ij}. Because the matrix (a_{ij}) is symmetric, it is sufficient to compute its upper triangular part. The values of $\bar{x}_i$ and a_{ij} begin at zero and are updated after reading each case. After reading the tth case $(x_{t1}, \ldots, x_{tm})$, the new values are:

$$\bar{x}_i^* = \frac{(t - 1)\bar{x}_i + x_{ti}}{t}$$

$$a_{ij}^* = a_{ij} + (x_{ti} - \bar{x}_i)(x_{tj} - \bar{x}_j^*) \qquad (17)$$

for $i = 1, \ldots, m$ and $j = i, \ldots, m$. Note that the last expression employs an old mean $\bar{x}_i$ and a new mean $\bar{x}_j^*$.

c. Development of the Regression Function

The stepwise development of the regression function and the corresponding output is dependent almost exclusively on the status matrix $(\tilde{a}_{ij})$. At the beginning of the first step the status matrix is the sums of cross-products matrix from the previous subsection. It is updated from step to step by means of the sweep operator. All steps, including the first, are formally identical. On any step a negative diagonal element $\tilde{a}_{ii}$ of the status matrix indicates that variable x_i is in the regression function.

Following Rules I and II of Section 1, a backward step is attempted first by seeking an index k such that $\tilde{a}_{kk} < 0$ and k maximizes the value of V_k as given by (11). If the corresponding F-to-remove value, given by (15), is below the F-to-remove threshold, variable x_k is removed from the regression function by means of an inverse sweep on the kth diagonal element of the status matrix $(\tilde{a}_{ij})$.

If it is not possible to execute a backward step, a forward step is attempted by seeking k to maximize V_k over all $k \neq d$ and such that the tolerance t_k of x_k given by (12) is at least as great as the tolerance threshold. If the corresponding F-to-enter value (13) is at least as great as the F-to-enter threshold, variable x_k is entered into the regression function by means of a forward sweep on the kth diagonal element of $(\tilde{a}_{ij})$.

If it is not possible to execute either a backward or a forward step, the stepping procedure terminates. Otherwise, the current step is completed by reporting a variety of output:

1. The residual degrees of freedom, sum of squares, and mean square:

$$df = n - p - 1, \qquad SS = \tilde{a}_{dd},$$

$$MS = \frac{SS}{df}.$$

2. The regression degrees of freedom, sum of squares, mean square, and F-value:

$$rdf = p, \qquad RSS = a_{dd} - \tilde{a}_{dd}$$

$$RMS = \frac{RSS}{p}, \qquad F = \frac{RMS}{MS}.$$

3. The residual standard deviation and the multiple correlation of the dependent variable with the entered variables:

$$s = \sqrt{MS}, \qquad R = \left(\frac{RSS}{a_{dd}} \right)^{1/2}.$$

4. The regression coefficient, standard error, and F-to-remove value for each variable x_i in the regression function:

$$b_i = \tilde{a}_{id}, \qquad s_i = (-\tilde{a}_{ii} MS)^{1/2},$$

$$F_i = \left(\frac{b_i}{s_i} \right)^2.$$

5. The regression intercept:

$$b_0 = \bar{x}_d - \sum_i^* b_i \bar{x}_i$$

where $\sum_i^*$ denotes summation over all i corresponding to variables x_i in the regression function.

6. The tolerance, partial correlation with the dependent variable, and F-to-enter value for each variable, x_i, $i \neq d$, which is not in the regression function:

$$t_i = \frac{\tilde{a}_{ii}}{a_{ii}}, \qquad R_i = \frac{\tilde{a}_{id}}{(\tilde{a}_{ii} \tilde{a}_{dd})^{1/2}},$$

$$F_i = \frac{(n - p - 2) R_i^2}{1 - R_i^2}.$$

d. Summary Output

After the stepping has terminated it may be summarized by giving a history of the variables entered and removed, their F-to-enter and remove values, their partial correlation with the dependent variable, changes in the residual sum of squares, and the multiple correlation with the dependent variable. In addition, predicted values and residuals,

$$\hat{y}_t = b_0 + \sum_i^* b_i (x_{ti} - \bar{x}_i)$$

$$\hat{e}_t = x_{td} - \hat{y}_t$$

may be printed and plotted against values of selected variables x_i.

4. FLOW CHART

The flow chart below describes a complete, though stripped down, stepwise regression program. It is essentially the core of BMD02R, a program in the BMD Biomedical Computer Programs Series [4]. The complete program which contains about 1500 Fortran statements is much too lengthy to describe in detail. Some of the things omitted include provisions for transforming the input data before analysis, provisions for reading parameters and allocating storage, the output of simple descriptive statistics such as means, standard deviations, and correlations, all detail on labeling and output formatting, the creation of a summary of the stepping procedure, provisions for forcing the entry of specified variables, provisions for plotting variables, residuals, and predicted values, and provisions for the execution of multiple problems.

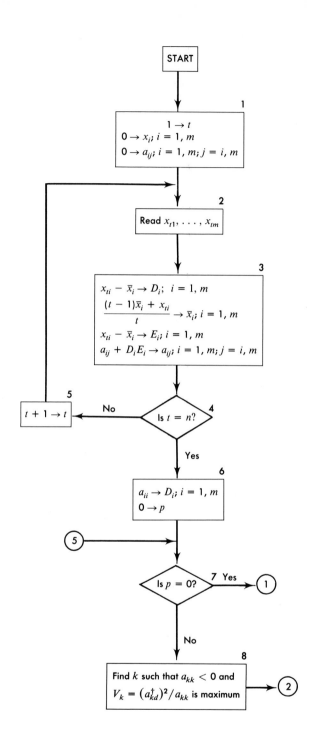

START

1
$$1 \to t$$
$$0 \to x_i; \ i = 1, m$$
$$0 \to a_{ij}; \ i = 1, m; j = i, m$$

2
Read $x_{t1}, \ldots, x_{tm}$

3
$$x_{ti} - \bar{x}_i \to D_i; \ i = 1, m$$
$$\frac{(t-1)\bar{x}_i + x_{ti}}{t} \to \bar{x}_i; \ i = 1, m$$
$$x_{ti} - \bar{x}_i \to E_i; \ i = 1, m$$
$$a_{ij} + D_i E_i \to a_{ij}; \ i = 1, m; j = i, m$$

4 Is $t = n$?

No

5 $t + 1 \to t$

Yes

6
$$a_{ii} \to D_i; \ i = 1, m$$
$$0 \to p$$

5

Is $p = 0$? **7** Yes → 1

No

8
Find k such that $a_{kk} < 0$ and
$V_k = (a_{kd}^{\dagger})^2 / a_{kk}$ is maximum → 2

66

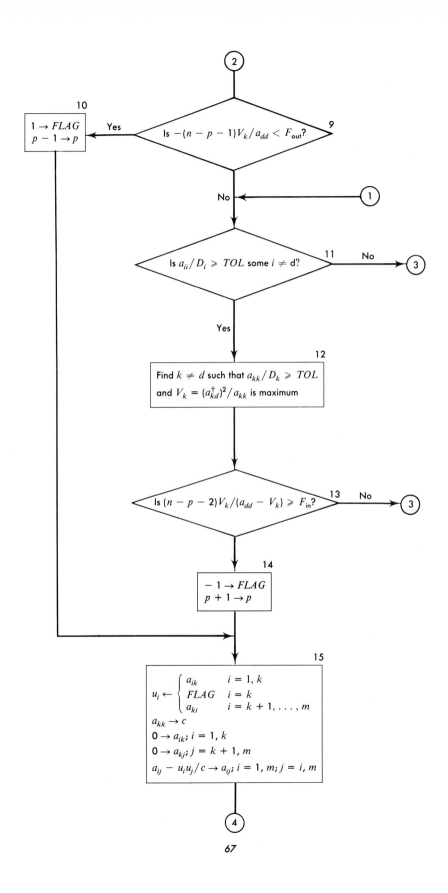

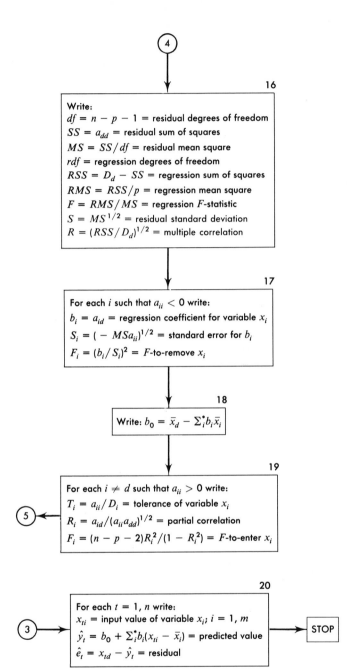

Write:
$df = n - p - 1$ = residual degrees of freedom
$SS = a_{dd}$ = residual sum of squares
$MS = SS/df$ = residual mean square
rdf = regression degrees of freedom
$RSS = D_d - SS$ = regression sum of squares
$RMS = RSS/p$ = regression mean square
$F = RMS/MS$ = regression F-statistic
$S = MS^{1/2}$ = residual standard deviation
$R = (RSS/D_d)^{1/2}$ = multiple correlation

For each i such that $a_{ii} < 0$ write:
$b_i = a_{id}$ = regression coefficient for variable x_i
$S_i = (-MSa_{ii})^{1/2}$ = standard error for b_i
$F_i = (b_i/S_i)^2$ = F-to-remove x_i

Write: $b_0 = \bar{x}_d - \Sigma_i^* b_i \bar{x}_i$

For each $i \neq d$ such that $a_{ii} > 0$ write:
$T_i = a_{ii}/D_i$ = tolerance of variable x_i
$R_i = a_{id}/(a_{ii}a_{dd})^{1/2}$ = partial correlation
$F_i = (n - p - 2)R_i^2/(1 - R_i^2)$ = F-to-enter x_i

For each $t = 1, n$ write:
x_{ti} = input value of variable x_i; $i = 1, m$
$\hat{y}_t = b_0 + \Sigma_i^* b_i(x_{ti} - \bar{x}_i)$ = predicted value
$\hat{e}_t = x_{td} - \hat{y}_t$ = residual

STOP

*Denotes sum over all i such that $a_{ii} < 0$.
†Indicates that $a_{kd}^{\dagger} = \begin{cases} a_{kd}, & k \leqslant d \\ a_{dk}, & k > d \end{cases}$.

5. DESCRIPTION OF THE FLOW CHART

Box 1: The case index t is set to one. The provisional means $\bar{x}_i$ and the provisional sums of cross-products a_{ij} are set to zero. Only the upper triangular part of (a_{ij}) is computed.

Box 2: The tth case $(x_{t1}, \ldots, x_{tm})$ is read. Since the data are needed only one case at a time, it is customary to keep the data in auxiliary storage. Except for the summary computations in Box 20, the data need be read only once.

Box 3: The provisional means $\bar{x}_i$ and sums of cross-products a_{ij} are stepped as described in Section 3b.

Box 4: If t is less than the number n of cases, a branch is made to read additional cases. Otherwise, the computation of the means $\bar{x}_i$ and sums of cross-products a_{ij} is complete and the program proceeds to the stepwise development of the regression function.

Box 5: The case number t is stepped in preparation for reading another case.

Box 6: The diagonal of the sums of cross-products matrix is stored for later use and the number of variables p in the regression function is set to zero.

Box 7: If $p = 0$, there are no variables in the regression function and control is passed to Box 11 where an attempt to enter a variable is initiated. Otherwise, control passes to Box 8 where an attempt to remove a variable is initiated.

Box 8: If $a_{kk} < 0$ then the kth variable is in the regression function and $V_k = a_{kd}^2 / a_{kk}$ is the negative of the increase in the residual sum of squares which would result from its removal. The index k of the variable whose removal would cause the least increase is found. Since the lower diagonal part of the matrix (a_{ij}) is not computed, lower diagonal values are obtained by symmetry from upper diagonal values.

Box 9: The value of the F-to-remove statistic for the variable k found in Box 8 is $-(n - q - 1)V_k / a_{dd}$. If this is less than the F-to-remove threshold F_{out}, control is passed to Box 10 where removal is initiated. Otherwise, it passes to Box 11 where an attempt to enter a new variable is begun.

Box 10: Setting $FLAG$ to 1 will produce an inverse sweep in Box 15 and the removal of the kth variable. In accordance, the variable count p is reduced by 1.

Box 11: If the ith variable is not in the regression function, then a_{ii} / D_i is its tolerance. If it is in the regression function this value is negative. If some value of a_{ii} / D_i other than that corresponding to the dependent variable is greater than or equal to the tolerance threshold TOL, control is passed to Box 12 where an attempt to enter a new variable is initiated. Otherwise, the stepping process is complete and control passes to Box 20.

Box 12: If $k \neq d$ and $a_{kk} / D_k \geq TOL$, then the kth variable is not in the regression function, is not the dependent variable, and satisfies the tolerance criterion for entry. Moreover, $V_k = a_{kd}^2 / a_{kk}$ is the reduction in the residual sum of squares which would result from its entry. The index k of the variable whose entry produces the greatest reduction in the residual sum of squares is found.

Box 13: The value of the F-to-enter statistic for the variable found in Box 12 is $(n - p - 2)V_k / (a_{dd} - V_k)$. If this value is greater than or equal to the F-to-enter threshold F_{in}, control passes to Box 14 where entry is initiated. Otherwise the stepping is complete and control passes to Box 20.

Box 14: Setting $FLAG$ to -1 will produce a forward sweep in Box 15 and the entry of the kth variable. In accordance, the number of variables in the regression function p is increased by 1.

Box 15: This box is an implementation of the sweep and inverse sweep operators given by (3) and (4) and modified so that only the upper triangular part of (a_{ij}) is used. A forward sweep is obtained when $FLAG = -1$ and an inverse sweep when $FLAG = 1$.

Box 16: This box is largely self-explanatory. It represents some of the statistical output which may be produced at each step. The regression F-statistic is that used for testing zero regression on all entered variables or, equivalently, zero multiple correlation with the entered variables.

Box 17: If $a_{ii} < 0$, then the ith variable is in the regression function. For each such variable, its regression coefficient, the standard error of its regression coefficient, and its F-to-remove are computed and reported.

Box 18: The regression coefficients obtained in Box 17 are used to compute the regression intercept b_0. The summation is over indices i corresponding to variables in the regression function.

Box 19: For each variable not in the regression function, its tolerance, partial correlation with the dependent variable given the entered variables, and F-to-enter values are computed and reported. At this point control is returned to Box 7 where an attempt to make another step is initiated.

Box 20: This box is executed at the conclusion of the stepping procedure. Predicted values $\hat{y}_t$ and residuals $\hat{e}_t$ are computed and written together with the input data. A summary table may also be given which includes a history of the variables entered and removed, their F-to-enter and remove values, changes in the residual sum of squares, and partial and multiple correlations with the dependent variable. The creation of such a table, however, requires recording the appropriate statistics as the stepping progresses.

6. THE PROGRAM

The Fortran code that follows is for three subroutines which implement the stepwise portions of the complete program described in the flow chart. The first, STPCRS, is used to compute means and sums of cross-products by the method of provisional means. It corresponds to Box 3 in the flow chart. The variables in its calling sequence are:

X Vector of data values for the Nth case
A Current value of the sums of cross products matrix
XB Current mean vector
M Number of variables
N Case number
U Scratch array

Starting with the values of A and XB for the first $N - 1$ cases, the subroutine updates A and XB to include the Nth case.

```
       SUBROUTINE STPCRS (X, A, XB, M, N, U)
       DIMENSION X(M), A(M, M), XB(M), U(M)
       DO 1 I = 1, M
       U(I) = X(I) − XB(I)
       XB(I) = ((N − 1)*XB(I) + X(I))/N
   1   X(I) = X(I) − XB(I)
       DO 2 I = 1, M
       DO 2 J = 1, M
   2   A(I, J) = A(I, J) + U(I)*X(J)
       RETURN
       END
```

The second subroutine, SELVAR, scans the status matrix to select a variable to enter or delete. It corresponds to Boxes 7 through 14 of the flow chart. The variables in its calling sequence are:

A Current status matrix
D Vector containing the corrected sum of squares for each variable
M Number of variables
N Number of cases
NP Number of variables in the regression function
TOL Tolerance threshold
FIN F-to-enter threshold
$FOUT$ F-to-remove threshold
ID Index of the dependent variable
$FLAG$ 1 to remove, -1 to enter, 0 to stop
K Index of variable to enter or remove

$FLAG$ and K are the only calling sequence variables modified by the subroutine.

```
      SUBROUTINE SELVAR (A, D, M, N, NP, TOL, FIN, FOUT, ID, FLAG, K)
      DIMENSION A(M, M), D(M)
      VN = -FOUT*A(ID, ID)
      VP = 0.0
      DO 1 I = 1, M
      IF (I.EQ.ID) GO TO 1
      IF (A(I, I).EQ.0.0) GO TO 1
      V = A(MIN0(I, ID), MAX0(I, ID))**2/A(I, I)
      IF (V.LE.VN) GO TO 1
      IF (V.LT.0.0) GO TO 2
      IF (V.LE.VP) GO TO 1
      IF (A(I, I)/D(I).LT.TOL) GO TO 1
      VP = V
      KP = I
      GO TO 1
2     VN = V
      KN = I
1     CONTINUE
      FLAG = 0.0
      IF ((N - NP - 2)*VP.GE.FIN*(A(ID, ID) - VP)) FLAG = -1.0
      IF (-(N - NP - 1)*VN.LT.FOUT*A(ID, ID)) FLAG = 1.0
      K = KP
      IF (FLAG.EQ.1.0) K = KN
      RETURN
      END
```

The final subroutine implements the sweep operator as described in Box 15. The calling sequence variables are:

A	Square matrix to be swept
M	Order of *A*
K	Index of the pivot element
FLAG	− 1 for sweep, 1 for inverse sweep
U	Scratch vector

The subroutine works with and modifies only the upper triangular part of *A*.

```
      SUBROUTINE SWP (A, M, K, FLAG, U)
      DIMENSION A(M, M), U(M)
      C = A(K, K)
      DO 1 I = 1, K
      U(I) = A(I, K)
1     A(I, K) = 0.0
      DO 2 I = K, M
      U(I) = A(K, I)
2     A(K, I) = 0.0
      U(K) = FLAG
      DO 3 I = 1, M
      DO 3 J = I, M
3     A(I, J) = A(I, J) - U(I)*U(J)/C
      RETURN
      END
```

7. SAMPLE PROBLEM

The output that follows was obtained from an execution of BMD02R. This program is available at about 500 computing facilities and is probably the most widely used stepwise regression program. Its coding follows that described here except that it contains numerous additional options. The write-up for BMD02R appears in [4] and Fortran source code may be obtained by writing: The Program Librarian, Health Sciences Computing Facility, University of California, Los Angeles, California 90024.

```
PROBLEM CODE                    TSTC2R
NUMBER OF CASES                    68
NUMBER OF ORIGINAL VARIABLES       6
NUMBER OF VARIABLES ADDED          0
TOTAL NUMBER OF VARIABLES          6
NUMBER OF SUB-PROBLEMS             1
THE VARIABLE FORMAT IS   (F6.2,F6.0,2F6.2,2F6.0)
```

VARIABLE		MEAN	STANDARD DEVIATION
AGE	1	6.99558	6.47375
WEIGHT	2	15.25000	9.35750
	3	10.42512	11.62698
HEIGHT	4	3.09955	5.99713
STATUS	5	25.39705	12.47935
	6	56.79411	43.54991

COVARIANCE MATRIX

VARIABLE NUMBER	1	2	3	4	5	6
1	41.909	-10.690	0.387	9.919	-15.809	23.134
2		87.563	94.437	5.652	102.660	305.484
3			135.187	8.776	109.104	398.026
4				35.966	-10.510	89.470
5					155.734	350.634
6						1896.595

CORRELATION MATRIX

VARIABLE NUMBER	1	2	3	4	5	6
1	1.000	-0.176	0.005	0.255	-0.196	0.082
2		1.000	0.868	0.101	0.879	0.750
3			1.000	0.126	0.752	0.786
4				1.000	-0.140	0.343
5					1.000	0.645
6						1.000

```
SUB-PROBLM     1
DEPENDENT VARIABLE            6
MAXIMUM NUMBER OF STEPS       6
F-LEVEL FOR INCLUSION    0.500000
F-LEVEL FOR DELETION     0.300000
TOLERANCE LEVEL          0.001000
```

```
STEP NUMBER    1
VARIABLE ENTERED    3

MULTIPLE R           0.7861
STD. ERROR OF EST.  27.1234
```

ANALYSIS OF VARIANCE

	DF	SUM OF SQUARES	MEAN SQUARE	F RATIO
REGRESSION	1	78517.063	78517.063	106.728
RESIDUAL	66	48554.734	735.678	

VARIABLES IN EQUATION					VARIABLES NOT IN EQUATION			
VARIABLE	COEFFICIENT	STD. ERROR	F TO REMOVE		VARIABLE	PARTIAL CORR.	TOLERANCE	F TO ENTER
(CONSTANT	26.09973)							
3	2.94427	0.28500	106.7276 (2)		AGE 1	0.12622	1.0000	1.0523 (2)
					WEIGHT 2	0.21933	0.2466	3.2847 (2)
					HEIGHT 4	0.39729	0.9842	12.1823 (2)
					STATUS 5	0.13276	0.4346	1.1662 (2)

```
STEP NUMBER    2
VARIABLE ENTERED    4

MULTIPLE R           0.8235
STD. ERROR OF EST.  25.0817
```

ANALYSIS OF VARIANCE

	DF	SUM OF SQUARES	MEAN SQUARE	F RATIO
REGRESSION	2	86180.875	43090.438	68.496
RESIDUAL	65	40890.934	629.091	

VARIABLES IN EQUATION					VARIABLES NOT IN EQUATION			
VARIABLE	COEFFICIENT	STD. ERROR	F TO REMOVE		VARIABLE	PARTIAL CORR.	TOLERANCE	F TO ENTER
(CONSTANT	21.74443)							
3	2.82756	0.26566	113.2883 (2)		AGE 1	0.02724	0.9340	0.0475 (2)
HEIGHT 4	1.79767	0.51504	12.1823 (2)		WEIGHT 2	0.24653	0.2465	4.1414 (2)
					STATUS 5	0.32179	0.3784	7.3926 (2)

```
STEP NUMBER    3
VARIABLE ENTERED    5

MULTIPLE R              0.8435
STD. ERROR OF EST.    23.9324

ANALYSIS OF VARIANCE
                    DF     SUM OF SQUARES    MEAN SQUARE     F RATIO
    REGRESSION       3         90415.063     30138.352      52.619
    RESIDUAL        64         36656.719       572.761
```

	VARIABLES IN EQUATION				VARIABLES NOT IN EQUATION		
VARIABLE	COEFFICIENT	STD. ERROR	F TO REMOVE		VARIABLE	PARTIAL CORR.	TOLERANCE	F TO ENTER
(CONSTANT	2.91C84)							
3	1.95842	0.40797	23.0441 (2)		AGE 1	0.11112	0.8832	0.7876 (2)
HEIGHT 4	2.31237	0.52664	19.2789 (2)		WEIGHT 2	0.01574	0.1134	0.0156 (2)
STATUS 5	1.03552	0.38C85	7.3926 (2)					

```
STEP NUMBER    4
VARIABLE ENTERED    1

MULTIPLE R              0.8456
STD. ERROR OF EST.    23.9722

ANALYSIS OF VARIANCE
                    DF     SUM OF SQUARES    MEAN SQUARE     F RATIO
    REGRESSION       4         90867.625     22716.906      39.530
    RESIDUAL        63         362C4.129       574.669
```

	VARIABLES IN EQUATION				VARIABLES NOT IN EQUATION		
VARIABLE	COEFFICIENT	STD. ERROR	F TO REMOVE		VARIABLE	PARTIAL CORR.	TOLERANCE	F TO ENTER
(CONSTANT	-1.25267)							
AGE 1	0.4272C	0.48139	0.7876 (2)		WEIGHT 2	0.05241	0.1029	0.1708 (2)
3	1.89679	0.41451	20.9399 (2)					
HEIGHT 4	2.23333	0.53499	17.4269 (2)					
STATUS 5	1.11673	0.39231	8.1028 (2)					

F-LEVEL OR TOLERANCE INSUFFICIENT FOR FURTHER COMPUTATION

SUMMARY TABLE

STEP NUMBER	VARIABLE ENTERED	REMOVED	MULTIPLE R	RSQ	INCREASE IN RSQ	F VALUE TO ENTER OR REMOVE	NUMBER OF INDEPENDENT VARIABLES INCLUDED
1	3		0.7861	0.6179	0.6179	106.7276	1
2	HEIGHT	4	0.8235	0.6782	0.0603	12.1823	2
3	STATUS	5	0.8435	0.7115	0.0333	7.3926	3
4	AGE	1	0.8456	0.7151	0.0036	0.7876	4

LIST OF RESIDUALS

CASE NUMBER	Y X(6)	Y COMPUTED	RESIDUAL	X(3)	X(4)	X(5)	X(1)
1	64.0000	88.5539	-24.5539	25.0000	1.5000	34.0000	2.5000
2	65.0000	86.2788	-21.2788	21.0000	0.8700	36.0000	13.0000
3	82.0000	88.7182	-6.7182	22.0000	0.4300	41.0000	3.5000
4	23.0000	22.7317	0.2683	1.3000	1.8000	15.0000	1.7500
5	64.0000	84.9738	-20.9738	23.0000	2.0000	33.0000	3.0000
6	16.0000	22.6273	-6.6273	0.6000	3.3000	13.0000	2.0000
7	12.0000	29.2135	-17.2135	1.4000	3.4000	16.0000	5.5000
8	27.0000	26.2787	0.7213	0.8000	5.0000	11.0000	6.0000
9	48.0000	28.9919	19.0081	2.7000	1.5000	19.0000	1.3000
10	50.0000	41.8835	8.1165	3.6000	1.8000	27.0000	5.0000
11	12.0000	21.5410	-9.5410	1.0000	1.4030	14.0000	5.0C00
12	13.0000	35.3018	-22.3018	2.7000	1.0000	25.0000	3.0C00
13	20.0000	32.C934	-12.0934	3.0000	1.5000	21.0000	2.0C00
14	23.0000	27.1830	-4.1830	1.0000	2.5000	18.0000	2.0C00
15	118.0000	94.7301	23.2699	22.0000	1.1000	46.0000	1.0C00
16	50.0000	50.3521	-0.3521	13.0000	2.8000	17.0000	4.0C00
17	63.0000	56.4705	6.5295	1.2000	0.7300	48.0000	0.5C00
18	150.0000	82.9059	67.0941	23.0000	0.1000	36.0000	0.2500
19	72.0000	20.0253	51.9747	1.0000	3.5000	5.0000	14.0000
20	54.0000	42.0347	11.9653	2.5000	0.2800	33.0000	2.5000
21	109.0000	78.1895	30.8105	14.0000	0.0100	46.0000	3.5000
22	10.0000	23.7146	-13.7146	0.6000	5.0000	10.0000	3.5000
23	125.0000	121.3686	3.6314	35.0000	5.7000	38.0000	2.5000
24	44.0000	28.2155	15.7845	2.0000	3.4000	16.0000	0.5000
25	48.0000	43.9177	4.0823	11.0000	0.5000	20.0000	5.0000
26	105.0000	119.6107	-14.6107	32.0000	6.6000	38.0000	7.0C00
27	9.0000	25.8037	-16.8037	1.0000	4.5000	12.0000	4.0C00
28	130.0000	103.8363	26.1637	23.0000	0.1500	49.0000	15.0C00
57	103.0000	53.1120	49.8880	8.0000	1.0000	22.0000	29.0C00
58	106.0000	89.9316	16.0684	24.0000	1.1000	38.0000	1.8C00
59	63.0000	99.8499	-36.8499	26.0000	1.7000	38.0000	13.0C00
60	208.0000	201.4559	6.5441	29.0000	48.0000	29.0000	19.0000
61	32.0000	67.1835	-35.1835	17.0000	1.6000	25.0000	11.0000
62	28.0000	41.5378	-13.5378	5.0000	3.5000	19.0000	10.0C00
63	32.0000	42.0628	-10.0628	5.0000	1.2000	26.0000	6.0C00
64	100.0000	88.8452	11.1548	22.0000	1.2000	39.0000	5.0C00
65	50.0000	42.8303	7.1697	5.0000	0.8000	29.0000	1.0C00
66	80.0000	51.9007	28.0993	3.0000	13.0000	10.0000	17.0C00
67	65.0000	134.0513	-69.0513	35.0000	0.9000	58.0000	5.0C00
68	25.C000	33.0357	-8.0357	1.3000	9.0000	10.0000	1.3C00

                                      73
```
```

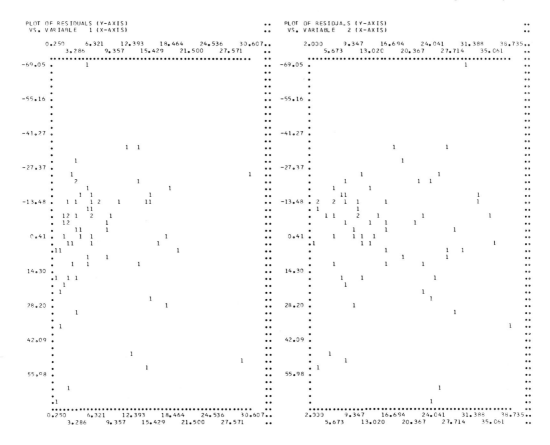

The first paragraph of the sample output identifies, among other things, the number of cases $n = 68$ and the total number of variables $m = 6$. The next three paragraphs give means, standard deviations, covariances, and correlations. The paragraph which follows these identifies the dependent variable $y = x_6$ together with threshold levels for F-to-enter, F-to-remove, and tolerance. All three thresholds are set fairly low. This is common practice on an early run because it allows the execution of a large number of steps. The specified tolerance threshold .001 corresponds to a squared multiple correlation of .999.

On step 1 variable x_3 entered the regression function. Scanning the correlation table reveals that x_3 has the highest correlation with the dependent variable and so should be the first to enter. The output at each step

includes the multiple correlation, the residual standard deviation, regression and residual sums of squares, mean squares, and an F-statistic. In addition, the left half of the page gives a regression coefficient, its standard error, and F-to-remove value for each variable in the regression function while the right half gives a partial correlation, tolerance, and F-to-enter value for each variable (except the dependent variable) not in the regression function. These are as described in Sections 3–5. The "2" in parentheses following each F-value is associated with the forced entry option in BMD02R. They indicate that no variable is being forced to enter.

Variables x_4, x_5, and x_1 are entered on the next three steps. After this the stepping ends with the message "F-level or tolerance insufficient for further computation." The only remaining variable, x_2, is not entered because its F-to-enter value 0.1708 falls below the F-to-enter threshold 0.5000.

The output concludes with a summary table, a list of residuals, and plots of residuals against variables x_1 and x_2.

8. ESTIMATED RUNNING TIME

The number of operations (additions, subtractions, multiplications, and divisions) required for each part of the computation are approximately:

$m(m + 6)n$ for sums of cross-products,

$\frac{3}{2} m^2(m + 1)$ for stepping,

$2mn$ for predicted values.

In most applications, the sums of cross-products require by far the greatest computational effort. Thus careful optimization of the other more difficult parts of the program is unnecessary. The computer time required to execute BMD02R on a typical 30-variable 100-case problem using an IBM 360/91 was 2 seconds which at the author's shop cost 44 cents.

9. REFERENCES

1. A. E. Beaton, *The Use of Special Matrix Operators in Statistical Calculus*, Ed.D thesis, Harvard University, Reprinted as Educational Testing Service Res. Bull. 64-51, Princeton, N.J., 1964.

2. M. A. Efroymson, "Multiple Regression analysis," in *Mathematical Methods for Digital Computers*, A. Ralston and H. S. Wilf (eds.) Ch. 17, Wiley, New York, 1960.

3. A. P. Dempster, *Elements of Continuous Multivariate Analysis*, Addison-Wesley, Reading, Mass., 1969.

4. W. J. Dixon (ed.), *BMD Biomedical Computer Programs*, University of California Press, Berkeley, Calif., 1970.

5. N. R. Draper and H. Smith, *Applied Regression Analysis*, Wiley, New York, 1966.

6. D. F. Morrison, *Multivariate Statistical Methods*, McGraw-Hill, New York, 1967.

7. S. N. Roy, *Some Aspects of Multivariate Analysis*, Wiley, New York, 1957.

Stepwise Discriminant Analysis

5

Robert I. Jennrich*
University of California (Los Angeles)

1. FUNCTION

Given a set of classification variables $x_1, \ldots, x_p$ defined over two or more groups, the basic purpose of linear discriminant analysis is to find linear discriminant functions

$$d = a + b_1 x_1 + \cdots + b_p x_p \qquad (1)$$

to be used for classifying cases into groups. In the case of two groups it is desirable to find a function d whose values over the two groups are as separated as possible (see Fig. 5.1). Following Fisher [3], this may be made precise by demanding that d have a maximum ratio

$$R(d) = \frac{T(d)}{W(d)} \qquad (2)$$

of total (T) to within group (W) sums of squares. Such a function d has the property that any other discriminant function which has zero within group correlation with d has zero separation power in the sense that it must have the same mean in each group.

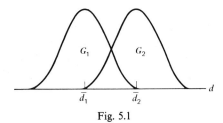

Fig. 5.1

This property may be used to generalize to the multigroup case. Given an arbitrary number of groups, a set of discriminant functions $d_1, \ldots, d_r$ is complete if every discriminant function d which has zero within group correlation with $d_1, \ldots, d_r$ has the same mean in each group. This is a precise way of saying that all the classification information in $x_1, \ldots, x_p$ is contained in $d_1, \ldots, d_r$.**

It is helpful to identify some specific complete sets. A sequence $d_1, \ldots, d_r$ of nonzero discriminant functions which have zero within group correlations is called a canonical sequence if

$$R(d_i) = \max_{d \in Z_i} R(d); \qquad i = 1, \ldots, r \quad (3)$$

*This work was supported by the National Institutes of Health Grant RR-3.

**For a discussion of alternate methods of discriminant analysis see Chapter 6, Section 2 of this volume.

where Z_i denotes the set of all discriminant functions having zero within group correlation with $d_1, \ldots, d_{i-1}$. If there are q groups, we will show that any canonical sequence of length $q - 1$ is complete.

Later a group classification function d_g will be introduced for each group g. A case will be classified into that group g for which the value of d_g is largest. We shall see that these functions $d_1, \ldots, d_q$ form another complete set. Moreover, for each g and h the difference

$$d_{gh} = d_g - d_h \qquad (4)$$

defines a hyperplane which separates group g from group h. All $q(q - 1)/2$ such differences form a third complete set. A good deal of confusion arises from the fact that all three types of discriminant functions are in common use and are referred to simply as discriminant functions. To avoid confusion we shall refer to them as canonical, group classification, and group separation functions, respectively, and use the term discriminant function to refer to an arbitrary linear function of the classification variables of the form given in (1).

We are concerned here with stepwise discriminant analysis. As in the case of stepwise regression, the set of classification variables to be used in the final analysis is often not known in advance and even when it is, useful insights can be obtained by looking at analyses based on subsets of classification variables. A stepwise discriminant analysis is a sequence of simple analyses that moves from one analysis to the next by adding, and sometimes deleting, a classification variable at each step.

The most commonly used method of selecting variables to be entered or deleted is based on the ratio of the within generalized dispersion to the total generalized dispersion for the selected variables. The within generalized dispersion is simply the determinant of the within groups cross-product matrix $W(\mathbf{x})$ for the variables $\mathbf{x} =$ $(x_1, \ldots, x_p)$ in the analysis and, similarly, the total generalized dispersion is the determinant of the total cross-product matrix $T(\mathbf{x})$ for these variables. This ratio

$$\Lambda(\mathbf{x}) = \frac{\det W(\mathbf{x})}{\det T(\mathbf{x})} \qquad (5)$$

is called Wilks' Λ-criterion. It has values between zero and one. Large values indicate poor separation between groups while small values indicate good separation between (at least some) groups. In the case of a single variable, Wilks' Λ is simply the reciprocal of $R(x)$. As such it may be viewed as a generalization of Fisher's ratio.

The multiplicative increment

$$\Lambda(u \cdot \mathbf{x}) = \frac{\Lambda((\mathbf{x}, u))}{\Lambda(\mathbf{x})} \qquad (6)$$

in $\Lambda(\mathbf{x})$ resulting from adding a variable u to the set $\mathbf{x} = (x_1, \ldots, x_p)$ is called a partial Λ-statistic. The corresponding F-statistic ([6], p. 470)

$$F = \frac{n - q - p}{q - 1} \cdot \frac{1 - \Lambda(u \cdot \mathbf{x})}{\Lambda(u \cdot \mathbf{x})} \qquad (7)$$

is used to test the significance of the change in $\Lambda(\mathbf{x})$ resulting from the addition of u. It will be used here to guide the selection of variables. The F-statistic in (7) is called either the F-to-enter statistic for the entry of u into the set $\mathbf{x} = (x_1, \ldots, x_p)$ or the F-to-remove statistic for the deletion of u from the set $(x_1, \ldots, x_p, u)$.

As in stepwise regression (See Chapter 4, Section 1) a number of entry and deletion inhibiting rules are employed:

a. Do not remove a variable if its F-to-remove value is greater than or equal to a specified threshold.

b. Do not enter a variable if its F-to-enter value is below a specified threshold.

c. Do not enter a variable if its tolerance value is below a specified threshold.

Tolerance for the entry of a classification variable is one minus the square of its within group multiple correlation with the currently entered variables.

The stepping process considered here proceeds as follows:

1. Remove the variable with the smallest F-to-remove value unless this value is greater than or equal to the F-to-remove threshold.

2. If it is not possible to remove a variable, find the variable with the largest F-to-enter value among all variables whose tolerance is greater than or equal to the tolerance threshold. Enter this variable unless its F-to-enter value is below the F-to-enter threshold.

3. If it is not possible to remove or enter a variable the stepping is complete.

2. MATHEMATICAL DISCUSSION

a. Symbols Used

m	Total number of variables
q	Number of groups
n	Total number of cases
n_g	Number of cases in group g
x_i	ith variable
x_{gti}	Value of the ith variable for the tth case in the gth group
$\bar{x}_{gi}$	Mean of the ith variable over the gth group
$\bar{x}_i$	Overall mean of the ith variable
$T(u, v)$	Total sum of cross-products for variables u and v
$W(u, v)$	Within group sum of cross-products for u and v
t_{ij}	$T(x_i, x_j)$
w_{ij}	$W(x_i, x_j)$
$\tilde{t}_{ij}$	Element in the total status matrix
$\tilde{w}_{ij}$	Element in the within status matrix
p	Number of variables currently in the analysis
V_k	Multiplicative increment in Wilks' Λ resulting from the entry or deletion of x_k

The W and T products are defined as follows. Given two arbitrary variables u and v defined over the q groups let:

$$W(u, v) = \sum_{g=1}^{q} \sum_{t=1}^{n_g} \left(u_{gt} - \bar{u}_g \right)\left(v_{gt} - \bar{v}_g \right)$$

$$\tag{8}$$

$$T(u, v) = \sum_{g=1}^{q} \sum_{t=1}^{n_g} \left(u_{gt} - \bar{u} \right)\left(v_{gt} - \bar{v} \right).$$

These are the usual within group and total sums of cross-products for u and v. Generalizing the W and T notation, let $\mathbf{u} = (u_1, \ldots, u_r)$ and $\mathbf{v} = (v_1, \ldots, v_s)$ be sequences of variables and let $W(\mathbf{u}, \mathbf{v})$ and $T(\mathbf{u}, \mathbf{v})$ be the matrices whose ijth elements are $W(u_i, v_j)$ and $T(u_i, v_j)$, respectively. Finally, let $W(\mathbf{u})$ and $T(\mathbf{u})$ be abbreviated notation for $W(\mathbf{u}, \mathbf{u})$ and $T(\mathbf{u}, \mathbf{u})$.

b. Variable Selection

As in stepwise regression, the sweep operator is used to control variable selection. The required properties of this operator are discussed in Chapter 4, Section 2. Two current status matrices are used, the within current status matrix ($\tilde{w}_{ij}$) and the total current status matrix ($\tilde{t}_{ij}$). The initial values of these matrices are the within sums-of-cross-products matrix (w_{ij}) and the total sums-of-cross-products matrix (t_{ij}).

Let $\mathbf{x} = (x_{i_1}, \ldots, x_{i_p})$ denote the classification variables which are currently in the discriminant analysis. Then ($\tilde{w}_{ij}$) and ($\tilde{t}_{ij}$) are the results of sweeping (w_{ij}) and (t_{ij}) on diagonal elements whose indices are in the index set $S = \{i_1, \ldots, i_p\}$. It follows from Theorem 2 of Chapter 4, Section 2 and the identity

$$det\ \mathbf{A} = det(\mathbf{A}_{11})\ det\left(\mathbf{A}_{22} - \mathbf{A}_{21}\mathbf{A}_{11}^{-1}\mathbf{A}_{12} \right)$$

for partitioned matrices ([4], p. 66) that if $j \notin S$, then

$$det\ W\left((\mathbf{x}, x_j) \right) = det\left(W(\mathbf{x}) \right)\tilde{w}_{jj}$$

$$det\ T\left((\mathbf{x}, x_j) \right) = det\left(T(\mathbf{x}) \right)\tilde{t}_{jj}.$$

Thus using (5) and (6),

$$\Lambda(x_j \cdot \mathbf{x}) = \frac{\tilde{w}_{jj}}{\tilde{t}_{jj}} \qquad (9)$$

gives the partial Λ-statistic for the entry of x_j, $j \notin S$. Because the effect of an inverse sweep on a diagonal element is to invert the element and change its sign, the partial Λ-statistic for removing a variable x_i, $i \in S$, is

$$\Lambda(x_i \cdot \mathbf{x}') = \frac{\tilde{t}_{ii}}{\tilde{w}_{ii}}$$

where $\mathbf{x}'$ is obtained from $\mathbf{x}$ by deleting x_i. Let

$$V_k = \frac{\tilde{w}_{kk}}{\tilde{t}_{kk}}; \qquad k = 1, \ldots, m \qquad (10)$$

Then V_j is the partial Λ for the entry of x_j and V_i^{-1} is the partial Λ for the removal of x_i.

The corresponding F-to-enter and F-to-delete statistics are:

$$F_j = \frac{n - p - q}{q - 1} \cdot \frac{1 - V_j}{V_j} \qquad (11)$$

for entry and

$$F_i = \frac{n - p - q + 1}{q - 1} (V_i - 1) \qquad (12)$$

for deletion. If $\mathbf{x}'$ is obtained from $\mathbf{x}$ by adding or removing a variable x_k, then

$$\Lambda(\mathbf{x}') = \Lambda(\mathbf{x})V_k. \qquad (13)$$

Finally, it follows from (12) of Chapter 4, that the within group tolerance for a variable x_j not in $\mathbf{x}$ is

$$t_j = \frac{\tilde{w}_{jj}}{w_{jj}}. \qquad (14)$$

The stepwise entry and removal of variables under the rules described in Section 1 may be carried out through the use of (11), (12), and (14). On each step the status matrices $(\tilde{w}_{ij})$ and $(\tilde{t}_{ij})$ are updated by sweeps on diagonal elements corresponding to the variable entered or removed.

c. Classification

We will be concerned here with finding discriminant functions, one for each group, which are particularly convenient for the purpose of classifying cases into groups. We call these group classification functions. Canonical discriminant functions discussed in the next section will be used mainly for the graphical display of results. Let

$$\bar{x}^{(g)} = \left(\bar{x}_{gi_1}, \ldots, \bar{x}_{gi_p} \right)$$

$$\bar{x} = \left(\bar{x}_{i_1}, \ldots, \bar{x}_{i_p} \right) \qquad (15)$$

be the gth group and overall mean vectors for the selected classification variables $\mathbf{x} = (x_{i_1}, \ldots, x_{i_p})$ and let $\hat{\Sigma} = (n - q)^{-1}W(\mathbf{x})$ denote the usual pooled within sample covariance matrix for the selected variables. Then

$$d_g(\mathbf{x}) = \left(\mathbf{x} - \tfrac{1}{2} \bar{x}^{(g)} \right) \hat{\Sigma}^{-1} \bar{x}^{(g)T} \qquad (16)$$

defines the group classification function for group g based on the selected classification variables.

THEOREM 1: *The functions $d_1, \ldots, d_q$ given in (16) are a complete set of discriminant functions.*

Proof: Let $d(\mathbf{x}) = a + \mathbf{x}b$ be any discriminant function that has zero within group correlation with $d_1, \ldots, d_q$. This together with (16) implies that

$$0 = (n - q)^{-1}W(d_g, d)$$

$$= (n - q)^{-1}W\left(\mathbf{x}\hat{\Sigma}^{-1}\bar{x}^{(g)T}, \mathbf{x}b \right)$$

$$= \bar{x}^{(g)}\hat{\Sigma}^{-1}\hat{\Sigma}b = \bar{x}^{(g)}b \qquad (17)$$

for $g = 1, \ldots, q$. But since $a + \bar{x}^{(g)}b$ is the mean of d over the gth group, d has the same mean a over each group. Thus $d_1, \ldots, d_q$ is complete.

We turn now to the problem of identifying approximate posterior probabilities to be used for classifying cases. Given that a random vector $z = (z_{i_1}, \ldots, z_{i_p})$ came with equal probability from each of q normal populations with means $\mu_1, \ldots, \mu_q$ and common covariance matrix Σ, the posterior probability that z is from the gth population is

$$P(g|z) = \text{const} \exp\left(-\tfrac{1}{2}(z - \mu_g)\right.$$
$$\left. \times \Sigma^{-1}(z - \mu_g)^T\right). \quad (18)$$

The constant will depend on z but not on g. Replacing μ_g by $\bar{x}_g$ and Σ by $\hat{\Sigma}$ leads to the natural estimate

$$p(g|z) = \text{const} \exp\left(-\tfrac{1}{2}(z - \bar{x}^{(g)})\right.$$
$$\left. \times \hat{\Sigma}^{-1}(z - \bar{x}^{(g)})^T\right). \quad (19)$$

Using (16) and choosing the constant so $\sum_{g=1}^{q} p(g|z) = 1$ gives

$$p(g|z) = \exp(d_g(z)) / \sum_{g=1}^{q} \exp(d_g(z)).$$
$$(20)$$

Thus the function d_g which has the largest value at z corresponds to the group with the largest (estimated) posterior probability given z. As mentioned earlier another reason for our interest in the group classification functions $d_1, \ldots, d_q$ is that for any groups g and h the difference $d_{gh} = d_g - d_h$ defines a hyperplane which bisects the segment from $\bar{x}^{(g)}$ to $\bar{x}^{(h)}$ and is, moreover, the classical discriminant function for separating groups g and h ([1], p. 149).

d. Canonical Functions

In this section let $W = W(x)$ and $T = T(x)$ where $x = (x_{i_1}, \ldots, x_{i_p})$ is the set of selected variables. Let $\lambda_1 \geqslant \cdots \geqslant \lambda_p$ and $b_1, \ldots, b_p$ be eigenvalues and vectors obtained from solving the generalized eigen-

value problem:

$$\mathbf{T}b_i = \lambda_i \mathbf{W}b_i, \qquad b_i^T \mathbf{W}b_i = \delta_{ij} \quad (21)$$

where δ_{ij} denotes the Kronecker delta. Use the b_i to define discriminant functions:

$$d_i(x) = xb_i; \qquad i = 1, \ldots, p. \quad (22)$$

THEOREM 2: *The discriminant functions $d_1, \ldots, d_p$ defined in* (22) *form a canonical set.*

Proof: Let $d(x) = a + xb$ be an arbitrary discriminant function. Then

$$\frac{T(d)}{W(d)} = \frac{b^T \mathbf{T}b}{b^T \mathbf{W}b}. \quad (23)$$

Maximizing this expression with respect to b leads to the eigenvalue problem given in (21). The maximum is λ_1 obtained when $b = b_1$. This implies that d_1, by itself, is a canonical sequence. Assume now that $d(x) = a + xb$ is an arbitrary discriminant function which has zero within group correlation with $d_1, \ldots, d_{r-1}$. This implies that

$$b_i^T \mathbf{W}b = 0; \qquad i = 1, \ldots, r - 1 \quad (24)$$

Maximizing (23) under this constraint leads again to the eigenvalue problem defined in (21). The constrained maximum is λ_r obtained when $b = b_r$, that is, when $d = d_r$. Thus, by induction, $d_1, \ldots, d_p$ is a canonical sequence of discriminant functions.

In general, the sequence $d_1, \ldots, d_p$ defined by (22) is longer than it need be. We show next that any canonical sequence of length $q - 1$ is complete. Let $\mathcal{D}$ be the space of all discriminant functions based on $x_{i_1}, \ldots, x_{i_p}$ and let $\mathcal{E}$ be the subspace of functions whose mean in each group is the same. These functions are characterized by the fact that their total and within group sums of squares are equal. Thus

$$\mathcal{E} = \{e \in \mathcal{D} : W(e) = T(e)\}. \quad (25)$$

Let $\mathcal{C}$ be the W-orthogonal complement of $\mathcal{E}$ in $\mathcal{D}$ so that

$$\mathcal{D} = \mathcal{C} \oplus \mathcal{E} \qquad (26)$$

is an orthogonal decomposition of $\mathcal{D}$. It is clear from its definition that any basis of $\mathcal{C}$ is a minimal complete set. Moreover, the span of any complete set must contain $\mathcal{C}$. For this reason $\mathcal{C}$ is called the minimal complete space.

THEOREM 3: *If the minimal complete space $\mathcal{C}$ has dimension r, then any canonical sequence of length r is a basis of $\mathcal{C}$.*

Proof: For any $e \in \mathcal{E}$ and $d \in \mathcal{C}$,

$$W(e) + W(d) = W(e + d) \leqslant T(e + d)$$

$$= T(e) + 2T(e,d) + T(d).$$

But since $W(e) = T(e)$,

$$W(d) - T(d) \leqslant 2T(e, d). \qquad (27)$$

The right side of this last expression is a linear function of e which is bounded below for all $e \in \mathcal{E}$. Since zero is the only such function,

$$T(e, d) = 0$$

for all $e \in \mathcal{E}$ and $d \in \mathcal{C}$. In other words the spaces $\mathcal{C}$ and $\mathcal{E}$ are T-orthogonal as well as W-orthogonal.

Let $d_1, \ldots, d_r$ be any canonical sequence of length r. Assume that $d_1, \ldots, d_{s-1} \in \mathcal{C}$, $\Delta \leqslant 2$ and let $d_s = d + e$ where $d \in \mathcal{C}$ and $e \in \mathcal{E}$. Then e, and as a consequence d, is W-orthogonal to $d_1, \ldots, d_{s-1}$. Now since d and e are both W and T-orthogonal and since $T(e) = W(e)$,

$$\frac{T(d_s)}{W(d_s)} = \frac{T(d) + W(e)}{W(d) + W(e)} . \qquad (28)$$

This ratio is clearly not a maximum unless $W(e)$ and hence $e = 0$. Thus $d_s = d \in \mathcal{C}$ and the theorem follows by induction on s.

Since the $d = a + xb$ in $\mathcal{E}$ are defined by $q - 1$ linear constraints of the form $\bar{x}^{(g)}b = \bar{x}^{(1)}b$, the space $\mathcal{C}$ has dimension at most $q - 1$. Thus by the theorem just proved, every canonical sequence of length $q - 1$ is complete. Unless the means $\bar{x}^{(g)}$ have very special positions (i.e., lie on a plane of dimension less than $q - 1$) any canonical sequence of length $q - 1$ is a minimal complete sequence.

We turn now to a result that provides a useful means of plotting discriminant analysis results. Let $d_1, \ldots, d_r$ be a canonical sequence. By definition it is W-orthogonal. Assume without loss of generality that the functions are scaled so $d_1, \ldots, d_p$ is actually W-orthonormal. If there are three groups, a plot of d_1 and d_2 will look like Fig. 5.2. The circles suggest that the pooled within cross-product matrix computed over all groups is the identity, that is, that d_1 and d_2 are W-orthonormal. There is a precise way to say that the groups displayed in Fig. 5.2 are separated as much as possible.

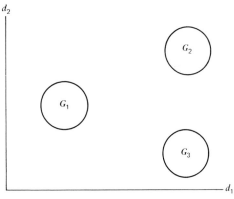

Fig. 5.2

The sum of the Euclidean distances of each value of $\mathbf{d} = (d_1, \ldots, d_r)$ from the grand mean $\bar{d}$ of all n such values is simply

$$\operatorname{tr} T(\mathbf{d}) = T(d_1) + \cdots + T(d_r) \qquad (29)$$

which we call the total dispersion for $\mathbf{d}$. The

following theorem asserts that for any W-orthonormal sequence $\mathbf{d} = (d_1, \ldots, d_r)$, the total dispersion is maximum when $\mathbf{d}$ is a canonical sequence. In particular no other W-orthonormal pair can have greater dispersion than that displayed in Fig. 5.2 for the canonical pair (d_1, d_2).

THEOREM 4: *If* $\mathbf{d} = (d_1, \ldots, d_r)$ *is a canonical sequence of* W-*orthonormal discriminant functions and if* $\tilde{\mathbf{d}} = (\tilde{d}_1, \ldots, \tilde{d}_r)$ *is another* W-*orthonormal sequence, then the total dispersion of* $\tilde{\mathbf{d}}$ *is not greater than that of* $\mathbf{d}$.

Proof: Let $\mathbf{d}^* = (d_1^*, \ldots, d_r^*)$ be a W-orthonormal basis for the span $\mathfrak{M}$ of $\tilde{\mathbf{d}} = (\tilde{d}_1, \ldots, \tilde{d}_r)$ chosen so that

$$W(d_i, d_j^*) = 0, \qquad i < j. \qquad (30)$$

This may be done by choosing d_r^* first and working back.

Since $\mathbf{d} = (d_1, \ldots, d_r)$ is a canonical sequence,

$$T(d_i^*) \leqslant T(d_i); \qquad i = 1, \ldots, r \quad (31)$$

and hence tr $T(\mathbf{d}^*) \leqslant$ tr $T(\mathbf{d})$. Since $T(\mathbf{d}^*)$ and $T(\tilde{\mathbf{d}})$ are the matrices of a symmetric product T defined on $\mathfrak{M}$ with respect to two W-orthonormal bases,

$$\text{tr } T(\tilde{\mathbf{d}}) = \text{tr } T(\mathbf{d}^*) \leqslant \text{tr } T(\mathbf{d}),$$

which completes the proof.

e. An F Approximation to Λ

The tabulation of the distribution of Wilks' Λ-statistic under normal sampling assumptions is quite incomplete and rather inaccessible. Rao [5] has given a useful approximation based on the F-distribution. In our notation, his result asserts that

$$F = \frac{df_2}{df_1} \cdot \frac{1 - \Lambda^{1/c}}{\Lambda^{1/c}} \qquad (32)$$

has an approximate F-distribution with df_1

and df_2 degrees of freedom where

$$df_1 = pa$$
$$df_2 = bc + 1 - \frac{pa}{2}$$

with

$$a = q - 1$$
$$b = n - 1 - \frac{p + q}{2}$$
$$c = \begin{cases} \left(\dfrac{p^2 a^2 - 4}{p^2 + a^2 - 5} \right)^{1/2} & \text{if } p^2 + a^2 \neq 5 \\[2mm] 1 & \text{if } p^2 + a^2 = 5 \end{cases}$$

We use this approximation in addition to Λ so that critical values may be obtained from easily accessible F-tables.

3. SUMMARY OF CALCULATION PROCEDURE

a. Sums of Cross-Products

Reading the data one case at a time, the method of provisional means (Chapter 4, Section 2c) is used to compute group means $\bar{x}_{gi}$ and within group sums of cross-products w_{ij}. The values of $\bar{x}_{gi}$ and w_{ij} begin at zero and are updated after reading each case. After reading the tth case in the gth group, $(x_{gt1}, \ldots, x_{gtm})$, the new values are:

$$\bar{x}_{gi}^* = \frac{(t - 1)\bar{x}_{gi} + x_{gti}}{t}$$

$$\tag{33}$$

$$w_{ij}^* = w_{ij} + \left(x_{gti} - \bar{x}_{gi} \right)\left(x_{gtj} - \bar{x}_{gi}^* \right)$$

for $i = 1, \ldots, m$ and $j = i, \ldots, m$. Note that the last expression employs an old mean $\bar{x}_{gi}$ and a new mean $\bar{x}_{gi}^*$ and that only the upper triangular part of (w_{ij}) is updated. Note also that $\bar{x}_{hi}$ is not modified for $h \neq g$. The final values of $\bar{x}_{gi}$ and w_{ij} after reading all n cases are the group means and pooled within group sums of cross-products for all m variables.

If the group means remain in high-speed storage, the overall means $\bar{x}_i$ and total sums of cross-products t_{ij} may be computed directly. Thus:

$$\bar{x}_i = \frac{1}{n} \sum_{g=1}^{q} n_g \bar{x}_{gi}$$

$$t_{ij} = w_{ij} + \sum_{g=1}^{q} n_g(\bar{x}_{gi} - \bar{x}_i)(\bar{x}_{gj} - \bar{x}_j) \tag{34}$$

for $i = 1, \ldots, m$ and $j = i, \ldots, m$.

b. Development of the Discriminant Functions

The stepwise development of the discriminant functions is dependent almost exclusively on the current values of the status matrices $(\tilde{w}_{ij})$ and $(\tilde{t}_{ij})$; actually on their upper triangular parts. At the begining of the first step these matrices are equal to the within and total sums of cross-products matrices (w_{ij}) and (t_{ij}) computed in the previous section. The status matrices are updated from step to step by means of the sweep operator of Chapter 4, Section 2a. All steps, including the first, are formally identical. On any step a negative value of $\tilde{w}_{ii}$ indicates that variable x_i is in the analysis.

Stepping is steered by the multiplicative increment V_k in Wilks' Λ resulting from the entry or removal of variable x_k as given by (10). First a backward step is attempted by seeking that index k which minimizes the value of V_k over all k such that $\tilde{w}_{kk} < 0$. If the corresponding F-to-remove value F_k given by (12) is below the F-to-remove threshold, variable x_k is removed by means of inverse sweeps on the kth diagonal elements of $(\tilde{w}_{ij})$ and $(\tilde{t}_{ij})$.

If it is not possible to execute a backward step, a forward step is attempted by seeking that index k which minimizes V_k over all k such that $\tilde{w}_{kk} > 0$ and such that the tolerance t_k given by (14) is at least as large as the tolerance threshold. If the corresponding F-to-enter value F_k given by (11) is not below the F-to-enter threshold, variable x_k

is entered by means of forward sweeps on the kth diagonal elements of $(\tilde{w}_{ij})$ and $(\tilde{t}_{ij})$.

If it is not possible to remove or enter a variable, the stepping terminates. Otherwise, the value of Λ, which is set to one before the first step, is updated by multiplying by V_k and the step goes on to give a variety of output including:

1. The F-to-delete value (12) for each variable in the analysis.
2. The F-to-enter value (11) for each variable not in the analysis.
3. Wilks' Λ and its degrees of freedom $(p, q - 1, n - q)$ together with the corresponding approximate F-statistic (32) and its degrees of freedom.

c. Post-Stepping Output

After the stepping is complete it may be summarized by giving a history of the variables entered and removed, together with their F-to-enter and remove values and Wilks' Λ-statistic at each step. Additional output (Sections 2c and 2d) which is included in the summary, but may also be produced at selected steps along the way, includes:

1. Group classification function coefficients for each selected variable x_i and each group $g = 1, \ldots, q$:

$$b_{ig} = -(n - q)\Sigma_j^* \tilde{w}_{ij}\bar{x}_{gj} \tag{35}$$

and for each group $g = 1, \ldots, q$ a classification function constant:

$$a_g = -\tfrac{1}{2}\Sigma_j^* \bar{x}_{gj}b_{jg}. \tag{36}$$

Here "*" indicates that the summation is over all j such that $\tilde{w}_{jj} < 0$.

2. Posterior probability that case t in group g came from group h:

$$p_h = \exp(d_h)/ \sum_{f=1}^{q} \exp(d_f);$$

$$h = 1, \ldots, q \tag{37}$$

where

$$d_h = a_h + \Sigma^*_i x_{gti} b_{ih}. \qquad (38)$$

3. A classification matrix that gives the number of cases n_{gh} in group g whose group h posterior probability was greatest; $g, h = 1, \ldots, q$.

d. Canonical Analysis

The coefficients of the ith canonical discriminant function are the components of the p-vector b_i obtained by solving the eigenvalue problem given by (21). This may be done by finding the lower triangular matrix $\mathbf{L}$ in the Cholesky factorization $\mathbf{LL}^T$ of $\mathbf{W}^{-1}$ and solving the eigenvalue problem

$$\mathbf{L}^T\mathbf{TL}v_i = \lambda_i v_i; \qquad v_i^T v_j = \delta_{ij} \qquad (39)$$

for eigenvalues $\lambda_1 \geqslant \cdots \geqslant \lambda_p$ and eigenvectors $v_1, \ldots, v_p$. Setting $b_i = \mathbf{L}v_i$ gives the required solution $\lambda_1 \geqslant \cdots \geqslant \lambda_p$; $b_1, \ldots, b_p$ to (21).

4. FLOW CHART

The flow chart that follows describes a stepwise discriminant analysis program which is similar to and contains the principal features of BMD07M, a program in the BMD Biomedical Computer Programs Series [2]. The complete program, which contains about 1400 Fortran statements, is too lengthy to describe in detail. Some of the things omitted include provisions for transforming the input data before analysis, provisions for reading parameters and allocating storage, the output of simple descriptive statistics such as means, standard deviations, and correlations, all detail on labeling and output formatting, the creation of a summary of the stepping procedure, provisions for forcing the entry of specified variables, details for plotting canonical variables, and provisions for the execution of multiple problems.

5. DESCRIPTION OF THE FLOW CHART

Box 1: The group index g, the case index t, and the current value of Λ are set to one. The provisional group means $\bar{x}_{gi}$ and provisional within group products w_{ij} are set to zero. Only the upper triangular part of (w_{ij}) is computed at this point.

Box 2: The tth case in the gth group $(x_{gt1}, \ldots, x_{gtm})$ is read. Since the data are needed only one case at a time, it is customary to keep the data in auxiliary storage. Except for the summary computations in Boxes 22 and 26, the data need be read only once.

Box 3: This box steps the provisional group means $\bar{x}_{gi}$ and the provisional within group products w_{ij} as described in Section 3a.

Box 4: If the case index t is not equal to the number of cases n_g in the gth group a branch is made to read another case. Otherwise, control passes to Box 6 where an attempt is made to read another group.

Box 5: The case index is stepped.

Box 6: If the group index g is not equal to the total number of groups q, a branch is made to read another group. Otherwise, the computation of the group means $\bar{x}_{gi}$ and within group products w_{ij} is complete and control passes to Box 8.

Box 7: The group index g is stepped and the case index set to one.

Box 8: The total number of cases n, the overall means $\bar{x}_i$, and the total products t_{ij} are computed as described in Section 3a.

Box 9: The lower diagonal parts of the symmetric matrices (w_{ij}) and (t_{ij}) are obtained from their upper diagonal parts, the diagonals of (w_{ij}) and (t_{ij}) are stored, and the current number p of classification variables in the analysis is set to zero.

Box 10: If $p = 0$ there are no variables in the analysis and control passes to Box 14 where an attempt to enter a variable is initiated. Otherwise, control passes to Box 11 where an attempt to remove a variable is initiated.

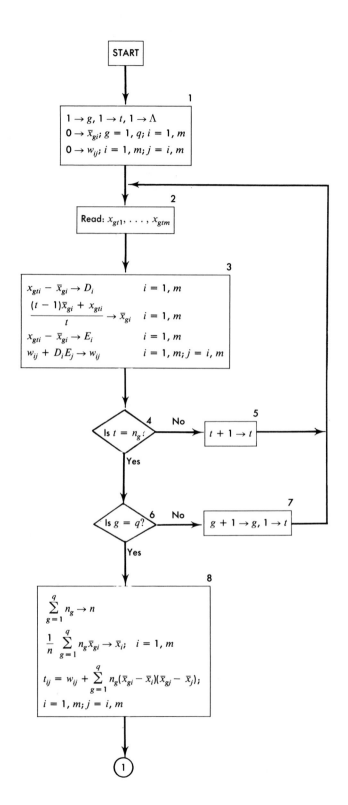

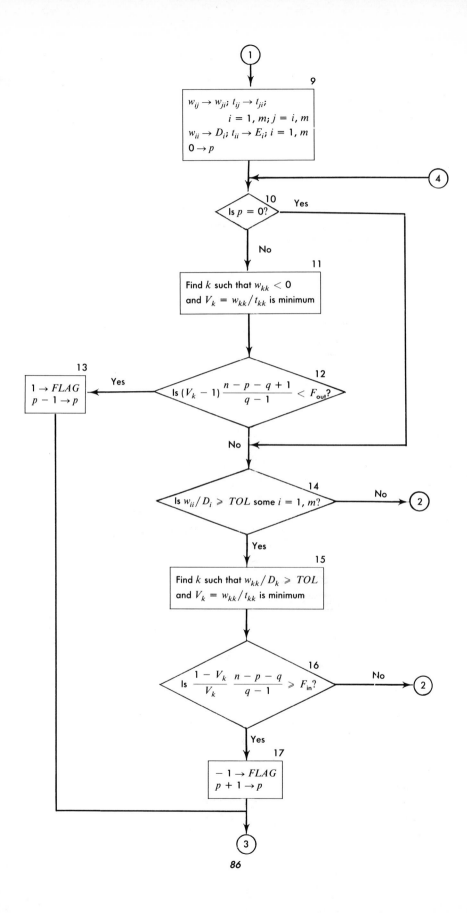

1

9

$w_{ij} \to w_{ji}$; $t_{ij} \to t_{ji}$;
    $i = 1, m$; $j = i, m$
$w_{ii} \to D_i$; $t_{ii} \to E_i$; $i = 1, m$
$0 \to p$

4

10   Is $p = 0$?   Yes

No

11

Find k such that $w_{kk} < 0$
and $V_k = w_{kk}/t_{kk}$ is minimum

13

$1 \to FLAG$
$p - 1 \to p$

Yes

12   Is $(V_k - 1) \dfrac{n - p - q + 1}{q - 1} < F_{\text{out}}$?

No

14   Is $w_{ii}/D_i \geqslant TOL$ some $i = 1, m$?   No   **2**

Yes

15

Find k such that $w_{kk}/D_k \geqslant TOL$
and $V_k = w_{kk}/t_{kk}$ is minimum

16   Is $\dfrac{1 - V_k}{V_k} \dfrac{n - p - q}{q - 1} \geqslant F_{\text{in}}$?   No   **2**

Yes

17

$-1 \to FLAG$
$p + 1 \to p$

3

86

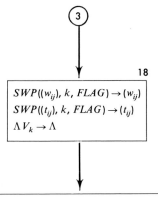

18

$$SWP((w_{ij}), k, FLAG) \rightarrow (w_{ij})$$
$$SWP((t_{ij}), k, FLAG) \rightarrow (t_{ij})$$
$$\Lambda V_k \rightarrow \Lambda$$

19

For each i such that $w_{ij} < 0$, write:

$$F_i = \frac{w_{ii} - t_{ii}}{t_{ii}} \; \frac{n - p - q + 1}{q - 1} = F\text{-to-remove}$$

For each i such that $w_{ii} > 0$ write:

$$F_i = \frac{t_{ii} - w_{ii}}{w_{ii}} \; \frac{n - p - q}{q - 1} = F\text{-to-enter}$$

20

$$q - 1 \rightarrow a, \; n - 1 - \tfrac{1}{2}(p + q) \rightarrow b$$

$$c \leftarrow \begin{cases} \left(\dfrac{p^2 a^2 - 4}{p^2 + a^2 - 5} \right)^{1/2} & \text{if } p^2 + a^2 \neq 5 \\[2mm] 1 & \text{if } p^2 + a^2 = 5 \end{cases}$$

$$pa \rightarrow df_1, \; bc + 1 - pa/2 \rightarrow df_2$$

Write:

Λ = Wilks' lambda

$(p, q - 1, n - q)$ = degrees of freedom for Λ

$$F = \frac{1 - \Lambda^{1/c}}{\Lambda^{1/c}} \; \frac{df_2}{df_1} = \text{approximate } F\text{-statistic}$$

(df_1, df_2) = degrees of freedom for F

4

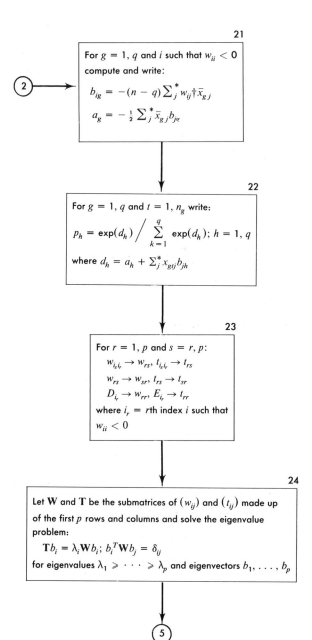

21

For $g = 1, q$ and i such that $w_{ii} < 0$ compute and write:

$$b_{ig} = -(n - q) \sum_j^* w_{ij}\dagger \bar{x}_{gj}$$

$$a_g = -\tfrac{1}{2} \sum_j^* \bar{x}_{gj} b_{jg}$$

22

For $g = 1, q$ and $t = 1, n_g$ write:

$$p_h = \exp(d_h) \Big/ \sum_{k=1}^{q} \exp(d_h); \quad h = 1, q$$

where $d_h = a_h + \sum_j^* x_{gtj} b_{jh}$

23

For $r = 1, p$ and $s = r, p$:

$$w_{i_s i_r} \to w_{rs}, \; t_{i_s i_r} \to t_{rs}$$

$$w_{rs} \to w_{sr}, \; t_{rs} \to t_{sr}$$

$$D_{i_r} \to w_{rr}, \; E_{i_r} \to t_{rr}$$

where $i_r = r$th index i such that $w_{ii} < 0$

24

Let **W** and **T** be the submatrices of (w_{ij}) and (t_{ij}) made up of the first p rows and columns and solve the eigenvalue problem:

$$\mathbf{T}b_i = \lambda_i \mathbf{W} b_i; \; b_i^T \mathbf{W} b_j = \delta_{ij}$$

for eigenvalues $\lambda_1 \geqslant \cdots \geqslant \lambda_p$ and eigenvectors $b_1, \ldots, b_p$

---

*Indicates that the summation is over all j such that $w_{jj} < 0$.

†Indicates that $w_{ij}\dagger = \begin{cases} w_{ij} \text{ if } i \leqslant j \\ w_{ji} \text{ if } i > j \end{cases}$.

(5)

25

For $j = 1, p$ write:

$b_j^T = (b_{ij}, \ldots, b_{pj})$ = coefficients for the jth canonical function

E_j / E_p = cumulative proportion of explained dispersion

where $E_j = \sum\limits_{i=1}^{j} (\lambda_i - 1)$

26

For $g = 1, q$ and $t = 1, n_q$ compute:

$d_{gtj} = \sum\limits_{r=1}^{p} x_{gti_r} b_{rj}; j = 1, 2$

And plot:

(d_{gt1}, d_{gt2}) = values of the first two canonical functions

STOP

Box 11: If $w_{kk} < 0$, then the kth variable is in the analysis and $V_k = w_{kk}/t_{kk}$ is the multiplicative increment in Wilks' Λ which would result from its removal. The index k of the variable whose V_k value is smallest among all variables in the analysis is found.

Box 12: If the F-to-remove statistic of the variable found in Box 11 is less than the F-to-remove threshold F_{out}, control passes to Box 13 where removal is initiated. Otherwise, it passes to Box 14 where an attempt to enter a variable is begun.

Box 13: Setting *FLAG* to 1 will produce inverse sweeps in Box 18 and the removal of the kth variable. The variable count is reduced by 1.

Box 14: If the ith variable is in the analysis, w_{ii}/D_i is negative. Otherwise, this value is the tolerance of the ith variable. If at least one of these values is as great as the tolerance threshold *TOL*, control passes to Box 15 where an attempt is made to add a new variable. Otherwise, the stepping is complete and control passes to Box 21.

Box 15: If $w_{kk}/D_k \geqslant TOL$, then the kth variable is not in the analysis but does satisfy the tolerance criterion for entry. For all such variables, the index k of the variable which gives the smallest multiplicative increment $V_k = w_{kk}/t_{kk}$ in Wilks' Λ is found.

Box 16: If the value of the F-to-enter statistic for the variable found in Box 15 is at least as great as the F-to-enter threshold, control passes to Box 17 where entry is initiated. Otherwise, the stepping is complete and control passes to Box 21.

Box 17: Setting *FLAG* to -1 will produce forward sweeps in Box 18 and entry of the kth variable. In accordance, the number of variables p is increased by 1.

Box 18: The sweep operator described in Chapter 4, Section 4, Box 15 is applied to the within and total cross-product matrices (w_{ij}) and (t_{ij}). A forward sweep on the kth diagonal element is obtained when *FLAG* = -1 and an inverse sweep when *FLAG* = 1. The value of Wilks' Λ is stepped.

Box 19: If $w_{ii} < 0$ the ith variable is in

the analysis. An F-to-remove value is printed for each variable in the analysis and an F-to-enter value for each variable not in the analysis.

Box 20: Wilks' Λ-statistic and its degrees of freedom are printed together with the corresponding approximate F-statistic and its degrees of freedom as described in Section 2e.

Box 21: The group classification function coefficients are computed and printed. The coefficient b_{ig} is the loading on classification variable i of the function for group g, and a_g is the constant term for this function. Since only the upper diagonal part of the status matrix is computed, only this part is used in evaluating the b_{ig}.

Box 22: Using the coefficients from Box 21, the values $d_1, \ldots, d_q$ of the group classification functions are computed and the corresponding posterior probabilities printed for each case in each group. This requires rereading the original data. A classification summary (not shown) as described in Section 3c, part 3 may be produced at this point.

Box 23: The within and total cross-products matrices for the selected variables are written in the upper left-hand corner of the (w_{ij}) and (t_{ij}) arrays. The off-diagonal components are obtained from the lower diagonal elements of the (w_{ij}) and (t_{ij}) arrays which up to this point have not been modified. The diagonal values are obtained from the (D_i) and (E_i) arrays.

Box 24: The eigenvalue problem $\mathbf{T}b_i = \lambda_i \mathbf{W} b_i$ is solved. See Section 3d.

Box 25: The coefficients of the canonical functions are written. The value b_{ij} is the ith component of the jth eigenvector computed in Box 24 and is also the loading of the jth canonical function on the ith selected classification variable. The value $\lambda_i - 1$ is the between (total minus within) sum of squares for the ith canonical function.

Box 26: The initial data are read again one case $(x_{gt1}, \ldots, x_{gtm})$ at a time. The values corresponding to the selected variables are used to evaluate the first two canonical discriminant functions. These values (d_{gt1}, d_{gt2}) are stored and plotted when the reading is complete.

6. THE PROGRAM

The Fortran code that follows implements the variable selection procedure corresponding to Boxes 10–17 of the flow chart. It is not, however, a one-to-one translation of the flow chart. The subroutine arguments are as follows:

T	Total status matrix
W	Within status matrix
D	Diagonal of the within sums of cross-products matrix
M	Order of T, W, and D
N	Total number of cases
NP	Current number of variables in the analysis
NQ	Number of groups
TOL	Tolerance threshold
FIN	F-to-enter threshold
$FOUT$	F-to-remove threshold
K	Index of the next variable to be entered or removed
$FLAG$	Flag to indicate entry, removal, or completion

The subroutine modifies only the last two arguments. If $FLAG$ has output value 1, the Kth variable should be removed; if $FLAG$ has output value -1, the Kth variable should be entered; and if $FLAG$ has output value 0, no variable qualifies for entry or removal and the stepping is complete.

```
      SUBROUTINE SELVAR(T, W, D, M, N, NP, NQ, TOL, FIN, FOUT, K, FLAG)
      DIMENSION T(M, M), W(M, M), D(M)
      VI = NQ*FOUT + 1
      VO = 1.0
      DO 1 I = 1, M
      IF (T(I, I).EQ.0.0) GO TO 1
      V = W(I, I)/T(I, I)
      IF (V.GE.VI) GO TO 1
      IF (W(I, I).LT.0.0) GO TO 2
      IF (W(I, I)/D(I).LT.TOL) GO TO 1
      IF (V.GE.VO) GO TO 1
      VO = V
      KO = I
      GO TO 1
2     VI = V
      KI = I
1     CONTINUE
      FLAG = 0.0
      IF (((1.0 - VO)/VO)*((N - NP - NQ)/(NQ - 1)).GE.FIN) FLAG = -1.0
      IF ((VI - 1.0)*(N - NP - NQ + 1)/(NQ - 1).LT.FOUT) FLAG = 1.0
      K = KO
      IF (FLAG.EQ.1.0) K = KI
      RETURN
      END
```

7. SAMPLE PROBLEM

The output that follows was obtained from an execution of BMD07M. This program is available at about 500 computing facilities. Its coding is similar to that described in our flow chart except that BMD07M contains a number of additional options. The write-up for BMD07M appears

BMD07M - STEPWISE DISCRIMINANT ANALYSIS - REVISED JUNE 2, 1972
HEALTH SCIENCES COMPUTING FACILITY, UCLA

PROBLEM CODE   IRIS

NUMBER OF VARIABLES   4

NUMBER OF GROUPS   3

NUMBER OF CASES IN EACH GROUP   50   50   50

PRIOR PROBABILITIES   0.3333   0.3333   0.3333

VARIABLE FORMAT   (4F3.1)

DATA INPUT FROM CARDS

MEANS   (THE LAST COLUMN CONTAINS THE GRAND MEANS OVER THE GROUPS USED IN THE ANALYSIS)

	GROUP			
	SETOSA	RVSCLR	VRGNCA	
VARIABLE				
1	5.00599	5.93598	6.58797	5.84332
2	3.42799	2.76999	2.97399	3.05733
3	1.46200	4.25999	5.55199	3.75799
4	0.24600	1.32599	2.02599	1.19933

STANDARD DEVIATIONS

	GROUP		
	SETOSA	RVSCLR	VRGNCA
VARIABLE			
1	0.35249	0.51617	0.63588
2	0.37906	0.31380	0.32250
3	0.17366	0.46991	0.55189
4	0.10539	0.19775	0.27465

WITHIN GROUPS CORRELATION MATRIX

	VARIABLES			
	1	2	3	4
VARIABLE				
1	1.00000			
2	0.53024	1.00000		
3	0.75616	0.37791	1.00000	
4	0.36451	0.47053	0.48446	1.00000

SUBPROBLEM   1
F-LEVEL FOR INCLUSION   1.0000
F-LEVEL FOR DELETION   1.0000
TOLERANCE LEVEL   0.0100
CONTROL VALUES   1111

****

STEP NUMBER   0
VARIABLE ENTERED

VARIABLES NOT INCLUDED AND F TO ENTER - DEGREES OF FREEDOM   2   147

  1 119.2625   2   49.1601   3 1180.1619   4 960.0061

****

STEP NUMBER   1
VARIABLE ENTERED   3

VARIABLES INCLUDED AND F TO REMOVE - DEGREES OF FREEDOM   2   147

  3 1180.1631

VARIABLES NOT INCLUDED AND F TO ENTER - DEGREES OF FREEDOM   2   146

  1 34.3238   2   43.0351   4 24.7671

U-STATISTIC   0.05863   DEGREES OF FREEDOM   1   2   147
APPROXIMATE F   1180.16187   DEGREES OF FREEDOM   2   147.00

F MATRIX - DEGREES OF FREEDOM   1   147

	GROUP	
	SETOSA	RVSCLR
GROUP		
RVSCLR	1056.87866	
VRGNCA	2258.26563	225.34641

****

STEP NUMBER   2
VARIABLE ENTERED   2

VARIABLES INCLUDED AND F TO REMOVE - DEGREES OF FREEDOM   2   146

  2 43.0351   3 1112.9509

VARIABLES NOT INCLUDED AND F TO ENTER - DEGREES OF FREEDOM   2   145

  1 12.2691   4   34.5702

U-STATISTIC   0.03688   DEGREES OF FREEDOM   2   2   147
APPROXIMATE F   307.10425   DEGREES OF FREEDOM   4   292.00

F MATRIX - DEGREES OF FREEDOM   2   146

	GROUP	
	SETOSA	RVSCLR
GROUP		
RVSCLR	804.51172	
VRGNCA	1473.23047	116.03792

```
*************************************************************************************************
STEP NUMBER         3
VARIABLE ENTERED    4

VARIABLES INCLUDED AND F TO REMOVE - DEGREES OF FREEDOM    2  145

  2  54.5765       3  38.7261        4  34.5703

VARIABLES NOT INCLUDED AND F TO ENTER - DEGREES OF FREEDOM    2  144

  1   4.7222

U-STATISTIC          0.02498     DEGREES OF FREEDOM    3    2  147
APPROXIMATE F      257.50488     DEGREES OF FREEDOM    6  290.00

F MATRIX - DEGREES OF FREEDOM    3  145

            GROUP
          SETOSA      RVSCLR
GROUP
RVSCLR   692.01416
VRGNCA  1381.16357   133.37375

*************************************************************************************************
STEP NUMBER         4
VARIABLE ENTERED    1

VARIABLES INCLUDED AND F TO REMOVE - DEGREES OF FREEDOM    2  144

  1   4.7222        2  21.5360        3  35.5933        4  24.9064

U-STATISTIC          0.02344     DEGREES OF FREEDOM    4    2  147
APPROXIMATE F      199.14853     DEGREES OF FREEDOM    8  288.00

F MATRIX - DEGREES OF FREEDOM    4  144

            GROUP
          SETOSA      RVSCLR
GROUP
RVSCLR   550.19019
VRGNCA  1098.27612   105.31296

F LEVEL INSUFFICIENT FOR FURTHER COMPUTATION

          FUNCTION
          SETOSA       RVSCLR       VRGNCA
VARIABLE
  1      23.54445     15.65827     12.44586
  2      23.58778      7.07253      3.68531
  3     -16.43080      5.21152     12.76666
  4     -17.39845      6.43420     21.07921

CONSTANT
         -86.30879    -72.85271   -104.36847

          NUMBER OF CASES CLASSIFIED INTO GROUP -
          SETOSA RVSCLR VRGNCA
GROUP
  SETOSA     50      0      0
  RVSCLR      0     48      2
  VRGNCA      0      1     49
```

```
SUMMARY TABLE

    STEP       VARIABLE        F VALUE TO        NUMBER OF        U-STATISTIC
   NUMBER   ENTERED  REMOVED   ENTER OR REMOVE   VARIABLES INCLUDED

     1         3               1180.1631              1              0.0586
     2         2                 43.0351              2              0.0369
     3         4                 34.5703              3              0.0250
     4         1                  4.7222              4              0.0234

          EIGENVALUES

            32.19211      0.28541      0.00004      0.00000

          CUMULATIVE PROPORTION OF TOTAL DISPERSION

             0.99121      1.00000      1.00000      1.00000

          CANONICAL CORRELATIONS

             0.98482      0.47121      0.00652      0.00142

          COEFFICIENTS FOR CANONICAL VARIABLE -

          ORIGINAL      1             2             3             4
          VARIABLE
             1       -0.82940      -0.02430       2.73640      -1.63318
             2       -1.53446      -2.16427      -2.65926      -0.35163
             3        2.20123       0.93221      -2.95625      -0.57914
             4        2.81047      -2.83961       3.68249       2.69253

          GROUP       CANONICAL VARIABLES EVALUATED AT GROUP MEANS
             1       -7.60762      -0.21513      -0.00002       0.0
             2        1.82506       0.72791       0.00005       0.00001
             3        5.78257      -0.51277      -0.00004      -0.00002

          CHECK ON FINAL U-STATISTIC        0.02344
```

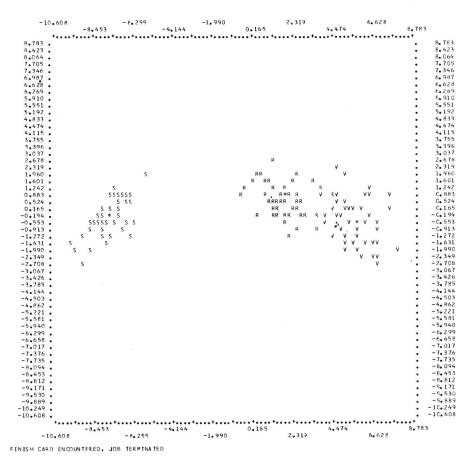

FINISH CARD ENCOUNTERED, JOB TERMINATED

in [2] and Fortran source code for the program itself may be obtained by writing: Program Librarian, Health Sciences Computing Facility, University of California, Los Angeles, California 90024.

The data are the well-known Fisher iris data [3]. There are 50 observations on each of four variables in each of three groups of iris. The variables are sepal length and width and petal length and width. The groups are *setosa*, *versicolor*, and *virginica*.

The first paragraph of the output gives the total number of variables, the number of groups, and the number of cases in each group. The next two paragraphs give the group means and standard deviations together with the overall mean of each variable. This is followed by the within group correlation matrix obtained by standardiz-

ing the within groups cross-product matrix.

The stepwise entry of variables begins on the second output page. The F-to-enter and delete thresholds are both 1.0 and the tolerance threshold is 0.01. These are moderate values chosen to allow all four variables to enter. The "control values" listed in the output represent perhaps the most important option we have not described. They allow the user to override the stepping algorithm by forcing the entry of some variables and preventing entry for others. The control value for each variable in the sample output is 1 which means that each variable is free and no overriding takes place.

Step 0 gives the F-to-enter value of each variable before the entry of any. Variable x_3 has the largest value and enters on the first step. This and all subsequent steps are of the same form. They include *F*-to-remove and *F*-to-enter values, Wilks' Λ-statistic (called the *U*-statistic in the output) for testing the equality of all three group means and the corresponding approximate *F*-statistic. Also given is a matrix of *F*-statistics, which we have not discussed, for testing the equality of the means in each pair of groups.

The stepping continues with the entry of a variable at each step until step 4 at which point no variable remains to enter and no *F*-to-remove value is small enough to require the removal of a variable.

The last part of the third output page gives the group classification function coefficients and constants. These are used to compute the posterior probabilities for each case in each group and these, in turn, are used to classify the cases into groups. The classification shown is nearly perfect.

The fourth output page begins with a history of the stepping. It then gives the canonical coefficients for each canonical function together with the cumulative proportion of explained dispersion. As Theorem 3 implies, when there are three groups, this proportion is 1 after the first two or more functions are included.

The last output page is a plot of the first two canonical functions. The cases in the three groups are indicated by the letters *S*, *R*, and *V*, the first letters of the group labels. The asterisks denote group means. As expected, the groups are well separated.

8. ESTIMATED RUNNING TIME

The number of operations (additions, subtractions, multiplications, or divisions) required for each part of the computation are approximately:

$m(m + 6)n$	for sums of cross-products,
$3m^2(m + 1)$	for stepping,
$2m(m + 1)$	for discriminant coefficients,
$nq(2m + 25)$	for posterior probabilities,
$7m^2(m + 1)$	for canonical coefficients,
$4mn$	for canonical plot.

As in stepwise regression, the majority of the computation in a typical problem is devoted to producing sums of cross-products. This, fortunately, implies that only this step needs to be coded with careful attention to computational efficiency.

The computer time required for a recent execution of BMD07M on a typical 30-variable 100-case 4-group problem using an IBM 360/91 was 3 seconds, which at the author's shop cost 48 cents.

9. REFERENCES

1. T. W. Anderson, *Introduction to Multivariate Statistical Analysis*, Wiley, New York, 1958.
2. W. J. Dixon (ed.), *BMD Biomedical Computer Programs*, University of California Press, Berkeley, Calif., 1970.
3. R. A. Fisher, "The Use of Multiple Measurements in Taxonomic Problems," *Annals of Eugenics*, **7**, 179–188 (1936).
4. D. F. Morrison, *Multivariate Statistical Methods*, McGraw-Hill, New York, 1967.
5. C. R. Rao, "An Asymptotic Expansion of the Distribution of Wilks' Criterion," *Bull. Int. Stat. Inst.*, **33**(2), 177–180 (1951).
6. C. R. Rao, *Linear Statistical Inference and Its Applications*, Wiley, New York, 1965.

A method of coalitions in statistical discriminant analysis

6

Herbert S. Wilf
University of Pennsylvania

1. FUNCTION

The purpose of this program is to compute the parameters of a set of statistical discriminant functions which can then be used for deciding to which one of a given set of populations a certain individual belongs. Such problems arise in the diagnosis of disease, in taxonomy and in many other areas.

2. MATHEMATICAL DISCUSSION

Suppose, as an example, that it is desired to distinguish between two species of insects based on two physical characteristics x_1, x_2, which can be measured on any given individual. Suppose further that eleven individuals who were known to belong to species A were measured, yielding the data in Table 1 below.

Next, suppose that twelve individuals known to be of species B are measured, giving Table 2.

Our task now is to use these data to construct a function, say $f(x_1, x_2)$, which will be used to discriminate between the two species *in the future* as follows: given any individual; measure his (x_1, x_2); if $f(x_1, x_2) > 0$ assign the individual to species A, otherwise to species B. Such a function is

Table 1*(SPECIES A)

x_1	6.36 5.92 5.92 6.44 6.40 6.56 6.64 6.68 6.72 6.76 6.72
x_2	5.24 5.12 5.36 5.64 5.16 5.56 5.36 4.96 5.48 5.60 5.08

Table 2* (SPECIES B)

x_1	6.00 5.60 5.64 5.76 5.96 5.72 5.64 5.44 5.04 4.56 5.48 5.76
x_2	4.88 4.64 4.96 4.80 5.08 5.04 4.96 4.88 4.44 4.04 4.20 4.80

*Data taken from [6], page 125.

called a *discriminant function* for the problem.

Evidently there is, in general, no unique way of constructing $f(x_1, x_2)$, and equally evidently, whatever f we construct will not be right every time, that is, it will occasionally assign an individual of species A to species B and *vice-versa*. Hence we cannot ask for perfection, but only that, statistically speaking, we do our best.

There are many methods in current use which will find an $f(x_1, x_2)$. We give here a brief summary and comparison of some of these methods.

First of all, we may divide the procedures into two major categories: the parametric methods, and the nonparametric methods. Roughly speaking, in a nonparametric method we work directly with the given data points in space, and we try to find some surface which separates the two populations as much as possible. In a parametric method, we use the data points to estimate the parameters of a statistical distribution function, such as the normal distribution, and then in the future, discriminations are made from the distribution function.

As an example of a nonparametric method we give

METHOD 1: THE CONVEX HULL METHOD

Suppose we plot, in the x_1, x_2 plane, the data points of Tables 1 and 2 above. We obtain Fig. 6.1, in which the points of species A are shown as small circles and those of species B as crosses. We notice that there is a straight line,

$$f(x_1, x_2) \equiv x_2 + 3.55x_1 - 7.20 = 0 \quad (1)$$

which *completely* separates the two sets of points. In other words, for each of the eleven members of species A we have $f(x_1, x_2) > 0$ whereas, for all twelve of species B it is true that $f(x_1, x_2) < 0$.

Geometrically what has happened here is that the convex hulls of the data sets are disjoint.

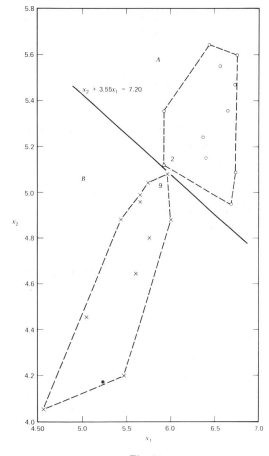

Fig. 6.1

These convex hulls are shown in Fig. 6.1 as the polygonal areas whose boundaries are the dotted lines. It happens that these two areas do not overlap, and we can separate them by a straight line. This fact holds true in spaces of any number of dimensions, namely if two convex sets A and B are disjoint then there is a hyperplane that separates them.

Since our discriminant function f in (1) distinguishes perfectly between the two data sets it is surely the "best" one for our problem. Or is it? The defects of such a function f become clear if we consider that it is extremely sensitive to the behavior of just a few outlying points. Indeed if the points labeled q and r in Fig. 6.1 are moved only very slightly, the convex hulls will overlap and the whole method will fail, whereas, on the other hand, the discriminant line is quite insensitive to large motions of the points that are well away from the boundaries. It is therefore, the outlying, or "far out," points which most strongly affect the decision line. Such points, as q and r, are outlying because they are unusual members of their classes.

Such a discriminant function is, therefore, largely determined by the behavior of the few most atypical data points, and consequently cannot be expected to provide a reliable predictor for future use.

This kind of unreliability is characteristic of nonparametric methods because of their sensitivity to the placement of a few unusual data points, rather than depending only on gross properties of the aggregate of all data points.

METHOD 2: SORTING BY COORDINATES

As another nonparametric method, we might consider trying to do the best possible separation on one coordinate at a time. If we arrange the values of x_1 in descending order we find:

Species A—6.76, 6.72, 6.72, 6.68, 6.64, 6.56, 6.44, 6.40, 6.36, 5.92, and 5.92.

Species B—6.00, 5.96, 5.76, 5.76, 5.72, 5.64, 5.64, 5.60, 5.48, 5.44, 5.04, and 4.56.

Thus the first step in discrimination would be to assert that "if $x_1 > 6.18$ (any value > 6.00 but less than 6.36 could be chosen here) assign to species A; if $x_1 < 5.84$, assign to species B." After this first step, we have not assigned the following four individuals:

Species A	Species B
(5.92, 5.36)	(6.00, 4.88)
(5.92, 5.12)	(5.96, 5.08)

As our second step in discrimination we assert that "if $x_2 > 5.10$, assign to species A, otherwise to species B."

In practice we would apply rule 1 to an individual always, and rule 2 only if the individual was left unclassified by rule 1.

This method obviously generalizes to more variables, and it is subject to the same criticism which was made of Method 1: for instance, if, by chance, a *single* individual were to appear in group B with an x_1 of, say, 6.70, the whole method would fail.

METHOD 3: LINEAR DISCRIMINANT ANALYSIS

We now turn from methods that treat all points individually and discriminate pointwise, towards a family of methods that assume the existence of an underlying statistical distribution function and which discriminate on the basis of that function.

It may be the case that in a particular application one knows that a certain particular distribution function is the appropriate one. In such a case, of course, that function would be used.

The normal distribution, however, occupies a distinguished niche in probability theory. Because of the central limit theorem [7] the normal distribution is the natural candidate whenever it is reasonable to suppose that the differences between individual members of a population are the result of the action of a large number of random phenomena whose cumulative effect is additive.

We shall, therefore, restrict this discussion to the normal distribution in N-dimensional space,* though many of the results will generalize to other density functions.

First of all, the normal probability density function in N variables $(x_1, \ldots, x_N) = \mathbf{x}$ is given by

$$f(\mathbf{x}) = (2\pi)^{-N/2} \left(\det \sum\right)^{-1/2}$$

$$\times \exp\left\{-\tfrac{1}{2}\left((\mathbf{x} - \boldsymbol{\mu}), \sum{}^{-1}(\mathbf{x} - \boldsymbol{\mu})\right)\right\}$$

$$\tag{2}$$

*For an excellent introduction, see [1].

In equation (2), $\boldsymbol{\mu}$ is the N-vector of *means* of the variables $x_1, \ldots, x_N$; Σ is an $N \times N$ matrix, the *covariance* matrix of the population; Σ^{-1} is the matrix inverse of Σ; and the parenthesis $(\ ,\ )$ denotes an inner product. Thus (2) is of the form

$$f(\mathbf{x})$$
$$= (\text{const}) \times e^{-\{\text{quadratic form in } \mathbf{x} + \text{linear terms in } \mathbf{x}\}}$$
$$(3)$$

The covariance matrix Σ is positive definite.

We henceforth shall make the

ASSUMPTION 1: The different populations among which we wish to discriminate each have a normal density function of the form (2).

Two questions remain. First, how shall we estimate the parameters $\boldsymbol{\mu}$, Σ of each of the normal populations involved, and second, supposing the parameters to be known, how shall we carry out the discrimination?

We consider the second question first. Precisely, then, we are given density functions $f_1(\mathbf{x}), f_2(\mathbf{x}), \ldots, f_M(\mathbf{x})$ of M normally distributed populations. We are also given a point $\mathbf{x}$ in space of N dimensions. How shall we decide to which of the populations $\mathbf{x}$ is to be assigned?

The most natural answer turns out to be the best: *assign the point* $\mathbf{x}$ *to the population i whose density function f_i has the largest value at* $\mathbf{x}$. It is not hard to prove (see [1], p. 142) that if the a priori probabilities of encountering points of each population are equal and if the costs of misclassifying the ith population as the jth are independent of i and j, then the decision procedure stated above actually minimizes the expectation of the cost of misclassification.

We consider the first question, that of estimating the parameters of the normal populations. At first sight this appears to be a straightforward matter. If we are given K samples

$$\left(x_1^{(k)}, x_2^{(k)}, \ldots, x_N^{(k)}\right) \equiv \mathbf{x}_k,$$
$$(k = 1, \ldots, K)$$

of a certain population, it is well known that the means $(\mu_1, \ldots, \mu_N) \equiv \mathbf{M}$ may be estimated by the averages

$$\hat{\mu}_n = \frac{1}{K} \sum_{k=1}^{K} x_n^{(k)} \qquad (n = 1, \ldots, N) \quad (4)$$

and that unbiased estimates of the elements of the covariance matrix Σ are given by

$$\left(\hat{\Sigma}\right)_{rs} = \frac{1}{K-1} \sum_{k=1}^{K} \left(x_r^{(k)} - \hat{\mu}_r\right)\left(x_s^{(k)} - \hat{\mu}_s\right),$$
$$(r, s = 1, \ldots, N) \quad (5)$$

We might, therefore, estimate $\hat{\boldsymbol{\mu}}$, $\hat{\Sigma}$ from K samples in each of the populations from (4) and (5), and then, given a point $\mathbf{x}$, assign it to the population i for which the density (2) is maximal. This discrimination procedure, in fact, is only rarely used, for reasons that are in part historical and in part statistical.

Historically, the classical discriminant function of R. A. Fisher [4] results from imposing on the theoretical structure that we have so far discussed one additional assumption, namely

ASSUMPTION 2: The normal density functions of the different populations among which we wish to discriminate all have the same covariance matrix Σ.

This assumption is only occasionally discussed critically in the literature, which is surprising in view of its sweeping nature. One advantage of this assumption is the great simplification that occurs in the form of the discriminant functions. Indeed, to discover the population to which a sample point $\mathbf{x}$ is to be assigned, we need to ask a series of questions of the type

$$\text{``Is } f_i(\mathbf{x}) > f_j(\mathbf{x})?\text{''} \quad (6)$$

If we inspect (2) in the case where the covariance matrices Σ of populations i and j

are *equal* then the question (6) becomes

$$\text{"Is } -\left((\mathbf{x} - \boldsymbol{\mu}^{(i)}),\ \textstyle\sum^{-1}(\mathbf{x} - \boldsymbol{\mu}^{(i)})\right)$$

$$> -\left((\mathbf{x} - \boldsymbol{\mu}^{(j)}),\ \textstyle\sum^{-1}(\mathbf{x} - \boldsymbol{\mu}^{(j)})\right)?\text{"}$$

where $\boldsymbol{\mu}^{(i)}$ is the vector of means in the *i*th population.

Next if we expand out the inner products on both sides and cancel common terms, we find that the question becomes

$$\text{"Is } \left(\mathbf{x},\ \textstyle\sum^{-1}\boldsymbol{\mu}^{(i)}\right) - \tfrac{1}{2}\left(\boldsymbol{\mu}^{(i)},\ \textstyle\sum^{-1}\boldsymbol{\mu}^{(i)}\right)$$

$$> \left(\mathbf{x},\ \textstyle\sum^{-1}\boldsymbol{\mu}^{(j)}\right) - \tfrac{1}{2}\left(\boldsymbol{\mu}^{(j)},\ \textstyle\sum^{-1}\boldsymbol{\mu}^{(j)}\right)?\text{"}$$

in which the terms of second degree in $\mathbf{x}$ have canceled out. Finally, if we define

$$\boldsymbol{\nu}^{(i)} = \textstyle\sum^{-1}\boldsymbol{\mu}^{(i)} \qquad (i = 1, \ldots, M)$$

and

$$\lambda_i = \tfrac{1}{2}\left(\boldsymbol{\mu}^{(i)},\ \textstyle\sum^{-1}\boldsymbol{\mu}^{(i)}\right) \qquad (i = 1, \ldots, M)$$

then our question takes the final form

$$\text{"Is } (\mathbf{x}, \boldsymbol{\nu}^{(i)}) - \lambda_i > (\mathbf{x}, \boldsymbol{\nu}^{(j)}) - \lambda_j?\text{"} \quad (7)$$

Thus *a consequence of assumption 2 is that a test point* $\mathbf{x}$ *will be assigned to that population i on which the linear function*

$$h_i(\mathbf{x}) = (\mathbf{x}, \boldsymbol{\nu}^{(i)}) - \lambda_i \qquad (8)$$

is maximal.

One of the main justifications for Fisher's method is the *linearity* of the discriminant functions (8) as contrasted to the quadratic forms which are involved in the original functions (2). If this were the sole justification there would be little reason for retaining the questionable assumption in this age of electronic computers.

A second justification, however, comes from the reliability of the estimates of the population covariance matrices. Take, for example, the case of just two populations,

with parameters $(\boldsymbol{\mu}^{(1)}, \Sigma_1), (\boldsymbol{\mu}^{(2)}, \Sigma_2)$. The estimators $\hat{\Sigma}_1, \hat{\Sigma}_2$ of the covariances will, of course, *appear* to be different. But if the sample sizes K_1, K_2 are small, then statistically *we may not be able to reject the hypothesis that the underlying covariance matrices Σ_1 and Σ_2 are equal.* In such a case, that is, if the estimators $\hat{\Sigma}_1, \hat{\Sigma}_2$ are statistically indistinguishable, then evidently we gain in the reliability of the estimates by pooling the data points of the two populations for the computation of a common estimator $\hat{\Sigma}$ based on a sample of $K_1 + K_2$ points, and then using Fisher's linear decision functions (8).

METHOD 4: THE METHOD OF COALITIONS

We have now said essentially all that can be said in favor of assumption 2. In opposition to that assumption we can, of course, offer a very weighty argument, namely that if the sample sizes are *large*, and the estimators $\hat{\Sigma}_1, \hat{\Sigma}_2$ are statistically quite *different*, then if we artificially decree that $\Sigma_1 = \Sigma_2$ and pool the data for a common estimator we may be throwing away a piece of individuality of the most vital importance for doing a good discrimination. For instance, if we are trying to distinguish between malignant and benign blood cells on the basis of N measurable quantities for each cell, it might just be that there is a considerably different covariance between length of cell and diameter of nucleus in a malignant cell than in a benign one, for fundamental (if unperceived) physiological reasons. This difference of covariance may considerably enhance the discrimination process if we do not artificially submerge it by pooling the data.

The method of coalitions, which we propose here, attempts to retain the best features of assumption 2 when justified, but to drop that assumption when the covariance matrices are statistically different. We do this by the simple device of testing the hypothesis that the estimated covariances were drawn from populations with the same underlying covariance matrix. This test is made following a method due to G. E. P. Box [5], as follows:

Let $S_1, \ldots, S_M$ denote the estimated covariance matrices of a certain set of M populations. We test the hypotheses that $S_1, \ldots, S_M$ are all sampled from normal populations with a common covariance matrix. First, if $K_1, K_2, \ldots, K_M$ are the sample sizes in each population, put $n_i = K_i - 1$ $(i = 1, \ldots, M)$, compute the weighted average matrix

$$S = \sum_{i=1}^{M} n_i S_i / \sum_{i=1}^{M} n_i \qquad (9)$$

then calculate the numbers

$$T = \left(\sum_{i=1}^{M} n_i \right) \log \det S - \sum_{i=1}^{M} n_i \log \det S_i \qquad (10)$$

$$C = 1 - \frac{2N^2 + 3N - 1}{6(N + 1)(M - 1)} \left[\sum_{i=1}^{M} \frac{1}{n_i} - \frac{1}{\sum_{i=1}^{M} n_i} \right] \qquad (11)$$

The quantity TC then has approximately the χ^2 distribution with

$$\frac{(M - 1)N(N + 1)}{2} \qquad (12)$$

degrees of freedom. If TC, therefore, is acceptable to the χ^2 distribution at, say, 95% confidence, we accept the hypothesis that the covariance matrices are equal, otherwise we reject it.

We can now describe the method of coalitions. Let $\varphi(i_1, \ldots, i_L)$, for convenience of exposition, denote the quantity TC described in (10), (11) above, computed for the L populations $i_1, \ldots, i_L$.

(i) We first calculate all of the numbers

$$\varphi(i, j) \qquad (i < j)$$

and suppose $\varphi(l_1, l_2)$ is the smallest of these (note that populations l_1 and l_2 will have the same covariance matrix, according to Box's test, if there is any pair of populations which do).

(ii) If $\varphi(l_1, l_2) < \chi^2_{.95}$ then l_1 and l_2 are decreed to have the same covariance matrix, that is, to belong to the same coalition. In this case, we fix l_1, l_2, and we search through all $l_3 \neq l_1, l_2$ to see if any of the $\varphi(l_1, l_2, l_3)$ are acceptable. In general, if groups $l_1, l_2, \ldots, l_p$ have already been assigned to a coalition, we test, for each remaining unassigned group l, in turn, the hypothesis that $l_1, l_2, \ldots, l_p, l$ have the same covariance matrix. If so, l joins the coalition. We arrive finally at a maximal coalition $l_1, l_2, \ldots, l_Q$ such that $\varphi(l_1, \ldots, l_Q)$ is acceptable, but no matter what l_{Q+1} we choose, $\varphi(l_1, \ldots, l_{Q+1})$ is unacceptable. Then populations $l_1, \ldots, l_Q$ constitute a single coalition.

(iii) We delete populations $l_1, \ldots, l_Q$ from our original list and repeat the whole process from step (i) on the remaining populations, if any.

(iv) The process halts when either every population has been entered into some coalition, or, for every pair $i < j$ of remaining populations, $\varphi(i, j)$ is unacceptable. In the latter case, each remaining population is put into a "coalition" consisting only of itself.

(v) When coalitions have been formed, the data for all populations contained in any single coalition is pooled and a common covariance matrix is computed for the coalition from the pooled data.

(vi) This common matrix is used in the normal density function of each population in the coalition for the purposes of discrimination.

Two limiting cases of this procedure, either of which can be forced as an option on the program which follows, are:

1. Each coalition consists of only a single population. In this case every pair of covari-

ance matrices is statistically distinguishable.

2. All populations belong to the same coalition. In this case all data will be pooled, and the process reduces to Fisher's linear discrimination.

3. SUMMARY OF CALCULATION PROCEDURE

To compute the parameters of the discrimination from a set of data points each of which is identified according to the population to which it belongs:

Let N = number of variables

M = number of different populations among which it is desired to discriminate

K_i = number of data points which belong to the ith population (i = 1, ..., M).

Then,

1. For each population i = 1, ..., M compute the mean vector $\boldsymbol{\mu}^{(i)}$ of the population, according to (4).

2. For each population i = 1, ..., M compute the estimated covariance matrix $S^{(i)}$ of the population, according to (5).

3. Calculate the determinant of each $S^{(i)}$, and the inverse of each $S^{(i)}$. The inverse will be used as the Σ^{-1} in (2) for the evaluation of the normal density of population i.

4. Group the given set of M populations into coalitions by forming maximal sets of populations with statistically indistinguishable covariance matrices, as described in (9)–(12) *et seq.* Let N_c denote the number of coalitions which result.

5. For each coalition j = 1, 2, ..., N_c compute the pooled covariance matrix $\Sigma^{(j)}$ of the coalition by using all of the data points from all of the populations belonging to the coalition.

6. Compute the determinant Δ_j, and the inverse $(\Sigma^{(j)})^{-1}$ of each $\Sigma^{(j)}$, j = 1, ..., N_c.

7. Punch out, on option, the parameters of the discrimination, which are (a) a list of the populations which belong to each coalition, (b) the mean vectors $\boldsymbol{\mu}^{(i)}$ for each

population i = 1, ..., M, (c) the matrix $(\Sigma^{(j)})^{-1}$ and the number Δ_j for each coalition j = 1, ..., N_c. These cards can be used as an input for future discrimination of new data points.

8. Use the parameters that have just been computed to sort out the original data points, that is, to find out to which populations the method would assign each of these data points, and with what probabilities, and compare with the actual population to which the data point is known to belong. This is done as follows: given a data point $\mathbf{x}$; for each population i = 1, 2, ..., M compute the value $f_i(x)$ of the normal density (2), in which $\boldsymbol{\mu}$ is the vector of means of the population i and Σ is the covariance matrix of the coalition to which population i belongs.

Let $f_p(\mathbf{x})$ be the largest of these numbers, and let $f_q(\mathbf{x})$ be the second largest. Then print out the fact that with probability

$$\frac{f_p(\mathbf{x})}{\sum\limits_{j=1}^{M} f_j(\mathbf{x})}$$

the point $\mathbf{x}$ is assigned to population p and with probability

$$\frac{f_q(x)}{\sum\limits_{j=1}^{M} f_j(x)}$$

it would be assigned to population q.

9. Print out the matrix whose i, j entry is the number of data points that really belong to population i and were assigned to population j (i, j = 1, ..., M). Hopefully this matrix will have large diagonal entries with a sprinkling of small numbers off the diagonal.

4. FLOW CHART

The flow chart for this program is given on pages 103–112.

5. DESCRIPTION OF FLOW CHART

The program operates in any of three modes and any of three options.

MODE 1: Compute discrimination parameters, use them on the original input data points.

MODE 2: Compute discrimination parameters and punch them out for future use.

MODE 3: Does both of the preceding.

OPTION 1: The method of coalitions as described previously.

OPTION 2: All populations put into the same coalition, therefore identical with classical linear discrimination.

OPTION 3: Each coalition consists of a single population, that is, pure "quadratic discrimination."

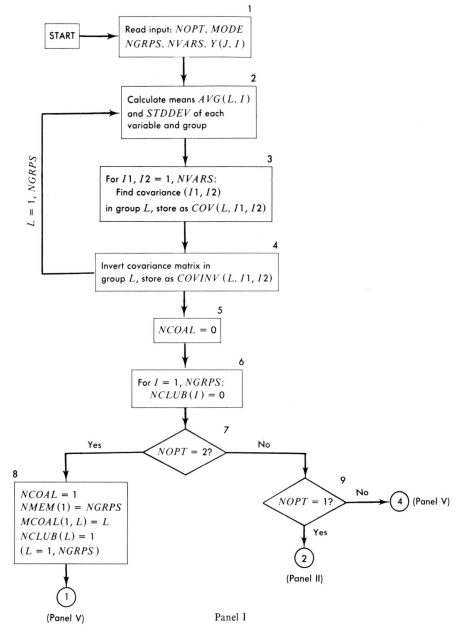

Panel I

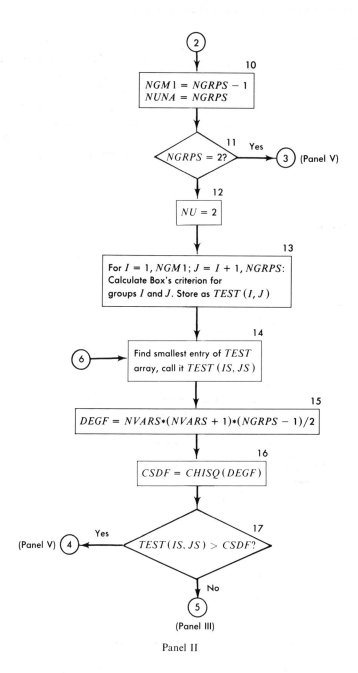

Panel II

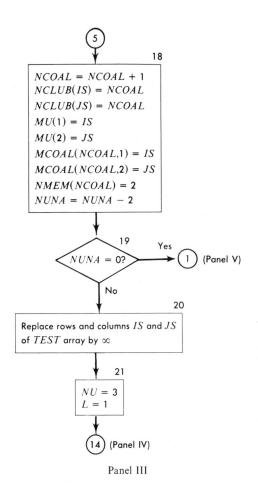

Panel III

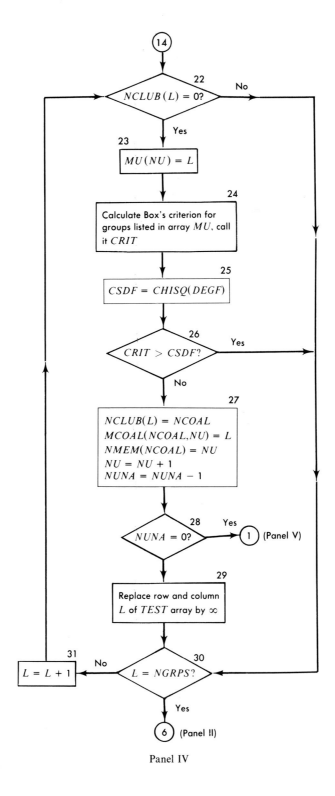

Panel IV

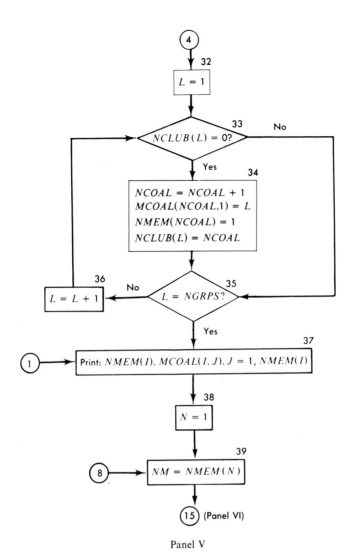

Panel V

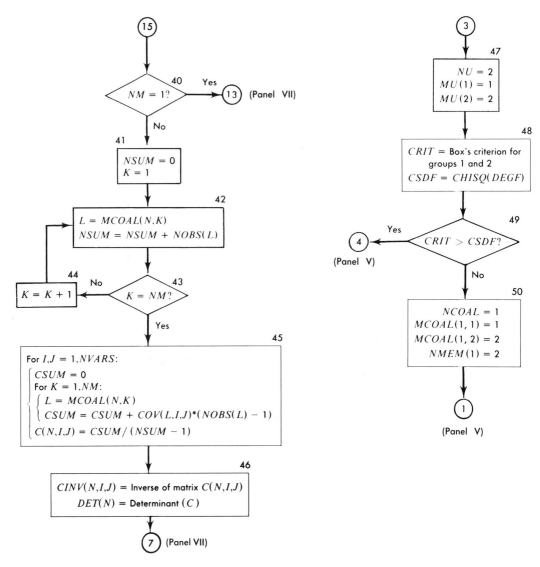

Panel VI

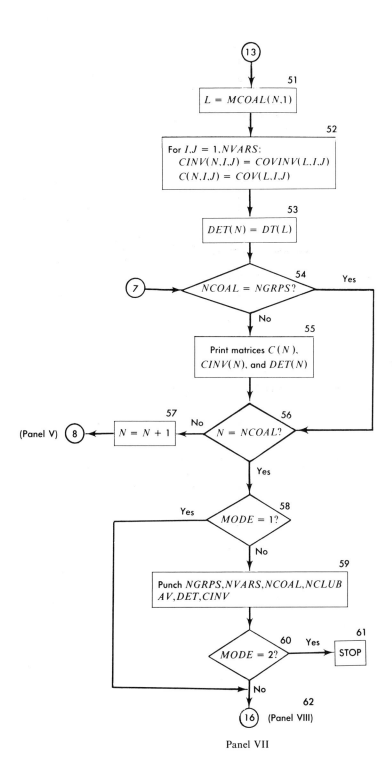

Panel VII

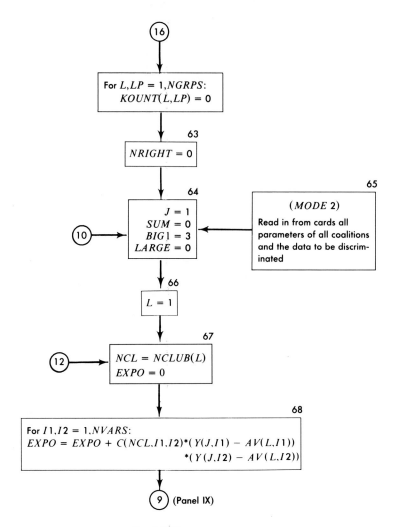

Panel VIII

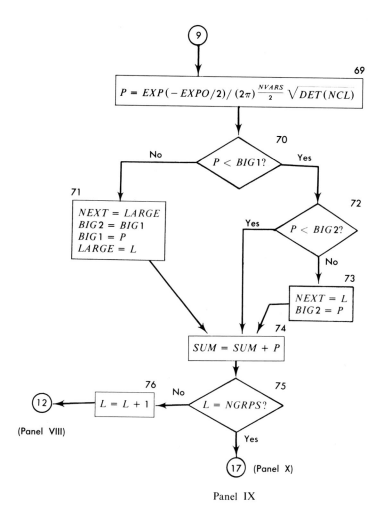

Panel IX

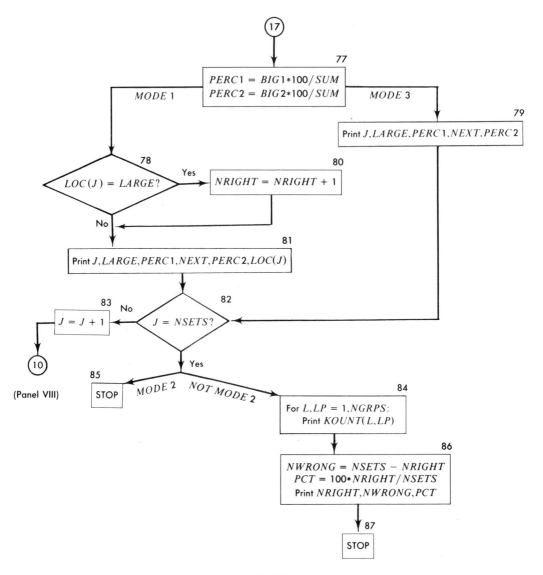

Panel X

Input data required:

1. Option (*NOPT*); FORMAT I3
2. Mode (*MODE*); FORMAT I3
3. Number of populations (*NGRPS*); FORMAT I3
4. Number of variables (*NVARS*); FORMAT I3
5. Number of data points in group *L* (*NOBS(L)*); FORMAT I3
6. Data points in group *L*; FREE FORMAT

The order is Card 1: *NOPT*; columns 1–3
Card 2: *MODE*; columns 1–3
Card 3: *NGRPS*; columns 1–3; *NVARS*; columns 4–6
Thereafter, 5, 6(*L* = 1), 5, 6(*L* = 2), . . . , 5, 6(*L* = *NGRPS*)

a. Box-by-Box Description of the Flow Chart (refer to directory of variable names, page 114)

Box 1: Input data are read in.

Boxes 2–4: Means, standard deviations, covariance matrices, their determinants and their inverses are calculated, for each variable and group.

Box 5: Begin forming coalitions. *NCOAL*, the number of coalitions so far found, is set to zero.

Box 6: *NCLUB(I)* are all set to zero.

Box 8: On option 2 all groups are put on the same coalition.

Box 10: On option 1 the coalitions will form themselves. *NUNA* is set to *NGRPS*.

Box 11: If there are only two groups a separate procedure is used (Box 47).

Boxes 12–13: For each pair of variables, the statistic *TC* of equations (10), (11) is computed and stored as *TEST(I, J)*.

Box 14: *IS*, *JS* are the row and column in which we find the smallest entry of *TEST*.

Boxes 14–17: χ^2 is computed for *DEGF* degrees of freedom, and the smallest *TEST* is compared with it for significance.

Box 18: Groups *IS*, *JS* are assigned to the same coalition.

Box 19: If all groups have been assigned to coalitions, exit to Box 37.

Box 20: *TEST(IS, J), TEST(I, JS)* are replaced by $+\infty$, for all *I, J*.

Boxes 21–31: Each unassigned group, *L*, in turn, is examined to see if it can be added to the coalition which is currently being formed. First group *L*, together with all already in the coalition, have their joint Box's criterion computed (Box 24). If significant (Box 26) group *L* is adjoined (Box 27) to the coalition. If unassigned groups remain (Box 28), the process is repeated on them to see if they can join the now augmented coalition.

Boxes 32–36: Each group is examined, in turn, to see if it has been assigned to a coalition. If not, it is assigned to a coalition consisting of only itself. In option 3, all groups are assigned here.

Box 37: All coalitions are formed. Print their structure.

Box 38: Begin forming pooled covariance matrices within each coalition.

Boxes 39–46: If only one group in coalition *N* (Box 40) exit to Box 51. Otherwise calculate total number *NSUM* of data points in the coalition and pool (Box 45) all data points of all groups in coalition *N* to form *C(N, I, J)*. The determinant and inverse of this matrix are calculated (Box 46).

Boxes 47–50: Special procedure if there are only two groups (*NGRPS* = 2), for forming coalitions.

Boxes 51–53: Special procedure for a coalition with just one member group.

Boxes 54–57: If some coalition contains more than one group the pooled matrices for the coalition just formed are printed.

Boxes 58–61: In modes 2 or 3 punch out the parameters just computed. In mode 2 the process is finished. In mode 1 omit the punch-out.

Box 62: Here begins the process of using the calculated parameters in order to discriminate the original input data to the problem.

Boxes 63–67: Prepare to find the largest and next-to-largest of the normal density functions of each group evaluated at the current data set J.

Boxes 68–69: Compute normal density function P of group L evaluated at current data set J.

Boxes 70–74: Logic associated with finding largest and second-largest.

Box 77: Probability that data point J belongs to group *LARGE* is *PERC*1. Probability that it belongs to group *NEXT* is *PERC*2.

Box 78: Actual group to which it belongs is *LOC(J)*.

Box 79: In mode 3, print identification of data set J.

Box 80: If identification is correct, increase *NRIGHT*.

Boxes 81–83: Print identification of data set J and do next set.

Boxes 84–87: In mode 2, stop. In mode 1, print the number of identifications of a member of group L as a member of group LP, the total number of correct and incorrect identifications, and stop.

b. Directory of Variable Names

AVG(L, I)	Average value of variable I in group L
C(N, I, J)	I, J entry of the pooled covariance matrix in coalition N
CINV(N, I, J)	I, J entry of the inverse of the pooled covariance matrix in coalition N
COV(L, I1, I2)	The $I1, I2$ entry on the covariance matrix in group L.
COVINV(L, I1, I2)	The $I1, I2$ entry in the inverse of the covariance matrix in group L.
DET(N)	Determinant of the pooled covariance matrix in coalition N
DT(L)	Determinant of the covariance matrix in group L
KOUNT(L, LP)	Number of input data sets of group L which were assigned to group LP by the discrimination process
LOC(J)	The group to which data set J belongs
MCOAL(I, J)	The group which is the Jth number of the Ith coalition
MODE	Mode of operation
NCLUB(I)	The coalition to which group I belongs
NCOAL	The number of coalitions so far formed
NGRPS	Number of populations among which we wish to discriminate
NMEM(I)	The number of groups in the Ith coalition
NOBS(L)	The number of observations (= data sets) of each variable in group L
NOPT	Chosen option
NRIGHT	Number of correct assignments of an input data set to its group.
NUNA	Number of groups so far unassigned to a coalition.
NVARS	The number of variables
Y(J, I)	Value of the Ith variable in the Jth data set. J counts continuously from 1 to $(NOBS(1) + \cdots + NOBS(NGRPS))$.

6. SUBROUTINES

The following subroutines are used by the program but they are not included in the flow chart. Several of these subroutines are of independent interest.

a. Subroutine AVG(K, S, AVE)

Computes the average of the K elements of the array $S(1), \ldots, S(K)$, leaving the answer in AVE.

b. Subroutine STDEV(K, S, AVE, SD)

Finds the standard deviation of the K elements of the array S, whose average is AVE, and stores it in SD.

c. Subroutine COVAR(A1, A2, K, T, CV)

Calculates the covariance of two variables. Each of the variables has K observations. The K observations of the first variable are stored as $T(1, J), J = 1, K$; and of the second are $T(2, J), J = 1, K$. $A1$ and $A2$ are the means of the two variables, and the answer is left in CV.

d. Subroutine EQCOV(NGRPS, K, MU, COV, DET, NVARS, NOBS, CRIT, DEGF)

Calculates quantity to test the hypothesis that a given set of covariance matrices are all equal. K is the number of matrices in the set. It is supposed that there is in storage a set of $NGRPS$ covariance matrices $COV(L, I, J)$ where $L = 1, NGRPS$; $I, J = 1, NVARS$. It is desired to test a certain subset of K of them for equality. The values of L corresponding to this subset are $MU(1), MU(2), \ldots, MU(K)$. The determinant of $COV(L, I, J)$ is $DET(L)$, $L = 1, NGRPS$. $NOBS(L)$ is the number of observations on which the Lth covariance matrix is based.

The subroutine calculates the quantity TC of Box's test as shown in Eqs. (10)–(11) above, stores it as $CRIT$, then calculates the degrees of freedom $DEGF$, as in (12) above, for a χ^2 test.

e. Subroutine MINV(A, N, D, L, M)

This is a matrix inversion routine from the IBM SSP package.

f. Function CHISQ(X)

This calculates the 95% confidence level for the χ^2 distribution with x degrees of freedom, as

$$CHISQ = X + 1.65\sqrt{2X} + 1$$

7. SAMPLE PROBLEM

Our sample problem is the famous example that was used by Fisher [4] in his original work and is shown on pages 116–120. The problem is to distinguish between three species of Iris (*setosa, versicolor, virginica*) on the basis of four variables

$$x_1 = \text{sepal length}$$
$$x_2 = \text{sepal width}$$
$$x_3 = \text{petal length}$$
$$x_4 = \text{petal width}$$

The given data are measurements of these four variables on 150 individuals, 50 of each of the three species. It will be noticed that in this case the program decided to put each species of Iris into a separate coalition, meaning that their covariance matrices were statistically quite different, and that the program in fact misclassified only three individuals out of the 150 given.

8. ACKNOWLEDGMENTS

My thanks are due first of all to Mr. William Ryan, of the University of Pennsylvania, who prepared the program itself, rapidly and accurately. Next, to Dr. Mortimer Mendelsohn, of the Radiology Department of the University of Pennsylvania I am indebted for several stimulating discussions, while to him and Dr. Brian Mayall of the same department go my appreciation for the opportunity to test the

```
                /GO
OPTION  1   MODE   1

OBSERVATIONS IN GROUP  1:


    1         5.1000        3.5000        1.4000        0.20000
    2         4.9000        3.0000        1.4000        0.20000
    3         4.7000        3.2000        1.3000        0.20000
    4         4.6000        3.1000        1.5000        0.20000
    5         5.0000        3.6000        1.4000        0.20000
    6         5.4000        3.9000        1.7000        0.40000
    7         4.6000        3.4000        1.4000        0.30000
    8         5.0000        3.4000        1.5000        0.20000
    9         4.4000        2.9000        1.4000        0.20000
   10         4.9000        3.1000        1.5000        0.10000
   11         5.4000        3.7000        1.5000        0.20000
   12         4.8000        3.4000        1.6000        0.20000
   13         4.8000        3.0000        1.4000        0.10000
   14         4.3000        3.0000        1.1000        0.10000
   15         5.8000        4.0000        1.2000        0.20000
   16         5.7000        4.4000        1.5000        0.40000
   17         5.4000        3.9000        1.3000        0.40000
   18         5.1000        3.5000        1.4000        0.30000
   19         5.7000        3.8000        1.7000        0.30000
   20         5.1000        3.8000        1.5000        0.30000
   21         5.4000        3.4000        1.7000        0.20000
   22         5.1000        3.7000        1.5000        0.40000
   23         4.6000        3.6000        1.0000        0.20000
   24         5.1000        3.3000        1.7000        0.50000
   25         4.8000        3.4000        1.9000        0.20000
   26         5.0000        3.0000        1.6000        0.20000
   27         5.0000        3.4000        1.6000        0.40000
   28         5.2000        3.5000        1.5000        0.20000
   29         5.2000        3.4000        1.4000        0.20000
   30         4.7000        3.2000        1.6000        0.20000
   31         4.8000        3.1000        1.6000        0.20000
   32         5.4000        3.4000        1.5000        0.40000
   33         5.2000        4.1000        1.5000        0.10000
   34         5.5000        4.2000        1.4000        0.20000
   35         4.9000        3.1000        1.5000        0.20000
   36         5.0000        3.2000        1.2000        0.20000
   37         5.5000        3.5000        1.3000        0.20000
   38         4.9000        3.6000        1.4000        0.10000
   39         4.4000        3.0000        1.3000        0.20000
   40         5.1000        3.4000        1.5000        0.20000
   41         5.0000        3.5000        1.3000        0.30000
   42         4.5000        2.3000        1.3000        0.30000
   43         4.4000        3.2000        1.3000        0.20000
   44         5.0000        3.5000        1.6000        0.60000
   45         5.1000        3.8000        1.9000        0.40000
   46         4.8000        3.0000        1.4000        0.30000
   47         5.1000        3.8000        1.6000        0.20000
   48         4.6000        3.2000        1.4000        0.20000
   49         5.3000        3.7000        1.5000        0.20000
   50         5.0000        3.3000        1.4000        0.20000


GROUP  1    VARIABLE  1      AVERAGE =   5.0060      STANDARD DEVIATION =   0.35249
GROUP  1    VARIABLE  2      AVERAGE =   3.4280      STANDARD DEVIATION =   0.37906
GROUP  1    VARIABLE  3      AVERAGE =   1.4620      STANDARD DEVIATION =   0.17366
GROUP  1    VARIABLE  4      AVERAGE =   0.24600     STANDARD DEVIATION =   0.10539

THE COVARIANCE MATRIX FOR GROUP   1 IS


   0.12425        0.99216E-01    0.16355E-01    0.10331E-01
   0.99216E-01    0.14369        0.11698E-01    0.92979E-02
   0.16355E-01    0.11698E-01    0.30159E-01    0.60694E-02
   0.10331E-01    0.92979E-02    0.60694E-02    0.11106E-01

THE DETERMINANT OF THE COVARIANCE MATRIX FOR GROUP 1 IS 0.21131E-05

THE INVERSE OF THE COVARIANCE MATRIX FOR GROUP 1 IS


   18.943        -12.405        -4.5003        -4.7761
  -12.405         15.571         1.1111        -2.1041
   -4.5002         1.1111        38.776        -17.935
   -4.7761        -2.1041       -17.935        106.05
```

Sample Problem (Continued)

```
OBSERVATIONS IN GROUP 2:

    1        7.0000        3.2000        4.7000        1.4000
    2        6.4000        3.2000        4.5000        1.5000
    3        6.9000        3.1000        4.9000        1.5000
    4        5.5000        2.3000        4.0000        1.3000
    5        6.5000        2.8000        4.6000        1.5000
    6        5.7000        2.8000        4.5000        1.3000
    7        6.3000        3.3000        4.7000        1.6000
    8        4.9000        2.4000        3.3000        1.0000
    9        6.6000        2.9000        4.6000        1.3000
   10        5.2000        2.7000        3.9000        1.4000
   11        5.0000        2.0000        3.5000        1.0000
   12        5.9000        3.0000        4.2000        1.5000
   13        6.0000        2.2000        4.0000        1.0000
   14        6.1000        2.9000        4.7000        1.4000
   15        5.6000        2.9000        3.6000        1.3000
   16        6.7000        3.1000        4.4000        1.4000
   17        5.6000        3.0000        4.5000        1.5000
   18        5.8000        2.7000        4.1000        1.0000
   19        6.2000        2.2000        4.5000        1.5000
   20        5.6000        2.5000        3.9000        1.1000
   21        5.9000        3.2000        4.8000        1.8000
   22        6.1000        2.8000        4.0000        1.3000
   23        6.3000        2.5000        4.9000        1.5000

   24        6.1000        2.8000        4.7000        1.2000
   25        6.4000        2.9000        4.3000        1.3000
   26        6.6000        3.0000        4.4000        1.4000
   27        6.8000        2.8000        4.8000        1.4000
   28        6.7000        3.0000        5.0000        1.7000
   29        6.0000        2.9000        4.5000        1.5000
   30        5.7000        2.6000        3.5000        1.0000
   31        5.5000        2.4000        3.8000        1.1000
   32        5.5000        2.4000        3.7000        1.0000
   33        5.8000        2.7000        3.9000        1.2000
   34        6.0000        2.7000        5.1000        1.6000
   35        5.4000        3.0000        4.5000        1.5000
   36        6.0000        3.4000        4.5000        1.6000
   37        6.7000        3.1000        4.7000        1.5000
   38        6.3000        2.3000        4.4000        1.3000
   39        5.6000        3.0000        4.1000        1.3000
   40        5.5000        2.5000        4.0000        1.3000
   41        5.5000        2.6000        4.4000        1.2000
   42        6.1000        3.0000        4.6000        1.4000
   43        5.8000        2.6000        4.0000        1.2000
   44        5.0000        2.3000        3.3000        1.0000
   45        5.6000        2.7000        4.2000        1.3000
   46        5.7000        3.0000        4.2000        1.2000
   47        5.7000        2.9000        4.2000        1.3000
   48        6.2000        2.9000        4.3000        1.3000
   49        5.1000        2.5000        3.0000        1.1000
   50        5.7000        2.8000        4.1000        1.3000


GROUP   2    VARIABLE    1      AVERAGE =    5.9360      STANDARD DEVIATION =   0.51617
GROUP   2    VARIABLE    2      AVERAGE =    2.7700      STANDARD DEVIATION =   0.31380
GROUP   2    VARIABLE    3      AVERAGE =    4.2600      STANDARD DEVIATION =   0.46991
GROUP   2    VARIABLE    4      AVERAGE =    1.3260      STANDARD DEVIATION =   0.19775

THE COVARIANCE MATRIX FOR GROUP   2 IS


   0.26643        0.85183E-01    0.18290        0.55779E-01
   0.85183E-01    0.98469E-01    0.82653E-01    0.41204E-01
   0.18290        0.82653E-01    0.22082        0.73102E-01
   0.55779E-01    0.41204E-01    0.73102E-01    0.39106E-01
```

117

```
THE DETERMINANT OF THE COVARIANCE MATRIX FOR GROUP 2 IS 0.18938E-04

THE INVERSE OF THE COVARIANCE MATRIX FOR GROUP 2 IS


    9.5028        -3.6762        -8.6317         6.4546
   -3.6762        19.711          2.1160        -19.480
   -8.6317         2.1160        19.804         -26.937
    6.4546        -19.480        -26.937         87.245

OBSERVATIONS IN GROUP 3:


    1        6.3000        3.3000        6.0000        2.5000
    2        5.8000        2.7000        5.1000        1.9000
    3        7.1000        3.0000        5.9000        2.1000
    4        6.3000        2.9000        5.6000        1.8000
    5        6.5000        3.0000        5.8000        2.2000
    6        7.6000        3.0000        6.6000        2.1000
    7        4.9000        2.5000        4.5000        1.7000
    8        7.3000        2.9000        6.3000        1.8000

    9        6.7000        2.5000        5.8000        1.8000
   10        7.2000        3.6000        6.1000        2.5000
   11        6.5000        3.2000        5.1000        2.0000
   12        6.4000        2.7000        5.3000        1.9000
   13        6.8000        3.0000        5.5000        2.1000
   14        5.7000        2.5000        5.0000        2.0000
   15        5.8000        2.8000        5.1000        2.4000
   16        6.4000        3.2000        5.3000        2.3000
   17        6.5000        3.0000        5.5000        1.8000
   18        7.7000        3.8000        6.7000        2.2000
   19        7.7000        2.6000        6.9000        2.3000
   20        6.0000        2.2000        5.0000        1.5000
   21        6.9000        3.2000        5.7000        2.3000
   22        5.6000        2.8000        4.9000        2.0000
   23        7.7000        2.8000        6.7000        2.0000
   24        6.3000        2.7000        4.9000        1.8000
   25        6.7000        3.3000        5.7000        2.1000
   26        7.2000        3.2000        6.0000        1.8000
   27        6.2000        2.8000        4.8000        1.8000
   28        6.1000        3.0000        4.9000        1.8000
   29        6.4000        2.8000        5.6000        2.1000
   30        7.2000        3.0000        5.8000        1.6000
   31        7.4000        2.8000        6.1000        1.9000
   32        7.9000        3.8000        6.4000        2.0000
   33        6.4000        2.8000        5.6000        2.2000
   34        6.3000        2.8000        5.1000        1.5000
   35        6.1000        2.6000        5.6000        1.4000
   36        7.7000        3.0000        6.1000        2.3000
   37        6.3000        3.4000        5.6000        2.4000
   38        6.4000        3.1000        5.5000        1.8000
   39        6.0000        3.0000        4.8000        1.8000
   40        6.9000        3.1000        5.4000        2.1000
   41        6.7000        3.1000        5.6000        2.4000
   42        6.9000        3.1000        5.1000        2.3000
   43        5.8000        2.7000        5.1000        1.9000
   44        6.8000        3.2000        5.9000        2.3000
   45        6.7000        3.3000        5.7000        2.5000
   46        6.7000        3.0000        5.2000        2.3000
   47        6.3000        2.5000        5.0000        1.9000
   48        6.5000        3.0000        5.2000        2.0000
   49        6.2000        3.4000        5.4000        2.3000
   50        5.9000        3.0000        5.1000        1.8000


GROUP  3    VARIABLE  1     AVERAGE =   6.5880        STANDARD DEVIATION =  0.63588
GROUP  3    VARIABLE  2     AVERAGE =   2.9740        STANDARD DEVIATION =  0.32250
GROUP  3    VARIABLE  3     AVERAGE =   5.5520        STANDARD DEVIATION =  0.55189
GROUP  3    VARIABLE  4     AVERAGE =   2.0260        STANDARD DEVIATION =  0.27465

THE COVARIANCE MATRIX FOR GROUP  3 IS


   0.40434        0.93763E-01   0.30329        0.49094E-01
   0.93763E-01    0.10400       0.71379E-01    0.47628E-01
   0.30329        0.71379E-01   0.30459        0.48824E-01
   0.49094E-01    0.47628E-01   0.48824E-01    0.75432E-01

THE DETERMINANT OF THE COVARIANCE MATRIX FOR GROUP 3 IS 0.13274E-03

THE INVERSE OF THE COVARIANCE MATRIX FOR GROUP 3 IS


   10.534        -3.4798        -9.9605         1.7882


   -3.4798        15.876         1.1028        -8.4729
   -9.9605         1.1028        13.406        -2.8909
    1.7882        -8.4729        -2.8909        19.314

                 TEST MATRIX
   66.810        109.30
   0000000000000  35.037

CHI-SQ( 20.000   )= 31.436        SMALLEST TEST =  35.037        TEST( 2, 3)

THERE ARE 3 COALITIONS

    COALITION 1 HAS 1 MEMBER(S). THEY ARE:


        1

    COALITION 2 HAS 1 MEMBER(S). THEY ARE:


        2

    COALITION 3 HAS 1 MEMBER(S). THEY ARE:


        3
```

Sample Problem (Continued)

DATA SET	GROUP	PROBABILITY	GROUP	PROBABILITY	ACTUAL GROUP
1	1	100.0000%	2	0.0000%	1
2	1	100.0000%	2	0.0000%	1
3	1	100.0000%	2	0.0000%	1
4	1	100.0000%	2	0.0000%	1
5	1	100.0000%	2	0.0000%	1
6	1	99.9999%	2	0.0000%	1
7	1	99.9999%	2	0.0000%	1
8	1	100.0000%	2	0.0000%	1
9	1	100.0000%	2	0.0000%	1
10	1	99.9999%	2	0.0000%	1
11	1	100.0000%	2	0.0000%	1
12	1	100.0000%	2	0.0000%	1
13	1	100.0000%	2	0.0000%	1
14	1	100.0000%	2	0.0000%	1
15	1	100.0000%	2	0.0000%	1
16	1	100.0000%	2	0.0000%	1
17	1	100.0000%	2	0.0000%	1
18	1	100.0000%	2	0.0000%	1
19	1	100.0000%	2	0.0000%	1
20	1	100.0000%	2	0.0000%	1
21	1	100.0000%	2	0.0000%	1
22	1	100.0000%	2	0.0000%	1
23	1	100.0000%	2	0.0000%	1
24	1	100.0000%	2	0.0000%	1
25	1	100.0000%	2	0.0000%	1
26	1	99.9999%	2	0.0000%	1
27	1	100.0000%	2	0.0000%	1
28	1	100.0000%	2	0.0000%	1
29	1	100.0000%	2	0.0000%	1
30	1	100.0000%	2	0.0000%	1
31	1	100.0000%	2	0.0000%	1
32	1	100.0000%	2	0.0000%	1
33	1	100.0000%	2	0.0000%	1
34	1	100.0000%	2	0.0000%	1
35	1	100.0000%	2	0.0000%	1
36	1	100.0000%	2	0.0000%	1
37	1	100.0000%	2	0.0000%	1
38	1	100.0000%	2	0.0000%	1
39	1	99.9999%	2	0.0000%	1
40	1	100.0000%	2	0.0000%	1
41	1	100.0000%	2	0.0000%	1
42	1	100.0000%	2	0.0000%	1
43	1	100.0000%	2	0.0000%	1
44	1	100.0000%	2	0.0000%	1
45	1	100.0000%	2	0.0000%	1
46	1	100.0000%	2	0.0000%	1
47	1	100.0000%	2	0.0000%	1
48	1	100.0000%	2	0.0000%	1
49	1	100.0000%	2	0.0000%	1
50	1	100.0000%	2	0.0000%	1
51	2	99.9956%	3	0.0044%	2
52	2	99.9650%	3	0.0350%	2
53	2	99.8386%	3	0.1614%	2
54	2	99.7221%	3	0.2779%	2
55	2	99.7344%	3	0.2656%	2
56	2	98.8829%	3	1.1172%	2
57	2	99.4709%	3	0.5291%	2
58	2	99.9994%	3	0.0006%	2
59	2	99.9787%	3	0.0213%	2
60	2	99.3656%	3	0.6344%	2
61	2	99.9938%	3	0.0062%	2
62	2	99.8549%	3	0.1450%	2
63	2	99.9986%	3	0.0014%	2
64	2	98.8481%	3	1.1520%	2
65	2	99.9989%	3	0.0011%	2
66	2	99.9987%	3	0.0013%	2
67	2	97.3369%	3	2.6631%	2
68	2	99.9866%	3	0.0133%	2
69	2	81.3094%	3	18.6906%	2
70	2	99.9964%	3	0.0036%	2
71	3	66.4082%	2	33.5917%	2
72	2	99.9990%	3	0.0010%	2
73	2	69.9321%	3	30.0678%	2
74	2	97.2111%	3	2.7889%	2
75	2	99.9979%	3	0.0021%	2
76	2	99.9968%	3	0.0032%	2
77	2	99.8466%	3	0.1534%	2
78	2	86.0996%	3	13.9004%	2
79	2	99.2145%	3	0.7855%	2
80	2	100.0000%	3	0.0000%	2
81	2	99.9970%	3	0.0030%	2
82	2	99.9994%	3	0.0006%	2
83	2	99.9989%	3	0.0011%	2
84	3	84.5654%	2	15.4346%	2
85	2	94.3427%	3	5.6572%	2
86	2	99.5999%	3	0.4000%	2
87	2	99.9393%	3	0.0607%	2
88	2	99.8898%	3	0.1102%	2
89	2	99.9764%	3	0.0236%	2
90	2	99.8944%	3	0.1056%	2
91	2	98.0653%	3	1.9347%	2
92	2	99.6970%	3	0.3030%	2
93	2	99.9960%	3	0.0041%	2
94	2	99.9996%	3	0.0004%	2
95	2	99.8638%	3	0.1362%	2
96	2	99.9727%	3	0.0273%	2
97	2	99.9574%	3	0.0425%	2
98	2	99.9932%	3	0.0067%	2
99	2	99.9999%	3	0.0001%	2
100	2	99.9760%	3	0.0240%	2
101	3	100.0000%	2	0.0000%	3
102	3	99.9544%	2	0.0456%	3
103	3	99.9946%	2	0.0054%	3
104	3	99.4158%	2	0.5842%	3
105	3	99.9997%	2	0.0003%	3
106	3	99.9998%	2	0.0002%	3
107	3	99.6122%	2	0.3878%	3

Sample Problem (Continued)

108	3	99.9955%	2	0.0044%	3
109	3	99.9870%	2	0.0130%	3
110	3	99.9999%	2	0.0000%	3
111	3	99.3949%	2	0.6050%	3
112	3	99.9049%	2	0.0951%	3
113	3	99.9935%	2	0.0065%	3
114	3	99.9998%	2	0.0002%	3
115	3	100.0000%	2	0.0000%	3
116	3	100.0000%	2	0.0000%	3
117	3	96.6898%	2	3.3102%	3
118	3	99.9740%	2	0.0260%	3
119	3	100.0000%	2	0.0000%	3
120	3	95.8899%	2	4.1101%	3
121	3	100.0000%	2	0.0001%	3
122	3	99.9975%	2	0.0025%	3
123	3	100.0000%	2	0.0000%	3
124	3	97.1915%	2	2.8084%	3
125	3	99.9105%	2	0.0895%	3
126	3	99.2653%	2	0.7346%	3
127	3	94.3361%	2	5.6639%	3
128	3	84.8872%	2	15.1128%	3
129	3	99.9994%	2	0.0006%	3
130	3	98.0183%	2	1.9817%	3
131	3	99.9848%	2	0.0152%	3
132	3	99.0766%	2	0.9234%	3
133	3	100.0000%	2	0.0000%	3
134	2	60.4965%	3	39.5035%	3
135	3	99.9784%	2	0.0216%	3
136	3	100.0000%	2	0.0000%	3
137	3	100.0000%	2	0.0000%	3
138	3	94.9811%	2	5.0189%	3
139	3	85.9297%	2	14.0703%	3
140	3	99.9811%	2	0.0189%	3
141	3	100.0000%	2	0.0000%	3
142	3	100.0000%	2	0.0000%	3
143	3	99.9544%	2	0.0456%	3
144	3	99.9999%	2	0.0001%	3
145	3	100.0000%	2	0.0000%	3
146	3	100.0000%	2	0.0000%	3
147	3	99.9834%	2	0.0166%	3
148	3	99.8932%	2	0.1068%	3
149	3	99.9999%	2	0.0001%	3
150	3	93.9184%	2	6.0816%	3

method with some of their data on various types of human blood cells. Finally, the research described herein was supported by a grant from the National Science Foundation.

9. REFERENCES

1. T. W. Anderson, *An Introduction to Multivariate Statistical Analysis*, Wiley, New York, 1958.

2. D. F. Morrison, *Multivariate Statistical Methods*, McGraw-Hill, New York, 1967.

3. P. R. Krishnaiah (ed.), *Multivariate Analysis (Symposium)*, Academic Press, New York, 1966.

4. R. A. Fisher, "The Use of Multiple Measurements in Taxonomic Problems," *Ann. Eugenics*, **7**, 179–188 (1937).

5. G.E.P. Box, "A General Distribution Theory for a Class of Likelihood Criteria," *Biometrika*, **36**, 317–346 (1949).

6. P. Hoel, *Introduction to Mathematical Statistics*, Wiley, New York, 1947.

7. W. Feller, *An Introduction to Probability Theory and Its Applications*, Wiley, New York, 1968.

PART III | PRINCIPAL COMPONENTS AND FACTOR ANALYSIS

Editorial Preface to Part III

Chapters 7–10 deal with principal components and factor analysis. The reader might wonder why we include several methods of factor analysis—Chapter 10 on multivariate analysis of variance and covariance really stands quite by itself.

Chapter 7 by Jöreskog presents a general, all-encompassing series of methods for orthogonal factor analysis by the least-squares and maximum likelihood methods. It uses a very elegant algorithm to switch between the three implemented methods. Harman's Chapter 8 is really an early and special implementation of the ULS algorithm of Jöreskog, arrived at by a totally independent path via a different algorithm. The reader will recall that a chapter by Harman on factor analysis was included in Volume 1 of this series. That chapter did not, among other variants, include the solution to the Heywood case, that is, an algorithm to treat the problem of a communality > 1.0.

Cattell's Chapter 9 is structurally different from the standard format of this volume. He discusses methods of interpretation of factor analytic results and what to do if one does not wish an orthogonal but rather an oblique solution. The latter is particularly useful in applications in psychology. Cattell thus concentrates on the uses of factor analysis and relates this scientific method to the art of discovering structure.

The reader may in fact wish to read the introductory sections of Chapters 7 and 9 first before proceeding to the more technical aspects of these two chapters and Chapter 8.

The editors were in a quandry as to whether these chapters could be unified in a different fashion but felt that this sequence would still preserve the greatest utility to the reader.

Just as for Chapters 3–6, we have felt it necessary to include a symbol equivalency table for these four chapters.

Chapter			
7	8	9	
Λ	A	V_0	Matrix of coefficients of common factors
	α_{jp}		Factor loading, i.e., coefficient of factor p in the linear expression of variable j in terms of the factors
	H		Diagonal matrix of "communalities"
k	m	k	Number of common factors
p	n	n	Number of variables
	r_{jk}		Correlation between variable j and variable k
r_{ij}			Correlation between variable i and variable j
e	u		Vector of n "unique" factors
x	z		Vector of observed variables
	μ		A Lagrange multiplier
μ			Mean vector of variables
$x_{\alpha i}$			Observed value of variable for individual α
A			A symmetric matrix, $S - \Psi^2$ or $\Psi S^{-1}\Psi$
H			Matrix of derivatives $\partial^2 f / \partial\sigma\,\partial\theta$

Factor Analysis by Least-squares and Maximum-likelihood Methods

7

K. G. Jöreskog
University Institute of Statistics
Uppsala, Sweden

1. FUNCTION

Factor analysis is the common term for a number of statistical techniques for the resolution of a set of variables in terms of a small number of hypothetical variables, called factors. Within the statistical framework, factor analysis belongs to the field of multivariate analysis. In fact, factor analysis may be formulated in terms of partial correlations.

Though the models and methods of factor analysis are of a statistical nature, factor analysis has been mainly developed by psychologists, particularly for the purpose of analyzing the observed scores of many individuals on a number of aptitude and achievement tests. The phenomenon that is continually observed in this situation is that such tests correlate with each other. Factor analysis attempts to "explain" these correlations by an analysis, which, when carried out successfully, yields underlying factors, smaller in number than the number of observed variables, that contain "all" the essential information about the linear interrelationships among the test scores.

Factor analysis is most often employed in the behavioral sciences, but the techniques of factor analysis are not limited to such applications only. It has been used in such diverse fields as meteorology, political science, medicine, geography, and business. For a general description of the concepts, theories and techniques of factor analysis, the reader is referred to [5]. For a statistical formulation and treatment of factor analysis, see [10].

2. MATHEMATICAL DISCUSSION

a. Symbols Used

Matrix notation and matrix algebra will be used. Matrices are denoted by uppercase letters and vectors by lowercase letters. For example, $A = [a_{ij}]$, $i = 1, 2, \ldots, p$, $j = 1, 2, \ldots, q$, will denote a matrix of order $p \times q$ and $b = (b_i)$, $i = 1, 2, \ldots, m$ a column vector of order m. The transpose of A is denoted by A' and that of b by b'. All vectors introduced are column vectors. A row vector is denoted as the transpose of a column vector. The identity matrix of order p is denoted I_p and the elements of any identity matrix are denoted δ_{ij}. If A is a square matrix, tr A denotes the trace of A, that is, the sum of the diagonal elements of A and $|A|$ denotes the determinant of A. If A is square and nonsingular, the inverse of A is denoted by A^{-1} and a typical element of A^{-1} is denoted a^{ij}.

If F is a scalar function of a matrix X, $\partial F / \partial X$ denotes the matrix derivative of F, that is, the matrix of derivatives $\partial F / \partial x_{ij}$, dF denotes the total differential of F and dX denotes the matrix of differentials dx_{ij}.

In what follows, we make use of various results from matrix algebra. For a detailed exposition of matrix algebra, the reader is referred to [3]. Most of the results on eigenvalues and eigenvectors may be found in [2].

b. Mathematical Background

The basic model in factor analysis is

$$x = \mu + \Lambda f + e \qquad (1)$$

where x is a column vector of observations on p variables, μ is the mean vector of x, f is a vector of k common factors, e is a vector of p residuals, which represent the combined effect of specific factors and random error, and $\Lambda = [\lambda_{ir}]$ is a $p \times k$ matrix of factor loadings.

The residuals e are assumed to be uncorrelated with each other and with the common factors f. The dispersion or covariance matrices of f, e, and x are denoted respectively by Φ, Ψ^2, and Σ. The matrix Ψ^2 is diagonal with elements ψ_{ii}^2 ($i = 1, \ldots, p$), which are termed either residual or unique variances. We further assume, without loss

of generality, that the common factors have unit variances, so that the diagonal elements of Φ are unities. If, in addition, for $k > 1$, the common factors are orthogonal or uncorrelated, then the nondiagonal elements of Φ are zeros and thus Φ becomes the identity matrix of order k. In view of equation (1) and of the assumptions that we have made, Σ is given in terms of the other matrices by the equation

$$\Sigma = \Lambda \Phi \Lambda' + \Psi^2 \qquad (2)$$

Equations (1) and (2) represent a model for a population of individuals. This population is characterized by the parameters μ, Λ, Φ, and Ψ^2. In practice, these parameters are unknown and must be estimated from data on N individuals. Let $x_{\alpha i}$ be the observed value of variable i for individual α. Then the available data may be written as a data matrix X of order $N \times p$.

From this we can compute the sample mean vector $\bar{x}' = (\bar{x}_1, \bar{x}_2, \ldots, \bar{x}_p)$ and the sample covariance matrix $S = (s_{ij})$, where

$$\bar{x}_i = \left(\frac{1}{N} \right) \sum_{\alpha=1}^{N} x_{\alpha i} \qquad (3)$$

$$s_{ij} = \left(\frac{1}{n} \right) \sum_{\alpha=1}^{N} (x_{\alpha i} - \bar{x}_i)(x_{\alpha j} - \bar{x}_j) \qquad (4)$$

with $n = N - 1$.

The information provided by S may also be represented by a correlation matrix $R = (r_{ij})$ and a set of standard deviations $s_1, s_2, \ldots, s_p$, where $s_i = \sqrt{s_{ii}}$ and $r_{ij} = s_{ij} / s_i s_j$.

In most applications the mean vector μ is unconstrained and one simply takes $\bar{x}$ as an estimate of μ. The remaining estimation problem is then to fit a matrix Σ of the form (2) to an observed covariance matrix S. In many applications both the origin and the unit in the scales of measurement are arbitrary or irrelevant and then only the correlation matrix R is of any interest. In such cases one takes S to be a correlation matrix R in what follows.

In the following sections, it is assumed that the number of factors k is known in advance. In most exploratory factor studies this is not the case, but the investigator wants to determine the smallest k for which the model fits the data. This is usually done by a sequential procedure testing increasing values of k until sufficient fit has been obtained (e.g., [10]).

Three different methods of fitting Σ to S will be considered here, namely the *unweighted least squares* (ULS), which minimizes

$$U = \tfrac{1}{2} \operatorname{tr}(S - \Sigma)^2, \qquad (5)$$

the *generalized least squares* (GLS), which minimizes

$$G = \tfrac{1}{2} \operatorname{tr}\left(I_p - S^{-1}\Sigma\right)^2, \qquad (6)$$

and the *maximum likelihood* method (ML), which minimizes

$$M = \operatorname{tr}(\Sigma^{-1}S) - \log|\Sigma^{-1}S| - p \qquad (7)$$

Each function is to be minimized with respect to Λ, Φ, and Ψ. Derivations and justifications of these methods are found in the literature [1, 7, 8, 10].

The GLS and ML methods are scale-free. When x has a multivariate normal distribution both GLS and ML yield estimates that have good properties in large samples. Both GLS and ML require a positive definite covariance matrix S or correlation matrix R; ULS will work even on a matrix which is non-Gramian.

The ULS solution is equivalent to the traditional iterated principal factor solution and the minres solution ([5], and Chapter 8, this volume). The minres method described in the next chapter of this volume is another algorithm for the same solution.

When $k > 1$, and there is more than one common factor, it is necessary to remove an element of indeterminacy in the basic model before the procedure for minimizing F can be applied. This indeterminacy arises from the fact that there exist nonsingular linear transformations of the common factors which change Λ, and in general also Φ, but leave Σ, and therefore also the function unaltered. Hence to obtain a unique set of parameters and a corresponding unique set of estimates, we must impose some additional restrictions. These have the effect of selecting a particular set of factors and thus of defining the parameters uniquely.

The usual way to eliminate this indeterminacy in exploratory factor analysis (e.g., [7, 9, 10]) is to choose $\Phi = I$, $\Lambda'\Lambda$ to be diagonal in ULS and $\Lambda'\Psi^{-2}\Lambda$ to be diagonal in GLS and ML and to estimate the parameters in Λ and Ψ subject to these conditions. This leads to an arbitrary set of factors which may then be subjected to a rotation or a linear transformation to another set of factors to facilitate a more meaningful interpretation. Criteria and techniques for rotation of factors are considered in Chapter 9 of this volume.

c. Derivation of the Method

All three functions U, G, and M may be minimized by basically the same algorithm. Each function U, G, and M is considered as a function $F(\Lambda, \Psi)$ of Λ and Ψ. The minimization of $F(\Lambda, \Psi)$ is done in two steps. First the conditional minimum of F for given Ψ is found. This gives a function $f(\Psi)$ which is then minimized numerically using the Newton–Raphson procedure. Function values and derivatives of f of first and second order are given in terms of the eigenvalues and eigenvectors of a certain matrix A.

MATRIX DERIVATIVES

In the following derivation we need to obtain certain matrix derivatives. To do so we make use of the following well-known result from calculus: If F is a scalar function of a matrix X then $dF = \operatorname{tr}(\partial F/\partial X \, dX')$. Hence if $dF = \operatorname{tr}(C \, dX') = \operatorname{tr}(C' \, dX)$, where C may depend on X but not on dX, then $\partial F/\partial X = C$. Furthermore we have the following general results (e.g.,

[3, Ch. 10]):

$$d(YX) = dYX + YdX, dX^{-1}$$

$$= -X^{-1} dXX^{-1}$$

$$d(\text{tr } X) = \text{tr}(dX), d \log|X| = \text{tr}(X^{-1} dX)$$

For ULS, we have with respect to variation in Λ,

$$dU = \tfrac{1}{2} d \text{ tr}(S - \Sigma)^2$$

$$= \tfrac{1}{2}\text{tr}\left[d(S - \Sigma)^2\right]$$

$$= -\text{tr}\left[(S - \Sigma) d\Sigma\right]$$

$$= -\text{tr}\left[(S - \Sigma)(\Lambda\, d\Lambda' + d\Lambda\Lambda')\right]$$

$$= -2\text{tr}\left[(S - \Sigma)\Lambda\, d\Lambda'\right]$$

where the last step follows from $\text{tr}(AB') = \text{tr}(B'A) = \text{tr}(A'B)$. Hence

$$\frac{\partial U}{\partial \Lambda} = 2(\Sigma - S)\Lambda \qquad (8)$$

Similarly, for GLS we have,

$$dG = \tfrac{1}{2} d\text{tr}\left(S^{-1}\Sigma - I_p\right)^2$$

$$= \tfrac{1}{2} \text{tr}\left[d\left(S^{-1}\Sigma - I_p\right)^2\right]$$

$$= \text{tr}\left[\left(S^{-1}\Sigma - I_p\right)d\left(S^{-1}\Sigma - I_p\right)\right]$$

$$= \text{tr}\left[\left(S^{-1}\Sigma - I_p\right)S^{-1} d\Sigma\right]$$

$$= \text{tr}\left[\left(S^{-1}\Sigma - I_p\right)S^{-1}(\Lambda\, d\Lambda' + d\Lambda\Lambda')\right]$$

$$= 2\text{tr}\left[\left(S^{-1}\Sigma - I_p\right)S^{-1}\Lambda\, d\Lambda'\right]$$

$$= 2\text{tr}\left[S^{-1}(\Sigma - S)S^{-1}\Lambda\, d\Lambda'\right]$$

Hence

$$\frac{\partial G}{\partial \Lambda} = 2S^{-1}(\Sigma - S)S^{-1}\Lambda \qquad (9)$$

Finally, for ML we have

$$dM = d \text{ tr}(\Sigma^{-1}S) - d \log|\Sigma^{-1}S|$$

$$= \text{tr}(d\Sigma^{-1}S) - \text{tr}(S^{-1}\Sigma\, d\Sigma^{-1}S)$$

$$= \text{tr}\left[(S - \Sigma) d\Sigma^{-1}\right]$$

$$= \text{tr}\left[(\Sigma - S)\Sigma^{-1} d\Sigma\Sigma^{-1}\right]$$

$$= \text{tr}\left[\Sigma^{-1}(\Sigma - S)\Sigma^{-1}(d\Lambda\Lambda' + \Lambda\, d\Lambda')\right]$$

$$= 2 \text{tr}\left[\Sigma^{-1}(\Sigma - S)\Sigma^{-1}\Lambda\, d\Lambda'\right]$$

Hence

$$\frac{\partial M}{\partial \Lambda} = 2\Sigma^{-1}(\Sigma - S)\Sigma^{-1}\Lambda \qquad (10)$$

It should be noted that for all three methods, $\partial F/\partial \Lambda$ has the form

$$\frac{\partial F}{\partial \Lambda} = 2Q(\Sigma - S)Q\Lambda$$

where $Q = I$ for ULS, $Q = S$ for GLS, and $Q = \Sigma$ for ML.

REDUCTION OF U

The minimum of U with respect to Λ, for given Ψ, is to be found among the solutions of $\partial U/\partial \Lambda = 0$, that is,

$$S\Lambda = \Sigma\Lambda$$

or from

$$(S - \Psi^2)\Lambda = \Lambda(\Lambda'\Lambda)$$

Since $\Lambda'\Lambda$ is assumed to be diagonal, this equation shows that the columns of Λ are eigenvectors of $S - \Psi^2$ and it is readily verified that the absolute minimum of U is obtained when the eigenvectors are chosen to correspond to the k largest eigenvalues of $S - \Psi^2$. Taking this for granted for the moment, let $\gamma_1 \geqslant \gamma_2 \geqslant \cdots \gamma_p$ be the eigenvalues of $S - \Psi^2$ and let $\omega_1, \omega_2, \ldots, \omega_p$ be an orthonormal set of corresponding eigenvectors. Let $\Gamma_1 = \text{diag}(\gamma_1, \gamma_2, \ldots, \gamma_k)$, $\Gamma_2 = \text{diag}(\gamma_{k+1}, \gamma_{k+2}, \ldots, \gamma_p)$, $\Omega_1 = [\omega_1,$

$\omega_2, \ldots, \omega_k]$ and $\Omega_2 = [\omega_{k+1}, \omega_{k+2}, \ldots, \omega_p]$. The conditional solution for Λ for given Ψ is, provided $\gamma_k \geqslant 0$,

$$\tilde{\Lambda} = \Omega_1 \Gamma_1^{\frac{1}{2}} \qquad (11)$$

with

$$U(\tilde{\Lambda}, \Psi) = \text{tr}(S - \Psi^2 - \tilde{\Lambda}\tilde{\Lambda}')^2$$

$$= \text{tr}(\Omega_1\Gamma_1\Omega_1' + \Omega_2\Gamma_2\Omega_2' - \Omega_1\Gamma_1\Omega_1')^2$$

$$= \text{tr}(\Omega_2\Gamma_2\Omega_2')^2$$

$$= \text{tr}(\Omega_2\Gamma_2^2\Omega_2')$$

$$= \text{tr}\,\Gamma_2^2$$

Hence the conditional minimum of $U(\Lambda, \Psi)$ is

$$u(\Psi) = \frac{1}{2} \sum_{m=k+1}^{p} \gamma_m^2 \qquad (12)$$

It is now evident from this derivation, that the choice of another set of k eigenvalues in (11), would have resulted in a conditional minimum larger than or equal to (12).

For the $\tilde{\Lambda}$ in (11) to be real and uniquely defined (up to sign changes in the columns) it is necessary that the largest eigenvalues $\gamma_1, \gamma_2, \ldots, \gamma_k$ be distinct and nonnegative. If two eigenvalues are equal the corresponding eigenvalues in Ω_1 are indeterminate. If an eigenvalue is negative this would correspond to an imaginary column of Λ. Fortunately, such cases are extremely rare in practice and would only be expected to occur for unusual values of Ψ^2 and/or very large values of k.

REDUCTION OF G

Here we shall assume that Ψ is nonsingular, that is, that no $\psi_i = 0$. The case when one or more of the ψ's are zero will be considered separately on pages 135–136. The partial derivative of G with respect to Λ set equal to zero and premultiplied by S gives

$$\Sigma S^{-1}\Lambda = \Lambda \qquad (13)$$

or

$$S^{-1}\Lambda = \Sigma^{-1}\Lambda \qquad (14)$$

From (2) we have

$$\Sigma^{-1} = \Psi^{-2} - \Psi^{-2}\Lambda(I_k + \Lambda'\Psi^{-2}\Lambda)^{-1}\Lambda'\Psi^{-2}$$

Substitution of this into (14) gives

$$S^{-1}\Lambda = \Psi^{-2}\Lambda(I_k + \Lambda'\Psi^{-2}\Lambda)^{-1}$$

which after premultiplication of Ψ becomes

$$(\Psi S^{-1}\Psi)\Psi^{-1}\Lambda = \Psi^{-1}\Lambda(I_k + \Lambda'\Psi^{-2}\Lambda)^{-1}$$

$$(15)$$

Since we have assumed the matrix $\Lambda'\Psi^{-2}\Lambda$ to be diagonal, the columns of the matrix on the right side of (15) become proportional to those of $\Psi^{-1}\Lambda$. Therefore, as in the ULS case, the columns of $\Psi^{-1}\Lambda$ are eigenvectors of $\Psi S^{-1}\Psi$ with corresponding eigenvalues given by the diagonal elements of $(I_k + \Lambda'\Psi^{-2}\Lambda)^{-1}$. As in the ULS case, it may be shown that the conditional minimum of G, for the given Ψ, is obtained when the columns of $\Psi^{-1}\Lambda$ are chosen as eigenvectors corresponding to the k smallest eigenvalues of $\Psi S^{-1}\Psi$.

Let $\gamma_1 \leqslant \gamma_2 \leqslant \cdots \leqslant \gamma_p$ be the eigenvalues of $\Psi S^{-1}\Psi$ and let $\omega_1, \omega_2, \ldots, \omega_p$ be an orthonormal set of corresponding eigenvectors. Let $\Gamma_1 = \text{diag}(\gamma_1, \gamma_2, \ldots, \gamma_k)$ and $\Gamma_2 = \text{diag}(\gamma_{k+2}, \ldots, \gamma_p)$ and let $\Omega = [\omega_1, \omega_2, \ldots, \omega_p]$ be partitioned as $\Omega = [\Omega_1\Omega_2]$ where Ω_1 consists of the first k vectors and Ω_2 of the last $p - k$ vectors. Then

$$\Omega_1'\Omega_1 = I_k, \ \Omega_1'\Omega_2 = 0, \ \Omega_2'\Omega_2 = I_{p-k}, \quad (16)$$

$$I_p = \Omega_1\Omega_1' + \Omega_2\Omega_2' \qquad (17)$$

$$\Psi S^{-1}\Psi = \Omega_1\Gamma_1\Omega_1' + \Omega_2\Gamma_2\Omega_2' \qquad (18)$$

and the conditional solution $\tilde{\Lambda}$ is given by

$$\tilde{\Lambda} = \Psi\Omega_1(\Gamma_1^{-1} - I_k)^{\frac{1}{2}} \quad (19)$$

Defining, from (2),

$$\tilde{\Sigma} = \tilde{\Lambda}\tilde{\Lambda}' + \Psi^2 \quad (20)$$

it is easily verified from (16) and (19) that

$$\Psi^{-1}\tilde{\Sigma}\Psi^{-1} = \Omega_1\Gamma_1^{-1}\Omega_1' + \Omega_2\Omega_2' \quad (21)$$

and that

$$I_p - S^{-1}\tilde{\Sigma} = \Psi^{-1}\left[\Omega_2(I_{p-k} - \Gamma_2)\Omega_2'\right]\Psi$$

so that

$$\mathrm{tr}\left(I_p - S^{-1}\tilde{\Sigma}\right)^2 = \mathrm{tr}\left(I_{p-k} - \Gamma_2\right)^2$$

$$= \sum_{m=k+1}^{p} (\gamma_m - 1)^2$$

Therefore, the conditional minimum of $G(\Lambda, \Psi)$, with respect to Λ for a given Ψ, is the function $g(\Psi)$ defined by

$$g(\Psi) = \frac{1}{2} \sum_{m=k+1}^{p} (\gamma_m - 1)^2 \quad (22)$$

One difficulty may arise in (19) if one or more eigenvalues in Γ_1 are greater than one, for then the corresponding columns of $\tilde{\Lambda}$ will be imaginary. However, this is the same situation as with equation (11) for ULS. If Ψ is nonsingular, $S - \Psi^2$ has as many negative eigenvalues as $\Psi S^{-1}\Psi$ has eigenvalues greater than one. The remarks made in connection with equation (11) for ULS apply to equation (19) for GLS as well. Thus it is assumed that the eigenvalues $\gamma_1, \gamma_2, \ldots, \gamma_k$ are all distinct and less than or equal to one.

REDUCTION OF M

The partial derivative of M with respect to Λ, set equal to zero and premultiplied by Σ gives

$$S\Sigma^{-1}\Lambda = \Lambda$$

or

$$S^{-1}\Lambda = \Sigma^{-1}\Lambda$$

which is identical to (14). The conditional ML solution is therefore identical to the conditional GLS solution in (19). However, the conditional minimum value of the function is different. From (21) we find the determinant and trace of $\tilde{\Sigma}^{-1}S$ to be equal to the determinant and trace of

$$\Psi\tilde{\Sigma}^{-1}\Psi\Psi^{-1}S\Psi^{-1} = (\Omega_1\Gamma_1\Omega_1' + \Omega_2\Omega_2')$$

$$\times (\Omega_1\Gamma_1^{-1}\Omega_1' + \Omega_2\Gamma_2^{-1}\Omega_2')$$

$$= \Omega_1\Omega_1' + \Omega_2\Gamma_2^{-1}\Omega_2'$$

This matrix has k eigenvalues equal to one and the remaining $p - k$ eigenvalues are $1/\gamma_{k+1}, 1/\gamma_{k+2}, \ldots, 1/\gamma_p$, so that the conditional minimum becomes

$$M(\tilde{\Lambda}, \Psi) = k + \sum_{m=k+1}^{p} \left(\frac{1}{\gamma_m}\right)$$

$$+ \sum_{m=k+1}^{p} \log \gamma_m - p$$

Hence

$$m(\Psi) = \sum_{m=k+1}^{p} \left(\log \gamma_m + \frac{1}{\gamma_m} - 1\right) \quad (23)$$

MATRIX DERIVATIVES OF EIGENVALUES AND EIGENVECTORS

We have shown how each function $F(\Lambda, \Psi)$ may be minimized with respect to Λ for a given Ψ, yielding a function $f(\Psi)$ expressed in terms of certain eigenvalues of a symmetric matrix $A(\Psi)$ which is $S - \Psi^2$ in ULS and $\Psi S^{-1}\Psi$ in GLS and ML. To minimize $f(\Psi)$ by the Newton–Raphson method, the derivatives of $f(\Psi)$ of first and second order are needed. These may be obtained from the derivatives of γ_m and ω_m with respect to Ψ as follows.

The eigenvalues γ_m and eigenvectors ω_m, $m = 1, 2, \ldots, p$, of A are defined by

$$A\omega_m = \gamma_m\omega_m \tag{24}$$

$$\left.\begin{matrix} \omega'_m\omega_m = 1 \\ \omega'_m\omega_n = 0, n \neq m \end{matrix}\right\} \quad m = 1, 2, \ldots, p \quad \begin{matrix} (25) \\ (26) \end{matrix}$$

Differentiation of these equations gives

$$dA\omega_m + A\,d\omega_m = d\gamma_m\omega_m + \gamma_m\,d\omega_m \tag{27}$$

$$\omega'_m\,d\omega_m = 0 \tag{28}$$

$$\omega'_m\,d\omega_n + d\omega'_m\omega_n = 0, n \neq m \tag{29}$$

Premultiplication of (27) by ω'_m and use of (24) and (25) gives

$$d\gamma_m = \omega'_m\,dA\,\omega_m \tag{30}$$

Let $\varepsilon_{mn} = \omega'_m\,dA\,\omega_n = \varepsilon_{nm}$ for $m, n = 1, 2, \ldots, p$. The premultiplication of (27) by ω'_n for $n \neq m$ and use of (24) and (26) gives

$$\varepsilon_{mn} = \gamma_m\omega'_n\,d\omega_m - \omega'_n A\,d\omega_m$$

$$= \gamma_m\omega'_n\,d\omega_m - \gamma_n\omega'_n\,d\omega_m$$

$$= (\gamma_m - \gamma_n)\omega'_n\,d\omega_m$$

or

$$\omega'_n\,d\omega_m = \frac{\varepsilon_{mn}}{\gamma_m - \gamma_n}, n \neq m \tag{31}$$

Multiplying this equation by ω_n, summing over $n \neq m$, using (28) and remembering that

$$\sum_{n \neq m} \omega_n\omega'_n = I - \omega_m\omega'_m$$

gives $d\omega_m$ as

$$d\omega_m = \sum_{n \neq m} \frac{\varepsilon_{mn}}{\gamma_m - \gamma_n}\omega_n \tag{32}$$

The merits of (30) and (32) are that they express the differentials of γ_m and ω_m in terms of the differentials of A.

In ULS we have $A = S - \Psi^2$ so that $dA = -2\Psi\,d\Psi$. Substitution of this into the definition of ε_{mn} gives

$$\varepsilon_{mn} = -2\omega'_m\Psi\,d\Psi\omega_n$$

$$= -2\,\mathrm{tr}(\Psi\,d\Psi\omega_n\omega'_m)$$

With this result we have

$$d\gamma_m = -2\,\mathrm{tr}(\Psi\,d\Psi\omega_m\omega'_m)$$

and

$$d\omega_m = -2\sum_{n \neq m} \frac{\omega_n}{\gamma_m - \gamma_n}\,\mathrm{tr}(\Psi\,d\Psi\omega_n\omega'_m)$$

Hence

$$\frac{\partial\gamma_m}{\partial\psi_i} = -2\psi_i\omega_{im}^2 \tag{33}$$

$$\frac{\partial\omega_{im}}{\partial\psi_j} = -2\psi_j\omega_{jm}\sum_{n \neq m} \frac{\omega_{in}\omega_{jn}}{\gamma_m - \gamma_n} \tag{34}$$

In GLS and ML we have $A = \Psi S^{-1}\Psi$ so that

$$dA = d\Psi S^{-1}\Psi + \Psi S^{-1}\,d\Psi$$

$$= d\Psi\Psi^{-1}A + A\Psi^{-1}\,d\Psi$$

Substitution of this into the definition of ε_{mn} gives

$$\varepsilon_{mn} = \omega'_m\,dA\,\omega_n$$

$$= \omega'_m\,d\Psi\Psi^{-1}A\omega_n + \omega'_m A\Psi^{-1}\,d\Psi\omega_n$$

$$= (\gamma_m + \gamma_n)\omega'_m\,d\Psi\Psi^{-1}\omega_n$$

$$= (\gamma_m + \gamma_n)\,\mathrm{tr}(\omega_n\omega'_m\Psi^{-1}\,d\Psi)$$

With this result we have

$$d\gamma_m = 2\gamma_m\,\mathrm{tr}(\omega_m\omega'_m\Psi^{-1}\,d\Psi)$$

and

$$d\omega_m = \sum_{n \neq m} \frac{\gamma_m + \gamma_n}{\gamma_m - \gamma_n}\,\mathrm{tr}(\omega_n\omega'_m\Psi^{-1}\,d\Psi)\omega_n$$

Hence the derivatives of γ_m and ω_{im} with respect to ψ_j are

$$\frac{\partial \gamma_m}{\partial \psi_j} = \frac{2\gamma_m}{\psi_j} \omega_{jm}^2 \qquad (35)$$

and

$$\frac{\partial \omega_{im}}{\partial \psi_j} = \frac{1}{\psi_j} \omega_{jm} \sum_{n \neq m} \frac{\gamma_m + \gamma_n}{\gamma_m - \gamma_n} \omega_{in}\omega_{jn} \qquad (36)$$

First and Second Derivatives
Using these results we obtain for ULS,

$$\frac{\partial u}{\partial \psi_i} = -2\psi_i \sum_{m=k+1}^{p} \gamma_m \omega_{im}^2 \qquad (37)$$

$$\frac{\partial^2 u}{\partial \psi_i \partial \psi_j} = 4\psi_i\psi_j \sum_{m=k+1}^{p} \left[\omega_{im}^2\omega_{jm}^2 + 2\gamma_m\omega_{im}\omega_{jm} \right.$$

$$\left. \sum_{n \neq m} \frac{\omega_{in}\omega_{jn}}{\gamma_m - \gamma_n} \right] - 2\delta_{ij} \sum_{m=k+1}^{p} \gamma_m \omega_{im}^2$$

$$(38)$$

for GLS,

$$\frac{\partial g}{\partial \psi_i} = \frac{2}{\psi_i} \sum_{m=k+1}^{p} (\gamma_m^2 - \gamma_m)\omega_{im}^2 \qquad (39)$$

$$\frac{\partial^2 g}{\partial \psi_i \partial \psi_j} = \frac{4}{\psi_i\psi_j} \sum_{m=k+1}^{p} \left\{ (2\gamma_m^2 - \gamma_m)\omega_{im}^2\omega_{jm}^2 \right.$$

$$+ (\gamma_m^2 - \gamma_m)\omega_{im}\omega_{jm} \sum_{n \neq m} \frac{\gamma_m + \gamma_n}{\gamma_m - \gamma_n} \omega_{in}\omega_{jn}$$

$$\left. - \frac{1}{2} \delta_{ij} (\gamma_m^2 - \gamma_m)\omega_{im}\omega_{jm} \right\} \qquad (40)$$

and for ML,

$$\frac{\partial m}{\partial \psi_i} = \frac{2}{\psi_i} \sum_{m=k+1}^{p} \left(1 - \frac{1}{\gamma_m} \right)\omega_{im}^2 \qquad (41)$$

$$\frac{\partial^2 m}{\partial \psi_i \partial \psi_j} = \frac{4}{\psi_i\psi_j} \sum_{m=k+1}^{p} \left\{ \frac{1}{\gamma_m} \omega_{im}^2\omega_{jm}^2 \right.$$

$$+ \left(1 - \frac{1}{\gamma_m} \right)\omega_{im}\omega_{jm} \sum_{n \neq m} \frac{\gamma_m + \gamma_n}{\gamma_m - \gamma_n} \omega_{in}\omega_{jn}$$

$$\left. - \frac{1}{2} \delta_{ij} \left(1 - \frac{1}{\gamma_m} \right)\omega_{im}\omega_{jm} \right\} \qquad (42)$$

When one or more of the ψ_i are close to zero the derivatives (39) – (42) are numerically unstable. For this reason the transformation

$$\theta_i = \log \psi_i^2, \quad \psi_i = +\sqrt{e^{\theta_i}} \qquad (43a\text{--}b)$$

from ψ_i to θ_i is made. This makes the derivatives stable even at $\psi_i = 0$. We now consider g and m as functions of $\theta_1, \theta_2, \ldots, \theta_p$ instead of $\psi_1, \psi_2, \ldots, \psi_p$. The new function is defined for all θ_i, $-\infty < \theta_i < +\infty$. Note that $\psi_i = 0$ corresponds to $\theta_i = -\infty$.

The derivatives $\partial g / \partial \theta_i$ and $\partial^2 g / \partial \theta_i \partial \theta_j$ are obtained from $\partial g / \partial \psi_i$ and $\partial^2 g / \partial \psi_i \partial \psi_j$ by

$$\frac{\partial g}{\partial \theta_i} = \frac{\psi_i}{2} \frac{\partial g}{\partial \psi_i}$$

$$\frac{\partial^2 g}{\partial \theta_i \partial \theta_j} = \frac{\psi_i\psi_j}{4} \frac{\partial^2 g}{\partial \psi_i \partial \psi_j} + \delta_{ij} \frac{\psi_i}{4} \frac{\partial g}{\partial \psi_i}$$

and the same holds with m instead of g.

Each of the second-order derivatives (38), (40), and (42) involves a double sum of the form $\sum_{m=k+1}^{p}\sum_{n \neq m} a_{mn} b_{ijmn}$, where $b_{ijmn} =$

$\omega_{im}\omega_{jm}\omega_{in}\omega_{jn} = b_{ijnm}$ and

$$
a_{mn} = \begin{cases} \dfrac{2\gamma_m}{\gamma_m - \gamma_n} & \text{(ULS)} \\[2ex] \dfrac{(\gamma_m^2 - \gamma_m)(\gamma_m + \gamma_n)}{\gamma_m - \gamma_n} & \text{(GLS)} \\[2ex] \dfrac{(\gamma_m - 1)(\gamma_m + \gamma_n)}{\gamma_m(\gamma_m - \gamma_n)} & \text{(ML)} \end{cases}
$$

This double sum may be written as

$$
\sum_{m=k+1}^{p} \sum_{n=1}^{k} a_{mn} b_{ijmn}
$$

$$
+ \sum_{m=k+1}^{p} \sum_{n=k+1}^{m-1} (a_{mn} + a_{nm}) b_{ijmn}
$$

Using all these results and the identity

$$
\sum_{m=k+1}^{p} \omega_{im}\omega_{jm} = \delta_{ij} - \sum_{n=1}^{k} \omega_{in}\omega_{jn} \quad (44)
$$

one obtains, after considerable simplification, the final derivatives used in the program as follows:

For ULS:

$$
\frac{\partial u}{\partial \psi_i} = -2\psi_i \sum_{m=k+1}^{p} \gamma_m \omega_{im}^2 \quad (45)
$$

$$
\frac{\partial^2 u}{\partial \psi_i \partial \psi_j} = 4 \left[\psi_i \psi_j \sum_{m=k+1}^{p} \omega_{im}\omega_{jm} \right.
$$

$$
\times \sum_{n=1}^{k} \frac{\gamma_m + \gamma_n}{\gamma_m - \gamma_n} \omega_{in}\omega_{jn}
$$

$$
\left. + \delta_{ij} \sum_{m=k+1}^{p} \left(\psi_i^2 - \frac{\gamma_m}{2} \right) \omega_{im}^2 \right] \quad (46)
$$

When $\gamma_{k+1}, \gamma_{k+2}, \ldots, \gamma_p$ are all close to zero, this is approximately

$$
\frac{\partial^2 u}{\partial \psi_i \partial \psi_i} \approx 4\psi_i\psi_j \left(\sum_{m=k+1}^{p} \omega_{im}\omega_{jm} \right)^2 \quad (47)
$$

For GLS:

$$
\frac{\partial g}{\partial \theta_i} = \sum_{m=k+1}^{p} (\gamma_m^2 - \gamma_m)\omega_{im}^2 \quad (48)
$$

$$
\frac{\partial^2 g}{\partial \theta_i \partial \theta_j} = \frac{\delta_{ij} \partial g}{\partial \theta_i} + \sum_{m=k+1}^{p} \gamma_m \omega_{im}\omega_{jm}
$$

$$
\times \left[\sum_{n=1}^{k} \gamma_n \frac{\gamma_m + \gamma_n - 2}{\gamma_m - \gamma_n} \omega_{in}\omega_{jn} + s^{ij}\psi_i\psi_j \right]
$$

$$(49)$$

When $\gamma_{k+1}, \gamma_{k+2}, \ldots, \gamma_p$ are all close to one, this is approximately

$$
\frac{\partial^2 g}{\partial \theta_i \partial \theta_j} \approx \left(\sum_{m=k+1}^{p} \omega_{im}\omega_{jm} \right)^2 \quad (50)
$$

For ML:

$$
\frac{\partial m}{\partial \theta_i} = \sum_{m=k+1}^{p} \left(1 - \frac{1}{\gamma_m} \right) \omega_{im}^2 \quad (51)
$$

$$
\frac{\partial^2 m}{\partial \theta_i \partial \theta_j} = \frac{-\delta_{ij} \partial m}{\partial \theta_i} + \sum_{m=k+1}^{p} \omega_{im}\omega_{jm}
$$

$$
\times \left[\sum_{n=1}^{k} \frac{\gamma_m + \gamma_n - 2}{\gamma_m - \gamma_n} \omega_{in}\omega_{jn} + \delta_{ij} \right]
$$

$$(52)$$

When $\gamma_{k+1}, \gamma_{k+2}, \ldots, \gamma_p$ are close to one, this is approximately

$$\frac{\partial^2 m}{\partial \theta_i \partial \theta_j} \approx \left(\sum_{m=k+1}^{p} \omega_{im} \omega_{jm} \right)^2 \quad (53)$$

BASIC MINIMIZATION ALGORITHM

Let θ denote a column vector with elements $\theta_1, \theta_2, \ldots, \theta_p$ (GLS and ML) or $\psi_1, \psi_2, \ldots, \psi_p$ (ULS), and let h and H denote the column vector and matrix of corresponding derivatives $\partial f / \partial \theta$ and $\partial^2 f / \partial \theta \partial \theta'$, respectively. Let $\theta^{(s)}$ denote the value of θ in the sth iteration and let $h^{(s)}$ and $H^{(s)}$ be the corresponding vector and matrix of first- and second-order derivatives. The Newton–Raphson iteration procedure may then be written

$$H^{(s)} \delta^{(s)} = h^{(s)} \quad (54)$$

$$\theta^{(s+1)} = \theta^{(s)} - \delta^{(s)}, \quad (55)$$

where $\delta^{(s)}$ is a column vector of corrections determined by (54). This procedure is, therefore, easy to apply, the main computations in each iteration being the computation of the eigenvalues and eigenvectors of A and the solution of the symmetric system (54). It has been found that the Newton–Raphson procedure is very efficient, generally requiring only a few iterations for convergence. The convergence criterion is that the largest absolute correction be less than a prescribed small number ε. The minimizing θ may be determined very accurately, if desired, by choosing ε very small.

In detail, the numerical method is as follows. The starting point $\theta^{(1)}$ is chosen as (e.g., [6, eq. 26], [9, eqs. 6.20 and 7.10]):

$$\theta_i^{(1)} = \log \left[\frac{(1 - k/2p)}{s^{ii}} \right] \quad \text{in GLS and ML}$$

$$(56a)$$

$$\psi_i^{(1)} = +\sqrt{\left[(1 - k/2p)/s^{ii} \right]} \quad \text{in ULS}$$

$$(56b)$$

$$\psi_i^{(1)} = .6 s_{ii} \quad \text{in ULS if } S \text{ is not positive definite} \quad (56c)$$

where s_{ii} and s^{ii} are the ith diagonal element of S and S^{-1}, respectively. The exact matrix H of second-order derivatives given by (46), (49), or (52) may not be positive definite in the beginning. Therefore, the approximation E given by (47), (50), or (53) is used in the first iteration and for as long as the maximum absolute correction is greater than a given constant ε_E. After that, H is used if it is positive definite. It has been found empirically that E gives good reductions in function values in the early iterations but is comparatively ineffective near the minimum, whereas H near the minimum is very effective.

In each iteration we compute the eigenvalues and eigenvectors of A by the Householder transformation to tridiagonal form, the QR method for the roots of the tridiagonal matrix and inverse iteration for the vectors. This is probably the most efficient method available [13]. There is only one difficulty and this is that computed eigenvectors corresponding to eigenvalues that are equal or very close tend to be identical rather than orthogonal. In factor analysis this is not likely to occur except when there are two or more Heywood variables (see below and next subsection).

The system of equations (54) is solved by the square-root factorization $H = TT'$, where T is lower triangular. This shows at an early stage whether H is positive definite or not.

In Heywood cases, when one or more of the $\theta_i \to -\infty$, that is, $\psi_i \to 0$, a slight modification of the above procedure is necessary to achieve fast convergence. This is due to the fact that the search for the minimum is then along a "valley" and not in a quadratic region. For ML and GLS, when $\theta_i \to -\infty$, then $\partial f / \partial \theta_i \to 0$, $\partial^2 f / \partial \theta_i \partial \theta_j \to 0$, $j = 1, 2, \ldots, p$, so that when θ_i is small the ith element of h and the ith row and column of H and E are also small. This tends to produce "bad" corrections even for $\theta_j, j \neq i$, and the objective function may increase instead of decrease. A simple and effective way to deal with this problem is to delete the ith equation in the system (54) and compute the corrections for all the other θ's from the reduced system. One then computes the correction for θ_i as

$$\delta_i = \frac{\partial f / \partial \theta_i}{\partial^2 f / \partial \theta_i^2} \qquad (57)$$

This procedure will decrease θ_i slowly in the beginning but faster the more evident it is that θ_i is a Heywood variable. When θ_i has become less than $\log(\varepsilon)$ it is not necessary to change θ_i any more unless $\partial f / \partial \theta_i$ is negative. For ULS, an analogous procedure is used. When ψ_i becomes less than $\sqrt{\varepsilon}$, ψ_i is not changed unless $\partial f / \partial \psi_i$ is negative. Thus the procedure corrects itself quickly if a variable is incorrectly taken as a Heywood variable.

THE CASE WHEN Ψ IS SINGULAR OR NEARLY SINGULAR

The minimization procedure described in the previous section gives the values $\hat{\psi}_1, \hat{\psi}_2, \ldots, \hat{\psi}_p$ of $\psi_1, \psi_2, \ldots, \psi_p$ that minimize the function $f(\Psi)$. The matrix $\hat{\Psi}^2$ is taken as an estimate of the unique variance matrix Ψ^2. The estimate $\hat{\Lambda}$ of the loading matrix Λ is computed from (11) for ULS and from (19) for GLS and ML.

Usually all the $\hat{\psi}_i^2$, $i = 1, 2, \ldots, p$ are positive and not very close to zero and then no problems arise. However, sometimes one or more of $\hat{\psi}$'s are zero or close to zero. This causes no problem for ULS. However, equation (19) needs modification for GLS and ML.

The following modification of (19) gives a conditional minimum of $G(\Lambda, \Psi)$ and $M(\Lambda, \Psi)$ for given Ψ which is valid even if one or more of the ψ_i are zero. Consider Eq. (13), which after substitution of Σ from (2), becomes

$$\Lambda\Lambda' S^{-1}\Lambda + \Psi^2 S^{-1}\Lambda = \Lambda$$

or

$$(I - \Psi^2 S^{-1})\Lambda = \Lambda\Lambda' S^{-1}\Lambda$$

This equation is equivalent to

$$(S - \Psi^2) S^{-1}\Lambda = \Lambda\Lambda' S^{-1}\Lambda \qquad (58)$$

Since S is assumed to be positive definite, S^{-1} is also positive definite and there is a lower triangular matrix T, with positive diagonal elements, such that

$$S^{-1} = TT'$$

Then

$$S = T'^{-1}T^{-1}$$

and Eq. (14) premultiplied by T' becomes

$$\left[T'(S - \Psi^2)T \right]T'\Lambda = T'\Lambda(\Lambda' S^{-1}\Lambda) \qquad (59)$$

It is clear from (59) that is is convenient to replace the assumption that $\Lambda'\Psi^{-2}\Lambda$ be diagonal, which was used to obtain (19), by the equivalent assumption that $\Lambda' S^{-1}\Lambda$ be diagonal. Then the columns of the matrix on the right side of (59) become proportional to those of $T'\Lambda$. Therefore, as before, the columns of $T'\Lambda$ are eigenvectors of $T'(S - \Psi^2)T$ with the corresponding eigenvalues in the diagonal of $\Lambda' S^{-1}\Lambda$.

Let $d_1 \geqslant d_2 \geqslant \cdots \geqslant d_p$ be the eigenvalues of $T'(S - \Psi^2)T = I_p - T'\Psi^2T$ and let $u_1, u_2, \ldots, u_p$ be an orthonormal set of corresponding eigenvectors. As before, let $D_1 = \text{diag}(d_1, d_2, \ldots, d_k)$ and let $U_1 = [u_1, u_2, \ldots, u_k]$. Then the conditional minimum $\tilde{\Lambda}$ is given by

$$\tilde{\Lambda} = T'^{-1}U_1 D_1^{1/2} \qquad (60)$$

When one of the ψ's are zero, one of the eigenvalues in D_1 is one, but $\tilde{\Lambda}$ in (60) is still well defined. If two or more of ψ's are zero, two or more of the eigenvalues will be one. The matrix $\tilde{\Lambda}$ may still be defined by (60) but two or more columns in U_1 are indeterminate.

The eigenvalues $d_1, d_2, \ldots, d_p$ of $I_p - T'\Psi^2T$ and the eigenvalues $\gamma_1, \gamma_2, \ldots, \gamma_p$ of $\Psi S^{-1}\Psi$ are related by

$$\gamma_m = 1 - d_m, m = 1, 2, \ldots, p$$

and, if all ψ_i are nonzero, $i = 1, 2, \ldots, p$, the corresponding eigenvectors are related by

$$d_m \omega_m = \Psi T u_m, \, m = 1, 2, \ldots, p$$

Hence (19) and (60) are equivalent. However, (60) is defined even when one or more of the ψ's are zero, whereas (19) is not.

In the program the following procedure is used. When the minimum of $f(\Psi)$ has been obtained, the minimizing values $\hat{\psi}_1$, $\hat{\psi}_2, \ldots, \hat{\psi}_p$ are examined. If all $\hat{\psi}_i^2 > \varepsilon$, $\hat{\Lambda}$ is computed by (19). If one or more of the ψ_i^2 are less than or equal to ε these are set equal to zero and Λ is computed by (60). When there are more than one ψ_i equal to zero, special care must be taken to make sure that the computed eigenvectors corresponding to zero or very close to zero eigenvalues are orthogonal. For this reason Jacobi's method (e.g., [4]) is used instead of the Householder–Wilkinson method, when this happens.

3. SUMMARY OF THE CALCULATION PROCEDURE

a. Subroutine NWTRAP

The program, which is written as a subroutine, performs a factor analysis of a given covariance or correlation matrix S of order p for a given number of factors k to compute the matrix of factor loadings Λ and the vector of unique variances Ψ^2. The user must write a main program that reads in the data, computes the matrix S and generates the printed output quantities that are desired. Alternatively, the user may use the general purpose main program described here in Section 3b.

Subroutine *NWTRAP* is called by the following statement *CALL NWTRAP (P, K, IND, IO, IS, S, EPS, EPSE, MAXIT, A, E, X, Y, FO, DET)*

INPUT PARAMETERS

P — Order of covariance or correlation matrix.

K — Number of factors.

IND — Determines which method of estimation is to be used.
$IND = 1$ for ULS.
$IND = 2$ for GLS.
$IND = 3$ for ML.

IO — Determines whether intermediate results are to be printed (see Section b).
$IO = 0$, if *no* intermediate results are to be printed.
$IO = 1$, if intermediate results are to be printed.

IS — Determines whether the starting point is defined by the program or read in by the user as data (see Section b).
$IS = 0$, if the starting point is defined by the program (see Basic Minimization Algorithm, Section 2c).
$IS = 1$, a starting vector ψ is read in as data with a format of 5D15.7 for each number of factors K.

S — Covariance or correlation matrix, stored row-wise as a vector. Should be singly dimensioned in the calling program by at least $P(P + 1)/2$.

EPS — Convergence criterion ε (see Basic Minimization Algorithm, Section 2c). For reasonable results use $\varepsilon \leqslant .005$.

$EPSE$ — If all elements of the correction vector are less than $EPSE$, the *exact* second-order derivatives are used in the minimization algorithm, otherwise the *approximate* second-order derivatives are used. From our experience $EPSE = .1$ seems reasonable.

$MAXIT$ — Maximum number of iterations allowed for each number of factors K. Program exits if this number is exceeded.

OUTPUT PARAMETERS

A — Matrix of unrotated factor loadings

Λ, stored row-wise as a vector. Should be singly subscripted in the calling program by at least $P \times K$.

E   Dummy vector. Should be dimensioned in the calling program by at least $(P \times (P + 1))/2$.

X   Vector of unique variances. Should be dimensioned in the calling program by at least P.

Y   Vector of eigenvalues of A at the minimum. Should be dimensioned in the calling program by at least P.

FO   The value of the function at the minimum.

DET   The determinant of the matrix S.

b. The Main Program

In this section we describe briefly what the program does. Details about the input are given in the first subsection.

The *input* data may be the raw data matrix X from which the matrix to be analyzed is computed, or it may be a covariance matrix, or it may be a correlation matrix or a correlation matrix followed by a vector of standard deviations. From these input matrices, variables may be selected to be included in the analysis, so that the matrices to be analyzed could be of smaller order than the input matrices. Variables may be interchanged with one another. The matrices to be analyzed may be dispersion matrices or correlation matrices. The user has the option to read in a starting point for ψ or have the program define a starting point (see Basic Minimization Algorithm, Section 2b). This option may be useful if convergence is slow and the user runs out of computer time. From the intermediate results, the last ψ can be read in as a new starting point and minimization can continue.

For the given matrix S of order p by p, and a given lower bound k_L and a given upper bound k_U for the number of factors, the program performs a sequence of factor analyses by the ML, ULS, or GLS method

of estimation chosen by the user and outlined in the previous section. The value of k_L may be zero. One such analysis is done for each number of factors

$$k = k_L, k_L + 1, \ldots, k_U$$

The *output* will consist of the title with parameter listing and the matrix to be analyzed. Then for each number of factors k the unrotated factor loadings, the unique variances and the varimax-rotated and/or promax-rotated factor loadings (e.g., [5]) are printed. For ML and GLS this is followed by various statistics useful for the determination of the best number of factors to use (e.g., [10]). These statistics are χ_k^2 and the corresponding degrees of freedom d_k, the probability level, that is, the probability of obtaining a larger value of χ^2 than that actually obtained given that the model and the assumptions hold, Tucker and Lewis' [12] reliability coefficient ρ_k, defined as follows

$$C_0 = N - 1 - \tfrac{1}{6}(2p + 5)$$

$$\chi_0^2 = C_0 \left[\sum_{i=2}^{p} \log s_{ii} - \log|S| \right]$$

$$d_0 = \tfrac{1}{2} p(p - 1)$$

$$M_0 = \frac{\chi_0^2}{d_0}$$

$$C_k = C_0 - \tfrac{2}{3} k$$

$$\chi_k^2 = C_k f_{\min}$$

$$d_k = \tfrac{1}{2} \left[(p - k)^2 - (p + k) \right]$$

$$M_k = \frac{\chi_k^2}{d_k}$$

$$\rho_k = \frac{M_0 - M_k}{M_0 - 1}$$

Finally, the latent roots and their first differences at the minimum and the matrix of residual correlations are printed. The user also has an option to print intermediate results consisting of the value of the function and the vector ψ at each iteration.

The program has dynamic storage allocation, which means that there are no limits set by the program on the number of variables or the number of factors that can be handled. The program is written in Fortran IV. Double precision is used in floating point arithmetic throughout the program. In computers with a single word length of 36 bits or more, single precision is probably sufficient.

INPUT DATA

For each set of data to be analyzed, the input consists of the following data cards:

1. Title card
2. Parameter card
3. Data matrix
4. Selection cards (optional)
5. Starting point (optional)
6. New data or a STOP card

The function and setup of each of the above quantities are described in general terms as follows.

Title Card Whatever appears on this card will appear on the first page of the printed output. All 80 columns of the card are available to the user.

Parameter Card All quantities on this card, except for the logical indicators, must be punched as integers right-adjusted within the field.

cols. 1–5   Number of observations N
cols. 6–10   Order of data matrix (p_0), before selection of variables
cols. 11–15   Lower bound for the number of factors k_L
cols. 16–20   Upper bound for the number of factors k_U
cols. 21–25   Maximum number of iterations allowed for each number of factors k
col. 31   Logical variable that determines whether selection of variables from the data matrix is desired

col. 31 = T, if selection of variables is wanted
col. 31 = F, if no selection of variables is wanted
col. 32   Logical variable that determines whether a covariance matrix or a correlation matrix is to be analyzed
col. 32 = T, if a dispersion matrix is to be analyzed
col. 32 = F, if a correlation matrix is to be analyzed
col. 41   Integer indicator that determines whether raw data, a covariance matrix, a correlation matrix or a correlation matrix with standard deviations are read in to determine the matrix to be analyzed
col. 41 = 1, read in raw data
col. 41 = 2, read in a dispersion matrix
col. 41 = 3, read in a correlation matrix
(followed by a vector of standard deviations if col. 32 is T)
col. 42   Integer indicator that determines which method of estimation is to be used
col. 42 = 1 for ULS
col. 42 = 2 for GLS
col. 42 = 3 for ML
col. 43   Integer indicator which determines whether intermediate results are to be printed
col. 43 = 0, if no intermediate results are to be printed
col. 43 = 1, if intermediate results are to be printed
col. 44   Integer indicator that determines whether a starting point is defined by the pro-

gram or is to be supplied by the user

cols. 44 = 0, if a starting point is defined by the program

col. 44 = 1, if a starting point is read in as data

cols. 46–55 Convergence criterion ε. For reasonable results use ε ≤ .005.

cols. 56–65 ε_E; if all elements of the correction vector are less than ε_E the *exact* second-order derivatives are computed in the minimization algorithm; otherwise the *approximate* second order derivatives are used. From our experience $\varepsilon_E = .1$ seems reasonable.

cols. 66–70 Logical tape (disk) number of *scratch tape* (disk) used for intermediate storage

Data Matrix The data matrix is preceded by a format card, containing at most 80 columns, beginning with a left parenthesis and ending with a right parenthesis. The format must specify floating point numbers consistent with the way in which the elements of the matrix are punched. Readers who are unfamiliar with Fortran are referred to a Fortran manual where format rules are given.

The input matrix can be any one of the following:

If col. 41 = 1 on the parameter card an $N \times p$ matrix of raw data is read in, one row at a time, starting a new card for each row. The matrix is preceded by a format card as described above.

If col. 41 = 2 the lower triangular part of a dispersion matrix, including the diagonal, is read in. The matrix should be punched row-wise as one long vector, that is, there is no need to go to a new card if a new row starts. Again the matrix should be preceded by a format card.

If col. 41 = 3 and col. 32 = F the lower triangular part of a correlation matrix, in-

cluding the diagonal, is read in. The matrix should be punched row-wise as one long vector, and should be preceded by a format card.

If col. 41 = 3 and col. 32 = T the lower triangular part of a correlation matrix, including the diagonal, is read in. The matrix should be punched row-wise as one long vector, and should be preceded by a format card. This matrix is then followed by a format card and a row-vector of standard deviations.

Selection Cards (optional) Omit if column 31 of the parameter card is *F*. Otherwise the *first card* will have an integer value *p* punched in columns 1–5, right-adjusted within the field. This integer will specify the new order of the data matrix after selection of variables ($p \leqslant p_0$).

The next card will contain integers, right-adjusted in five-column fields (i.e., 16 such values will fit on one card), specifying which columns (rows) are to be *included*. For example, if $p_0 = 6$, $p = 3$ and the first, second, and fifth columns (rows) are to be excluded, this card would have a 3 punched in column 5, a 4 punched in column 10, and a 6 punched in column 15.

Note that if $p = p_0$ there will be no reduction in the size of the data matrix but columns (rows) can be interchanged.

Starting Point (optional) Omit if column 44 on the parameter card is zero. Otherwise read in a starting ψ vector punched according to a format of 5D15.7 for each number of factors *k*.

Stacked Data In the preceding paragraphs we have described how each set of data should be set up. Any number of such sets of data may be stacked together and analyzed in one run. *After the last set of data in the stack, there must be a card with the word STOP punched in columns 1–4.*

4. FLOW CHARTS

The flow charts appear on pages 140–149.

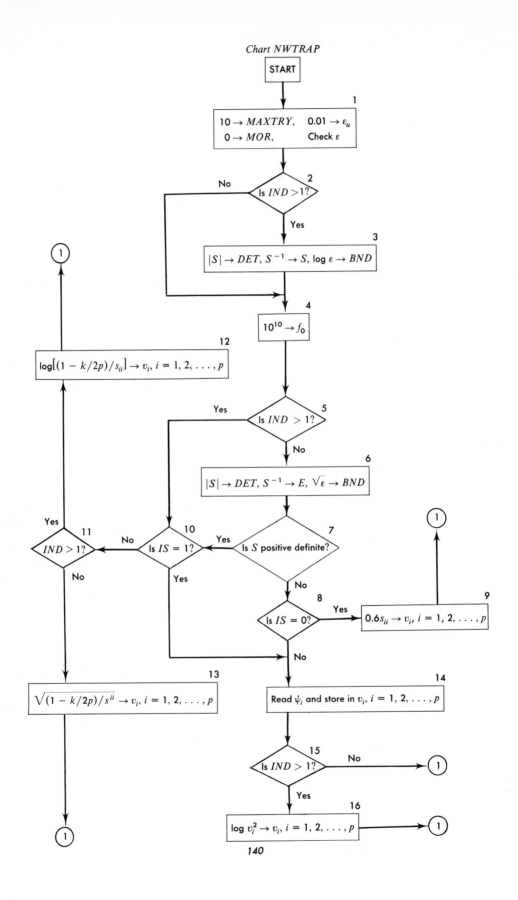

Chart NWTRAP

START

1
$10 \to MAXTRY, \quad 0.01 \to \varepsilon_u$
$0 \to MOR, \quad$ Check ε

2
Is $IND > 1$?

No

Yes

3
$|S| \to DET, S^{-1} \to S, \log \varepsilon \to BND$

4
$10^{10} \to f_0$

12
$\log[(1 - k/2p)/s_{ii}] \to v_i, i = 1, 2, \ldots, p$

5
Is $IND > 1$?

Yes

No

6
$|S| \to DET, S^{-1} \to E, \sqrt{\varepsilon} \to BND$

11
$IND > 1$?

10
Is $IS = 1$?

No

Yes

7
Is S positive definite?

Yes

No

Yes

Yes

8
Is $IS = 0$?

Yes

9
$0.6 s_{ii} \to v_i, i = 1, 2, \ldots, p$

No

13
$\sqrt{(1 - k/2p)/s^{ii}} \to v_i, i = 1, 2, \ldots, p$

14
Read ψ_i and store in $v_i, i = 1, 2, \ldots, p$

15
Is $IND > 1$?

No

Yes

16
$\log v_i^2 \to v_i, i = 1, 2, \ldots, p$

140

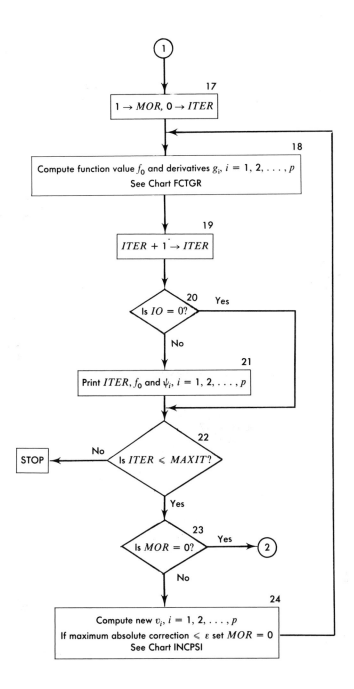

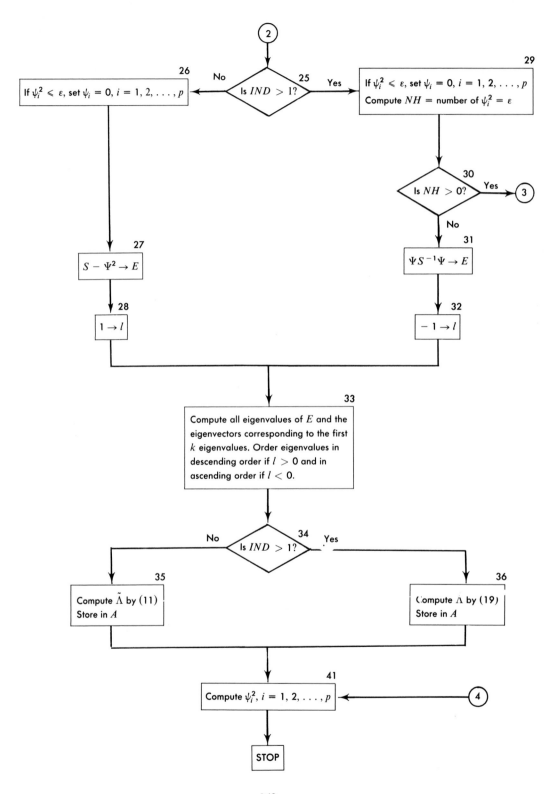

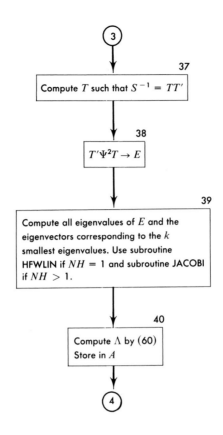

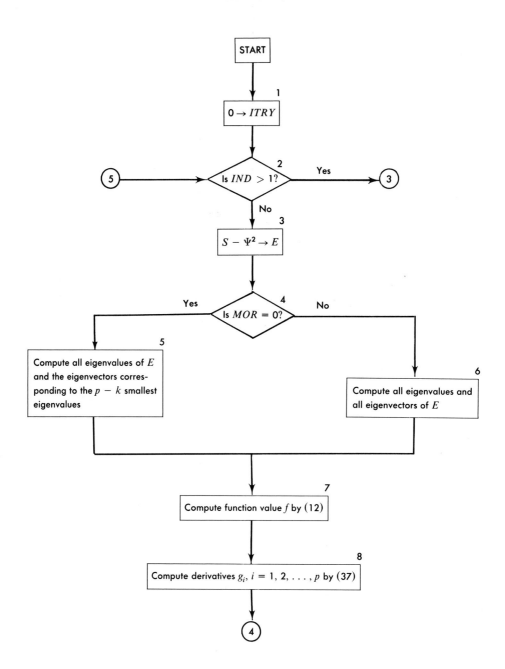

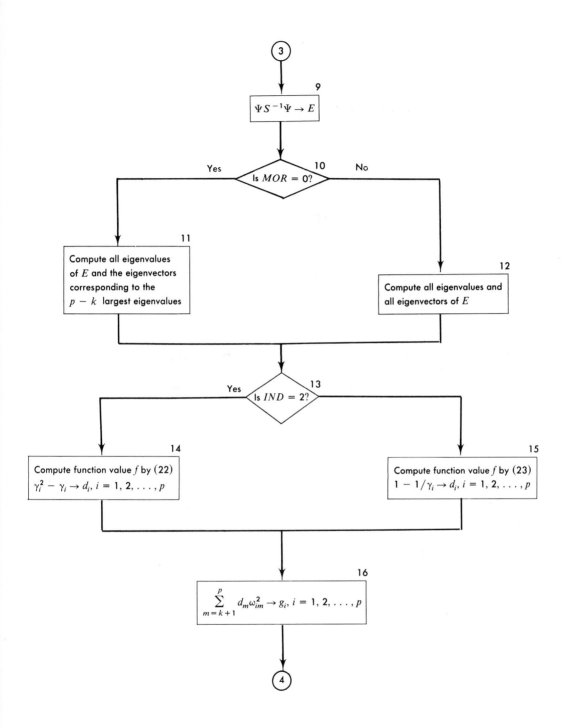

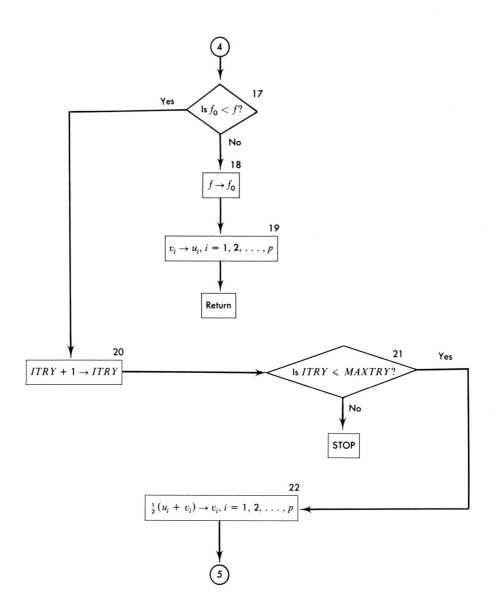

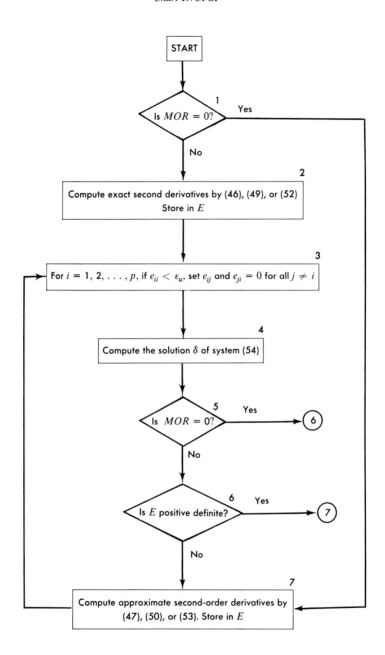

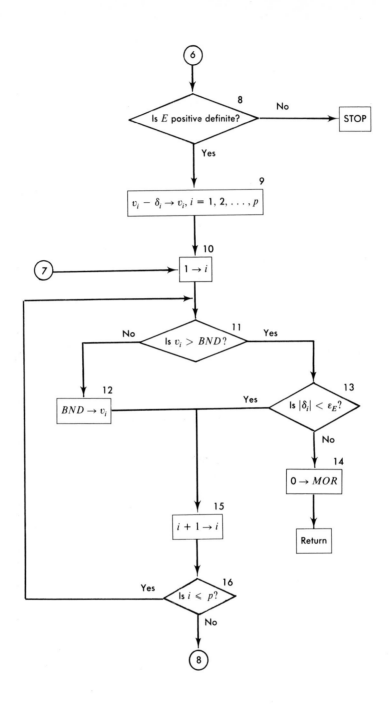

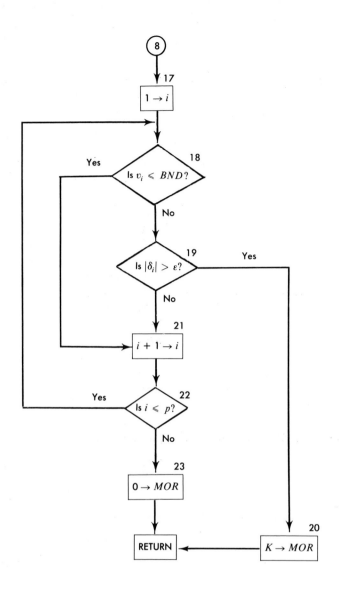

5. DESCRIPTION OF THE FLOW CHARTS

a. Chart NWTRAP

Box 1: In this box various quantities are defined and initialized. In each iteration, when $\theta^{(s+1)}$ have been computed from $\theta^{(s)}$ by (54) and (55), the new function value $f(\theta^{(s+1)})$ is compared with the old function value $f(\theta^{(s)})$. Usually $f(\theta^{(s+1)}) < f(\theta^{(s)})$, but if this is not the case, the midpoint $\theta_1^{(s+1)} = \frac{1}{2}(\theta^{(s)} + \theta^{(s+1)})$ is used instead of $\theta^{(s+1)}$ and the function value $f(\theta_1^{(s+1)})$ is compared with $f(\theta^{(s)})$. If $f(\theta_1^{(s+1)}) \geqslant f(\theta^{(s)})$ a new midpoint $\theta_2^{(s+1)} = \frac{1}{2}(\theta^{(s)} + \theta_1^{(s+1)})$ is computed, and so on. At most *MAXTRY* such midpoints will be tried. If after *MAXTRY* such halvings the function value is still greater than or equal to $f(\theta^{(s)})$, the computations are terminated. In the program we use *MAXTRY* equal to 10 but other values may also be used.

The quantity ε_u is used in connection with Heywood variables in the GLS and ML methods. If, for an $i = 1, 2, \ldots, p$, $\partial^2 f / \partial \theta_i^2 < \varepsilon_u$, the correction δ_i is computed by (57) instead of by (54) and (55) as described in Section 2.c. If ε_u is too large, variables will be mistakenly taken as Heywood variables and if ε_u is too small, difficulties may arise in the solution of the system (54) causing "bad" corrections and slow convergence. Our experience is that ε_u should be around 0.01.

The convergence criterion ε should not be larger than 0.005. The indicator *MOR* is used as follows. If *MOR* = 0, the approximate second-order derivatives will be used; otherwise the exact second-order derivatives will be used (see Basic Minimization Algorithm, Section 2c).

Boxes 2–5: Compute $|S|$ and S^{-1}. If *IND* is 2 or 3, S^{-1} is used in the computations. Hence store S^{-1} in the same locations as S and define $BND = \log \varepsilon$. If *IND* is 1, S will be used in the computations. Hence store S^{-1} in E and define $BND = \sqrt{\varepsilon}$. BND is the lower bound for $\theta_1, \theta_2, \ldots, \theta_p$.

Also set initial function value to some large number.

Box 9: If S is not positive definite and $IS = 0$ (see Input Parameters, Section 3a) compute start values as $0.6s_{ii}$ and store in v_i, $i = 1, 2, \ldots, p$.

Boxes 12–13: If S is positive definite and $IS = 0$, start values for θ_i are computed as $\sqrt{(1 - k/2p)/s^{ii}}$ if *IND* is 1 or as $\log[(1 - k/2p)/s^{ii}]$ if *IND* is 2 or 3 (see Basic Minimization Algorithm, Section 2c). These start values are stored in v_i, $i = 1, 2, \ldots, p$.

Box 14: If $IS = 1$ start values for ψ_i are read in instead of computed (see Input Parameters, Section 3a).

Box 16: The ψ_i is transformed to θ_i, $i = 1, 2, \ldots, p$, by (43a).

Box 17: *ITER* is an iteration counter. The indicator *MOR* is used to test for convergence. If all corrections for ψ_i^2 are less than ε in magnitude, *MOR* will be set equal to 0; otherwise it will remain equal to 1.

Box 22: The iterations are terminated after *MAXIT* iterations (see Input Parameters, Section 3a).

Boxes 25–41: The iterations have now converged. Small ψ_i^2 are replaced by zero. For ULS, the solution is computed by (11). For GLS and ML, the solution is computed by (19) if there are no ψ_i^2 equal to zero, and by (60) if one or more of the ψ_i^2 are zero.

b. Chart FCTGR

Subroutine FCTGR is used to compute the function value $f(\theta^{(s)})$ and the gradient vector $h^{(s)}$.

Box 1: *ITRY* is a counter for the number of halvings in each iteration (see explanation to Box 1 of Chart NWTRAP).

Boxes 2–8: This is the ULS method.

Boxes 9–16: These are the GLS and ML methods.

Boxes 10–12: If MOR = 0, the approximate second derivatives are used. Therefore, only the eigenvectors corresponding to the $p - k$ largest eigenvalues are needed. Otherwise, all the eigenvectors are needed. The second derivatives are computed in subroutine INCPSI.

Boxes 14–16: The first derivatives are computed from (48) for GLS and (51) for ML.

Boxes 17–22: Here the new function value f is compared with the old one f_0 and if $f > f_0$, successive halvings are made until $f \leqslant f_0$ (see explanation to Box 1 of NWTRAP).

c. Chart INCPSI

This subroutine is used to compute the correction vector $\delta^{(s)}$ and the new parameter vector $\theta^{(s+1)}$.

Boxes 1–7: If *MOR* is zero, the approximate second derivatives are used; otherwise the exact second derivatives are used.

Box 3: If $\partial^2 f / \partial \theta_i^2 < \varepsilon_u$ we set all off-diagonal elements in the ith row and column of H to zero. The ith correction δ_i determined by the system (54) will then automatically be that given by (57).

Box 8: We know here that the matrix of approximate second derivatives was used and this is always positive definite.

Boxes 10–16: The elements of the new vector $\theta^{(s+1)}$ are examined as follows. If an element is less than *BND* it is set equal to *BND*. If any correction was larger than ε_E in magnitude, we continue to use the approximate second derivatives.

Boxes 17–23: Test for convergence. If for all θ_i which are not equal to *BND*, the

correction δ_i is less than or equal to ε in magnitude, convergence has been obtained and *MOR* is set to zero. Otherwise, we know that all corrections are smaller than or equal to ε_E so we continue iteration using the exact derivatives.

6. SAMPLE PROBLEMS

Two sample problems are given, one which illustrates the behavior of the subroutine NWTRAP and one which illustrates the use of the whole program.

The first problem is based on the correlation matrix of order 9×9 given in Table 1. This is analyzed with $k = 3$ using the GLS and ML methods. The start values for ψ_i^2, computed as $(1 - k/2p)/s^{ii}$, are as follows: 0.424, 0.414, 0.566, 0.250, 0.380, 0.267, 0.394, 0.595, 0.290.

The final unrotated solutions are shown in Table 3, and Table 2 gives details about the GLS minimization. Column 2 of Table 2 shows what kind of second-order derivative matrix was used, E = approximate, H = exact. The function values in each iteration are shown in column 3. In column 4, the maximum absolute corrections are given and in column 5, the maximum absolute derivatives.

The second sample problem uses some data on intelligence tests administered to 286 senior high-school students at Hyde Park High School in Chicago in 1937. The

Table 1. CORRELATION MATRIX FOR PROBLEM 1

1	2	3	4	5	6	7	8	9
1.000	0.523	0.395	0.471	0.346	0.426	0.576	0.434	0.639
	1.000	0.479	0.506	0.418	0.462	0.547	0.283	0.645
		1.000	0.355	0.270	0.254	0.452	0.219	0.504
			1.000	0.691	0.791	0.443	0.285	0.505
				1.000	0.679	0.383	0.149	0.409
					1.000	0.372	0.314	0.472
						1.000	0.385	0.680
							1.000	0.470
								1.000

Table 2. Details of the GLS minimization for Problem 1

Iteration	Type	Function	Max. Correction	Max. Gradient
0	—	0.1170246	—	2.45×10^{-1}
1	E	0.04017278	6.64×10^{-1}	5.04×10^{-2}
2	E	0.03341929	1.71×10^{-1}	1.06×10^{-2}
3	E	0.03321625	2.73×10^{-2}	7.36×10^{-4}
4	H	0.03321503	2.91×10^{-3}	3.64×10^{-6}
5	H	0.03321503	2.67×10^{-5}	2.37×10^{-10}

Table 3. Unrotated solutions for Problem 1

		GLS					ML		
i	λ_{i1}	λ_{i2}	λ_{i3}	ψ_i^2	λ_{i1}	λ_{i2}	λ_{i_3}	ψ_i^2
1	.662	.325	−.082	.445	.664	.321	−.073	.450
2	.688	.255	.191	.416	.689	.247	.193	.427
3	.491	.310	.225	.600	.493	.302	.222	.617
4	.839	−.286	.041	.208	.837	−.292	.035	.212
5	.708	−.309	.162	.370	.705	−.315	.153	.381
6	.823	−.376	−.106	.168	.819	−.377	−.105	.177
7	.660	.404	.073	.387	.662	.396	.078	.400
8	.454	.290	−.484	.473	.458	.296	−.491	.462
9	.763	.434	.001	.227	.766	.427	.012	.231

Table 4. Correlation matrix for Problem 2

Test Name	Original No.	Recode No.	1	2	3	4	5	6	7	8	9
Addition	1	1		.684	.284	.177	.072	.227	.288	.029	.321
Multiplication	18	2	.684		.368	.186	.091	.232	.421	.141	.352
Arithmetic	3	3	.234	.368		.332	.358	.415	.096	.149	.120
Figures	9	4	.177	.186	.332		.727	.577	.099	.305	.306
Cards	4	5	.072	.091	.358	.727		.519	.052	.304	.178
Squares	31	6	.227	.232	.415	.577	.519		.240	.320	.322
Identical Numbers	11	7	.288	.421	.096	.099	.052	.240		.342	.500
Identical Forms	10	8	.029	.141	.149	.305	.304	.320	.342		.401
Repeated Letters	27	9	.321	.352	.120	.306	.178	.322	.500	.401	

data was originally gathered and analyzed by Thurstone [11]. Nine tests are used here for illustration. The names of these tests are given in the first column of Table 4 and their original code numbers are given in column 2. Table 4 also shows all the intercorrelations between the nine tests.

The correlation matrix in Table 4 was run with the ML method for one, two, and three factors. Table 5 shows the value of χ^2, the corresponding degrees of freedom and the

reliability coefficient. It is seen that one and two factors are not sufficient to reproduce the correlations. For $k = 3$, χ^2 is still significant but the reliability coefficient is sufficiently large. It is probably best to stop with three factors to avoid overfitting and the capitalization on chance.

The varimax-rotated factor loadings for three factors are given in Table 6. This factor matrix can be given a clear interpretation. The first factor has high loadings for

Table 5. TESTS FOR NUMBER OF FACTORS FOR PROBLEM 2

k	χ^2	Degrees of Freedom	Reliability Coefficient
1	414.00	27	0.41
2	135.99	19	0.75
3	32.83	12	0.93

Table 6. VARIMAX SOLUTION FOR PROBLEM 2

	Spatial	Numerical	Perceptual Speed	Unique Variance
Addition	.086	.747	.151	.411
Multiplication	.079	.856	.252	.198
Arithmetic	.411	.371	.012	.693
Figures	.837	.091	.167	.264
Cards	.845	−.002	.081	.279
Squares	.613	.157	.279	.522
Identical Numbers	−.022	.282	.673	.466
Identical Forms	.289	−.038	.533	.631
Repeated Letters	.174	.216	.667	.478

tests 4–6 and may be interpreted as a spatial or geometric factor. The second factor has high loadings for tests 1–3 and is interpreted as a numerical factor. The third factor being highly loaded for tests 7–9 is best interpreted as a perceptual speed factor. An oblique rotation would make the simple structure even more clear.

7. REFERENCES

1. T. W. Anderson, "Some Scaling Models and Estimation Procedures in the Latent Class Model," in *Probability and Statistics*, The Harald Cramér Volume, U. Grenander (ed.), Wiley, New York, 9–38 (1959).

2. R. Bellman, *Introduction to Matrix Analysis*, McGraw-Hill, 1960.

3. F. A. Graybill, *Introduction to Matrices with Applications in Statistics*, Wadsworth Publishing Co., Belmont, California, 1969.

4. J. Greenstadt, "The Determination of the Characteristic Roots of a Matrix by the Jacobi Method," in *Mathematical Methods for Digital Computers*, Vol. I, Ch. 7, Ralston and Wilf (eds.), Wiley, New York, 1960.

5. H. H. Harman, *Modern Factor Analysis*, (2nd ed.), Univ. of Chicago Press, Chicago, 1967.

6. K. G. Jöreskog, *Statistical Estimation in Factor Analysis*, Almqvist & Wiksell, Stockholm, 1963.

7. ——, "Some Contributions to Maximum Likelihood Factor Analysis," *Psychometrika*, **32**, 443–482 (1967).

8. K. G. Jöreskog and A. S. Goldberger, "Factor Analysis by Generalized Least Squares," *Psychometrika*, **37**, 243–259 (1972).

9. K. G. Jöreskog and D. N. Lawley, "New Methods in Maximum Likelihood Factor Analysis," *Brit. J. Math. Statist. Psychol.*, **21**, 85–96 (1968).

10. D. N. Lawley and A. E. Maxwell, *Factor Analysis as a Statistical Method*, 2nd edit., Butterworth, London, 1971.

11. L. L. Thurstone, "Experimental Study of Simple Structure," *Psychometrika*, **5**, 153–168 (1940).

12. L. R. Tucker and C. Lewis, "A Reliability Coefficient for Maximum Likelihood Factor Analysis," *Psychometrika*, **38**, 1–10 (1973).

13. J. H. Wilkinson, *The Algebraic Eigenvalue Problem*, Oxford Univ. Press, Oxford 1965.

Minres Method of Factor Analysis*

8

Harry H. Harman
Educational Testing Service

1. FUNCTION

Although component analysis is designed to account for the total variance optimally with the least number of principal components, the objective of factor analysis is to explain the interrelationships among the variables optimally in terms of as few *common* factors as possible. That can be accomplished by the usual statistical approaches: the maximum-likelihood method as employed in the preceding chapter; and the least-squares method of the present chapter. The factorization, in either case, shows the degree of fit of a model to empirical data. Although formal tests of significance for the number of common factors are presented, applied factor analysts more often are content in selecting a small number of factors that have "practical" significance.

The word "minres" is a contraction of "minimum residuals" and represents a

method long sought by factor analysts. This objective can be traced to Thurstone [6, p. 61]: "The object of a factor problem is to account for the tests, or their intercorrelations, in terms of a small number of derived variables, the smallest possible number that is consistent with acceptable residual errors." Conceptually, the idea of getting a factor solution by minimizing the residual correlations is an obviously direct approach. The first practical solution, however, was not developed until 1965 by Harman and Jones [4]. The idea certainly is not new—its accomplishment, however, was dependent on the high-speed computer. No doubt it must have crossed the minds of many workers in factor analysis over the years. The first theoretical treatment appeared in 1936, when Eckart and Young [1, p. 211] noted that "if the least-squares criterion of approximation [of one matrix by another of lower rank] be adopted, this problem has a general solution which is relatively simple in a theoretical sense, though the amount of numerical work involved in applications may be prohibitive." Of course, the numeri-

*This chapter is based in part on Chapter 9 of H. H. Harman, "*Modern Factor Analysis*", and is produced here with the kind permission of the publishers, The University of Chicago Press.

cal work is feasible now. (The minres method is akin to the ULS (unweighted least-squares) method described in Chapter 7.)

In obtaining a minres (or a maximum-likelihood) factorization of a given correlation matrix the basic question of factor analysis is answered, namely, how well the model fits the given data. However, this is only the initial step in applied uses of factor analysis. Following this, the applied scientist is usually concerned with a meaningful interpretation of the results and, to assist in that, he may wish to transform the direct factor analysis results to a new basis—a "confirmatory" solution (see Chapter 7) or a "simple structure" solution (see Chapter 9). Still another aspect of factor analysis involves the estimation of actual factor measurements. For a detailed description of these concepts as they arise in the basic theory and techniques of factor analysis the reader is referred to Harman [2], upon which the present chapter is based.

2. MATHEMATICAL DISCUSSION

a. Symbols Used

A — Matrix of coefficients of common factors

A_{-j} — Factor matrix A with the elements in row j replaced by zeros

a_{jp} — Factor loading, that is, coefficient of factor p in the linear expression of variable j in terms of the factors

b_{jp} — $= a_{jp} + \varepsilon_p$ Modified factor loadings for Gauss–Seidel process

b — Vector of the m modified factor loadings

c_p — Constants (a fixed point) derived in the course of simplifying transformations

D — Diagonal matrix of coefficients of "unique" factors

f — Vector of m "common" factors

f_j — Part of objective functions $f(A)$ due to variable j

$f(A)$ — Function of the factor loadings that is to be minimized

H — Diagonal matrix of "communalities"

h_j^2 — Communality of variable j, that is, the variance of the variable that is due to the common factors

K — A constant derived in the course of simplifying transformations

m — Number of common factors

N — Number of sample elements

n — Number of variables

Q — Matrix of eigenvectors of W

R — Matrix of correlations among n observed variables

$R^\dagger$ — Matrix of correlations produced from the factor model (1)

r_{jk} — Correlation between variable j and variable k

r_{jk}^* — $= r_{jk} - \sum_{p=1}^{m} a_{jp} a_{kp}$ Residual correlation between variables j and k

r^0 — Vector of residual correlations of variable j with all other variables, with the self-residual zero

x_p — Functions of the desired quantities b_{jp} that simplify the computations

U_m — Asymptotic χ^2 statistic for testing significance of m factors

u — Vector of n "unique" factors

W — Symmetric matrix developed in the course of simplifying the quadratic form in (8)

z — Vector of n variables

ε_j — Vector of incremental changes in the m factor loadings of variable j

ε_p — Increments added to the m factor loadings for a particular row of A in the Gauss–Seidel process

$\Lambda = (\lambda_p)$ Diagonal matrix of eigenvalues of W

μ A Lagrange multiplier

ν Number of degrees of freedom for asymptotic χ^2 test

b. Mathematical Background

The classical factor analysis model, in contrast to the principal-components model, may be put as follows:

$$z = Af + Du \qquad (1)$$

where the vector z represents the n observed variables, the vector f represents m common factors, the vector u represents n error or unique factors, the $n \times m$ matrix A represents the common-factor loadings (a_{jp}) that are the parameters to be estimated, and D is an $n \times n$ diagonal matrix of coefficients of the unique factors to account for the unexplained variance of each variable. Once a solution A is obtained, the fundamental theorem of factor analysis gives (assuming, without any loss of generality, that the factors are uncorrelated):

$$R^\dagger = AA^T \qquad (2)$$

where $R^\dagger$ is the matrix of correlations produced from the model (1) but with the self-correlations reduced by deleting the unique variance. The resulting "communalities" are represented by the diagonal matrix

$$H = I - D^2 = \text{diag}(AA^T) \qquad (3)$$

The problem, then, is to get a "best" fit to the observed correlation matrix R by the reproduced correlations $R^\dagger$ employing model (1).

A least-squares fit can be obtained for the entire correlation matrix, which leads to the principal-component method. On the other hand, by fitting the off-diagonal values only, we arrive at the minres method. This condition may be expressed in the form:

$$\min \left\| [R - I] - [AA^T - \text{diag}(AA^T)] \right\| \qquad (4)$$

Writing the norm in (4) algebraically, we obtain:

$$f(A) = \sum_{k=j+1}^{n} \sum_{j=1}^{n-1} \left(r_{jk} - \sum_{p=1}^{m} a_{jp}a_{kp} \right)^2 \qquad (5)$$

which is the objective function to be minimized.

It should be noted that this function involves the $n(n-1)/2$ off-diagonal residual correlations which are dependent upon the elements in the factor matrix A. The objective of minres is to minimize the function $f(A)$, for a specified m, by varying the values of the factor loadings. The diagonal matrix of communalities is obtained as a by-product of the method.

Without further constraint on the matrix A, an occasional solution may be obtained for which the communality of a variable exceeds unity. Such a solution is known as a "Heywood" case [2, p. 117]. In order to assure that the resulting communalities will be within the acceptable range, the following side conditions on the objective function (5) are introduced:

$$h_j^2 = \sum_{p=1}^{m} a_{jp}^2 \leqslant 1 \qquad (j = 1, \ldots, n) \quad (6)$$

Once the problem has been formulated in terms of minimizing the objective function (5), there are several approaches that would yield an appropriate solution but with varying degrees of efficiency. Some of the methods investigated by Harman and Jones [4] include (1) principal-factor iterations and (2) gradient methods. In the first instance an arbitrary matrix H of communalities is selected, and by successive calculations of a principal-factor matrix A and its associated communalities H, improvements in $f(A)$ are obtained. The gradient methods start from the purely mathematical criterion for a minimum value of a nonlinear function $f(A)$, namely, that its partial derivatives with respect to the nm independent variables must be zero and its matrix of second-order derivatives must be positive definite. A minimum value of the function $f(A)$ is obtained, iteratively, by proceeding from a trial solution to the next approximation in the direction (the gradient) of maximal change in the function.

Although either of these approaches can produce acceptable solutions, they are generally too time consuming. In searching for more efficient methods, Harman and Jones [4] adapted the Gauss–Seidel process to produce an effective solution to the problem. The basic mathematics for the minres method is developed first and this is followed by the resolution of the Heywood case as worked out by Harman and Fukuda [3].

c. Derivation of the Method

BASIC PROCEDURE

As will be recalled, the Gauss–Seidel method involves an iterative process in which small changes are made in the variables and the corresponding new variables replace the original ones. Thus if small changes or displacements are made in only one row of A, the reproduced correlations, as given by (2), will be linear functions of these displacements; the objective function (5) will be quadratic in the displacements. This is in contrast to fourth-degree polynomials that arise in the gradient methods [4].

Designating the increments that are added to the m factor loadings for any row j of A by ε_p, the new loadings become:

$$b_{jp} = a_{jp} + \varepsilon_p \qquad (p = 1, \ldots, m) \quad (7)$$

The impact on the objective function of a variable j that is modified in this manner may be represented by

$$f_j = \sum_{\substack{k=1 \\ k \neq j}}^{n} \left(r_{jk} \sum_{p=1}^{m} a_{kp} b_{jp} \right)^2 \qquad (j \text{ fixed}) \quad (8)$$

or, upon separating the incremental

changes, by

$$f_j = \sum_{\substack{k=1 \\ k \neq j}}^{n} \left(r_{jk}^* - \sum_{p=1}^{m} a_{kp} \varepsilon_p \right)^2 \qquad (j \text{ fixed}) \quad (9)$$

where $r_{jk}^* = r_{jk} - \sum_{p=1}^{m} a_{kp} b_{jp}$ are the unmodified residual correlations.

To determine values of the ε's that will minimize the objective function $f(A)$, we take partial derivatives of (9) with respect to each of these, and set these equal to zero, obtaining

$$\sum_{p=1}^{m} \left[\sum_{\substack{k=1 \\ k \neq j}}^{n} a_{kp} a_{kq} \right] \varepsilon_p = \sum_{\substack{k=1 \\ k \neq j}}^{n} r_{jk}^* a_{kq}$$

$$(q = 1, \ldots, m) \quad (10)$$

This may be put in matrix form,

$$\varepsilon_j A_{-j}^T A_{-j} = r_j^0 A \quad (11)$$

where ε_j is the row vector of incremental changes of the factor loadings for variable j, A_{-j} is the factor matrix A with the elements in row j replaced by zeros, and r_j^0 is the row vector of residual correlations of variable j with all other variables (and 0 for the self-residual). Then the solution for the displacements to the factor loadings (for a given variable) that will minimize the objective function, is:

$$\varepsilon_j = r_j^0 A \left(A_{-j}^T A_{-j} \right)^{-1} \quad (12)$$

The foregoing process is carried out systematically for all variables. In this way successive approximations of the rows of A are obtained that produce a value of $f(A)$ as close to the minimum as the computing accuracy will permit.

RESOLUTION OF THE HEYWOOD CASE

The basic procedure does not guarantee that the resulting elements of A will remain in the acceptable range, that is, that (6) will be satisfied. For the minres method to produce proper solutions it is necessary that the objective function as expressed in (8) be minimized subject to

$$\sum_{p=1}^{m} b_{jp}^2 \leqslant 1 \qquad (13)$$

that is, the new values of the factor loadings must satisfy the constraints (6) as well. At this stage of the process the r_{jk} and the a_{kp} are known; only the b_{jp} may vary.

If the minimum of f_j, as defined in (8), is obtained at a point $(b_{j1}, \ldots, b_{jm})$ in the region (13) there is no problem. However, if the point does not belong to the region then the problem becomes complicated, primarily because of the *inequality* in the side condition. This inequality may be removed by means of the following:

THEOREM 1: If the minimum of f_j is attained outside of the region defined by (13), then the minimum of f_j under the constraint (13) will be attained at a boundary point of the region, so that the constraint may be replaced by

$$\sum_{p=1}^{m} b_{jp}^2 - 1 \qquad (14)$$

The proof [3] involves the rewriting of the quadratic form in (8) to facilitate its diagonalization into eigenvalues and associated eigenvectors as indicated in the descriptions of Boxes 8–9 of the flow chart. Then, additional transformation leads to the simplified expression

$$f_j = \sum_{p=1}^{m} (x_p - c_p)^2 + K \qquad (15)$$

subject to the constraint

$$\sum_{p=1}^{m} \frac{x_p^2}{\lambda_p^2} \leqslant 1 \qquad (16)$$

in which the x_p are functions of the original

b_{jp} and are the quantities to be determined; while the λ_p (eigenvalues of the $m \times m$ matrix introduced in the simplification of the quadratic form), the c_p, and K are all constants determined from the known r_{jk} and a_{kp} and the intervening transformations. In this simplified form it is evident that f_j is the sum of a constant K and a square of the distance between a fixed point $(c_1, \ldots, c_m)$ and a variable point $(x_1, \ldots, x_m)$ belonging to the region defined by (16). Then, minimization of f_j is equivalent to locating a point satisfying (16) that is at the minimum distance from the given point $(c_1, \ldots, c_m)$.

If the given point belongs to the region, that is,

$$\frac{c_1^2}{\lambda_1^2} + \cdots + \frac{c_m^2}{\lambda_m^2} \leqslant 1 \qquad (17)$$

then this point itself is the minimizing point, and the solution is

$$x_p = c_p \qquad (p = 1, \ldots, m) \qquad (18)$$

On the other hand, if the given point is *outside* the region, then a point $(x_1, \ldots, x_m)$ belonging to the region must lie on its boundary in order to be at a minimum distance from the given point. Furthermore, since the x_p/λ_p were obtained by an orthogonal transformation from the original variables, distance is preserved and a point on the boundary of the region can be expressed in terms of the b_{jp} as in (14).

In the course of proving Theorem 1 additional information became available that facilitates the solution of the problem. When the minimum of f_j is attained in the region (13) its value is given by K in (15) and the minimizing point is (18). For the crucial case of the minimum of f_j falling outside this region, a more tractable approach than that originally implied—minimizing (8) under the constraint (14)—follows from (15) and (16), namely, minimize

$$(x_1 - c_1)^2 + \cdots + (x_m - c_m)^2 \qquad (19)$$

under the constraint

$$\frac{x_1^2}{\lambda_1^2} + \cdots + \frac{x_m^2}{\lambda_m^2} = 1 \qquad (20)$$

To get solutions for the x_p, the method of Lagrange multipliers can be applied by creating a new function $(19) - \mu(20)$, setting its partial derivatives with respect to the m variables x_p equal to zero, and solving this set of equations together with (20). The parameter μ, determined from any one of the first m equations, is given by

$$\mu = \frac{\lambda_p^2(x_p - c_p)}{x_p} \qquad (p = 1, \ldots, m)$$

(21)

and μ may be eliminated by setting any one of the m values equal to any other. Thus they may all be expressed in terms of the first variable so that the remaining unknowns in terms of the first become:

$$x_p = \frac{\lambda_p^2 c_p x_1}{(\lambda_p^2 - \lambda_1^2)x_1 + \lambda_1^2 c_1}$$

$$(p = 2, \ldots, m) \quad (22)$$

Substitution of these values into (20) gives rise to a polynomial equation in x_1 of degree $2m$. A solution of this equation, involving a numerical method of successive approximations is employed, which rests on the following:

THEOREM 2: For a given x_1 between 0 and $\min(c_1, \lambda_1)$, with x_p ($p = 2, \ldots, m - 1$) determined by (22) and x_m by (20), if

$$\lambda_m^2\left(1 - \frac{c_m}{x_m}\right) \gtrless \lambda_1^2\left(1 - \frac{c_1}{x_1}\right) \qquad (23)$$

then

$$x_1 \gtrless x_1^* \qquad (24)$$

where x_1^* designates the true solution for x_1.

The proof begins with the fact that x_p is an increasing function of x_1 (the c's being assumed positive without loss of generality) which can easily be shown by differentiation. Then the two conclusions are reached by the following reasoning: If $x_1 < x_1^*$ then x_p ($p = 2, \ldots, m$) is less than its solution x_0^*, and, consequently x_m determined by (20) is larger than its solution x_m^*. Therefore, using (21)

$$\lambda_1^2\left(1 - \frac{c_1}{x_1}\right) < \lambda_1^2\left(1 - \frac{c_1}{x_1^*}\right)$$

$$= \lambda_m^2\left(1 - \frac{c_m}{x_m^*}\right) < \lambda_m^2\left(1 - \frac{c_m}{x_m}\right)$$

If $x_1 > x_1^*$ then a similar argument leads to

$$\lambda_1^2\left(1 - \frac{c_1}{x_1}\right) > \lambda_m^2\left(1 - \frac{c_m}{x_m}\right)$$

completing the proof. This theorem facilitates the determination of a modified factor matrix A as indicated in the descriptions of Boxes 11–13 of the flow chart.

d. Test of Significance for Number of Factors

The foregoing mathematical methods lead to the factor loadings that yield a minimum value of $f(A)$ for a specified number of common factors (m). Of course, the fit to the data improves with increasing size of m; the question is, what value of m is justified on the basis of the sample. A large-sample criterion for judging the completeness of factorization was developed by Rippe [5] and is adapted to the minres solution.

The test involves the basic assumption that the original variables have a multivariate normal distribution, from which it follows that the correlations have a Wishart distribution and the sample values are maximum-likelihood estimates of the population correlations. While Rippe's development is explicitly in terms of the sample covariance matrix, the results are equally applicable to a factor analysis of the sample correlation matrix.

The statistic for testing the significance of m factors may be put in the form:

$$U_m = (N - 1)\log_e \frac{|AA^T + D^2|}{|R|} \quad (25)$$

which is asymptotically distributed as χ^2 with degrees of freedom equal to

$$\nu = \tfrac{1}{2}\left[(n - m)^2 + n - m\right] \quad (26)$$

The test procedure is to reject the hypothesis of m common factors if U_m exceeds the value of χ^2 for the desired significance level; otherwise it would be accepted. Of course, if the hypothesis is rejected an alternate hypothesis of some larger number of factors may be assumed to explain the observed correlations.

It should be noted that the derivation was based upon the sampling variation of the observed correlation matrix R (and consequently on the sampling variation of the factor matrix A). The variability of the individual correlations is, of course, dependent on the sample size N. Since a correlation matrix would be subject to extreme variation for small samples, it is standard practice to apply factor analysis only to large samples. Hence, the large-sample approximations made in the course of arriving at (25) are not really additional constraints on good experimental practice.

3. SUMMARY OF CALCULATION PROCEDURE

The calculation of the factor matrix A so as to minimize the objective function (5) subject to the side conditions (6) is accomplished according to the mathematical development of the last section, and is presented in a flow chart and described in the following three sections. In the present section a general overview of the process is presented.

a. Input Quantities

To run the program, the following input cards are required, exclusive of system control cards for the particular computer. These cards are described in terms of the symbols used in the program (and sometimes parenthetically related to the symbols of the mathematical development) in order to facilitate its use.

1. Parameter card (format 5I5,E10.0,3I5) showing:
   - (a) N = number of variables ($n \leqslant 100$);
   - (b) $M1$ and $M2$ = lower and upper bound of range of factors ($m \leqslant 20$);
   - (c) $ITMAX$ = maximum number of iterations (usually 1000);
   - (d) IND = initial factor matrix option: 0, principal components, based on 1's in the diagonal of the correlation matrix (default option); 1, principal factors, based on communality values for the diagonal as given in (5);
   - (e) EPS = convergency criterion (usually $\varepsilon = .001$);
   - (f) NPR = print switch (0, final values only; > 0, critical values at each iteration; > 10, critical plus detailed values at each iteration);
   - (g) $NSAMP$ = sample size (N); test of significance is omitted if blank;
   - (h) $IPNCH$ = punch switch (0, punched output produced; $\neq 0$, punched output omitted).

2. Title card (format 20A4), giving name of the problem.

3. Format card, indicating the format of the data according to Fortran specification.

4. Data cards, following format in (3), giving the complete correlation matrix (with unities in diagonal) with each variable starting a new card.

5. Communality values, following format in (3), if the IND parameter in (1) $\neq 0$.

If more than one problem is to be run at the

same time, the specific input for each problem as enumerated above, is repeated before the closing control cards that may be required by the computer system.

b. Order of Calculation

Although the flow chart in the next section gives a more detailed plan of the minres program, it is the intent here to present a general overview of the calculations.

The procedure starts out by calculating the eigenvalues and eigenvectors of a real symmetric matrix (R) leading to the initial factor matrix A_0. The incremental changes ε_j of the Gauss–Seidel process are calculated and a new factor matrix A_1, is determined. This process is continued until the changes in the factor loadings stabilize to any desired degree. Along the way, a test is made to determine whether the computed communality for any variable is greater than one. If such a Heywood case arises, a special computing loop modifies the results so that they conform to an acceptable factor matrix. Before the results are output, the factor matrix is put in canonical form [2, pp. 169–171].

c. Output Quantities

The basic output for each problem consists of a printout of the input parameters and correlation matrix, and the following results for each value of m desired: initial factor matrix, minres solution, along with derived communalities; value of the objective function $f(A)$ for the solution; matrix of residual correlations; frequency distribution of the residuals; frequency distribution of the differences in factor loadings between the final iteration and the preceding one; test of significance for the number m of common factors specified; and the cumulative time for the calculations.

4. FLOW CHART

The flow chart appears on page 162.

5. DESCRIPTION OF FLOW CHART

The flow chart, although somewhat abbreviated, is described in greater detail in the following steps.

Box 1: Stored are the input for each problem, consisting of the correlation matrix R and such parameters as the number of variables n, number of factors m (or m_1 to m_2), the maximum number of iterations t, the convergence criterion ε (not to be confused with the vector ε_j of incremental changes), and the number of cases N, if the significance test for u's is to be performed.

Box 2: A subroutine for the calculation of the eigenvalues and eigenvectors of a real symmetric matrix.

Box 3: At this point the subroutine has calculated and stored the arbitrary factor matrix A_0 with which the minres method is started, consisting of the first m principal components (or m principal factors if communality input). Actually, the program computes a minres solution (and correspondingly, an initial solution) for each value of m from m_1 to m_2, but that detail is not shown in the abbreviated flow chart.

Box 4: The incremental changes ε_j are calculated, according to (12) using the subroutine of Box 5. The iteration process is started with the calculation of increments ε_1 for the first variable from the initial factor matrix A_0 and the first row of observed correlations r_1^0.

Box 5: A subroutine for the solution of a system of linear equations.

Box 6: At this point a new factor matrix A_1 has been determined in which the loadings in the first row have been replaced by the computed values (7). This constitutes iteration 1. For each iteration i, a new factor matrix A_i is determined (the subscript of the A represents the iteration number, not the pivot variable).

Box 7: Each communality h_j^2 (of the new row j of A) is tested to see if it is greater than one. If $h_j^2 > 1$ proceed to Box 8, otherwise to Box 15.

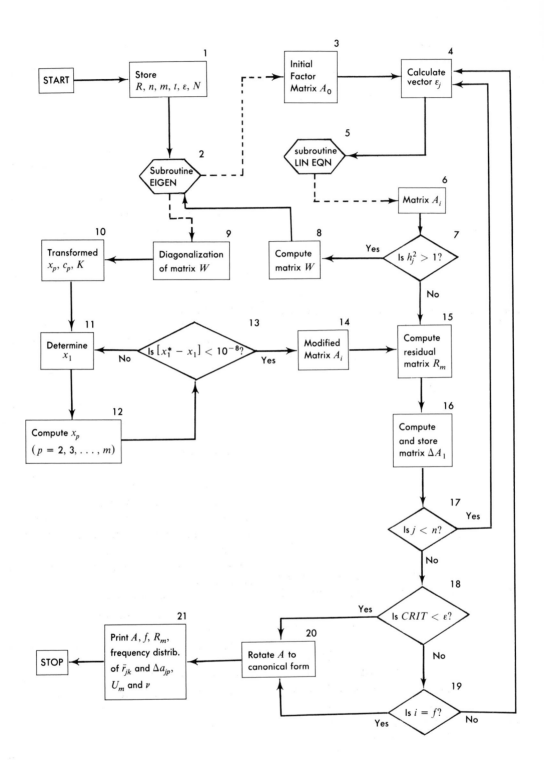

Box 8: The objective function (8) is expressed as

$$f_j = b^T W b + \sum_{p=1}^{m} 2v_p b_{jp} + K$$

in which b is a column vector of the m unknown variables b_{jp} (j fixed, $p = 1, \ldots, m$), and the matrix W, the coefficients v_p, and K are constants determined from the known r_{jk} and a_{kp}. The symmetric matrix W is determined at this stage.

Box 9: Diagonalization of the matrix W is accomplished by means of the subroutine of Box 2, yielding.

$$Q^T W Q = \Lambda$$

where Λ is a diagonal matrix with elements $\lambda_1^2, \ldots, \lambda_m^2$ that are the eigenvalues of W, and the orthogonal transformation matrix Q contains in its columns the eigenvectors of W.

Box 10: Additional transformations which lead to the derived unknowns x_p as functions of the original b_{jp}, and to the derived constants c_p and K as functions of the known r_{jk} and a_{kp}. The result of this step leads to (15) for the objective function, subject to the condition (16).

Box 11: The process pivots on the first unknown x_1 and employs an iterative scheme implied by Theorem 2 for the determination of the remaining x's. The initial value for x_1 was taken to be

$$x_1^0 = c_1 \bigg/ \sqrt{\sum_{p=1}^{m} \left(\frac{c_p}{\lambda_p} \right)^2}$$

Box 12: The remaining x_p ($p = 2, \ldots, m - 1$) are computed by means of (22) and x_m by (20).

Box 13: The convergence of x_1 to x_1^*, according to Theorem 2, is tested. The iteration process for this distance optimization routine (Boxes 11–13) is continued until x_1 converges to its solution within 10^{-8}.

Box 14: The modified matrix A_i is determined. This completes the modification loop, Boxes 8–14, to correct for $h_j^2 > 1$.

Box 15: The residual matrix R_m (with zeros in the diagonal) is computed from the factor matrix A_i and the original correlation matrix R. The designation R_m calls attention to the fact that the residual matrix is based upon m common factors, but the iteration number is omitted for the sake of simplicity.

Box 16: Computes the matrix of changes in factor loadings (from preceding to current iteration), and stored for later use.

Box 17: Test to see if each row of the factor matrix has been subjected to the Gauss–Seidel process. The loop, Boxes 4–17, for $j = 1, \ldots, n$ constitutes a major iteration cycle. Thus, in the first major iteration cycle, the successive factor matrices $A_1, \ldots, A_n$ are determined from the vectors $\varepsilon_1, \ldots, \varepsilon_n$ representing the incremental changes in the loadings for the n variables.

Box 18: At the conclusion of each major iteration cycle, the following convergence criterion is applied:

$$\max_{j,p} |_{(i)} a_{jp} - _{(i-1)} a_{jp}| < \varepsilon$$

$$(j = 1, \ldots, n; p = 1, \ldots, m)$$

where the iteration number i is a multiple of n.

Box 19: If the factor loadings have not converged, a test is made to see whether the present maximum number of iterations has been reached.

Box 20: When the factor loadings have converged, or the maximum number of iterations reached, the last determined factor matrix is rotated to "canonical" form. This is a reference basis having many of the properties of the principal-factor method [2, p. 169]. The subroutine of Box 2 is again employed in this process.

Box 21: The output is printed for the specified m, and the procedure starts over again for additional values of m or for additional problems.

In testing the significance of the number of factors, the computer program determines U_m according to (25) and the associated number of degrees of freedom. However, the table lookup of χ^2 for comparison must be done manually.

6. THE PROGRAM

In addition to the main minres program there is a function F to compute the sum of squares of residuals, a subroutine LEQN to solve a system of linear equations, and two subroutines PRTR and PRTA to print the correlation and factor matrices.

What must be provided is a subroutine to compute eigenvalues and eigenvectors corresponding to the referenced *EIGEN* 3 (B, C, EV, M), in which B is 100×100 for the input matrix, C is a 100×100 work matrix, EV is a 100-element array for the eigenvalues, and M is the dimension of the input matrix. The eigenvectors are returned in place of matrix B. In addition provision must be made for the function *DETE* (A, N), which computes the determinant of the 100×100 matrix in A of order N and returns it as the value of the function. It should be noted that minres is a fixed dimension program even though the sizes of the matrices may have any values up to 100. Hence, the dimensions of both these subroutines should be compiled as 100. (It would be possible to restructure this program to use only that amount of core needed for the actual number of variables in a given problem).

7. SAMPLE PROBLEM

A simple example [2, pp. 13–14] involving only $n = 5$ variables provides an illustration of the process without consuming too much space. It was set up to compute a minres solution for one to four factors. Some of the detailed output, rearranged to save space, is shown for the case of $m = 2$. The symmetric correlation matrix R and the symmetric residual residual matrix R_2 (based on two factors) are both shown in the following compositie matrix (with R in the upper triangle and R_2 in the lower triangle):

$$R_2 \begin{bmatrix} & .010 & .972 & .439 & .022 \\ -.017 & & .154 & .691 & .863 \\ .002 & .019 & & .515 & .122 \\ .005 & -.002 & -.005 & & .778 \\ .001 & -.000 & -.013 & .002 & \end{bmatrix} R$$

The minres solution for two common factors is given in the table,

Variable	a_{j1}	a_{j2}	h_j^2
1	.621	−.784	1.000
2	.701	.522	.764
3	.702	−.683	.958
4	.881	.144	.797
5	.781	.605	.976
Variance	2.756	1.739	4.495

along with the derived communalities and the variance accounted for by each factor. For this solution the objective function $f(A)$ = .00095 (having dropped from .96419 for $m = 1$). A frequency distribution of the residuals is a standard output, but there is no need to print it here. Neither is it necessary to print the frequency distribution of changes in factor loadings ΔA. The statistic (25) has the value $U_2 = 35.42$, with 6 degrees of freedom, while the corresponding

χ^2's (from manual table lookup) are 22.5 for $P = .001$, 16.5 for $P = .01$, and 12.6 for $P = .05$. The hypothesis of $m = 2$ common factors would be rejected at all levels, and it must be assumed that at least 3 common factors are required for statistical explanation of the observed data based on $N = 120$.

For $m = 3$, all 10 residuals were zero to 3 decimal places, and the objective function was also zero to more than 5 places. The test for $m = 3$ leads to $U_3 = .05$ with 3 degrees of freedom and a $\chi^2 = 7.8$ for $P = .05$; certainly 3 common factors are adequate.

8. ESTIMATION OF RUNNING TIME

The time for a problem depends largely on the number of variables (n) and the number of factors (m). Of course it is closely related to the number of iterations, which could be affected by the initial factor matrix selected. Perhaps the best way to give a rough indication of running time is by way of a few illustrations, all on an IBM 360/65. The problems in the table are purposely grouped, but the estimated time is for a single problem (i.e., for a given n and a given m).

Problem Size		Time
n	m	Estimates
5–8	2–6	1–12 sec
24	2–4	4–10 sec
24	5–11	7–38 sec
30	2–4	4–15 sec
30	5–8	12–48 sec
40	2–4	8–23 sec
40	5–7	19–49 sec
50	5	2.2 min
100	5	10 min

9. REFERENCES

1. C. Eckart and G. Young, "The Approximation of One Matrix by Another of Lower Rank," *Psychometrika*, **1**, 211–218 (1936).

2. H. H. Harman, *Modern Factor Analysis*, 2nd edit., Univ. of Chicago Press, 1967.

3. H. H. Harman and Y. Fukuda, "Resolution of the Heywood Case in the Minres Solution," *Psychometrika*, **31**, 563–571 (1966).

4. H. H. Harman and W. H. Jones, "Factor Analysis by Minimizing Residuals (Minres)," *Psychometrika*, **31**, 351–368 (1966).

5. D. D. Rippe, "Application of a Large Sampling Criterion to Some Sampling Problems in Factor Analysis," *Psychometrika*, **18**, 191–205 (1953).

6. L. L. Thurstone, *Multiple Factor Analysis*, Univ. of Chicage Press, 1947.

Principles and Procedures for Unique Rotation in Factor Analysis

9

Raymond B. Cattell
University of Illinois

and

Dev K. Khanna
Genesee Computer Center

1. FUNCTION

This chapter concerns itself primarily with the procedures *following* the delivery to the investigator of a principal axis factor analysis. These procedures lead, via rotation, to the ultimately desired unique, meaningful solution.

At the outset, we must recognize the difference between *component analysis*, which yields as many factors as there are variables, and *factor analysis*, which inserts communalities in the diagonal of the factor matrix in an attempt to reduce the matrix to a number of factors decidedly smaller than the number of variables. In rotation in component analysis one simply applies an orthonormal transformation matrix which shifts the orthogonal framework to some new orthogonal position, decided by whatever the component analyst considers the position he wishes to reach. On the other hand, in factor analysis, there is always an implied scientific model, requiring a unique resolution, which demands that the rotation conform to a number of conditions to be discussed further on in this chapter.

2. MATHEMATICAL DISCUSSION AND SURVEY OF STATE OF THE ART

Symbols Used

V_0 — Unrotated $n \times k$ orthogonal matrix

L or Λ — Transformation matrix

V_{rs} — Reference vector structure matrix

τ_p Pattern similarity coefficient
V_0' Transposed V_0 matrix
V_{fp} Procrustes fit matrix
W Eigenvector matrix
P Eigenvector matrix
D_s Diagonal matrix of eigenvalues
R Reference vector

As a result from factor analysis, (Chapters 7 and 8 of this volume) the investigator finds himself with an $n \times k$ orthogonal matrix (n variables, k factors), and may wish to rotate the axes either to a new position that is internally orthogonal or to a new position in which factors are mutually oblique, that is, nonorthogonal. (Incidentally, while considering transformations of the original matrix in the broadest context the reader might raise the question also whether there could also be a shift of origin. It is quite possible to shift the origin, and the matter has been adequately discussed by Ross [28], but the situations in which this is a meaningful thing to do are so rare—virtually only the alignment of R- and Q-analysis and of ordinary and ipsative scoring—that we may dismiss it). We are, therefore, concerned with taking the $n \times k$ matrix, which we will call V_0 (defining an *unrotated orthogonal* matrix), and shifting it by a transformation matrix, which we will call L, to a new position which will be called V_{rs} (*reference* vector *structure* matrix) as follows:

$$V_{rs} = V_0 L \qquad (1)$$

The notation V is used throughout this chapter for all *variable-dimension* matrices with subscripts added according to the particular meaning. V_0 refers to the pristine matrix from the factor extraction process itself, with orthogonal factors of unit length. Though the ideal reference axes are of equal unit length the variance contribution (to variables) of the factors will, in general, diminish from left to right in this matrix, that is, the factors will be ordered in diminishing contribution to total variance. The L matrix is normalized by columns, but

can be either orthonormal, that is, with its columns uncorrelated, or oblique, and in the latter case it will yield the V_{rs} matrix as oblique. The subscript *rs* for this obtained matrix denotes *reference vector structure*, because the new axes will be reference vectors, not factors in the ordinary sense. This distinction between factors and reference vectors is necessary for the oblique case but vanishes in the orthogonal, and since we may consider the orthogonal case as a special instance of the general oblique case, we retain for generality the same subscript here for every rotated product. The distinction between the reference vector system and the factor system, which is due to Thurstone [32] and the earlier workers in oblique factoring (Holzinger; see [2]) will become evident as we proceed.

a. Approaches to Factor Rotation

The *decision* concerning the position to which the original orthogonal V_0 should be rotated must rest upon some principle or model. It is easy to think of a number of purely mathematical principles that *might* be set up, such as spreading the loading variance equally across the factors, or some other abstract mathematical principle, but, in fact, since the use of factor analysis is for scientific purposes, rotation according to some scientific model is more important. Broadly, models can be based either on the effect they produce on the distribution of *test loadings* (variable loadings), or the effect they produce with regard to the distribution of *factor scores of people*. An instance of the latter would be criterion rotation [6, 19].

The latter has been used to rotate until the first factor gives maximum separation of certain groups of people, but in principle could be used parallel to a discriminant function to give maximum separation on some combination of factors. Another development of the criterion-oriented rotation procedure is available in canonical factor analysis, where we might rotate to yield maximum prediction from one set of axes to another set of axes, the variances of these factors being unrestricted.

Yet another kind of criterion rotation arises when a second factorization on the same variables with another group is involved. We might then want to rotate to some kind of agreement between them—usually maximum agreement. There are two main principles at present in use for such rotation across studies, namely, Cattell's *confactor* principle [9, 11] and Tucker's synthesis method [33]. These will be discussed later on, but it must be pointed out at the outset that the main stream of interest in factor rotation has rested on the obtaining of a unique structure *within a particular matrix*, and to this aim, "*simple structure*," we must therefore give our main consideration. In "zeroing in" on the simple structure principle let us nevertheless recognize that a considerable number of scientific models *could* theoretically be invoked, as a basis for a rational rotational solution, but in fact (provided we keep within the linear model) the only approaches worthy of serious consideration are three, as follows:

1. The rotation of one or more factors to align with some particular external predefined criteria which are themselves also representable as dimensions (criterion rotation, canonical factoring).

2. The use of factor analysis as a *classificatory* system only, in which case it generally means rotation to either given maximum separation of person-groups or to attempt alignment with some logical system imposable on the variables themselves.

3. The use of rotation to locate underlying *determiners or influences* responsible for the empirically observed correlations, by applying conditions that distinguish determiners from mere dimensions.

Examples of the first have been cited. Examples of the second may be seen particularly in the work of Burt [3], who has perhaps been the most consistent defender of the purely classificatory use. However, there are also instances in Eysenck, Comrey,

and the work of some sociologists, and especially in the numerous uses of Q-technique [26, 30] in which the aim has been to classify people or other objects into groups. There are arguments against this usage. In the first place, as Burt points out [3], Q-technique yields *dimensions* like R-technique, not groups, and, as Cattell, Coulter, and Tsujioka [12] and Bolz [2] have pointed out, a quite different approach is needed for grouping people into types. Locating types calls for first rotating (on approach (3) above) bringing meaning to the factors as scientific entities, and then grouping the people by the pattern similarity coefficient, r_p, and the use of the taxonome program [12] into naturally dense clusters. Burt's argument that Q-technique is really only R-technique transposed does not prevent his regarding R-technique as classificatory of *variables*. In our opinion there are no compelling empirical examples of factor analysis suggesting any particular *logical* classification of variables, and even if there were we would argue that this usage misses the real potency of the method, which lies in the third approach.

Examples of the successful use of factor analysis according to the third approach, in relation to scientific models supported by other kinds of evidence, are now very numerous. They can be found in psychology, sociology, neurology, physiology, geology, economics, and even chemistry and physics. Here the investigators are seeking the underlying determiners that could account for the correlations, positing that the factor locations when correctly guided will correspond to some "real" entity in the scientific domain, for example, intelligence, thyroxin level, anxiety, or length of carbon side chain.

Under the third approach, the principal problem lies in discovering and defining the rotational requirements for distinguishing a scientific determiner from a "neutral" mathematical dimension. Before pursuing this topic, let us note that, even within this conception, there are two possible sub-approaches equally fitting the use of factor analysis as a discoverer of underlying influences. They consist of the use of factor analysis as (a) a *hypothesis-testing* or (b) a *hypothesis-creating* procedure. The search for simple structure or for the unique confactor solution has no other hypothesis than that distinct scientific influences acting roughly in linear fashion exist in the given data. They are therefore hypothesis-creating uses, in any sense of a specific hypothesis. Here then the investigator is prepared to take the position that he knows nothing about what actual factors are at work (though, in fact, he may have a number of hunches), and that he simply wishes to find them. After finding them, he is likely, of course, to repeat the experiment, and *then* use factor analysis as a *hypothesis testing or checking* method.

The greatest contributions to science through factor analysis have probably been through its use as a hypothesis-creating approach, since there is no other method that will so powerfully indicate the probable main determiners in a given system. And the determination in such subjects as psychology, sociology, economics, and physiology is so multivariate that wise investigators will not risk a hypothesis until they have seen *some* picture of the factors at work. Factor analysis may, in this respect, deliver to us in a couple of factor analyses and a year of work concepts which could otherwise, by a pedestrian series of bivariate correlational investigations, take many years and still leave much doubt as to the validity of the hypothesis.

Since the hypothesis-testing usage, as it concerns rotational resolution, is comparatively simple, we will describe and dismiss it briefly. It has, unfortunately, been not unusual for an investigator merely to "eyeball" the patterns of the factors that he gets from some rotation and say that they agree with his hypothesis. However, if hypothesis testing is to be rigorously employed in factor analysis, then the investigator, taking some n variables into a factor analysis, should state his hypothesis beforehand and in much more definite form, by setting down (1) the number of factors k that he believes exists, (2) the particular loading patterns that he believes they possess, and (3) the correlations among the factors, whether oblique or orthogonal, and so on.

Assuming that he is right as to the number of factors (since our concern here is only with the rotational part), he then needs to find a rotation that will bring the system as close as possible to the hypothetical loading pattern that he has prescribed, and, lastly, to examine the goodness of fit to that pattern. Examination of the goodness of fit belongs to procedures beyond rotation, but the rotation itself can be performed by a program called PROCRUSTES [21]. This program aims to bring the rotation to a position that will give the best least-squares fit of the loadings to the loadings specified in what we may call the "hypothesis target" matrix. There are two forms of the PROCRUSTES program, one of which allows the axes to become oblique, and therefore, tests both the statement of hypothesis in terms of the loading and the statement in terms of the expected correlation among the factors, and the orthogonal PROCRUSTES [29] which gets as near as possible to the hypothesis statement of the loading pattern under the assumption that the factors must be orthogonal.

The name PROCRUSTES comes, of course, from classical Greek mythology, this being the name of the exacting innkeeper whom Theseus met on the cliff path. The innkeeper fitted all guests to his beds no matter what their stature, by lopping them off or stretching them. The program has the same kind of ruthlessness, and in the oblique case, will sometimes produce an astonishingly good fit, but at the cost of severe obliqueness of the axes. It is, therefore, almost meaningless to evaluate any hypothesis (either by this or other rotations) without stating, not only the loading pattern but also the expected obliqueness of the factors, as indicated above. Methods for evaluating the relative goodness of fit of the same data to different targets seem not yet to have been sufficiently dismissed due to the problem of simultaneously evaluating pattern and factor correlation fit, but some χ^2 derivative is indicated.

b. Basic Rotation Formulae

The formulae for the PROCRUSTES programs themselves are briefly as follows, and their alternatives may be read in more detail in the sources indicated [21, 29].

Premultiplying (1) above by V_0' we have:

$$V_0'V_0L = V_0'V_{rs} \qquad (2)$$

whence:

$$L = (V_0'V_0)^{-1}V_0'\overline{V}_{rs} \qquad (3)$$

where $\overline{V}_{rs}$ is now the target matrix. The program thus (1) transposes V_0; (2) multiplies out $V_0'V_0$; (3) inverts the result; (4) multiplies by $V_0'\overline{V}_{rs}$; (5) normalizes the columns of the resulting L; and (6) performs the multiplication in (1).

Schonemann's [29] orthogonal PROCRUSTES fit differs as follows:

Let $S = V_0'V_{fp}$ where the orthogonal matrix V_0 is to be rotated to V_{fp} the target matrix for the PROCRUSTES fit (fp). Then L is found so that trace $\{(V_{fp} - V_0L)'(V_{fp} - V_0L)\}$ is minimized. If we set

$$S'S = PD_sP' \quad \text{and} \quad SS' = WD_sW' \qquad (4)$$

where D_s is a diagonal matrix of eigenvalues and W and P are matrices of eigenvectors, then it can be shown that $L = WP'$.

In the use of factor analysis as a hypothesis-creating method, that is, a method of discovery, it is necessary to stipulate what seem the necessary characteristics of de-

terminers in the scientific domain in general. If such widely applicable criteria for the action of influences can be stated, then the application of these conditions to any given data would be likely to converge toward the rotation in which the factors correspond to the underlying influences. As indicated above, there are essentially two known expressions of the characters of determiners, and though they may seem independent in their mathematico–statistical formulations, they are essentially consistent in principle.

The first expression is simple structure which applies to *a single experimental* matrix. Its argument is, essentially, that if one takes a deliberately wide array of variables, chosen on some principle of stratified sampling from the domain of variables, then it is extremely unlikely that any one factor will influence more than a minority of such variables. Thus, one would expect each factor to have significant and possibly high loadings on a minority of variables, and zero loadings on the rest. It will be recognized at once that this must be a different position from that in which the principal axis is simply derived from principal components, for in that solution almost every variable is loaded on almost every factor, and certainly on the first. Another way of justifying simple structure is through the basic principle in science, as stated by Newton in the terms *natura est simplex* (which relates also to Occam's razor) that when in doubt we choose the explanation that is the simplest. In fact, it was more with this general simplicity principle in mind that Thurstone originally stated simple structure [32], though in later uses by Cattell [6], and his associates the emphasis has been placed not on generalized simplicity, but on the notion that factors are determiners, and that the matrix should express properties, as stated in "minority loading" above, consistent with determiners. The difference between the two emphases is not great, but it appears in such matters as (a) that Thurstone's interpretation explicitly required (i) that each factor should leave many variables unloaded and (ii) that each variable should arise from relatively few factors. Cattell's determiner principle would agree on (i) but not require the (ii). (There is, of course, an inevitable tendency for a matrix simplified by columns also to be simplified by rows but this does not require, as in Thurstone, that *every* variable have several zero loadings). (b) The simplicity concept *might* argue for orthogonal rather than oblique factors, whereas the determiner concept demands that factors be allowed to be oblique. It does so on the grounds (not the simplest) that any two or more influences in an interacting universe are quite unlikely to be unrelated and precisely orthogonal. (Parenthetically this applies only to the primary factors, i.e., the first order.) Once we have disentangled higher and lower order factors there is a good argument that they should all be orthogonal [13].

The second point (b) has proved to be one of the slowest to receive general recognition. To the extent that factor analysis began in mathematics (actually it was developed about equally by psychologists and mathematicians), or to the extent that purely mathematical considerations take priority of prestige, many early investigators started with orthogonal rotations. The arguments of Thurstone, Cattell, and others for oblique factors, based on a scientific model, encountered the passive indifference of most users and the active resistance of a few psychologists of considerable prestige, such as Burt and Guilford (not to mention general surprise and incomprehension by mathematical statisticians, such as Horst) who liked the simplicity of orthogonality. However, over some 20 years, almost a majority of substantively experienced psychologists, as illustrated, for example, by Eysenck, have moved over from the orthogonal to the oblique camp. The movement has occurred through (1) acceptance of the general principle that influences in nature are unlikely to be uncorrelated, (2) recognition that if they *do* happen to be uncorrelated in a given population they will not be uncorrelated in a given sample, and (3) partly through the good sense yielded by oblique rotations in substantive findings. Among the latter is the recognition that the second- and higher order domains in factor analysis, which open up only if one accepts obliquity of the primaries, yield scientifically valuable concepts. Unfortunately, in the computer world, there has been a severe lag in recognizing this, inasmuch as Kaiser's quick and cheap orthogonal Varimax program has had mass appeal and is probably the most widely disseminated rotation program in computer libraries. The word "unfortunately" is used because so long as the less well-equipped computer centers continue to present it as the only available program, exasperated investigators will be compelled to present rough orthogonal solutions when they would prefer an oblique solution. However, in the list of programs that follows, both orthogonal and oblique alternatives are set out.

The second expression or *confactor rotation principle* requires *two* factor analyses instead of one—and, of course, on the same variables but different subjects or situations. The assumption is that since any factor at work in one must be at work in the other—but probably with a different variance in the first from that existing in the second sample—then the loading pattern of each factor in the first study will be *parallel and proportional to that of a corresponding factor in the second* once the uniquely correct rotation in both is achieved. That is to say, if we can find a rotation position in the first study which gives a particular factor with loadings proportional to those of some factor rotated in the second study, then we may conclude that we have the same underlying influence in these two instances. The same, of course, will apply to all the other factors. Part of the proof necessary for this inference [5] is that if such a rotation position exists, then any deviation from that rotation position in either study will destroy the relationship. In short, this proportionality can be achieved *only in one unique position simultaneously possible in the two researches*. Further, it has been shown [11] that this position can be found by solving the following equations. From (1), supposing V_{0A} to come from the first experiment and V_{0B} from the other, we may write:

$$V_{0A} L_A = V_{0B} L_B D \qquad (5)$$

where D is the diagonal matrix that expresses the proportionality of the size (variance) of factors between one experiment and the other. Assuming for the moment an inverse for V_{0B} we may write:

$$V_{0B}^{-1} V_{0A} = L_B D L_A^{-1} = L_B D L_A' = K \quad (6)$$

where $V_{0A} = V_{0B} K$. Thus

$$K'K = \left(V_{0B}^{-1} V_{0A} \right)' \left(V_{0B}^{-1} V_{0A} \right)$$

$$= L_A D L_B' L_B D L_A'$$

$$= L_A D^2 L_A' \qquad (7)$$

The expression on the right is a latent roots and vectors solution, which the program now carries out upon the matrix $K'K$. With D thus obtained the unique position is known. Worked examples are in [11] and with discussion of related issues and improvements in [13].

A solution depends on the factors actually having *different* variances in the two samples, so that, ideally, one seeks the situation where a real difference of population or a real difference of experimental situations (in psychological data) exists to produce such a difference. Incidentally, the aim and the method of confactor rotation is sometimes confused in the literature with the aim and method of Tucker's synthesis method, probably because a formula involved at one stage is the same. Tucker's synthesis method

aims to bring two studies to the closest possible agreement in their factor patterns. The prime aim is not to get proportionality of loadings, though this is a by-product of applying some standards for maximum agreement of the two. However, in principle, the two studies could be very close without being proportional. Furthermore, the inter-battery rotation method has as its aim, first, bringing the two studies into lockstep, and then rotating them together according to some other principle, generally maximum simple structure, whereas in confactor rotation the converse priorities hold-first to find the unique confactor position to determine the unique position. The program for confactor rotation works quite well, so long as the factors are orthogonal or approximately so, but 20 years of discussion of the problem has failed to yield a unique solution for the oblique case. A monograph on this topic has recently been published [13]. This, at least, sets out some partial solutions. Meanwhile, however, the confactor rotational solution can be used with confidence only when there is reason to believe that the real factors are near orthogonality or only moderately correlated, say, up to about .2 or .3.

c. Simple Structure

After this wider survey of the various possibilities, aims, and resources in factor rotation, we come back to the recognition that the real workhorse rotation in everyday hypothesis-creation is simple structure. Probably, about 95% of all factor-analytic researches in psychology and related areas are brought to a meaningful resolution by a search for simple structure. It should go without saying that the search for simple structure must be "blind." Human nature being what it is, if an investigator knows what he hopes to get, and can see in the plots what he is rotating (by the descriptions of the test vectors), there is danger that he will distort rotation in the direction of his theory. Of course, if an entirely automatic program is used, in which no plots appear, this cannot happen, but as will be pointed out below, there are good reasons for not letting a program decide at what point to cease rotation. There is also guidance in a plot not easily quantitatively represented in any matrix, but *the variables must appear only as nameless points*, plotted in the factor space created by the axes, if rotation is to be blind and unbiased by specific theories.

Before we proceed now to focus on the techniques of search for simple structure, it is necessary, in the interest of perspective, to refer to other background features in the total experimental design that are likely to affect this search. In the first place, we have the fairly obvious—yet, nevertheless, frequently overlooked—principle that if the variables are so chosen that *all* are likely to load on one factor then there will be no hyperplane available by which to rotate that factor. For example, if we take 20 mechanical aptitude tests in a search for the factors in mechanical aptitude, there could well be a general factor *across all 20* of these which would leave absolutely no points in the hyperplane. Since the reference vector finds its position as the perpendicular to the hyperplane, this absence of a hyperplane, or the appearance of only a fragmentary hyperplane, makes unique rotation impossible. Consequently, if by the nature of the experimental data, one would not get a sufficient number of variables unloaded by the factor, then one must deliberately plan to put in "hyperplane stuff." An instance where failure to do this held up psychological ideas for about 20 years is that of general intelligence, where the failure to put in nonintelligence variables into many ability variable factorizations resulted in failure to separate the two distinct factors of fluid and crystallized intelligence [8].

The due role of the hyperplane will be clearer from Fig. 9.1, which is necessarily restricted to two dimensions, but shows a not unusual disposition of points in a typical factor analysis of psychological tests. The fact that must never be forgotten is that we rotate the reference vector (RV_w or RV_s in Fig. 9.1). not by putting *it* through clusters, but by making it a normal to a hyperplane which goes through the line of points representing the variables that would be unloaded on the ideally placed factor reference vector. The initial factor plot on the axes that resulted from the computation of the principal axes might be as shown in the dotted lines. Having plotted the points according to their projections on the first two principal components, the investigator begins to search for lines of points (such a line representing a hyperplane seen on edge), as indicated at X and Y. Actually, it is impossible to see these hyperplanes immediately in the *first* plot, because of the quite special "genealogical" relationship between the first and second factor, so Fig. 9.1 must be considered as what emerges after a few random shifts. Parenthetically, however, one must point out that there is no possible meaningful uniqueness about the first two components as they come from principal component analysis since, whether by the weighted or the unweighted summation method, they place the first component axis through the (weighted) center of gravity of the total array of variables in the study. Since the particular totality of variables in a factor analysis cannot usually be insightfully chosen with regard to the true structure of the influences at work, the first principal component is merely an average across variables likely to represent several factors. Even if one is aiming largely at one factor, as Spearman did at intelligence, different investigators will choose sufficiently different sets to make this first component, unrotated, change direction and meaning from study to study. To summarize, then, from a catholic choice of variables one rotates to discover a hyperplane, and having found it, erects a normal vector to it; this is called the reference vector. The items in the hyperplane will have zero or near zero loading on the reference vector. The factor derived from this reference vector is then said to

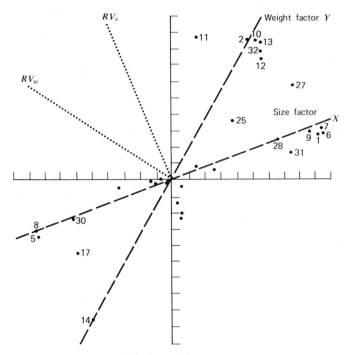

Fig. 9.1. Identification of variables by number;

1. Diameter	13. Springboard depression
2. Weight	14. Angular momentum
5. Rotations rolling	17. Croquet blow up in inclined plane
6. Distance from eye to cover circle	25. Inclined plane carpet friction
7. Diameter of shadow cast	27. Weight of splash
8. Rotations to one rotation of tire	28. Inclined plane impulse distance
9. Number of squares covered by ball	30. Winding necessary to use up string
10. Distance of weight from ball	31. Size of eclipse shadow
11. Collision displacement	32. Impact displacement by pendulum
12. Paddle wheel rotations	

have the best possible simple structure position.

It is true that in an *orthogonal* rotation, the hyperplane of one reference vector forms, as it were, a cluster through which the reference vector to the *other* hyperplane inevitably passes. But (a) in the oblique case this is not true, and (b) there may be *other* clusters, which do not constitute hyperplanes at all, but which have as many as or more variables in them than the hyperplane. Such clusters can often be seen in factor plots, standing out on their own as in *A*, *B*, *C*, *D*, *E*, and *F* in Fig. 9.2. It is the basic distinction between, what we shall call in a moment, analytical and topological pro-

grams that the former are commonly designed to chase clusters with the reference vectors, whereas the latter scrupulously fix the rotation first by the hyperplanes, to which the normals of the reference vectors are then attached. Parenthetically, as Fig. 9.1 shows, even the true "cluster" one might be pursuing—the other hyperplane—is unlikely to be orthogonal to the hyperplane of the reference vector in question.

Correlation clusters of the ordinary kind (not the unusual shapes we call hyperplanes) have been called surface traits in psychology, because they represent what is actually seen on the surface, namely, a group of highly intercorrelated manifestations, as, for

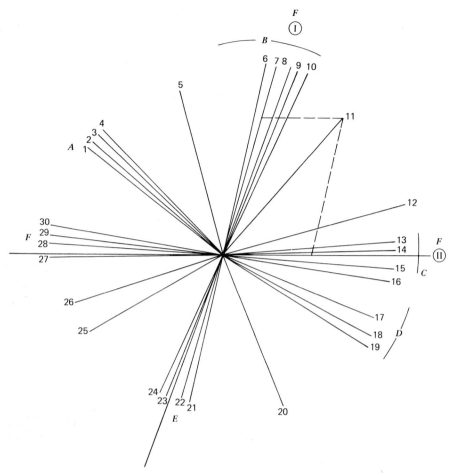

Fig. 9.2. Diagrammatic representation of correlation clusters and factors, among variables representing specific measured behaviors.

example, in a clinical syndrome. They are often factorially complex (as in Fig. 9.2) and in many fields it can easily be shown that it is virtually the rule for surface traits to be composite. For example, the particular syndromes we see in schizophrenia, hysteria, and so on, though easily visible as a correlated set of variables, are almost certainly due to the *overlapping action* of two or more contributing determiners. The outcome is a single cluster, but the causative influences are not simple. Similarly, in economic data, we might get a cluster of variables which, factored over time, describe a stock market crash, but any economist is likely to suggest

that two or three or more distinct trend factors enter into causing a stock market crash. Or again, crystallized intelligence begins as a cluster [8], combining a factor of "years of education" and another of "fluid intelligence." If we keep this scientific model in mind, then we shall be less likely to fall into the error of simple-minded "cluster chasing" in our factor analytic rotations. This point will be taken up again in connection with the program constructions that follow.

In summary, in preparing an experiment with an eye to simple structure rotation one cannot avoid clusters occurring in the data, but one can avoid such foresightless choices of distribution of variables as will fail to make good hyperplanes available. Avoidance of wild goose chases due to clusters must come through the design of the resolution programs themselves.

A second source of indeterminacy that the procedures of rotation may face as a result of unfortunate prior steps in the factor analysis, concerns the earlier decisions on communalities and the choice of the number of factors. In the normal procedure one will decide the number of factors by, for example, the scree test [7] or the maximum-likelihood method [25], or the Tucker method [32], or Sokal's procedure [31], and the communalities will then be adjusted to leave no residuals when that number of factors is taken out. If the investigator fails to make a thorough test for the number of factors and takes out the wrong number, or if, with the right number, he solves with unities in the diagonal instead of communalities, *then the real simple structure is no longer obtainable*. Demonstration of the kind of distortion that results has been presented in several plasmodes, that is, examples made up with a known number of factors, from which a correlation score matrix is then calculated, so that the factor analyst can work back from the raw scores to the factors with definite knowledge of what they should be [13].

An instance is presented in Table 1 from the Cattell–Dickman ball problem, in which it will be seen that when the correct number of factors is extracted (5 instead of 4) the hyperplane count on the first four goes up from 72 to 81. Simple structure is poorer with the wrong number of factors, and incidentally, there are sometimes extreme correlations among factors when the factor number is not correctly assessed (−.81 in Table 1).

Granted however, that the factor analytic procedures up to the point of rotation have been sensibly carried out and checked, then there is no doubt that simple structure is, in general, a way of arriving at a unique rotational position, at which we are entitled to infer that the factors found are determiners or influences. This has been shown by physical instances, for example the Cattell–Dickman ball problem in which some 32 variables measuring the behavior of balls, for instance, the distance they will roll or bounce, shows that the factoring leads to the same determiners as would be accepted by a physicist, such as weight, volume, elasticity, and length of pendulum on which the ball swings.

d. Survey of Rotation Programs

In the early days of factor analysis the discovery of maximum simple structure (say, the greatest number of points in the ±.10 hyperplane across all factors, assuming a loading standard error of 0.05) was pursued by successive visual plot trial and error rotations of one or all of the axes. This has always proved very time consuming and investigators were driven to find automatic computer programs that would approach the same result. At least a dozen of these have proliferated and the most important of them are listed in Table 2.

Automatic programs can be divided into two types, analytical and topological. By an *analytical program*, one means a program that takes some mathematical function of the loadings of *all* the variables and, typically by differential calculus, discovers a maximum or minimum value. By a *topological program*, one means a program that defines certain spaces in the geometrical representation of the data, and maximizes the number of variables in some particular subspace leaving the other loadings free to be what they will. To clarify the special value of the latter immediately, let us recognize that although a hyperplane loading theoretically means a loading of zero, in practice a variable that really lies in the hyperplane may have a loading varying between, say, +.10 and −.10. There is a standard error to a loading, just as there is a standard error to

Table 1. EFFECT ON SIMPLE STRUCTURE OF OPERATING WITH THE WRONG NUMBER OF FACTORS[a]

(Data from Cattell–Dickman Ball Problem)

		4 Factors Insufficient Number for the Substantive (Physical) Factors				5 Factors Number According to Scree Test				
		1	2	3	4	1	2	3	4	5
	1				.65				.59	−.11
	2		.56				.62			.12
	3	.81	−.23		.10	.85				.14
	4			.99				.98		
	5				−.50				−.38	.47
	6		−.12		.67				.60	−.11
	7				.64				.59	
	8				−.50		.11		−.39	.48
	9		−.12		.62	.10			.63	.10
	10		.56				.61			.11
	11		.75		−.30		.63		−.35	
	12		.50				.41			−.19
	13		.52				.54			
V_{fp}'s 14			−.56				−.61			−.11
	15	.71	−.15			.77				.22
	16	.81	−.23		.11	.84	−.10		.13	.10
	17	.59	−.16		−.34	−.56	−.20		−.31	
	18	.86				.86				
	19	.85	.16		−.14	.83	.11		−.17	
	20			.98	−.11			.97		
	21			.97	−.13			.96		
	22			.98				.97		
	23			−1.00				−.98		
	24			−.94				−.95		.11
	25	.54	.25			.48				−.37
	26	.80			.12	.80				
	27		.19		.39		.22		.33	−.12
	28	.52			.36	.54			.31	
	29	.78		.11		.75				−.15
	30			.58	−.39			.54	−.25	.35
	31		−.13	−.42	.54			−.43	.47	
	32	.14	.47	.32		.16	.47	.29		
No. in hyperplane		21	15	22	14	20	20	23	18	15

		1	2	3	4		1	2	3	4	5
	1	1.00				1	1.00				
R_{f}'s 2		.31	1.00			2	.34	1.00			
	3	−.06	−.03	1.00		3	−.10	−.17	1.00		
	4	−.37	−.81	.03	1.00	4	−.29	−.56	.11	1.00	
						5	.22	.60	−.13	.03	1.00

[a]The factors here are weight, volume, length of pendulum cord, elasticity coefficient, and rotational inertial of ball.

Table 2. THE MOST COMMONLY USED AUTOMATIC PROGRAMS FOR ATTAINING
ROTATIONAL SIMPLE STRUCTURE

Analytical	Topological (All Oblique)

Analytical

(1) QUARTIMAX [35]. During 1952–53, four separate groups of researchers, independently, proposed analytical orthogonal rotational methods. This first was QUARTIMAX.
The most used nowadays is
(2) VARIMAX [22].
(3) OBLIMAX [27]. The four versions of QUARTIMAX are not precisely equivalent nor are they easily generalizable to the oblique case. Pinzka and Saunders generalized Saunders' orthogonal criterion into OBLIMAX.
(4) QUARTIMIN. Generalization of Carroll's version of QUARTIMAX.
(5) OBLIMIN. Oblimin is actually a term applied to a whole *class* of procedures, involving oblique factor and minimization of a function (Carroll, [4]).
(6) COVARIMIN [4]. An oblique generalization of VARIMAX, an oblimin solution.
(7) BIQUARTIMIN (Carroll). QUARTIMIN produced factors too oblique and COVARIMIN not oblique enough, so BIQUARTIMIN is an average of the other two methods.
(8) BINORMAMIN. BIQUARTIMIN provides arbitrarily an unweighted average of quartimax and covarimin. BINORMAMIN combines the two criteria so that the arbitrary weights problem is eliminated [23].
(9) PROMAX [34]. This starts with a VARIMAX solution, accentuates it, and uses PROCRUSTES to get the oblique solution closest thereto [21].
(10) VARISIM. Similar to PROMAX, but keeping orthogonal [29].
(11) HARRIS–KAISER. This pursues initially an orthogonal solution maximizing the projection of clusters on axes. It then converts to an oblique solution (see below).

Topological (All Oblique)

(1) MAXPLANE [16, 18].
(2) PRESCRIBED MAXPLANE [18].

(3) ROTOPLOT[a] [14].

---

[a]This is a semi-automatic program in that it is hitched to a human decision but cuts out all the heavy labor of plotting and calculating in "hand rotation."

a correlation coefficient, and if that sigma should be, say, .04, then, by taking ±.10 as the limits, we should hope to encompass 99/100 of the variables that really lie in the hyperplane. To maximize the count in this subspace would therefore amount to encompassing the essential hyperplane. In the analytical programs, on the other hand, there is no such precise delimitation of the hyperplane space but only a general tendency to maximize low loadings. Thus a couple of loadings at, say, .15 might be considered as good, by the analytical programs, as putting one at say, .08 and another at .20, which would not be the case in the topological programs.

The analytical programs were actually the first types to appear, beginning with the QUARTIMAX program of Wrigley and Neuhaus [35] and followed closely by the VARIMAX program of Kaiser. Both of these restricted rotation to orthogonal solutions only. Since all analytical programs hinge essentially on the same principle as used in the above, we will pause to explain the rationale. As Fig. 9.3 illustrates with just two points: (1) the sum of squares of the loadings of a set of points, summed for all factors simultaneously, will remain constant under any orthogonal transformation. That is to say, if we square the loadings in the columns, and add them up, this total will remain unchanged under orthogonal rotation. On the other hand, (2) if we take some higher power of the loading—and the fourth power is the first to suggest itself since one does not want to get involved with negative numbers—then this value will increase if points 1 and 2 lie on the axes instead of in spaces between them, as shown in Fig. 9.3.

Another way of saying this is that a rotation to maximize the sum of the fourth powers will tend to "spread out" the loadings. For the sum of the fourth powers will benefit from the position in which a few are very high and a few are very low relative to a more even or normal distribution of the loadings. In other words, analytical pro-

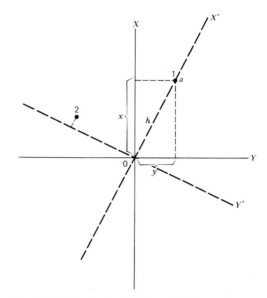

Fig. 9.3. The basic principle in analytical rotation programs. The sum of squares of the loading of point *a* on *X* and *Y* will remain constant when they are shifted to any other position, such as *X'* or *Y'*, namely, h^2. But the ratio of the sum of fourth powers will be greatest in the position *X'*, as testable by

$$\frac{(x^2 + y^2)^2}{x^4 + y^4} = \frac{h^4}{x^4 + y^4}$$

grams aim primarily to increase the standard deviation among the loadings on each and every factor, though they evaluate it necessarily by the summed effect over all factors. It will thus become clear why we stated above that the effect is to thrust the low loadings down to lower values, but not necessarily to the values required by being actually in the hyperplane (within a really small value like ±.10).

After the first two analytical programs, there appeared a number of more developed and ingenious programs chiefly concerned with adapting to the problem of finding the best *oblique* solution. Except for very rare instances, *simple structure and orthogonality are incompatible goals*. It is unquestionably empirically true that the single-minded pursuit of maximum simple structure almost invariably yields oblique factors, and restriction to orthogonality prevents natural simple structure from being attained. Fig. 9.1 represents the attempt of the VARIMAX program to reach simple structure in the Cattell–Dickman ball problem, and it was seen that it failed dismally. In most cases the obliquities are not great, the correlations among factors commonly being around .2 or .3, but occasionally rising to .5. In certain kinds of data, for example, the *P*-technique, longitudinal factorization of psychological states, however, the factor correlations may be decidedly higher because events that cause one emotion to arise frequently happen to provoke another also, and the temporal correlation of state factors is, therefore, likely to be high. In this case, an orthogonal rotation yields a very crude approximation indeed to the true structure.

A list of the principal analytical types of programs that have now accumulated is given in Table 2.

Dielman, Wagner, and one of the present writers (R. C.) have investigated the relative successes of these programs on a far more exhaustive array of material and criteria than in any other published study. Six representative programs from Table 2—two of them in different designs to yield eight rotational approaches in all—were applied to four different types of problem, in a factorial type of design, with evaluation of the success of the programs in (a) producing the highest possible percentage of loadings in the hyperplane, (b) producing factor patterns agreeing from one sample to another, and (c) reaching the known factor structure. The weak spot is the last point, since, with real data, we never really know what the number of factors should be. Consequently, we have designed several "plasmodes" for which the number of factors is known, but in which the similarity to real data, in terms of the natural distributions of error and the natural departures from the ideal linear model is not, of course, as realistic as in real data. In short, one has the alternatives of working with real data and

not being sure of the factors, or working with artificial data and not being sure that conditions are the same as with real data. The data for the four studies was in each case split into two samples and factor analyses and rotations were done on each to see how much sampling error might influence the comparison of methods.

Actually, with the exception of questionnaire material (which in any case should probably not be factored by items) the results are so similar that one kind of data will suffice for illustration, as in Table 3, which takes plasmode 30–10–5–2 [15], that is, known to have 30 variables, 10 primaries, 5 secondaries, and so on. Both MAXPLANE and PROMAX were tried with and without a Landahl [24] spin, that is, spun to equal factor variance before rotation versus working directly from the principal axes output without spin. The third column in Table 3 is an attempt to give greater weight to values in the center ($\pm.05$) of the hyperplane. By adding columns (1) and (2) we in fact give weight to the $\pm.05$s which are already in the $\pm.10$s. It will be seen that the differences between samples reach 5 at most, whereas those between methods reach 24. Consequently the ranking of goodness of methods in column 4 has meaning, and we see that MAXPLANE-ROTOPLOT is best, followed by MAXPLANE with spin, and the HK method. OBLIMAX and PROMAX follow, being about equal, and VARIMAX is the poorest of all.

Another example of interest because, though a plasmode, it is on real physical data and because we *know* that the factors in two instances have decided natural obliquity is the Cattell–Dickman ball problem shown in Table 4 (and also depicted in one actual plot in Fig. 9.1).

Here there is again a general tendency for MAXPLANE-ROTOPLOT and HARRIS-KAISER to be the two best, but the main lesson from the data is that the orthogonal type of rotation (VARIMAX) fails con-

Table 3. RELATIVE GOODNESS OF HYPERPLANE FIT BY DIFFERENT AUTOMATIC PROGRAMS

Rotational Method	Sample	Hyperplane Goodness			
		(1) At ±.05	(2) At ±.10	(3) Weighted	(4) Rank on (3)
Topological					
MAXPLANE	1	30%	61%	91	
No spin	2	25%	63%	88	3
MAXPLANE	1	32%	62%	94	
W/Spin	2	27%	63%	89	2
MAXPLANE-	1	31%	66%	97	
ROTOPLOT	2	29%	67%	96	1
Analytical					
PROMAX	1	29%	53%	82	
no spin	2	32%	55%	87	
PROMAX	1	29%	53%	82	
W/Spin	2	32%	55%	87	4
OBLIMAX	1	29%	53%	82	
No spin	2	26%	51%	87	
VARIMAX	1	24%	48%	72	
No spin	2	26%	47%	73	5
HARRIS–KAISER	1	31%	59%	90	
No spin	2	33%	60%	93	2

Table 4. GOODNESS OF HYPERPLANES BY AUTOMATIC PROGRAMS ON A PHYSICAL EXAMPLE
(Ball Problem)

Rotational Method	Hyperplane Goodness (%)		
	At ±.05	At ±.10	At ±.15
MAXPLANE	35	54	65
MAXPLANE-ROTOPLOT[a]	44	59	66
PROMAX	34	58	64
OBLIMAX	43	58	66
VARIMAX	28	41	48
HARRIS–KAISER	38	61	65

[a]MAXPLANE-ROTOPLOT here reaches the highest value for a really tight hyperplane, such as would be appropriate for the relatively error-free physical measurements.

spicuously when factors demonstrably oblique (volume and weight of balls) are involved. (For despite throwing in golf balls and large, light beach balls, there is still an appreciable correlation between the weight of a ball and the size of a ball in this population.) The compromise by VARIMAX, after some neurotic hesitation between two equally attractive hyperplanes both of which it cannot have at once (see Fig. 9.1), was to take neither of them! In the MAXPLANE oblique rotation of the same data (which can be plotted from Table 1) it will be found that the hyperplanes are actu-

ally better than those in the interrupted lines in Fig. 9.1.

The differences in hyperplane count between the topological programs and the better analytical programs is generally, as shown above, percentagewise small. But the associated differences in interpretation by the verdict of applying a matching index to a factor in another study, in the form of the congruence coefficient [3] or the *s* index (salient variable similarity index [10]) can be quite important. The final polishing given by ROTOPLOT has in our experience frequently made the difference between a good

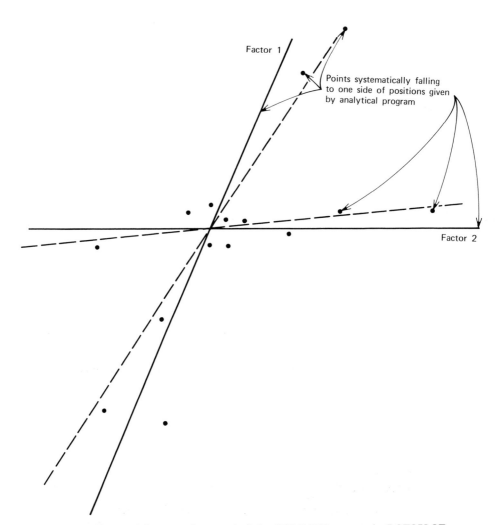

Fig. 9.4. Characteristic correction required in **OBLIMAX** program by ROTOPLOT.

and a poor match, and a statistically significant and nonsignificant structure, as evaluated by Bargmann's criterion [1].

Parenthetically, experience will help the rotator in getting to know and correct some of the vices in analytical programs—by ROTOPLOT tidyings. For example, the OBLIMAX program has the very minor vice of running its axes a little bit outside the line of points that should be involved, as shown in Fig. 9.4. On the other hand, OBLIMIN does just the opposite. Thus, in both of these programs, one gets very near to the ideal solution, and a relatively quick tidy-up by the ROTOPLOT visual program, recognizing what the deviations are likely to be, will produce a good final result.

The design of a topological program is to demarcate the required subspaces, and to count and maximize the variables appearing in a required subspace. It will be recognized that what we call a hyperplane is, in fact, a subspace, not a plane. It is a subspace because the standard error of a zero loading has to be recognized as blurring the plane. The particular value on which custom has almost uniformly settled in the last 20 years is that of $\pm.10$. Thus the MAXPLANE program, which is, as yet, the only thoroughly developed and practical program using this approach, sets out to find the position of the hyperplane indicated (on edge) by a blurred line of points centering close to zero but extending to $\pm.10$ on either side. It does so, not by an analytical program but by repeated trial and error shifts and counts, identical in intention with those used by the human brain in finding hyperplanes by visual inspection (but equally blind as to the particular individual nature of the variables.

The more specific steps are indicated in the program section below. It is a more costly program than most analytical programs especially compared with say, PROMAX, VARIMAX, or the HK and the choice of one or the other of these must depend upon whether one wants to travel

first class to the true position or go cheaply to a destination that is not quite right, and then "walk" by ROTOPLOT. The ROTOPLOT program is a topological one, but is a step-by-step, human judgment procedure, that is, one rotation at a time, whereas the MAXPLANE program runs through all such trial and error rotations in one computer session. In the ROTOPLOT program the investigator has the computer plot output before him, and makes his shifts by a quick pencil mark indicating a move of a certain tangent value on each axis. His tangent values are transferred to a matrix S shift and applied to Eq. (1) above, as follows:

$$L_{(+1)} = LS \tag{8}$$

$$V_{rs(+1)} = V_0 L_{(+1)} \tag{9}$$

This iterative process is continued until the solution hill is climbed to such a point that there can only be a decline in performance if the solution is disturbed in any direction.

3. SUMMARY OF THE CALCULATION PROCEDURE

We consider here the procedure used with MAXPLANE program discussed in Section 2d.

MAXPLANE rotates an orthogonal factor matrix to oblique simple structure. Simple structure is defined by the position which maximizes the number of points in the hyperplanes of the factors (i.e., it maximizes a weighted or unweighted function of the number of points (variables) whose loading on the factor lies within a narrow interval about zero in the reference vector structure). The program uses a systematic *search* procedure. Each factor is in turn rotated in the plane of the other factors, in the normal case first with angular intervals of 6° and then, when there is no improvement with 6° shifts, 2° shifts are used. For each trial shift position the (weighted) hyperplane count is calculated and finally the best shift for the factor is actually made. Rotation proceeds in this way until one of four criteria are met:

1. A specified number of cycles (rotations of each factor on every other factor) have been done.
2. No factor was moved during a cycle (i.e., the best position has been found).
3. The percent of variables in the hyperplane did not increase by at least a specified amount.
4. There was insufficient time to complete another cycle.

When one of these criteria is met the program either changes to 2° shifts, if these remain to be done, or goes to output.

The input consists of an orthogonal factor matrix V_0 (*VZERO*). The transformation matrix Λ (*CLAM*) is always the identity matrix at the start of a run but is an input parameter so that a run terminated for lack of time may be continued from where it left off. If a transformation matrix is not input to the program, the matrix *CLAM* is set equal to the identity matrix. Once *CLAM* is no longer an identity matrix, the angles between the reference vectors are no longer necessarily orthogonal.

Since the factors are bipolar and negative values are equivalent to positive, the total space available for rotation of any factor K against another factor L is 180°. Unless set otherwise, the limit of approach of any K toward L (*ANIFMIN*) is set at 60°, positive or negative, so that the remaining space in which K is free to move is 60°.

The variable *NSH* (number of shifts) is 60°/*KANG* where *KANG* is the number of degrees in each shift. In radians

$$NSH = \frac{3.14159 - 2*(.174533)*ANIFMIN}{KANG}$$

Once a factor, K, has been selected to be rotated, MAXPLANE calculates the existing angle between K and all other factors L. These values are stored in an array

EXANG(L) where

$$EXANG(L) = ATAN(SQRT(1.$$
$$- COSN(K, L)**2)/COSN(K, L))$$

subject to the following:

1. In the nearly orthogonal case when *COSN(K, L)* is very small, *EXANG(L)* = 1.57079 (90°).
2. If the arc-tangent formula yields a negative angle when *COSN(K, L)* is negative, the corresponding positive angle used is *EXANG(L)* = *EXANG(L)* + 3.141594.

Now given any K and L, *EXANG(L)* − *ANIFMIN* defines the largest positive approaching shift. *NPOS* = (*EXANG(L)* − *ANIFMIN*)/*KANG* represents the number of permissible steps K can take toward L.

Now when the hyperplane count is to be maximized, a static criterion, simply the highest count, can be used, but strategic considerations are better served by a dynamic criterion. To achieve this, the value of *KPREV* (a counter) is set at zero, and redefined later, only if the present position of K with respect to L forms an acceptable angle.

Since the angle limitations always permit *NSH* trial positions *KANG* degrees apart, MAXPLANE proceeds with the selected K − L pair to define *NSH* positions for K. If, and only if, the existing angle between K and L is an acceptable one (greater than 60°), one of the *NSH* positions will be the existing one. In that case, *KPREV* will be redefined as the existing hyperplane count.

For each trial position, MAXPLANE calculates the K-projections and proceeds to count the hyperplanes. The proper value is added for each point whose K-loading is within the limit set by ± *WID*.

Thus this part of the procedure terminates when a hyperplane count has been defined for each of *NSH* trial positions, and the count corresponding to the existing position has been stored in *KPREV* if, and only if, the existing position has an acceptable angle between *K* and *L*. Otherwise, *KPREV* is left as zero.

The hyperplane counts are next converted to improvements by subtraction of *KPREV* from them. Obviously, in the case where the existing position is untenable, the improvements will be very large.

MAXPLANE next selects the one of the *NSH* trial positions with the largest improvement value and stores the value as *LKOUNT(L)*.

The entire procedure of definition of trial shifts, evaluation, and selection is next repeated pairing *K* with each other possible *L*. At this point, a best shift for each *L* has been defined. It should be noted that the best shift may be a zero shift, which means simply that no improvement was possible for *K* with a particular *L*. If no improvement was possible for any *L*, MAXPLANE proceeds to the next *K*. If no improvement was possible for any *K*, the program exits.

Assuming that at least one best shift is a nonzero shift, MAXPLANE searches the *LKOUNT(L)* vector for the one best shift, and then stores the corresponding *SHIFT(L)* as *TEM(L)*. Next *TEM(K)* is defined as unity, and straightforward matrix multiplication and column normalization produces the new values for the *K*th column of *CLAM*. All cosine values involving *K* are recalculated and used to replace the existing row and column of *COSN*.

4. FLOW CHARTS

Flow charts are on pages 186–193.

5. DESCRIPTION OF FLOW CHART

a. Program MAXPLANE

The main program MAXPLANE reads in the input parameters of Type 1 and calls the various routines to perform oblique rotation.

Box 1:   The program reads in parameters used for control flexibility. The numbers to the left of the following variable names refer

to the first page of the example, and are in an arbitrary sequence.

1. *TOTIM*   The maximum time in minutes for which the program is to run.

8. *IPLOT*   0 = No plot required.
   1 = Plot required.
   2 = Do not rotate but go to output and plot.

9. *KANG*   0 = Do 6 degree shifts, then do 2 degree shifts.
   1 = Do 6 degree shifts only.
   2 = Do 2 degree shifts only.

10. *KSTART*   Rotation starts with this factor and factors before it are not moved.

11. *NCYCLE*   The number of cycles to be run. (If this stopping criterion is not desired, leave blank.)

12. *KCYCLE*   The number of cycles already completed.

13. *WID*   The hyperplane width.

14. *SIG*   Values below this are set to zero in the second printing of the reference structure matrix. (Otherwise set to .25.)

15. *ANIFMIN*   The minimum angle that must exist between vectors. If this parameter is not set the next two take their standard values even if other values are punched on the card.

16. *NCLCY*   The number of cycles that the minimum angle restriction is to be kept before being set to 30°.

17. *XCLHC*   The hyperplane percent at which the angle restriction is to be changed.

18. *NCLSP*   Cycle number at which the spread across the hyperplane is to be weighted 1 in full width, 5 in $\frac{2}{3}$ of width, 15 in $\frac{1}{2}$ of width.

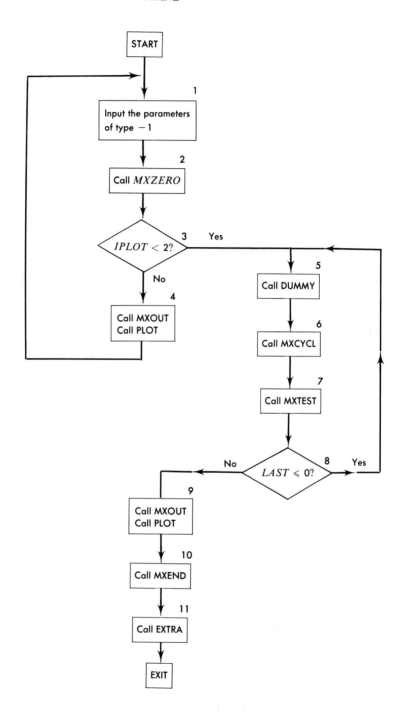

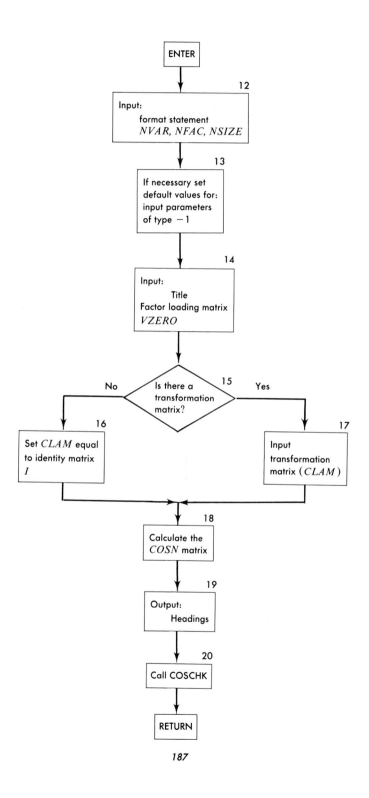

Subroutine MXCYCL

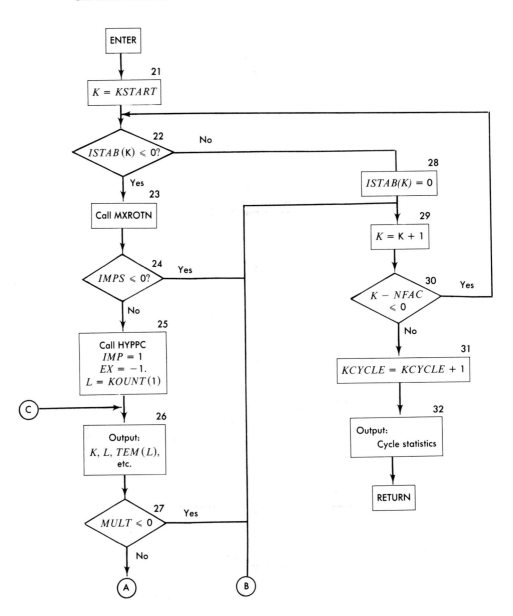

Subroutine MXCYCL (cont.)

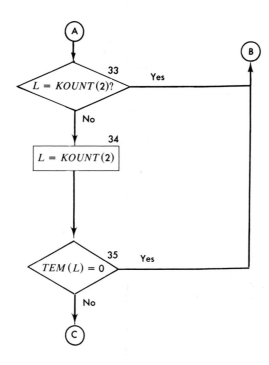

Subroutine COSCHK

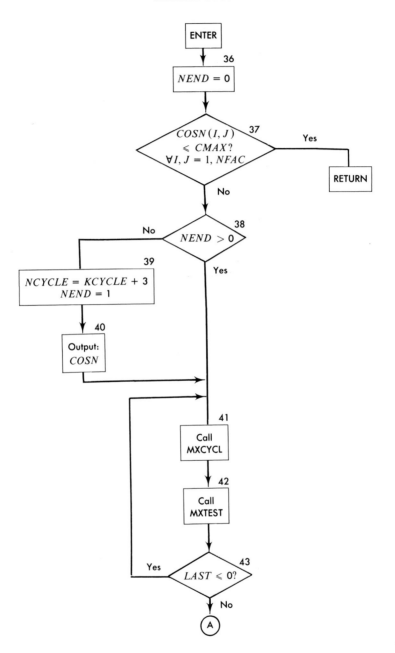

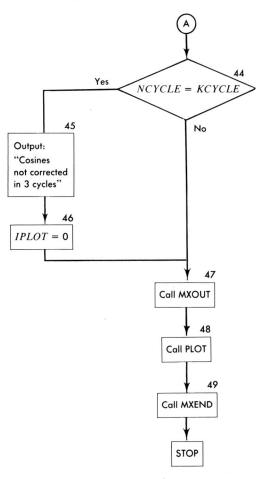

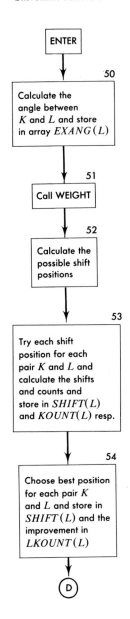

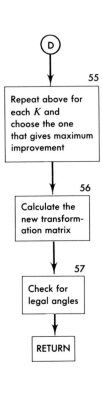

Subroutine HYPPC

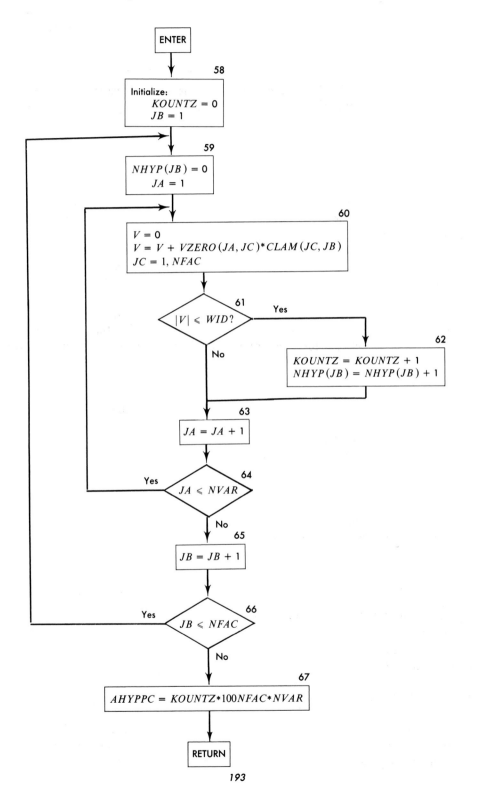

19. *NCLHO*   Cycle number at which outlying points are weighted by $(2.*V/3.*WID)$ $**(KSWT + 1)$ where V is the distance out in the hyperplane. N. B. If neither is to apply set each to -1. The two weightings are additive.

20. *UP*   The percent hyperplane increase that is necessary in 3 cycles if rotation is not to be terminated.

23. *KHWT*   Hyperplane spread weighting indicator (set to -5 if *NCLSP* is $-VE$).

24. *KSWT*   Hyperplane outlier weighting index (set to -5 if *NCLHO* is $-VE$).

26. *KRAP*   After exit criterion is reached the program will go back for a final scan to see if a better hyperplane has appeared. Set to 1 if not desired.

27. *MULT*   0 = Program will make best 2 shifts when doing multiple shifts.
                    1 = Program will make best 3 shifts when doing multiple shifts.

Box 2: Call routine MXZERO to read the factor loading matrix and the transformation matrix.

Box 3: Test to decide whether only a plot is desired or rotation is to be done.

Box 4: Call MXOUT and PLOT to output the data and give a plot.

Boxes 5–7: Perform a rotation cycle by calling routine MXCYCL and test for end conditions by calling MXTEST.

Box 8: Test whether last cycle performed.

Boxes 9–11: Call MXOUT and PLOT to output the results. Call MXEND to print some time of computation statistics.

Note. Routines DUMMY and EXTRA are included for special uses, if the user so desires.

b. Subroutine MXZERO

This routine reads in the factor matrix and reads in or generates an identity transformation matrix. It also sets the parameters that are unspecified to standard values and calculates the cosine of the angles between the various factors.

Box 12: Input format statement and *NVAR*, *NFAC*, and *NSIZE*, where:

     NVAR: number of variables in the problem

     NFAC: number of factors

     NSIZE: maximum number of variables.

Box 13: Set the unspecified parameters to their default values.

Boxes 14–16: Input the problem title, factor loading matrix *VZERO* and if given the transformation matrix, *CLAM*. If *CLAM* not given set it to identity matrix.

Box 18: Calculate the matrix of the cosine of the angle between the reference vectors:

$$V_{rs} = V_0 \Lambda$$

Thus

$$COSN = V_{rs'} V_{rs}$$
$$= \Lambda' V_0' V_0 \Lambda$$
$$= \Lambda' \Lambda$$
$$= (CLAM)'(CLAM)$$

Box 19: Output the headings for the problem.

Box 20: Call *COSCHK* to check for the angles being within the accepted range. This is a check to see whether the angles between any two factors are less than 60°.

c. Subroutine MXCYCL

This subroutine controls the cycling of the factor K and does the actual rotation by calling MXROTN.

Box 21: Initialize K, the factor number from which rotation cycling starts.

Box 22: Test for whether K was removed at the previous cycle.

Box 23: If yes, call *MXROTN* for factor rotation.

Box 24: Test *IMPS* to determine if there is any improvement in hyperplane count. (i.e. there is improvement $-IMPS > 0$)

Box 25: If no, call *HYPCC* to obtain the count and set pointers *IMPEX* and *L*.

Box 26: Output K, L and *TEM(L)* etc.

Box 27: Test for multiple shifts.

Box 28: Set $ISTAB(K) = 0$

Box 29: Increment the factor counter by 1, i.e., go to the next factor.

Box 30: Test whether all factors have been tried. If not go to Box 20 and start again.

Box 31: If yes, increment the cycle count by one.

Box 32: Output the cycle statistics.

Box 33: Test if the previous shift was a multiple shift.

Box 34: If the previous shift was not a multiple shift select the second best shift.

Box 35: Test whether the second (best) shift is zero.

Subroutine COSCHK

This subroutine checks to see that the cosines of the angles between the factors are within the limits set by the minimum angle restriction. If not, 3 cycles are allowed to adjust the angles. If there still are invalid angles after 3 cycles, the program proceeds to output and termination.

Box 36: Initialize *NEND* to zero.

Box 37: If all cosine (*COSN(I, J)*) are within the range, program return control to the main program. Else go to box 38.

Box 38: Test whether this is the first clean up cycle.

Boxes 39–40: If yes, increment the permissible cycles up by 3, set $NEND = 1$ and output the matrix *COSN*.

Box 41: Call MXCYCL to perform the rotation cycling to remove the angle violation.

Box 42: Call MXTEST to test for any end conditions being violated.

Box 43: Test whether this is the last cycle. If not go back to Box 40, else go to Box 43.

Boxes 44–46: If correction not possible, output "cosines not corrected in 3 cycles," set $IPLOT = 0$ and go to Box 46.

Boxes 47–49: Call MXOUT, PLOT, and MXEND routines to output necessary data, plots and end the program.

e. Subroutine MXROTN

This routine rotates factor K against factor L. All shift positions that do not violate the angle restriction are tried and if any of these is better than the original position the factor is shifted to the best of these.

Box 50: The angle between any two factors K and L is calculated as follows:

$$EXANG(L) = ATAN\big((SQRT(1.$$
$$- COSN(K, L)**2))/COSN(K, L)\big)$$

where if *EXANG(L)* is negative it is replaced by $EXANG(L) + \pi$ and if

$$COSN(K, L) < .0349$$

then $EXANG(L) = \pi/2$ (i.e., $COS(\pi/2) = 0.$)

Box 51: The routine on option weighs the distant points in the hyperplane of K and L with the following weighting function:

$$\{5.0 \times |v|\}^{(KSWT+7)}$$

where v is the distance.

Boxes 52–53: The various shift positions are calculated. Each shift is in turn tried and stored in *SHIFT(L)* and the corresponding hyperplane count in *KOUNT(L)*.

Box 54: Choose the best position for each pair *K* and *L* and store in *SHIFT(L)* and the improvement in *LKOUNT(L)*.

Box 55: Repeat Boxes 49–53 for each *K* and select the position that gives the maximum improvement.

Boxes 56–57: Calculate the new transformation matrix and check for legal angles.

f. Subroutine HYPCC

This subroutine calculates the hyperplane count for each factor and also the count and percent value of points for the total.

Box 58: Initialize *KOUNTZ* to zero and *JB* = 1, where *KOUNTZ* is the total hyper-

plane count and *JB* is a counter for the number of factors.

Box 59: Initialize the hyperplane count for factor *JB*, i.e., *NHYP(JB)* = 0.

Boxes 60–64: Count the number of variables for the factor *JB*, *NHYP(JB)* and the total for all factors, *KOUNTZ*.

Boxes 65–66: Check to see whether all the factors have been accounted for.

Box 67: Calculate the percent total hyperplane count, and return control to the calling program.

6. SAMPLE PROBLEM

The printout of a MAXPLANE program is shown on pages 196–201.

M A X P L A N E

TEST PROBLEM FROM MODERN FACTOR ANALYSIS HARMAN PP214 TABLE 10.13

ROTATION TO SIMPLE STRUCTURE
WITH 24 VARIABLES   4 FACTORS
HYPERPLANE WIDTH TAKEN AS .150

FACTOR	SHIFTED ON FACTOR	ANGLE	HYPERPLANE COUNT THIS FACTOR	ALL FACTORS	HYPERPLANE PER CENT
2	1	.445	12	34	35.4
3	1	-.325	14	38	39.6
4	2	.213	13	39	40.6

CYCLE NO. 1 WITH   39 HYPERPLANE VARIABLES (40.63 PERCENT).

3	2	.542	15	40	41.7
4	3	.463	15	43	44.8

CYCLE NO. 2 WITH   43 HYPERPLANE VARIABLES (44.79 PERCENT).

1	2	-.813	7	50	52.1
3	4	-.314	16	51	53.1
4	2	-.722	16	51	53.1

CYCLE NO. 3 WITH   51 HYPERPLANE VARIABLES (53.13 PERCENT).

*** DOUBLE SHIFTS STARTED
***MINIMUM ANGLE OF SEPARATION SET AT 30 DEGREES
***POINTS WEIGHTED 1 IN 1/1, 5 IN 2/3, 15 IN 1/3 OF HYPERPLANE WIDTH

1	2	-.257	8	52	54.2
2	4	.712	16	56	58.3
3	4	-.330	12	52	54.2
4	2	-.210	15	51	53.1

CYCLE NO. 4 WITH   51 HYPERPLANE VARIABLES (53.13 PERCENT).

1	3	1.226	10	53	55.2
2	1	.106	14	51	53.1
3	1	-.427	14	53	55.2
4	1	.208	17	55	57.3

CYCLE NO. 5 WITH   55 HYPERPLANE VARIABLES (57.29 PERCENT).

1	2	-.817	11	56	58.3
2	4	.613	13	55	57.3
3	4	.108	15	56	58.3
4	2	-.120	18	55	57.3

CYCLE NO. 6 WITH   55 HYPERPLANE VARIABLES (57.29 PERCENT).

***OUTLYING HYPERPLANE POINTS WEIGHTED

1	2	.849	11	55	57.3
2	4	-.500	14	56	58.3
3	1	.109	15	56	58.3
4	2	.105	17	57	59.4

CYCLE NO. 7 WITH   57 HYPERPLANE VARIABLES (59.38 PERCENT).

1	4	-.116	11	57	59.4

CYCLE NO. 8 WITH   57 HYPERPLANE VARIABLES (59.38 PERCENT).

CYCLE NO. 9 WITH 57 HYPERPLANE VARIABLES (59.38 PERCENT).

```
                        ***NO IMPROVEMENT IN STRUCTURE
                        ***SS HAS BEEN REACHED. BEGINNING FINAL SCAN.
    1      2    -.211              13        59        61.5
    2      1    -.109              15        60        62.5
    3      1     .232              19        63        65.6
    4      2     .215              18        64        66.7
CYCLE NO.  10 WITH    64 HYPERPLANE VARIABLES ( 66.67 PERCENT).

                        *** DOUBLE SHIFTS STARTED
                        ***MINIMUM ANGLE OF SEPARATION SET AT 30 DEGREES
                        ***POINTS WEIGHTED 1 IN 1/1, 5 IN 2/3, 15 IN 1/3 OF HYPERPLANE WIDTH
    1      2     .208               9        60        62.5
    1      4    -.508               9        60        62.5
    2      4     .521              14        59        61.5
    2      1     .105              14        59        61.5
    3      1    -.120              17        58        60.4
    3      2     .112              17        58        60.4
    4      2    -.233              16        56        58.3
    4      3     .216              16        56        58.3
CYCLE NO.  11 WITH    56 HYPERPLANE VARIABLES ( 58.33 PERCENT).
```

```
                        ***LESS THAN  1.0 PERCENT IMPROVEMENT IN 3 CYCLES

                        ***MAXIMUM SIMPLE STRUCTURE HAS BEEN REACHED

                        ***ROTATION TERMINATED

                        ***TRANSFORMATION MATRIX AND NEW PARAMETER CARD HAVE BEEN PUNCHED
```

```
                        VECTOR COSINES  (MAXIMUM COSINE ALLOWED BETWEEN VECTORS IS    .966)

    1.000 -.147  .456  .002

    -.147 1.000  .408  .538

     .456  .408 1.000  .205

     .002  .538  .205 1.000

                        TRANSFORMATION MATRIX (LAMBDA)

     .915  .163 -.211 -.294

    -.177  .431  .555 -.387

     .659  .476  .774  .634

    -.602  .750 -.220  .602
```

PER CENT OF VARIABLES IN .050 HYPERPLANE IS 27.1

PER CENT OF VARIABLES IN .100 HYPERPLANE IS 47.9

PER CENT OF VARIABLES IN .150 HYPERPLANE IS 58.3

PER CENT OF VARIABLES IN .200 HYPERPLANE IS 66.7

PER CENT OF VARIABLES IN .250 HYPERPLANE IS 70.8

```
                        REFERENCE STRUCTURE  V(RS)

          1      2      3      4

    1    .594  -.011   .058  -.099

    2    .431  -.036   .054  -.043

    3    .415   .044  -.015   .093

    4    .446   .000  -.044   .027

    5    .027  -.096  -.588  -.233

    6    .002   .041  -.564  -.079

    7   -.032  -.076  -.657  -.150

    8    .198  -.064  -.403  -.199

    9   -.006   .080  -.576  -.009

   10    .020  -.145  -.116  -.700

   11    .060   .072  -.100  -.486

   12    .340  -.216   .052  -.569

   13    .402  -.187  -.050  -.512

   14   -.053   .429  -.041   .022

   15    .038   .410   .050   .040

   16    .341   .329   .142   .054
```

```
        17  .005  .410  .044 -.111

        18  .320  .325  .234 -.178

        19  .231  .199  .063 -.103

        20  .306  .171 -.130  .011

        21  .398  .011  .017 -.300

        22  .326  .167 -.101 -.000

        23  .410  .081 -.136 -.076

        24  .164  .051 -.164 -.402

             9    14    17    18
```

PER CENT OF VARIABLES IN .150 HYPERPLANE IS 58.3

REFERENCE VECTOR STRUCTURE V(RS) WITH NON-SALIENT VALUES LESS THAN .250 SUPPRESSED

```
         1    2    3    4
   1    59    0    0    0
   2    43    0    0    0
   3    41    0    0    0
   4    45    0    0    0
   5     0    0  -59    0
   6     0    0  -56    0
   7     0    0  -66    0
   8     0    0  -40    0
   9     0    0  -58    0
  10     0    0    0  -70
  11     0    0    0  -49
  12    34    0    0  -57
  13    40    0    0  -51
  14     0   43    0    0
  15     0   41    0    0
  16    34   33    0    0
  17     0   41    0    0
  18    32   33    0    0
  19     0    0    0    0
  20    31    0    0    0
  21    40    0    0  -30
  22    33    0    0    0
  23    41    0    0    0
  24     0    0    0  -40
```

X AXIS IS FACTOR 1   Y AXIS IS FACTOR 3
COSINE OF ANGLE BETWEEN AXES IS .456

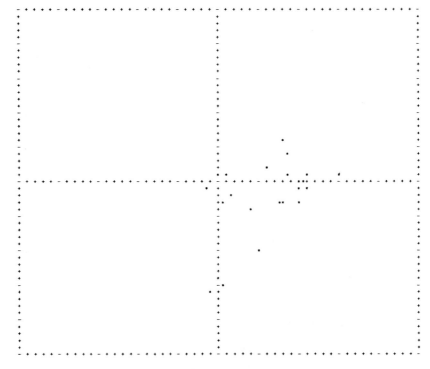

X AXIS IS FACTOR 1   Y AXIS IS FACTOR 2
COSINE OF ANGLE BETWEEN AXES IS -.147

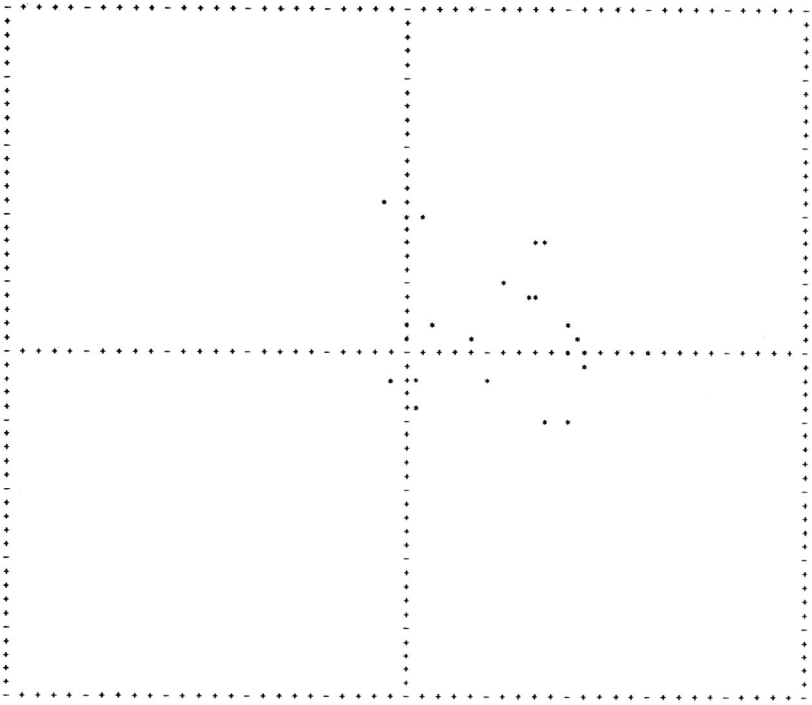

X AXIS IS FACTOR 1   Y AXIS IS FACTOR 4
COSINE OF ANGLE BETWEEN AXES IS .002

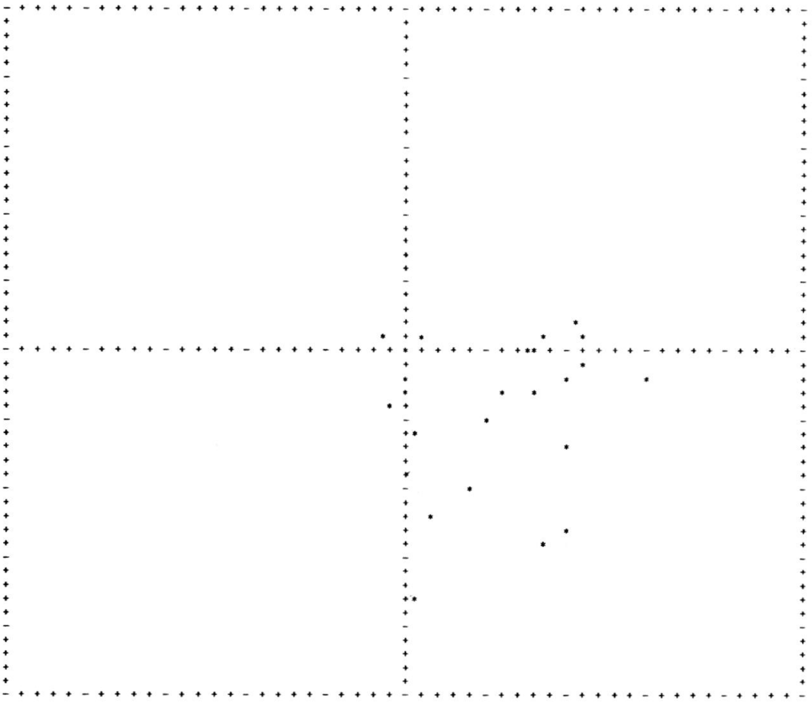

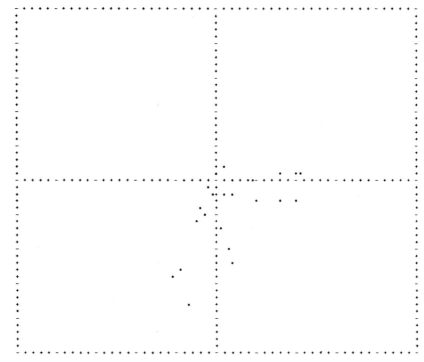

X AXIS IS FACTOR 2   Y AXIS IS FACTOR 4
COSINE OF ANGLE BETWEEN AXES IS   .538

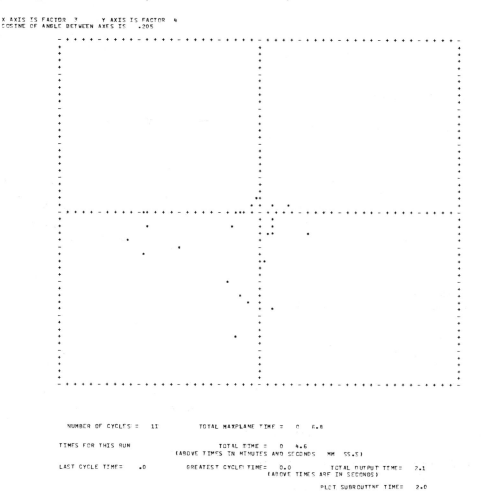

X AXIS IS FACTOR 3   Y AXIS IS FACTOR 4
COSINE OF ANGLE BETWEEN AXES IS   .205

NUMBER OF CYCLES =   11   TOTAL MAXPLANE TIME =   0   6.8

TIMES FOR THIS RUN   TOTAL TIME =   0   4.6
                          (ABOVE TIMES IN MINUTES AND SECONDS   MM SS.S)

LAST CYCLE TIME=   .0   GREATEST CYCLE TIME=   0.0   TOTAL OUTPUT TIME=   2.1
                                      (ABOVE TIMES ARE IN SECONDS)

                                              PLOT SUBROUTINE TIME=   2.0

7. REFERENCES

1. R. Bargmann, "Signifikanz unter 2 Suchangen der einfachen Stauktar in der Faktor analyse," *Mittle, Bl. Math. Stat.*, 1–24 (1955).

2. C. R. Bolz, "Types of Personality," in *Multivariate Personality Research*, R. M. Dreger (ed.), Claitor's Publishing Division, Baton Rouge, 1972.

3. C. L. Burt, *Factors of the Mind*, Univ. of London Press, London, 1940.

4. J. B. Carroll, *IBM 704 Program for Generalized Analytic Rotation Solution in Factor Analysis*, Unpublished manuscript, Harvard Univ., 1960.

5. R. B. Cattell, "Psychological Measurement; Normative, Ipsative, Interactive," *Psychol. Rev.*, **51**, 292–303 (1944).

6. R. B. Cattell, *Factor Analysis*, Harper, New York, 1952.

7. R. B. Cattell, "The Scree Test for the Number of Factors," *MBR*, **1**, 2, 140–161 (1966).

8. R. B. Cattell, *Abilities, Their Structure, Growth and Action*, Houghton Mifflin, Boston, 1970.

9. R. B. Catell, "Real Base, True Zero Factor Analysis," *Multiv. Behav. Res. Monogr.* No. 72-1, 1-151, IPAT, Champaign, Illinois, 1972.

10. R. B. Catell, K. R. Balcar, J. L. Horn, and J. R. Nesselroade, "Factor Matching Procedures: An Improvement of the *s* Index; with Tables," *Educational and Psychological Measurement*, **24**, 3, 348–360 (1969).

11. R. B. Cattell, and A. K. S. Cattell, "Factor Rotation for Proportional Profiles: Analytical Solution and an Example," *Brit. Statist. Psychol.*, **8**, 83–92 (1955).

12. R. B. Cattell, M. A. Coulter, and B. Tsujioka, "The Taxonometric Recognition of Types and Functional Emergents, in *Handbook of Multivariate*

Experimental Pscyhology, R. B. Cattell (ed.) Rand McNally, Chicago, 1966.

13. R. B. Cattell, and K. W. Dickman, "A Dynamic Model of Physical Influences Demonstrating the Necessity of Oblique Simple Structure," *Psychol. Bull.*, **59**, 389–400 (1962).

14. R. B. Cattell, and M. J. Foster, "The Rotoplot Program for Multiple Singleplane, Visually Guided Rotation," *Behav. Sci.*, **8**, 156–165 (1963).

15. R. B. Cattell, and J. Jaspers, "A General Plasmode (no. 30-10-5-2) for Factor Analytic Exercises and Research," *MBR Monographs*, **67**, 3, 1–212 (1967).

16. R. B. Cattell, and J. L. Muerle, "The MAXPLANE Program for Factor Rotation to Oblique Simple Structure," *Educat. Psychol. Measurement*, **20**, 569–590 (1960).

17. R. B. Cattell, A. Wagner, and M. D. Cattell, "Adolescent Personality Structure in *Q*-data, Checked in the High School Personality Questionnaire," *Brit. J. Psychol.*, **61**, 1, 39–54 (1970).

18. H. W. Eber, "Toward Oblique Simple Structure: A New Version of Cattell's MAXPLANE Rotation Program for the 7094," *Multiv. Behav. Res.*, **1**, 112–125 (1966).

19. H. J. Eysenck, "Criterion Analysis: An Application of the Hypothetico-deductive Method to Factor Analysis," *Psychol. Rev.*, **57**, 38–53 (1950).

20. H. Harman, *Modern Factor Analysis*, Univ. of Chicago Press, Chicago, 1960.

21. J. R. Hurley, and R. B. Cattell, "The PRO-CRUSTES Program: Producing Direct Rotation to Test a Hypothesized Factor Structure," *Behav. Sci.*, **7**, 258–262 (1962).

22. H. F. Kaiser, "The VARIMAX Criterion for Analytic Rotation in Factor Analysis," *Psychometrika*, **23**, 187–260 (1958).

23. H. F. Kaiser, and K. W. Dickman, *Analytic Determination of Common Factors*, Unpublished manuscript, Univ. of Illinois, 1959.

24. H. D. Landahl, "Centroid Orthogonal Transformations," *Psychometrika*, **3**, 219–223 (1938).

25. D. N. Lawley, "The Application of the Maximum Likelihood Method to Factor Analysis," *Brit. J. Pscyhol.*, **33**, 172–175 (1943).

26. J. C. Nunnally, *Pscyhometric Theory*, McGraw-Hill, New York, 1967.

27. C. Pinzka, and D. R. Saunders, *Analytic Rotation to Simple Structure, II. Extension to an Oblique Solution* (R. B. - 5431), Educational Testing Service, (Multilithed) Princeton, N. J., 1954.

28. J. A. Ross, *A Factor Test of a Memory Model*, (R. B. - 61-14), Educational Testing Service, Princeton, N. J., 1961.

29. P. H. Schonemann, "A Generalized Solution of the Orthogonal PROCRUSTES Problem," *Psychometrika*, 1–10 (1966).

30. W. Stephenson, *The Study of Behavior*: *Q-technique and its Methodology*. Univ. of Chicago Press, Chicago, 1953.

31. R. R. Sokal, "A Comparison of Five Tests for Completeness of Factor Extraction," *Trans. Kansas Acad. Sci.*, **62**, 141–152 (1959).

32. L. L. Thurstone, *Multiple Factor Analysis*, University of Chicago Press, Chicago, 1937.

33. L. R. Tucker, "The Objective Definition of Simple Structure in Linear Factor Analysis", *Psychometrika*, **20**, 209–225 (1955).

34. A. E. Hendrickson and P. O. White, "PROMAX: a quick method for rotation to oblique simple structure", *Brit. J. Statis. Psychol.*, **17**, 65 (1964).

35. C. Wrigley, and J. O. Neuhaus, "The Matching of two Sets of Factors," *Amer. Psychologists*, **10**, 418–419 (1955).

Multivariate Analysis of Variance and Covariance

Jeremy D. Finn*
State University of New York at Buffalo

1. FUNCTION

The multivariate general linear model can be expressed as the sum of matrix products,

$$Y = A\Theta^* + X\mathrm{B} + \mathrm{E} \qquad (1)$$

Y is a matrix of observed outcome scores for N subjects on p random variables. A is an analysis-of-variance model matrix defining the group to which each observation belongs. Θ^* is a matrix of parameters associated with the experimental group (μ, α_j, β_k, etc.). X is a regression model matrix containing scores on $q(\geqslant 1)$ *measured* independent or predictor variables, for the N observations. B is the

*I am indebted to Professor R. Darrell Bock for his teachings in multivariate analysis, and to Dr. Thomas Shuell for allowing me to use his data to exemplify the procedures described in this chapter. Mrs. Jacqueline Rance and my wife, Joyce, gave valuable assistance in the preparation of the manuscript.

The flow charts presented in this chapter have been prepared by Ms. Sharon Ward, then at Genesee Computer Center, from more detailed specifications prepared by Mr. Finn. The author is deeply indebted to Ms. Ward for the many hours of work spent.

matrix of regression weights relating the p outcome variables to the q predictors. E is the ($N \times p$) matrix of random errors.

Linear estimates of the parameters in Θ^* and B and related functions, may be obtained either by least squares or maximum likelihood. Univariate and multivariate tests on subsets or on all of the parameters may be conducted as special cases of general test criteria.

Specific forms of (1) include common analysis-of-variance, covariance, and linear regression models. When there are no measured predictor variables (X null) the model is the analysis-of-variance model. Differences among group means are estimated and tested for departure from zero. If all observations represent a single population of subjects, then A is null and the model is the linear regression model. The regression weights are estimated, and hypotheses are tested about the contribution of some or all of the predictors to variation in the outcome measures. When there are both group-membership and measured antecedents (neither A nor X null), the model is the analysis-of-covariance model. The predictor variables in X are termed covariates. Hypotheses are tested about the contribution of the covariates to criterion variation, and about mean differences after eliminating variation attributable to the covariates. Also the equality of the covariates' effects across the experimental groups may be tested.

As special cases of (1), analysis-of-variance designs may be complete or incomplete (missing observations from one or more groups). The most general solution yields exact tests and confidence intervals, without restricting the group sizes to being equal or proportional. In all cases, the order of the independent and dependent variables is assumed fixed.

Univariate and simultaneous multivariate test criteria are presented. When Y, Θ^*, B, and E have a single column (one criterion measure) the simultaneous test statistics reduce the common univariate form. Additional results are easily computed as by-products of the simultaneous tests. These include step-down test criteria for variates having a natural order by time or complexity. Canonical analyses (discriminant analysis, canonical correlation) are obtained through direct transformation of the model and error sum of cross-products matrices. The univariate mixed-model solution for repeated measures data [19] may be conducted as a special case of fitting (1). The multivariate solution is obtained by a pre-analysis transformation of Y, or by appending a post-matrix model to Θ^*; that is, $Y = A\Theta^*Q + X\mathrm{B} + \mathrm{E}$ [8, 24].

2. MATHEMATICAL DISCUSSION

a. Symbols Used

Matrices are represented by uppercase Greek and Roman letters, and vectors by boldface lowercase letters. Italic lowercase letters are scalars. The (i, j) element of A is denoted by a_{ij}; the ith element of $\mathbf{v}$ by v_i. A' is the transpose of A. Untransposed vectors

are in column form; transposed vectors are rows. $A \otimes B$ is the Kronecker product of A and B, that is, $C = A \otimes B$ is a supermatrix with submatrix elements $C_{ij} = a_{ij}B$.

The following representations are used.

O and $\mathbf{0}$	Null matrix and null vector, respectively.
$\mathbf{1}_n$	n-element unit vector, $\mathbf{1}' = \begin{bmatrix} 1 & 1 \cdots 1 \end{bmatrix}$.
$\char`\^$	Sample value (estimate); e.g., $\hat{\Theta}$ is the estimate of Θ.
$\perp$	An orthonormal matrix. $A^\perp$ means $A^{\perp\prime}A^\perp = I$.
$\lvert A \rvert$	Determinant of matrix A.
c	Rank of analysis-of-variance model to be estimated ($c \leqslant l$).
$\mathrm{diag}_i(A)$	The ith diagonal element of A, i.e., a_{ii}.
$\mathscr{E}(\mathbf{v})$	Expected value of a vector variable.
I_c	Identity matrix of order c.
l	Rank of analysis-of-variance model (between-group degrees of freedom, $l \leqslant n_0$).
m	Total number of parameters in analysis-of-variance model.
n	Number of subclasses in complete analysis-of-variance design.
n_e or n_e^*	Degrees of freedom for error.
n_h	Degrees of freedom for hypothesis.
N	Total number of observations.
n_j or n_{jk}	Number of observations in subclass j or jk.
n_0	Number of subclasses in analysis-of-variance design with at least one observation ($n_0 \leqslant n$).
nz	Number of empty subclasses ($nz = n - n_0$).
$\mathscr{N}_p$	p-variate multivariate normal distribution.
p	Number of dependent (criterion) variates.
q	Number of measured predictor variables, or covariates.
$r(A)$	Rank of matrix A.
$\mathscr{V}(\mathbf{v})$	Variance–covariance matrix of a vector variable.

$\mathcal{V}(y|X)$ Conditional variance of y, given the values of X-variables.

b. Mathematical Background

ANALYSIS OF VARIANCE

The multivariate analysis-of-variance model is efficiently represented in vector notation. For example, a two-way $(A \times B)$ p-variate fixed-effects model with interactions may be represented as

$$\mathbf{y}'_{ijk} = \boldsymbol{\mu}' + \boldsymbol{\alpha}'_j + \boldsymbol{\beta}'_k + (\boldsymbol{\alpha}\boldsymbol{\beta})'_{jk} + \boldsymbol{\varepsilon}'_{ijk} \quad (2)$$

All terms are $1 \times p$ vectors, with an element for each outcome measure. $\mathbf{y}_{ijk}$ is the vector of criterion scores for observation i in subclass jk. $\boldsymbol{\mu}$ is the grand mean common to all observations. $\boldsymbol{\alpha}_j$ is the fixed mean deviation from $\boldsymbol{\mu}$ due to the observation belonging to level j of the A factor $(j = 1, 2, \ldots, J)$. $\boldsymbol{\beta}_k$ is the deviation for level k of the B factor $(k = 1, 2, \ldots, K)$. $(\boldsymbol{\alpha}\boldsymbol{\beta})_{jk}$ is the unique interaction for group jk.

$\boldsymbol{\varepsilon}_{ijk}$ vectors are random errors assumed independently distributed in p-variate normal fashion, with expectation $\mathscr{E}(\boldsymbol{\varepsilon}_{ijk}) = \mathbf{0}$ and covariance matrix $\mathcal{V}(\boldsymbol{\varepsilon}_{ijk}) = \Sigma$. That is,

$$\boldsymbol{\varepsilon}_{ijk} \sim \mathscr{N}_p(\mathbf{0}, \Sigma) \quad (3)$$

As an example, let $J = K = 2$. The model for an observation in group 1,1 is

$$\mathbf{y}'_{i11} = \boldsymbol{\mu}' + \boldsymbol{\alpha}'_1 + \boldsymbol{\beta}'_1 + (\boldsymbol{\alpha}\boldsymbol{\beta})'_{11} + \boldsymbol{\varepsilon}'_{i11}$$

$$= \begin{bmatrix} 1 & 1 & 0 & 1 & 0 & 1 & 0 & 0 & 0 \end{bmatrix}$$

$$\begin{bmatrix} \boldsymbol{\mu}' \\ \boldsymbol{\alpha}'_1 \\ \boldsymbol{\alpha}'_2 \\ \boldsymbol{\beta}'_1 \\ \boldsymbol{\beta}'_2 \\ (\boldsymbol{\alpha}\boldsymbol{\beta})'_{11} \\ (\boldsymbol{\alpha}\boldsymbol{\beta})'_{12} \\ (\boldsymbol{\alpha}\boldsymbol{\beta})'_{21} \\ (\boldsymbol{\alpha}\boldsymbol{\beta})'_{22} \end{bmatrix} + \boldsymbol{\varepsilon}'_{i11}$$

$$= \mathbf{a}'_{11}\Theta^* + \boldsymbol{\varepsilon}'_{i11}$$

N vector observations $\mathbf{y}'_{ijk}$ may be juxtaposed to form the rows of an $(N \times p)$ data-matrix, Y. The models can be explicitly written for each observation, and expressed as the sum of matrix terms, in the form

$$Y = A\Theta^* + E \quad (4)$$

This is expression (1) with matrix X null.

A is the $(N \times m)$ analysis-of-variance model matrix, having all elements 0 or 1 [7, 9, 19, 30]. Rows of A are the vectors $\mathbf{a}'_{jk}$ as in the 2×2 example. Θ^* is the $(m \times p)$ parameter matrix, where m is the total number of parameters in the model. For the general two-way case,

$$[\Theta^*]' = \begin{bmatrix} \boldsymbol{\mu} & \boldsymbol{\alpha}_1 & \boldsymbol{\alpha}_2 \cdots \boldsymbol{\alpha}_J & \boldsymbol{\beta}_1 & \boldsymbol{\beta}_2 \end{bmatrix}$$

$$\cdots \boldsymbol{\beta}_K \ (\boldsymbol{\alpha}\boldsymbol{\beta})_{11} \cdots (\boldsymbol{\alpha}\boldsymbol{\beta})_{JK} \big] \quad (5)$$

E is the $(N \times p)$ matrix of random errors, with rows $\boldsymbol{\varepsilon}'_{ijk}$.

Concern is usually with differences of group means. Since rows of A are identical for all observations of any one group or subclass, the models are more efficiently written for only the subclass means. The model for the mean of subclass jk, having n_{jk} observations, is

$$\mathbf{y}'_{\cdot jk} = \boldsymbol{\mu}' + \boldsymbol{\alpha}'_j + \boldsymbol{\beta}'_k + (\boldsymbol{\alpha}\boldsymbol{\beta})'_{jk} + \boldsymbol{\varepsilon}'_{\cdot jk} \quad (6)$$

$\mathbf{y}_{\cdot jk}$ is the vector mean, $\mathbf{y}_{\cdot jk} = (1/n_{jk})\Sigma_i \mathbf{y}_{ijk}$. Also $\boldsymbol{\varepsilon}_{\cdot jk} = (1/n_{jk})\Sigma_i \boldsymbol{\varepsilon}_{ijk}$. Errors are independently distributed as p-variate normal vectors,

$$\boldsymbol{\varepsilon}_{\cdot jk} \sim \mathscr{N}_p\left(\mathbf{0}, \frac{1}{n_{jk}}\Sigma\right) \quad (7)$$

Like the vector observations, means $\mathbf{y}'_{\cdot jk}$ and $\boldsymbol{\varepsilon}'_{\cdot jk}$ may be juxtaposed for the n subclasses yielding $(n \times p)$ matrices $Y.$ and $E.$, respectively. Mean models for all juxtaposed subclasses may be written in the form of (4). A becomes the $(n \times m)$ model matrix for means only, and all rows of A are unique. For example, if there are J levels of the first factor and K levels of a second crossed factor, $m = 1 + J + K + JK$. The matrix model for $J = K = 2$ is:

$$
\begin{bmatrix} \mathbf{y}'_{\cdot 11} \\ \mathbf{y}'_{\cdot 12} \\ \mathbf{y}'_{\cdot 21} \\ \mathbf{y}'_{\cdot 22} \end{bmatrix} = \begin{bmatrix} 1 & 1 & 0 & 1 & 0 \\ 1 & 1 & 0 & 0 & 1 \\ 1 & 0 & 1 & 1 & 0 \\ 1 & 0 & 1 & 0 & 1 \end{bmatrix} I_4 \begin{bmatrix} \boldsymbol{\mu}' \\ \boldsymbol{\alpha}'_1 \\ \boldsymbol{\alpha}'_2 \\ \boldsymbol{\beta}'_1 \\ \boldsymbol{\beta}'_2 \\ (\boldsymbol{\alpha\beta})'_{11} \\ (\boldsymbol{\alpha\beta})'_{12} \\ (\boldsymbol{\alpha\beta})'_{21} \\ (\boldsymbol{\alpha\beta})'_{22} \end{bmatrix}
$$

$$
+ \begin{bmatrix} \boldsymbol{\varepsilon}'_{\cdot 11} \\ \boldsymbol{\varepsilon}'_{\cdot 12} \\ \boldsymbol{\varepsilon}'_{\cdot 21} \\ \boldsymbol{\varepsilon}'_{\cdot 22} \end{bmatrix} \qquad (8)
$$

with $m = 1 + 2 + 2 + 4 = 9$. The unit elements of each row of A serve to select the parameters from Θ^* which are contained in the corresponding mean model. In the discussion following, we assume that A is the $(n \times m)$ model matrix for subclass means.

The general representation of mean models like (8) for any crossed or nested design is

$$
\underset{(n \times p)}{Y.} = \underset{(n \times m)}{A} \; \underset{(m \times p)}{\Theta^*} + \underset{(n \times p)}{E.} \qquad (9)
$$

The distributional assumption is that rows of E. are independently and identically distributed as in (7). Together, the rows have distribution

$$
\text{E.} \sim \mathfrak{N}_{np}(O, D^{-1} \otimes \Sigma) \qquad (10)
$$

O is an $(n \times p)$ null matrix, and D is a diagonal matrix of subclass frequencies,

$$
D = \text{diag}(n_{11}, n_{12}, \ldots, n_{JK}) \qquad (11)
$$

Since A and Θ^* are both matrices of con-

stants, it follows that $\mathfrak{V}(Y.) = \mathfrak{V}(E.) = D^{-1} \otimes \Sigma$.

To avoid complex subscripts for many-way or nested designs, we shall generally subscript vector observations, means, and frequencies only once, that is, $\mathbf{y}_{ij}$, $\mathbf{y}_{\cdot j}$, or n_j $(j = 1, 2, \ldots, n)$. So for example, we denote the subscripts in (11) as $1, 2, \ldots, n$ [cf. (12) below].

Least-squares estimation of Θ^* is accomplished by minimizing the sum of squared, equal-variance residuals for all p-variates. The mean residuals do not have equal variance across groups, but the variances and covariances are inversely proportional to n_j. Rows of E. multiplied by respective elements n_j have equal variance–covariance matrices. Thus the sum of squared elements of $Q = D^{1/2}(Y. - A\Theta^*) = D^{1/2}\text{E.}$ is minimized, where

$$
D^{1/2} = \text{diag}(\sqrt{n_1}, \sqrt{n_2}, \ldots, \sqrt{n_n}) \qquad (12)
$$

The sum of squares is

$$
q = \sum_{i,j} [q_{ij}]^2
$$

$$
= \text{trace}(\text{E}'. \, D\text{E}.) \qquad (13)
$$

In the univariate case, E. is the $(n \times 1)$ column vector $\boldsymbol{\varepsilon}.$ and expression (13) becomes

$$
q = \boldsymbol{\varepsilon}'. \, D\boldsymbol{\varepsilon}.
$$

$$
= (\mathbf{y}. - A\boldsymbol{\theta}^*)' D (\mathbf{y}. - A\boldsymbol{\theta}^*)
$$

$$
= \mathbf{y}'. \, D\mathbf{y}. - 2(\boldsymbol{\theta}^*)'A' D\mathbf{y}. + (\boldsymbol{\theta}^*)'A' DA\boldsymbol{\theta}^*
$$

$$
\qquad (13a)
$$

The vector of derivatives of q with respect to each element of $(\boldsymbol{\theta}^*)'$ is

$$
\frac{\partial q}{\partial (\boldsymbol{\theta}^*)'} = -2A' D\mathbf{y}. + 2A' DA\boldsymbol{\theta}^*.
$$

Setting the derivatives to zero yields the equations in $\boldsymbol{\theta}^*$ which keep q minimal.

These are the analysis-of-variance *normal equations*,

$$A'DA\theta^* = A'Dy. \tag{14}$$

In the multivariate case, expression (13a) must be minimized for p separate measures. When the univariate criterion is satisfied for each variable, then their sum (13) will also be minimal. The resulting normal equations are similar to (14) but with Θ^* having a column for each dependent variable;

$$(A'DA)\Theta^* = A'DY. \tag{14a}$$

In general, $m > n$, and columns of A are linear functions of one another. Analysis-of-variance models have more parameters than groups; each mean is decomposed into at least a general effect, plus a specific treatment deviation. As a result, $A'DA$ cannot be inverted, and there is no unique solution for Θ^*. At most, n parameters may be estimated, of the m parameters defined in Θ^*.

Common solutions to (14a) are obtained by restricting the parameters, for example, $\Sigma_j \alpha_j = \Sigma_k \beta_k = \Sigma_j(\alpha\beta)_{jk} = \Sigma_k(\alpha\beta)j_k = \mathbf{O}$ or constructing a *generalized inverse* of $A'DA$ [14, 25, 30]. Alternately we may define $l (\leqslant n)$ linear functions of the m parameters. These functions are usually suggested by the research hypotheses. They define the rows of an $(l \times m)$ contrast matrix L, such that the l alternate parameters are $L\Theta^* = \Theta$ with $r(L) = l$.

Θ is an $(l \times p)$ substitute parameter matrix whose rows are linear combinations of the rows of Θ^*. Usually, the leading row of Θ is a constant which absorbs scaling factors in the criterion measures. Subsequent rows are contrasts among the parameters, for example, $\alpha_1' - \alpha_2'$ or $\beta_1' - \beta_2'$. All rows of L except the first sum to zero. Θ may be uniquely estimated through least squares, as long as contrasts are chosen which are not linear functions of one another, that is, L must be of full rank (l).

This *reparameterization* to full rank requires an alternate model matrix. Replacing (9), we have

$$Y. = KL\Theta^* + E.$$
$$= K\Theta + E. \tag{15}$$

The substitution is equivalent to factoring the original matrix,

$$A = KL \tag{16}$$

K is an $(n \times l)$ *column basis* for the design, or model matrix for substitute parameters Θ, with $r(K) = l$.

Factoring A in (16) requires that rows of L be linear functions of rows of A. K may be determined from A and L, since

$$AL' = KLL'$$

and

$$AL'(LL')^{-1} = K \tag{17}$$

The usual procedure is to construct A from the experimental design, to define L (and Θ) according to the research hypotheses, and then to determine K by (17). The technical note at the end of this section gives suggested procedures for computing K.

The least-squares criterion (13) may be minimized to solve for Θ in (15). The normal equations are

$$(K'DK)\Theta = K'DY. \tag{18}$$

Since K is of full rank, (18) may be pre-multiplied by $(K'DK)^{-1}$ and

$$\hat{\Theta} = (K'DK)^{-1}K'DY.$$
$$= GK'DY. \tag{19}$$

Elements of $\hat{\Theta}$ are minimum-variance unbiased estimates, with covariance matrix

$$\mathcal{V}(\hat{\Theta}) = \mathcal{V}(GK'DY.)$$
$$= GK'D\,\mathcal{V}(Y.)D'KG$$
$$= GK'D(D^{-1} \otimes \Sigma)DKG$$
$$= G \otimes \Sigma \tag{20}$$

The standard error of $\hat{\theta}_{ij}$ is the square-root of the corresponding diagonal element of (20), that is $(g_{ii}\hat{\sigma}_j^2)^{1/2}$. If $\mathbf{y}$ is normally distributed, then $(\hat{\theta}_{ij} - \theta_{ij})/(g_{ii}\sigma_j^2)^{1/2}$ follows a standard normal distribution.

Least-squares estimation does not yield a unique value for Σ. However, the conditions for estimating Σ are set when the sum of squared residuals is minimized in estimating Θ.

The variance–covariance matrix is a function of the sums of squares and cross-products of the residuals. The unbiased estimate is

$$\hat{\Sigma} = \frac{1}{N - l} (Y'Y - \hat{\Theta}'K'DK\hat{\Theta})$$

$$= \frac{1}{N - l} (S_T - S_M)$$

$$= \frac{1}{N - l} S_E \qquad (21)$$

S_T is the $(p \times p)$ total sum of squares and cross-products of the N vector observations; S_M is the sum of squares and cross-products due to the model, or to mean differences. The difference S_E is the residual or error sum of squares and cross-products.

When $l = n$, all estimable between-group effects are included in the model. Then (21) reduces to the *pooled within-group variance–covariance matrix*

$$\hat{\Sigma} = \frac{1}{N - n} (Y'Y - Y.'DY.)$$

$$= \frac{1}{N - n} S_E \qquad (22)$$

In (22), S_E is the sum of squares and cross products of deviations from separate sub-group vector means, that is, $\sum (\mathbf{y}_{ij} - \mathbf{y}._{j})(\mathbf{y}_{ij} - \mathbf{y}._{j})'$.

$\hat{\Sigma}$ may be substituted for Σ in (20) to estimate the precision of $\hat{\Theta}$, and to construct confidence intervals. The t-distribution with $N - l$ degrees of freedom is used instead of the standard normal.

Σ is transformed to a residual or within-group correlation matrix by standardizing all variates. Let the vector of p standardized variables for subject i in group j be

$$\mathbf{z}_{ij} = \Delta^{-1/2}[\mathbf{y}_{ij} - \mathcal{E}(\mathbf{y}_{ij})] \qquad (23)$$

Δ is a diagonal matrix of variance from Σ, $\Delta = \text{diag}(\sigma_1^2, \sigma_2^2, \ldots, \sigma_p^2)$, and $\Delta^{-\frac{1}{2}}$ is the matrix of inverse standard deviations,

$$\Delta^{-1/2} = \text{diag}\left(\frac{1}{\sigma_1}, \frac{1}{\sigma_2}, \ldots, \frac{1}{\sigma_p} \right) \qquad (24)$$

The covariance matrix of $\mathbf{z}$ is the $(p \times p)$ matrix of intercorrelations.

$$\mathcal{V}(\mathbf{z}) = \Delta^{-1/2}\mathcal{V}(\mathbf{y})\Delta^{-1/2}$$

$$= \Delta^{-1/2}\Sigma\Delta^{-1/2}$$

$$= \mathcal{R} \qquad (25)$$

$\mathcal{R}$ is estimated by substituting $\hat{\Sigma}$ for Σ in (24) and (25). Elements $\hat{\rho}_{ij}$ may be adjusted for bias, as described in [9].

Means may be predicted or estimated from the l terms of the analysis-of-variance model. From (15), the predicted means for n groups are

$$\hat{Y}. = K\hat{\Theta} \qquad (26)$$

$\hat{Y}.$ is an $(n \times p)$ unbiased estimate of $Y.$, and has variance–covariance matrix

$$\mathcal{V}(\hat{Y}.) = K\mathcal{V}(\hat{\Theta})K'$$

$$= KGK' \otimes \Sigma \qquad (27)$$

Mean residuals are

$$\hat{E}. = Y. - \hat{Y}. \qquad (28)$$

with expectation O and covariance matrix

$$\mathcal{V}(\hat{E}.) = [I - KGK'] \otimes \Sigma$$

$$= H \otimes \Sigma \qquad (29)$$

With normal $\mathbf{y}$, $\hat{\varepsilon}._{ij}/(h_{ii}\hat{\sigma}_j^2)^{1/2}$ follows a t-distribution with $N - l$ degrees of freedom.

Rows of Θ are not independent if contrasts in L are not orthogonal, or if subclass frequences are unequal. This can be seen in the variance–covariance matrix among the estimates (20). $G = (K'DK)^{-1}$ will be non-diagonal (nonzero covariances) if K is not orthogonal or if D does not have equal elements. For the latter, the elements n_j must be equal; for the former, contrasts in L must be orthogonal (see 17). In general, research designs may not and need not meet either condition.

Orthogonal effects may be estimated for a fixed order of columns of K, as follows. Let T be the Cholesky or square-root triangular factor of $K'DK$. That is,

$$K'DK = TT' \qquad (30)$$

The *orthogonal estimates* are

$$T'\hat{\Theta} = U \qquad (31)$$

with expectation $T'\Theta$, and variance–covariance matrix

$$\mathcal{V}(U) = T'\mathcal{V}(\hat{\Theta})T$$

$$= I \otimes \Sigma \qquad (32)$$

Alternately, U may be obtained through the Gram–Schmidt orthonormal factorization of K,

$$T'\hat{\Theta} = T'(K'DK)^{-1}K'DY.$$

$$= T'(TT')^{-1}K'DY.$$

$$= K^{\perp\prime}DY. \qquad (33)$$

$K^{\perp}$ is an orthogonal basis, determined from K in a prespecified order of columns. $K^{\perp}$ satisfies

$$K^{\perp}T' = K \qquad (34a)$$

and

$$K^{\perp\prime}DK^{\perp} = I \qquad (34b)$$

In orthogonal designs (equal frequencies, or-

thogonal contrasts) the columns of $K^{\perp}$ are identical or simply proportional to columns of K, and the factoring is unnecessary.

Hypotheses about one or more rows of Θ, eliminating all effects in preceding rows, may be tested from U. Assume Θ to be partitioned into Θ_0, the leading $l - n_h$ rows, and Θ_h, the final n_h rows. The hypothesis is

$$\underset{(n_h \times p)}{H_0 : \Theta_h = O} \qquad (35)$$

that the final n_h effects or contrasts in Θ are null, for all p criterion measures.

To test H_0 (35), two sum of squares and cross-products matrices are compared. The *hypothesis sum of products* (S_H) reflects the extent to which criterion variation can be attributed to the n_h effects in Θ_h. The *error sum of products* (S_E) reflects the extent to which criterion variation cannot be attributed to any of the terms in Θ. S_H and S_E are measures of the extent to which mean differences in Θ_h are nonzero, and the extent to which mean differences are not important to the model, respectively.

The orthogonal estimates U, estimate the same contrasts as Θ but at each step eliminating any correlation with preceding effects. The final n_h rows of U estimate the n_h effects in Θ_h, eliminating any mean differences that can be attributed to terms in Θ_0. Represent the final n_h rows of U as U_h. Then the hypothesis sum of squares and cross-products is the sum of products of the terms in U_h.

$$\underset{(p \times p)}{S_H} = \underset{(p \times n_h)}{U_h'} \underset{(n_h \times p)}{U_h} \qquad (36)$$

S_H has n_h degrees of freedom.

The error sum of squares and cross-products may have several forms. The general residual matrix is given by (21). With U in place of $\hat{\Theta}$

$$S_E = Y'Y - U'U$$

$$= (N - l)\hat{\Sigma} \qquad (37)$$

S_E has $n_e = N - l$ degrees of freedom.

When $l = n$ and all between-group differences are included in the model, the residual becomes the within-group sum of products as in (22). The degrees of freedom are $n_e = N - n$. A third class of error terms is constructed from the final n_e effects in U. This is a "special effects" error term, of use in mixed models and nested designs. Let U_E comprise the final n_e rows of U. Then the $(p \times p)$ error matrix is

$$S_E = U_E' U_E \qquad (37a)$$

As in univariate anova, the error term is selected from the expected sums of squares (and cross-products) for all effects. The selection depends upon the crossing and nesting of experimental factors, and whether the model has fixed effects, random effects, or is a mixed model with both. In all cases when $p = 1$, S_H and S_E are the univariate sums of squares for hypothesis and error, respectively.

The expected values of S_E and S_H are

$$\mathcal{E}(S_E) = (N - l)\Sigma \qquad (38a)$$

and

$$\mathcal{E}(S_H) = n_h\Sigma + \Theta_h'(K_h' D K_h)\Theta_h \qquad (38b)$$

with K_h being the final n_h columns of K. Under H_0, Θ_h is null and both sample matrices estimate Σ.

Test criteria depend on the characteristic roots of $S_E^{-1}S_H$. There are as many nonzero roots as the rank of the product. Since S_E is of full rank, the product has rank equal to that of S_H. This is $r = \min(n_h, p)$. Represent the roots by λ_i, $i = 1, 2 \ldots, r$. Wilk's likelihood-ratio criterion is

$$\Lambda = \frac{|S_E|}{|S_E + S_H|}$$

$$= \prod_{i=1}^{r} \frac{1}{(1 + \lambda_i)} \qquad (39)$$

Tables of Λ are given in [31]. For large N,

Bartlett has proposed a test statistic which approximately follows a χ^2-distribution.

$$\chi^2 = -\left[n_e - \tfrac{1}{2}(p + 1 - n_h) \right]\log \Lambda$$

$$= -M \log \Lambda \qquad (40)$$

χ^2 is compared to upper percentage points of the χ^2-distribution with pn_h degrees of freedom. H_0 is rejected with confidence $1 - \alpha$ if χ^2 exceeds the 100α upper percentage point of $\chi^2_{pn_h}$.

Rao [26] derived a more accurate approximation by expanding the same series as Bartlett to an additional term. Rao's test statistic is

$$F = \left[\frac{(1 - \Lambda^{1/s})}{\Lambda^{1/s}} \right] \cdot \left[\frac{(Ms + 1 - n_h p/2)}{n_h p} \right]$$

$$(41)$$

with

$$s = \left[\frac{(p^2 n_h^2 - 4)}{(p^2 + n_h^2 - 5)} \right]^{1/2} \qquad (41a)$$

and M as in (40). F is compared to upper percentage points of the F-distribution with $n_h p$ and $Ms + 1 - n_h p/2$ degrees of freedom. For p or n_h values of 1 or 2, (41) follows the corresponding F-distribution exactly, and is not an approximation.

Tests may be conditionally conducted on all roots minus the largest, all minus the largest two, and so on. Assume the λ_i to be ordered from largest to smallest. The likelihood-ratio criterion for roots j through r is

$$\Lambda_j = \prod_{i=j}^{r} \frac{1}{(1 + \lambda_i)} \qquad (42)$$

Λ_j may be tested by either the χ^2 or F transformation. n_e and n_h are reduced by one for each larger root removed.

The characteristic vectors associated with the λ_i are the *discriminant function coefficients.* These may be inspected for identifying patterns among criteria that contribute to group mean discrimination. The associated vectors $\mathbf{v}_i$ may be adjusted to standard metric $\Delta^{1/2}\mathbf{v}_i$ to remove scale effects. Group-mean differences may also be inspected in the discriminant metric, by rescaling Θ_h; that is, by multiplying $\hat{\Theta}_h\mathbf{v}_i$.

Other multivariate test criteria have been developed. Among them is the *largest root criterion* [29], with test statistic $\lambda_1/(\lambda_1 + 1)$. The *trace criterion*, due to Hotelling, has statistic $\mathrm{tr}(S_E^{-1}S_H) = \sum_{i=1}^{r} \lambda_i$. Tables of both are given in [15, 21–23], with arguments

$$m = \tfrac{1}{2}(|n_h - p| - 1) \qquad (43a)$$

and

$$n = \tfrac{1}{2}(n_e - p - 1) \qquad (43b)$$

The largest-root statistic is more sensitive than Wilk's, to departures from H_0 in a single dimension. The criterion may be applied conditionally to roots 2 through r, reducing n_e and n_h by one for each larger root removed.

Univariate F-statistics may be computed from the diagonal elements of S_E and S_H, with degrees of freedom n_e and n_h, respectively. However, the univariate statistics for p intercorrelated measures are not independent of one another. The Roy–Bargmann step-down analysis [27, 28] provides p ordered but independent F-statistics for the test of H_0. H_0 is accepted if and only if all statistics fail to reach significance. The "step-down" analysis involves determining residual hypothesis and error variation in p stages. At each step, variation due to all prior variates is eliminated. This process is accomplished through the triangular factorization of S_E and $S_E + S_H$, by the Cholesky method. Represent these factorizations by

$$S_E = T_E T_E' \qquad (44a)$$

and

$$(S_E + S_H) = TT' \qquad (44b)$$

The squared diagonal elements of T_E and T are the conditional variances, eliminating all preceding measures. The step-down statistics are

$$F_j^* = \frac{\left[t_{jj}^2 - (t_e)_{jj}^2 \right]/n_h}{(t_e)_{jj}^2/(n_e - j + 1)} \qquad (45)$$

F_j^* is referred to the F-distribution with n_h and $n_e - j + 1$ degrees of freedom. Under H_0, $F_1^*, F_2^* \cdots F_{j-1}^*$ are independent of $F_j^*, F_{j+1}^* \cdots F_p^*$. F_p^* provides the test of between-group differences or regression effects for y_p, eliminating y_1 through y_{p-1}. If the critical value is not exceeded, the test of y_{p-1}, eliminating y_1 through y_{p-2} is conducted, with F_{p-1}^*. Testing stops and H_0 is rejected if one significant F^*-ratio is encountered. Unlike the other test criteria discussed, the step-down results are not invariant under a permutation of criterion measures.

Testing of Sequential Hypotheses. If H_0 is accepted, S_H and n_h may be ignored or pooled with S_E and n_e, respectively. Remaining rows of Θ may be partitioned into a new Θ_0 and Θ_h, and test statistics computed for the next hypothesis. In this manner a series of hypotheses about main effects and interactions, or specific planned comparisons, may be tested sequentially [1].

If H_0 is rejected, all prior, as yet untested rows of Θ are confounded with variation due to Θ_h. To test leading terms, the non-zero final effects in Θ_h must be ordered *before* those yet untested, and K re-orthogonalized and re-partitioned as in (30)–(35). Then the leading terms may be tested, *eliminating* the significant effects in the original Θ_h. In general, the number of alternate orders in which orthogonal effects are estimated, beyond the first or original order is represented as a.

At the completion of testing, only the

leading c significant terms remain. The rejected $l - c$ terms may be ignored, and Θ, $Y.$, and $E.$ re-estimated from K_c, the leading columns of K, as in (19), (26), and (28).

Note on the Construction of Design Bases. The means $Y.$, frequencies D, and mean-model basis K, are necessary to the estimation of Θ. For computation, the model matrix A may be bypassed entirely.

The basis for a one-way design with n groups is determined directly from the contrast matrix L. The contrast matrix for a one-way design has the form:

$$L = \begin{bmatrix} 1 & \dfrac{1}{N} & \dfrac{1}{N} & \cdots & \dfrac{1}{N} \\ 0 & & & & \\ 0 & & & & \\ 0 & & & L_c & \\ \vdots & & & & \\ 0 & & & & \end{bmatrix}$$

The l rows of L each multiply the parameter

matrix with terms $\mu, \alpha_1, \alpha_2, \ldots \alpha_n$. The total numbers of parameters is $m = n + 1$.

The leading row of L contains the weights for the constant or scaling term in the reparameterized model, $\mu + \dfrac{1}{n} \Sigma_j \alpha_j$. L_c is the $(l-1 \times n)$ submatrix containing the weights which define contrasts among the parameters α_j. Rows of L_c sum to zero by definition. Given these conditions, Bock [3] has shown that a column basis is obtained by:

$$K = [\mathbf{1}_n, K_c] \qquad (46)$$

where

$$K_c = L_c'(L_c L_c')^{-1} \qquad (46a)$$

For some commonly employed contrasts, K has a regular form and can be constructed without performing (46a). For example, with orthogonal contrasts, rows of K_c are simply rescaled rows of L_c since $(L_c L_c')^{-1}$ is diagonal. These include *orthogonal polynomials*, and *Helmert contrasts*, of the form

$$L_c = \begin{bmatrix} 1 & -\dfrac{1}{n-1} & -\dfrac{1}{n-1} & \cdots & -\dfrac{1}{n-1} & -\dfrac{1}{n-1} \\ 0 & 1 & -\dfrac{1}{n-2} & \cdots & -\dfrac{1}{n-2} & -\dfrac{1}{n-2} \\ & & & \vdots & & \\ 0 & 0 & 0 & \cdots & 1 & -1 \end{bmatrix} \begin{matrix} H1 \\ H2 \\ \vdots \\ H(n-1) \end{matrix} \qquad (47)$$

Symbolically, orthogonal polynomial contrast vectors may be represented as $P1, P2, \ldots P(n-1)$, Helmert vectors as $H1, H2, \ldots, H(n-1)$. The columns of the basis correspond to the same effects, and may be given the same symbolic representation. Also, $P0$, or $H0$, may be used to represent the "zero'th" effect or unit vector of K.

Two other contrast types yield regular

bases. When comparing group means to a control or standard, *simple contrasts* have the form

$$L_c = \begin{bmatrix} 1 & -1 & 0 & 0 & 0 \\ 0 & -1 & 1 & 0 & 0 \\ 0 & -1 & 0 & 1 & 0 \\ 0 & -1 & 0 & 0 & 1 \end{bmatrix} \begin{matrix} C1 \\ C3 \\ C4 \\ C5 \end{matrix} \qquad (48)$$

The corresponding basis vectors may be

designated $C0, C1, \ldots, C(n)$. The index omitted indicates the control level. For example, in (48), group means are contrasted with those of group two. The resulting basis vectors may be represented symbolically as

$$
L_c = \begin{bmatrix} 1 - \dfrac{1}{n} & -\dfrac{1}{n} & \cdots & -\dfrac{1}{n} & -\dfrac{1}{n} \\[2mm] -\dfrac{1}{n} & 1 - \dfrac{1}{n} & \cdots & -\dfrac{1}{n} & -\dfrac{1}{n} \\[2mm] \vdots & & & & \vdots \\[2mm] -\dfrac{1}{n} & -\dfrac{1}{n} & \cdots & 1 - \dfrac{1}{n} & -\dfrac{1}{n} \end{bmatrix} \begin{matrix} D1 \\[2mm] D2 \\[2mm] \vdots \\[2mm] D(n-1) \end{matrix} \qquad (49)
$$

The resulting basis vectors are represented $D0, D1, \ldots, D(n-1)$.

The basis matrix for deviation contrasts has the form of (48), whereas the basis resulting from simple contrasts has form (49). Either may be constructed directly, without computation of (46) and (46a). Thus the symbolic representation alone is sufficient to determine K. This representation was developed in Bock [3], and parallels the symbolic design specification of Kurkjian and Zelen [18]. Other contrasts for which the basis may not be regular, require evaluation by (46). These are termed *arbitrary contrasts* and generally denoted $L0, L1, \ldots, L(n-1)$.

Bases for crossed and nested designs may be constructed from those for separate classification factors. Assume a two-way crossed design with J levels of factor A, and K levels of B. The total number of groups is $n = JK$. Simple contrasts $[C0, C1, C3, C4, \ldots, C(J)]$, are to be employed for factor A. Levels of B are to be compared through Helmert contrasts, $H0, H1, \ldots, H(K-1)$. The columns of the basis for the entire design are JK-element Kronecker products of a single vector from each one-way matrix. Assume the A vector always to be the pre-factor. Representing all vectors symbolically, the products

$C0$ for the grand mean, and contrasts $C1$, $C3$, $C4$, and $C5$.

Deviation contrasts involve the comparison of $n - 1$ groups with the mean of all n groups. The contrast weights have the form are:

$C0 \otimes H0$	Grand mean
$C1 \otimes H0$	A effects
$C3 \otimes H0$	
$\vdots$	
$C(J) \otimes H0$	
$C0 \otimes H1$	B effects
$C0 \otimes H2$	
$\vdots$	
$C0 \otimes H(K-1)$	
$C1 \otimes H1$	Interactions
$\vdots$	
$C(J) \otimes H(K-1)$	

$$ (50) $$

Similarly, r-way designs have column bases whose vectors are r-order Kronecker products of r one-way design basis vectors. Each symbolic code represents a single-degree-of-freedom source of variation in the analysis of-variance model. Altogether, l codes represent the entire reparameterized model. Multiple examples of the symbolic representation are given by Finn [9].

REGRESSION ANALYSIS

The multivariate multiple linear regression model is

$$\mathbf{y}'_i = \boldsymbol{\alpha}' + x_{i1}\boldsymbol{\beta}'_1 + x_{i2}\boldsymbol{\beta}'_2 + \cdots$$
$$+ x_{iq}\boldsymbol{\beta}'_q + \boldsymbol{\varepsilon}'_i \qquad (51)$$

$\mathbf{y}'_i$ is the vector of criterion scores on p random variables, for observation i. $\boldsymbol{\alpha}$ is the vector of scaling constants for the p variates; its inclusion in the model is to equate the right and left side of (51); $\boldsymbol{\beta}_j (j = 1, 2, \ldots, q)$ are the p-element vectors of partial regression coefficients for predicting $\mathbf{y}'_i$ from predictor variables x_j. $\boldsymbol{\varepsilon}_i$ is the vector random error, independently and identically distributed as in (3).

Models for N observations are juxtaposed to yield the matrix model,

$$\underset{(N \times p)}{Y} = \underset{(N \times q+1)}{X} \underset{(q+1 \times p)}{B} + \underset{(N \times p)}{E} \qquad (52)$$

Y is the $(N \times p)$ data matrix of scores on the criterion variables. X is the regression model matrix. Each row of X has a unit element followed by q predictor scores for the particular observation. B is the matrix of unknown parameters with rows $\boldsymbol{\alpha}'$ and $\boldsymbol{\beta}'_j$ $(j = 1, 2, \ldots, q)$. E is the matrix of random errors with rows $\boldsymbol{\varepsilon}'_i$. The entire matrix has distribution

$$\mathbf{E} \sim \mathfrak{N}_{np}(O, I \otimes \Sigma) \qquad (53)$$

Since X is generally of full rank $(q + 1)$, estimation of B directly parallels the estimation of Θ in (15), (18), and (19). X replaces K, and the rank of the model is $q + 1$ rather than l. D is the identity matrix. Likewise, the $(p \times p)$ residual matrices for Y (Σ and $\mathfrak{R}$) may be estimated as in (21)–(25). Tests on rows or sections of B are conducted exactly as tests on Θ in (30)–(45).

Substituting in (19) and (21) respectively,

$$\hat{\mathbf{B}} = (X'X)^{-1}X'Y \qquad (54)$$

and

$$\hat{\Sigma} = \frac{1}{N - q - 1}(Y'Y - \hat{\mathbf{B}}'X'X\hat{\mathbf{B}}) \qquad (55)$$

$$= \frac{1}{N - q - 1}S_E \qquad (55a)$$

$\hat{\Sigma}$ is the $(p \times p)$ estimate of the variance–covariance matrix of $\boldsymbol{\varepsilon}_i$, or of $\mathbf{y}_i$ given X. $\hat{\mathbf{B}}$ is unbiased and has covariance matrix $\mathcal{V}(\hat{\mathbf{B}}) = (X'X)^{-1} \otimes \Sigma$.

$\hat{\mathbf{B}}$ and $\hat{\Sigma}$ are easily found from the covariance matrix of the (p) y-variates and the (q) x-variables. Let $\mathbf{v}_i$ be the vector of all $(p + q)$ measures for observation i. That is

$$\mathbf{v}'_i = [\mathbf{y}'_i, \mathbf{x}'_i] \qquad (56)$$

where $\mathbf{x}'_i = [x_{i1}, x_{i2} \cdots x_{iq}]$. Let S_v be the matrix of sums of squares and cross-products of mean deviations.

$$S_v = \sum_{i=1}^{N} (\mathbf{v}_i - \mathbf{v}_\cdot)(\mathbf{v}_i - \mathbf{v}_\cdot)' \qquad (57)$$

where $\mathbf{v}'_\cdot = \frac{1}{N}\sum_{i=1}^{N}\mathbf{v}'_i$. The $(p + q)$-square matrix may be partitioned into sections for the y and x-variables alone, and for the cross-products of the two.

$$S_v = \begin{bmatrix} S^{(yy)} & | & S^{(yx)} \\ \hline S^{(xy)} & | & S^{(xx)} \end{bmatrix} \begin{array}{l} p \text{ rows} \\ q \text{ rows} \end{array} \qquad (57a)$$

$$p \text{ columns} \quad q \text{ columns}$$

The sections of S_v correspond to the terms in (54) and (55). $S^{(yy)}$ is the same as $Y'Y$ except that all variables are expressed as mean deviations before the squares and cross-products are computed. $S^{(xx)}$ is the sum of products of mean deviations of the x-variables. It is similar to $X'X$ of (54) and (55) except that mean deviations are used in lieu of the original x-measures. The need for the unit vector is obviated. Also $S^{(xy)}$ is like $X'Y$, but obtained from mean-deviation variables.

The estimate of B derived from (57a) is

$$\hat{B} = \left[S^{(xx)} \right]^{-1} S^{(xy)} \qquad (58)$$

$\hat{B}$ is the $(q \times p)$ matrix of estimates, excluding the constant $\boldsymbol{\alpha}$. This term is unnecessary since all variables are expressed as mean deviations in obtaining (57). The terms of (58) are identical to the final q rows of (54).

The *unconditional* variance–covariance matrix for all measures is estimated by

$$\hat{\Sigma}_v = \frac{1}{N-1} S_v \qquad (59)$$

An estimate of Σ, the conditional covariance matrix of y given X, equivalent to (55) but using S_v is

$$\hat{\Sigma} = \frac{1}{N-q-1} \left[S^{(yy)} - \hat{B}'(S^{(xx)})\hat{B} \right]$$

$$= \frac{1}{N-q-1}$$

$$\times \left[S^{(yy)} - S^{(yx)}(S^{(xx)})^{-1} S^{(xy)} \right]$$

$$= \frac{1}{n_e} \left[S^{(yy)} - S_R \right] \qquad (60)$$

S_R is the *sum of products for regression*, $S_R = S^{(yx)}\hat{B}$.

If the x_{ij} are values of random variables $x_1, x_2, \ldots, x_q$, correlations of the y and x-variates may also be estimated. *Simple correlations* are obtained by reducing (59) to correlational form as in (24)–(25). The *squared multiple correlation* of criterion variable y_i with all q predictors x_j, is the proportion of decrease in y_i variation when the x_j are held constant. That is,

$$R_i^2 = \frac{\left[\mathcal{V}(y_i) - \mathcal{V}(y_i|X) \right]}{\mathcal{V}(y_i)} \qquad (61)$$

$\mathcal{V}(y_i)$ is the unconditional variance of criterion y_i, estimated by the ii diagonal element of $\hat{\Sigma}_v$. $\mathcal{V}(y_i|X)$ is the conditional variance of y_i given the (q) x-measures, estimated by the ii diagonal element of $\hat{\Sigma}$.

Thus the estimate of R_i^2 is

$$\hat{R}_i^2 = \frac{\text{diag}_i \left\{ S^{(yy)} - \left[S^{(yy)} - S^{(yx)}(S^{(yx)})^{-1} S^{(xy)} \right] \right\}}{\text{diag}_i \left[S^{(yy)} \right]}$$

$$= \frac{\text{diag}_i \left[S_R \right]}{\text{diag}_i \left[S^{(yy)} \right]} \qquad (62)$$

Test of $H_0 : R_i = 0$, may be obtained through likelihood-ratio procedures. The test statistic is

$$F_i = \frac{\hat{R}_i^2 (N - q - 1)}{(1 - \hat{R}_i^2)q} \qquad (63)$$

F_i follows an F-distribution with q and $N - q - 1$ degrees of freedom. If the y_i are intercorrelated, tests of the p multiple correlations are not independent. Multivariate tests of regression (30)–(45) or canonical correlation analysis should be employed.

The *canonical correlations* of variable sets y and x are product-moment correlations of composites

$$c_i = \boldsymbol{\alpha}_i^{(y)\prime} y \qquad (64a)$$

and

$$d_i = \boldsymbol{\alpha}_i^{(x)\prime} x \qquad (64b)$$

where $\boldsymbol{\alpha}_i^{(y)}$ and $\boldsymbol{\alpha}_i^{(x)}$ are chosen to maximize the correlation $\rho_{c_i d_i}$ (represented by ρ_i). There are as many unique vectors of weights $\boldsymbol{\alpha}_i^{(y)}$ and $\boldsymbol{\alpha}_i^{(x)}$ as $s = \min(p, q)$. The vectors are chosen to be mutually orthogonal, and of unit length with respect to the variance–covariance matrix metric.

The properties of the correlations and corresponding weight vectors may be defined as follows. Let Σ_v be partitioned as is S_v in (57a); let $A^{(y)}$ be a $(p \times s)$ matrix with columns $\boldsymbol{\alpha}_i^{(y)}$; let $A^{(x)}$ be a $(q \times s)$ matrix with columns $\boldsymbol{\alpha}_i^{(x)}$; let the s correlations be the diagonal elements of an $(s \times s)$

diagonal matrix P. Then

$$A^{(y)'}\Sigma^{(yy)}A^{(y)} = I \qquad (65a)$$

$$A^{(x)'}\Sigma^{(xx)}A^{(x)} = I \qquad (65b)$$

$$A^{(y)'}\Sigma^{(yx)}A^{(x)} = P \qquad (66)$$

Maximum values of ρ_i and associated vectors $\alpha_i^{(y)}$ are the solutions of the homogeneous equations,

$$\left[\Sigma^{(yx)}(\Sigma^{(xx)})^{-1}\Sigma^{(xy)} - \rho_i^2\Sigma^{(yy)}\right]\alpha_i^{(y)} = 0 \qquad (67)$$

where ρ_i satisfies

$$\left|\Sigma^{(yx)}(\Sigma^{(xx)})^{-1}\Sigma^{(xy)} - \rho_i^2\Sigma^{(yy)}\right| = 0 \quad (67a)$$

The weights $A^{(x)}$ are obtained by

$$A^{(x)} = BA^{(y)}P^{-1} \qquad (68)$$

Estimates of ρ_i and the associated vectors are obtained by substituting $\hat{\Sigma}_v$ for Σ_v.

The likelihood-ratio principle may be employed to test

$$H_0 : \rho_i = 0 \qquad (69)$$

for all s correlations simultaneously. The test criterion is

$$\Lambda = \prod_{i=1}^{s} \left(1 - \hat{\rho}_i^2\right) \qquad (70)$$

Λ may be transformed to any of the distributional referents (40)–(41a) and (43a)–(43b) with q substituted for n_h. Test of all correlations minus the largest j values, has criterion

$$\Lambda = \prod_{i=j+1}^{s} \left(1 - \hat{\rho}_i^2\right) \qquad (71)$$

Test parameters $(p - j)$ and $(q - j)$ are substituted for p and q, respectively.

ANALYSIS OF COVARIANCE

The analysis-of-covariance model has both group-membership variables and measured predictor variables. It combines the analysis-of-variance model (2) and the linear regression model (51). The model for observation i in subclass jk is

$$y'_{ijk} = \mu' + \alpha'_j + \beta'_k + (\alpha\beta)'_{jk} + x'_{ijk}B + \varepsilon'_{ijk}. \qquad (72)$$

μ, α_j, β_k, and $(\alpha\beta)_{jk}$ are $(p \times 1)$ vector effects, as in (2); x_{ijk} is the $(q \times 1)$ vector of mean deviation scores on the concomitant measures (covariates); B is the $(q \times p)$ matrix of regression weights as in (52). ε_{ijk} are assumed independently normally distributed with expectation 0, and covariance matrix Σ^*. This is the covariance matrix of y_{ijk}, conditional upon both sets of independent variables, A and X.

Models may be written for N observations (1) or for the subclass means. The mean model for n groups is

$$\begin{matrix} Y. & = & K & \Theta & + & (X. - 1x'..) \\ (n \times p) & & (n \times l) & (l \times p) & & (n \times q)(n \times 1)(1 \times q) \end{matrix}$$

$$\begin{matrix} & \times & B & + & E. \\ & & (q \times p) & & (n \times p) \end{matrix} \qquad (73)$$

K and Θ comprise the group membership part of the model. $X.$ is the matrix of subclass means on the q covariates, and $x..$ is the $(q \times 1)$ vector of grand means for the covariates, that is,

$$x'.. = (1/n)1'_n X. \qquad (74)$$

Group means on the covariates are expressed as deviations from the grand mean $x..$.

Estimation of Θ and B is accomplished by treating both outcome measures and covariates as comprising a single vector observation. Let v_{ij} be the $(p + q)$-element vector of scores on both sets of variables as in (56).

$$v'_{ij} = \left[y'_{ij}, x'_{ij}\right] \qquad (75)$$

V is the complete $[N \times (p + q)]$ data-matrix, with rows $\mathbf{v}'_{ij}$.

$$V = \underset{(N \times p)(N \times q)}{(Y, X)} \qquad (75a)$$

The means for n subclasses comprise the $[n \times (p + q)]$ matrix $V. = (Y., X.)$.

Between-group effects are first estimated for all $(p + q)$ variables, and then adjusted for the $\mathbf{x}$ values. From (19) we have

$$\hat{\Theta}_v = (K'DK)^{-1}K'DV.$$

$$= \underset{(l \times p) \quad (l \times q)}{\left[\hat{\Theta}^{(y)} \mid \hat{\Theta}^{(x)} \right]} \qquad (76)$$

The $(p + q)$-square covariance matrix for all measures, given group membership effects, follows from (21).

$$\hat{\Sigma}_v = \frac{1}{N - l} \left(V'V - \hat{\Theta}'_v [K'DK]\hat{\Theta}_v \right)$$

$$= \frac{1}{N - l} S_v \qquad (77)$$

S_v and $\hat{\Sigma}_v$ may be partitioned like the sum of products in (57a). From the partitioned form, the estimate of B in (73), given group-membership effects, is

$$\hat{B} = \left[S^{(xx)} \right]^{-1} S^{(xy)} \qquad (78)$$

The expectation of $\hat{B}$ is B. The variance–covariance matrix is

$$\mathcal{V}(\hat{B}) = \left[S^{(xx)} \right]^{-1} \otimes \Sigma^* \qquad (79)$$

The estimate of Θ in (73), given regression effects, is determined from (76) and (78).

$$\underset{(l \times p)}{\hat{\Theta}} = \underset{(l \times p)}{\hat{\Theta}^{(y)}} - \underset{(l \times q)}{\hat{\Theta}^{(x)}} \underset{(q \times p)}{\hat{B}} \qquad (80)$$

The expectation of $\hat{\Theta}$ is Θ. The covariance matrix is

$$\mathcal{V}(\hat{\Theta}) = \mathcal{V}(\hat{\Theta}^{(y)}) + \mathcal{V}(\hat{\Theta}^{(x)}B) \qquad (81)$$

Since $\hat{\Theta}^{(x)}$ is fixed,

$$\mathcal{V}(\hat{\Theta}^{(x)}\hat{B}) = \Theta^{(x)} \left[S^{(xx)} \right]^{-1} \Theta^{(x)'} \otimes \Sigma^*$$

and thus

$$\mathcal{V}(\hat{\Theta}) = \left[(K'DK)^{-1} \right.$$

$$\left. + \Theta^{(x)} (S^{(xx)})^{-1} \Theta^{(x)'} \right] \otimes \Sigma^* \qquad (81a)$$

The residual covariance matrix Σ^*, is adjusted for both regression and group-membership effects. The covariance matrix of $\mathbf{y}$ *and* $\mathbf{x}$, adjusted for group-mean differences, is given by (77). To further adjust for regression on $\mathbf{x}$, we follow (60). The adjusted variances and covariances of $\mathbf{y}$ comprise the $(p \times p)$ matrix

$$\hat{\Sigma}^* = \frac{1}{N - q - l}$$

$$\times \left[S^{(yy)} - S^{(yx)}(S^{(xx)})^{-1}S^{(xy)} \right]$$

$$= \frac{1}{N - q - l} \left[S^{(yy)} - S_R \right]$$

$$= \frac{1}{n_e^*} S_E^* \qquad (82)$$

$\hat{\Sigma}^*$ may be reduced to correlational form in the usual manner to yield the $(p \times p)$ matrix of *partial correlations* among the y-variates, removing the effects of the (q) x-measures, and l group-mean effects.

All regression hypotheses of the preceding section may be tested utilizing S_v, $\hat{B}$, and $\hat{\Sigma}^*$, adjusted for mean differences. The adjusted error degrees of freedom are $n_e^* = N - q - l$, replacing n_e in (60)ff.

To test that regression planes are parallel for all n groups, S_E^* may be compared to the sum of separately adjusted subgroup covariance matrices. Let S_j be the within-group sum of squares and cross-products for all $(p + q)$ measures, in subgroup j only. S_j may be partitioned as in (57a). $S_j^{(yy)}$ is adjusted for x-variables by

$$S_j^* = S_j^{(yy)} - S_j^{(yx)} \left[S_j^{(xx)} \right]^{-1} S_j^{(xy)} \qquad (83)$$

The error sum of products for the parallel-ism test is

$$S^* = \sum_{j=1}^{n} S_j^* \qquad (84)$$

having $n^* = n_e - nq$ degrees of freedom. The hypothesis matrix is

$$S_H = S_E^* - S^* \qquad (85)$$

with

$$n_h = n_e^* - n^*$$
$$= q(n - 1) \qquad (86)$$

degrees of freedom. All test criteria (39)–(45) may be employed.

Hypotheses about means are tested, after adjusting for covariates. The adjusted error sum of products is S_E^*, which substitutes for S_E in (39)–(45). To adjust the hypothesis sum of products, an $[l \times (p + q)]$ matrix of orthogonal estimates may be computed by (31) for both the x and y variables, using $\hat{\Theta}_v$ from (76). The hypothesis sum of products for all variables is the $(p + q)$-square matrix $S_H = U_h' U_h$. The covariate adjustment is performed on the sum,

$$S_T = S_H + S_v \qquad (87)$$

Partitioning S_T into the same sections as S_v in (57a), the adjusted "total sum of prod-ucts" is the $(p \times p)$ matrix

$$S_T^* = S_T^{(yy)} - S_T^{(yx)} \left[S_T^{(xx)} \right]^{-1} S_T^{(xy)} \qquad (88)$$

The adjusted hypothesis sum of products is then

$$S_H^* = S_T^* - S_E^* \qquad (89)$$

All test criteria for between-group effects may be employed, with $(p \times p)$ error and hypothesis matrices S_E^* and S_H^* respectively, and error degrees of freedom n_e^*. If a sequence of covariance hypotheses are tested, each S_H must be individually adjusted as in (87)–(89).

Adjusted treatment means are functions of observed means $Y.$ and $X..$ The $(n \times p)$ matrix of means adjusted for covariates, is

$$Y.^* = \hat{Y}. - (\hat{X}. - 1_n \hat{x}..')\hat{B}$$
$$= K\hat{\Theta} \qquad (90)$$

Predicted means from the rank-l analysis of variance model, plus the rank-q regression model, are obtained by substituting in (73). The $(n \times p)$ matrix is

$$\hat{Y}.^* = K\hat{\Theta} + (X. - 1x..')\hat{B} \qquad (91)$$

with $\hat{\Theta}$ estimated by (80). Mean residuals, adjusted for covariates, are the differences

$$\hat{E}.^* = Y. - \hat{Y}.^* \qquad (92)$$

c. Computing Notes

ACCUMULATING SUMMARY STATISTICS

Sufficient summary statistics for all analyses in Section 2b, are: $Y.$, the matrix of means for n groups on p dependent vari-ables; $X.$, the means for the n groups on q predictor variables or covariates; D, the $(n \times n)$ diagonal matrix of subclass frequen-cies; S_v, the $[(p + q) \times (p + q)]$ symmetric matrix of sum of squares and cross products for all measures. In analysis-of-variance models, q is zero and $X.$ is not computed.

Youngs and Cramer [33] suggest that for accuracy all sums of squares and cross-products should be accumulated in double precision, and should be computed employ-ing a correction-term algorithm. On large word computers (more than 36 bits) the need for the correction-term algorithm is generally obviated. However, double preci-sion should still be employed until the error covariance matrix is computed.

STORAGE CONSERVATION

For computers with limited core memory, matrices may be stored in packed form as one continuous vector. Nonzero elements of a diagonal matrix may be stored in consecutive locations. Triangular and symmetric matrices may be packed by rows, that is, $a_{11}, a_{21}, a_{22}, a_{31}, a_{32}, a_{33}, a_{41}, \ldots, a_{nn}$. Only the lower half of the matrix is necessary. Most vector and matrix manipulations (addition, multiplication, partitioning of matrices) are performed repeatedly. Subroutines such as those available from IBM [17], or National Educational Resources, Inc. [6] may be employed to operate on matrices stored in packed form.

Data matrices Y and X need not be constructed. The summary matrices $Y.$, $X.$, D, and S_v may be accumulated from each data vector as it is read. If n_0 $(< n)$ subclasses have observations and $n - n_0$ groups are empty, then $Y.$ and $X.$ may be collapsed to only n_0 rows, and D to an $(n_0 \times n_0)$ diagonal matrix.

ORTHONORMALIZATION

To obtain the orthogonal estimates (31), the design basis is orthonormalized as in (34a) and (34b). The Gram–Schmidt algorithm normalizes the first column of K, determines a second column orthogonal to the first, a third column orthogonal to the first two, and so on. At each stage, the resulting orthogonal column is normalized to unit length. The normalizing constants and the inner products from the orthogonalization comprise the triangular factor T.

In large problems, the accuracy of the Gram–Schmidt procedure is not sufficient, even in double precision. Either the Householder procedure [16] or a modification of the Gram–Schmidt algorithm [2] will increase precision to an acceptable level. A flow chart and Fortran coding for the modified Gram–Schmidt algorithm are given in a following section.

INVERSION

A three-stage Cholesky factoring and inversion algorithm provides a unified procedure for several aspects of the analysis. Any symmetric positive-definite matrix can be factored into the product of a lower-triangular positive-definite matrix, and its trans-

pose. The factoring may be represented as

$$A = TT' \tag{93}$$

A is $(n \times n)$ symmetric, and T is $(n \times n)$ with zero elements above the principal diagonal.

Since a triangular matrix is easily inverted by common sweep-out procedures, its inverse may be utilized to find A^{-1}. Thus at stage two we find T^{-1}, such that $T^{-1}T = I$. At stage three multiply,

$$(T^{-1})'T^{-1} = A^{-1} \tag{94}$$

The three-step procedure results in an efficiently computed and accurate inverse for A [11, Ch. 4], [12]. A Fortran routine for the three stages is given in the following section, similar to that used in MULTIVARIANCE [10]. It is useful to avoid condensing the three steps. Each can be used for separate facets of the analysis, as well as the complete inversion process.

The Cholesky factors of sum-of-products matrices are the basic data for the step-down analysis in (44a) and (44b) and for determining the orthogonal estimates in (30) and (31). If T is constructed by Gram–Schmidt orthonormalization (34a), its inverse provides $\hat{\Theta}$ from U, by

$$\hat{\Theta} = (T^{-1})'U \tag{95}$$

The determinants required for Λ in (39) may be obtained at the same time as the step-down F^*-statistics. Since $A = TT'$

$$|A| = |T|\,|T'| \tag{96}$$

The determinant of a triangular matrix is the product of its diagonal elements. Thus

$$|A| = \prod_{i=1}^{n} t_{ii}^2 \tag{97}$$

For even moderate n, only $\log|A|$ will have

sufficient computed accuracy.

$$\log|A| = 2 \sum_{i=1}^{n} \log(t_{ii}) \qquad (98)$$

Equation (98) may be obtained as a by-product while factoring to obtain T and T_E in (44a) and (44b). Thus computation of the characteristic roots for (39) is obviated.

The discriminant function coefficients and the canonical correlation weights (67) require determining nonzero solutions of equations,

$$(A - \lambda B)\mathbf{x} = 0 \qquad (99)$$

B is assumed symmetric positive-definite. To simplify from a two-matrix to single-matrix problem, the equation may be pre-multiplied by B^{-1}, and the roots and vectors of $B^{-1}A$ computed.

The equation may also be converted into a single symmetric matrix problem, by using stages one and two of the Cholesky inversion. Let

$$\mathbf{x} = (T^{-1})'\mathbf{w} \qquad (100)$$

and factor

$$B = TT' \qquad (101)$$

Then (99) becomes

$$(A - \lambda TT')(T^{-1})'\mathbf{w} = \mathbf{0} \qquad (102)$$

Pre-multiplying both sides by T^{-1}, we have

$$\left[T^{-1}A(T^{-1})' - \lambda I \right]\mathbf{w} = \mathbf{0} \qquad (103)$$

The characteristic roots λ, and vectors $\mathbf{w}$, of $T^{-1}A(T^{-1})'$ may be calculated by the method of Jacobi, or by more efficient procedures of Householder [16], Ortega [20], and Wilkinson [32]. $\mathbf{x}$ is determined from $\mathbf{w}$ by (100).

3. SUMMARY OF CALCULATION PROCEDURE

The calculation procedure is given in three phases to parallel the phases of the

MULTIVARIANCE program [10]. These are (a) Input, in which simple summary matrices are computed; (b) Estimation, in which analysis-of-variance effects are estimated and combined to give predicted means and residuals; (c) Analysis, in which tests of analysis-of-variance and covariance hypotheses are made, and regression effects are estimated and tested. In the first two phases, no distinction is made between the p criterion measures and the q measured predictor variables (covariates). q is assumed zero for analysis-of-variance models. When q is nonzero, the x-variables are identified in the third phase, and employed as regression predictors, or as covariates for testing between-group differences. Each phase has its own input quantities as well as utilizing all output from the prior phases.

a. Input

INPUT QUANTITIES

1. t = total number of measured input variables $(t = p + q)$.

2. f = number of factors (ways of classification) in analysis-of-variance design. Also names for factors.

3. $f_i (i = 1, 2, \ldots, f)$ = number of levels of each factor in analysis-of-variance design.

4. n_j = numbers of observations in group j. [This is the jj diagonal element of D.]

5. $\mathbf{v}'_{ij} = (\mathbf{y}'_{ij}, \mathbf{x}'_{ij})$. Data vector for all observations i in all subclasses j.

ORDER OF CALCULATION

1. Total number of groups in design, $n = \prod_{i=1}^{f} f_i$. Number of groups with at least one observation, n_0.

2. Total number of observations, $N = \sum_{j=1}^{n} n_j$.

3. Sum of score vectors for each group, $\mathbf{v}'_{+j} = \Sigma_i \mathbf{v}'_{ij} \, (1 \times t)$; total sum of squares and cross-products for each group, $S_j = \Sigma_i \mathbf{v}_{ij}\mathbf{v}'_{ij}$ $(t \times t)$. [The sum of all S_j is the total sum of products $Y'Y$ in (21), for all t measures].

4. Mean vector for each group, $\mathbf{v}_{\cdot j} = (1/n_j)\mathbf{v}_{+j}$ [$\mathbf{v}'_{\cdot j}$ is one row of $V_{\cdot\cdot}$. The matrix of means for all t measures]; mean-adjusted sum of products for each group, $S_{w_j} = S_j - n_j\mathbf{v}_{\cdot j}\mathbf{v}'_{\cdot j}$ [The sum of all S_{w_j} is the pooled within-group sum of products, S_E in (22), for all t measures]; Variance–covariance matrix for each group, $V_j = (1/n_j - 1)S_{w_j}$; standard deviations for each group $D_j = \text{diag}(V_j)^{1/2}$; correlation matrix for each group, $R_j = D_j^{-1}V_jD_j^{-1}$.

5. Mean matrix $V_{\cdot\cdot}$. ($n \times t$) with row vectors $\mathbf{v}'_{\cdot j}$; combined observed "row and column means" from rows of $V_{\cdot\cdot}$, weighted by corresponding elements of D; total sum of products, $S_T = \Sigma_j S_j$; pooled within-group sum of cross-products, $S_W = \Sigma_j S_{w_j} = S_T - V'_{\cdot\cdot}DV_{\cdot\cdot}$; within-group degrees of freedom, $n_w = \Sigma_j(n_j - 1) = N - n$; within-group variance–covariance matrix, $V_W = (1/n_w)S_W$; diagonal matrix of standard deviations, $D_W = \text{diag}(V_W)^{1/2}$; within-group correlation matrix, $R_W = D_W^{-1}V_WD_W^{-1}$.

OUTPUT QUANTITIES

1. Input parameters
2. n, n_0, N.
3. j, V_j, $D_j(j = 1, 2, \ldots, n)$.
4. $V_{\cdot\cdot}$, combined row and column observed means.
5. S_T, S_W, V_W, D_W, R_W, n_w.

b. Estimation of Analysis-of-Variance Parameters

INPUT QUANTITIES

1. Rank of analysis-of-variance contrast matrix $l(0 \leqslant l \leqslant n_0)$; rank of model for estimation, $c(c \leqslant l)$; error term parameter e; [$e = 0$ for within-groups S_E; $e = 1$ for residual; $e = 2$ for "special effects"]; number of alternate orders for orthogonalization, a; number of factors having arbitray contrasts, g; number of factors having orthogonal polynomials, o.

2. Names of factors for arbitrary contrasts, and one-way contrast matrix for each.

3. Names of factors for orthogonal polynomial contrasts.

4. l symbolic contrast vectors (SCV's), indicating between-group contrasts to be tested. [SCV conventions are given in (47)–(50).]

5. a reordering keys, indicating alternate orders in which orthogonal effects are to be estimated.

ORDER OF CALCULATION

1. For each factor having arbitrary contrasts, compute one-way basis, according to (46) and (46a).

2. For each factor having orthogonal polynomial contrasts, generate orthogonal polynomial matrix.

3. For each SCV, generate corresponding f-way basis vector $\mathbf{k}_i$, from Kronecker products of one-way basis vectors, as in (50). $\mathbf{k}_i$ is of order ($n \times 1$). If there are reordering keys, store original order of basis vectors and all alternate orders on scratch $I/0$ file.

4. Orthogonalize the design basis in the original order; obtain the triangular factor of the decomposition as in (34a); find the orthogonal estimates, $U = K^{\perp\prime}DV_{\cdot\cdot}$. ($l \times t$). Put rows of U on scratch $I/0$ file.

5. Error sum of products ($t \times t$). If $e = 0$, error matrix is within-groups sum of products, $S_E = S_W$ from input phase; $n_e = N - n$. If $e = 1$, error matrix is residual sum of products, $S_E = S_T - U'U$; $n_e = N - l$. If $e = 2$, error matrix is formed from the last n_e rows of U. Let $\mathbf{u}'_i$ be the i'th row of $U(1 \times t)$. Then $S_E = \sum_{i=k}^{l} \mathbf{u}_i\mathbf{u}'_i$, where $k = l - n_e + 1$; n_e is an additional input parameter.

6. Error variance-covariance matrix, $\hat{\Sigma}_v = V_E = (1/n_e)S_E$; error mean squares, $D_E = \text{diag}(V_E)$; error standard deviations, $D_E^{1/2}$; error correlation matrix $R_E = D_E^{-1/2}V_ED_E^{-1/2} = \hat{\mathcal{R}}$.

7. Least-squares estimates of leading c effects in model, $\hat{\Theta} = (T_c^{-1})'U_c$. T_c is leading ($c \times c$) submatrix of T from (34a). U_c is the leading c rows of U. Variance–covari-

ance factors of estimates from (20), $G = (T_c^{-1})'T_c^{-1}$; correlations among estimates, by reducing G to correlational form; standard errors of estimates, $\text{diag}[G \otimes \hat{\Sigma}]^{1/2}$. These may be put in $(c \times t)$ matrix form.

8. Estimated means, $\hat{V}. = K_c\hat{\Theta}$, where K_c are the leading c columns of the basis; mean residuals, $\hat{E}. = V. - \hat{V}.$; standard errors of residuals, from (29), $\text{diag}[(I - K_cGK_c') \otimes \hat{\Sigma}]^{1/2}$; combined estimated row and column means, from equally weighted rows of $\hat{V}..$.

9. Orthogonalize basis in any complete or partial alternate orders, compute orthogonal estimates for analysis phase, store on scratch I/O file.

OUTPUT QUANTITIES

1. Input parameters.
2. S_E, V_E, $D_E^{1/2}$, R_E, n_e.
3. $\hat{\Theta}$, variance-covariance factors and correlations among estimates, standard errors.
4. $\hat{V}.$, $\hat{E}.$, standard errors $\hat{E}.$, combined row and column estimated means.

c. Analysis

INPUT QUANTITIES

1. Number of dependent variables, p.
2. Number of covariates, or predictors for regression, q $(q \geqslant 0)$.
3. Key for grouping predictors, for tests of Q successive regression hypotheses (see next paragraph).
4. Key for grouping rows of U, for tests for analysis-of-variance or covariance hypotheses. The key defines the between-group degrees of freedom $[n_h$ of (35)] for a sequence of hypotheses about sections of Θ. The first element on the key (n_{h_1}) indicates that the leading n_{h_1} rows of U form the first hypothesis matrix as in (36). The second element (n_{h_2}) indicates that the subsequent n_{h_2} rows of U form the next hypothesis matrix, and so on. The additional subscript on n_h is necessary to distinguish the "degrees of freedom" of one hypothesis from another. The sum of the elements cannot exceed l, the total number of rows of Θ. One additional key for each of a alternate orders of estimating orthogonal effects.

ORDER OF CALCULATION

IF $q > 0$, PERFORM REGRESSION ANALYSIS AND COVARIATE ADJUSTMENTS.

1. Partition S_E into $S_E^{(yy)}$ $(p \times p)$, $S_E^{(yx)} = S_E^{(xy)'}(p \times q)$, $S_E^{(xx)}$ $(q \times q)$; D_E into $D_E^{(yy)}$ $(p \times p)$, $D_E^{(xx)}$ $(q \times q)$.
2. Regression coefficients, $\hat{B} = [S_E^{(xx)}]^{-1}S_E^{(xy)}$; standardized regression coefficients $\hat{\bar{B}} = [D_E^{(xx)}]^{1/2}\hat{B}[D_E^{(yy)}]^{-1/2}$; sum of products for regression, $S_R = S_E^{(yx)}\hat{B}$.
3. Residual sum of products, $S_E^* = S_E^{(yy)} - S_R$; residual degrees of freedom, $n_e^* = n_e - q$; residual variance-covariance matrix $\hat{\Sigma}^* = V_E^* = (1/n_e^*)S_E^*$; adjusted variances $D_E^* = \text{diag}(V_E^*)$; partial correlations, $R_E^* = [D_E^*]^{-1/2}V_E^*[D_E^*]^{-1/2}$.
4. Variance-covariance factors of regression coefficients, $G = [S_E^{(xx)}]^{-1}$; correlations among regression coefficients, by reducing G to correlational form; standard errors of regression coefficients, $\text{diag}[G \otimes \hat{\Sigma}^*]^{1/2}$. These may be put in $(q \times p)$ matrix form.

IF $c > 0$, ADJUST GROUP-MEAN ESTIMATES

5. Partition Θ_v into $\hat{\Theta}^{(y)}$ $(c \times p)$, $\hat{\Theta}^{(x)}$ $(c \times q)$; adjust $\hat{\Theta} = \hat{\Theta}^{(y)} - \hat{\Theta}^{(x)}\hat{B}$; covariance factors among adjusted estimates, $G = [(T_c^{-1})'T_c^{-1} + \hat{\Theta}^{(x)}(S_E^{(xx)})^{-1}\hat{\Theta}^{(x)'}]$; correlations among adjusted estimates, by reducing G to correlational form; standard errors of adjusted estimates, $\text{diag}[G \otimes \hat{\Sigma}^*]^{1/2}$. These may be put in $(c \times p)$ matrix form.
6. Adjusted treatment means. Partition $\hat{V}.$ into $\hat{Y}.$ $(n \times p)$, $\hat{X}.$ $(n \times q)$; $Y.^* = K\hat{\Theta} = \hat{Y}. - (\hat{X}. - 1\hat{x}..')\hat{B}$, where $\hat{x}..' = (1/n)\sum_{j=1}^{n}\hat{x}.'_j$; predicted means under analysis-of-covariance model. Partition $V.$ into $Y.$ $(n \times p)$, $X.$ $(n \times q)$; $\hat{Y}.^* = Y.^* + (X. - 1x..')\hat{B}$. Combined adjusted and adjusted predicted row and column means, from equally weighted rows of $Y.^*$ and $\hat{Y}.^*$ respectively;

mean residuals, adjusted for covariates, $\hat{E}.*$ $= Y. - \hat{Y}.*$.

REGRESSION TESTS

7. Parallelism of regression planes, if more than one group of subjects. Error sum of products for this test: partition each S_{w_j} into $S_{w_j}^{(yy)}$ $(p \times p)$, $S_{w_j}^{(xx)}$ $(q \times q)$, $S_{w_j}^{(yx)} = S_{w_j}^{(xy)\prime}(p \times q)$; $S = \Sigma_j[S_{w_j}^{(yy)} - S_{w_j}^{(yx)}(S_{w_j}^{(xx)})^{-1} \times S_{w_j}^{(xy)}]$ Error degrees of freedom are $n_e - nq$. Hypothesis sum of products, $S_E^* - S$; hypothesis degrees of freedom are $(n - 1)q$. Univariate and multivariate test statistics are computed as listed below for analysis-of-variance hypotheses.

8. Multiple correlation for each dependent variable, $\hat{R}_i^2 = \text{diag}_i(S_R)/\text{diag}_i$ $(S_E^{(yy)})$; F-statistic, $F_i = \hat{R}_i^2 n_e^*/(1 - \hat{R}_i^2)q$. Step-down tests are computed as for analysis-of-variance hypotheses with hypothesis and error matrices S_R and S_E^*, respectively.

9. Multivariate stepwise regression tests (assuming a fixed order of predictor variables). Orthogonal estimates, $U = [S_E^{(xx)}]^{-1/2}S_E^{(xy)}$, where $[S_E^{(xx)}]^{-1/2}$ is the inverse Cholesky factor of $S_E^{(xx)}$. The sum of products for regression for the ith predictor eliminating all preceding, is $S_H = \mathbf{u}_i\mathbf{u}_i'$, where $\mathbf{u}_i'$ is the $(1 \times p)$ ith row of U. The sum of products for a set of n_h consecutive predictors, eliminating all preceding, is S_H $= U_h'U_h = \sum_{i=k}^{k+n_h-1} \mathbf{u}_i\mathbf{u}_i'$, where U_h is the corresponding $n_h \times p$ submatrix of U. Predictor x_k is the first of the set. The grouping of predictors for regression tests can be indicated on a grouping key, entered for the analysis phase. For each element on the key, the corresponding number of rows of U (n_h rows) give $S_H(p \times p)$. For each S_H, the error matrix is $S_E^{(yy)} - \sum_{i=1}^{k+n_h-1} \mathbf{u}_i\mathbf{u}_i'$. This is S_E^* plus sums of products for all predictors following those being tested. Degrees of freedom for hypothesis and error are n_h and $n_e - (k + n_h - 1)$, respectively. Univariate,

multivariate, and step-down test criteria are the same as those for testing analysis-of-variance hypotheses.

10. Canonical correlation analysis. The squared correlations are the nonzero characteristic roots of $[(S_E^{(yy)})^{-1/2} S_R \times (S_E^{(yy)})^{-1/2}]$, where $[S_E^{(yy)}]^{-1/2}$ is the inverse Cholesky factor of $S_E^{(yy)}$. The weight vectors for the dependent variables are the corresponding characteristic vectors W, multiplied by a scaling factor and the triangular transformation, that is, $\hat{A}^{(y)} = \sqrt{n_e}[S_e^{(yy)}]^{-1/2\prime}W$ $(p \times s)$. The weights for the independent variables are $\hat{A}^{(x)} = \hat{B}\hat{A}^{(y)}\hat{P}^{-1}$. The weights may be put in standard metric by $[D_E^{(yy)}]^{1/2}\hat{A}^{(y)}$ and $[D_E^{(xx)}]^{1/2}\hat{A}^{(x)}$. The correlations of the original measures and the canonical variates are $(1/n_e) [D_E^{(yy)}]^{-1/2}S_E^{(yy)}\hat{A}^{(y)}$, and $(1/n_e)[D_e^{\text{nxx}}]^{-1/2}S_E^{(xx)}\hat{A}^{(x)}$. Successive tests of all correlations, all minus the largest, and so on, are obtained directly from (70) and (71). The percentage of variation in the criterion measures accounted for by correlation $\hat{\rho}_i$ is $100\hat{\rho}_i^2/p$.

Analysis of Variance (or covariance).

FOR EACH ORDER OF EFFECTS IN ANALYSIS-OF-VARIANCE MODEL ($a + 1$ ORDERS):

1. Identify consecutive elements of the "grouping key" for U (degrees of freedom between groups). For each element taken individually, form S_H as the sum of cross-products of the corresponding number of rows (n_{h_j}) of U, as in (36), and perform the following steps. S_H is the ($t \times t$) sum of products for n_h effects, eliminating all preceding effects. n_h is the degrees of freedom for the hypothesis matrix.

2. If $q > 0$, adjust S_H for covariates. S_E^* is the adjusted error sum of cross-products, from regression. Form $S_T = S_H + S_E$. Partition S_T into $S_T^{(yy)}$ $(p \times p)$, $S_T^{(yx)} = S_T^{(xy)\prime}$ $(p \times q)$, and $S_T^{(xx)}$ $(q \times q)$. Adjust S_T by $S_T^* = S_T^{(yy)} - S_T^{(yx)}(S_T^{(xx)})^{-1}S_T^{(xy)}$. The adjusted hypothesis matrix is $S_H^* = S_T^* - S_E^*$. S_E^* with n_e^* degrees of freedom, and S_H^*,

substitute for S_E with n_e degrees of freedom, and S_H, respectively, to test analysis-of-variance hypotheses.

TEST CRITERIA.

3. Multivariate likelihood ratio test. Represent the hypothesis and error matrix by S_H and S_E, respectively, regardless of whether regression, variance, or covariance hypotheses are tested. The respective degrees of freedom for significance tests are represented as n_h and n_e. Find the Cholesky factors of S_E and $(S_E + S_H)$; that is, factor $S_E = T_E T_E'$ and $(S_E + S_H) = TT'$. The log of the likelihood ratio is

$$\lambda = 2 \left[\sum_{i=1}^{p} \log(t_e)_{ii} - \sum_{i=1}^{p} \log(t_{ii}) \right]$$

The likelihood ratio is $\Lambda = e^\lambda$. The corresponding F-statistic and degrees of freedom are computed directly from (41) and (41a). When s is undefined ($pn_h = 2$), substituting $s = 1$ will provide an appropriate test value.

4. Univariate and step-down test statistics. Univariate:

$$F_i = \frac{\left[(s_h)_{ii} / n_h \right]}{\left[(s_e)_{ii} / n_e \right]} = \frac{(m_h)_i}{(m_e)_i}$$

($i = 1, 2, \ldots, p$). m_h and m_e are hypothesis and error mean squares. Degrees of freedom are n_h and n_e for each ratio.

Step-down:

$$F_i^* = \frac{\left\{ \left[t_{ii}^2 - (t_e)_{ii}^2 \right] / n_h \right\}}{\left[(t_e)_{ii}^2 / (n_e - i + 1) \right]}$$

$$= \frac{(m_h^*)_i}{(m_e^*)_i}, \qquad (i = 1, 2, \ldots, p)$$

Degrees of freedom are n_h and $n_e - i + 1$, for F_i^*

5. Variances of the discriminant variables are the r nonzero characteristic roots of $S_E^{-1/2} S_H (S_E^{-1/2})'$ where $S_E^{-1/2}$ is the inverse Cholesky factor of S_E. Represent roots

by λ_i ($i = 1, 2, \ldots, r$). The weight vectors are the corresponding characteristic vectors W, multiplied by the scaling factor n_e, and the triangular transformation, that is, $\hat{A} = \sqrt{n_e} (S_E^{-1/2})' W$. $\hat{A}$ and W are ($p \times r$) matrices. The standardized weights are $[D_{iE}]^{1/2} \hat{A}$. Roy's criterion for λ_i is $\lambda_i / (1 + \lambda_i)$. The trace criterion is $\sum_{i=1}^{r} \lambda_i$. The m and n arguments for the trace and largest root criteria are given by (43a) and (43b). Roots two through r are tested, reducing n_e and n_h by one for each previous root excluded. Successive likelihood ratio criteria are computed exactly as in (42). Between-group effects may be estimated for the discriminant variables by transforming $\hat{\Theta}_h$. $\hat{\Theta}_h \hat{A}$ is the ($n_h \times r$) matrix of contrast estimates. Mean differences are in within-group standard deviation units for the discriminant functions.

OUTPUT QUANTITIES

Regression Analysis.

1. $\hat{B}$, $\hat{B}$, standard errors, variance–covariance factors and correlations among regression coefficients, S_R, S_E^*, n_e^*, $\hat{\Sigma}^*$, R_E^*, $[D_E^*]^{1/2}$.

2. $\hat{\Theta}$ adjusted, standard errors, variance–covariance factors, and correlations among adjusted estimates.

3. $Y.^*$, $\hat{Y}.^*$ for all groups, for rows and columns of design; $\hat{E}.^*$ adjusted, rank of analysis-of-covariance model.

4. Univariate, multivariate, and step-down tests of regression parallelism, degrees of freedom for hypothesis and error.

5. $\hat{R}_i^2$, $\hat{R}_i$, F_i, step-down F_i^* for multiple correlations.

6. For each predictor or set, multivariate F-statistic, p univariate and step-down F-statistics, degrees of freedom for hypothesis and error.

7. Canonical correlations, squared correlations, weights for both sets of variables in raw, standardized, and correlational form; s successive test statistics and degrees of freedom, for all canonical correlations, all

minus the largest, and so on; proportion of criterion variation attributable to each correlation.

Analysis of Variance or Covariance.

1. For each hypothesis, multivariate F-statistic, likelihood ratio, log likelihood, degrees of freedom; p univariate F-statistics, hypothesis mean squares; p step-down F-statistics, hypothesis and error mean squares, degrees of freedom for hypothesis and error.

2. Variance of r discriminant variables; r weight vectors in raw and standarized form; Roy's criterion, m and n arguments for each discriminant function; Hotelling's trace criterion; r successive test statistics, and degrees of freedom, for all discriminant functions, all minus the largest, all minus the largest two, and so on; estimated contrasts in discriminant variable metric.

3. Results of 1 and 2 in a alternate orders of effects.

4. FLOW CHART

The flow chart is given on pages 229–240. The three phases conform to those of the MULTIVARIANCE program [10]: Input, Estimation of analysis-of-variance parameters, Analysis-of-variance hypothesis testing and regression analysis. Details are not provided for simple operations. In actual computation, an accurate and efficient matrix subroutine package such as the MATCAL system [6], is indispensable. Program listings for the Gram–Schmidt and Cholesky operations are included. For further description of these techniques, see Bock [5, Ch. 2] and [9]. A flow chart for generating the vectors of a design basis from "symbolic contrast vectors" (*SCV*s) is given by Bock [4, pp. 90–92] and is not reproduced here.

5. DESCRIPTION OF FLOW CHART

Box 1: Parameters read:
t = total number of measured input variables

f = number of factors
f_i = number of levels for factor i ($i = 1, 2, \ldots, f$)

Parameters initialized:

$$n = \prod_{i=1}^{f} f_i = \text{total number of cells}$$

n_0 = number of cells with at least one observation

Box 2: $\mathbf{v}_{ij} = t \times 1$ vector containing values for all variables, observation i, cell j

Box 3: Cell sums: $\mathbf{v}_{+j}$
Cell frequencies n_j
Total sum of squares and cross products:

$$S_T = \sum_j S_j \, (t \times t)$$

where $S_j = \sum_i \mathbf{v}_{ij} \mathbf{v}'_{ij}$

Box 4: Cell means: $\mathbf{v}_{+j}/n_j = \mathbf{v}_{\cdot j}$ where $\mathbf{v}_{+j} = \sum_j \mathbf{v}_{ij} \, (t \times 1)$
Matrix of means: $V.$ ($n \times t$) Total number of observations: $N = \sum_j n_j$, where n_j = number of observations in cell j

Box 5: Transformation matrix: A ($t' \times t$), where t' is the number of new variables

Box 6: Transformed means: $V.A'$
Transformed total sum of cross products: AS_TA'

Box 7: Parameters read:
l = rank of analysis-of-variance model matrix
c = rank of model for estimation ($c \leqslant l$)
e = error term parameter
a = number of alternative orders of the basis matrix
g = number of factors having arbitrary contrasts
o = number of factors having orthogonal polynomials

Box 8: Basis matrices (46) and (46a)

Box 9: Basis matrices (46) and (46a)

Box 10:
(a) Matrix of basis vectors K (50)
(b) Triangular factor of decomposition T (30); T satisfies $K'DK = TT'$, where D is a diagonal matrix of cell frequencies

(c) Orthogonal estimates, U (33); $U = (K^\perp)'DY$. where

(1) $K^\perp$ is orthonormal and satisfies $K^\perp T' = K$

(2) D is as above

(3) Y. is the matrix of means

Box 11:   Orthogonal estimates, U (33)

Box 12:   Error sum of cross products $S_{E'}$

(a) If the error term is within, S_E is given by (22)

(b) If the error term is residual, S_E is given by (37)

(c) If the error term is special effects, S_E is given by (37a)

Box 13:   Variances: D_E, where $D_E = \text{diag}(1/n_e)S_e$; $n_E = $ degrees of freedom for error

Standard deviations: $D_E^{1/2}$

Correlation matrix: $R_E = D_E^{-1/2}S_E D_E^{-1/2}/n_e$

Box 14:   Least-squares estimates of effects, $\hat{\Theta}$ (95)

$$\hat{\Theta} = (T^{-1})'U$$

Box 15:   Variance–covariance factors of estimates, G (20)

Box 16:   Standard errors of least-squares estimates (20) and (21)

Box 17:   Variance–covariance factors of estimates, G (see Box 15)

Correlations among estimates: G in correlation form

Box 18:   Estimated cell means, $\hat{V}. = K_c\hat{\Theta}$, where K_c constitutes the leading c columns of the basis

Box 19:   Raw residuals, $\hat{E}. = V. - \hat{V}.$; standardized residuals, elements of $\hat{E}.$ divided by variable standard deviations, residuals as t-statistics. $\hat{E}.$ elements divided by standard errors from (29)

Box 20: $D = $ diagonal matrix of eigenvalues of S_E, the error sum of products in covariance or correlation form.

$V = $ matrix of eigenvectors of S_E in covariance or correlation form.

Box 21: $VD^{1/2} = $ Principal components;

$\text{Diag}_i(D^{1/2}) = $ square root of the ith eigenvalue

$$\frac{100 D_{ii}}{p} = \% \text{ of variation for the } i\text{th eigenvalue}$$

Box 22: $S_H = U_h'U_h = $ hypothesis sum of cross products (Eq. 36), where U_h is n_h rows of orthogonal estimates

$n_h = $ degrees of freedom for the hypothesis

Box 23: $S_{H_0} = S_T - U_{h_0}'U_{h_0} = $ sum of cross-products for last hypothesis, where

$U_{h_0} = $ all but the last n_{h_0} rows of orthogonal estimates

$n_{h_0} = $ degrees of freedom for the last hypothesis

Box 23a: see (87)–(89)

Box 24: $F = \dfrac{S_H/n_h}{S_e/n_e} = F - $ statistic for hypothesis where $S_H/n_h = $ hypothesis mean square, $S_E/n_e = $ error mean square

Box 25: $\Lambda = \prod\limits_{i=1}^{p} \left(\dfrac{(t_e)_{ii}}{t_{ii}}\right)^2 = $ Wilks' Λ

for this hypothesis (39) where

$(t_e)_{ii} = \text{diag}_i(T_E)$, $S_E = T_E T_E'$

$t_i = \text{diag}_i(T)$, $S_E + S_H = TT'$

T_E and T are triangular Cholesky factors

$F = $ multivariate F statistic is based on this Λ (41, 41a)

For each dependent variable:

$$(m_h)_i = \frac{(s_h)_{ii}}{n_h} = \text{hypothesis mean square, variable } i$$

where $(s_h)_{ii} = \text{diag}_i(S_H)$

$$F_i = \frac{(m_h)_i}{(s_e)_{ii}/n_e} = \text{univariate } F, \text{ variable } i$$

where $(s_e)_{ii} = \text{diag}_i(S_E)$

$$F_i^* = \frac{\left[t_{ii}^2 - (t_e)_{ii}^2 \right]/n_h}{(t_e)_{ii}^2/(n_e - i + 1)} = \text{step-down } F,$$
variable i

where t_{ii} and $(t_e)_{ii}$ are as above; n_h and $n_e - i + 1$ are the degrees of freedom

Box 26: $M_H = S_H/n_h = $ hypothesis mean squares and cross-products

Box 27: $\lambda_i = i$th nonzero characteristic root of $T_E^{-1}S_H(T_E^{-1})' = $ variance of the ith discriminant variable $(i = 1, 2, \ldots, r)$; T_E is as in Box 25.

Box 28: $100\lambda_i/\Sigma\lambda_i = \%$ canonical variation, discriminant variable i

$\lambda_i/1 + \lambda_i = $ Roy's criterion

$A = \sqrt{n_e}\ T_E^{-1}W = $ discriminant function coefficients, where $W = $ matrix of eigenvectors of $T_E^{-1}S_H(T_E^{-1})'$

$(D_E^{1/2})A = $ standardized discriminant function coefficients

Box 29: $\Sigma\lambda_i = $ Hotelling's trace criterion

$$\chi^2 = -M \sum_{i=j}^{r} \log\left(\frac{1}{1 + \lambda_i} \right)$$

$= $ Bartlett's chi-square test for roots j through r (40, 42)

Box 30: $\hat{\Theta}_h A = $ Canonical form of least-square estimates, for one hypothesis only where $\hat{\Theta}_h$ consists of n_h rows of estimated effects

Box 31: $S_E = $ error sum of cross products

$S_E^{(yy)} = $ sum of cross products for dependent variables

$S_E^{(xy)} = $ sum of cross products for independent $\times$ dependent variables

$S_E^{(xx)} = $ sum of cross products for independent variables

Box 32: $\hat{B} = [S_E^{(xx)}]^{-1}S_E^{(xy)} = $ regression coefficients

$\hat{B} = [D_E^{(xx)}]^{1/2}\hat{B}[E_E^{(yy)}]^{-1/2} = $ standardized regression coefficients

$S_R = S_E^{(yx)}\hat{B} = $ regression sum of cross-products

$S_E^* = S_E^{(yy)} - S_R = $ residual error sum of cross-products

Box 33: $\text{Diag}(G \times \hat{\Sigma}^*)^{1/2} = $ standard errors of regression coefficients where $G = (S_E^{(xx)})^{-1}$

$\hat{\Sigma}^* = (1/n_e^*) S_E^* = V_E^* = $ residual variance-covariance matrix

$n_e^* = n_e - q = $ residual degrees of freedom

Box 34: $D_E^* = \text{diag}(V_E^*) = $ adjusted variances

$R_E^* = [D_E^*]^{-1/2}V_E^*[D_E^*]^{-1/2} = $ partial correlations among criteria

Box 35: $\hat{\Theta} = \hat{\Theta}^{(y)} - \hat{\Theta}^{(x)}\hat{B} = $ adjusted least-squares estimates

Box 36: $\text{Diag}(G \times \hat{\Sigma}^*)^{1/2} = $ standard errors of adjusted estimates, where $\hat{\Sigma}^* = V_E^*$ $G = \text{variance} - \text{covariance factors among}$ adjusted estimates (81a)

Box 37: $G = $ Variance-covariance factors among adjusted estimates (81a); correlations among estimates: G in correlation form

Box 38: $Y_{\cdot}^* = \hat{Y}_{\cdot} - (\hat{X}_{\cdot} - 1\hat{x}'_{\cdot\cdot})\hat{B} = $ adjusted estimated cell means

Box 39: $\hat{E}_{\cdot}^* = Y_{\cdot} - \hat{Y}_{\cdot}^* = $ adjusted residuals where $\hat{Y}_{\cdot}^* = Y_{\cdot}^* + (X_{\cdot} - 1x'_{\cdot\cdot})\hat{B}$

Box 40: $$\Lambda = \prod_{i=1}^{p} \frac{(t_e)_{ii}^2}{t_{ii}^2} = \text{Wilks' } \Lambda \text{ for}$$

parallelism test where $(t_e)_{ii} = \text{diag}_i(T_E)$ and T_E is the triangular Cholesky factor of

$S = \Sigma_j[S_{w_j}^{(yy)} - S_{w_j}^{(yx)}(S_{w_j}^{(xx)})^{-1}S_{w_j}^{(xy)}]$

$S_{w_j}^{(yy)} = $ sum of products of mean deviations for the jth group, dependent variables

$S_{w_j}^{(xy)} = $ sum of products of mean deviations for the jth group, dependent $\times$ independent variables

$S_{w_j}^{(xx)} = $ sum of products of mean deviations for the jth group, independent variables

$t_{ii} = \text{Diag}_i(T)$, $S_E^* = TT'$

Multivariate F-statistic is based on this Λ.

$$F_i = \frac{(s_h)_{ii}/(n-1)q}{s_{ii}/n_e - nq} = \text{univariate } F, \text{ variable } i$$

where $(s_h)_{ii} = \text{diag}_i(S_E^* - S)$
$\quad s_{ii} = \text{diag}_i(S)$
$\quad n = $ total number of groups
$\quad q = $ number of covariates

$$F_i^* = \frac{[t_{ii}^2 - (t_e)_{ii}^2]/(n-1)q}{(t_e)_{ii}^2/(n_e - nq - i + 1)}$$

$= $ Step-down F for variable i

Box 41: $\hat{R}_i^2 = \text{diag}_i(S_R)/\text{diag}_i(S_E^{(yy)}) = $ square multiple correlation coefficient

$\hat{R}_i = \sqrt{\hat{R}_i^2} = $ multiple correlation coefficient
$F_i = \hat{R}_i^2 n_e^* /(1 - \hat{R}_i)^2 q = $ univariate F

$$F_i^* = \frac{[t_{ii}^2 - (t_e)_{ii}^2]/q}{(t_e)_{ii}^2/(n_e^* - i + 1)} = \text{step-down } F$$

where $t_{ii} = \text{diag}_i(T)$, $S_E^{(yy)} = TT'$
$(t_e)_{ii} = \text{diag}_i(T^*)$, $S_E^* = T^*T^{*'}$
T and T^* are triangular Cholesky factors (Eq. 45)
$\quad \Lambda = |S_E^*|/|S_E^{(yy)}| = $ Wilks' Λ for association between dependent and independent variables.
Multivariate F statistic is based on this Λ (41).

Box 42: $\hat{\rho}_i^2 = i$th characteristic root of $T^{-1}S_R(T^{-1})' = i$th squared canonical correlation [Eqs. (67), (67a)], where $S_E^{(yy)} = TT'$; T is the triangular Cholesky factor
$W = $ matrix of eigenvectors of $T^{-1}S_R(T^{-1})'$ [Eqs. (67), (67a)]
$\hat{\rho}_i = \sqrt{\hat{\rho}_i^2} = i$th canonical correlation
$\hat{A}^{(y)} = \sqrt{n_e}(T^{-1})'W = $ coefficients for dependent variables
$\hat{A}^{(x)} = \hat{B}\hat{A}^{(y)}\hat{P}^{-1} = $ coefficients for independent variables where $\text{diag}_i(\hat{P}) = \hat{\rho}_i$
$(D_E^{(yy)})^{1/2}\hat{A}^{(y)} = $ standardized coefficients for dependent variables
$(D_E^{(xx)})^{1/2}\hat{A}^{(x)} = $ standardized coefficients

for independent variables
$100\hat{\rho}_i^2/p = \%$ variation accounted for by the ith canonical correlation $\chi^2 = -M \log \Lambda_j$. where M is given by Eq. (40) and Λ_j is given by Eq. (71). χ^2 is the test statistic for all correlations minus the j largest values.

Box 43:   For the ith group of covariates

$$\Lambda = \frac{|S_{H_i}|}{|S_{H_{i-1}}|} = \text{Wilks' } \Lambda \text{ for adding this group of covariates}$$

where $S_{H_i} = $ Error sum of products with covariates in groups 1 through i removed
$S_{H_0} = S_E^{(yy)}$
F-Test for adding this group of covariates is based on this Λ.

$$\frac{100[\text{Diag}_j(S_{H_{i-1}}) - \text{Diag}_j(S_{H_i})]}{\text{Diag}_j(S_E^{(yy)})}$$

$= $ percent additional variance accounted for, variable j

$$F_j = \frac{[\text{Diag}_j(S_{H_{i-1}}) - \text{Diag}_j(S_{H_i})]/n_i'}{\text{Diag}_j(S_{H_i})/\left(n_e - \sum_{k=1}^{i} n_k\right)}$$

$= $ univariate F − statistic for variable j

where
$\quad n_i = $ number of covariates in group i
$\quad n_e = $ degrees of freedom for error, with no covariate adjustment

$$F_j^* = \frac{t_{jj}^2 - (t_e)_{jj}^2/n_i}{(t_e)_{jj}^2/\left(n_e - \sum_{k=1}^{i} n_i - j + 1\right)}$$

$= $ Step-down F for variable j (45)

where $t_{jj} = \text{Diag}_j(T)$, $S_{H_{i-1}} = TT'$
$\quad (t_e)_{jj} = \text{Diag}_j(T_E)$, $S_{H_i} = TT'$
T and T_E are triangular Cholesky factors

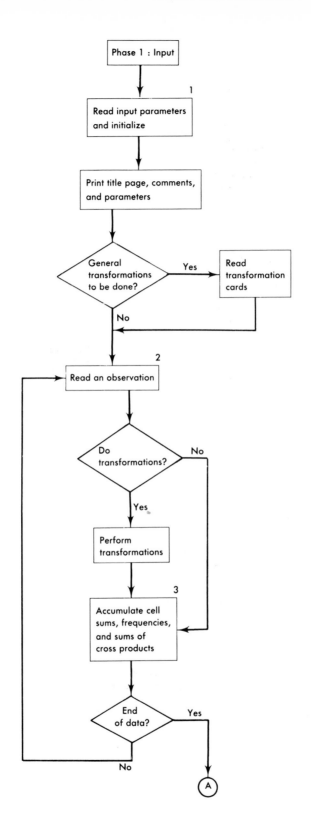

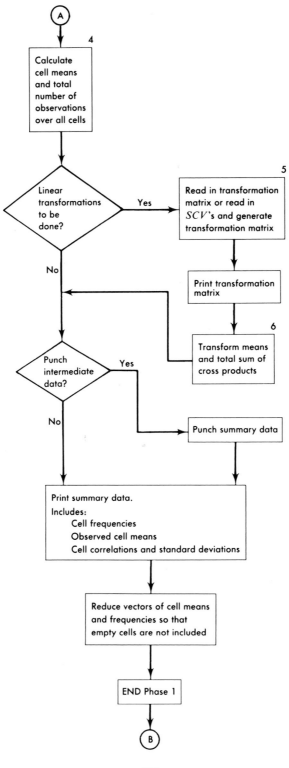

230

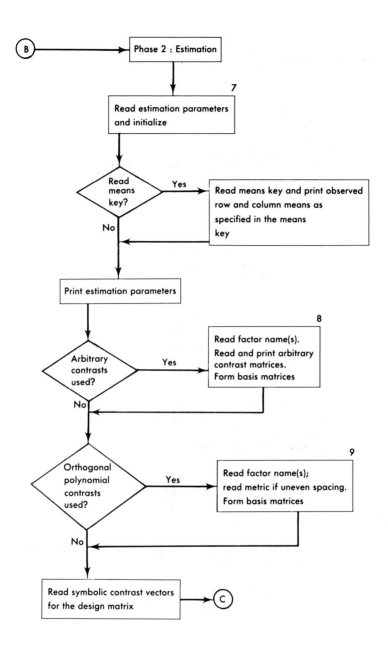

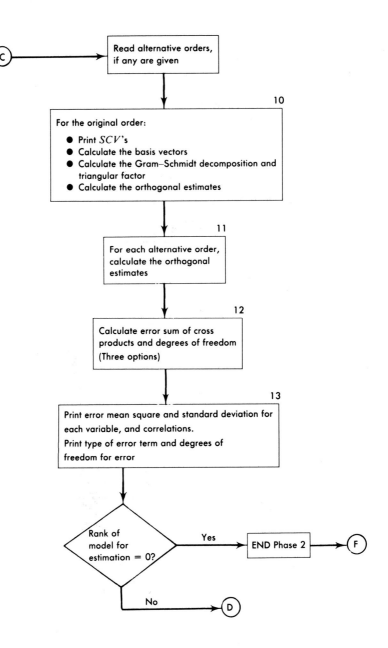

C

Read alternative orders,
if any are given

10

For the original order:

- Print SCV's
- Calculate the basis vectors
- Calculate the Gram–Schmidt decomposition and triangular factor
- Calculate the orthogonal estimates

11

For each alternative order, calculate the orthogonal estimates

12

Calculate error sum of cross products and degrees of freedom (Three options)

13

Print error mean square and standard deviation for each variable, and correlations.
Print type of error term and degrees of freedom for error

Rank of model for estimation = 0?

Yes → END Phase 2 → F

No → D

232

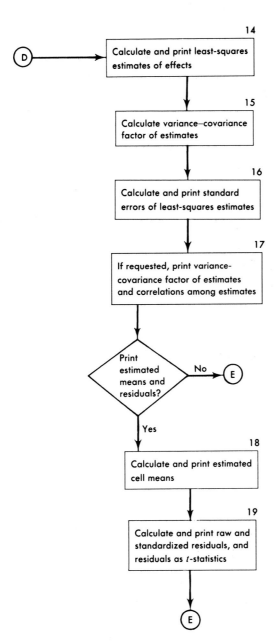

14 Calculate and print least-squares estimates of effects

15 Calculate variance–covariance factor of estimates

16 Calculate and print standard errors of least-squares estimates

17 If requested, print variance-covariance factor of estimates and correlations among estimates

Print estimated means and residuals? — No → E

Yes

18 Calculate and print estimated cell means

19 Calculate and print raw and standardized residuals, and residuals as t-statistics

E

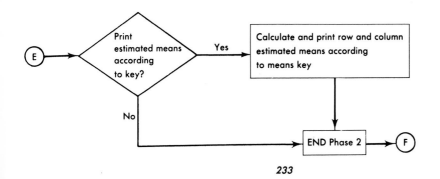

E → Print estimated means according to key? — Yes → Calculate and print row and column estimated means according to means key

No

END Phase 2 → F

233

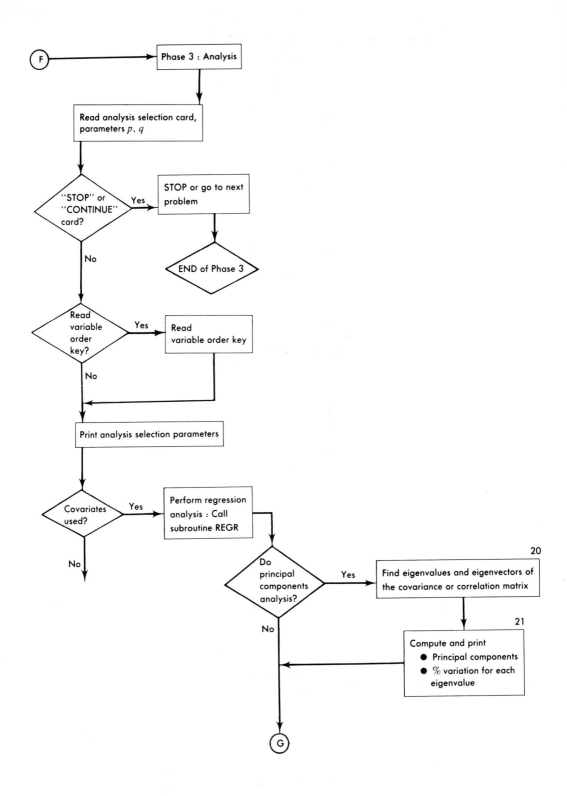

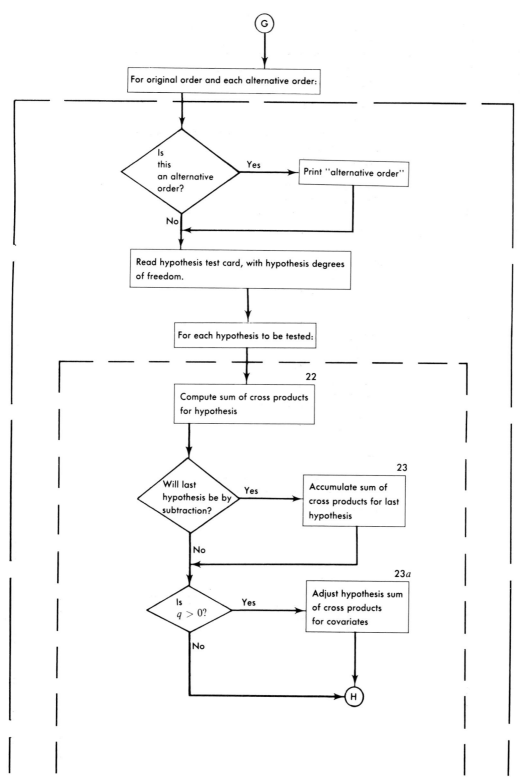

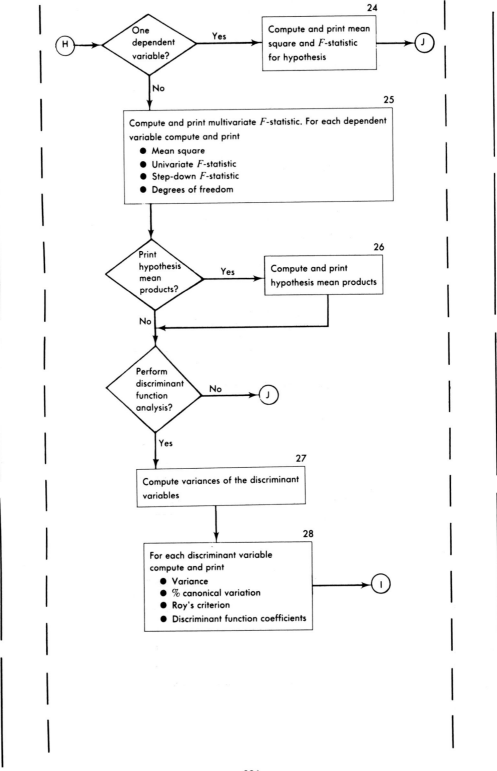

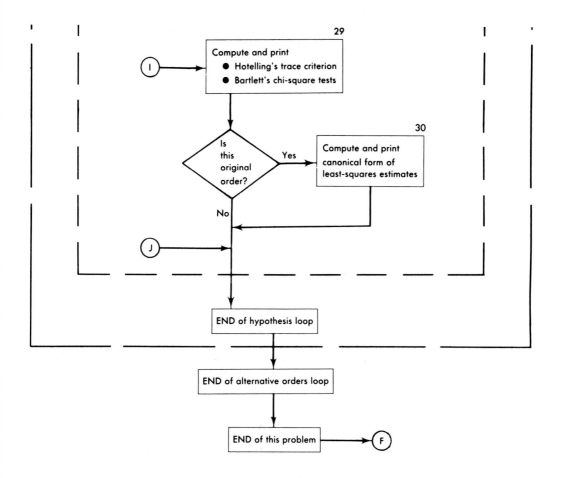

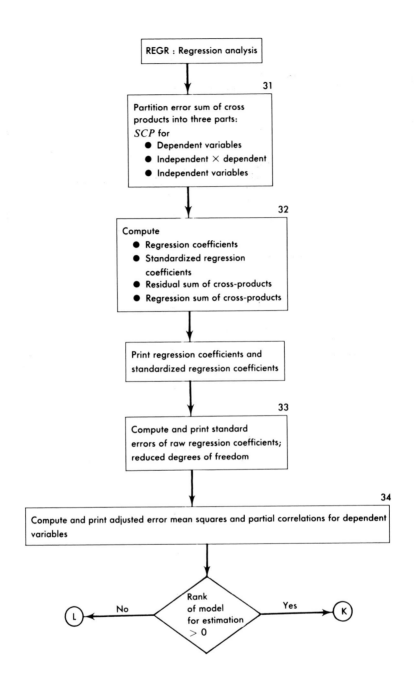

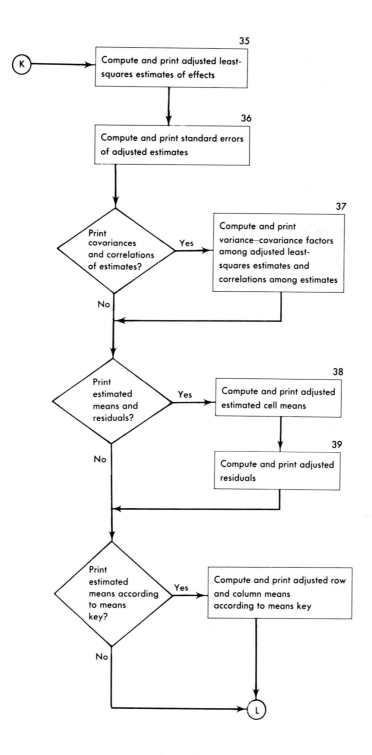

239

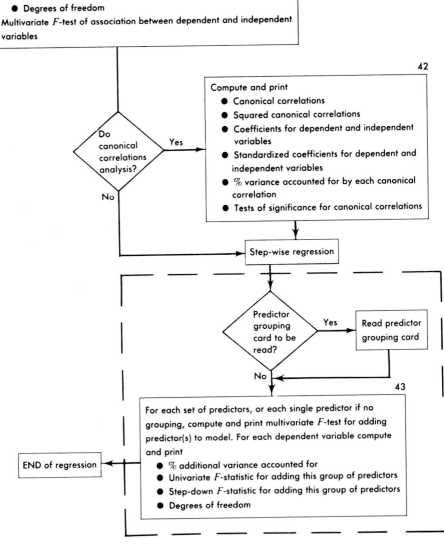

6. THE PROGRAM

Fortran routines for the modified Gram–Schmidt and Cholesky factorizations are provided here.

7. SAMPLE PROBLEM

Annotated computer output listings are given for a one-way, four-level analysis of variance and covariance problem. The output listings were produced by the MULTI-

VARIANCE program, Version 5 [10]. Since all data and problem parameters are printed, input listings are not included.

8. ESTIMATION OF RUNNING TIME

Running time is a function of the parameters of the particular problem run. The problem of Section 7 requires about 7.8 seconds of central processing time on the Control Data Corporation 6400 computer, under the Kronos operating system.

```
* * * * * * * * * M U L T I V A R I A N C E * * * * * * * * *
       *                                           *
     *       UNIVARIATE AND MULTIVARIATE ANALYSIS OF     *
       *       VARIANCE, COVARIANCE AND REGRESSION       *
         *        VERSION 5          MARCH 1972        *
           *                                       *
           * * * * * * * * * * * * * * * * *

                         PROBLEM
         - - - - - - - - - - - - - - - - - - - - - - - - -

         EXAMPLE PROBLEM  ---  ONE-WAY ANALYSIS OF VARIANCE,

         ANALYSIS OF COVARIANCE  ---  EQUAL SAMPLE SIZES

         - - - - - - - - - - - - - - - - - - - - - - - - -

  THE DATA CARDS ARE PUNCHED AS FOLLOWS-
     CARD COLUMN 1      EXPERIMENTAL CONDITION (1,2,3,4,)
               2-3      WORD LIST (1,2)
               4-6      SUBJECT IDENTIFICATION
               7-8      SEX (1=M)
                           (2=F)
               9-13     NUMBER OF WORDS RECALLED TRIAL 6
               14-18    NUMBER OF EXPERIMENTERS CATEGORIES RECONSTRUCTED TRIAL6
               19-21    NUMBER OF CATEGORIES IN PROBLEM
                           (10 FOR GROUPS 1 AND 2)
                           ( 5 FOR GROUPS 3 AND 4)
               22-27    TIME TRIAL 1 (SECONDS)
               28-33    TIME TRIAL 2
               34-39    TIME TRIAL 3
               40-45    TIME TRIAL 4
               46-51    TIME TRIAL 5
               52-57    TIME TRIAL 6

                      INPUT PARAMETERS
                      ================

         NUMBER OF VARIABLES IN INPUT VECTORS=           6

         NUMBER OF FACTORS IN DESIGN=                    1

           NUMBER OF LEVELS OF FACTOR 1 (TASK  ) =     4

         NUMBER OF VARIABLES AFTER TRANSFORMATIONS=      6

         INPUT IS FROM CARDS. DATA OPTION 3

         DATA WILL BE LISTED

         MINIMAL PAGE SPACING WILL BE USED

         ADDITIONAL OUTPUT WILL PRINTED

         DEBUG OUTPUT WILL BE PRINTED

         FORMAT OF DATA
           (8X2F5.0,F3.0,3(6XF6.0))              VARIABLE FORMAT CARD

                      TRANSFORMATIONS
```

```
- - - - - - - - - - - - - - - - - - - - - - - - - - - - - - - - - - - - - -

                    VARIABLE    2 WILL BE FORMED BY APPLYING TRANSFORMATION (    X/Y    ) TO
                    INPUT VARIABLES V(I):  X=V(    2), Y=V(   3), Z=V(  -0), C=    -0.00000.

- - - - - - - - - - - - - - - - - - - - - - - - - - - - - - - - - - - - - -



   SUBJECT    1 , CELL   1
      BEFORE TRANSFORMATIONS =    50.0000    10.0000    10.0000    83.0000    77.0000    75.0000
      AFTER TRANSFORMATIONS =     50.0000     1.0000    10.0000    83.0000    77.0000    75.0000
   SUBJECT    2 , CELL   1
      BEFORE TRANSFORMATIONS =    36.0000    10.0000    10.0000   136.0000   106.0000   116.0000
      AFTER TRANSFORMATIONS =     36.0000     1.0000    10.0000   136.0000   106.0000   116.0000
   SUBJECT    3 , CELL   1
      BEFORE TRANSFORMATIONS =    31.0000     9.0000    10.0030   144.0000   111.0000   115.0000
      AFTER TRANSFORMATIONS =     31.0000      .9000    10.0000   144.0000   111.0000   115.0000
   SUBJECT    4 , CELL   1
      BEFORE TRANSFORMATIONS =    35.0000     9.0000    10.0000   133.0000   102.0000    91.0000
      AFTER TRANSFORMATIONS =     35.0000      .9000    10.0000   133.0000   102.0000    91.0000
   SUBJECT    5 , CELL   1
      BEFORE TRANSFORMATIONS =    43.0000    10.0000    10.0000   201.0000   125.0000   147.0000
      AFTER TRANSFORMATIONS =     43.0000     1.0000    10.0000   201.0000   125.0000   147.0000
   SUBJECT    6 , CELL   1
      BEFORE TRANSFORMATIONS =    49.0000    10.0000    10.0000   161.0000   164.0000   129.0000
      AFTER TRANSFORMATIONS =     49.0000     1.0000    10.0000   161.0000   164.0000   129.0000
   SUBJECT    7 , CELL   1
      BEFORE TRANSFORMATIONS =    31.0000     9.0000    10.0000   178.0000   169.0000   135.0000
      AFTER TRANSFORMATIONS =     31.0000      .9000    10.0000   178.0000   169.0000   135.0000
   SUBJECT    8 , CELL   1
      BEFORE TRANSFORMATIONS =    33.0000     9.0000    10.0000   338.0000   129.0000   103.0000
      AFTER TRANSFORMATIONS =     33.0000      .9000    10.0000   338.0000   129.0000   103.0000
   SUBJECT    9 , CELL   1
      BEFORE TRANSFORMATIONS =    36.0000    10.3000    10.0000   112.0000    91.0000    86.0000
      AFTER TRANSFORMATIONS =     36.0000     1.0000    10.0000   112.0000    91.0000    86.0000
   SUBJECT   10 , CELL   1
      BEFORE TRANSFORMATIONS =    41.0000    10.0000    10.0000   126.0000   133.0000    74.0000
      AFTER TRANSFORMATIONS =     41.0000     1.0000    10.0000   126.0000   133.0000    74.0000
   SUBJECT   11 , CELL   1
      BEFORE TRANSFORMATIONS =    45.0000    10.0000    10.0000   126.0000   100.0000    94.0000
      AFTER TRANSFORMATIONS =     45.0000     1.0000    10.0000   126.0000   100.0000    94.0000
   SUBJECT   12 , CELL   1
      BEFORE TRANSFORMATIONS =    48.0000    10.0000    10.0000   129.0000    85.0000   118.0000
      AFTER TRANSFORMATIONS =     48.0000     1.0000    10.0000   129.0000    85.0000   118.0000

            GROUP   TASK   1
            =================================================


                                                        SUBCLASS COVARIANCE MATRIX
                           ----------------------------------------------------------------

                          1          2          3          4          5          6
                       WORDS       CATS       NCAT     TIME 2     TIME 4     TIME 6

          1   WORDS     49.788
          2   CATS        .267      .002
          3   NCAT        .000      .000      .000
          4   TIME 2   -176.348    -1.552      .000   4229.356
          5   TIME 4    -50.455     -.427      .000    864.818    848.727
          6   TIME 6    -16.779     -.148      .000    566.598    365.545    557.174



                                                        SUBCLASS CORRELATION MATRIX



                           ----------------------------------------------------------------

                          1          2          3          4          5          6
                       WORDS       CATS       NCAT     TIME 2     TIME 4     TIME 6

          1   WORDS    1.000000
          2   CATS      .767572  1.000000
          3   NCAT      .000000  0.000000  1.000000
          4   TIME 2   -.384702  -.484541   .000000  1.000000
          5   TIME 4   -.245445  -.297874   .000000   .456461  1.000000
          6   TIME 6   -.098339  -.127761   .000000   .369099   .531572  1.000000


   SUBJECT   13 , CELL   2
      BEFORE TRANSFORMATIONS =    50.0000    10.0000    10.0000   130.0000   110.0000   101.0000
      AFTER TRANSFORMATIONS =     50.0000     1.0000    10.0000   130.0000   110.0000   101.0000
   SUBJECT   14 , CELL   2
      BEFORE TRANSFORMATIONS =    49.0000    10.0000    10.0000   317.0000   302.0000   212.0000
      AFTER TRANSFORMATIONS =     49.0000     1.0000    10.0000   317.0000   302.0000   212.0000
   SUBJECT   15 , CELL   2
      BEFORE TRANSFORMATIONS =    44.0000    10.0000    10.0000   140.0000   119.0000   110.0000
      AFTER TRANSFORMATIONS =     44.0000     1.0000    10.0000   140.0000   119.0000   110.0000
   SUBJECT   16 , CELL   2
      BEFORE TRANSFORMATIONS =    31.0000     7.0000    10.0000   139.0000   131.0000   138.0000
      AFTER TRANSFORMATIONS =     31.0000      .7000    10.0000   139.0000   131.0000   138.0000
   SUBJECT   17 , CELL   2
      BEFORE TRANSFORMATIONS =    47.0000    10.0000    10.0000    95.0000   142.0000    94.0000
      AFTER TRANSFORMATIONS =     47.0000     1.0000    10.0000    95.0000   142.0000    94.0000
```

```
SUBJECT    18 , CELL   2
    BEFORE TRANSFORMATIONS =   38.0000   10.0000   10.0000   228.0000   228.0000   136.0000
    AFTER TRANSFORMATIONS =    38.0000    1.0000   10.0000   228.0000   228.0000   136.0000
SUBJECT    19 , CELL   2
    BEFORE TRANSFORMATIONS =   38.0000   10.0000   10.0000   145.0000   160.0000   151.0000
    AFTER TRANSFORMATIONS =    38.0000    1.0000   10.0000   145.0000   160.0000   151.0000
SUBJECT    20 , CELL   2
    BEFORE TRANSFORMATIONS =   48.0000   10.0000   10.0000   112.0000   112.0000   127.0000
    AFTER TRANSFORMATIONS =    48.0000    1.0000   10.0000   112.0000   112.0000   127.0000
SUBJECT    21 , CELL   2
    BEFORE TRANSFORMATIONS =   45.0000   10.0000   10.0000    91.0000    93.0000   128.0000
    AFTER TRANSFORMATIONS =    45.0000    1.0000   10.0000    91.0000    93.0000   128.0000
SUBJECT    22 , CELL   2
    BEFORE TRANSFORMATIONS =   48.0000   10.0000   10.0000   145.0000   122.0000   102.0000
    AFTER TRANSFORMATIONS =    48.0000    1.0000   10.0000   145.0000   122.0000   102.0000
SUBJECT    23 , CELL   2
    BEFORE TRANSFORMATIONS =   35.0000    8.0000   10.0000   123.0000   133.0000   129.0000
    AFTER TRANSFORMATIONS =    35.0000     .8000   10.0000   123.0000   133.0000   129.0000
SUBJECT    24 , CELL   2
    BEFORE TRANSFORMATIONS =   33.0000    8.0000   10.0000   156.0000   192.0000   141.0000
    AFTER TRANSFORMATIONS =    33.0000     .8000   10.0000   156.0000   192.0000   141.0000

        GROUP  TASK   2
        ===============================================
```

SUBCLASS COVARIANCE MATRIX

		1 WORDS	2 CATS	3 NCAT	4 TIME 2	5 TIME 4	6 TIME 6
1	WORDS	45.970					
2	CATS	.602	.012				
3	NCAT	.000	.000	.000			
4	TIME 2	21.773	.793	.000	3938.386		
5	TIME 4	-30.394	.297	.000	3523.455	3603.879	
6	TIME 6	-32.682	-.352	.000	1561.659	1501.455	974.023

SUBCLASS CORRELATION MATRIX

		1 WORDS	2 CATS	3 NCAT	4 TIME 2	5 TIME 4	6 TIME 6
1	WORDS	1.000000					
2	CATS	.818713	1.000000				
3	NCAT	.000000	0.000000	1.000000			
4	TIME 2	.051170	.116637	.000000	1.000000		
5	TIME 4	-.074673	.045651	.000000	.935243	1.000000	
6	TIME 6	-.154449	-.104164	.000000	.797338	.801387	1.000000

```
SUBJECT    25 , CELL   3
    BEFORE TRANSFORMATIONS =   44.0000    5.0000    5.0000   123.0000   104.0000    98.0000
    AFTER TRANSFORMATIONS =    44.0000    1.0000    5.0000   123.0000   104.0000    98.0000
SUBJECT    26 , CELL   3
    BEFORE TRANSFORMATIONS =   41.0000    5.0000    5.0000    96.0000    83.0000    70.0000
    AFTER TRANSFORMATIONS =    41.0000    1.0000    5.0000    96.0000    83.0000    70.0000
SUBJECT    27 , CELL   3
    BEFORE TRANSFORMATIONS =   34.0000    5.0000    5.0000   122.0000   111.0000    93.0000
    AFTER TRANSFORMATIONS =    34.0000    1.0000    5.0000   122.0000   111.0000    93.0000
SUBJECT    28 , CELL   3
    BEFORE TRANSFORMATIONS =   35.0000    5.0000    5.0000   124.0000   108.0000    95.0000
    AFTER TRANSFORMATIONS =    35.0000    1.0000    5.0000   124.0000   108.0000    95.0000
SUBJECT    29 , CELL   3
    BEFORE TRANSFORMATIONS =   40.0000    5.0000    5.0000    97.0000    78.0000    83.0000
    AFTER TRANSFORMATIONS =    40.0000    1.0000    5.0000    97.0000    78.0000    83.0000
SUBJECT    30 , CELL   3
    BEFORE TRANSFORMATIONS =   44.0000    5.0000    5.0000   184.0000   210.0000   172.0000
    AFTER TRANSFORMATIONS =    44.0000    1.0000    5.0000   184.0000   210.0000   172.0000
SUBJECT    31 , CELL   3
    BEFORE TRANSFORMATIONS =   39.0000    5.0000    5.0000   115.0000   150.0000   130.0000
    AFTER TRANSFORMATIONS =    39.0000    1.0000    5.0000   115.0000   150.0000   130.0000
SUBJECT    32 , CELL   3
    BEFORE TRANSFORMATIONS =   39.0000    5.0000    5.0000   105.0000    86.0000    94.0000
    AFTER TRANSFORMATIONS =    39.0000    1.0000    5.0000   105.0000    86.0000    94.0000
SUBJECT    33 , CELL   3
    BEFORE TRANSFORMATIONS =   45.0000    5.0000    5.0000    85.0000    65.0000    58.0000
    AFTER TRANSFORMATIONS =    45.0000    1.0000    5.0000    85.0000    65.0000    58.0000
SUBJECT    34 , CELL   3
    BEFORE TRANSFORMATIONS =   41.0000    5.0000    5.0000   105.0000    81.0000    80.0000
    AFTER TRANSFORMATIONS =    41.0000    1.0000    5.0000   105.0000    81.0000    80.0000
SUBJECT    35 , CELL   3
    BEFORE TRANSFORMATIONS =   46.0000    5.0000    5.0000   115.0000   105.0000    97.0000
    AFTER TRANSFORMATIONS =    46.0000    1.0000    5.0000   115.0000   105.0000    97.0000
SUBJECT    36 , CELL   3
    BEFORE TRANSFORMATIONS =   32.0000    5.0000    5.0000   144.0000    91.0000    73.0000
    AFTER TRANSFORMATIONS =    32.0000    1.0000    5.0000   144.0000    91.0000    73.0000


        GROUP  TASK   3
        ===============================================
```

----

		1 WORDS	2 CATS	3 NCAT	4 TIME 2	5 TIME 4	6 TIME 6
1	WORDS	20.182					
2	CATS	.000	.000				
3	NCAT	.000	.000	.000			
4	TIME 2	-16.364	.000	.000	679.902		
5	TIME 4	18.636	.000	.000	854.455	1548.182	
6	TIME 6	23.727	.000	.000	603.386	1153.000	910.750

SUBCLASS CORRELATION MATRIX
----

		1 WORDS	2 CATS	3 NCAT	4 TIME 2	5 TIME 4	6 TIME 6
1	WORDS	1.000000					
2	CATS	0.000000	1.000000				
3	NCAT	.000001	0.000000	1.000000			
4	TIME 2	-.139694	.000000	.000000	1.000000		
5	TIME 4	.105431	.000000	.000000	.832827	1.000000	
6	TIME 6	.175012	.000000	.000000	.766784	.970999	1.000000


```
SUBJECT   37 , CELL   4
    BEFORE TRANSFORMATIONS =   33.0000    5.0000    5.0000   107.0000   112.0000   107.0000
    AFTER TRANSFORMATIONS =    33.0000    1.0000    5.0000   107.0000   112.0000   107.0000
SUBJECT   38 , CELL   4
    BEFORE TRANSFORMATIONS =   36.0000    5.0000    5.0000   107.0000   116.0000   110.0000
    AFTER TRANSFORMATIONS =    36.0000    1.0000    5.0000   107.0000   116.0000   110.0000
SUBJECT   39 , CELL   4
    BEFORE TRANSFORMATIONS =   37.0000    5.0000    5.0000    60.0000    66.0000    42.0000
    AFTER TRANSFORMATIONS =    37.0000    1.0000    5.0000    60.0000    66.0000    42.0000
SUBJECT   40 , CELL   4
    BEFORE TRANSFORMATIONS =   42.0000    5.0000    5.0000   132.0000   147.0000   111.0000
    AFTER TRANSFORMATIONS =    42.0000    1.0000    5.0000   132.0000   147.0000   111.0000
SUBJECT   41 , CELL   4
    BEFORE TRANSFORMATIONS =   33.0000    5.0000    5.0000    85.0000   159.0000   100.0000
    AFTER TRANSFORMATIONS =    33.0000    1.0000    5.0000    85.0000   159.0000   100.0000
SUBJECT   42 , CELL   4
    BEFORE TRANSFORMATIONS =   33.0000    4.0000    5.0000   117.0000   113.0000   114.0000
    AFTER TRANSFORMATIONS =    33.0000     .8000    5.0000   117.0000   113.0000   114.0000
SUBJECT   43 , CELL   4
    BEFORE TRANSFORMATIONS =   41.0000    5.0000    5.0000   114.0000    72.0000    85.0000
    AFTER TRANSFORMATIONS =    41.0000    1.0000    5.0000   114.0000    72.0000    85.0000
SUBJECT   44 , CELL   4
    BEFORE TRANSFORMATIONS =   33.0000    5.0000    5.0000    87.0000    80.0000    96.0000
    AFTER TRANSFORMATIONS =    33.0000    1.0000    5.0000    87.0000    80.0000    96.0000
SUBJECT   45 , CELL   4



    BEFORE TRANSFORMATIONS =   38.0000    5.0000    5.0000    94.0000   126.0000   125.0000
    AFTER TRANSFORMATIONS =    38.0000    1.0000    5.0000    94.0000   126.0000   125.0000
SUBJECT   46 , CELL   4
    BEFORE TRANSFORMATIONS =   39.0000    5.0000    5.0000    88.0000   114.0000   100.0000
    AFTER TRANSFORMATIONS =    39.0000    1.0000    5.0000    88.0000   114.0000   100.0000
SUBJECT   47 , CELL   4
    BEFORE TRANSFORMATIONS =   28.0000    4.0000    5.0000    84.0000    90.0000   124.0000
    AFTER TRANSFORMATIONS =    28.0000     .8000    5.0000    84.0000    90.0000   124.0000
SUBJECT   48 , CELL   4
    BEFORE TRANSFORMATIONS =   42.0000    5.0000    5.0000   125.0000   130.0000   133.0000
    AFTER TRANSFORMATIONS =    42.0000    1.0000    5.0000   125.0000   130.0000   133.0000

        GROUP   TASK   4
        ==================================================
```

SUBCLASS COVARIANCE MATRIX
----

		1 WORDS	2 CATS	3 NCAT	4 TIME 2	5 TIME 4	6 TIME 6
1	WORDS	19.1136					
2	CATS	.2091	.0061				
3	NCAT	.0000	.0000	.0000			
4	TIME 2	42.1818	-.0182	.0000	423.8182		
5	TIME 4	21.7045	.3242	.0000	259.0909	833.5379	
6	TIME 6	-6.7045	-.5485	.0000	287.4545	393.2197	561.5379

SUBCLASS CORRELATION MATRIX
----

		1 WORDS	2 CATS	3 NCAT	4 TIME 2	5 TIME 4	6 TIME 6
1	WORDS	1.000000					
2	CATS	.614335	1.000000				
3	NCAT	.000001	0.000000	1.000000			
4	TIME 2	.468666	-.011345	.000000	1.000000		
5	TIME 4	.171956	.144261	.000000	.435913	1.000000	
6	TIME 6	-.064715	-.297315	.000000	.589237	.574755	1.000000

CELL SUMS - ALL GROUPS - BEFORE TRANSFORMATION MATRIX
----

	1 WORDS	2 CATS	3 NCAT	4 TIME 2	5 TIME 4	6 TIME 6
1	478.000	11.600	120.000	1867.000	1392.000	1283.000
2	506.000	11.300	120.000	1821.000	1844.000	1569.000
3	480.000	12.000	60.000	1415.000	1272.000	1143.000
4	435.000	11.600	60.000	1200.000	1325.000	1247.000

CELL IDENTIFICATION AND FREQUENCIES

CELL	FACTOR LEVELS TASK	N
1	1	12
2	2	12
3	3	12
4	4	12

TOTAL N=   48

TOTAL SUM OF CROSS-PRODUCTS
----

		1 WORDS	2 CATS	3 NCAT	4 TIME 2	5 TIME 4	6 TIME 6
1	WORDS	76.831000E+03					
2	CATS	18.509000E+02	45.290000E+00				
3	NCAT	14.415000E+03	34.700000E+01	30.000000E+02			
4	TIME 2	24.983800E+04	60.860000E+02	49.955000E+03	95.564900E+04		
5	TIME 4	23.166900E+04	56.370000E+02	45.345000E+03	83.940900E+04	80.114500E+04	
6	TIME 6	20.783700E+04	50.546000E+02	40.470000E+03	73.039800E+04	68.632400E+04	61.381400E+04

OBSERVED CELL MEANS --- ROWS ARE CELLS-COLUMNS ARE VARIABLES
----

	1 WORDS	2 CATS	3 NCAT	4 TIME 2	5 TIME 4	6 TIME 6
1	39.8333	.9667	10.0000	155.5833	116.0000	106.9167
2	47.1667	.9417	10.0000	151.7500	153.6667	130.7500
3	40.0000	1.0000	5.0000	117.9167	106.0000	95.2500
4	36.2500	.9667	5.0000	100.0000	110.4167	103.9167

OBSERVED CELL STD DEVS--ROWS ARE CELLS-COLUMNS VARIABLES
----

	1 WORDS	2 CATS	3 NCAT	4 TIME 2	5 TIME 4	6 TIME 6
1	7.05605	.04924	0.00000	65.03350	29.13292	23.60454
2	6.78010	.10836	0.00000	62.75656	60.03231	31.20934
3	4.49242	0.00000	0.00000	26.07492	39.34694	30.17863
4	4.37191	.07785	0.00000	20.58684	28.87106	23.69679

ESTIMATION PARAMETERS
========================

RANK OF THE BASIS = RANK OF MODEL FOR SIGNIFICANCE TESTING =   4

RANK OF THE MODEL TO BE ESTIMATED IS   4

ERROR TERM TO BE USED IS (WITHIN CELLS)

NUMBER OF FACTORS WITH ARBITARY CONTRASTS IS   1

VARIANCE-COVARIANCE FACTORS AND CORRELATIONS AMONG ESTIMATES WILL BE PRINTED

ESTIMATED COMBINED MEANS WILL BE PRINTED

245

OPTIONAL CONTRAST MATRIX--ROWS ARE CONTRASTS, COLUMNS SUBCLS

	1	2	3	4
1	1.000000	-1.000000	-0.000000	-0.000000
2	-0.000000	1.000000	-1.000000	-0.000000
3	-0.000000	-0.000000	1.000000	-1.000000

BASIS MATRIX FOR OPTIONAL CONTRASTS, BY COLUMNS

	1	2	3
1	.750000	.500000	.250000
2	-.250000	.500000	.250000
3	-.250000	-.500000	.250000
4	-.250000	-.500000	-.750000

FACTOR (TASK)

SYMBOLIC CONTRAST VECTORS
==============================

(1)
    LO,   CONST.

   BASIS VECTOR (NOT CONTRAST VECTOR) =
     1.00000000E+00 1.00000000E+00 1.00000000E+00 1.00000000E+00

  VECTOR OF T - TRIANGULAR FACTOR OF BASIS, FROM GRAM-SCHMIDT
    6.92820323E+00

  VECTOR OF ORTHONORMALIZED BASIS
    1.44337567E-01 1.44337567E-01 1.44337567E-01 1.44337567E-01

= =
(2)
    1,   INFORMATION ON HIERARCHY   T1-T2

   BASIS VECTOR (NOT CONTRAST VECTOR) =
     7.50000000E-01-2.50000000E-01-2.50000000E-01-2.50000000E-01

  VECTOR OF T - TRIANGULAR FACTOR OF BASIS, FROM GRAM-SCHMIDT
    0.   3.00000000E+00

  VECTOR OF ORTHONORMALIZED BASIS
    2.50000000E-01-8.33333333E-02-8.33333333E-02-8.33333333E-02

= =
(3)
    2,   MORE GLOBAL CATEGORIES   T2-T3

   BASIS VECTOR (NOT CONTRAST VECTOR) =
     5.00000000E-01 5.00000000E-01-5.00000000E-01-5.00000000E-01

  VECTOR OF T - TRIANGULAR FACTOR OF BASIS, FROM GRAM-SCHMIDT
    0.   2.00000000E+00 2.82842712E+00

  VECTOR OF ORTHONORMALIZED BASIS
    -8.37382645E-16 2.35702260E-01-1.17851130E-01-1.17851130E-01

= =
(4)
    3,   BUILT IN HIERARCHY   T3-T4

   BASIS VECTOR (NOT CONTRAST VECTOR) =
     2.50000000E-01 2.50000000E-01 2.50000000E-01-7.50000000E-01

  VECTOR OF T - TRIANGULAR FACTOR OF BASIS, FROM GRAM-SCHMIDT
    0.   1.00000000E+00 1.41421356E+00 2.44948974E+00

  VECTOR OF ORTHONORMALIZED BASIS
    -7.25194643E-16-4.83463095E-16 2.04124145E-01-2.04124145E-01

= =

246

EFFECT 1
    2.74097040E+02 6.71169688E+00 5.19615242E+01 9.09759687E+02 8.41921030E+02 7.56617528E+02

EFFECT 2
    1.08333333E+00-8.33333333E-03 1.00000000E+01 9.70833333E+01-2.20833333E+01-9.16666667E+00

EFFECT 3
    1.14315596E+01-1.17851130E-01 1.41421356E+01 1.21033111E+02 1.28575583E+02 8.81526454E+01

EFFECT 4
    9.18558654E+00 8.16496581E-02 1.48331870E-14 4.38866912E+01-1.08185797E+01-2.12289111E+01

ERROR SUM OF CROSS-PRODUCTS
----

		1 WORDS	2 CATS	3 NCAT	4 TIME 2	5 TIME 4	6 TIME 6
1	WORDS	14.855833E+02					
2	CATS	11.850000E+00	22.250000E-02				
3	NCAT	15.697310E-11	-99.191766E-14	23.419489E-12			
4	TIME 2	-14.163333E+02	-85.416667E-01	55.615601E-11	10.198608E+04		
5	TIME 4	-44.558333E+01	21.333333E-01	50.877702E-11	60.520000E+03	75.177583E+03	
6	TIME 6	-35.241667E+01	-11.541667E+00	44.835247E-11	33.210083E+03	37.545417E+03	33.038333E+03

ERROR VARIANCE -COVARIANCE MATRIX
----

		1 WORDS	2 CATS	3 NCAT	4 TIME 2	5 TIME 4	6 TIME 6
1	WORDS	33.763					
2	CATS	.269	.005				
3	NCAT	.000	-.000	.000			
4	TIME 2	-32.189	-.194	.000	2317.866		
5	TIME 4	-10.127	.048	.000	1375.455	1708.581	
6	TIME 6	-8.009	-.262	.000	754.775	853.305	750.871

ERROR CORRELATION MATRIX
----

		1 WORDS	2 CATS	3 NCAT	4 TIME 2	5 TIME 4	6 TIME 6
1	WORDS	1.000000					
2	CATS	.651786	1.000000				
3	NCAT	.000001	0.000000	1.000000			
4	TIME 2	-.115066	-.056703	.000000	1.000000		
5	TIME 4	-.042163	.016495	.000000	.691169	1.000000	
6	TIME 6	-.050304	-.134615	.000001	.572124	.753362	1.000000

VARIABLE	VARIANCE (ERROR MEAN SQUARES)	STANDARD DEVIATION
1 WORDS	33.763258	5.8106
2 CATS	.005057	.0711
3 NCAT	.000000	.0000
4 TIME 2	2317.865530	48.1442
5 TIME 4	1708.581439	41.3350
6 TIME 6	750.871212	27.4020

D.F.=   44

ERROR TERM FOR ANALYSIS OF VARIANCE (WITHIN CELLS)

INVERSE OF T - TRIANGULAR FACTOR OF BASIS FROM GRAM-SCHMIDT

		1 CONST.	2 T1-T2	3 T2-T3	4 T3-T4
1	CONST.	.144338			
2	T1-T2	0.000000	.333333		
3	T2-T3	0.000000	-.235702	.353553	
4	T3-T4	0.000000	-.000000	-.204124	.408248

LEAST SQUARE ESTIMATES OF EFFECTS -- EFFECTS X VARIABLES

		1 WORDS	2 CATS	3 NCAT	4 TIME 2	5 TIME 4	6 TIME 6
1	CONST.	39.5625	.9687	7.5000	131.3125	121.5208	109.2083
2	T1-T2	-2.3333	.0250	.0000	3.8333	-37.6667	-23.8333
3	T2-T3	2.1667	-.0583	5.0000	33.8333	47.6667	35.5000
4	T3-T4	3.7500	.0333	.0000	17.9167	-4.4167	-8.6667

ESTIMATES OF EFFECTS IN STANDARD DEVIATION UNITS-EFF X VARS

		1 WORDS	2 CATS	3 NCAT	4 TIME 2	5 TIME 4	6 TIME 6
1	CONST.	6.80866	13.62301	0.00000	2.72748	2.93990	3.98541
2	T1-T2	-.40156	.35156	0.00000	.07962	-.91125	-.86977
3	T2-T3	.37288	-.82031	0.00000	.70275	1.15318	1.29552
4	T3-T4	.64537	.46875	0.00000	.37215	-.10685	-.31628

STANDARD ERRORS OF LEAST-SQUARES ESTIMATES--EFFECTS BY VARS

		1 WORDS	2 CATS	3 NCAT	4 TIME 2	5 TIME 4	6 TIME 6
1	CONST.	.83869	.01026	.00000	6.94902	5.96619	3.95514
2	T1-T2	2.37217	.02903	.00000	19.65479	16.87494	11.18683
3	T2-T3	2.37217	.02903	.00000	19.65479	16.87494	11.18683
4	T3-T4	2.37217	.02903	.00000	19.65479	16.87494	11.18683

VARIANCE-COVARIANCE FACTORS OF ESTIMATES

		1 CONST.	2 T1-T2	3 T2-T3	4 T3-T4
1	CONST.	.020833			
2	T1-T2	0.000000	.166667		
3	T2-T3	0.000000	-.083333	.166667	
4	T3-T4	0.000000	-.000000	-.083333	.166667

INTERCORRELATIONS AMONG THE ESTIMATES

		1 CONST.	2 T1-T2	3 T2-T3	4 T3-T4
1	CONST.	1.000000			
2	T1-T2	0.000000	1.000000		
3	T2-T3	0.000000	-.500000	1.000000	
4	T3-T4	0.000000	-.000000	-.500000	1.000000

ESTIMATED COMBINED MEANS BASED ON FITTING A MODEL OF RANK   4
==

- -

FACTORS   1 (TASK)

    LEVEL   1

        MEANS   WORDS = 39.83   CATS = .9667   NCAT = 10.000   TIME 2= 155.6   TIME 4= 116.0
        -------   TIME 6= 106.9

    LEVEL   2

        MEANS   WORDS = 42.17   CATS = .9417   NCAT = 10.000   TIME 2= 151.7   TIME 4= 153.7
        -------   TIME 6= 130.7

    LEVEL   3

        MEANS   WORDS = 40.00   CATS = 1.0000   NCAT = 5.000   TIME 2= 117.9   TIME 4= 106.0
        -------   TIME 6= 95.25

    LEVEL   4

        MEANS   WORDS = 36.25   CATS = .9667   NCAT = 5.000   TIME 2= 100.00   TIME 4= 110.4
        -------   TIME 6= 103.9

ANALYSIS OF VARIANCE

====================

====================

2 DEPENDENT VARIABLE(S)

1 WORDS
2 CATS

DISCRIMINANT ANALYSIS WILL BE PERFORMED FOR EACH BETWEEN CELL HYPOTHESIS

ERROR SUM OF CROSS-PRODUCTS (SE)
----

		1 WORDS	2 CATS
1	WORDS	1485.583	
2	CATS	11.850	.223

CHOLESKY FACTOR SE
----

		1 WORDS	2 CATS
1	WORDS	38.54327	
2	CATS	.30745	.35774

LOG-DETERMINANT ERROR SUM OF CROSS-PRODUCTS = 5.24765436E+00

HYPOTHESIS   1   1 DEGREE(S) OF FREEDOM
===

     L0,   CONST.

- -

SUM OF CROSS-PRODUCTS FOR HYPOTHESIS
----

		1 WORDS	2 CATS
1	WORDS	75129.19	
2	CATS	1839.66	45.05

```
                    (SCP HYP + SCP ERROR) - ADJUSTED FOR ANY COVARIATES (STI*)
                    ------------------------------------------------------------

                   1          2
                 WORDS      CATS

1   WORDS     76614.77
2   CATS       1851.51     45.27



                                 CHOLESKY FACTOR STI*
                    ------------------------------------------------------------

                   1          2
                 WORDS      CATS

1   WORDS     276.7937
2   CATS        6.6891      .7246

        LOG-DETERMINANT SCP HYPOTHESES + SCP ERROR, ADJUSTED FOR ANY COVARIATES, =  1.06023036E+01



              F-RATIO FOR MULTIVARIATE TEST OF EQUALITY OF MEAN VECTORS=   4527.6794

                    D.F.=    2   AND     43.0000     P LESS THAN  .0001



                 (LIKELIHOOD RATIO =  4.72612704E-03     LOG = -5.35464922E+00)
```

VARIABLE	HYPOTHESIS MEAN SQ	UNIVARIATE F	P LESS THAN	STEP DOWN F	P LESS THAN
1 WORDS	75129.1875	2225.1759	.0001	2225.1759	.0001
				STEP-DOWN MEAN SQUARES =(75129.1875/ 33.7633)	
2 CATS	45.0469	8908.1461	.0001	133.4199	.0001
				STEP-DOWN MEAN SQUARES =(.3971/ .0030)	

```
                         DEGREES OF FREEDOM FOR HYPOTHESIS=    1
                         DEGREES OF FREEDOM FOR ERROR=       44




                    HYPOTHESIS MEAN PRODUCTS, ADJUSTED FOR ANY COVARIATES
                    ------------------------------------------------------------

                   1          2
                 WORDS      CATS

1   WORDS     75129.19
2   CATS       1839.66     45.05



                         DISCRIMINANT ANALYSIS FOR HYPOTHESIS    1
                         ========================================



  VARIANCE OF CANONICAL VARIATE    1 =    210.5897      PER CENT OF CANONICAL VARIATION= 100.00      ROY#S CRITERION=  .9953
                                                                                                     M= 0.0      N=  20.5

                              --DISCRIMINANT FUNCTION COEFFICIENTS--

                              VARIABLE     RAW COEFFICIENT     STANDARDIZED

                              1 WORDS         -.044592           -.2591
                              2 CATS         16.163168           1.1494


                         HOTELLING#S TRACE CRITERION=    210.5897
                         ----------------------------------------


            BARTLETT#S CHI SQUARE TEST FOR SIGNIFICANCE OF SUCCESSIVE CANONICAL VARIATES
            -------------------------------------------------------------------------------

       FOR ROOTS   1 THROUGH   1 CHI SQUARE=    230.2499   WITH    2 DEGREES OF FREEDOM    P LESS THAN  .0001

                      (LIKELIHOOD RATIO =  4.72612704E-03     LOG = -5.35464922E+00)
```

CANONICAL FORM OF LEAST SQUARE ESTIMATES-VARIATES X EFFECTS

```
                     1
                  CONST.

        1         13.89391
```

HYPOTHESIS   2   3 DEGREE(S) OF FREEDOM
===== ===

```
        1,        INFORMATION ON HIERARCHY                        T1-T2


        2,        MORE GLOBAL CATEGORIES                          T2-T3
        3,        BUILT IN HIERARCHY                              T3-T4
```
- -

SUM OF CROSS-PRODUCTS FOR HYPOTHESIS

```
                     1          2
                  WORDS       CATS

1   WORDS        216.2292
2   CATS          -.6062      .0206
```


(SCP HYP + SCP ERROR) - ADJUSTED FOR ANY COVARIATES (STI*)

```
                     1          2
                  WORDS       CATS

1   WORDS        1701.813
2   CATS          11.244      .243
```


CHOLESKY FACTOR STI*

```
                     1          2
                  WORDS       CATS

1   WORDS        41.25303
2   CATS          .27256      .41090
```

LOG-DETERMINANT SCP HYPOTHESES + SCP ERROR, ADJUSTED FOR ANY COVARIATES, = 5.66063573E+00

F-RATIO FOR MULTIVARIATE TEST OF EQUALITY OF MEAN VECTORS=   3.2874

D.F.=   6 AND   86.0000   P LESS THAN .0059

(LIKELIHOOD RATIO = 6.61674606E-01   LOG = -4.12981375E-01)

VARIABLE	HYPOTHESIS MEAN SQ	UNIVARIATE F	P LESS THAN	STEP DOWN F	P LESS THAN
1 WORDS	72.0764	2.1348	.1095	2.1348	.1095
2 CATS	.0069	1.3596	.2676	STEP-DOWN MEAN SQUARES =(72.0764/ 33.7633) 4.5765	.0073
				STEP-DOWN MEAN SQUARES =(.0136/ .0030)	.0136/

DEGREES OF FREEDOM FOR HYPOTHESIS=   3
DEGREES OF FREEDOM FOR ERROR=   44

HYPOTHESIS MEAN PRODUCTS, ADJUSTED FOR ANY COVARIATES

```
                     1          2
                  WORDS       CATS

1   WORDS        72.07639
2   CATS          -.20208     .00688
```

DISCRIMINANT ANALYSIS FOR HYPOTHESIS   2
==

VARIANCE OF CANONICAL VARIATE   1 =   .4410   PER CENT OF CANONICAL VARIATION= 90.03   ROY#S CRITERION=   .3060
                                                                                                         M= 0.0   N= 20.5

                                    --DISCRIMINANT FUNCTION COEFFICIENTS--

                            VARIABLE   RAW COEFFICIENT   STANDARDIZED

                            1 WORDS   -.213849   -1.2426
                            2 CATS   16.093501   1.1444

VARIANCE OF CANONICAL VARIATE   2 =   .0488   PER CENT OF CANONICAL VARIATION= 9.97   ROY#S CRITERION=   .0465
                                                                                                         M= -.5   N= 20.0

                                    --DISCRIMINANT FUNCTION COEFFICIENTS--

                            VARIABLE   RAW COEFFICIENT   STANDARDIZED

                            1 WORDS   .075911   .4411
                            2 CATS   9.209365   .6549

                            HOTELLING#S TRACE CRITERION=   .4898

BARTLETT#S CHI SQUARE TEST FOR SIGNIFICANCE OF SUCCESSIVE CANONICAL VARIATES

FOR ROOTS 1 THROUGH   2 CHI SQUARE=   18.1712   WITH   6 DEGREES OF FREEDOM   P LESS THAN .0059

                        (LIKELIHOOD RATIO = 6.61674607E-01   LOG = -4.12981374E-01)

FOR ROOTS 2 THROUGH   2 CHI SQUARE=   2.0969   WITH   2 DEGREES OF FREEDOM   P LESS THAN .3505

                        (LIKELIHOOD RATIO = 9.53461784E-01   LOG = -4.76559345E-02)

CANONICAL FORM OF LEAST SQUARE ESTIMATES-VARIATES X EFFECTS
----

            1   2   3
          T1-T2   T2-T3   T3-T4

1   .901318   -1.402127   -.265483
2   .053108   -.372739   .591646

                                    ANALYSIS OF VARIANCE

                                    ====================

                                    ====================

                                    2 DEPENDENT VARIABLE(S)

                                        1 WORDS
                                        2 CATS

                                    3 INDEPENDENT VARIABLE(S)
                                  (PREDICTOR VARIABLES, COVARIATES)

                                        4 TIME 2
                                        5 TIME 4
                                        6 TIME 6

CANONICAL CORRELATION ANALYSIS WILL BE PERFORMED

DISCRIMINANT ANALYSIS WILL BE PERFORMED FOR EACH BETWEEN CELL HYPOTHESIS

REGRESSION PARALLELISM TEST REQUESTED

```
                                   ERROR SUM OF CROSS-PRODUCTS  (SE)
                        ----------------------------------------------------------------

                            1               2               3               4               5
                         WORDS           CATS           TIME 2          TIME 4          TIME 6


         1  WORDS      14.855833E+02
         2  CATS       11.850400E+00   22.250000E-02
         3  TIME 2    -14.163333E+02  -85.416667E-01  10.198608E+04
         4  TIME 4    -44.558333E+01   21.333333E-01  60.520000E+03  75.177583E+03
         5  TIME 6    -35.241667F+01  -11.541667E+00  33.210083E+03  37.545417E+03  33.038333E+03

                                           REGRESSION ANALYSIS

                                         =====================

                                            =============

                                               =====


                                   SUM OF PRODUCTS CRITERIA
                        ----------------------------------------------------------------

                            1               2
                         WORDS           CATS

         1  WORDS      1485.583
         2  CATS         11.850           .223




                                   SUM OF PRODUCTS - PREDICTORS BY CRITERIA
                        ----------------------------------------------------------------

                            1               2
                         WORDS           CATS

         1  TIME 2    -1416.333          -8.542
         2  TIME 4     -445.583           2.133
         3  TIME 6     -352.417         -11.542




                                   SUM OF PRODUCTS - PREDICTORS
                        ----------------------------------------------------------------

                            1               2               3
                         TIME 2          TIME 4          TIME 6

         1  TIME 2    10.198608E+04
         2  TIME 4    60.520000E+03  75.177583E+03
         3  TIME 6    33.210083E+03  37.545417E+03  33.038333E+03




                                   INVERSE SUM OF PRODUCTS OF PREDICTORS (X≠X)INV
                        ----------------------------------------------------------------

                            1               2               3
                         TIME 2          TIME 4          TIME 6




         1  TIME 2     18.996171E-06
         2  TIME 4    -13.310317E-06  40.085879E-06
         3  TIME 6    -39.688146F-07 -32.174877E-06  70.821485E-06




                                   SUM OF PRODUCTS - REGRESSION
                        ----------------------------------------------------------------

                            1               2
                         WORDS           CATS

         1  WORDS      23.99398
         2  CATS         .25123           .01229
    GROUP     1
    ====================================


                                   INVERSE SUM OF PRODUCTS PREDICTORS FOR THIS SUBCLASS ONLY
                        ----------------------------------------------------------------

                            1               2               3
                         TIME 2          TIME 4          TIME 6

         1  TIME 2     27.938757E-06
         2  TIME 4    -22.624782F-06  16.762113E-05
         3  TIME 6    -13.567876E-06 -86.963776E-06  23.401269E-05
```

SUM OF PRODUCTS ADJUSTED FOR PREDICTORS , THIS SUBCLASS ONLY
----

		1 WORDS	2 CATS
1	WORDS	458.8981	
2	CATS	2.1600	.0199

GROUP   2
======================================

INVERSE SUM OF PRODUCTS PREDICTORS FOR THIS SUBCLASS ONLY
----

		1 TIME 2	2 TIME 4	3 TIME 6
1	TIME 2	19.410030E-05		
2	TIME 4	-16.802291E-05	21.595459E-05	
3	TIME 6	-52.195627E-06	-63.501076E-06	27.490616E-05

SUM OF PRODUCTS ADJUSTED FOR PREDICTORS , THIS SUBCLASS ONLY
----

		1 WORDS	2 CATS
1	WORDS	414.2334	
2	CATS	5.5008	.1124

GROUP   3
======================================

INVERSE SUM OF PRODUCTS PREDICTORS FOR THIS SUBCLASS ONLY
----

		1 TIME 2	2 TIME 4	3 TIME 6
1	TIME 2	48.498272E-05		
2	TIME 4	-49.636998E-05	15.352942E-04	
3	TIME 6	30.709045E-05	-16.148134E-04	19.407025E-04

SUM OF PRODUCTS ADJUSTED FOR PREDICTORS , THIS SUBCLASS ONLY
----

		1 WORDS	2 CATS
1	WORDS	174.5865	
2	CATS	.0000	.0000

GROUP   4
======================================

INVERSE SUM OF PRODUCTS PREDICTORS FOR THIS SUBCLASS ONLY
----

		1 TIME 2	2 TIME 4	3 TIME 6
1	TIME 2	33.585023E-05		
2	TIME 4	-34.776988E-06	16.646699E-05	
3	TIME 6	-14.757095E-05	-98.766794E-06	30.659745E-05

SUM OF PRODUCTS ADJUSTED FOR PREDICTORS , THIS SUBCLASS ONLY
----

		1 WORDS	2 CATS
1	WORDS	120.9136	
2	CATS	1.5297	.0494

```
STATISTICS FOR PARALLELISM TEST WITH   4 SUBCLASSES OF OBSERVATIONS
===============================================================
```

VARIABLE	HYPOTHESIS MEAN SQ	UNIVARIATE F	P LESS THAN	STEP DOWN F	P LESS THAN
1 WORDS	32.5509	.8913	.5437	.8913	.5437
2 CATS	.0032	.5567	.8216	.2734	.9773

```
                    DEGREES OF FREEDOM FOR HYPOTHESIS=   9
                    DEGREES OF FREEDOM FOR ERROR=     32


       F-STATISTIC FOR TEST OF PARALLELISM OF REGRESSION HYPERPLANES =      .5576

              D.F.=   18 AND      62.0000    P LESS THAN  .9159

           (LIKELIHOOD RATIO = 7.40758960E-01    LOG = -3.00079997E-01)




                    RAW REGRESSION COEFFICIENTS - INDEPENDENT X DEPENDENT VARS
                    -----------------------------------------------------------

                         1              2
                       WORDS           CATS

 1  TIME 2   -19.575378E-03 -14.484756E-05
 2  TIME 4    12.329208E-03  57.056054E-05
 3  TIME 6   -50.009183E-04 -85.213742E-05



                    STANDARDIZED REGRESSION COEFFICIENTS - INDEP X DEPENDENT VAR
                    -----------------------------------------------------------

                         1              2
                       WORDS           CATS

 1  TIME 2    -.162193       -.098066
 2  TIME 4     .087706        .331651
 3  TIME 6    -.023584       -.328363




                    STANDARD ERRORS OF RAW REGRESSION COEFS-IND X DEP VARIABLES
                    -----------------------------------------------------------

                         1              2
                       WORDS           CATS

 1  TIME 2   26.022786E-03  31.208168E-05
 2  TIME 4   37.802147E-03  45.334722E-05
 3  TIME 6   50.246206E-03  60.258424E-05



                    ERROR SUM OF PRODUCTS ADJUSTED FOR PREDICTORS
                    -----------------------------------------------------------

                         1              2
                       WORDS           CATS

 1  WORDS    1461.589
 2  CATS       11.599        .210



                    ERROR VAR-COV MATRIX ADJUSTED FOR PREDICTORS
                    -----------------------------------------------------------

                         1              2
                       WORDS           CATS

 1  WORDS    33.64852
 2  CATS       .28290        .00513



                    MATRIX OF CORRELATIONS WITH PREDICTORS ELIMINATED
                    -----------------------------------------------------------

                         1              2
                       WORDS           CATS

 1  WORDS    1.000000
 2  CATS      .661717       1.000000
```

255

```
                VARIABLE          VARIANCE          STANDARD DEVIATION
                               (ERROR MEAN SQUARES)

                1 WORDS           35.648521              5.9706
                2 CATS              .005127               .0716


                              D.F.=      41

             ERROR TERM FOR ANALYSIS OF COVARIANCE (WITHIN CELLS)



                     3 COVARIATE(S) HAVE BEEN ELIMINATED



             LEAST SQUARE ESTIMATES ADJUSTED FOR COVARIATES-EFFECT X VARS
             ----------------------------------------------------------

                         1          2
                       WORDS      CATS

        1  CONST.    41.18088    1.01150
        2  T1-T2     -1.91308     .02674
        3  T2-T3      2.41881    -.05038
        4  T3-T4      4.11184     .03106

                                  3 COVARIATE(S) ELIMINATED



             ESTIMATES IN ADJUSTED STANDARD DEVIATION UNITS- EFFS X VARS
             ----------------------------------------------------------

                         1          2
                       WORDS      CATS

        1  CONST.     6.89723   14.12631
        2  T1-T2      -.32042     .37340
        3  T2-T3       .40512    -.70357
        4  T3-T4       .68868     .43382



             STANDARD ERRORS OF ADJUSTED ESTIMATES - EFFECTS X VARIABLES
             ----------------------------------------------------------

                         1          2
                       WORDS      CATS

        1  CONST.     3.740037    .044853
        2  T1-T2      2.741609    .032879
        3  T2-T3      2.719020    .032608
        4  T3-T4      2.531311    .030357



             VARIANCE-COVARIANCE FACTORS AMONG ADJUSTED ESTIMATES
             ----------------------------------------------------------

                         1          2          3          4
                       CONST.     T1-T2      T2-T3      T3-T4

        1  CONST.      .392383
        2  T1-T2      -.062325    .210848
        3  T2-T3       .113666   -.115996    .207388
        4  T3-T4      -.018958    .019746   -.094449    .179742
                                  3 COVARIATE(S) ELIMINATED



             CORRELATIONS AMONG ADJUSTED ESTIMATES
             ----------------------------------------------------------

                         1          2          3          4
                       CONST.     T1-T2      T2-T3      T3-T4

        1  CONST.     1.000000
        2  T1-T2      -.216682   1.000000
        3  T2-T3       .398458   -.554712   1.000000
        4  T3-T4      -.071384    .101433   -.489195   1.000000
                                  3 COVARIATE(S) ELIMINATED
```

ESTIMATED COMBINED MEANS BASED ON FITTING A MODEL OF RANK   4
===

- -

FACTORS   1 (TASK)

   LEVEL   1

      MEANS   WORDS = 40.37   CATS = .9714

   LEVEL   2

      MEANS   WORDS = 42.28   CATS = .9446

   LEVEL   3

      MEANS   WORDS = 39.86   CATS = .9950

   LEVEL   4

      MEANS   WORDS = 35.75   CATS = .9640
      ----

                      3 COVARIATE(S) ELIMINATED

ESTIMATED COMBINED MEANS INCLUDING COVARIATE TERM - MODEL OF RANK   7
===

- -

FACTORS   1 (TASK)

   LEVEL   1

      MEANS   WORDS = 39.83   CATS = .9667

   LEVEL   2

      MEANS   WORDS = 42.17   CATS = .9417

   LEVEL   3

      MEANS   WORDS = 40.00   CATS = 1.0000

   LEVEL   4

      MEANS   WORDS = 36.25   CATS = .9667
      ----

                      3 COVARIATE(S) ELIMINATED

CHOLESKY FACTOR ERROR SCP ADJUSTED FOR PREDICTORS
----

		1 WORDS	2 CATS
1	WORDS	38.23074	
2	CATS	.30339	.34375

CHOLESKY FACTOR ERROR SCP BEFORE PREDICTOR ADJUSTMENT
----

		1 WORDS	2 CATS
1	WORDS	38.54327	
2	CATS	.30745	.35774

LOG-DETERMINANT ERROR SUM OF PRODUCTS BEFORE ADJUSTMENT FOR PREDICTORS = 5.24765436E+00   AFTER = 5.15161317E+00

STATISTICS FOR REGRESSION ANALYSIS WITH   3 PREDICTOR VARIABLE(S)
==

VARIABLE	SQUARE MULT R	MULT R	F	P LESS THAN	STEP DOWN F	P LESS THAN
1 WORDS	.0162	.1271	.2244	.8790	.2244	.8790
2 CATS	.0552	.2350	.7990	.5016	1.1070	.3576

DEGREES OF FREEDOM FOR HYPOTHESIS=   3
DEGREES OF FREEDOM FOR ERROR=   41

257

F VALUE FOR TEST OF HYPOTHESIS OF NO ASSOCIATION BETWEEN DEPENDENT AND INDEPENDENT VARIABLES=   .6559

D.F.=   6 AND   80.3000   P LESS THAN .6853

(LIKELIHOOD RATIO = 9.08426604E-01   LOG = -9.60411829E-02)

INVERSE CHOLESKY FACTOR (X≠X)
----

		1 TIME 2	2 TIME 4	3 TIME 6
1	TIME 2	31.313351E-04		
2	TIME 4	-29.947454E-04	50.466351F-04	
3	TIME 6	-47.160489E-05	-38.232648E-04	84.155502E-04

SEMI-PARTIAL REGRESSION COEFICIENTS - REGRESSION ANALYSIS
----

		1 WORDS	2 CATS
1	TIME 2	-4.435014	-.026747
2	TIME 4	1.992861	.036346
3	TIME 6	-.594247	-.101257

CANONICAL CORRELATION ANALYSIS
================================

CANONICAL CORRELATION 1 = .2774   SQUARE CORRELATION= .0770

ACCOUNTS FOR 3.8475 PERCENT OF VARIATION IN DEPENDENT VARIABLES

COEFFICIENTS FOR DEPENDENT VARIABLES

VARIABLE	RAW	STANDARDIZED	CORRELATION WITH CANONICAL VARIATE
1 WORDS	-.135277	-.7860	.0712
2 CATS	18.495146	1.3152	.8029

COEFFICIENTS FOR INDEPENDENT VARIABLES

	RAW	STANDARDIZED	
3 TIME 2	-.000111	-.0054	.0572
4 TIME 4	.032029	1.3239	.1977
5 TIME 6	-.054376	-1.4900	-.4957

CANONICAL CORRELATION 2 = .1259   SQUARE CORRELATION= .0158

ACCOUNTS FOR .7921 PERCENT OF VARIATION IN DEPENDENT VARIABLES

COEFFICIENTS FOR DEPENDENT VARIABLES

VARIABLE	RAW	STANDARDIZED	CORRELATION WITH CANONICAL VARIATE
1 WORDS	.182192	1.0586	.9975
2 CATS	-1.320088	-.0939	.5961

COEFFICIENTS FOR INDEPENDENT VARIABLES

	RAW	STANDARDIZED	
3 TIME 2	-.026817	-1.2911	-.9255
4 TIME 4	.011863	.4904	-.3669
5 TIME 6	.001698	.0465	-.3227

TOTAL PERCENTAGE OF VARIATION IN DEPENDENT VARIABLES ACCOUNTED FOR= 4.6396

TEST OF SIGNIFICANCE OF CANONICAL CORRELATIONS

FOR CORRELATIONS 1 THROUGH   2, CHI SQUARE=   3.9377   WITH   6 DEGREES OF FREEDOM   P LESS THAN .6852

(LIKELIHOOD RATIO = 9.08426612E-01   LOG = -9.60411735E-02)

FOR CORRELATIONS 2 THROUGH   2, CHI SQUARE=   .6547   WITH   2 DEGREES OF FREEDOM   P LESS THAN .7209

(LIKELIHOOD RATIO = 9.84158529E-01   LOG = -1.59682882E-02)

STEP-WISE REGRESSION TO ANALYZE THE CONTRIBUTION OF EACH INDEPENDENT VARIABLE
==

SUM OF PRODUCTS ERROR - PARTIALLY ADJUSTED
----

		1 WORDS	2 CATS
1	WORDS	1465.914	
2	CATS	11.731	.222

```
                              CHOLESKY FACTOR PARTIALLY ADJUSTED SCP
                    ------------------------------------------------------------

                         1          2
                       WORDS      CATS

       1  WORDS       38.28726
       2  CATS          .70640     .35763

                         (LIKELIHOOD RATIO =  9.86177916E-01     LOG = -1.39184986E-02)


              ADDING VARIABLE   1 (TIME 2) THROUGH    1( TIME 2) TO THE REGRESSION EQUATION



                    F=      .2943  WITH    2   AND      42.0000   D.F.    P LESS THAN  .7466

                                                                               PERCENT OF ADDITIONAL
          VARIABLE         UNIVARIATE F          P LESS THAN        STEP DOWN F       P LESS THAN    VARIANCE ACCOUNTED FOR
          --------      ----------------------    -----------    --------------------   -----------   ----------------------

       1  WORDS              .5770                  .4517              .5770               .4517              1.3240
                                                           STEP-DOWN MEAN SQUARES =(   19.6694/   34.0910)
       2  CATS               .1387                  .7115              .0248               .8757                .3215
                                                           STEP-DOWN MEAN SQUARES =(    .0001/    .0030)
                                                   D.F.=   1 AND     43
```

- -

```
                              SUM OF PRODUCTS ERROR - PARTIALLY ADJUSTED
                    ------------------------------------------------------------

                         1          2
                       WORDS      CATS

       1  WORDS       1461.942
       2  CATS          11.659     .220



                              CHOLESKY FACTOR PARTIALLY ADJUSTED SCP
                    ------------------------------------------------------------

                         1          2
                       WORDS      CATS

       1  WORDS       38.23536
       2  CATS          .30493     .35705

                         (LIKELIHOOD RATIO =  9.94037691E-01     LOG = -5.98015499E-03)


              ADDING VARIABLE   2 (TIME 4) THROUGH    2( TIME 4) TO THE REGRESSION EQUATION
                    F=      .1230  WITH    2   AND      41.0000   D.F.    P LESS THAN  .8847

                                                                               PERCENT OF ADDITIONAL
          VARIABLE         UNIVARIATE F          P LESS THAN        STEP DOWN F       P LESS THAN    VARIANCE ACCOUNTED FOR
          --------      ----------------------    -----------    --------------------   -----------   ----------------------

       1  WORDS              .1141                  .7373              .1141               .7373                .2673
                                                           STEP-DOWN MEAN SQUARES =(    3.9715/   34.8082)
       2  CATS               .2517                  .6186              .1342               .7161                .5937
                                                           STEP-DOWN MEAN SQUARES =(    .0004/    .0031)
                                                   D.F.=   1 AND     42
```

- -

```
                              SUM OF PRODUCTS ERROR - PARTIALLY ADJUSTED
                    ------------------------------------------------------------

                         1          2
                       WORDS      CATS

       1  WORDS       1461.589
       2  CATS          11.599     .210



                              CHOLESKY FACTOR PARTIALLY ADJUSTED SCP
                    ------------------------------------------------------------

                         1          2
                       WORDS      CATS

       1  WORDS       38.23074
       2  CATS          .30339     .34375
```

(LIKELIHOOD RATIO = 9.26684118E-01   LOG = -7.61425292E-02)

ADDING VARIABLE   3 (TIME 6) THROUGH   3(TIME 6) TO THE REGRESSION EQUATION
      F=   1.5823   WITH   2   AND   40.0000   D.F.   P LESS THAN .2181

	VARIABLE	UNIVARIATE F	P LESS THAN	STEP DOWN F	P LESS THAN	PERCENT OF ADDITIONAL VARIANCE ACCOUNTED FOR
1	WORDS	.0099	.9213	.0099	.9213	.0238
				STEP-DOWN MEAN SQUARES =(	.3531/ 35.6485)	
2	CATS	1.9998	.1649	3.1542	.0834	4.6081
				STEP-DOWN MEAN SQUARES =(	.0093/ .0030)	

D.F.=   1 AND   41

- -

ANALYSIS OF COVARIANCE

=========================

================

=======

HYPOTHESIS   1   1 DEGREE(S) OF FREEDOM
==

        LO,   CONST.

- -

SUM OF CROSS-PRODUCTS FOR HYPOTHESIS

----

		1 WORDS	2 CATS	3 TIME 2	4 TIME 4	5 TIME 6
1	WORDS	75.129187E+03				
2	CATS	18.396562E+02	45.046875E+00			
3	TIME 2	24.936244E+04	61.060312E+02	82.766269E+04		
4	TIME 4	23.076806E+04	56.507187E+02	76.594581E+04	70.883102E+04	
5	TIME 6	20.738662E+04	50.781875E+02	68.834012E+04	63.701221E+04	57.247008E+04

SUM OF PROD. FOR HYPOTHESIS,ADJUSTED FOR COVARIATES
----

		1 WORDS	2 CATS
1	WORDS	4321.962	
2	CATS	106.157	2.607

(SCP HYP + SCP ERROR) - ADJUSTED FOR ANY COVARIATES (STI*)
----

		1 WORDS	2 CATS
1	WORDS	5783.551	
2	CATS	117.756	2.818

CHOLESKY FACTOR STI*
----

		1 WORDS	2 CATS
1	WORDS	76.04966	
2	CATS	1.54841	.64815

LOG-DETERMINANT SCP HYPOTHESES + SCP ERROR, ADJUSTED FOR ANY COVARIATES, = 7.79551624E+00

F-RATIO FOR MULTIVARIATE TEST OF EQUALITY OF MEAN VECTORS=   261.3601
       D.F.=   2 AND   40.0000   P LESS THAN .0001

(LIKELIHOOD RATIO = 7.10832849E-02   LOG = -2.64390306E+00)

VARIABLE	HYPOTHESIS MEAN SQ	UNIVARIATE F	P LESS THAN	STEP DOWN F	P LESS THAN
1 WORDS	4321.9620	121.2382	.0001	121.2382	.0001
				STEP-DOWN MEAN SQUARES =(4321.9620/	35.6485)
2 CATS	2.6075	508.5661	.0001	102.2078	.0001
				STEP-DOWN MEAN SQUARES =(.3019/	.0030)

```
                    DEGREES OF FREEDOM FOR HYPOTHESIS=   1
                    DEGREES OF FREEDOM FOR ERROR=      41

                       3 COVARIATE(S) ELIMINATED
```

HYPOTHESIS MEAN PRODUCTS, ADJUSTED FOR ANY COVARIATES

	1 WORDS	2 CATS
1 WORDS	4321.962	
2 CATS	106.157	2.607

```
                       3 COVARIATE(S) ELIMINATED
```

DISCRIMINANT ANALYSIS FOR HYPOTHESIS   1

VARIANCE OF CANONICAL VARIATE   1 =   13.0680   PER CENT OF CANONICAL VARIATION= 100.00   ROY#S CRITERION= .9289

M= 0.0   N=   19.0

--DISCRIMINANT FUNCTION COEFFICIENTS--

VARIABLE	RAW COEFFICIENT	STANDARDIZED
1 WORDS	-.050353	-.3006
2 CATS	16.384682	1.1732

HOTELLING#S TRACE CRITERION=   13.0680

BARTLETT#S CHI SQUARE TEST FOR SIGNIFICANCE OF SUCCESSIVE CANONICAL VARIATES

FOR ROOTS   1 THROUGH   1 CHI SQUARE=   105.7561   WITH   2 DEGREES OF FREEDOM   P LESS THAN .0001

(LIKELIHOOD RATIO = 7.10832849E-02   LOG = -2.64390306E+00)

CANONICAL FORM OF LEAST SQUARE ESTIMATES-VARIATES X EFFECTS

	1 CONST.
1	14.49946

HYPOTHESIS   2   3 DEGREE(S) OF FREEDOM

1,	INFORMATION ON HIERARCHY	T1-T2
2,	MORE GLOBAL CATEGORIES	T2-T3
3,	BUILT IN HIERARCHY	T3-T4

- -

SUM OF CROSS-PRODUCTS FOR HYPOTHESIS

	1 WORDS	2 CATS	3 TIME 2	4 TIME 4	5 TIME 6
1 WORDS	216.23				
2 CATS	-.61	.02			
3 TIME 2	1891.90	-11.49	26000.23		
4 TIME 4	1346.52	-15.85	12943.19	17136.40	
5 TIME 6	802.79	-12.05	8847.79	11766.37	8305.58

SUM OF PROD. FOR HYPOTHESIS,ADJUSTED FOR COVARIATES
----

		1 WORDS	2 CATS
1	WORDS	230.5623	
2	CATS	-.2753	.0127

(SCP HYP + SCP ERROR) - ADJUSTED FOR ANY COVARIATES (STI*)

		1	2
		WORDS	CATS
1	WORDS	1692.152	
2	CATS	11.323	.223

CHOLESKY FACTOR STI*
----

		1 WORDS	2 CATS
1	WORDS	41.13577	
2	CATS	.27527	.38361

LOG-DETERMINANT SCP HYPOTHESES + SCP ERROR, ADJUSTED FOR ANY COVARIATES, = 5.51751248E+00

F-RATIO FOR MULTIVARIATE TEST OF EQUALITY OF MEAN VECTORS=   2.6767

D.F.=   6 AND   80.0000   P LESS THAN .0204

(LIKELIHOOD RATIO = 6.93572639E-01   LOG = -3.65899302E-01)

VARIABLE	HYPOTHESIS MEAN SQ	UNIVARIATE F	P LESS THAN	STEP DOWN F	P LESS THAN
1 WORDS	76.8541	2.1559	.1080	2.1559	.1080
				STEP-DOWN MEAN SQUARES =(76.8541/	35.6485)
2 CATS	.0042	.8271	.4866	3.2714	.0309
				STEP-DOWN MEAN SQUARES =(.0097/	.0030)

DEGREES OF FREEDOM FOR HYPOTHESIS=   3
DEGREES OF FREEDOM FOR ERROR=   41

3 COVARIATE(S) ELIMINATED

HYPOTHESIS MEAN PRODUCTS, ADJUSTED FOR ANY COVARIATES
----

		1 WORDS	2 CATS
1	WORDS	76.85412	
2	CATS	-.09177	.00424

3 COVARIATE(S) ELIMINATED

DISCRIMINANT ANALYSIS FOR HYPOTHESIS   2
==

VARIANCE OF CANONICAL VARIATE   1 =   .3819   PER CENT OF CANONICAL VARIATION= 89.81   ROY≠S CRITERION=   .2764
M= 0.0   N=   19.0

--DISCRIMINANT FUNCTION COEFFICIENTS--

VARIABLE	RAW COEFFICIENT	STANDARDIZED
1 WORDS	-.217640	-1.2994
2 CATS	15.156570	1.0853

VARIANCE OF CANONICAL VARIATE   2 =   .0433   PER CENT OF CANONICAL VARIATION= 10.19   ROY#S CRITERION=   .0415
                                                                                                   M= -.5   N= 18.5

                              --DISCRIMINANT FUNCTION COEFFICIENTS--

                     VARIABLE   RAW COEFFICIENT   STANDARDIZED

                     1 WORDS   .050351   .3006
                     2 CATS   10.828141   .7753

                      HOTELLING#S TRACE CRITERION=   .4253

         BARTLETT#S CHI SQUARE TEST FOR SIGNIFICANCE OF SUCCESSIVE CANONICAL VARIATES

    FOR ROOTS 1 THROUGH 2 CHI SQUARE=   15.0019   WITH   6 DEGREES OF FREEDOM   P LESS THAN .0203

                       (LIKELIHOOD RATIO = 6.93572638E-01   LOG = -3.65899304E-01)

    FOR ROOTS 2 THROUGH 2 CHI SQUARE=   1.7386   WITH   2 DEGREES OF FREEDOM   P LESS THAN .4193

                       (LIKELIHOOD RATIO = 9.58481708E-01   LOG = -4.24048006E-02)

                CANONICAL FORM OF LEAST SQUARE ESTIMATES-VARIATES X EFFECTS
                ----

               1   2   3
             T1-T2   T2-T3   T3-T4

     1   .821605 -1.289994   -.424086
     2   .193187   -.423715   .543395

CORE USED FOR DATA= 151 LOCATIONS OUT OF 3000 AVAILABLE

9. REFERENCES

1. T. W. Anderson, "The choice of the Degree of Polynomial Regression as a Multiple Decision Problem," *Ann Math Stat* **33**, 255–265 (1962).

2. Å. Björck, "Solving Linear Least Squares Problems by Gram–Schmidt Orthonormalization," *BIT*, **7**, 1–21 (1967).

3. R. D. Bock, "Programming Univariate and Multivariate Analysis of Variance," *Technometrics*, **5**, 95–117 (1963).

4. R. D. Bock, "A Computer Program for Univariate and Multivariate Analysis of Variance," in *Proceedings of Scientific Symposium on Statistics*," Thomas J. Watson Research Center, Yorktown Heights, 69–111 (1965).

5. R. D. Bock, *Multivariate Statistical Methods in Behavioral Research*, McGraw-Hill, New York, 1975.

6. R. D. Bock, *MATCAL: Double Precision Matrix Operations Subroutines*, National Educational Resources, Inc., Chicago, 1973.

7. N. R. Draper and N. Smith, *Applied Regression Analysis*, Wiley, New York, 1966.

8. J. D. Finn, "Multivariate Analysis of Repeated Measures Data," *Multivariate Behav. Res.*, **4**, 391–413 (1969).

9. J. D. Finn, *A General Model for Multivariate Analysis*, Holt, Rinehart, and Winston, New York, 1974.

10. J. D. Finn, *Multivariance: Univariate and Multivariate Analysis of Variance, Covariance, and Regression*. Version, 5.2, Chicago: National Educational Resources, Inc., (Box A-3650, Chicago, Illinois 60690), October, 1974.

11. L. Fox, *An Introduction to Numerical Linear Algebra*, Oxford Univ. Press, New York, 1965.

12. G. H. Golub, "Matrix Decompositions and Statistical Calculations," in *Statistical Computation*, R. C. Milton and J. A. Nelder (eds.), Academic Press, New York, 365–397 (1969).

13. G. H. Golub and G. P. H. Styan, "Numerical Computations for Univariate Linear Models," *Research memorandum number SU326 P30-13*, Computer Sciences Department, Stanford Univ., September 1971.

14. F. A. Graybill, *An Introduction to Linear Statistical Models*, Vol. I, McGraw-Hill, New York, 1961.

15. D. L. Heck, "Charts of Some Upper Percentage Points of the Distribution of the Largest Characteristic Root," *Annals Math. Statist.*, **31**, 625–642 (1960).

16. A. S. Householder, *The Theory of Matrices in Numerical Analysis*, Blaisdell Press, New York, 1964.

17. International Business Machines Corp., *System 360 Scientific Subroutine Package Programmer's Manual*, Manual 360A-CM-03X. Corporation, White Plains, N. Y., 1966.

18. B. Kurkjian and M. Zelen, "A Calculus for Factorial Arrangements," *Annals Math. Statist.*, **33**, 600–619 (1962).

19. W. Mendenhall, *Introduction to Linear Models and the Design and Analysis of Experiments*, Wadsworth Publishing Company, Belmont, Calif., 1968.

20. J. M. Ortega, "On Sturm Sequences for Tridiagonal Matrices" *J. Assoc. Comput. Mach.*, **7**, 260–263 (1960).

21. K. C. S. Pillai, *Statistical Tables for Tests of Multivariate Hypotheses*, University of the Philippines Statistical Center, Manila, 1960.

22. K. C. S. Pillai, "On the Distribution of the Largest Seven Roots of a Matrix in Multivariate Analysis," *Biometrika*, **51**, 270–275 (1964).

23. K. C. S. Pillai, "On the Distribution of the Largest Characteristic Root of a Matrix in Multivariate Analysis," *Biometrika*, **52**, 405–414 (1965).

24. R. F. Potthoff and S. N. Roy, "A Generalized Multivariate Analysis of Variance Model Useful Especially for Growth Curve Problems," *Biometrika*, **51**, 313–326 (1964).

25. S. J. Press, *Applied Multivariate Analysis*, Holt, Rinehart and Winston, New York, 1972.

26. C. R. Rao, *Advanced Statistical Methods in Biometric Research*, Wiley, New York, 1952.

27. J. Roy, "Step-down Procedure in Multivariate Analysis," *Annals Math. Statist.*, **29**, 1177–1187 (1958).

28. J. Roy and R. E. Bargmann, "Test of Multiple Independence and the Associated Confidence Bounds," *Annals Math. Statist.*, **29**, 491–503 (1958).

29. S. N. Roy, *Some Aspects of Multivariate Analysis*, Wiley, New York, 1967.

30. S. R. Searle, *Linear Models*, Wiley, New York, 1971.

31. F. J. Wall, *The Generalized Variance Ratio of U-Statistic*, The Dikewood Corp., Albequerque, N. M., 1968.

32. J. H. Wilkinson, *The Algebraic Eigenvalue Problem*, Oxford Univ. Press, London, 1965.

33. E. A. Youngs and E. M. Cramer, "Some Results Relevant to Choice of Sum and Sum-of-product Algorithms," *Technometrics*, **13**, 657–665 (1971).

PART IV | CLUSTER ANALYSIS AND PATTERN RECOGNITION

Editorial Introduction to Part IV

What is classification?—Nothing more than the assignment of an object to a group. Classification methods can be broken down into two groups: classification *with* and classification *without* a teacher. Classification *with* a teacher means that the categories are preestablished prior to the assignment of objects to classes. Discriminant analysis (Chapter 5) could be considered classification with a teacher.

In classification *without* a teacher, the classification scheme attempts to define "natural" populations on the basis of parametric or nonparametric criteria. Examples of classification without a teacher are the hierarchical clustering and ISODATA techniques described in this volume in Chapters 11 and 13.

Some of the applications for which classification techniques have been used are the following:

- The classification of chest X-rays into normal and abnormal categories.
- The classification of electrocardiograms into normal and abnormal categories.
- The finding of cases with chronic obstructive lung disease and their classification into specific disease entities.
- The karyotyping of human chromosomes.
- The assignment of patients in shock to various severity states.
- The classification of white cells (leukocytes) into differential categories.
- The partitioning of animals, or flowers, into species.

Hierarchical Classificatory Methods

11

W. T. Williams and G. N. Lance
Commonwealth Scientific and Industrial Organization
Townsville & Canberra, Australia

1. FUNCTION

"Numerical classification" (often called "numerical taxonomy") is not concerned with the allocation of individuals to an existing classification, which is the province of discriminant analysis and related methods; its function is to set up a classification where none has existed previously, or where it is desired to ignore previous work and reexamine data *de novo*. Its purpose is almost invariably to simplify a data matrix too extensive for the human mind to process intuitively. An ecological survey, for example, may produce data consisting of some hundreds of sample areas of land specified by the presence or absence of over a thousand plant species, and matrices on this scale are no longer exceptional. In any case, however, the human mind is very inefficient at elucidating patterns in even quite small matrices, and numerical assistance is increasingly in demand. The objects for classification may be almost anything; recent examples have included genera, species or varieties of living organisms, towns, water samples, limestones, chemical firms—the list is virtually endless. Fortunately, the numerical methods (which we shall here refer to as *strategies*) are almost completely independent of the nature of the material to be classified. There is, however, no single "correct" classification of any set of data; different numerical strategies will usually produce quite different results. It therefore becomes necessary for numerical consultants to advise on the types of classification available, and for a user to decide which type he requires. The most highly developed set of classificatory strategies comprises those known as *hierarchical* (for definition, see following); in this chapter we summarize the present state of knowledge concerning these strategies, with a view to providing information that will enable a numerical consultant to write the necessary programs and offer the appropriate advice concerning their use.

For general accounts see Cole [4], Cormack [5], Jardine and Sibson [10], Macnaughton-Smith [17], Sokal and Sneath

[20], Williams and Dale [27], and Williams [24]. In the mathematical discussion which follows we have not attempted to describe every strategy that has at some time been used; we confine ourselves to those strategies that we ourselves have found useful over a wide range of applications.

2. MATHEMATICAL DISCUSSION

a. Introduction and Definitions

THE BASIC MODEL

The data normally consist of a set of elements, variously known as *individuals* or *operational taxonomic units* (O.T.Us.), each defined by a set of attributes; the term "attribute" is in this context always used *sensu lato* to include variables. The set is postulated as being discontinuous, in that it can profitably be regarded as comprising an unknown number of distinct subsets, which are to be found. The members of any one subset are to be more similar to each other than they are to the members of any other subset; the term "similar" here includes a number of different mathematical relationships which are set out below. This is usually described as a *minimum variance model*, even though variance, in the statistical sense, may not be the measure used. The solution is in general not unique; it is best regarded as a pattern which is not an objective property of the data, but is *pattern-for-an-agent* [16] in that it is intended to elicit, from a data-matrix too extensive for intuitive processing, those properties of interest to the particular user. Two extreme types of user interest can usefully be distinguished:

1. The user wishes to ascertain the extent to which, within the numerical model chosen, distinct subsets exist; the system is to be distorted as little as possible, so that if no distinct subsets exist, none will be found. This type of process is relatively stable under change of numerical strategy.

2. The user suspects that truly distinct subsets do not exist; but in order to facilitate his understanding of a very large set of elements, wishes such diffuse subsets as can be found to be artificially sharpened. This process, sometimes called *dissection*, is very sensitive to change of numerical strategy and hence is disliked by mathematicians; it does, however, appear to be the commoner user requirement.

It may sometimes be desirable to transpose the data matrix and classify the attributes by reference to the individuals. Such a classification is said to be *inverse*, in contrast to the *normal* classification of individuals.

TYPES OF ATTRIBUTE

There are three main types. *Nominal* attributes (sometimes known as "disordered multistates") are defined by a series of states (e.g., sandstone, granite, basalt, chalk) such that, although the states may be numbered serially, no meaning is to be attached to the order in which the states are taken; in the standard case any one element can be in only one state of a given attribute. A special case is the *binary* (sometimes called "qualitative") attribute, a nominal attribute with only two states (present or absent, yes or no). *Ordinal* attributes (sometimes known as "ordered multistates") are defined by an ordered series of states (e.g., rare, occasional, common, abundant); the order in which the states are taken is meaningful, but the distances between states are undefined. *Numerical* attributes (sometimes called "metric" or "quantitative") are measured or counted quantities (weight in grams, number of leaves); the term "metric" is older, but in this context may cause confusion with its restricted topological meaning as applied to certain measures. Not all observations fit neatly into these categories, and prior discussion with the user concerning the method of defining and scoring his attributes is often desirable. In a general-purpose program provision must also be made for missing attributes to cover the case in which it has proved impossible to record a particular element.

Two special cases require special attention. *Linked* attributes comprise a set of attributes such that the contribution from the whole set must not exceed that which can be provided from a single attribute; a common example is a soil measurement at a single location taken at several levels. If the linked attributes are binary (e.g., presence or absence of particular types of hair on a plant stem) the complete set resembles a single nominal attribute such that an element can be in more than one state at a time, and is often collectively known as a "nonexclusive disordered multistate." Linked attributes usually require special mathematical treatment. *Serially dependent* attributes (sometimes known as "conditionally defined" or "hierarchically ordered") arise when, if one attribute is in a particular state, the question implied by other attributes cannot be answered, for example, wings present or absent; if wings are present, a further set of descriptive attributes relating to wings can be scored; if they are absent the latter attributes cannot be scored and are said to be *inapplicable*. In most programs inapplicable attributes are simply treated as missing, but in theory this can have undesirable consequences; the problem is treated in detail by Kendrick [11], Williams [23], and McNeill [18].

Lastly, cases arise in which attributes as such do not exist, or are not provided. The material submitted for classification in these cases consists of a symmetric matrix of pair-functions, that is, some numerical comparison calculated or recorded between all pairs of individuals. The methods of handling such material are dealt with later.

TYPES OF CLASSIFICATION

Numerical classification includes a number of different numerical processes, from which an appropriate choice must be made for each application The successive choices are summarized in Fig. 11.1, in which the

choices are numbered in order; the strategies enclosed in the box, and any choices internal to them, are outside the scope of this chapter. We deal with the relevant decisions in order:

(1) Exclusive/Nonexclusive. In an exclusive classification, a given element can occur in one, and only one, subset; in the nonexclusive case the same element can occur in more than one subset. (In a classification of hospital patients based on diseases, a single patient can have more than one disease.) Nonexclusive classifications are used in particular forms of information retrieval, particularly in library work and medical diagnosis; they are never hierarchical, and will not be considered further in this article.

(2) Intrinsic/Extrinsic. Formally, in the intrinsic case the classification is to be effected solely by reference to the attribute-set provided, all attributes initially possessing equal status. In the extrinsic case one of the attributes is designated as "external"; the problem is then to produce, by manipulation of the internal set only, a classifica-

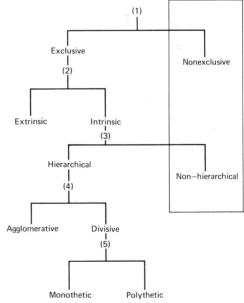

Fig. 11-1 The choices available for selection of classification methods.

tion that reflects the external attribute as closely as possible. To take an actual case: We had a large group of schoolchildren about whom much information had been collected concerning their home background, racial origin, health, and so on; we also knew whether they had left school early. The problem was to find out whether the other information could be used to sort the children into groups such that some of these were likely to leave school early, whereas others were not. "Leaving school early" had here been designated as an external attribute, and any other structure in the population was without interest; this is therefore a typical extrinsic case. Only one extrinsic algorithm is known; it is hierarchical, and will be considered in due course.

(3) Hierarchical / Nonhierarchical. In a nonhierarchical classification groups are selected such that each is individually as homogeneous as possible; the relationship between groups is not in issue. In the hierarchical case groups are considered in pairs, as possible candidates for fusion; and the criterion for fusion is that the *decrease* in homogeneity on fusion shall be as small as possible. Formally, this is usually expressed by saying that a nonhierarchical classification optimizes the internal properties of subsets; a hierarchical classification optimizes a *route* between individuals and the complete population. Nonhierarchical classifications are always iterative, and will not be further considered here. Almost all hierarchical strategies are computationally determinate, and consequently less extravagant of computer time than their nonhierarchical counterparts.

(4) Agglomerative / Divisive. These differ only in the direction of the route. In an agglomerative classification the individuals are progressively fused into subsets of increasing size until the entire population is in a single set; in a divisive classification the whole population of elements is progressively subdivided (in practice, always di-

chotomously) until an acceptable degree of subdivision is obtained.

(5) Monothetic / Polythetic. In a monothetic classification, division is effected by reference to a single attribute of maximal information-content; in the polythetic case all attributes are equally concerned. Agglomerative strategies are always polythetic.

Each of these major types still contains within itself a variety of strategies based on different numerical models, the choice of which is data dependent; it is with these individual models that the remainder of this chapter is largely concerned.

ANCILLARY REQUIREMENTS

At the beginning of the classificatory process, in almost all applications, all attributes are regarded as equivalent, but it is invariably found when the process is completed that the separate attributes have contributed very unequally to the final configuration. From this arises a requirement for a *diagnostic* system which shall simulate the course of a polythetic classification and provide an ordered list of attribute-contributions for each successive fusion or fission. A requirement may also arise for the interrelationships of the final subsets to be mapped into an efficiently reduced Euclidean space, the process known as *ordination*. For the problems arising in the ordination of an already-classified set, see [28]; all ordination programs ultimately rest on principal component, or principal coordinate, analysis, and will not be considered further here.

b. General Computational Considerations

The most striking feature of modern hierarchical classificatory programs is the contrast between the extreme mathematical simplicity of the basic algorithms, and the complexity of the production programs; for example, the algorithms of the program MULTBET (see later) can be encompassed in a few lines, but the program itself comprises about 1500 Fortran statements. All classificatory programs involve carrying out a relatively simple process a very large number of times, and storing a substantial proportion of the results; if there are n individuals to be classified it will usually be necessary initially to store $\frac{1}{2}n(n-1)$, or in some cases n^2, quantities, and it may also be necessary to retain the basic data from which these have been calculated. For all except small problems, or computers with a very large core-store, it will thus usually be necessary to initiate frequent transfers between core and auxiliary stores; and in order that these shall be reduced to a minimum, fairly complicated "tag and search" subroutines are required to ensure that only immediately relevant information is transferred. Furthermore, the provision of information for ancillary requirements, such as diagnostic programs or plotters, makes additional demands on the core-store. Such "housekeeping" routines are usually highly system dependent, and it is unlikely that a large-scale classificatory program will run on any installation other than that for which it was written, at least without considerable modification. Such modification is seldom profitable; we maintain that it is almost always preferable to return to the basic algorithms, and to write housekeeping routines *de novo* appropriate to the installation for which the program is required. This section deals only with the basic algorithms themselves.

c. Measures of Similarity or Dissimilarity

INTRODUCTION

These are measures of the degree of likeness between two individuals (or, less commonly, attributes). Strictly, an increasingly positive measure implies increased likeness in a similarity measure, decreased likeness in a dissimilarity measure; but the distinction is not always maintained, and both are frequently referred to as *similarity measures* (or, in earlier works, "similarity coefficients"). In practice, all modern systems operate on dissimilarity measures. Two main classes can be distinguished. The first,

the (i, j) measures, are such that when the characteristics of two elements, or groups of elements, are known, the measure can be calculated prior to fusion. The other, (ij, k) measures, relate the characteristics of the groups before, to those after, the fusion. A few measures can be defined in either form; but true (ij, k) measures, such as the information statistics, possess no known (i, j) counterparts. It will be shown later that such measures present special computational problems. The literature contains an enormous number of suggested measures, some of them frankly bizarre, but four main classes of measure will suffice for a standard battery of programs. These are (i) the correlation coefficient, (ii) measures based on the Euclidean metric, (iii) those based on the Manhattan (city-block or lattice) metric, and (iv) a variety of information statistics, and we shall consider these in turn. As symbols we shall use x_{1j} and x_{2j} for values of the jth numerical attribute for two individuals; where binary attributes are at issue we shall use the (a, b, c, d) notation, wherein a is the number of attributes possessed by both individuals, d the number possessed by neither, and b and c are the number possessed by one but not the other. We shall refer to a quantity $(1 - x)$ as the "ones-complement of x"; other symbols and terms will be defined as needed.

THE CORRELATION COEFFICIENT

This is used in classical statistics to define a relationship between two continuous variables. Let x_{ij}, x_{ik} represent the values of the ith of n individuals for the jth and kth attribute, respectively; let $\bar{x}_j$ and $\bar{x}_k$ be the means of the two attributes over all individuals. Then the correlation coefficient between j and k is given by

$$r_{jk} = \frac{\sum_i (x_{ij} - \bar{x}_j)(x_{ik} - \bar{x}_k)}{\sqrt{\sum_i (x_{ij} - \bar{x}_j)^2 \cdot \sum_i (x_{ik} - \bar{x}_k)^2}}$$

Note: it would never be computed in precisely this form, because of cumulative errors associated with subtraction of the means; use is made of the identity

$$\sum_i (x_{ij} - \bar{x}_j)(x_{ik} - \bar{x}_k)$$

$$= \sum_i x_{ij} x_{ik} - \left\{ \left(\sum_i x_{ij} \right)\left(\sum_i x_{ik} \right) \right\} / n$$

In the binary case, where all x_{ij}, $x_{ik} = 1$ or 0, we can use the (a, b, c, d) notation. The measure, then usually known as the Pearson ϕ-coefficient, takes the form

$$\frac{ad - bc}{\sqrt{(a + b)(a + c)(b + d)(c + d)}}$$

This binary form has found some use in plant ecological survey, and presents no difficulties. Two problems arise, however, in the use of the continuous form in classification programs. First, it may be desired to define the measure between two individuals instead of between two attributes. In the all-numerical case this presents no difficulty providing the attributes are all of the same dimensions: it is simply equivalent to transposing the data-matrix. This application is appropriate when the interest lies in similarity of proportions, not in absolute values; it has been found useful in anthropology (comparison of primate skulls) and in soil chemistry.

A more serious problem arises in certain mixed-data divisive programs (see Programs 5–7 in Section 6b), in which it may be necessary to define a squared correlation coefficient between *any* pair of attributes, not necessarily continuous or binary variables; the resulting r^2 values are to be summed into a vector with one entry for each numerical or ordinal attribute and for each state of a nominal attribute. Ordinals can be treated as numericals, and so present no difficulty; the problems arise with nominal/numerical or nominal/nominal comparisons. The only extant suggestion for handling such comparisons appears to be

that of Lance and Williams [15], and is as follows:

Nominal / Numerical. The nominal attribute, of m states, is regarded as a set of m independent binary attributes, whose state-symbols (0 and 1) are taken as real numbers. Correlations between the separate states of the nominal attribute are of no interest, so m binary/numerical r^2 values are calculated; the values are accumulated into the locations for the states of the nominal attribute, but only the largest is accumulated into the numerical location.

Nominal / Nominal. Consider two nominal attributes, *M1* with m states and *M2* with n states. Again regarding the states as independent binaries, and neglecting intra-attribute correlations, we have an $(m \times n)$ matrix of crosscorrelations, where we take the m rows as the r^2 values generated by the states of *M1*, and the n columns as those generated by the states of *M2*. The highest value in each row is accumulated into the appropriate state of *M1*, and the highest value in each column is accumulated into the appropriate state of *M2*.

The statistic χ^2, related in the all-binary case to the correlation coefficient (in this case $\chi^2 = nr^2$), is of historic interest in that it was the basis of the first successful divisive monothetic program ("association analysis"); but in this context it is now obsolete, having been superseded by an information statistic.

The Euclidean Metric

This, the Minkowski metric of order 2, is conventionally defined as

$$\left(\sum_j |x_{1j} - x_{2j}|^2 \right)^{\frac{1}{2}}.$$

Since it is desirable that classificatory strategies should where possible be additive over attributes, it is commonly used in the form of its square, and notated $\sum_j (x_{1j} - x_{2j})^2$; to avoid the value becoming inconveniently large, it is usual to divide by the number of attributes.

Numerical Attributes. If the attributes are of different physical dimensions, they must be made dimensionless before the addition can have any meaning; if they are of the same dimensions but of very different numerical ranges, they must be standardized if wide-ranging attributes are not completely to dominate the system. It is customary to fulfil both requirements by dividing the raw values by some quantity of the same dimensions which will in some sense equalize the contributions of individual attributes; it is desirable that the quantity chosen should be reasonably robust under alterations and errors of sampling. Three such quantities have been suggested. The semi-interquartile range is very robust over change of sampling; but since it involves a sorting process for every attribute it is cumbersome in practice and is never used. At the other extreme is the range; it is easily computed, but is very sensitive to sampling variations and is not, therefore, in common use. It is, therefore, usual to employ the standard deviation (or variance in the squared case), which is fairly stable under sampling variation and fairly easy to compute. It is unnecessary to compute both the variances and the complete set of distances, since the former can be obtained from the latter. As before, let x_{ij} be the value of the ith individual for the jth attribute, where $i = 1, 2, \ldots, p, q, \ldots, n$. It can be shown that

$$\frac{\sum\limits_{p < q}^{n-1} \sum\limits_{}^{n} (x_{pj} - x_{qj})^2}{\frac{1}{2} n(n-1)}$$

$$= \frac{2}{n-1} \left\{ \sum\limits_{i}^{n} x_{ij}^2 - \frac{1}{n} \left(\sum\limits_{i}^{n} x_{ij} \right)^2 \right\}$$

It follows that, for a given attribute, the arithmetic mean of its contributions to the upper triangle of all interindividual distances is equal to twice its sample variance.

For a rigorous examination of Euclidean standardization, see [2].

Ordinal Attributes. If the population were sufficiently large it would theoretically be possible to apply a normalizing transformation; but this would be cumbersome and it is current practice to regard the states as equidistant and to treat ordinals as numericals.

Nominal Attributes. If there are n elements, f_s of which are in state s of a nominal attribute, the general expression for the variance is

$$\frac{1}{2} \left(n \sum\limits_{s} f_s - \sum\limits_{s} f_s^2 \right) / (n^2 - n)$$

This includes the "nonexclusive multistate" case; for the exclusive case the term $n \sum\limits_{s} f_s$ in the numerator collapses into n^2.

Finally, it should be noted that in the all-binary case the unstandardized Euclidean distance collapses into $(b + c)/(a + b + c + d)$, the ones-complement of the "simple matching coefficient" of earlier writers.

Transformation. Data may be highly skewed; in the numerical case this arises from the occasional out-of-scale outlying value, in the binary case from the occasional presence of a rare attribute or the absence of a common one. Variance standardization then tends to exaggerate the importance of such abnormal values. For the all-binary case it is preferable to use a different model, such as an information statistic (see below). For the numerical case, prior transformation of the data is usually desirable. Current experience suggests that the aggregation-normalizing transformation of Taylor [21] is too drastic; square-root, cube-root and logarithmic transformations have been used with success, but further work is needed.

THE MANHATTAN METRIC

This, sometimes called the city-block or lattice metric, is the Minkowski metric of order 1, defined simply as $\sum\limits_{j} |x_{1j} - x_{2j}|$; it is again usual to divide by the number of attributes.

Numerical Attributes. Three forms of standardization are in use:

GOWER METRIC. This is range-standardized, and its properties have been examined in detail by Gower [9]. Its use is not indicated if the data are very highly skewed.

BRAY-CURTIS MEASURE. This is the quantity

$$\left(\sum_j |x_{1j} - x_{2j}|\right) \bigg/ \left(\sum_j x_{1j} + \sum_j x_{2j}\right).$$

Although constrained between 0 and 1, it can obviously be dominated by wide-ranging attributes; it is usual to prestandardize the raw data before applying it (it was originally intended for use when all x_j were percentages). The data after standardization must be nonnegative, or the constraint will fail. It is less used than formerly, though it still has its advocates. The form in which it is here given is computationally convenient, but may be unfamiliar to users. If we write w_j for the smaller of the two values x_{1j} and x_{2j}, and put $W = \Sigma w_j$, $a = \Sigma x_{1j}$ and $b = \Sigma x_{2j}$, the ones-complement of the expression above becomes $2W/(a + b)$; this is the form in which the measure is usually quoted in ecological texts.

CANBERRA METRIC. This is the quantity $\sum_j \{(|x_{1j} - x_{2j}|)/(x_{1j} + x_{2j})\}$. It is self-standardizing and, provided all x_j are nonnegative, is constrained between 0 and 1. Its insensitivity to large outlying values makes it peculiarly suitable for highly skewed data. It has a singularity at zero, in that if $x_{1j} = 0$, the measure takes its maximum value of 1 irrespective of the value of x_{2j}; it is usual to counter this by trapping all zero/nonzero comparisons and replacing x_{1j}, for that comparison only, by a quantity somewhat smaller than the smallest value of x_{ij} in the data-matrix. Double-zero comparisons can easily be neglected, the measure then being averaged over such comparisons as remain. For use with signed data Adkins has sug-

gested replacing the denominator by $(|x_{1j}| + |x_{2j}|)$, but in this form it takes its maximum value of 1 whenever x_{1j} and x_{2j} are of opposite sign.

Ordinal Attributes. These are invariably treated as numericals.

Nominal Attributes. The only case of interest is the comparison involving a nominal attribute if the contribution is to be 1 if the states nowhere overlap; for this purpose the Bray-Curtis measure is the most convenient. In the all-binary case the Bray-Curtis measure collapses into $(b + c)/(2a + b + c)$, the ones-complement of the Czekanowsi measure; the Canberra metric similarly collapses into $(b + c)/(a + b + c)$, the ones-complement of the Jaccard measure.

The LINKED Algorithm. Consider the case of the multilevel numerical attribute such that the complete set of levels is only to contribute as much as would a single numerical attribute. If all attributes are of this type, all have the same number of levels, and there are no missing values, it is permissible to regard the levels as independent attributes, since only a scaling factor is then involved. In all other cases it is better to make level-by-level comparisons for each attribute, averaging the resulting measures over such levels as are not missing on one side or the other. The Gower or Canberra metrics are commonly used, according to the degree of skewness of the data.

INFORMATION STATISTICS

These need to be treated somewhat differently, since counts and genuinely continuous variables cannot be processed in the same way; it will be convenient to begin with the all-binary case. The formulation may be that of Shannon (based on $n \ln n$) or Brillouin ($\ln(n!)$); for most purposes the distinction is unimportant, and the Shannon formulation is more commonly used.

Binary Attributes. Let there be a group of n elements defined by the presence or absence of s attributes, and let there be a_j elements possessing the jth attribute. We define an information content, I, for the group as

$$I = sn \ln n$$
$$- \sum_j \{ a_j \ln a_j + (n - a_j)\ln(n - a_j) \}$$

Let the information content of two groups A and B be I_A and I_B, respectively; let the two groups be fused to form a composite group C with information content I_C; then we define an information gain for the fusion, ΔI, as

$$\Delta I = I_C - (I_A + I_B)$$

The information content of a single element, or of a group of identical elements, is always zero in this model.

Counts. Let a single element for classification be itself a population of n true individuals falling into a number of distinct categories (e.g., plant or animal species) such that there are a_j individuals in the jth category, and $\sum_j a_j = n$. We define the information content of the complete element (also known as the *diversity*) as

$$\left(\sum_j a_j \right) \ln \left(\sum_j a_j \right) - \sum_j (a_j \ln a_j)$$

and we define an information gain as before. It is useful to state this gain in explicit form. Let two such elements for fusion be represented by two row-vectors (a_{1j}) and (a_{2j}); let r_i be a row sum ($i = 1, 2$) and c_j a column sum; let N be the grand sum. Then we shall have

$$\Delta I = N \ln N - \sum_j (c_j \ln c_j) - \sum_i (r_i \ln r_i)$$
$$+ \sum_i \sum_j (a_{ij} \ln a_{ij})$$

This is also known as the *transmitted information*. The diversity model takes no account of zero entries, and appears to have

unsatisfactory properties for certain types of data; the problem has been reexamined by Williams [25], who has suggested an alternative model for which there is as yet little experience.

Multistate Nominal Attributes. Consider a group of elements with a_j elements in the jth state. This is regarded as a row-vector, and the information gain for the fusion of two such groups is simply the transmitted information as calculated in the previous paragraph. The information gain from a nominal attribute of many states is often uncomfortably large, and may tend to dominate a classification; in this model it is thus advisable to keep the number of states small (say, 5) where possible.

Ordinal Attributes. The only extant solution is that of Lance and Williams [14]. An s-state ordinal will generate a $2 \times s$ contingency table; we partition the degrees of freedom and pick out that associated with the largest ΔI. By dichotomizing at each state in turn we obtain a set of $(s - 1)$ 2×2 contingency tables; ΔI for each table is calculated, and the largest taken as the contribution of this attribute to the fusion. The dichotomy may not be quite optimal, as it is strictly the optimal dichotomy for a restricted set, but it has been believed to be effective in practice. Its main disadvantage is that an s-state attribute implies the same amount of computation as $(s - 1)$ separate attributes, and the process is computationally slow.

Experience suggests that this partition concept is unfamiliar, and we therefore append a numerical example. Assume a four-state nominal attribute, with states tagged A, B, C, and D, and two groups, one of 11, the other of 12, individuals, disposed between the states as follows:

A	B	C	D	Total
2	5	0	4	11
3	1	4	4	12

The partitions used in current programs are A/BCD, AB/CD, and ABC/D; the resulting 2×2 tables and their associated information gains are as follows:

Partition	2×2 Table		ΔI
A/BCD	2	9	0.0789
	3	9	
AB/CD	7	4	1.0723
	4	8	
ABC/D	7	4	0.0117
	8	4	

We, therefore, choose the AB/CD partition, as having the largest gain. However, for s states there are in all, not $(s - 1)$, but $(2^{s-1} - 1)$ partitions; in this case, there are therefore 4 partitions we have not examined. These with their associated gains, are as follows:

B/ACD	2.1701
C/ABD	2.9897
AC/BD	2.0288
AD/BC	0.1179

It is clear that, in this example, the existing algorithm is seriously suboptimal. With the advent of faster computers it will almost certainly be desirable to examine all possible partitions, even though this may involve placing a restriction on s.

Continuous Variables. Three solutions exist in the literature. The message-length model of Wallace and Boulton [22] requires that the variables be normally distributed, an assumption unrealistic for much classificatory work. Lance and Williams [14] divide the range into 8 equal parts, and "chop" the variable into an 8-state ordinal; this discards much information and is computationally slow. Dale et al. [7] point out that if the variable can be treated as a count (e.g., percentage frequency of occurrence of a plant species), a percentage p can be treated as if it were a group of 100 elements, p of which possess a binary attribute. If this solution is not available, it is better to avoid information-statistic models where the data-matrix is largely numerical.

Missing Values. It is not permissible to average information gains over known comparisons, and use must be made of the variations in degrees of freedom associated with a given comparison; a binary, ordinal, or continuous attribute is associated with a single degree of freedom, whereas an s-state nominal contributes $(s - 1)$ degrees. We take advantage of the facts that $2\Delta I$ is asymptotically distributed as χ^2 with the same number of degrees of freedom; and that, if there are d degrees of freedom, $\sqrt{(2\chi^2)}$ tends to be normally distributed around a mean of $\sqrt{(2d - 1)}$ with unit variance if d is large. Since this is true in most mixed-data applications, it follows that the quantity $2\sqrt{(\Delta I)} - \sqrt{(2d - 1)}$ can be regarded as an approximation to a normal deviate with zero mean and unit variance. The ΔI values are therefore transformed into this form, which is used as the decision function for comparing information gains associated with different degrees of freedom; this difference can only arise when some values are missing.

d. Fusion Strategies (Agglomerative Systems)

INTRODUCTION

The Basic Algorithm. All agglomerative systems begin in the same way. For n individuals all $\frac{1}{2}n(n - 1)$ dissimilarity measures are computed, and that pair of individuals with the smallest measure are fused into a two-membered group. It is then immediately necessary to define a compatible measure between this group and the remaining $(n - 2)$ individuals; and at a later stage it will clearly be necessary to define a measure between an individual and a group of any size, and between two groups. At every step in the classification that fusion (individual-/individual, individual/group, or group/group) is made for which the measure is the smallest remaining in the system. The measure defined must be such that an individual can be processed as if it were a one-membered group. It is the nature of the resulting group/group measure which determines the fusion strategy; at the end of the process a total of $(n - 1)^2$ measures will have been computed.

Space Distortion. We consider the individuals as points in a multidimensional space defined by the attributes as axes. Certain fusion strategies operate in effect by erecting boundaries between groups of points, but do not change the relative positions of the points in the original space. Such strategies are said to be *space conserving*. In other strategies the space around a group appears to stretch as the group grows, so that the group appears to recede from other points as it grows. Such strategies are said to be *space dilating*; they cluster intensely, and the groups appear to be more distinct than is really the case. In still other strategies the space appears to contract around a group as it grows (*space-contracting* strategies); inherent clustering is reduced, and there may be much "chaining"—the successive addition of single individuals. For a comparative example, see [24]; for a mathematical examination of "group-size dependence" see [26]; for a discussion of the controversy which has arisen over the use of space-dilating strategies, see [29].

Combinatorial Solutions. If, given the initial interindividual dissimilarity matrix, all subsequent individual/group and group/group measures can be calculated from this alone by a recursive process, the system is said to be *combinatorial*; once the initial matrix has been computed the raw data can be overwritten. Lance and Williams [12] have shown that all (i, j) measures in common use can be encompassed within a single linear combinatorial model. We assume two groups (i) and (j) with n_i and n_j elements respectively and intergroup dissimilarity d_{ij}. We further assume that d_{ij} is the smallest measure remaining in the system, so that (i) and (j) fuse to form a new group (k) with $n_k(= n_i + n_j)$ elements. Consider a third group (h) with n_h elements. Before the fu-

sion the values of d_{hi}, d_{hj}, d_{ij}, n_h, n_i, and n_j are all known. Then we set

$$d_{hk} = \alpha_i d_{hi} + \alpha_j d_{hj} + \beta d_{ij} + \gamma |d_{hi} - d_{hj}|$$

where the parameters α_i, α_j, β, and γ determine the nature of the strategy. In a few cases these parameters may be actual numbers; in most, however, they are simple algebraic functions of some or all of n_i, n_j, n_k, and n_h. The actual values or expressions are given below in connection with the individual strategies.

The information statistics, being true (ij, k) measures, possess no known combinatorial solution and in their case the data must be retained for intergroup calculations throughout the entire classificatory process.

Monotonicity. For the complete process to be visually represented, the individuals (or intermediate groups if the presentation is to be truncated) can be arranged in convenient order along an abscissa; but the string of fusions (the *hierarchy* or *dendrogram*) then requires each fusion to be associated with an ordinate value. It is customary to use the dissimilarity measure of the fusion for this purpose, though in the space-dilating strategies this can give rise to errors in interpretation. The plot of the dendrogram will be extremely difficult to follow unless it rises with each successive fusion; this is equivalent to requiring that the string of dissimilarities associated with the successive fusions shall rise monotonically (as is the case in the two worked examples provided in Section 7). The only known combinatorial strategies with $\gamma \neq 0$ are in any case monotonic; the remainder are monotonic if $(\alpha_i + \alpha_j + \beta) \geqslant 1$. Although Burr [3] has shown that the information-statistic strategies are not necessarily monotonic, monotonicity failure in these cases is so rare that it can be disregarded.

Disadvantages. In most applications only the higher levels (i.e., the last few fusions) are of practical interest, but, to obtain these, the complete set of fusions, beginning with individuals, must be effected. As a result, agglomerative programs are relatively slow, and much of their computing time is employed obtaining results of little inherent interest. Secondly, fusions begin at the lowest information-level, where the possibility of error is highest. Since hierarchical fusions are irrevocable, some early fusions may later prove to have been unprofitable; some degree of "misclassification" in this sense is not uncommon, particularly if there are missing items of data.

INDIVIDUAL FUSION STRATEGIES

The information-statistic measures imply their own fusion strategies and need no separate description. They are intensely space-dilating and, though very popular, need to be interpreted with caution. A worked example is given in Section 7 below.

Of the several combinatorial strategies which have been proposed, six are (or have been) in common use. We examine these separately; the combinatorial parameters are given in each case.

Nearest-Neighbor. The distance between two groups is defined as the distance between those two individuals (one in each group) which are nearest. The parameters are $\alpha_i = \alpha_j = +\frac{1}{2}$; $\beta = 0$; $\gamma = -\frac{1}{2}$. It is a monotonic, intensely space-contracting strategy, with a number of theoretical mathematical advantages [10]. Its use is indicated if something in the nature of a minimum spanning tree, rather than a set of groups, is desired. It has also proved useful in cases where contiguity is relevant; for example, whether two flocks of sheep will behave as two units or a single unit depends on the distance between their two nearest neighbors. However, in our experience its space-contracting properties render it unsuitable for use in standard cases of classification. As a result, we never advocate its use unless there are special reasons for doing so, though not all analysts would agree with us.

Furthest-Neighbor. The distance between two groups is defined as the distance between their two most remote individuals; it is a monotonic, intensely space-dilating strategy which has been largely superseded by the *flexible* strategy (q.v.). The parameters are $\alpha_i = \alpha_j = +\frac{1}{2}$; $\beta = 0$; $\gamma = +\frac{1}{2}$.

Group-Average. If there are m_1 individuals in one group and m_2 in the other, the distance between them is defined as the arithmetic mean of all $m_1 m_2$ interindividual distances. The parameters are $\alpha_i = n_i/n_k$; $\alpha_j = n_j/n_k$; $\beta = \gamma = 0$. It is monotonic and substantially space-conserving, and is indicated when artifical sharpening of group boundaries is not required.

Centroid. In a Euclidean model, the distance between two groups is defined as the distance between their centroids, and the parameters are $\alpha_i = n_i/n_k$; $\alpha_j = n_j/n_k$; $\beta = -\alpha_i\alpha_j$; $\gamma = 0$. It is strictly space-conserving but is not monotonic; reversals are frequent and troublesome, and the strategy is almost obsolete.

Incremental Sum of Squares. In a Euclidean model, the intergroup distance is defined as the increase in the total within-group sum of squares (of distances from the respective centroids) on fusion. The parameters are $\alpha_i = (n_h + n_i)/(n_h + n_k)$; $\alpha_j = (n_h + n_j)/(n_h + n_k)$; $\beta = -n_h/(n_h + n_k)$; $\gamma = 0$. It is monotonic and space-dilating.

Flexible. This is applicable to *any* dissimilarity measure, and is defined by the quadruple constraint $(\alpha_i + \alpha_j + \beta = 1$; $\alpha_i = \alpha_j$; $\beta < 1$; $\gamma = 0)$. It is monotonic and its properties depend entirely on β. If $\beta = 0$ the strategy is space-conserving; as β becomes positive, the strategy becomes increasingly space-contracting; as β becomes negative the strategy becomes increasingly space-dilating. In practice a value of $\beta = -0.25$ is commonly used; a worked example using this value is provided in Section 7.

e. Fission Strategies (Divisive Systems)

INTRODUCTION.

General Characteristics. The theoretical advantages of divisive over agglomerative strategies are (i) the process begins at maximum information-content, (ii) division need not be continued until the population is fragmented into single individuals, and (iii) if there are fewer attributes than individuals, the computation needed is less, because, for n individuals and s attributes, the time for an agglomerative process depends roughly on n^2, for a divisive process on s^2. However, until very recently all divisive programs were monothetic, dichotomizing the population by reference to a single attribute at each step. Such a system is sensitive to errors in recording or coding the division-attribute; and individuals with aberrant values of the division attribute are taken down the "wrong" branch of the hierarchy. Monothetic systems can be converted into polythetic by a process of iterative reallocation of all individuals at each division, but in the mixed-data case much work still needs to be done in this field. Monothetic divisive methods, however, still remain the only computationally realistic solution for the classification of a very large number of individuals specified by a modest set of attributes. For a general account of mixed-data divisive programs see [15].

Dichotomizing. A monothetic divisive system requires an algorithm for dichotomizing a population on any type of attribute. The binary case is trivial; a multistate nominal attribute is treated as a string of binaries, and dichotomy is on a specified state. The ideal dichotomy of a continuous variable would be that which maximized the between-group sum of squares on fission; but for n individuals there are $(2^{n-1} - 1)$ possible splits, which is computationally impracticable. It is therefore usual to adopt the restricted procedure of Dale [6]: The string of values is sorted into order; two locations are nominated, one initially zero, the other initially Σx_i; values are transferred from one location to the other singly, and dichotomy is at that point where the between-group sum of squares is maximum. The process may be summarized algebraically as follows. Let the sorted string of values be represented by x_i, where $i = 1, 2,..,r,..,n$ (it is immaterial whether the order is ascending or descending). We shall call the two locations P and Q, and shall also use these symbols to denote the numerical value contained in the locations. We require a "correction term" C, defined as $C = \left(\sum_1^n x_i\right)^2 / n$; and an "uncorrected total sum of squares" T, defined as $T = \sum_1^n x_i^2$; we shall use D to denote a quantity that is to be calculated. At each stage the between-group sum of squares will be given by $(D - C)$, and the residual will be $(T - D)$. In all, $(n - 1)$ of the values are transferred; the contents of P and Q, and the value of D, at each stage will be as follows:

	P	Q	D
Initially	0	$\sum_1^n x_i$	—
1st transfer	x_1	$\sum_2^n x_i$	$P^2/1 + Q^2/(n-1)$
2nd transfer	$(x_1 + x_2)$	$\sum_3^n x_i$	$P^2/2 + Q^2/(n-2)$
rth transfer	$\sum_1^r x_i$	$\sum_{r+1}^n x_i$	$P^2/r + Q^2/(n-r)$
$(n-1)$th transfer	$\sum_1^{n-1} x_i$	x_n	$P^2/(n-1) + Q^2/1$

The quantity D will frequently rise, fall, and later rise again; it is therefore necessary to transfer the entire string to find the true maximum. If only a single division is needed, it is obvious that only D need be calculated, since T and C are invariant. However, for certain applications it may be desirable to perform successive splits of this type; the relative efficacy of such splits can then be estimated by examination of the between-group and residual sums of squares.

Finally, it should be noted that no satisfactory procedure for the dichotomizing of an ordinal attribute has yet been suggested.

Stopping Rules. In the nonhierarchical divisive program of Boulton and Wallace [1], a rigorous probabilistic test exists to define the point at which further fission is undesirable, though experience suggests that the test is too stringent. Many attempts have been made to define probabilistic stopping-rules for the divisive hierarchical programs, but none has proved satisfactory in practice. It is now usual to terminate the process at a predetermined number of "final" groups. Arbitrary though this procedure appears, it is satisfactory in practice; from 10 to 25 groups are commonly specified, according to the size of the problem.

INDIVIDUAL FISSION STRATEGIES

Association Analysis. This is a monothetic strategy for all-binary data. It begins by comparing attributes in all possible pairs. For the jth and kth attribute we set up a 2×2 contingency table; and, if N is the size of the population under study, we calculate χ^2/N. In the (a, b, c, d) notation of Section 2c this is given by

$$\frac{(ad - bc)^2}{(a + b)(a + c)(b + d)(c + d)}$$

This is not stored, but is added by attributes into a previously cleared vector, which ultimately contains a quantity of the form $\sum_{k \neq j} \chi_{jk}^2/N$. Some workers have preferred to

store the (unsigned) square-root of this quantity, which has the same form as the product-moment correlation coefficient; the quantity stored is then $\sum_{k \neq j} |r_{jk}|$. Division is on that attribute for which this quantity is maximum. The hierarchy is not monotone, and the algorithm is very sensitive to skewness of distribution; as a result the strategy is tending to fall into disuse. A mixed-data version exists, but has been little used.

Divisive Information Analysis. This is now the standard monothetic divisive system for large sets of binary data. The information content of the population is calculated in accordance with the expression given on page 277; we will call this I. For each attribute in turn the population is now divided into those members which contain the attribute and those which do not. The information content of each of these two subpopulations is then calculated; for division on the jth attribute, let the two such information contents be represented by I_{+j} and I_{-j}. We calculate the information fall, ΔI, in the form

$$\Delta I = I - \left(I_{+j} + I_{-j}\right)$$

The division chosen is that for which ΔI is maximum. If information content (instead of fall) is taken as a measure of hierarchical level the dendrogram is necessarily monotonic; the strategy is relatively insensitive to skewness. A mixed-data version exists, but has not proved satisfactory.

The POLYDIV System. This is a polythetic divisive system suitable where the data-matrix consists of a large number of individuals specified by a fairly small number of continuous variables as attributes. The matrix is first standardized to bring each attribute to zero mean and unit variance; this standardized matrix is premultiplied by its own transpose to produce the interattribute correlation matrix; the eigenvector corresponding to the largest eigenvalue of the correlation matrix is extracted by any standard roots-and-vectors subroutine; the standardized data-matrix is postmultiplied by this eigenvector to produce the scores on the first principal component of the system. The resulting vector of individual scores is dichotomized by the Dale method (page 281) and the population dichotomized accordingly. The process is repeated on the subpopulations as often as is appropriate.

Predictive Attribute Analysis. This, the only known extrinsic strategy, is due to Macnaughton–Smith [17]. The population is divided at random into two halves, the *construction* and the *validation* sets. An external attribute, which is to be predicted, is nominated. In the all-binary case, χ^2 is computed between the external attribute and all internal attributes in turn; the construction set is dichotomized on that internal attribute associated with the highest χ^2. The subpopulation means of the external attribute for the resulting two subpopulations are biased estimates; the system is said to be *over-fitted*. The validation set is dichotomized on the same attribute, providing unbiassed estimates; these will normally diverge less than those from the construction set, a phenomenon known as *shrinkage*. The process is repeated on the subpopulations. The system is particularly valuable if the prediction required is associated with high-order interactions of the internal attributes; for a detailed account of a practical case, see [19]. A mixed-data analog has been devised, though it has been little used.

3. SUMMARY OF CALCULATION PROCEDURE

a. Input Information

CONTROL CARDS

A set of control cards will always precede the data. There will always be one, followed by a title card (which is simply copied for record purposes onto the output); there may be more. These cards have five functions:

1. *Size of problem.* The control card will always contain information concerning the number of individuals, and the number and types of attributes. For any given program and installation it is immediately possible to calculate whether the problem can be accommodated in the machine; if it cannot, a suitable diagnostic is printed out and the run is terminated.

2. *Dimensioning.* We assume the program is written mainly in Fortran, in which there are no facilities for dimensioning variables in the main program at run-time. It would be impracticable to specify the precise dimensions of every array for every problem; but since a data-matrix may have many rows and few columns, or *vice versa*, it is equally impracticable to declare arrays large enough to accommodate a wide variety of problems. It is thus desirable to declare only a single master array, of a length equal to all the core left after the program has been loaded. A subroutine is then called which computes, from the control-card information, the sizes of all arrays required, and then defines the starting and finishing addresses of these arrays within the single main array. Once this is done, these subarrays can be passed through the usual variable-dimensioning facilities of Fortran and treated as normal arrays.

3. *Data checking.* Classificatory runs tend to be time-consuming and therefore expensive, and the data need to be carefully checked. In our experience it is particularly easy to miscode nominal or ordinal attributes. It is, therefore, usual to check (i) that the correct number of individuals has been read, (ii) that the correct number of nominal or ordinal attributes has been read for each individual, (iii) that no individual is in a nonexistent state of such an attribute, and (iv) that no alien alphanumeric characters appear on the input medium. The information necessary for this checking should be obtainable from the control card(s).

4. *Algorithm selection.* Programs frequently offer different measures or fusion strategies as alternative options. The option required must then be declared on the control card(s).

5. *Ancillary requirements.* These will depend on the level of sophistication of the individual programs, and this in turn will depend on the particular installation for which they have been written. Possible examples are (i) a statement of whether the data are to be read from a card-reader or from, for example, a specified logical unit on a backing-store, (ii) instructions whether to print, punch, or write away the matrix of interindividual measures in agglomerative programs, (iii) instructions to terminate a divisive process, or to summarize an agglomerative process, at a given number of groups, (iv) to print or punch out cards containing this summary information in a form suitable for later use in a diagnostic program, and (v) to pass such information to plotting routines which will draw out the dendrogram.

DATA

The format in which data are prepared is not critical. There would in principle be no difficulty in reading in a FORMAT statement on each occasion; but since this would complicate the control we have preferred, in the programs written for the Control Data 3600 computer in Canberra, to use fixed formats.[†] These are as follows:

Binary Data. For mixed-data programs with provision for missing values the FORMAT is essentially (72R1), with 1 for "present", 0 for "absent," and * for missing or inapplicable. For the case (common in plant ecology) in which the data-matrices are large, with many zeros but no missing values, we use a compressed format; if attributes 2, 4, 8, 9, 10, 11, and 35 were present in a particular individual it would be punched: 2/4/8-11/35. We use . as terminator for an individual, * as terminator for the data-deck. Such data are always "packed," one attribute to a single bit; so that, if 1 represents the presence of a bit, this individual would appear in the 48-bit word of the Control Data 3600 computer in the form:

.1.1...1111......................1............

It follows that input programs for data of this type are word-length dependent.

Multistate Nominal Data. If, for four successive attributes, a particular individual was in states 3, 2, unknown, and 5, it would be punched 3/2/*/5/ with no terminator. A "nonexclusive multistate" attribute uses, as terminator between states, for example, 2, 4/3/1, 2/.

Numerical Data. We use FORMAT (10F7), with * in the seventh column of the field for a missing value. For the LINKED algorithm we use a free-format read with, as separator for levels, / for attributes, and $ as terminator for individuals.

Interindividual Measures (for all-combinatorial programs). We present the upper triangle of the matrix in (7(F9.5, X)).

Name or Number Tags. When data are read in by individuals, it is theoretically possible to associate each individual with a name or number tag. In most cases this requires space that can ill be spared; we, therefore, recommend that individuals be serially numbered in the order in which they are read.

MASK-CARDS

A user frequently asks that a run be repeated disregarding certain attributes; it is, therefore, advisable to make provision for this by reading in "mask-cards" which specify the attributes to be disregarded. In the case of complete binary data it is also convenient to make provision for the deletion of certain individuals from the matrix.

b. Calculation Procedure

We shall consider only the agglomerative procedures; the variations required for setting up a divisive system will be sufficiently obvious.

[†] *Note added in proof*: Since this chapter was written, all programs have been converted to run on the Control Data Cyber 76 machine, but the data formats are unchanged.

The Basic Fusion Cycle

We use the formulation of Burr [3]:

STEP 1: Regarding each element as a cluster of size one, compute an initial matrix D of intercluster distances. (This step is omitted if distances have been calculated in another program, and are to be read in as such.)

STEP 2: Scan D to locate its smallest term. Call this term D_{ij}.

STEP 3: Fuse the two clusters i, j determined by Step 2. Call the new cluster J. Print information concerning this fusion. If only one cluster remains, stop.

STEP 4: Update D by computing new distances D_{Jk} between the new cluster J and every other remaining cluster k. Go to Step 2.

Notes on the Fusion Cycle

Group Numbering. If there are n elements, the cluster or group formed by the first fusion is numbered $(n + 1)$; at each successive fusion the new group is allocated the next available serial number. In general, when there are g groups left in the system the last group formed will have been numbered $(2n - g)$. If summaries of group constitution are required, it will be necessary to associate with each group number a list of the serial numbers of the individuals that it contains; this information can be printed out when a specified value of $(2n - g)$ is attained.

Individual Fusions. For the information statistics, for which no combinatorial solution is known, the fusions must be physically effected within the computer by addition of the appropriate individuals over all attributes. This process is unnecessary with combinatorial solutions.

Over-writing. It would be possible to define a new vector of measures corresponding to each completed fusion. Since, however, this expands the original n vectors to a total of $(2n - 1)$, it is a computationally unacceptable solution. When (in the symbolism of Step 3 above) i and j have been fused, physically or notationally, into a new group J, and when the vector of d_{Jk} values has been computed, the old vectors i and j are no longer needed, and the new J vector can be written over one of them. When g groups have been formed, only $(n - g)$ vectors remain in the system; the matrix can, therefore, be "closed up" by suitable housekeeping routines. The advantage of this procedure is that, even if the original matrix cannot all be held in core, a stage will be reached when this is possible.

c. Output Information

Essential

For each fusion it is essential to print out the serial numbers of the individuals or groups fusing, the serial number of the new composite group thus formed, and the value of the measure at which fusion took place. A convenient form is:

$$23 + 42 = 97 \qquad 0.5284$$

For the mixed-data information statistics with missing values it is usual to print out, in place of the single measure, the actual information gain, the number of degrees of freedom with which it is associated, and the value of the decision-function computed from these.

If the program offers several alternative options it is also essential to print out, before the string of fusions, a suitable title for the option selected.

Desirable

Since queries concerning a run frequently arise long after the run has been performed, it is wise to copy the control card(s) onto the output. It is also usual to print out the data matrix, since this provides a check that the matrix has been coded and read correctly.

Optional

Most of our own programs offer four additional facilities:

1. *Initial measures* (D) *matrix.* In those

programs which accept raw data the upper triangle of the D matrix can be printed and punched out for use in a subsequent ordination procedure. The format will depend on the ordination program to be used; we find that $(7(F9.5, 1H,))$ is convenient.

2. *Group summaries*. If summaries at the g-group level have been requested, the serial numbers of the groups remaining in the system at this level will be printed out, with a list for each group of the serial numbers (in ascending order) of the individuals it contains. This facility is invaluable if the original data-matrix contains many individuals.

3. *Group comparisons*. The constitution of the g groups can be punched out in a form suitable for a diagnostic program which will compute and order the contributions of each attribute for any given fusion; it is also possible to punch out cards defining the order of the later fusions, so that the diagnostic program can simulate the remainder of the classificatory process.

4. *Plotting*. The hierarchical fusions, from the specified number of groups (or in some case from the original individuals) to the top of the hierarchy are defined in a form which can be passed to plotting routines, so that the dendrogram is plotted automatically.

4. THE FLOW CHART

Of the many flow charts that could in principle be illustrated, we have elected to show the commonest, that is, the flow chart for a combinatorial fusion cycle with provision for summarizing the classification at a pre-set number of groups. This is shown in Fig. 11.2.

5. DESCRIPTION OF FLOW CHART

Boxes 1–5: We assume n individuals to be classified, the classifications to be summarized at the level of NG groups; it is conventional, if the *entire* classification is to be plotted without group summaries, to put

$NG = 0$. We use IG for the serial number of the last group formed, and assume the existence of an array $GMAT$, which stores the string of serial numbers of the individuals which constitute each group. Initially, $IG = (n + 1)$, the first available new serial number. In all cases n and NG must be read in; but the data presented may be raw data (individuals × attributes) or precalculated interindividual measures. If the former, information concerning the attributes is also required; although this is shown in Box 5 as a separate operation, it would in practice be read in at the same time as n and NG.

Box 6: Calculation of the D matrix will depend on the measure in use.

Boxes 7–8: The calculated interindividual measures may be required for a subsequent ordination procedure, in which case they can be punched out as indicated, or be stored on a disc for use by a subsequent program.

Box 9: Detection of the minimum value of d_{ij} is the beginning of the fusion cycle.

Box 10: Relevant output.

Box 11: Are group summaries required?

Box 12: If group summaries are required (i.e., if $NG \neq 0$), has the specified summary level yet been achieved?

Boxes 13–19: If summaries are required, but the specified summary level has not yet been achieved, the summaries are updated.

Box 20: Update IG.

Box 21: Update the D matrix; the method of so doing will depend on the fusion algorithm in use.

Box 22: If the summary level has been achieved, so that no further updating of $GMAT$ is required, it is necessary to test whether the classificatory process has been completed.

Boxes 23–25: If the classification is not yet complete, it may be necessary to begin storing information for plotting the dendrogram.

Boxes 26–28: If the classification is completed, the flow passes to the final summary output and plot.

If an information statistic were in use, the chart would be slightly more complex. A *GMAT*-type summary must be kept throughout the entire procedure, since it is needed for updating the *D* matrix; the operation symbolized by Box 21 would require both this summary and the original raw data.

6. PROGRAMS

a. General Principles

It is impracticable to present actual classificatory programs, because of their length and their dependence on individual installations. It is, however, important to consider the *type* of programs that should be provided by any installation proposing to offer classificatory services. First, we regard the concept of the general-purpose program as computationally unrealistic. Both space and time are at a premium in classificatory programs, and an efficient program must have as little redundant code as is compatible with its functions. The combination of mutually incompatible algorithms—such as combinatorial and noncombinatorial strategies—in the same program results in a considerable area of store devoted to code which on any one occasion is not in use. Furthermore, it is our experience that individual programs fall rather sharply into two groups: those that are in almost daily use, and those that are required only occasionally. In this section we outline a suitable battery of classificatory programs; the names given are those of the programs written for the Control Data 3600 computer in C.S.I.R.O., Canberra. These have recently been converted to Control Data Cyber 76.

b. The Basic Program Set

AGGLOMERATIVE PROGRAMS

Program 1. An information-statistic program which will accept all-binary data without missing values; it must be able to accept data punched in compressed format either by individuals or attributes, and to carry out either normal or inverse analyses. (CENTCLAS.)

Program 2. The mixed-data analog of Program 1, able to accept binary, multistate nominal, ordinal, or numerical attributes with provision for missing or inapplicable values. It will be used when the data are not predominantly numerical. (MULTBET.)

Program 3. A Euclidean-metric program with combinatorial fusion strategies. It must be able to accept nominal attributes with provision for missing data; it will be used when the data are predominantly numerical and not excessively skewed. At least the "group average" and "incremental sum of square" strategies must be available. (MULTCLAS.)

Program 4. An all-combinatorial program which accepts only the upper triangle of a similarity or (more usually) dissimilarity matrix, and offers a wide variety of combinatorial strategies, especially the "flexible" strategy with provision for varying β. (CLASS.)

DIVISIVE PROGRAMS

Program 5. The monothetic divisive analog of Program 1, for use with very large datasets. (DIVINF.)

Program 6. Some form of divisive mixed-data program is desirable. Monothetic programs (MULASS using χ^2 and MULTDIV using information statistics) have been developed, but are relatively unsatisfactory in practice. The most promising solution is effect a monothetic split followed by iterative reallocation across the split. (REMUL.)

Program 7. The divisive analog of Program 3, normally setting up a correlation matrix and dichotomising the first principal component. Such programs are suitable only for all-numerical data with a relatively small number of attributes. (POLYDIV.)

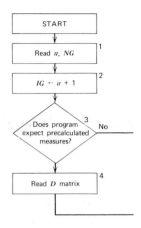

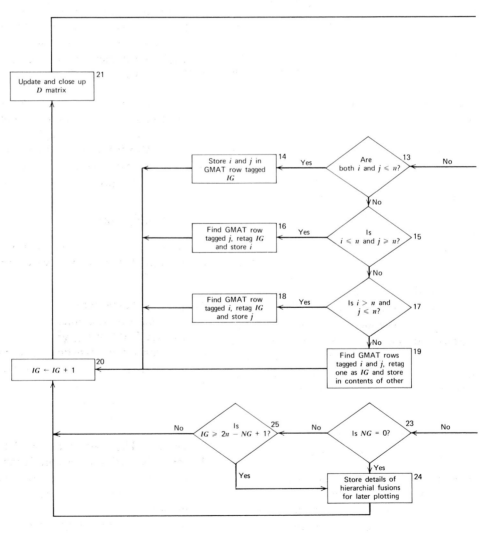

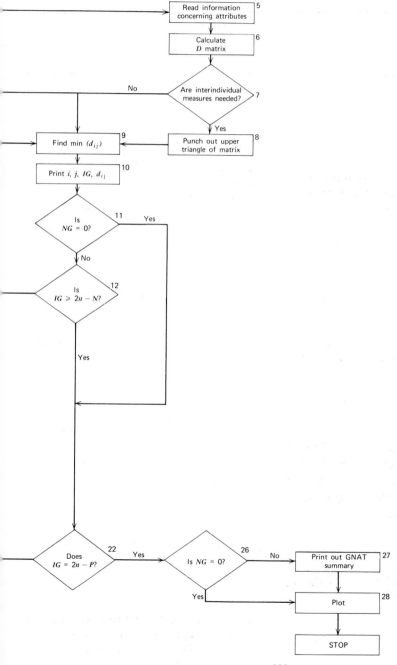

Diagnostic Programs

Program 8. A program that can simulate the measure used in *any* program available in the main battery; for a specified fusion the attribute contributions are computed and printed out in descending order. Must have complete facilities for mixed data and missing values. (GROUPER.)

c. Special-Purpose Programs

Programs that implement the following algorithms are in regular but relatively infrequent use in Canberra; their provision should normally await completion of the basic set:

Program 9. The LINKED algorithm of Lance and Williams [13]; it is most commonly used for soil data taken at a number of levels with an appreciable proportion of missing values. The Canberra and Gower metrics would normally be provided, and the interindividual measures punched out for entry to Program 4.

Program 10. The TRANSMAT algorithm of Dale et al. [8]. This sets up or accepts transition matrices which are then classified by an information-statistic model. The interindividual measures may be punched out for use in an ordination program.

Program 11. The CENTPERC algorithms of Dale, Lance, and Albrecht [7]. This is equivalent in its commonest option to entering Program 1 after an initial set of groups has been formed. It is used as an information-statistic model capable of processing percentages, and finds its commonest use in vegetation surveys in agricultural experiments.

Program 12. An extrinsic, monothetic program which implements the "predictive attribute analysis" of Macnaughton–Smith [17]. (ASSOPRED.)

Program 13. The mixed-data analog of Program 12, as defined by Lance and Williams [15]. (GENPRED.)

7. SAMPLE PROBLEMS

We provide two contrasting examples. The first is a combinatorial strategy, employing "flexible" fusion, as an example of Program 4 of the previous section. The second simulates the more difficult information-statistic program, Program 1 of the previous section.

a. Combinatorial (Flexible Strategy) Program

We assume five individuals for which the set of dissimilarity measures d_{ij} is given (i.e., the matrix D of Section 3b) as follows:

	1	2	3	4	5
1	—	0.227	0.250	0.422	0.897
2	0.227	—	0.492	0.387	0.917
3	0.250	0.492	—	0.356	1.000
4	0.422	0.387	0.356	—	0.773
5	0.897	0.917	1.000	0.773	—

The set is to be classified by the "flexible" fusion strategy with the cluster-intensity coefficient, $\beta = -0.25$. From Section 2d, Individual Fusion Strategies, we have $\alpha_i = \alpha_j = 0.625$.

The smallest value is $d_{12} = 0.227$. We therefore are to fuse 1 and 2, and number the group $(1 + 2)$ as 6. We require the values of d_{36}, d_{46} and d_{56}, and we have

$$d_{36} = 0.625(0.250 + 0.492) - 0.250(0.227)$$

$$= 0.407$$

$$d_{46} = 0.625(0.422 + 0.387) - 0.250(0.227)$$

$$= 0.449$$

$$d_{56} = 0.625(0.897 + 0.917) - 0.250(0.227)$$

$$= 1.077$$

We now delete column and row 1, write the values for column and row 6 over those for column and row 2, and close up the matrix.

This now reads:

	6	3	4	5
6	—	0.407	0.449	1.077
3	0.407	—	0.356	1.000
4	0.449	0.356	—	0.773
5	1.077	1.000	0.773	—

The smallest value remaining in the system is now $d_{34} = 0.356$. We therefore fuse 3 and 4 and number the group $(3 + 4)$ as 7, and we now need the values of d_{57} and d_{67}; these are given by

$$d_{57} = 0.625(1.000 + 0.773) - 0.250(0.356)$$

$$= 1.019$$

$$d_{67} = 0.625(0.407 + 0.449) - 0.250(0.365)$$

$$= 0.446$$

We delete column and row 3, write the values for column and row 7 over those for column and row 4 and close up the matrix. This now reads:

	6	7	5
6	—	0.446	1.077
7	0.446	—	1.019
5	1.077	1.019	—

The smallest value left is now $d_{67} = 0.446$. We therefore fuse 6 and 7, numbering the resulting $(6 + 7)$ as 8. We now need only d_{58}, given by:

$$d_{58} = 0.625(1.077 + 1.019) - 0.250(0.446)$$

$$= 1.198$$

5 and 8 fuse to give 9, the next available serial number; only one group remains in the system, so the process ends.

The print-out will appear as follows:

$1 + 2 = 6$	0.227
$3 + 4 = 7$	0.356
$6 + 7 = 8$	0.446
$5 + 8 = 9$	1.198

The corresponding dendrogram, or hierarchy, will appear as in Fig. 11.3.

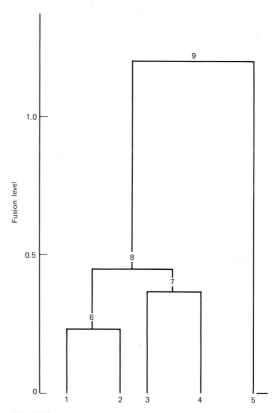

Fig. 11.3

b. Noncombinatorial Information-Statistic Program

We begin by recapitulating the calculation of the information content for a binary set. If there are n individuals, a_j of which possess the jth binary attribute, the information content contributed by that attribute is $n \ln n - a_j \ln a_j - (n - a_j)\ln(n - a_j)$; and we remember that $1 \ln 1 = 0 \ln 0 = 0$. Assume a population of 5 individuals specified by 4 binary attributes, such that 3 of the individuals possess the first attribute, 2 the second, 4 the third, and all 5 the fourth. We shall denote such a population by (3-2-4-5). The information contributed by the first attribute is $5 \ln 5 - 3 \ln 3 - 2 \ln 2$, that is, $8.0472 - 3.2958 - 1.3863$, that is, 3.3651.

That from the second attribute is the same. For the third, it is $5 \ln 5 - 4 \ln 4 - 1 \ln 1$, that is, $8.0472 - 5.5452 - 0$, that is, 2.5020. For the fourth, it is $5 \ln 5 - 5 \ln 5 - 0 \ln 0$, which is zero. (Note that if $a_j = n$ or 0 the information contribution is always zero, so that the information content of a single individual, or of a group of all-identical individuals, is also zero). The total information content is thus

$$3.3651 + 3.3651 + 2.5020 + 0.0000 = 9.2322$$

We now assume a set of 5 individuals specified by 10 binary attributes, which are to be classified; in practice the individuals would as before be numbered, but it will simplify the exposition if instead we letter them A to E. The set we shall operate on is then specified as follows:

A	(1-1-0-1-0-0-1-1-1-1)
B	(1-0-1-1-0-1-0-1-1-1)
C	(0-0-1-0-1-0-1-0-0-1)
D	(0-0-0-1-0-1-1-1-0-0)
E	(1-1-1-0-1-1-0-0-1-0)

At each step in the process we need to know (i) the constitution of all groups remaining in the system, (ii) the number of individuals in each group, and (iii) the information content of each group. We then need to examine all possible fusions (intergroup, inter-individuals, or individual–group). For each fusion we need to know (i) the groups from which it has been constituted, (ii) the number of individuals (n) after the fusion, (iii) the information content after fusion, and (iv) the information gain when the information contents of the two fusing elements have been subtracted.

Table 1 illustrates the process for initial groups A–E. At each step some fusions may remain in the system, and need not be recalculated; these are marked with an asterisk. "Information gain" refers to fusions only.

The following should be noted about the system in Table 1:

STEP 1: Since the individuals A–E have zero information content, the gain on fusion is, for example, $I_{AB} - I_A - I_B$, that is, $5.5452 - 0 - 0$; so that for this initial fusion the gain is the same as the content. Note the possibility of ambiguities, which in a small set can be troublesome; their resolution is discussed in Williams et al. [29].

We require to fuse that pair with the smallest information gain. This is the A–B fusion, so we fuse A and B to form a new group F, with two members and information content 5.5452. The individuals A and B, and any fusion involving them, can now be deleted from the system.

STEP 2: Note that the information gain for FC, for example, is obtained from its content (17.1855) by subtracting the content of F (5.5452) and of C (zero). The smallest gain remaining in the system is that associated with FD; so we fuse these to make a new group G (with 3 individuals), and delete from the system anything involving F or D.

STEP 3: The smallest remaining gain is that associated with CE; so we fuse these to make a new group H (with 2 individuals). Anything involving C and E is now deleted from the system.

STEP 4: The process is now completed. As before, the computer print-out would number, not letter, the individuals and groups; and it is usual to print the gain first, followed by the information content.

The print-out would then appear as follows:

1 + 2 = 6	5.5452	5.5452
4 + 6 = 7	7.8213	13.3665
3 + 5 = 8	8.3178	8.3178
7 + 8 = 9	11.9667	33.6510

The dendrogram is normally plotted with information gain as ordinate for each fusion, though information content is occasionally used.

Table 1

	n	Specification	Inf. content	Inf. gain
		Step 1		
		Groups initially in system		
A	1	(1-1-0-1-0-0-1-1-1-1)	0.0000	—
B	1	(1-0-1-1-0-1-0-1-1-1)	0.0000	—
C	1	(0-0-1-0-1-0-1-0-0-1)	0.0000	—
D	1	(0-0-0-1-0-1-1-1-0-0)	0.0000	—
E	1	(1-1-1-0-1-1-0-0-1-0)	0.0000	—
Fusion				
AB	2	(2-1-1-2-0-1-1-2-2-2)	5.5452	5.5452
AC	2	(1-1-1-1-1-0-2-1-1-2)	9.7041	9.7041
AD	2	(1-1-0-2-0-1-2-2-1-1)	6.9315	6.9315
AE	2	(2-2-1-1-1-1-1-1-2-1)	9.7041	9.7041
BC	2	(1-0-2-1-1-1-1-1-1-2)	9.7041	9.7041
BD	2	(1-0-1-2-0-2-1-2-1-1)	6.9315	6.9315
BE	2	(2-1-2-1-1-2-0-1-2-1)	6.9315	6.9315
CD	2	(0-0-1-1-1-1-2-1-0-1)	8.3178	8.3178
CE	2	(1-1-2-0-2-1-1-0-1-1)	8.3178	8.3178
DE	2	(1-1-1-1-1-2-1-1-1-0)	11.0904	11.0904
		Step 2		
		Groups remaining in system		
C	1	(0-0-1-0-1-0-1-0-0-1)	0.0000	—
D	1	(0-0-0-1-0-1-1-1-0-0)	0.0000	—
E	1	(1-1-1-0-1-1-0-0-1-0)	0.0000	—
F	2	(2-1-1-2-0-1-1-2-2-2)	5.5452	—
Fusions				
*CD	2	(0-0-1-1-1-1-2-1-0-1)	8.3178	8.3178
*CE	2	(1-1-2-0-2-1-1-0-1-1)	8.3178	8.3178
*DE	2	(1-1-1-1-1-2-1-1-1-0)	11.0904	11.0904
FC	3	(2-1-2-2-1-1-2-2-2-3)	17.1855	11.6403
FD	3	(2-1-1-3-0-2-2-3-3-3)	13.3665	7.8213
FE	3	(3-2-2-2-1-2-1-2-3-2)	15.2760	9.7308
		Step 3		
		Groups remaining in system		
C	1	(0-0-1-0-1-0-1-0-0-1)	0.0000	—
E	1	(1-1-1-0-1-1-0-0-1-0)	0.0000	—
G	3	(2-1-1-3-0-2-2-3-3-3)	13.3665	—
Fusions				
*CE	2	(1-1-2-0-2-1-1-0-1-1)	8.3178	8.3178
CG	4	(2-1-2-3-1-2-3-3-2-3)	24.5868	11.2203
EG	4	(3-2-2-3-1-3-2-3-3-2)	24.5868	11.2203
		Step 4		
		Groups remaining in system		
G	3	(2-1-1-3-0-2-2-3-3-3)	13.3665	—
H	2	(1-1-2-0-2-1-1-0-1-1)	8.3178	—
Fusions				
GH	5	(3-2-3-3-2-3-3-3-3-3)	33.6510	11.9667

8. ESTIMATION OF RUNNING TIME

a. General Principles

Running time is extremely data dependent, and the following general principles should be borne in mind: We suppose there to be n individuals specified by s attributes.

1. The normal number of operations required by the three types of agglomerative program are as follows:

Noncombinatorial (e.g., Program 2 of Section 6): $s(n-1)^2$.

Requiring raw data, but with combinatorial solution (e.g., Program 3):

$$\tfrac{1}{2}\,sn(n-1) + \tfrac{1}{2}(n-1)(n-2)$$

Combinatorial, accepting precalculated measures (e.g., Program 4):

$$\tfrac{1}{2}(n-1)(n-2)$$

It will be clear from this that the noncombinatorial information statistic programs will always be the slowest running.

2. If a divisive program were required to subdivide a population completely into individuals, the total number of operations required could always be encompassed within $\tfrac{1}{2}ns(s-1)(t-1)$, where $t = 2^s$ or n, whichever is the smaller. However, it would be most unusual to continue the subdivision to its ultimate limits, and in any case an appreciable number of attributes are likely to become indeterminate and be "masked out" en route; the expression therefore represents a gross overestimate of the work required. It will usually suffice to remember that divisive programs are fast, and roughly dependent on some function of ns^2.

3. If the problem is large, considerable time may be expended on disc-core or similar transfers.

4. It is essential that the operations such as plotting shall be available on a time-sharing or multiprogramming basis, or the cost of C.P.U. time may be prohibitive.

b. Specific Examples

We give a few examples for the Control Data 3600 computer with the DAD monitor.

Program 3 (our MULTCLAS)

n	s	t(seconds)
13	66	18
80	100	33
124	100	65

n	t(seconds)
120	34

Program 4 (our CLASS)

At the other end of the scale the information-statistic Program 2 (our MULTBET), with 299 individuals specified by 10 binary, 13 numerical, 5 multistate nominal and 16 ordinal attributes, required $2\tfrac{1}{2}$ hours.

9. REFERENCES

1. D. M. Boulton and C. S. Wallace, "A Program for Numerical Classification," *Comput. J.*, **13**, 63–69 (1970).

2. E. J. Burr, "Cluster Sorting with Mixed Character Types. I. Standardization of Character Values," *Aust. Comput. J.*, **1**, 97–99 (1968).

3. E. J. Burr, "Cluster Sorting with Mixed Character Types. II. Fusion Strategies," *Aust. Comput. J.*, **2**, 98–103 (1970).

4. A. J. Cole (ed.), *Numerical Taxonomy*, Academic Press, London, 1969.

5. R. M. Cormack, "A Review of Classification," *J. Roy. Statist. Soc.*, Ser. A, **134**, 321–367 (1971).

6. M. B. Dale, *The Application of Multivariate Methods to Heterogeneous Data*, Ph.D. Thesis, Univ. Southampton, 1964.

7. M. B. Dale, G. N. Lance, and L. Albrecht, "Extensions of Information Analysis," *Aust. Comput. J.*, **3**, 29–34 (1971).

8. M. B. Dale, P. Macnaughton–Smith, W. T. Williams, and G. N. Lance, "Numerical Classification of Sequences," *Aust. Comput. J.*, **2**, 9–13 (1970).

9. J. C. Gower, "A General Coefficient of Similarity and Some of its Properties," *Biometrics*, **27**, 857–871 (1971).

10. N. Jardine and R. Sibson, *Mathematical Taxonomy*, Wiley, London, 1971.

11. W. B. Kendrick, "Complexity and Dependence in Computer Taxonomy," *Taxon*, **14**, 141–154 (1965).

12. G. N. Lance and W. T. Williams, "A General Theory of Classificatory Sorting Strategies. I. Hierarchical Systems," *Comput. J.*, **9**, 373–380 (1967).

13. G. N. Lance and W. T. Williams, "Note on the Classification of Multi-level Data," *Comput. J.*, **9**, 381–382 (1967).

14. G. N. Lance and W. T. Williams, "Mixed-data Classificatory Programs. I. Agglomerative Systems," *Aust. Comput. J.*, **1**, 15–20 (1967).

15. G. N. Lance and W. T. Williams, "Mixed-data Classificatory Programs. II. Divisive Systems," *Aust. Comput. J.*, **1**, 82–85 (1968).

16. D. M. Mackay, "Recognition and Action," in *Methodologies of Pattern Recognition*, S. Watanabe (ed.), 409–416. Academic Press, London, 1969.

17. P. Macnaughton–Smith, *Some Statistical and Other Numerical Techniques for Classifying Individuals*, Home Office Research Unit Report No. 6. H.M.S.O., London (1965).

18. J. McNeill, "The Hierarchical Ordering of Characters as a Solution to the Dependent Character Problem in Numerical Taxonomy," *Taxon*, **21**, 71–82 (1972).

19. F. H. Simon, *Prediction Methods in Criminology*, Home Office Research Unit Report No. 7. H.M.S.O., London, 1971.

20. R. R. Sokal and P. H. A. Sneath, *Principles of Numerical Taxonomy*, W. H. Freeman & Co., San Franciso and London, 1963.

21. L. R. Taylor, "Aggregation, Variance and the Mean," *Nature, Lond.*, **189**, 732–735 (1961).

22. C. S. Wallace and D. M. Boulton, "An Information Measure for Classification," *Comput. J.*, **11**, 185–194 (1968).

23. W. T. Williams, "The Problem of Attribute-weighting in Numerical Classification," *Taxon*, **18**, 369–374 (1969).

24. W. T. Williams, "Principles of Clustering," *Ann. Rev. Ecol. Syst.*, **2**, 303–326 (1971).

25. W. T. Williams, "Partition of Information," *Aust. J. Bot.* **20**, 135–240 (1972).

26. W. T. Williams, H. T. Clifford, and G. N. Lance, "Group-size Dependence: a Rationale for Choice between Numerical Classifications," *Comput. J.*, **14**, 157–162 (1971).

27. W. T. Williams and M. B. Dale, "Fundamental Problems in Numerical Taxonomy," *Adv. Bot. Res.*, **2**, 35–68 (1965).

28. W. T. Williams, M. B. Dale, and G. N. Lance, "Two Outstanding Ordination Problems," *Aust. J. Bot.*, **19**, 251–258 (1971).

29. W. T. Williams, G. N. Lance, M. B. Dale and H. T. Clifford, "Controversy concerning the Criteria for Taxonometric Strategies," *Comput. J.*, **14**, 162–164 (1971).

Multidimensional Scaling and Other Methods for Discovering Structure

12

Joseph B. Kruskal
Bell Laboratories (Murray Hill)

1. INTRODUCTION

a. Function of Multidimensional Scaling

We define *multidimensional scaling* to mean any method for constructing a configuration of points in low-dimensional space from interpoint distances which have been corrupted by random error, or from rank order information about the corrupted distances. The typical input consists of a matrix, or part of a matrix, of numbers that we interpret as interpoint distances corrupted by random error and perhaps distorted by an unknown order-preserving transformation. The primary typical output consists of several points in a low-dimensional space (provided both in graphical form and as coordinates), together with the relationship between the input values and distances among the points (provided both in graphical form and numerically). Replicated measurements of the distances are

sometimes used. Characteristically, this method is used in situations where it is not known in advance whether a meaningful configuration of points underlies the data at hand, nor in what dimensionality. Note that many people use the term multidimensional scaling to cover a far broader area, which is difficult to define precisely.

Characteristic of "individual differences scaling" is the use of several matrices of interpoint distances. Also characteristic is the concept that the coordinate axes are differentially weighted while calculating the interpoint distances, and that the pattern of weights is different for each matrix of interpoint distances. We define *individual differences scaling* to mean any method for reconstructing a pattern of weights and a configuration of points in low-dimensional space from several matrices of weighted interpoint distances. We consider individual differences scaling to be a special type of multidimensional scaling, but one which deserves special attention because of its great importance.

The central focus of this chapter is ordinary multidimensional scaling. Although no computer program is explained in its entirety, the chapter should be particularly useful in connection with KYST, M-D-SCAL, and TORSCA.* It should also be of some use in connection with some other programs for multidimensional scaling, such as MINISSA, MINITRI, PARSCL, and SSA. We also give some useful coverage to individual differences scaling. In this connection, the chapter should be of use in connection with INDSCAL, CANDE-COMP, and PARAFAC. We only regret that limitations of space and time have not permitted us to treat this topic as fully as ordinary multidimensional scaling.

Also falling within our definition of ordinary multidimensional scaling, though historically of independent origin, is multidimensional unfolding (or at least those versions of multidimensional unfolding which are of greatest practical importance).

b. Computation for a Wide Variety of Other Data Analysis Situations Similar to Multidimensional Scaling

Increasingly often, social scientists and others find it necessary to devise methods of data analysis, as a way of applying their conceptions and models to actual data. As they attempt to devise suitable computational procedures, the problems they face are often quite similar to those that were involved in implementing multidimensional scaling. Thus the principles involved in this specific problem may usefully point the way for a larger class of problems.

In addition to describing the computational methods actually used in multidimensional scaling, we also seek in this chapter to

*For further information about the authors and background papers for all computer programs mentioned in this chapter, see the Reference section.

give an overview of the computational methods that are useful in many similar data analysis situations, and to present some guiding principles for choosing among alternative procedures. Although the illustrations are primarily from multidimensional scaling, we believe that the overview and the guiding principles have a much wider validity.

c. On Choosing a Method of Data Analysis with the Right Degree of Formality

Methods for analyzing data can be ordered along a rough spectrum, having to do with their "formality." This spectrum should be better known, since the real scientific value of analysis can be greatly increased by properly matching the degree of formality of the methods used to the needs of the situation. Near the formal end of the spectrum are the much-studied models of classical mathematical statistics, which include a detailed specification of the stochastic (or probabilistic) elements of the situation. Near the informal end of the spectrum are such methods as plotting a scatter diagram or a histogram. Note that some techniques, such as the analysis of variance, are referred to by a single name and may perhaps be thought of as a single method, but contain many methods of data analysis at varying levels of formality.

For any given problem or application, it is important to select methods of analysis which have the right degree of formality. The penalty for too informal an approach is loss of power, depth, and precision which more formal methods can at their best make available. The penalty for too formal an approach is loss of breadth and the capacity to notice the unexpected which more informal methods can at their best make available. The appropriate degree of formality tends to increase as we learn more about the problem.

As we move along the spectrum in the direction of increasing formality, we encounter the following characteristics, roughly in this order (though there is no claim of completeness in this description).

1. There is a definite numerical or graphical procedure; for example, draw a scatter diagram.

2. There is a definite conception of what the data should look like (in the absence of obscuring events such as random error); for example, y is linear in x, or y is a low-order polynomial in x.

3. The procedure is based in some fairly explicit way on the conception of what the data should look like; for example, we conceive y to be linear in x and in consequence we draw a straight line through the points by eye.

4. One or more evaluation functions are used to measure how well the data fit the conception of what they should look like; for example, a correlation, or a sum of squared residuals.

5. The procedure is closely related to one or more of the evaluation functions; for example, draw a straight line through the points by eye, and evaluate the linearity of the relationship by the correlation.

6. The procedure is based explicitly on optimizing some particular evaluation function, for example, least-squares fitting.

7. There is a definite conception of the nature of the obscuring events; for example, independent normal errors.

8. The procedure is based explicitly on the conception of the obscuring events; for example, maximum-likelihood fitting.

Generally, characteristics further along this scale only assume importance as we acquire confidence in the characteristics before them. Thus, when the conception in (2) is seriously unclear, the idea of (3) or the conception in (7) is generally not very important. At the same time, when the situation realistically permits the addition of greater formality, this addition can sometimes add greatly to the value or power of the method.

All the methods we discuss seriously in this chapter include characteristics (1)–(4). Characteristic (5) generally applies, characteristic (6) sometimes applies, and (7) seldom applies. My belief is that for the large majority of applications of multidimensional scaling, we have good ways to implement (6), and we benefit by using a method that includes it. For the same majority of applications, I believe that good ways to implement (7) have not yet been demonstrated, but that they will come soon, and the analysis of data will benefit by their inclusion.

d. Some Historical Remarks on the Methodology

Disregarding some precursors in 1927 and 1936, the history of multidimensional scaling may be said to start with Warren Torgerson [24], who invented the name and contributed importantly to the idea. However, the method did not really gain wide currency until the substantial improvements introduced in 1962 by Roger Shepard [22] which included the concept and first practical demonstration through a successful computer program that a rank ordering of interpoint distances was adequate to determine a low-dimensional configuration. Building directly on Shepard's work, the present writer made further improvements, both conceptual and computational, and named the computer program M-D-SCAL.

Forest Young implemented Torgerson's procedure in a program he called TORSCA for "Torgerson Scaling," to which he added procedures of his own and procedures based on M-D-SCAL. Working with Louis Guttman, James Lingoes wrote a program called SSA for "Smallest Space Analysis," and subsequently several related programs. J. Douglas Carroll and Jih-Jie Chang made an important generalization to the analysis of several matrices simultaneously, which they implemented in a program called INDSCAL for "Individual Differences Scaling." A program called KYST (pronounced "kissed"), from the initials of Kruskal, Young, Shepard, and Torgerson, was subsequently developed to combine the best features of TORSCA and M-D-SCAL by a cooperative effort of Kruskal, Young, and Judith Seery.

2. MATHEMATICAL BACKGROUND

a. Symbols Used

Table 1 first lists some special symbols, then some numerical symbols, and finally alphabetic symbols. The alphabetical symbols are *approximately* in alphabetical order (with the Roman and Greek alphabets intermixed), but with some minor deviations to simplify the explanation.

Not every symbol in the chapter is listed in the table. About 10% of the symbols, which are used only briefly and explained fully at their place of occurrence, are omitted, since their presence would disrupt the smooth flow of explanation for the remaining symbols, and would require a disproportionate amount of space. For each symbol, the table indicates which sections it may occur in, and explains its meaning.

Table 1. SYMBOLS

Symbol	Sections	Explanation
$\approx$	General	Means "equal except for the presence of random error in the observations"
$\| \ \|$	General	Indicates the norm or length of a vector, equal to the root-sum-square of its components
$\| \ \|$	General	Indicates absolute value
$\equiv$	General	Means "identically equal to"
$'$	General	Indicates the transpose of a matrix
$'$	General	Prime, used to distinguish similar quantities
0_R	2k	A vector with R components, all 0
1_I	4, 5	A vector with I components, all 1
α	2i	Order of convergence
a, b	General	Coefficients of a linear function
A, B	2k	Matrix and vector which are input to linear regression
A, C	2c	Orthogonal matrix and matrix with constant columns
B	2f	Matrix obtained from matrix of squared distances by simple operations
b_{ij}	2f, 2g	Element of B, which in fact equals $x_i \cdot x_j$ if $\bar{x} = 0$
b_{ijk}	2g	Similar to b_{ij}, for kth data matrix
β_{ijk}	2g	Analogous to b_{ijk}, but resulting from operations on observed data

(Continued next page)

Table 1. (*Continued*)

Symbol	Sections	Explanation
β	General	Vector (a, b)
β_i	2e	Successive values of β
β_o	2k	Optimum value of β, as function of X
δ_{ij}	General	Dissimilarity (or similarity) between objects i and j; data which is input to multidimensional scaling
$\delta_{ij\nu}$	General	Replicated measurements of δ_{ij}
δ_{ijk}	2g	Value of δ_{ij} for individual or treatment k
δ_m	General	Abbreviation for $\delta_{i(m), j(m)}$
DATA	General	Array that holds values of $\delta_{i(m), j(m)}$
d_{ij}	General	Distance between point i and point j
d_{ijk}	2g	Distance between points i and j, calculated using weights for individual k
d_m	General	Abbreviation for $d_{i(m), j(m)}$
DIST	General	Array that holds values of $d_{i(m), j(m)}$
$\hat{d}_{ij}$	General	Pseudodistance between points i and j; found by regression of the d_{ij} over the δ_{ij}
$\hat{d}_m$	General	Abbreviation for $d_{i(m), j(m)}$
d_n	2i	Distance of nth configuration from true optimum configuration. Not related to other uses of d.
d	2k	Used in the ordinary manner to indicate differentiation
∂	2k	Used in the ordinary manner to indicate partial differentiation of a function
	2k	Abbreviation of ∂_{ir} where the indices are not important
∂_{ir}	2k	Abbreviation for $\partial / \partial x_{ir}$
∇	General	Indicates the gradient of a function
∇_X	2k	Indicates the partial gradient of a function with respect to the elements x_{ir} of X
ε_{ij}	2k	Identifies matrix or Kronecker symbol; ε used instead of the more usual δ because δ is so heavily used for other purposes

(*Continued next page*)

Table 1. (*Continued*)

Symbol	Sections	Explanation
E_i	General	Operator from R-space to IR-space which places argument vector in ith "block" of otherwise all-zero vector; though awkward to describe mathematically, very easy to deal with computationally.
f	General	Univariate regression function, usually with δ_{ij} as argument and $\hat{d}_{ij}$ as value
	General	An arbitrary function of many variables which we seek to optimize. (Which meaning of f is intended is always clear from context.)
f_i	2b	Same as first meaning of f, but used only for dissimilarities from ith row of matrix of dissimilarities
G	General	$\nabla\, S'(X)$
G_L	4, 5	Value G on last preceding iteration
θ	General	The angle between the gradients on two successive iterations
I	General	The number of objects being scaled
$\begin{matrix} i \\ j \end{matrix}$	General	An index that runs from 1 to I, and indicates which object or point is referred to
$(i(m), j(m))$	General	The subscript combination (i, j) corresponding to the mth element in a listing of all observations $\delta_{ij\nu}$
IJ	General	Array that holds the subscript pairs $(i(m), j(m))$, with a subscript pair packed together into a single word
K	2g	The number of square $I \times I$ matrices which constitute the data for individual differences scaling; the number of subjects or treatments
k	General	Index that indicates which iteration the procedure has reached
	2g	Index that runs from 1 to K, and which indicates which square matrix (which subject, which treatment) is being referred to
	2c	Arbitrary positive constant
λ	General	Step-size used in moving from one configuration X to the next during one iteration
$\lambda^{(k)}$	General	Value of λ on the kth iteration

(*Continued next page*)

Table 1.   (*Continued*)

Symbol	Sections	Explanation
L	2k	The scale factor used as the denominator of S (L stands for "lower")
M	General	The total number of data values $\delta_{ij\nu}$ which are actually present in the data
m	General	An index that runs from 1 to M, and which indicates which data value is being referred to
ν	General	Index to indicate which replication is being referred to
P	General	When polynomial regression is used, the degree of the polynomial; when monotonic regression is used, $P = \pm 1$ to indicate ascending or descending regression
p	2j	Power to which $|\cos \theta|$ is put in older version of step-size procedure
R	General	Dimensionality of the space in which the multidimensional scaling is being carried out; hence the number of components in many of the vectors we deal with, and the number of columns in many of the matrices we deal with
r	General	Index that runs from 1 to R, and which indicates which coordinate of the scaling space is being referred to
$\left.\begin{array}{l}R_{\max}\\ R_{\mathrm{mim}}\end{array}\right\}$	General	When several scalings are carried out successively on the same data in different dimensionalities, $R_{\max}$ is the largest (and the first) dimensionality used, and $R_{\min}$ is the smallest (and the last) dimensionality used
ρ	General	A constant involved in the step-size procedure, and used in connection with the value or the average value of $\cos \theta$; generally set equal to 4
S	General	The evaluation quantity used in KYST (and in several other scaling programs) as a function of the configuration X and the regression parameters (β for the linear scaling example used throughout this paper); S stands for "stress," but stress is also used for S' and several other closely related meanings; in a few places, S is used loosely to indicate the value of the function
	2g	An evaluation quantity used in INDSCAL, as a function of X and W

(*Continued next page*)

Table 1. (*Continued*)

Symbol	Sections	Explanation
S'	General	A function of X which is found by minimizing S over the regression parameters; "stress" often refers to S', as well as the minimum value of S' over all X, and other closely related meanings
	2g	A function of U, V, and W used in INDSCAL which slightly generalizes $S(X, W)$
signum	2j	The univariate function which is $+1$ for positive arguments, -1 for negative arguments, and 0 at 0
t	8	The average computer time per data value per iteration
τ	4, 5	Used to indicate one of several "temporary" quantities, which are needed only briefly during computation
U	2k	The numerator of S ("U" stands for upper)
U, V	2g	Two $I \times R$ matrices which replace X when the function S of INDSCAL is generalized to S'
W	2g	A $K \times R$ matrix of weight, used in INDSCAL
w	2j, 4	A weight used in making the running average of $\cos \theta$; usually $w = \frac{2}{3}$
$\bar{w}$	2j	A weight used in making the running average of $|\cos \theta|$; usually, $\bar{w} = \frac{2}{3}$
x_{ir} x'_{ir}	General	The rth coordinate of the ith point of the configuration X and of the configuration X'
x_i x'_i	General	The ith point $x_i = (x_{i1}, \ldots, x_{iR})$ of the configuration X, and of the configuration X'
X X'	General	An $I \times R$ matrix of values x_{ir} thought of as a configuration of I points in R-space; the ith row constitutes the ith point; in Section 2k, X is rearranged as a vector with IR coordinates
X^k	General	The value of X on iteration k
$\{x_i\}_1^I$ $\{x'_i\}_1^I$	2c	The configuration x, thought of as a set of I labeled points; and the same for X'

b. Some Models For Multidimensional Scaling

The models described below all share a common approach and have much in common with one another. Although these models are not the only ones in use, they underlie at least three publicly available programs (KYST by Kruskal, Young, and Seery; M-D-SCAL by Kruskal; and TORSCA by Young) and are relatively simple to explain. Except as otherwise stated, all the models described can actually be fitted by KYST, though a few can be used only awkwardly and with severe limitations on the size of the data.

For one simple situation, the data form an $I \times I$ matrix of values δ_{ij}, which we call dissimilarities. The very simplest structural model represents these as distances d_{ij} between I points in R-space. In other words, we assume there are I points $x_i = (x_{i1}, \ldots, x_{iR})$ such that

$$\delta_{ij} \approx d_{ij} \equiv \sqrt{\sum_{r=1}^{R} (x_{ir} - x_{jr})^2}$$

$$\text{for all} \quad (i, j)$$

Here the sign for approximate equality is meant to indicate that although we do not specifically describe any random error in the data values δ_{ij}, we expect the data to contain such error and hence do not expect precise equality. In practice, multidimensional scaling is able to tolerate surprisingly large random error.

More generally the dissimilarities δ_{ij} should be thought of as either the distances or some monotone increasing distortion of the distances, such as the square, square-root, logarithm, or whatever. Each value should also be thought of as containing random error. The data values might also consist of a monotone *decreasing* distortion of the distances, such as the reciprocal, corrupted by random error, in which case we call them similarities. (However, we must know whether the data are similarities or dissimilarities.) We shall talk henceforth

only of dissimilarities, but everything is meant to apply also to similarities with obvious trivial modifications.

Not all dissimilarities may be present, either due to missing observations, or for other reasons. Sometimes the self-dissimilarities δ_{ii} are meaningless, and hence absent. Sometimes δ_{ij} and δ_{ji} are intrinsically the same, so that we are given only a half matrix for which $i < j$ (or for which $i > j$). Sometimes there are replicated observations of the same value, so that we have δ_{ijv}. We shall cover all these situations implicitly by a simple device. When we indicate that some equation holds "for all available (i, j)," this is meant to cover the pairs for which we have an observation δ_{ij}. Furthermore, if we have replicated measurements δ_{ijv}, it is meant to hold for every replication, though we do not include the extra subscript. Likewise, a summation over ij is meant to cover all the observations which are present. Note that where replicated measurements occur (so that the dissimilarities need an extra subscript), δ_{ijv} corresponds to the same distance d_{ij} for every v.

Now we generalize the structural model beyond the simplest case above. For "linear scaling" we suppose that the dissimilarities δ_{ij}, after transformation by some (presumably increasing) linear function, may be represented as interpoint distances d_{ij} among the I points x_j. In other words, we assume that for some a and for some b (presumably > 0) we have the structural equation

$$a + b\delta_{ij} \approx d_{ij} \quad \text{for all available} \quad (i, j)$$

More generally, for "polynomial scaling" we assume that

$$f(\delta_{ij}) \approx d_{ij}$$

where f is a polynomial of specified degree, and where f is assumed to be increasing over the region containing the δ_{ij}. (The condition that a polynomial be increasing over a given range is a difficult one to work with computationally, unless the polynomial is of first degree. Hence this condition is almost always handled by special indirect means which may achieve it only approximately. Furthermore, since linear scaling in several existing programs is treated simply as polynomial scaling for which the degree $P = 1$, without any special provisions, the requirement that the linear polynomial be increasing is treated by the same special indirect means, though in principle there would be no difficulty in requiring $b > 0$.)

Another kind of scaling is based on the structural equation

$$f(\delta_{ij}) \approx d_{ij} \quad \text{for all available} \quad (i, j)$$

where f is permitted to be any monotone increasing function. It turns out that arbitrary monotone functions are computationally easy to deal with in this context, so this kind of scaling can be handled with mathematical rigor.

Note that for this structural model it is only the rank order of the dissimilarities which is important: The actual numerical values make no difference. For multidimensional scaling and related methods, the word "nonmetric" is used to indicate this. Thus scaling based on this structural equation is one kind of "nonmetric scaling." Likewise, polynomial scaling as described previously is one kind of metric scaling.

Still further generalizations are possible and useful. Classes of relationships may be used other than linear increasing, polynomial increasing, or monotonic increasing. Particularly natural (and available in KYST) is any class of the type appropriate for multivariate linear regression, namely, any finite-dimensional linear space of functions.

Our structural equations set $f(\delta) \approx d$, whether f is linear, polynomial, or monotonic. Turning this around, it would be just as natural to set $\delta \approx f(d)$ instead (though KYST cannot handle this case). There is a computational reason why this is far more difficult when f is merely assumed mono-

tonic increasing, however: The most natural badness-of-fit functions (see the next section) are piecewise constant, so that gradient methods are not available to minimize them. This is one major reason why KYST, whose early history included a strong nonmetric element, does not include these possibilities.

Another element of generality may be combined with either linear, polynomial, or nonmetric scaling be assuming not just one transformation but several. For example, one model that is sometimes appropriate is based on the structural equations

$$f_i(\delta_{ij}) \approx d_{ij} \quad \text{for all available} \quad (i, j)$$

where each f_i is permitted to be any monotone increasing function. (The linear and polynomial analogues are equally sensible.) Notice that a separate relationship is assumed for each row of the matrix. The analog for columns is just as natural, of course.

This generalization is based on breaking up the matrix into subsets (rows or columns), and assuming a separate relationship for each subset. There are useful generalizations to other subsets, which may overlap. For example, one might sensibly have one relationship for each row *and* one relationship for each column. Also, one might have one relationship for each triple of the form (d_{ij}, d_{ik}, d_{jk}), and indeed Roskam's program MINITRI is specially adapted to this purpose. Similarly, one might have one relationship for each pair of the form (d_{ij}, d_{kl}), and Johnson's program PARSCL is specially adapted to this purpose. Guttman and Lingoes also have programs akin to Johnson's, and Guttman uses the phrase "absolute value principle" to describe this approach.

c. Indeterminacies in Models for Multidimensional Scaling

The only information that is used as input to multidimensional scaling relates to interpoint distances. Therefore if two different solutions (i.e. sets of I points in R-space) produce precisely the same interpoint distances there is no valid reason for considering one better than another. We call this the rigid motion indeterminacy, and ask when two configurations of points in R-space, $\{x_i\}_1^I$ and $\{x_i'\}_1^I$, have the same interpoint distances. Fortunately, geometry provides a complete and fairly simple answer to this question in Euclidean space. Informally, this happens only when one configuration can be obtained from the other by translation and rotation.

To describe this more formally, we rewrite any configuration $\{x_i\}$ as a matrix X, using x_i as the ith row. Thus a configuration of I points in R-space is now written as an $I \times R$ matrix. Then X' has the same interpoint distances as X if and only if there is an $I \times R$ matrix C with constant values down each column, and an $R \times R$ orthogonal matrix A, such that

$$X' = XA + C$$

Addition of a matrix C with constant columns is a translation, and multiplication by an orthogonal matrix A is a rotation.

When solutions to a problem contain indeterminacy, it is often advantageous to add constraints which reduce or eliminate the indeterminacy, in order to permit easier comparison of different solutions, and for other reasons. To eliminate the free translation, it is conventional to add the constraint that the centroid (or mean) of the configuration is 0, namely, $(1/I)\Sigma x_i = 0$.

To reduce the rotational indeterminacy, it is common to rotate the configuration to principal components. A full explanation of principal components (or coordinates) may be found in [10]. Briefly, the first principal component is (any) vector (commonly taken to have length 1) such that the perpendicular projections of the points onto that vector have the largest possible variance. The second principal component is (any) vector orthogonal to the first principal component, such that the projections of the points onto the vector yield the largest possible vari-

ance, subject to the orthogonality constraint. The third principal component must be orthogonal to the first two, and maximizes the variance subject to that restriction; and so on. Rotation to principal components means rotation to a position such that the rth principal component can be taken along the rth coordinate axis. It is a mathematical theorem that after rotation to principal components, the projections onto different coordinate axes are uncorrelated.

Another indeterminacy, called the dilatational indeterminacy, arises in most forms of scaling (but not in the simplest kind of scaling which was introduced first). Suppose the structural equation is $f(\delta_{ij}) \approx d_{ij}$. If we define

$$f'(\delta) = kf(\delta)$$
$$x_i' = kx_i$$

then

$$d_{ij}' \equiv \text{distance}(x_i', x_j') = kd_{ij}$$

and the $f'(\delta_{ij})$ will match the d_{ij}' as well as the $f(\delta_{ij})$ match the d_{ij} in any reasonable sense. To eliminate this common form of indeterminacy, it is common to add a constraint such as

$$\sum \|x_i\|^2 = I$$

or

$$\sum d_{ij}^2 = \text{number of available pairs } (i, j)$$

Still other ways of handling this indeterminacy also exist.

d. Systematic Optimization: Picking a Measure of Fit Such as Stress

Given data and a structural model, there are many approaches to "fitting the model to the data," that is, to finding values for parameters in the model which make the structural equations hold "as closely as possible." Later on we shall survey several different approaches. One of these, which is often desirable, we call *systematic optimization*. This has two parts: picking a measure of fit, and optimizing it. We illustrate the first part, using linear multidimensional scaling for the purpose.

Looking at the structural equations for linear scaling,

$$a + b\delta_{ij} \approx d_{ij} \qquad \text{for all available} \quad (i, j)$$

one natural way to measure how far from correct these equations are is by the root-sum square of the residuals,

$$\sqrt{\sum \left[d_{ij} - (a + b\delta_{ij}) \right]^2}$$

Recalling the dilatational indeterminacy, however, we see that this expression can be made as small as desired simply by shrinking the configuration and shrinking a and b to match. To cure this we divide by a suitable scale factor. Thus one plausible badness-of-fit function is

$$S(X, a, b)$$

$$= \sqrt{\sum \left[d_{ij} - (a + b\delta_{ij}) \right]^2} \Big/ \sqrt{\sum d_{ij}^2}$$

where we use an $I \times R$ matrix X to denote the configuration as in the preceding section.

This badness-of-fit expression, and others like it, are often called "stress" in multidimensional scaling, since the expression indicates how badly the distances have to be "stressed" to make them a linear function of the δ_{ij}. Other kinds of evaluation functions are also used in multidimensional scaling, under other names. One which is widely used is Guttman's "coefficient of alienation." De Leeuw [5] has contributed useful new functions, and insight into the advantages and disadvantages of old and new functions.

We are going to be minimizing S over X, a, and b. If we hold X fixed temporarily, this comes to minimizing the numerator,

which in turn simply constitutes ordinary least-squares univariate regression. KYST and M-D-SCAL are based directly on the use of regression to measure the relationship between d_{ij} and δ_{ij}. Alternative types of regression may be used in place of linear, with very little conceptual change. KYST and M-D-SCAL permit the use of polynomial regression up to degree 4, with or without a constant term, and the use of monotonic regression (explained below). To permit easier notation for these and other generalizations, it is helpful to introduce a general notation $\hat{d}_{ij}$ for the quantity which we want approximately equal to d_{ij}. Thus we let

$$\hat{d}_{ij} \equiv a + b\,\delta_{ij} \qquad \text{for linear scaling}$$

$$\hat{d}_{ij} \equiv f(\delta_{ij}) \qquad \text{in general}$$

where f is the fitted polynomial or the fitted monotone function or the fitted function of whatever type, according to what type of regression we are using. We call $\hat{d}_{ij}$ the *pseudodistances*. In this notation, we can write the above formula for stress S as

$$S(X, a, b) = \sqrt{\sum \left(d_{ij} - \hat{d}_{ij} \right)^2} \Big/ \sqrt{\sum d_{ij}^2}$$

When monotonic regression is used, the computation depends only on the *rank order* of the dissimilarities, not on their numerical values. The surprising use of rank-order only was first introduced by Shepard [22a, b] and labeled by the word "nonmetric" (though his own original procedure is only approximately nonmetric). It has attracted a great deal of attention, and the nonmetric options of KYST and M-D-S-CAL are probably used more often than the metric options. For this reason, monotonic regression is explained briefly. Further information may be found in [1, Ch. 2] under the name "isotone regression" and in the literature cited there, as well as in Kruskal [15] and other sources.

The least-squares *linear* regression function of d_{ij} over δ_{ij} may be defined as the *linear* function f which minimizes $\Sigma(d_{ij} - f(\delta_{ij}))^2$. The definition of (ascending) *monotonic* regression is obtained by substituting the phrase "(ascending) monotonic" twice for the word "linear" in the preceding sentence. Although the linear regression function can be thought of as being defined everywhere, the monotonic regression function is in general only defined at the given values δ_{ij}. Calculating the monotonic regression function comes to minimizing a quadratic function of the variables

$$\hat{d}_{ij} = f(\delta_{ij})$$

subject to the linear inequalities which define monotonicity. Rapid, finite, special purpose procedures are available to perform this minimization. It is very easy to incorporate weights, so as to minimize a weighted sum of squared residuals. It turns out that if the d_{ij} are arranged in order of increasing δ_{ij}, and partitioned into the correct consecutive blocks, then each $\hat{d}_{ij}$ is the average (in general, weighted average) of the d_{ij} in its block. The key computational problem is to find out what blocks to use. Most procedures for this purpose start with blocks of size 1, and proceed by successive mergers. The existence of tied values among the δ_{ij} introduces both conceptual and computational complications, which we do not go into here.

Another plausible stress function is obtained in the same manner but with the addition of weighting of the residuals inversely by d_{ij}^2:

$$S = \sqrt{\Sigma \frac{(d_{ij} - \hat{d}_{ij})^2}{d_{ij}^2}}.$$

In this case no scale factor is needed. Other functions could be obtained by using other weightings, with appropriate scale factors to match. A somewhat different measure of fit is a goodness-of-fit function defined by

$$S = \text{correlation coefficient}$$

$$\text{of the pairs } (\hat{d}_{ij}, d_{ij})$$

Obviously, a great many other such formulae are possible.

To choose a good measure of fit requires both an intuitive feeling for what sort of discrepancies from the model are more important than others, plus some careful investigation of the properties of the formulas. A discussion of this topic is given by Kruskal and Carroll [16].

e. Systematic Optimization: Methods for Calculating the Optimum

Suppose we have picked some measure of fit for a given problem. For example, consider the first formula for stress $S(X, a, b)$ in the preceding section. The next step is to choose some systematic method of optimizing the measure of fit.

In seeking a good method, the first thing is to see what special properties the measure of fit has which can be exploited to reduce or simplify this calculation. Indeed the measure of fit and even the structural model may be influenced by such possibilities. After taking advantage of such reductions and simplifications, there may be left a "hard-core" optimization problem which must be solved by brute-force iterative numerical methods. For the kinds of problems that occur most often in the area we are dealing with, the best, iterative numerical methods available at the time this is written are various first derivative methods, such as the method of gradients, and the quasi-Newton methods [3]. Both types have been used successfully in this area. We shall come back to choice of iterative numerical calculation later.

How can the optimization calculation be reduced and simplified by exploiting special properties of the measure of fit function? The possibilities are endless and very diverse. They include exploitation of any existing method, such as linear regression, linear programming, principal components, singular value decomposition, and so forth.

We discuss here only one general principle which seems often to recur. In many cases, the variables over which we are optimizing split up naturally into several classes. For example, in linear multidimensional scaling, there are two obvious classes: the variables x_{ir} which we denote jointly by the matrix X, and the variables a and b, which we denote jointly by the vector $\beta = (a, b)$. Such a natural split is often associated with special properties of value. In particular, if we fix all the variables except those in one class, optimizing the measure of fit with respect to the remaining class may be simple to accomplish by some special method. For linear multidimensional scaling, we see that optimizing the stress $S(X, \beta)$ over all β with X fixed comes to nothing more than a very simple least-squares linear regression, which can be accomplished by a well-understood and rapid procedure (namely, solving the corresponding linear normal equations). We may call such a class of variables "nice."

Sometimes every natural class of variables for the measure of fit is nice. Examples are provided by the measures of fit used for Carroll's program CANDECOMP, Harshman's program PARAFAC, and this author's program MONANOVA (if the data are complete). We discuss exploitation of this situation in a later section on individual differences scaling. Sometimes just one of the classes is nice, as for linear multidimensional scaling. We illustrate here a way to exploit this property.

Define a new measure of fit (which we also ambiguously call stress) as follows:

$$S'(X) \equiv \min_{\beta} S(X, \beta)$$

and apply a brute-force numerical iterative optimization procedure to S' rather to S. In the present example, the advantage gained is relatively mild, partly because the number of variables in β is so small. In other cases, such as nonmetric scaling, the advantage can be very great. What optimizing S' iteratively comes to in practice is the following procedure. We start with some initial guess X^0 for the value of X. On each iteration, we start with X^k and calculate the corresponding optimum value β^k of β given X^k (using linear regression as described above). At this point we are ready to calculate $S'(X^k)$ and take one step of whatever iterative procedure we are using with S'. This yields a new value X^{k+1}, and we are ready to start the next iteration.

f. Classical Scaling: Fitting Simple Multidimensional Scaling by Neglecting Errors

One approach to fitting a model to data may be called "neglecting errors." We illustrate this approach with the simple type of multidimensional scaling first described. The data are a complete matrix of dissimilarities δ_{ij} (all entries are available, and there is just one replication), and the structural equation is

$$\delta_{ij} \approx d_{ij} \quad \text{for } i \text{ and } j = 1 \text{ to } I$$

The approach by "neglecting errors" is based on finding equations or relationships that would correctly specify the desired solution in terms of the given data if there were no errors in the data. In this case, we obtain the desired relationship in two steps. The first step is based on the following. (Most of the terminology introduced here will not be used outside this section.)

THEOREM: Suppose I points x_i in R-space have mean $\bar{x}$. Suppose that D is the matrix whose entries are d_{ij}^2, where d_{ij} is the (ordinary Euclidean) distance between x_i and x_j. Suppose we obtain D^* from D by what statisticians describe as removing the grand mean and the row and column effects, and what psychometricians describe as double-centering D; and suppose $B = -\frac{1}{2} D^*$. To express this in another way, suppose m is the grand mean of the elements of D, and a_i is the mean of the elements of row i (and also naturally of column i). Then

$$b_{ij} = -\tfrac{1}{2}\left(d_{ij}^2 - a_i - a_j + m\right)$$

Under these conditions, it follows that

$$b_{ij} = \left(x_i - \bar{x}\right) \cdot \left(x_j - \bar{x}\right)$$

(scalar product) for all i and j.

In the section on indeterminacies we noted that a configuration may be subjected to an arbitrary translation without changing it in any essential way. If we let $x_i' = x_i - \bar{x}$, then $b_{ij} = x_i' \cdot x_j'$ and the mean of the x_i' is 0. Thus we may assume that $b_{ij} = x_i \cdot x_j$ and $\bar{x} = 0$ without real loss of generality.

Another way of writing $b_{ij} = x_i \cdot x_j$ is $B = XX'$, where X is the matrix whose ith row is given by x_i, and X' indicates X transpose. The second step consists of determining the configuration of the x_i, which we may now refer to more briefly as X; it is based on the well-known theorem that any symmetric matrix can be factored into the form $Y \Lambda Y'$, where Y is orthogonal and Λ is diagonal, and that in any such factorization Λ is nonnegative if and only if the original matrix is positive semidefinite. Furthermore, procedures for performing the factorization are standard and well-known under the name of eigenvector calculation.

Since B satisfies all the requirements, we may calculate orthogonal Y and nonnegative diagonal Λ with $B = Y \Lambda Y'$. If we let $\Lambda^{\frac{1}{2}}$ have the obvious meaning, and let $Z = Y \Lambda^{\frac{1}{2}}$, then $ZZ' = B = XX'$. Obviously this is not enough to show that $X = Z$. However it can be proved by an argument we do not present here that X and Z differ only by a rotation, and hence that X and Z are essentially the same in a sense already discussed. Thus without real loss of generality we can take X to be Z.

Thus given some unknown points x_i and their known interpoint distances d_{ij}, we have defined a constructive procedure which can recover the x_i up to a rigid motion. In other words, we can find points y_i which differ from the x_i only by a rigid motion. This procedure starts with the d_{ij}, forms the b_{ij}, and then the y_i. This procedure constitutes

the relationship needed for the approach by neglecting errors. This approach is simply to disregard the errors and treat the δ_{ij} as if they were d_{ij}. There is no guarantee that this will be possible. For example, the matrix B may not turn out to be positive semidefinite in general, so it may not be possible to take the square-root of Λ. Even if it is possible, there is no guarantee that the resulting configuration of y_i will at all resemble the original configuration of x_i. In fact, the history of numerical analysis is filled with examples of the approach by neglecting errors which do not work, or do not work well. Later on we will mention one.

However, the present example of this approach is an outstanding success. Essentially, it is what many people now call the "classical" method of multidimensional scaling, which was first described by Richardson [19] and popularized by Torgerson [24], who introduced the name "multidimensional scaling." Classical scaling requires some way to handle B matrices which are not positive semidefinite, since they frequently occur. Also classical scaling is usually based on the structural equation $\delta_{ij} + a \approx d_{ij}$, and the parameter a must be estimated somehow: This is called the "additive constant" problem. However, reasonably effective answers to these and other difficulties have been developed.

An empirical fact is that classical scaling is amazingly robust. The solution is surprisingly little affected by random error or monotonic distortion in the δ_{ij}. Robustness is definitely not a characteristic that can be expected to hold for the approach by neglecting errors in general. To this writer's knowledge, no one has ever given a satisfactory account of why it holds in this case.

Classical scaling still remains of practical use today, despite the later developments. Both TORSCA and KYST use it to provide an initial configuration with which to start the iterative optimization procedure. Sometimes the iterative procedure does not change this initial configuration very much.

The chief virtue of classical scaling is rapidity and low cost. Its chief limitations are (1) that it cannot handle an incomplete set of dissimilarities without some ad hoc device which may substantially degrade its performance or increase its cost, and (2) that its theoretical foundation is somewhat less satisfactory than that of some other kinds of scaling.

g. Individual Differences Scaling: Model and Systematic Optimization

The data are dissimilarities δ_{ijk}, with i and $j = 1$ to I and $k = 1$ to K, which we consider as forming K square $I \times I$ matrices. We assume $K \geqslant 2$, and $\delta_{ijk} = \delta_{jik}$ for all i, j, k. Our structural model represents the dissimilarities as weighted distances among I points x_i in R-space, with weight vectors w_k. In other words, we assume there are I points $x_i = (x_{i1}, \ldots, x_{iR})$ and K points $w_k = (w_{k1}, \ldots, w_{kR})$ such that

$$\delta_{ijk} \approx d_{ijk} \equiv \sqrt{\sum_{r=1}^{R} w_{kr}(x_{ir} - x_{jr})^2}$$

$$\text{for all} \quad (i, j, k)$$

Although this is a great generalization of ordinary multidimensional scaling, in one respect it is more limited, in that it corresponds to the simplest structural model for multidimensional scaling, which was explained at the beginning of Section 2b. More general structural models for individual differences scaling have been used, which introduce the same kinds of generality we introduced into ordinary multidimensional scaling. However, the model given here has been dominant in applications. It is the basis for the INDSCAL program of Carroll and Chang and for the scaling applications of the Harshman program PARAFAC. It should be noted in this connection, however, that the INDSCAL program includes important provisions for preliminary transformation of the data by an additive constant, chosen separately for each matrix of dissimilarities, which greatly extends the range of situations for which the simple model above is appropriate.

The dominant approach to fitting this model to data combines two of the approaches we mentioned previously, namely neglecting errors and systematic optimization. Recall that the classical method of multidimensional scaling, which is based on neglecting errors, starts by performing a transformation which if applied to true distances d_{ij} would yield dot products b_{ij} of vectors from the centroid (mean vector). This same transformation is used here for each of the K matrices of dissimilarities, to yield K matrices of values which we call β_{ijk}.

If we applied the preliminary step to

$$d_{ijk} = \sqrt{\sum_r \left(x_{ir}\sqrt{w_{kr}} - x_{jr}\sqrt{w_{kr}} \right)^2}$$

where the vectors x_i have centroid (mean) 0, then according to the theorem cited in the section on classical scaling, we would get

$$b_{ijk} \equiv \sum_r \left(x_{ir}\sqrt{w_{kr}} \right)\left(x_{jr}\sqrt{w_{kr}} \right)$$

$$= \sum_r x_{ir}x_{jr}w_{kr}$$

Thus by neglecting errors we are led to the derived set of structural equations

$$\beta_{ijk} \approx \sum_r x_{ir}x_{jr}w_{kr} \qquad \text{for all} \quad (i, j, k)$$

where the vectors x_i have centroid (mean) 0.

To fit this derived structural model, the approach used is systematic optimization, based on the following measure of fit, which we wish to minimize:

$$S(X, W) = \sum_{i, j, k} \left(\beta_{ijk} - \sum_r x_{ir}x_{jr}w_{kr} \right)^2$$

Here W is the $K \times R$ matrix of values w_{kr}. To perform the optimization calculation, we first generalize the function S to

$$S'(U, V, W) = \sum_{i,j,k} \left(\beta_{ijk} - \sum_r u_{ir} v_{jr} w_{kr} \right)^2$$

This generalization offers an important advantage which we will describe below. First, however, we note that for an optimum of S' to yield a solution to the problem we are really concerned with, U and V of the optimum must be the "same" in some sense, and the centroid of the u_i (the rows of U) must be 0 to meet the centroid condition on the x_i. Fortunately, this all works out all right. [It is not hard to prove that the condition $U = VD$, with D a strictly positive diagonal matrix, is necessary and sufficient for the optimum of S' to yield an optimum of S, and that $X = UD^{\frac{1}{2}} = VD^{-\frac{1}{2}}$ and W then provide the desired optimum, where $D^{\frac{1}{2}}$ is the positive square-root of D. Fortunately, the symmetry assumed for δ_{ijk} generally yields the same kind of symmetry for β_{ijk}, and this together with other properties automatically yields that $U = VD$ at the optimum (at least in practice). The construction of the β_{ijk} shows that $\sum_i \beta_{ijk} = 0$ for all j and k, and from this it is elementary to show that the solution U to the normal equations has zero centroid (that is, zero column means).]

The variables in S' split up naturally into the three obvious classes U, V, and W. In the terminology of an earlier section, each of these classes is nice: With the other variables fixed, S' may be minimized over the variables in one class by the well-known methods of linear least-squares, namely, by solving the associated normal equations. (This is the advantage of changing from S to S'.) For example, to find the best U with V and W fixed we must solve I separate sets of R linear equations in R unknowns; each set of unknowns forms one row of the matrix U. Furthermore, all I sets of equations involve the same $R \times R$ matrix of coefficients. Since R, the dimensionality of

the space, is small (9 or 10 is a very large value for R), solving the normal equations is a simple matter.

How is the niceness of the classes U, V, and W exploited? One plausible procedure is to take any initial guess for U and V, U_0 and V_0, and find the optimum W_0. (In practice, we take $U_0 = V_0$.) Then we fix V_0 and W_0 and find the optimum U_1. Then we fix U_1 and W_0 and find the optimum V_1. This completes one cycle of an iteration, which goes cyclically around W, U, and V in that order. It is plausible to guess that this procedure will converge to a minimum value of S'. For an arbitrary continuous function S', this might not work: Counterexamples are not hard to construct, though they look quite artificial. For the actual function S' we are working with, and no doubt for many other natural measures of fit one might work with, it can be proved that the procedure does converge to at least a local minimum of S'. In principle, the procedure might converge to some local minimum other than the global minimum (this is known to be possible for the actual function S'), but in practice this seems to be a very rare event.

h. Approaches to Model Fitting

Several different approaches to model fitting may be observed in the area covered by this chapter.

SYSTEMATIC OPTIMIZATION

In one approach, an explicit measure of fit is defined and a computational procedure with some known type of mathematical effectiveness is used simply to find the parameter values which optimize the fit. This approach has already been illustrated in Section 2g for linear multidimensional scaling.

This approach is called systematic optimization. Within this approach we may distinguish varieties according to what type of effectiveness is known for the computational procedure.

1. Rarely, a procedure is used which is guaranteed to produce the true optimum in a finite number of steps. Examples in this area include MUMP, by Srinivasan and Shocker, which makes use of linear programming to optimize fit, and monotone (or isotone) regression, which is used as a subsidary procedure for nonmetric scaling and MONANOVA, but is also of interest in itself.

2. Much more commonly used are procedures for optimizing an unconstrained function of many variables, for which it is possible to prove convergence to a local optimum (though little attention has been paid in this area to actually providing such proofs). This is probably the major variety. (In rare special cases such procedures are used with a goodness-of-fit function which is convex, so that convergence to the global optimum is guaranteed.)

3. For some methods used in this area, notably among clustering methods, combinatorial optimization procedures are used. In most cases, it can be proved by elementary arguments that the probability of such a procedure finding the global optimum approaches 1 as the number of starting configurations approaches infinity.

NONSYSTEMATIC OPTIMIZATION

In another approach an explicit measure of fit is defined but an intuitive or ad hoc method of optimizing is devised for which it is difficult to make any clear mathematical statement of effectiveness. This approach may be called nonsystematic optimization. In cases where such procedures have been compared with systematic procedures, the intuitive methods may do reasonably well, sometimes very well. It is possible, in principle, that such an ad hoc procedure may later turn out to be a systematic optimization procedure either because it can be derived from some measure of fit, or because it uses some new principle not yet exploited by professional numerical analysts, and that further research might promote the procedure to the systematic optimization class. We shall cite such an example in a moment. More commonly, however, specific defects can be demonstrated in such procedures (even though they may have a high degree of practical effectiveness).

This writer believes that the SSA-1 program of Guttman and Lingoes (which falls within his definition of multidimensional scaling, though they prefer other terminology) is an example of nonsystematic optimization, though it is not at all clear that the authors would agree. In Appendix II some relevant evidence is presented. Also strongly relevant in this connection is [18].

One striking example is the scaling method introduced by Shepard in his path-breaking paper [22]. Many of us have considered this to be a method of nonsystematic optimization, since Shepard's paper does not derive his computational procedure from any measure of fit, though he does explicitly introduce and use a measure of fit. However discussions between J. D. Carroll and the present author, stimulated by the writing of this chapter, led to the surprising discovery of a very reasonable measure of fit (presented briefly in Appendix I) for which Shepard's computation procedure is the method of gradients. This discovery clearly indicates the sure strength and deftness of Shepard's approach.

A significant part of this author's improvement (first incorporated in M-D SCAL) of Shepard's method consisted of introducing a measure of fit (similar to that shown above for linear scaling) which is computationally better than the measure of fit explicitly introduced by Shepard, and of introducing a systematic method of optimizing it, so that the resulting method was explicitly displayed as an example of systematic optimization.

In some cases several measures of fit are used, which in itself is perfectly sensible and may be quite helpful. However in nonsystematic optimization it is often unclear which measure of fit is to be optimized. This tends to cause conceptual confusion.

In some cases *no* measure of fit is explicitly defined, though the elements for one may be present. In this case, the intuition of the model builder is used directly in forming the (generally iterative) procedure. (An advantage of systematic optimization over this situation results from splitting apart what-we-want from how-to-find-it, so that both parts may be approached more effectively.) This situation is not dignified as a separate approach since there are no obvious important examples of it.

NEGLECTING ERRORS

One approach that is often used to form computational procedures requires no measure of fit definition at all. One famous example of this approach is classical multidimensional scaling, discussed in Section 2f for simple multidimensional scaling. Another example of this approach, closely related to classical scaling, is the method invented by Schöneman [21] to solve one version of the metric unfolding problem.

This approach is very unpredictable. In some cases it works very well, and in other cases very poorly. Classical scaling, which works amazingly well with large amounts of error, is a strong success story. On the other hand, Schöneman's method reportedly does not do so well.

It might be possible to trace such failure and success to identifiable properties of the algorithm, and hence to predict failure and success. However numerical analysis has not yet reached the stage where useful analysis of this sort is practical for algorithms as complex as the two mentioned. Such analysis would be very welcome.

One important point should be mentioned here. Sometimes an algorithm can be changed in apparently very minor ways which do not affect how it works with error-free data. By analogy with other situations in numerical analysis, it is surely true that such apparently minor changes can have major effects for general data.

i. Numerical Procedures for Systematic Optimization

Systematic optimization is applied to models with ordinary continuous parameters, to models with combinatorial parameters (such as permutations, trees, and partitions), and to mixed models that have parameters of both types. A discussion of the latter two types is beyond the scope of this chapter; thus we restrict our discussion to models with ordinary real parameters. Nevertheless, it should be noted that within the field covered by this chapter combinatorial optimization is practiced, particularly for clustering methods. Two particularly effective examples within this field are demonstrated by Kernighan and Lin [12] and Hartigan [9].

For optimization over models with continuous parameters, there is a major split into constrained and unconstrained optimization. Constrained optimization refers to optimization when the parameters are subject to equations or inequalities which constrain them. The presence of constraints can add greatly to the computational difficulty. Fortunately, in this field there has been very little need to deal with genuine constraints, but there is one interesting example that has genuine constraints which cannot be removed or handled in some special trouble-avoiding manner. (The example, already mentioned above, is MUMP by Srinavasan and Shocker, and is so completely linear that it can be handled by standard linear programming.) Many of the constraints mentioned in this chapter are constraints added deliberately to reduce indeterminacy, and this type of constraint seldom causes much trouble. Some other constraints mentioned here are associated with monotonicity requirements, that is, a requirement that one set of variables have the same rank order as another set. While such constraints are genuine, it is generally possible to handle them in some special way.

Unconstrained optimization methods may be divided into three classes, 0, 1, and 2.

Class 0 consists of procedures in which the first partial derivatives are never calculated. Such procedures are generally used only where mathematical expressions for the first partial derivatives are impossible or extremely awkward, since their use is so helpful. Classes 1 and 2 consist of all other procedures, and include gradient, Newton, quasi-Newton, and other procedures. The distinction between them has to do with the amount of memory needed. If n is the number of variables in the function being optimized, Class 1 procedures (such as the gradient procedure) require memory space which is only linear in n, while Class 2 procedures (such as the Newton and quasi-Newton procedures) require memory space which is more than linear (typically quadratic). Class 1 procedures appear unable to achieve better than first-order convergence. (This means that, as convergence towards a particular optimum proceeds, the distance d_n from that optimum only decreases by a constant factor per iteration in the limit, that is, d_{n+1}/d_n approaches a constant as $n \to \infty$. To the author's knowledge, there is no general theorem to this effect, but first-order convergence has been proved for many particular Class 1 procedures, subject to certain minor technical restrictions.) Class 2 methods generally achieve better than first-order convergence. (This means that as convergence towards a particular optimum proceeds, d_{n+1}/d_n^α approaches a constant with $\alpha > 1$.) Although this may yield a great improvement in speed of convergence, the memory cost can be substantial when n is in the hundreds or even thousands.

Although Classes 1 and 2 have both been used in this field, Class 1 has been used much more often. In addition to the high cost of memory during computing, this may be due to the fact that high accuracy solutions are almost never needed in this field due to the substantial random error which we typically find in the data. Since the solution is meaningful only up to a certain level

due to random error in the input, there is no need to obtain a solution which is accurate to a much higher level. Hence the higher speed of convergence for Class 2 methods does not have so great an attraction.

Class 1 methods form a large topic in themselves, too extensive to cover in this chapter. In this field the predominant Class 1 method has been the method of gradients (the method of steepest ascent or descent). Relatively little use has been made of other Class 1 methods.

The method of gradients is very simple in principle. Suppose we are optimizing $f(X)$, where X is a vector of n variables. Let $\nabla f(X)$ indicate the gradient of f at X. We start with some guess X^0 of X. We then proceed to form $X^1, X^2, \ldots$ iteratively by the rule

$$X^{k+1} = X^k \pm \lambda^{(k)} \nabla f(X^k)$$

$$\begin{cases} + & \text{for maximizing} \\ - & \text{for minimizing} \end{cases}$$

where $\lambda^{(k)}$ is determined according to some step-size rule. Choice of the rule is the primary distinction among different versions of the gradient method. The word "step-size" has two different meanings in common use. Some authors use it to refer to the multiplier $\lambda^{(k)}$. However, we shall follow the other usage, in which the step-size refers to the length of the step $\|\lambda^{(k)} \nabla f(X^k)\|$.

j. The Step-Size Procedure in M-D-SCAL and KYST: An Innovation

One widely used procedure in gradient methods generally is to let the step-size be proportional to the magnitude of the gradient (that is, to use a constant value of λ). However in experimentation with the earliest versions of M-D-SCAL this did not work well, and an innovation was introduced. The step-size was made to depend entirely on the angle between the present gradient and the gradient on the preceding step. Since no full explanation of the rationale behind this angle-dependent step-size has ever been published, and essentially the same procedure is also used in KYST, it is explained here.

In many gradient methods, the gradient is used to define a direction in space, and then considerable exploration is done along that direction to find the one-dimensional optimum along that line. This may involve evaluating the function at several points along the line, and fitting them with a polynomial, for example. These methods are appropriate and sensible when the computer cost of evaluating the function is much less than the computer cost of evaluating the gradient, since it uses several cheap function evaluations to get the most good out of one expensive gradient evaluation. However, when the function evaluation cost is not small in relation to the gradient evaluation cost, or when there is substantial overlap between these two costs, the situation is rather different. Let us consider the situation we actually face.

In our situation, most of the computation required for function evaluation and for gradient evaluation is shared between these two calculations. (For example, consider the evaluation S' and $\nabla S'$ for linear multidimensional scaling in the skeleton computer program shown on page 322. Shared costs, needed to compute either S' and $\nabla S'$, include the linear regression. If we substitute more complex types of scaling, the linear regression is replaced by more time-consuming calculation such as monotonic regression instead of linear, and perhaps many regressions instead of just one.) Since the shared computation is so large, the cost of gradient evaluation is only slightly larger than the cost of function evaluation. Furthermore, once the function is evaluated, the extra cost required for gradient evaluation is very small.

Suppose we have just evaluated the function f and its gradient at X^k, and wish to decide the value of $\lambda^{(k)}$ to use in $X^{k+1} = X^k + \lambda^{(k)} \nabla f(X)$. Suppose we consider a strategy like the previous one, which involves evaluating f and ∇f for several possible values of λ, to decide what the optimum value of $\lambda^{(k)}$ is. Presumably we start by evaluating at our best guess λ_0 for what $\lambda^{(k)}$ will turn out to be. Unless this guess is quite bad, the function value will be better at $X^k + \lambda_0 \nabla f(X)$ than at X^k. Why spend one or two more evaluations along the present line? Why not let $X^{k+1} = X^k + \lambda_0 \nabla f(X)$, and spend the next one or two evaluations on the line from X^{k+1}? It seems intuitively that this would yield faster convergence. In the absence of any investigation, this intuition has been followed.

Now we get down to the question of determining $\lambda^{(k)}$ from the information available just after we have evaluated $f(X^k)$ and $\nabla f(X^k)$. The first principle we use is that a good step-size is in most cases approximately the same as a good step-size on the preceding iteration. (It is a common observation, for reasonably effective gradient procedures of all kinds, that the step-size may vary over many orders of magnitude during the course of iteration, but the step-sizes on adjacent iterations are generally not very different.) Thus if the preceding step size was about right, we want to use about the same value; if it was too large, we want to use a smaller value; and if it was too small, we want to use a larger value.

Now we need a way to determine whether the preceding step-size was too large or too small. Referring to Fig. 12.1, we determine this by the angle θ between $\nabla f(X^k)$ and

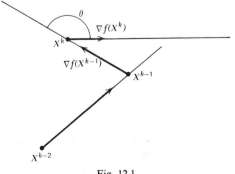

Fig. 12.1

$\nabla f(X^{k-1})$, the present gradient and the previous gradient. Suppose the preceding step-size, $\|\lambda^{(k-1)} \nabla f(X^{k-1})\|$, was about the right size. Then X^k should be near the one-dimensional minimum along the line from X^{k-1}. At the minimum position itself, θ must be precisely 90°, a right-angle. Thus if θ is near 90° we take the preceding step-size to have been about right.

Now suppose the preceding step-size was far too small. Then the gradient at X^k would be almost the same as the gradient at X^{k-1}, so the angle θ would be almost 0°. Thus if θ is near 0°, we take the preceding step-size to be too small, and use a larger step-size now. Conversely, suppose the preceding step-size was several times too large. Then we have moved well past the one-dimensional minimum along the line, so the new gradient $\nabla f(X^k)$ should point almost back along the line, and θ is near 180°. Thus if θ is near 180° we take the preceding step-size to be too large, and use a smaller step-size now.

At this point we are naturally led to take an empirical approach. It seems natural to make the new step-size a continuous function of θ. One plausible formula which presents itself after some thought is

$$\text{new step-size} = \text{old step-size} \cdot \rho^{\cos\theta}$$

Then the greatest change in the step-size is multiplication or division by ρ. At first it seemed natural to use $\rho = 2$, by analogy with the common practice in numerical analysis of doubling or halving step sizes in other situations (such as in the solution of differential equations and quadrature). However empirical investigation with early versions of M-D-SCAL revealed that $\rho = 2$ is too small, perhaps because $\cos\theta$ seldom gets close enough to ± 1 to make $2^{\cos\theta}$ very close to 2 or $\frac{1}{2}$. Work with larger values of ρ showed that $4^{\cos\theta}$ changed the step-size rapidly enough for $\cos\theta$ near ± 1, but too rapidly for moderate values of $\cos\theta$. This led to investigation of formulas like

new step-size

$$= \text{old step-size} \cdot \rho^{|\cos\theta|^p \cdot \text{signum}(\cos\theta)},$$

with p greater than 1. Although it certainly was not possible to pin down "optimum values" for ρ and p in any sense, $\rho = 4$ and $p = 3$ did reasonably well, and permitted the multiplier to be written more simply as

$$4^{(\cos\theta)^3}$$

Later on, a running average of the $\cos\theta$ values was substituted for $(\cos\theta)^3$. This running average is maintained by the formula

(new average of $\cos\theta$)

$$= w(\cos\theta) + (1 - w)(\text{old average of } \cos\theta)$$

with $0 < w < 1$, generally $w = \frac{2}{3}$. This running average is easily seen to be an exponentially weighted average of all the $\cos\theta$ values back to the first one, which is taken by convention to be 0.

A good-luck factor is also used, though it is of very minor importance. Once in a while, by chance, the stress will drop very sharply from one iteration to the next. Presumably this reflects good luck in getting near the minimum. If this happens, we don't want to jump away from this low stress region, which we might very well do by taking as large a step on the next iteration. For this purpose, we calculate the "stress ratio," which is the present stress value divided by the previous stress value. Usually, this is smaller than 1, but generally not much smaller than 1. If it is smaller than 1, we use $\sqrt{\text{stress ratio}}$ as a factor in forming the new step-size. By arbitrary convention, we take the stress ratio to be 0.8 on the very first iteration.

A bias factor is also used. To understand the purpose of this factor, first note that during the later stages of convergence, the function being optimized can be approximated by a positive semidefinite quadratic function whose minimum occurs at the minimum position we are seeking. Such an approximation is provided by the first few terms of a Taylor series at the minimum position. (The approximation is valid since the optimum of our evaluation function typically occurs where the function is analytic. For mathematical discussion of the behavior of such evaluation functions at the optimum values see [5, 17]. For discussion of an evaluation function used in SSA-1 which in some cases is not even differentiable at the optimum, see Appendix II of this chapter.) In the quadratic region the gradient is a reasonably good direction in which to move, though subject to some well-understood limitations. At this stage of the computation, there is no particular reason to tend towards particularly large or particularly small steps, though a slight tendency towards small steps might seem more conducive to final precise convergence.

However, during the early stages of the computation we are well outside the "quadratic valley," in a region where the function is probably very "irregular." In this region the gradient is not so useful a pointer. (More concretely, the angle between the gradient and the direction to the minimum probably would tend to be larger outside the quadratic valley than in it.) Furthermore, we do not wish to explore the shape of the function in detail in this region. It would seem sensible to take large steps, and if need be "jump around" quickly, to cover as much ground as possible, looking for the quadratic valley.

In an effort to make the steps larger outside the quadratic valley, and smaller inside it, we also multiply the old step-size by a bias factor in calculating the new step-size. Of course, our method for guessing whether we are in the quadratic valley or not is inevitably very crude. We maintain a running geometric average of the stress ratio by the formula

(new average stress ratio)

$$= \text{(stress ratio)}^{\frac{1}{3}} \text{(old average stress ratio)}^{\frac{2}{3}}$$

When the average stress ratio is near 1, so convergence is slow, we consider it likely that we are in the quadratic valley, whereas when the average stress ratio is a good bit smaller than 1, we consider it likely that we are outside the quadratic valley. An average stress ratio larger than 1 is abnormal, but conceivable, so we truncate at 1. After that we use the factor

$$\frac{1.6}{1 + \text{(average stress ratio)}^5}$$

When the average stress ratio is .9 or larger, this factor is smaller than 1, otherwise larger. When the average stress ratio approaches 1, this factor approaches 0.8.

However, the bias factor contains one final nicety, based on the empirical observation that in the final stages of convergence, $\cos \theta$ often takes on values which are all very close to $+1$ or -1. This suggests that the final convergence is taking place almost along a one-dimensional subspace of configuration space, and presumably in the quadratic valley.

A running average of $|\cos \theta|$ is maintained by the formula

$$\text{(new average of } |\cos \theta|) = \bar{w}(|\cos \theta|)$$

$$+ (1 - \bar{w})(\text{old average of } |\cos \theta|)$$

with $0 < \bar{w} < 1$, generally $\bar{w} = \frac{2}{3}$.

The bias factor also contains the factor

$$\frac{1}{1 + \text{(average of } |\cos \theta|) - |\text{average of } \cos \theta|}$$

This factor is always between $\frac{1}{2}$ and 1, but tends to decrease as $\cos \theta$ varies more widely around 0. The constant 1.6 is sensitive to the presence of this factor, and was adjusted to its present value by experiment after this factor was introduced.

Thus finally we have

(new step-size) = (old step-size)

$\times$ (angle factor)

$\times$ (good luck factor)

$\times$ (bias factor)

where

$$(\text{angle factor}) = \rho(\text{average } \cos \theta)$$

$$(\text{good luck factor}) = \sqrt{\min(1, \text{stress ratio})}$$

$$(\text{bias factor}) =$$

$$\frac{1.6}{\left[1 + (\text{average stress ratio})^5\right]}$$

$$\times \left[1 + (\text{average } |\cos \theta| - |\text{average } \cos \theta|)\right]$$

Finally, one clear improvement was introduced in later versions of M-D-SCAL. Occasionally, as we have mentioned before, a particular step-size will turn out to be much too large. This can happen merely by chance during normal iteration, though it does not occur that way frequently. However when the iterative procedure is first started the initial guess of the step-size is inevitably very crude. (The exact details of how the initial step-size is chosen hardly matter, because they are not and probably cannot be very good. This initial guess must cover both random starting configurations which fit the data very poorly, and configurations previously arrived at by scaling which fit fairly well and we wish to polish a little further. In the latter situation it has even legitimately been observed that the initial step-size is sometimes more than 1000 times as large as it should be.) If we are trying to converge more exactly to a previously obtained solution, an excessively large step may cause us to jump away from it and defeat the purpose entirely.

To avoid taking a step which is much too large, a "step-back" procedure has been incorporated. If the stress increases by 20% or more, or if $-0.95 \geqslant \cos \geqslant -1$, the program decides that the step-size was much too large, and steps back from X^k to X^{k-1} and proceeds again with a step-size $\frac{1}{10}$ as large as that used before. Up to four consecutive repetitions of the step-back are permitted, so that a step-size can be reduced by a factor of 10^4 before proceeding, if necessary. This step-back procedure is most often used for an initial configuration, but is always available, and is used occasionally to take a single step back during ordinary convergence. (The converse situation of an initial step-size which is much too small is much less serious, so that no mechanism has been installed to handle it. If the situation arises, the ordinary feed-back mechanism only takes one or two iterations to start multiplying the step-size by nearly $\rho = 4$ on each iteration, which brings the step-size up to a useful level fairly rapidly. Meanwhile no damage is done; just a little computer time is wasted.)

k. Calculating the Gradient for Linear Multidimensional Scaling

We base this section on the formula

$$S(X, \beta) = \sqrt{\sum (d_{ij} - \hat{d}_{ij})^2} \Big/ \sqrt{\sum d_{ij}^2}$$

where $\hat{d}_{ij} \equiv a + b\delta_{ij}$ are the pseudodistances. We recall that the problem of minimizing S iteratively was reduced above to the problem of minimizing S' iteratively, where $S'(X) = \min_\beta S(X, \beta)$. Many iterative methods of optimizing S', including gradient and quasi-Newton methods, require use of the gradient of S'. Aside from mathematical technicalities which need not concern us here, the gradient of S' may be thought of as the vector of first partial derivatives with respect to all the variables. Although it is possible to estimate the gradient numerically, it is generally more efficient to derive and use an explicit expression for the gradient, if this is feasible. It is worthwhile to illustrate this calculation, and the skeleton of the computer program it leads to, since it involves elements which have caused some difficulty.

The first step is to express the relationship between S' and S more explicitly. Because of the properties of linear regression, there is a unique value of β which minimizes $S(X, \beta)$ for given X. Let us call that value $\beta_0(X)$. Since the two components of β are called a and b, we denote the two components of $\beta_0(X)$ by $a_0(X)$ and $b_0(X)$. Now from the various definitions we immediately obtain that

$$S'(X) = S(X, \beta_0(X))$$

$$\equiv S(X, a_0(X), b_0(X)) \text{ for all } X \quad (1)$$

Furthermore, because the partial derivatives of a function are zero at a minimum value, we have that

$$\frac{\partial S}{\partial a}(X, \beta_0(X)) = 0, \quad \frac{\partial S}{\partial b}(X, \beta_0(X)) = 0$$

This last point is quite important, and though it appears elementary, failure to realize it in closely related situations has caused much confusion. The principle involved is of great generality.

Now we start calculating the partial derivatives of S'. The first step is to express them in terms of S.

$$\frac{\partial S'}{\partial x_{ir}}(X) = \frac{d}{dx_{ir}} S'(X) = \frac{d}{dx_{ir}} S(X, \beta_0(X))$$

$$= \sum_j \sum_s \frac{\partial S}{\partial x_{js}}(X, \beta_0(X)) \frac{dx_{js}}{dx_{ir}}$$

$$+ \frac{\partial S}{\partial a}(X, \beta_0(X)) \frac{da_0(X)}{dx_{ir}}$$

$$+ \frac{\partial S}{\partial b}(X, \beta_0(X)) \frac{db_0(X)}{dx_{ir}}$$

$$= \frac{\partial S}{\partial x_{ir}}(X, \beta_0(X)) \quad \text{for all } i \text{ and } r$$

To take the last step, we use the equations above to drop the last two terms, and we use the trivial equation

$$\frac{dx_{js}}{dx_{ir}} = \begin{cases} 1 & \text{if } (i, r) = (j, s) \\ 0 & \text{otherwise} \end{cases}$$

Note that if we omit the derivation and write simply

$$\frac{\partial S'}{\partial x_{ir}}(X) = \frac{\partial S}{\partial x_{ir}}(X, \beta_0(X))$$

it might appear as if we are ignoring certain terms, which we have actually dropped because they vanish. Many readers of Kruskal [15] have been misled into thinking certain terms were simply neglected in this way, since that paper, without any derivation at all, gives a formula at the top of page 136 for the gradient of the badness-of-fit function for nonmetric scaling which is analogous to the one we are working with here for linear scaling.

The next step is to calculate the partial derivatives of S. To simplify notation we let $\partial_{ir} = \partial/\partial x_{ir}$ and use merely ∂ when the indices are unimportant. Now

$$S = \frac{U}{L} \text{ where}$$

$$\left. U = \sqrt{\sum (d_{ij} - \hat{d}_{ij})^2} \right\} \quad (2)$$

$$L = \sqrt{\sum d_{ij}^2}$$

so

$$\partial S = \frac{1}{L} \partial U - \frac{U}{L^2} \partial L$$

$$= \frac{1}{2UL} \left[\partial(U^2) - \frac{U}{2L^3} \partial(L^2) \right] \quad (3)$$

Next we wish to express this in terms of $\partial(d_{ij}^2)$. Obviously

$$\partial L^2 = \sum \partial(d_{ij}^2)$$

$$\partial U^2 = 2 \sum (d_{ij} - \hat{d}_{ij})(\partial d_{ij} - \partial \hat{d}_{ij})$$

But $\partial \hat{d}_{ij} = 0$. (In case this is not clear, recall that $\hat{d}_{ij} \equiv a + b\delta_{ij}$, and a and b are being treated as constant since we are engaged in calculating, for some k and s,

$$\partial S \equiv \partial_{ks} S(x_{11}, \ldots, x_{IR}, a, b)$$

These details are emphasized here since the disappearance of these terms has caused confusion closely linked with that mentioned previously.) Since

$$\partial d_{ij} = \frac{1}{2d_{ij}} \partial(d_{ij}^2)$$

and $U^2/L^2 = S^2$, we have using (3)

$$\partial S = \frac{1}{2UL} \sum \left\{ \frac{d_{ij} - \hat{d}_{ij}}{d_{ij}} - S^2 \right\} \partial \left(d_{ij}^2 \right)$$

Now we write the matrix X as a long vector,

$$X = (x_{11}, \ldots, x_{1R}, \ldots, x_{I1}, \ldots, x_{IR})$$

We let ∇ be the gradient operator on any function, and we let

$$\nabla_X = (\partial_{11}, \ldots, \partial_{1R}, \ldots, \partial_{I1}, \ldots, \partial_{IR})$$

so that

$$\nabla S(X, a, b) \equiv \left(\nabla_X, \frac{\partial}{\partial a}, \frac{\partial}{\partial b} \right) S$$

$$\equiv \left(\nabla_X S, \frac{\partial S}{\partial a}, \frac{\partial S}{\partial b} \right)$$

and

$$\nabla S'(X) \equiv \nabla_X S'$$

What we proved earlier connecting the derivatives of S' and S can now be written

$$\nabla S'(X) = \nabla_X S(X, \beta_0(X)) \qquad (4)$$

and what we proved in the last paragraph can be written

$$\nabla_X S(X, \beta)$$

$$= \frac{1}{2UL} \sum \left\{ \frac{d_{ij} - \hat{d}_{ij}}{d_{ij}} - S^2 \right\} \nabla_X d_{ij}^2$$

Before proceeding further we change the notation slightly to make it more convenient for programming purposes. Recall that the summation signs we have been using refer to summations over "all available (i, j)." Because the set of available pairs (i, j) may be rather irregular for reasons given earlier, it is necessary to list the available pairs (i, j). Thus it is both necessary and convenient to perform such summations by running over a single index m. We arrange the pairs (i, j) in some definite order (the order makes no difference for linear scaling) and let the pairs be

$$(i(1), j(1)), (i(2), j(2)), \ldots, (i(m), j(m)), \ldots$$

We let m range from 1 to M, where M is the number of available pairs. Where the values of i and j are not important, we shall use merely m. Thus we may write δ_m rather than $\delta_{i(m), j(m)}$, d_m rather than $d_{i(m), j(m)}$, and so forth. In this notation

$$\nabla_X S(X, \beta)$$

$$= \frac{1}{2UL} \sum_{m=1}^{M} \left\{ \frac{d_m - \hat{d}_m}{d_m} - S^2 \right\} \nabla_X d_m^2$$

We now proceed to the calculation of $\nabla_X d_{ij}^2$. Let

$$\varepsilon_{ij} = \begin{cases} 1 & \text{if } i = j \\ 0 & \text{otherwise} \end{cases}$$

(We avoid the more common notation δ, since that letter is already in use for another purpose.) Then

$$\partial_{ks} d_{ij}^2 = \partial_{ks} \sum_{r=1}^{R} (x_{ir} - x_{jr})^2$$

$$= 2 \sum_r (x_{ir} - x_{jr}) \partial_{ks} (x_{ir} - x_{jr})$$

$$= 2(x_{is} - x_{js})(\varepsilon_{ki} - \varepsilon_{kj})$$

so

$$(\partial_{k1}, \ldots, \partial_{kR}) d_{ij}^2 = 2(x_i - x_j)(\varepsilon_{ki} - \varepsilon_{kj})$$

Now if we think of the long vector $\nabla_X d_{ij}^2$ broken up into pieces like that above for $k = 1$ to I, then this formula states that these pieces are 0 except where $k = i$ or $k = j$, and that the ith and jth pieces respectively are $2(x_i - x_j)$ and $-2(x_i - x_j)$. To write this in a computationally convenient manner, we introduce more notation. If y is an R-vector (for example, a "piece"), then

$$E_i(y) = \left(0_R, \ldots, 0_R, \overset{i\text{th position}}{y}, 0_R, \ldots, 0_R \right)$$

where 0_R is the zero vector with R components. Thus E_i is a function or operator from R-space into IR-space. Though it is awkward to describe in mathematical symbolism, it is very easy to handle in a computer program.

Now we have that

$$\nabla_X d_{ij}^2 = \left\{ \sum_{k=1}^{I} E_k(\partial_{k1}, \ldots, \partial_{kR}) \right\} d_{ij}^2$$

$$= \sum_k 2E_k(x_i - x_j)(\varepsilon_{ki} - \varepsilon_{kj})$$

$$= 2\{ E_i(x_i - x_j) - E_j(x_i - x_j) \}$$

$$= 2(E_i - E_j)(x_i - x_j)$$

From this, we get our final formula for $\nabla_x S$,

$$\nabla_X S(X, \beta) =$$

$$\frac{1}{UL} \sum_m \left\{ \frac{d_m - \hat{d}_m}{d_m} - S^2 \right\}$$

$$\times (E_{i(m)} - E_{j(m)})(x_{i(m)} - x_{j(m)}) \quad (5)$$

To write a computer program using the formulas we have developed is very simple. To make this plain, we show such a skeleton program for one complete iteration of the type described at the end of the preceding section. The key formulas are (1), (2), (4), and (5) from above, together with the well-known normal equations for linear regression which we must solve for $a_0(X)$ and $b_0(X)$:

$$a_0(X)M + b_0(X)\sum_m \delta_m = \sum_m d_m$$

$$a_0(X)\sum_m \delta_m + b_0(X)\sum_m \delta_m^2 = \sum_m d_m\delta_m$$

In the skeleton program, we denote the matrix of coefficients by A, the vector of right-hand-sides by B, and the solution by β, so these equations become $\beta A = B$. Also we denote the gradient $\nabla S'(X)$ by G.

SKELETON PROGRAM

Known or calculated prior to all iterations:

$$M, \{i(m), j(m), \delta_m\}_1^M, \sum \delta_m, \sum \delta_m^2$$

Known at start of iteration: X

PREPARATION FOR LINEAR REGRESSION

Set $A(1, 1) = M$, $A(1, 2) = A(2, 1)$
$= \sum \delta_m$, $A(2, 2) = \sum \delta_m^2$
Set $B(1) = B(2) = 0$
For $m = 1$ to M
    Set $y = x_{i(m)} - x_{j(m)}$
    Set $d_m = \|y\|$
    Set $B(1) = B(1) + d_m$
    Set $B(2) = B(2) + d_m\delta_m$

FIND $\beta_0(X)$ BY SOLVING NORMAL EQUATIONS OF LINEAR REGRESSION

Solve $\beta A = B$ for $\beta = (a, b)$

CALCULATE U, L, AND $S'(X) = S(X, \beta_0(X))$

Set $U = L = 0$

For $m = 1$ to M
    Set $\hat{d}_m = a + b\delta_m$
    Set $U = U + (d_m - \hat{d}_m)^2$
    Set $L = L + d_m^2$
    Set $U = \sqrt{U}$, $L = \sqrt{L}$, and $S = U/L$

CALCULATE $S'(X) = \nabla_X S(X, \beta_0(X))$

For $i = 1$ to I and for $r = 1$ to R
    Set $G(i, r) = 0$
For $m = 1$ to M
    Set

$$y = \frac{1}{UL} \left\{ \frac{d_m - \hat{d}_m}{d_m} - S^2 \right\}(x_{i(m)} - x_{j(m)})$$

    Add y into the $i(m)$-th row of G
    Add $-y$ into the $j(m)$-th row of G

CALCULATE A NEW X

Use the old X and the gradient G to calculate a new X.
(This is explained in a later section.)

3. SUMMARY OF THE CALCULATION PROCEDURE

a. Nature of the Example

This description and the flow chart describe the essential features of the method of multidimensional scaling used in KYST and in M-D-SCAL (all versions). However, this description does not include some very important elements of generality in KYST, such as the possibility of non-Euclidean metrics, and provision for matching dissimilarities to distances by several regressions rather than one. Also it deemphasizes the use of monotonic regression, even though monotonic regression has received much wider use than polynomial regression in this context.

It would be neither feasible nor desirable to describe here in full any of the actual programs which this description pertains to, since their great bulk (for example, about 3000 lines for KYST, including comments) is devoted largely to elaborate input and output, and a great variety of conceptually elementary options. For example, just to read the input values (denoted by δ_{ijk} below) KYST uses approximately 90 executable statements (in Fortran IV), of which only one is a READ statement.

b. Input Quantities

I Number of points being placed. Order of the square input matrix.

K (Maximum) number of replications for any cell in the square input matrix.

δ_{ijk} (i and j = 1 to I, k = 1 to K); the kth replication of the dissimilarity or similarity of objects i and j.

c Cutoff value. A value δ_{ijk} that is smaller than c is not to be treated as a data value, but merely as an indication that this data value is missing.

R_{max} Dimensionality of the solution space on the first scaling.

R_{min} ($\leqslant R_{max}$); dimensionality of the solution space on the final scaling (R goes from R_{max} to R_{min} by steps of -1, so that $R_{max} - R_{min} + 1$ successive scalings are carried out).

P Degree of the polynomial to be used in the regression (if polynomial regression is used); equals $+1$ or -1 to indicate ascending or descending regression (if monotonic regression is used).

c. Order of Calculation

1. The data are read in. The δ_{ijk} are stored in the form of a one-dimensional array called *DATA* (see Fig. 12.2). Values of δ_{ijk} which are smaller than the cutoff c are noted during the read-in process and discarded. In order to identify the data values, a second one-dimensional array called *IJ* is filled with pairs (i, j) (that is, two integers i and j are packed into a single memory location in the array). The value of subscript k is ignored. Corresponding positions in *DATA* and *IJ* contain associated values. Let M be the number of data values finally retained. Then $M \leqslant I^2 K$, and both *DATA* and *IJ* contain M values.

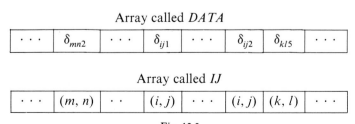

Fig. 12.2

2. The M values in *DATA* are sorted in ascending order, and the corresponding values in *IJ* are permuted to maintain the correspondence. For monotonic regression, sorting is essential, since it is only the rank order of the δ_{ijk} which is used. (This is reflected by the fact that for nonmetric scaling the calculation never subsequently uses the array *DATA* except for certain niceties of output. After sorting, the rank order is reflected by the values in *IJ*, and is used directly from that array. The possibility of ties, that is, equal values among the δ_{ijk}, causes complications both in the theory and the procedure, but we ignore this here.) For polynomial regression, the sorting makes no difference one way or the other to the subsequent calculation, but is retained for a minor nicety in the output.

R is set to R_{max}.

3. I points x_i are selected in R-space for use as an initial configuration, to start the iterative procedure. Several options are possible for this purpose.

   a. Use points evenly spaced along the R coordinate axes (sometimes called the L-configuration, from its appearance when $R = 2$).

   b. Use a pseudorandom number generator to pick points approximately from a spherical normal distribution (actually, a logistic distribution is used for each coordinate).

   c. Use the "classical" scaling of Torgerson, as described in Section 3f, after preprocessing the data suitably. The first step is to average over replicated measurements, so that each pair of stimuli is represented by at most one data value. The second step is to add a constant to make the data values more "distance-like." In particular they must all be positive. Beyond this, KYST sets the smallest transformed value to $1/10$ of the largest one, whereas INDSCAL adds the smallest constant which makes the transformed values satisfy the triangle inequality ($\delta_{ik} \leqslant \delta_{ij} + \delta_{jk}$). The third step is to fill in missing val-

ues with the average of the nonmissing values. The fourth step is to apply classical scaling.

   d. Use a procedure similar to one invented by Forrest Young, and first implemented in TORSCA. This starts with the preceding option, and then performs several "pre-iterations" which are quite different in nature from the primary iterative procedure. For further information, see [26].

4. The configuration of points x_i is normalized (by translation and dilation) so that the x_i have mean 0 and mean-square-length 1.

5. For each entry (i, j) in *IJ*, the distance between x_i and x_j is calculated and stored in the corresponding position of *DIST*.

6. A regression is performed for the values in *DIST* (as "dependent" variable) over the values in *DATA* (as "independent" variable). For monotonic regression, this does not require any use of the array *DATA*. [In fact, if it were not for the complication caused by ties in the data, the monotonic regression would not require any information other than the array *DIST*, the value of M, and the value of $P = \pm 1$ (to indicate whether the regression is ascending or descending). In actuality, information about ties is packed into the entries of *IJ* along with the subscripts, and forms another input to the monotonic regression procedure.]

For polynomial regression, the procedure used is the common one of solving the normal equations. For monotonic (or isotonic) regression, the procedure used may be found in [15]. Much literature is now available dealing with this topic; see particularly [1, Ch. 2].

7. The value and gradient of S' are calculated.

8. A decision is made whether to continue iterating or not. If so, the next step-size is calculated, and a new configuration is formed. Then control is returned to Step 4. If not, control goes to the following step.

9. The configuration of points x_i may be rotated to principal coordinates (optional),

and the results of the scaling are printed, including extensive printer-plotting. If $R > R_{min}$, the last coordinate x_{iR} is dropped from each point x_i, R is set to $R - 1$, and control returns to Step 4.

10. As an important summary, the final minimum stress S' for each R is printed, or is plotted versus R.

d. Output Quantities

The configuration of points x_i is the focus of interest for the user of multidimensional scaling. In most cases it is vital for him to have one or more graphical displays of these points. For this reason the output usually includes one or more printer plots of the configuration, and always includes numerical printout of the coordinates. The relationship between the dissimilarities and the distances is next most important. The output always includes a numerical measure of how good a relationship was achieved, namely, the final (minimum) value of the stress S. It usually includes a printer plot showing both a scatter diagram of this relationship and the fitted regression function. It may include the same information in numerical form. If linear or polynomial regression was used the fitted coefficients are always printed.

The output also includes a lot of other information of secondary value, such as a listing of the input cards (excluding the dissimilarities themselves) as a record of the options chosen, diagnostic remarks, an optional history of the calculation in case difficulties are suspected in the convergence process, and so on.

4. FLOW CHART

Figure 12.3 shows the flow chart of a program similar to KYST.

5. DESCRIPTION OF THE FLOW CHART

This flow chart shows one complete iteration of a multidimensional scaling program resembling KYST. We assume that the following quantities, which do not change during the iteration procedure, have already

been read in or calculated in advance:

I	Number of points x_i in the configuration
R	Dimensionality of the points x_i
M	Number of available pairs = the number of data values
δ_m	For $m = 1$ to M, the data values
$(i(m), j(m))$	For $m = 1$ to M, the subscripts that identify δ_m; for i and $j = 1$ to I, $A(i, j) = \sum \delta_m^{i+j-2}$ (needed only for polynomial regression)

We assume that the following quantities, which do change during the iteration procedure, already have values at the start of the iteration:

the configuration $X(i, r)$, an $I \times R$ matrix, whose ith row is the point x_i;

the gradient $G(i, r)$ which was used in forming $X(i, r)$, also an $I \times R$ matrix;

the norm $\|G\|$ of G;

step, stressratioav, cosav, and *abcosav*.

Box 1: The first step in normalizing X is to subtract the column means from every column. 1_I denotes a column vector of all 1's with I components.

Box 2: The second step in normalizing X is to make the root-mean-square of its row lengths 1.

Box 3: Since we are going to calculate the angle-cosine between two successive gradients, we save the preceding gradient in G_L (L for "last") as we clear G in preparation for calculating the new gradient. For the same reason we save $\|G\|$, the norm of G, in $\|G_L\|$ as we clear $\|G\|$.

Box 4: Calculate all the relevant interpoint distances.

Box 5: Choose the regression type designated by the user.

Box 6: Preparation for polynomial regression.

Box 7: Solve normal equations of linear regression, to estimate the coefficients $(b_0, \ldots, b_P) = \beta$.

Box 8: Calculate the polynomial pseudo-distance $\hat{d}_m$.

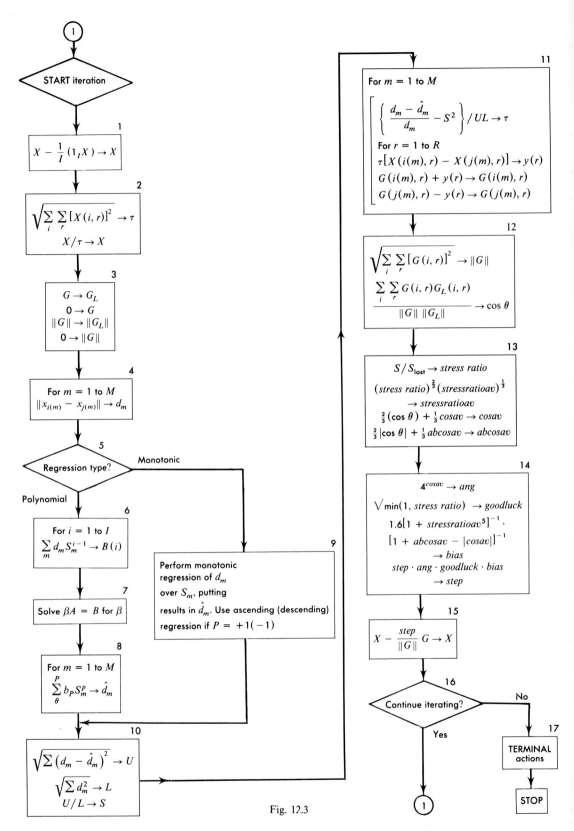

Fig. 12.3

Box 9: We do not give a program for performing monotonic regression here, since this topic is thoroughly covered elsewhere [1, Ch. 2].

Box 10: Calculate the stress *S*.

Box 11: Calculate the gradient *G*.

Box 12: Calculate the norm $\|G\|$ of *G* and the angle-cosine between *G* and G_L.

Box 13: Calculate the *stress ratio* and update the *stressratioav*, the *cosav*, and the *abcosav*.

Box 14: Calculate *ang*, *goodluck*, and *bias*, and use them to update *step*.

Box 15: Move to new configuration.

Box 16: Decide whether to continue iterating. The details of this decision are not given here.

Box 17: Terminal actions include normalizing the configuration, optionally rotating it to principal axes, and suitable printout.

6. THE PROGRAM

The present author is not familiar with any multidimensional scaling program which is suitable for listing here. Many of the programs are far too long. However, various multidimensional scaling programs are available from several sources. It should be noted that a "stripped-down" program, with minimal options and limited output, could quite feasibly be included here, if a suitable one were available. At a guess, such a program might include about 250 lines of code in Fortran IV.

7. SAMPLE PROBLEM

Figure 12.4 shows the complete input to KYST for a sample problem, and Fig. 12.5 shows the complete output. [This example, based on data from Curt McFarland, is taken with slight changes from an interesting paper by Paul Black (1975).] For this particular input, the first six cards happen to be "control cards," which are used to specify options in a free-format input which permits great freedom of rearrangement. The first two specify R_{max} and R_{min}. The

third specifies that descending monotonic regression will be used (for monotonic regression, this corresponds to $P = -1$). The fourth and fifth are self-explanatory descriptions of the data. The sixth card, containing the word *DATA*, is considered to be the first card of the data deck (which is only part of the input), and signals that the remainder of the data deck will follow in a fixed arrangement and format. The seventh card is the title of the data. The eighth specifies the size of the data matrix and the number of replications (of two types). The ninth card is a Fortran format statement for reading the rows of the data matrix, which immediately follow. The next to last card indicates that all the relevant input has been provided, and that computation is to start. The last card indicates that no further sets of data are to be provided.

Based on the options specified and the "standard" (or "default") options which are

```
dimmax=3
dimmin=2
regression=descending
lowerhalfmatrix
diagonal=absent
data
curt mcfarland's data on 12 bikol dialects
  12   1   1
(12x,11f3.3)
   2 virac      76
   3 naga       67 81
   4 legaspi    67 83 88
   5 daraga     68 72 78 83
   6 oas        64 67 74 75 86
   7 libon      64 67 73 73 83 85
   8 buhi       63 67 73 73 79 79 80
   9 iriga      61 67 73 70 77 78 80 78
  10 sorsogon   64 67 69 71 73 69 67 66 65
  11 gubat      64 66 66 69 69 66 64 64 63 79
  12 masbate    57 55 57 57 60 58 57 57 57 79 70
compute
stop
```

Fig. 12.4

```
DIMMAX=3

DIMMIN=2

REGRESSION=DESCENDING

LOWERHALFMATRIX

DIAGONAL=ABSENT

DATA

CURT MCFARLAND'S DATA ON 12 BIKOL DIALECTS
  12   1   1

(12X,11F3.3)

COMPUTE
```

Fig. 12.5

CURT MCFARLAND'S DATA ON 12 BIKOL DIALECTS

INITIAL CONFIGURATION COMPUTATION: NO. PTS.= 12   DIM=   3

PRE-ITERATION	STRESS
0	0.0996
1	0.0936

MAXIMUM NUMBER OF PRE-ITERATIONS 1, REACHED.

THE BEST INITIAL CONFIGURATION OF 12 POINTS IN 3 DIMENSIONS HAS STRESS 0.094 FORMULA 1

HISTORY OF COMPUTATION. N= 12.   THERE ARE   66   DATA VALUES, SPLIT INTO   1   LISTS.   DIMENSION =   3

ITERATION	STRESS	SRAT	SRATAV	CAGRGL	COSAV	ACSAV	SFGR	STEP
0	0.092	0.800	0.800	-0.000	-0.000	0.000	0.0030	0.0068
1	0.089	0.972	0.854	0.999	0.659	0.659	0.0028	0.0185
2	0.083	0.924	0.877	0.994	0.880	0.880	0.0024	0.0634
3	0.064	0.772	0.840	0.815	0.837	0.837	0.0014	0.2007
4	0.065	1.010	0.893	-0.613	-0.120	0.689	0.0027	0.1104
5	0.043	0.670	0.812	-0.610	-0.443	0.637	0.0010	0.0485
6	0.040	0.936	0.851	-0.754	-0.648	0.714	0.0007	0.0198
7	0.038	0.941	0.880	0.301	-0.022	0.441	0.0002	0.0138
8	0.037	0.984	0.913	0.347	0.221	0.379	0.0002	0.0157
9	0.037	0.990	0.938	-0.179	-0.043	0.247	0.0003	0.0113
10	0.037	0.988	0.955	-0.238	-0.172	0.241	0.0002	0.0074
11	0.036	0.993	0.967	0.180	0.060	0.201	0.0002	0.0061
12	0.036	0.994	0.976	0.505	0.354	0.402	0.0001	0.0080
13	0.036	0.993	0.981	0.372	0.366	0.382	0.0001	0.0109
14	0.036	0.995	0.986	-0.188	0.000	0.254	0.0002	0.0072
15	0.035	0.993	0.988	-0.075	-0.050	0.136	0.0001	0.0051
16	0.035	0.996	0.991	0.454	0.283	0.346	0.0001	0.0058
17	0.035	0.996	0.992	0.404	0.363	0.384	0.0001	0.0076
18	0.035	0.996	0.994	0.032	0.144	0.152	0.0001	0.0075
19	0.035	0.996	0.995	-0.323	-0.164	0.265	0.0002	0.0044
20	0.035	0.996	0.995	0.307	0.147	0.293	0.0001	0.0038
21	0.035	0.997	0.996	0.889	0.636	0.686	0.0001	0.0071
22	0.034	0.994	0.995	0.803	0.746	0.763	0.0001	0.0158
23	0.034	0.994	0.995	-0.103	0.185	0.328	0.0003	0.0144
24	0.034	1.002	0.997	-0.816	-0.475	0.650	0.0003	0.0051
25	0.034	0.987	0.994	0.932	0.454	0.836	0.0002	0.0056
26	0.034	0.995	0.994	-0.031	0.134	0.305	0.0001	0.0047
27	0.034	0.996	0.995	0.390	0.303	0.361	0.0001	0.0054
28	0.033	0.995	0.995	0.419	0.380	0.400	0.0001	0.0073
29	0.033	0.994	0.995	0.121	0.209	0.216	0.0002	0.0078
30	0.033	0.995	0.995	-0.219	-0.074	0.218	0.0002	0.0050
31	0.033	0.994	0.994	0.311	0.180	0.279	0.0001	0.0047
32	0.033	0.994	0.994	0.836	0.613	0.646	0.0001	0.0086
33	0.032	0.989	0.993	0.692	0.665	0.677	0.0001	0.0173
34	0.032	0.994	0.993	-0.234	0.072	0.384	0.0004	0.0118
35	0.032	0.984	0.990	-0.634	-0.394	0.549	0.0002	0.0048
36	0.031	0.992	0.991	0.452	0.165	0.485	0.0001	0.0037
37	0.031	0.995	0.992	0.990	0.709	0.818	0.0001	0.0074
38	0.031	0.989	0.991	0.984	0.891	0.928	0.0001	0.0198
39	0.030	0.972	0.985	0.718	0.777	0.789	0.0001	0.0471
40	0.034	1.126	1.030	-0.496	-0.063	0.595	0.0011	0.0225
41	0.028	0.846	0.964	0.616	0.385	0.609	0.0002	0.0252
42	0.030	1.037	0.988	-0.676	-0.315	0.653	0.0005	0.0100
43	0.028	0.949	0.975	0.873	0.469	0.798	0.0002	0.0120
44	0.028	0.995	0.982	-0.629	-0.256	0.686	0.0002	0.0049
45	0.028	0.990	0.984	0.545	0.273	0.593	0.0001	0.0045
46	0.028	0.996	0.988	0.484	0.412	0.521	0.0001	0.0059
47	0.027	0.996	0.991	0.100	0.206	0.243	0.0001	0.0062
48	0.027	0.998	0.993	-0.474	-0.243	0.395	0.0001	0.0031
49	0.027	0.996	0.994	0.527	0.266	0.482	0.0001	0.0030
50	0.027	0.998	0.995	0.935	0.707	0.781	0.0001	0.0060

MAXIMUM NUMBER OF ITERATIONS WERE USED

THE FINAL CONFIGURATION HAS BEEN ROTATED TO PRINCIPAL COMPONENTS.

THE FINAL CONFIGURATION OF 12 POINTS IN 3 DIMENSIONS HAS STRESS 0.027 FORMULA 1

LABEL FOR CONFIGURATION PLOTS	FINAL CONFIGURATION		
		1	2	3
A	1	0.046	-1.252	0.555
B	2	0.365	-0.842	-0.273
C	3	0.490	-0.321	-0.413
D	4	0.185	-0.251	-0.296
E	5	0.267	0.118	0.214
F	6	0.300	0.425	0.332
G	7	0.429	0.653	0.099
H	8	0.808	0.423	0.382
I	9	0.736	0.658	-0.384
J	10	-0.846	0.115	0.041
K	11	-0.996	-0.137	-0.403
L	12	-1.784	0.412	0.146

DATA GROUP(S)

SERIAL COUNT STRESS REGRESSION COEFFICIENTS (FROM DEGREE 0 TO MAX OF 4)
    1   66 0.027 DESCENDING

Fig. 12.5 (*Continued*)

DIST(D) AND DHAT(-) (Y-AXIS) VS. DATA (X-AXIS), FOR 3 DIMENSIONS. STRESS,FORMULA 1,= 0.0272
CURT MCFARLAND'S DATA ON 12 BIKOL DIALECTS

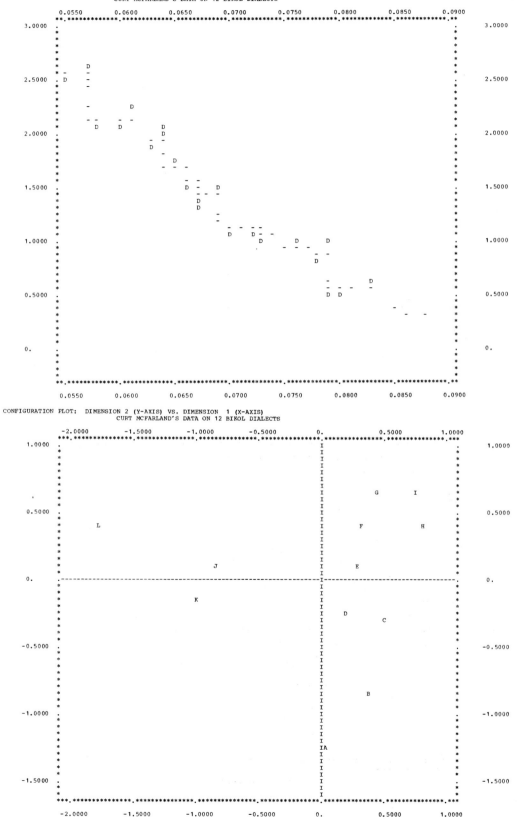

CONFIGURATION PLOT: DIMENSION 2 (Y-AXIS) VS. DIMENSION 1 (X-AXIS)
CURT MCFARLAND'S DATA ON 12 BIKOL DIALECTS

Fig. 12.5 (*Continued*)

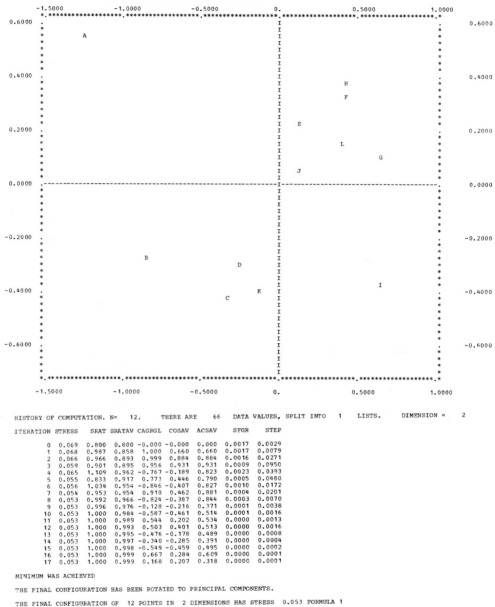

HISTORY OF COMPUTATION. N= 12.   THERE ARE   66   DATA VALUES, SPLIT INTO   1   LISTS.   DIMENSION =   2

ITERATION	STRESS	SRAT	SRATAV	CAGRGL	COSAV	ACSAV	SFGR	STEP
0	0.069	0.800	0.800	-0.000	-0.000	0.000	0.0017	0.0029
1	0.068	0.987	0.858	1.000	0.660	0.660	0.0017	0.0079
2	0.066	0.966	0.893	0.999	0.884	0.884	0.0016	0.0271
3	0.059	0.901	0.895	0.956	0.931	0.931	0.0009	0.0950
4	0.065	1.109	0.962	-0.767	-0.189	0.823	0.0023	0.0393
5	0.055	0.833	0.917	0.773	0.446	0.790	0.0005	0.0480
6	0.056	1.034	0.954	-0.846	-0.407	0.827	0.0010	0.0172
7	0.054	0.953	0.954	0.910	0.462	0.881	0.0004	0.0201
8	0.053	0.992	0.966	-0.824	-0.387	0.844	0.0003	0.0070
9	0.053	0.996	0.976	-0.128	-0.216	0.371	0.0001	0.0038
10	0.053	1.000	0.984	-0.587	-0.461	0.514	0.0001	0.0016
11	0.053	1.000	0.989	0.544	0.202	0.534	0.0000	0.0013
12	0.053	1.000	0.993	0.503	0.401	0.513	0.0000	0.0016
13	0.053	1.000	0.995	-0.476	-0.178	0.489	0.0000	0.0008
14	0.053	1.000	0.997	-0.340	-0.285	0.391	0.0000	0.0004
15	0.053	1.000	0.998	-0.549	-0.459	0.495	0.0000	0.0002
16	0.053	1.000	0.999	0.667	0.284	0.609	0.0000	0.0001
17	0.053	1.000	0.999	0.168	0.207	0.318	0.0000	0.0001

MINIMUM WAS ACHIEVED

THE FINAL CONFIGURATION HAS BEEN ROTATED TO PRINCIPAL COMPONENTS.

THE FINAL CONFIGURATION OF 12 POINTS IN 2 DIMENSIONS HAS STRESS 0.053 FORMULA 1

LABEL FOR CONFIGURATION PLOTS   FINAL CONFIGURATION
                                            1   2
                        A   1 -0.149   1.426
                        B   2 -0.479   0.843
                        C   3 -0.523   0.232
                        D   4 -0.246   0.204
                        E   5 -0.234   -0.172
                        F   6 -0.305   -0.454
                        G   7 -0.303   -0.650
                        H   8 -0.851   -0.387
                        I   9 -0.720   -0.818
                        J   10   0.909   -0.171
                        K   11   1.097   0.360
                        L   12   1.804   -0.413

DATA GROUP (S)

SERIAL   COUNT STRESS REGRESSION COEFFICIENTS (FROM DEGREE 0 TO MAX OF 4)
    1   66 0.053 DESCENDING

Fig. 12.5 (*Continued*)

DIST(D) AND DHAT(-) (Y-AXIS) VS. DATA (X-AXIS), FOR 2 DIMENSIONS. STRESS,FORMULA 1,= 0.0531
CURT MCFARLAND'S DATA ON 12 BIKOL DIALECTS

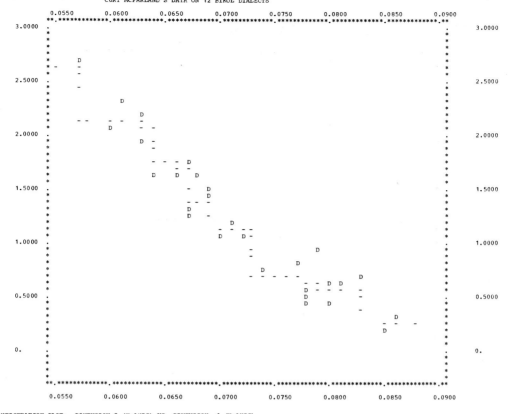

CONFIGURATION PLOT: DIMENSION 2 (Y-AXIS) VS. DIMENSION 1 (X-AXIS)
CURT MCFARLAND'S DATA ON 12 BIKOL DIALECTS

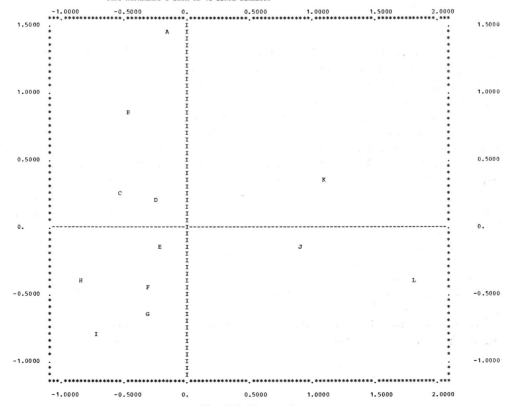

Fig. 12.5 (*Continued*)

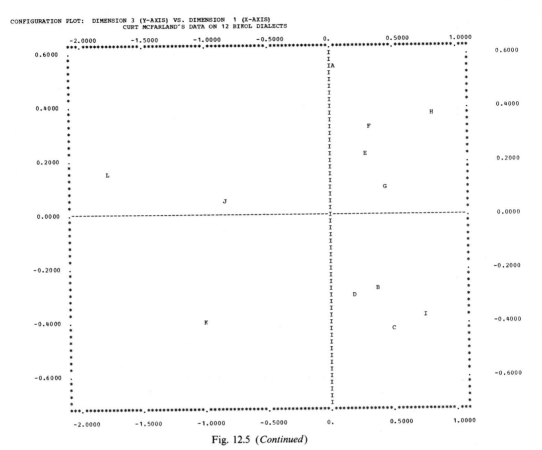

Fig. 12.5 (*Continued*)

assumed unless otherwise specified, these data will be scaled first in 3-dimensional space, and then in 2-dimensional space, and the spatial distances will be related to the data values by monotone descending regression. The "initial configuration" for the iterative process in 3-dimensional space will be provided by the "TORSCA" option, which starts with the classical Torgerson scaling, and then performs a few iterations of a "preliminary" iterative process due to Young, distinct from the main iterative process discussed in this article. The initial configuration for the iterative process in 2-dimensional space will be provided by dropping the last coordinate from the solution found in 3-dimensional space.

The output shows all of the input cards except the data values themselves. Then it shows the stress values achieved in 3-dimensional space by the classical scaling and the pre-iterations. It is not generally valid to compare these preliminary stress values with those achieved during the main calculation. Following this, the output shows the stress values found during the main iterative process, along with the values of other variables pertinent to the process. This constitutes a history of the iterative procedure. We list the variables shown, together with the mnemonic headings.

ITERATION Indicates how many iterations of the gradient procedure have taken place before this line was printed.

STRESS Indicates the stress value (badness-of-fit value) for

	the current configuration, as explained in Section 2d.
SRAT	Indicates the "stress ratio," that is, the ratio between the present and the preceding values of stress. On iteration 0, this is arbitrarily set to 0.8.
SRATAV	Indicates the "stress ratio average," that is, the exponentially weighted geometric average of all the stress ratios from the beginning up to the present one. On each iteration, the new value is computed as the old value to the $\frac{1}{3}$ times the stress ratio to the $\frac{2}{3}$.
CAGRGL	Indicates the "cosine of the angle between the gradient and the gradient-last," that is, the cosine of the angle between the present and the previous gradient.
COSAV	Indicates the "cosine average," that is, the exponentially weighted average of all the angle-cosines from the beginning to the present one, as explained in Section 2j. On each iteration, the new value is computed as $\frac{1}{3}$ the old value plus $\frac{2}{3}$ the angle-cosine.
ACSAV	Indicates the "absolute cosine average," that is, the exponentially weighted average of the absolute value of the angle-cosines, as explained in Section 2j. This is calculated in a similar manner to *COSAV*.

SFGR	Indicates the "scale factor of the gradient." This is the length of the gradient vector, divided by the number of points *I*.
STEP	Indicates the size of the step to be used in taking the next iteration.

The remaining output for the 3-dimensional solution is largely self-explanatory. However, it may be worth making a few comments about the printer plots. First is the scatter diagram, sometimes called the "Shepard" diagram. This displays the character **D** at the position $(\delta_{ij\nu}, d_{ij})$ for each data value $\delta_{ij\nu}$, where the data values correspond to the horizontal axis and the distances to the vertical axis. Also displayed is the character – at position $(\delta_{ij\nu}, \hat{d}_{ij\nu})$ for each data value. Where both – and **D** occur at precisely the same printer position, the – is displayed. The next three plots show two coordinates at a time of the final 3-dimensional configuration. Under the standard options, this has been rotated so that its principal components lie along the coordinate axes. Unfortunately, the computer program does not make the scale the same along both axes of each plot. *If* the two scales happen to be rather different, then visual distances *in the plot* do not correspond well to the distances as used by the model and the computer program, and the plot gives a deceptive appearance; in this case, it is advisable to replot using the same scale for all dimensions.

The output for the 2-dimensional solution is generally similar to that for the 3-dimensional solution. However, the initial configuration, as mentioned above, is derived from the final 3-dimensional solution (after rotation to principal components, if that option is used), so there is no use of the TORSCA option and no pre-iterations to be shown here. At the very end occurs the word STOP: this is the final control card, printed out when it is reached.

8. ESTIMATION OF RUNNING TIME

Typically, one set of data scaled in several different dimensionalities requires a few minutes of central processor time on machines such as an IBM 360/65. However, wide variations either way are possible.

Experience indicates that the most important factors controlling the running time for KYST and similar programs on a given computer are the number of data values, M, and the number of iterations. As a crude approximation,

running time for a single dimensionality

$$= t \cdot M \cdot \text{number of iterations}$$

where for KYST on the Honeywell 6070 t is roughly 3 milliseconds. However, t can vary by more than a factor of 2, depending on other aspects of the computation which this formula does not take into account. Although the number of iterations cannot be predicted precisely in advance, since the program itself decides when the calculation has converged to an adequate degree of approximation, typical problems require from 15 to 50 iterations for scaling in one dimensionality. However the number of iterations for one dimensionality is limited by an explicit bound, regardless of convergence: Unless set to another value by the user, the bound used by KYST is 50 iterations.

We mention here some other factors that affect t. Since monotone regression takes longer than polynomial regression, t tends to be larger for nonmetric than for polynomial scaling. The use of "classical" scaling to obtain a starting configuration generally reduces the total running time, by greatly reducing the number of iterations. However, it also increases t since overhead time is increased substantially and is allocated among fewer iterations. Higher dimensionality causes a mild increase in t. Use of metrics other than Euclidean and city-block substantially increases t, since it

greatly increases the computation for every d_{ij}. Obviously, there are many other factors also.

9. REFERENCES

a. Computer Programs

- CANDECOMP (CANonical DECOMPosition). Carroll and Chang. Described in [2] primarily as a subsidiary computational technique for INDSCAL. Essentially the same as PARAFAC. Program and manual available.
- INDSCAL (INdividual Differences SCALing). Carroll and Chang. Described in [2]. Many applications have been published. Program and manual available.
- KYST (Kruskal, Young, Shepard, Torgerson). Kruskal, Yound, and Seery. A merger of M-D-SCAL (5M) and TORSCA which combines best features of both, plus some improvements. There is no complete background paper on KYST, but Refs. [14, 15] may be helpful. Program and very complete manual available. Widely used.
- M-D-SCAL (MultiDimensional SCALing). Kruskal. The theory of the earliest versions is fully covered in [14, 15]. Many applications have been published. Program and very complete manual available. Widely used.
- MINISSA (Michigan Israel Netherlands Integrated Smallest Space Analysis). Roskam. Full description available.
- MINITRI (*MINI*SSA for TRIadic data). Roskam. Theory fully described in [20].
- MONANOVA (MONOtone ANalysis Of VAriance). Kruskal. Theory fully described in [13]. Program and manual available.
- MUMP (Multidimensional Unfolding by Mathematical Programming). Srinivasan and Shocker. Theory fully described in [23]. The computer program linear programming.
- PARAFAC (PARAllel FACtors). Harsh-

man. Full description of theory is available. Though invented independently of and subsequent to CANDECOMP, their theory and algorithms are virtually identical. The computer programs have important differences. Use of PARAFAC akin to INDSCAL was also reached independently by Harshman.

- POLYCON (POLYnomial CONjoint Measurement). Young. Full description, manual and program available.
- PARSCL (PAiRwise SCaLing). Johnson. Fully described in [11].
- SSA (Smallest Space Analysis). Guttman and Lingoes. At least four programs (SSA-1 through SSA-4). SSA-1 is fully described in [8]. Program and manual available. Widely used.
- TORSCA (TORgerson SCAling). Young. Full description, several versions of program, and manual available. Widely used.

b. Papers and Books

1. Barlow, Bartholomew, Bremner, and Brunk, *Statistical Inference under Order Restrictions*, Wiley, New York, 1972.

2. J. D. Carroll and J. J. Chang, "Analysis of Individual Differences in Multidimensional Scaling Via an *N*-Way Generalization of Eckart-Young Decomposition," *Psychometrika*, **35** (3): 283–319 (1970).

3. J. M. Chambers, "Fitting Nonlinear Models: Numerical Techniques," *Biometrika*, **60**, 1, 1 (1973).

4. Jan De Leeuw, *The Positive Orthant Method for Nonmetric Dimensional Scaling*, Department of Data Theory, University of Leiden, Research Note 001-70, 1970.

5. Jan De Leeuw, *Smoothness Properties of Nonmetric Loss Functions*, (1975a) (In press).

6. Jan De Leeuw, *Nonmetric Scaling with Rearrangement Methods* (1975b) (In press).

7. Jan De Leeuw, *Alternative Reparametrizations in Euclidean Multidimensional Scaling* (1975c) (In press).

8. L. Guttman, "General Nonmetric Technique for Finding Smallest Coordinate Space for a Configuration of Points," *Psychometrika*, **33** (4), 469–506 (1968).

9. J. A. Hartigan, "Representation of Similarity Matrices by Trees," *J. Amer. Statist. Assoc.*, **A62**, 1140–58 (1967).

10. H. Hotelling, "Analysis of a Complex of Statistical Variables into Principal Components," *J. Educat. Psychol.*, **26**, 139–42 (1935).

11. R. Johnson, "Pairwise Nonmetric Multidimensional Scaling," *Psychometrika*, **38** 11–18 (1973).

12. B. W. Kernighan, and S. Lin, "An Efficient Heuristic Procedure for Partitioning Graphs," *The Bell System Technical Journal*, **49**, No. 2 (1970).

13. J. B. Kruskal, "Analysis of Factorial Experiments by Estimating Monotone Transformations of the Data," *J. Roy. Statist. Soc.* **B27** (2), 251–63 (1965).

14. ———, "Multidimensional Scaling by Optimizing Goodness of Fit to a Nonmetric Hypothesis," *Psychometrika* **29** (2), 1–27 (1964).

15. J. B. Kruskal, "Nonmetric Multidimensional Scaling: A Numerical Method," *Psychometrika*, **29** (2), 115–29 (1964).

16. J. B. Kruskal, and J. D. Carroll, *Geometric Models and Badness-of-Fit Functions*, Academic Press, New York, 696 (1969).

17. Joseph B. Kruskal, "Monotone Regression: Continuity and Differentiability Properties," *Psychometrika*, **36**, 57–63 (1971).

18. James Lingoes and Edward E. Roskam, "A Mathematical and Empirical Analysis of Two Multidimensional Scaling Algorithms," *Psychometrika*, Monograph 19, **38** (4) pt. 2 (1973).

19. M. W. Richardson, "Multidimensional Psychophysics," *Psychol. Bull.*, **35**, 659–60 (1938).

20. E. E. Roskam, "The Method of Triads for Nonmetric Multidimensional Scaling," *Nederlands Tydskrift voor de Psychologie*, **25**, 404–417 (1970).

21. P. H. Schönemann, "Metric Multidimensional Unfolding," *Psychometrika*, **35**, 349–66 (1970).

22. R. N. Shepard, "Analysis of Proximities: Multidimensional Scaling with an Unknown Distance Function," *Psychometrika*, **27** (2), 125–40; **(27)** (3) 219–46 (1962).

23. V. Srinivasan and A. D. Shocker, "Estimating the Weights for Attributes in a Composite Criterion Using Pairwise Judgements," *Psychometrika*, **38**, 473–493 (1973).

24. W. S. Torgerson, "Theory and Methods of Scaling," Wiley, New York, 460 (1958).

25. F. W. Young, *Conjoint Scaling*, L. L. Thurstone Psychometric Laboratory Report 118, Univ. of North Carolina, Chapel Hill, N.C., April 1973.

26. F. W. Young, *A FORTRAN IV Program for Nonmetric Multidimensional Scaling*, L. L. Thurstone

Psychometric Laboratory Report 56, Univ. of North Carolina, Chapel Hill, N.C., March 1968.

APPENDIX I

Shepard's Iterative Procedure for Multidimensional Scaling Is a Gradient Procedure*

Shepard [22] invented and presented his iterative numerical process for multidimensional scaling as a direct way for making the configuration bear a suitable relationship to the data. We have now discovered for the first time, many years later, that there is a reasonable loss function for which his procedure constitutes a gradient method of minimization. We shall present this function, and indicate in part why a gradient method based on it is the same as Shepard's procedure.

Following Shepard's notation in part, we shall call the similarities used during the scaling computation s_{ij}. (Of course, a similar development can be carried out for dissimilarities.) Since these data may constitute either a whole or a half matrix, and may be incomplete, we shall take sums over "all available (i, j)" as in Section 2b.

To construct the loss function, we introduce some notation. If X is the configuration of points, and d_{ij} is the distance between points i and j, let

$$T(X) = \sum s_{ij} d_{ij}$$

If π is any permutation of the available (i, j), let

$$T^-(X) = \min_\pi \sum s_{\pi(i,j)} d_{ij}$$

By classical rearrangement inequalities, the minimum occurs for any permutation that makes $s_{\pi(i,j)}$ weakly descending over the distances d_{ij}. Let π be any fixed minimizing permutation, and let

$$s_{i,j}^* = s_{\pi(i,j)}$$

*This appendix was co-authored by J. Douglas Carroll.

(Shepard calls this $s(d_{ij})$.) Let

$$U(X) = \sum (s_{ij} - \bar{s}) d_{ij}$$

where $\bar{s}$ is the mean of all available s_{ij}, let

$$V(X) = \sqrt{\sum d_{ij}^2}$$

let

$$w = \frac{\beta}{\alpha}$$

where α and β are the two positive parameters used by Shepard to control his iterative procedure, and let

$$W(X) = (T(X) - T^-(X)) + wU(X),$$

$$= \sum \left[(s_{ij} - s_{ij}^*) + w(s_{ij} - \bar{s}) \right] d_{ij}$$

Now define the loss function by

$$S(X) = \frac{W(X)}{V(X)}$$

From Shepard's paper, it is plain that small values of $T(X) - T^-(X)$ indicate a more nearly monotonic relationship between the s_{ij} and the d_{ij}, while small values of $U(X)$ tend to go with configurations nearly in a low dimensional subspace.

Dividing by $V(X)$ puts these quantities in a scale-free form, and $S(X)$ is a weighted sum of the scale-free quantities, hence a very plausible loss function when seeking a low-dimensional configuration (in high-dimensional space) whose distances are nearly monotonic with the s_{ij}. When working with configurations already in low-dimensional space, Shepard takes $\beta = 0$, hence $w = 0$, and the loss function reflects only the monotonicity.

To make the connection between minimizing this loss function and Shepard's procedure, first note that minimizing $S(X)$ is equivalent to minimizing $W(X)$ subject to $V(X) = $ constant (since both W and V are homogeneous of degree 1 in the components of X). To minimize W subject to this constraint, one step of a gradient procedure is to subtract some positive constant times the gradient from the present configuration, and then project the resulting configuration onto the constraint surface, that is, find the nearest configuration satisfying the constraint. It can be proved that the "vectors" that Shepard adds to the configuration are proportional to the gradient of W, and Shepard's " 'similarity' transformation to re-center the centroid at the origin and to re-scale all the distances so that the mean interpoint separation is maintained at unity" does in fact project the configuration onto the nearest configuration satisfying the constraint.

APPENDIX II

"Two-Phase" Method in Guttman–Lingoes SSA-I Program Does Not Truly Optimize the Coefficient of Alienation

Despite a common misconception to the contrary, the so-called "two-phase" method used in SSA-I does not in principle truly optimize Guttman's "coefficient of alienation" K. Now it is true, as a practical matter, that this method does reduce K to a small value, generally quite close to the optimum value. Thus the present author is concerned only with clarifying this matter at the conceptual level, and makes no criticism of the "two-phase" method as a practical tool. However, the solution to which the "two-phase" method will in principle converge (after infinitely many iterations, using infinitely precise arithmetic) is not the minimum of K. Furthermore, the "two-phase"

method of SSA-I will systematically move away from the optimum configuration if started there. Since this question has been involved in controversy, we will examine the evidence substantiating this differing view before fully presenting it. (However, the evidence given in pages 36–47 of Ref. [18] is also helpful, though the discussion can be questioned.)

As evidence that the "two-phase" method of SSA-I does not minimize K, we start with numerical results kindly provided to this author by Professor James Lingoes. Using SSA-I to analyze this upper half-matrix of disimilarities,

$$\begin{array}{ccc} 1 & 2 & 6 \\ & 5 & 3 \\ & & 4 \end{array}$$

he obtained the results shown in the first line of Table 2. The first part of the line shows the coordinates of the four points in one-dimensional space. The latter part of the line shows the value of μ and K for this configuration, where

$$K = \left(1 - \mu^2\right)^{\frac{1}{2}}$$

$$\mu = \frac{\left(\sum d_m d_m^*\right)}{\left(\sum d_m^2\right)}$$

d_m = distance corresponding to the mth smallest dissimilarity

d_m^* = the mth smallest distance (this is the "rank-image")

Table 2

	Configuration				μ	K
Provided by Professor Lingoes	$-.52869$	$.26384$	-1	1	$.94581$	$.32471\ldots$
APL refinement of above	$-.5251372$	$.255153$	-1	1	$.94507$	$.32686$
Pencil and paper	$-(\sqrt{2}-1) = -.41421\ldots$	$(\sqrt{2}-1) = .41421\ldots$	-1 -1	1 1	$\frac{1}{4}+\frac{1}{2}\sqrt{2} =$	$.28974$
"One-phase" MINISSA	$-.41421$	$.41421$	-1	1		

Using APL informally to further refine this solution, to get closer to the ultimate solution to which the "two-phase" method would in principle converge, yields the results shown in the second line of the table. Evidence that this solution is in fact closer to the ultimate "two-phase" solution will be given below. Meanwhile, we note that this solution fits the data slightly worse than the solution provided by Professor Lingoes, in that μ is slightly smaller and K slightly larger.

For this tiny data set, it is possible to find the true minimum value of K by algebraic analysis. Carrying this out with pencil and paper, we find the solution shown in the third line of the table. The "one-phase" MINISSA solution for these data, taken from page 56, Table 17, No. 21 of Ref. [18] is displayed on the fourth line. (Thanks is due to Professor Jan De Leeuw for bringing this to our attention when he read a first draft of this appendix, long after the algebraic solution had been worked out.) The agreement between the third and fourth lines tends to confirm the correctness of the algebraic analysis, and also tends to confirm the fact that the "one-phase" method of MINISSA does in principle optimize K, unlike the "two-phase" method. From the fact that the (identical) values of μ and K on the third and fourth lines are better than the values on the first two lines, we see that the "two-phase" method has not reduced K as much as it might. Furthermore, when the APL program was used, starting with the solution shown on lines three and four, it moved back to the solution shown on line two, despite the fact that this increases K, which clearly shows that the "two-phase" method does not in principle minimize K.

What is the explanation for this behavior? Basically, it is because the "two-phase" method of SSA-I does not use the actual true gradient of K, but rather what might be considered an approximation to it, namely, the partial gradient, calculated by treating

the d_m^* as constant. To make this plainer, let X be a vector indicating the entire configuration, and consider the gradient

$$G(X) = \nabla_X K(X)$$

The gradient method works only with the "vector field" or "vector function" $G(X)$, seeking an X_0 such that $G(X_0) = 0$ and (informally speaking) such that $G(X)$ points away from X_0 for X near X_0 (this latter condition is so that we find a minimum, not a maximum or some other type of stationary point). Now the "two-phase" method of SSA-I carries out exactly this procedure, except that instead of using $G(X)$, it uses an approximation, call it $G_1(X)$. It finds an X where $G_1(X) = 0$, which is of course not quite where $G(X) = 0$.

This brings us to the evidence, promised above, that line two is closer than line one to the ultimate solution of the "two-phase" method. The APL program, like the "two-phase method", was based on trying to make $G_1(X)$ zero. The solution on line one already yields $G_1(X)$ quite small. However, APL used double-precision where SSA-I used single precision (both on IBM 360 computers), and the APL program used a method having second-order convergence (feasible for a tiny problem) where SSA-I used a method having first-order convergence, so it is not surprising that the APL program was able to reduce the magnitude of $G_1(X)$ by a factor of about 10^5 starting from the solution on line one. Informal numerical analysis, using APL, established that this solution was practically as close to the true minimum position as the double-precision accuracy would permit (probably good to about 15 significant digits, though the results have been rounded off here.)

When the APL program was applied to $G(X)$ rather than $G_1(X)$, it did converge toward the pencil and paper solution, though it was not possible to get this program to converge to full double-precision accuracy, due to a property of this solution that was already quite clear at the pencil and paper stage. The true gradient $G(X)$ does not, properly speaking, exist at the true minimum of K.

The reason for this is of interest. For almost any data set, the function K has the property that its gradient exists and is continuous within each of a finite number of regions. However, at a boundary point between two regions, the limiting value of the gradient from one side is generally not equal to the limiting gradient value from the other side. The present data set is probably not unusual in having the minimum value of K occur at such a boundary point between two regions. This phenomenon, which is well known in numerical analysis, requires a more subtle approach to minimization than the methods commonly used to locate a zero value of the gradient, since the gradient literally does not exist, and hence is not 0, at the desired minimum point. In the present case, once the minimum was narrowed down algebraically by pencil and paper to the boundary between two regions, the minimum was located by finding the boundary point at which the limiting gradients from both sides are normal to the boundary, and each points into its own region. (As a result of the continuity of K, the limiting gradient from one side must be normal to the boundary precisely where the same is true for the limiting gradient from the other side.)

The ISODATA Method Computation for the Relative Perception of Similarities and Differences in Complex and Real Data

13

David J. Hall
Stanford Research Institute

with

Dev. K. Khanna
Genesee Computer Center

1. FUNCTION

The function of the ISODATA computer program is to implement on a computer, as far as mechanization allows, the human process we call clustering. As we define clustering here, it is a subjective and intuitive ability that allows us to perceive many important aspects of our environment [1].*

*"These cluster processings are so fundamental that they affect the workings of the higher perceptual processes. For instance, the breaking up of clusters reduces the perception of symmetries and repetitions. Finally, it was noted that at a higher level of mental activity humans are very efficient in clumping complex items into clusters. The further generalization of similarity and proximity measures extends the usefulness of cluster notions into cognitive processes."

Clustering is a fundamental function that precedes the ability to count, for it enables us to separate things into distinct and consistent groups. Without such separation, counting is not meaningful. For example, if we wish to count the number of leaves hanging on a branch of a tree, we must first isolate each leaf from its surrounding environment of foreground and background leaves. In this example, as with most clustering applications, we must process some data collected from the environment. Measurements could be made of the three-dimensional positions of many points on each leaf, and we could cluster these data points. Because of the spaces between the leaves, the data points would cluster at the center of each leaf, and the number of such clusters would count the number of leaves. (This assumes that each leaf is at the center of a space that is approximately spherical. We shall later discuss cases in which these simple assumptions do not hold.) Clustering thus involves the fundamental ability to estimate central tendency, to summarize or agglomerate, to find average values, and get to the essence or origin of many specifics taken as a whole. Extending our example, all the leaves of a tree, taken together, stem from the trunk of the tree, and this trunk is their origin or cluster center—it is the place around which the leaves cluster. This example represents, in brief, the spirit of clustering.

When we come to implement clustering as a mechanical computation, we lose many of the subtle human abilities and must be content with only an approximation to human clustering. There is also a danger of relegating to a machine, a human function that might be easily accomplished by sensitive human judgement, and thereby also making it technologically expensive. However, we gain some technological advantages in mechanizing this process, such as objectivity, repetitiveness, and consistency with tirelessness; and by means of the computer program, we can specify the process explicitly. The main value of mechanizing clustering, in these authors' opinion, is to allow us to discuss the human perceptual process explicitly, and thus refine these computations concerning relative perception. The value of the explicit computation is expressed by such documentation as this, which is supported by a working computer program that can perform a function similar to a human observer, and thus constitutes a working model of the human perceptual process we call clustering. The program is explicit and detailed, whereas this discussion is only a summary of the computer code, but it is comparably precise, we claim, as we have been "debugging" it for as many years as we have been writing computer code. In fact, such discussion as this, may be looked upon as the forerunner, generator, or specifying vehicle for the code, rather than only as a post-facto documentation.

More specifically, clustering programs allow us to extract multiple mean values from large amounts of recorded data, automatically, and thus allow us to attribute objective significance to the data, which might otherwise be merely a bewildering array of numbers. The particular problem of producing an effective and efficient clustering program is complex. Many criteria have to be met, so we have a multivariate design problem in providing a good program to meet enough diverse requirements of many users to justify the many man-years of effort that have gone into refining this program.

The most general output from a clustering program is the complete clustering characteristic of the data, as shown in Fig. 13.1. This curve starts at the overall or one-cluster level, and proceeds to as many clusters as the user wishes to pay for (in computer time), or, until every individual data point is in a cluster by itself, whichever occurs first. (Both extremes of the clustering curve are trivial results.) Thus the first questions a user must face are, how many clusters am I searching for? Do I have bounds on the number of clusters that will be acceptable? What level of discrimination is appropriate for my problem? The answer to these questions will allow one to guide the program's search and thus reduce one's computer-running expenses. Once the user has the complete clustering characteristic of the data, one can usually state with greater confidence than before, how many clusters exist in the data. For example, in Fig. 13.1, the curve for artifically generated, structured Gaussian clusters in two dimensions, shows a distinct "knee" or point of diminishing return, at 9 clusters. This data was generated to have 9 clusters. Thus, the counting capability of clustering is demonstrated and validated. Note that, in contrast, data without any structure, that is, uniform random data, does not exhibit this "knee" at any particular number of clusters, illustrat-

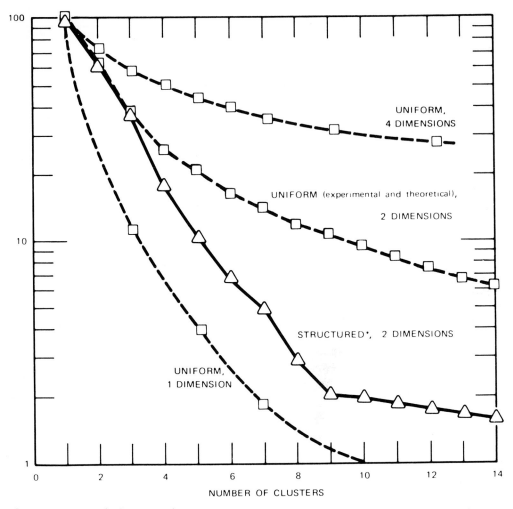

Gaussian clusters artifically generated

CLUSTERING CHARACTERISTICS FOR UNIFORM AND STRUCTURED DATA

Fig. 13.1. Clustering characteristics for uniform and structured data.

ing its formlessness or lack of structure. Thus the simplest output from the use of ISODATA, regardless of the multivariate complexity of the input data, is this single quality—the number of clusters that exist in the data. Associated with this single number are a set of numerical qualifiers of this number, giving the position or mean value for each cluster. The position of each cluster is also known as the cluster center—the place in space around which the specific activity of the cluster occurs. The dimensionality of

these qualifiers, or the number of components in each cluster center, is the same as the number of dimensions or components in the input measurement data. For example, if we clustered the positions of the leaves in a row of trees, we could obtain from the complete clustering characteristic, the number of trees in the row. (We would also obtain the number of branches at various levels of branching or detail.) The numbers associated with the number of trees (i.e., trunks) would be the positions of the trunks.

In addition to position, ISODATA printout gives the spread or standard deviation of each positional component. This number indicates how far each cluster extends along each component or direction. Referring to our example, it would give the size or extent of each tree.

In summary, the function of ISODATA is to provide the number of clusters in the data, and to give their positions and extents. ISODATA also gives the distribution or cluster membership of the data points in each cluster, as well as many other quantities of minor importance to be discussed later. We refer generally to these outputs of the program as a data description. Clustering, as a fundamental human cognitive (computational) ability, enables us to isolate different items into separate groups whose members (items) are similar. This is a way of ordering or formularizing relative perception.

2. MATHEMATICAL DISCUSSION

This mathematical discussion is mainly of academic, descriptive, and historical interest only, since the mathematical concepts are very simple and basic. The ISODATA computer program itself—the "listing" of the source code—is the actual repository for the precise formulation of the program. Mathematical conventions and formulations are more arbitrary and subjective than computer compilers, that either compile or do not compile a program, although this test does not guarantee a correct answer. If anyone is deeply interested in the detailed workings of the program, there is no substitute for reading and "compiling" the program oneself. The program contains extensive comments intended for human readers, between the lines of code to be compiled by the machine. Because the program is written in a language more suitable for a machine than for the typical mathematical reader, we provide this mathematical discussion. This chapter summarizes and describes (technically called "documentation") the complete workings of the clustering program and gives corresponding mathematical formulations where normally useful.

An important issue we face in describing the ISODATA program is that it has gone through many versions and modes of operation on many computers since its first use in 1965. It has also been modified in many special-purpose ways to suit specific applications. This issue is both a problem, in describing a nonconstant program, and also a benefit, in that many variations of this computation, adding "experience" to the evolution of the program, have been tested.

a. Mean, Variance, and Distance

The central mathematical concept in clustering is the computation of central tendency, or mean value, to use statistical terms; or center of gravity, to use physical, mechanical, or gravitational terms. The mathematical computation of a mean (i.e., average) value in statistics, and a center of gravity in physics, is formulated identically. This is an important asset of the program, in that it can handle *both* problems where the data may be collected from precise and deterministic measurments on "hard" objects, *and* also, it can handle (metaphysical) data or psychological problems such as are more usually collected statistically in the "soft" sciences such as psychology. Thus, the program is general in that it can serve both of these broad fields without specialization for either being needed. (In this chapter we consider only the pre-relativity or Newtonian formulation of center of gravity.) The average value ($\bar{x}$) of n numbers (x_i being the ith number) is given by:

$$\bar{x} = \frac{1}{n} \sum_{i=1}^{i=n} x_i$$

$\bar{x}$ is also the position of the center of gravity of n point-size unit masses situated at positions x_i in a one-dimensional arrangement. We can now extend the above one-dimensional formulation to d dimensions, and the data array (or matrix) X, can be written as:

$$X =$$

$$\begin{bmatrix} x_{11} & x_{21} & x_{31} & \cdots\cdots & x_{i1} & \cdots\cdots & x_{d1} \\ x_{12} & x_{22} & x_{32} & \cdots\cdots & x_{i2} & \cdots\cdots & x_{d2} \\ \vdots & & & & & & \vdots \\ x_{1j} & x_{2j} & x_{3j} & \cdots\cdots & x_{ij} & \cdots\cdots & x_{dj} \\ \vdots & & & & & & \vdots \\ x_{1n} & x_{2n} & x_{3n} & \cdots\cdots & x_{in} & \cdots\cdots & x_{dn} \end{bmatrix}$$

We can again find the mean value of these n observations for a typical ith column of the array of $d \times n$ dimensions, using a similar (matrix) formulation:

$$\bar{x}_j = \frac{1}{n} \sum_{i=1}^{n} x_{ij} \qquad \text{(where } \bar{x} \text{ is now a (row)} \\ \text{vector of } d \text{ dimensions)}$$

Whenever a cluster center is computed, this is the form used, and this formulation defines the cluster center in mathematical terms.

The other main mathematical concept is one of statistical spread or deviation, also known as variance. The mean value ($\bar{x}$) is the first moment and variance (v) is the second moment, expressed by:

$$v = \sigma^2 = \frac{1}{n-1} \sum_{i=1}^{n} (x_i - \bar{x})^2$$

where σ is the standard deviation and its calculation is dependent on knowing the value of $\bar{x}$.*

*Note that we do not formulate these quantities in the usual matrix terms using the covariance matrix, because we are primarily interested in computation, not mathematical notation. We hope for the widest class of readers and users, and do not wish to specialize the understanding of the program to only those familiar with matrix notation. Furthermore, we do not compute the covariance matrix in our program (it would require considerable memory space and computer time), and, therefore, to discuss it here would be a misrepresentation.

These two quantities, the mean and standard deviation, are the two basic mathematical quantities derived within the program. They are also output quantities. The program is thus very simple and appealing to intuition without special or mathematical sophistication.

In a one-dimensional uniform arrangement (scale), the distance between any two data points is merely the difference in their individual values anywhere on the scale. In a nonuniform space, the distance between any two points depends on the configuration of the space where the two points are located. We usually consider here a reference space that is uniform, relative to any nonuniform measurement space. These concepts of relativistic scaling are beyond the scope of this chapter, but have been dealt with in recent research for the Air Force [2]. We shall confine our attention in this chapter to Euclidean spaces and uniform, cartesian coordinate systems of measurement. In these cases, we can define the distance, D, between the kth cluster center vector $\bar{\mathbf{x}}_k$ and the jth pattern or data vector, $\mathbf{x}_j$, as:

$$D_{kj} = \sqrt{\sum_{i=1}^{i=d} \left(\bar{x}_{ik} - x_{ij} \right)^2}$$

This formulation of Euclidean distance assumes that the scales of all measurement dimensions are uniform and comparable. For example, in measuring the positions of leaves on a tree, the height, depth, and width measurements must all be in the same units (e.g., feet, inches, or meters). We later discuss cases in which noncomparable measurements are mixed together in this formulation.

Having defined the three basic quantities: (1) the mean, (2) the deviation, and (3) the distance, we need no further mathematical concepts, and can proceed to discuss the validity of the algorithm or process by which the data are sorted.

b. Validity and Error Analysis

In a typical clustering application problem, the data come from some remote application measurement system. Thus, we usually have little or no control over the data. To fully understand the structure of the data, it is necessary to understand the data generation process, the configuration of the measuring equipment, and the viewpoint or status of the data collection equipment at the time that the data patterns are collected. An effective way to achieve this type of system overview for research, is to generate artificial data and to recognize these patterns in a closed-loop system in which we have full control of all the data-generating parameters. In this way, we can work from a mathematical model of the system whose data structure we are investigating, write computer algorithms that implement this model, and control the data-sampling process. Therefore, in our validation experiments using computers and displays, we generate data from a model and use this data to exercise the ISODATA clustering algorithm. In this way we can analyze the errors of clustering objectively, which we cannot do for real data because in these cases there is usually no absolutely correct clustering answer.

In a typical clustering application, the choice of data observation instruments or transducers will affect the nature of the clustering. For example, if the source of data patterns is generating wide-band signals, but the measuring instrument is narrow-band, the source of signals will appear to be narrow-band because that is the only manner in which the transducers can respond. For accurate observations, therefore, a "wide-open" measuring system is required. In psychological terms, the observer must be free of preconceived notions and biases to perceive the reality of his environment. Any form of observer bias will distort his perception of the environment so that he will not be able to see the environment as it

is [5]. This same argument applies to any clustering algorithm when it gives undue weight to an irrelevant factor in the data. To measure and test clustering performance, and to discover the relative importance of various factors in the data, we developed the approach of a closed-loop clustering and data generation system and the following experimental methodology.

c. Experimental Methodology for Error Analysis

In our experiments, we test the hypothesis that the current computer algorithm (Version A) works well on the current test data set (Set A). The meaning of "works well" is that the machine algorithm performs at a certain acceptable level of error compared to a human clusterer. We say that a clustering program has rigor or validity if it can produce the same results as an intelligent human. This is an entirely practical approach to program validation, not resting upon any mathematical or theoretical abstraction. Thus, to measure the performance of the computer algorithm, we must ultimately compare the results from a human. To compare man and machine, we must have them perform similar tasks and give outputs in a comparable format. The input data to man and machine must also be similar. Our experiments start at a simple level, using easily described data to begin with, but we carefully investigate the accuracy of the responses and the detailed nature of the judgment criteria.

If any discrepancies arise between man and machine clustering performance, then we may modify the algorithm or the experimental procedure used for the human task. Once satisfactory closure or cross-comparison of results has been obtained with data Set A, we may proceed to data Set B, which has more complex characteristics, to see whether the algorithm can keep pace with the gestalt of human performance. If it cannot, we may try to improve the algorithm, using our insight into the human clustering task as a guide to the required modification. To make the human performance measures independent of personal idiosyncrasies, we included many human observers in the perceptual experiments.

d. The Clustering Language for Generation and Description of Data

In applying the above principles in practice, we implemented a particular computer language to allow convenient generation and clustering (i.e., description) of data. By valid clustering, in this context, we mean the recovery of a data description statement that corresponds to a statement in the data generation language. For example, the basic data description of clustering is the number of clusters in the data, and this number should equal the number of clusters specified in the data-generating language. Thus, clustering performance can be evaluated in specific cases by comparing the generating language statement with the description language statement. The development of this clustering language was necessary to allow the comparison between description and generation, both by human and by machine, and to allow evolutionary development of algorithms in a closed-loop process.

If these descriptions that are being compared match, we have closed-loop recognition and generation of data. By matching, we mean that the input and output descriptions must correspond in syntax and semantics, including vocabulary and quantitative values. In this way, we can check the accuracy of recognition by the degree of match. However, the degree of match may not have to be exact for the establishment of acceptable performance in a particular application. The term "closed-loop" is derived from the simple system block diagram shown in Fig. 13.2 in which the presence of the closed loop is evident, and the implication of circular completeness is intended by traveling one turn around the loop. Going

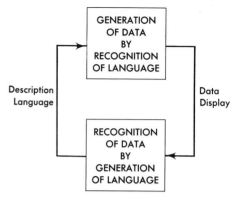

Fig. 13.2. The closed-loop generation and recognition methodology.

one turn around the loop is a universal process (uni = one, vertere = to turn). By this process, we imply that all things in this system have been considered and the system is complete, closed, or verified, when the beginning and the end states are in sufficiently close agreement.

The closed loop has advantages over the open loop in the research context because the beginning and end states are at the same place or state. This allows us to attribute any differences in the beginning and end states to the looping process. We can compare either the data displays or the description languages at beginning and end states. In contrast, the open loop has different starting and ending places; that is, the termination or goal is removed from the beginning, and differences may be due to either the process of getting from beginning to end or to the different states or places at the beginning and end. This does not provide a common basis for comparing results, but it is the usual mode of operation in working applications after the system has been designed and calibrated.

The methodology is verified by starting at any part of the loop, traveling around the loop for one turn to reach the starting place, and comparing the starting state with the result of the process around the loop. If the whole of this seems confusing, yet no part of it is difficult to understand, this seems to be the nature of significant proof or validation. Confusion arises when comparing opposite aspects across the whole loop, but this type of comparison is taking these aspects out of their local context. However, for global completeness of the whole conception, this type of contradiction must also be comprehended.

We have subjected the ISODATA clustering algorithm to this validation methodology and find that errors between generated and described data languages are generally small, particularly for data that is highly clustered. For random data (least clustered), we have derived a theoretical clustering characteristic curve (as given in Fig. 13.1) and find that ISODATA's performance is close to this theoretical value [3]. The current limitations to proving the validity of the algorithm are in generating data that is more "realistic," and this limitation is linked to the need for a more realistic clustering language so that more complex scenes or processes can be described or generated.

3. SUMMARY OF CALCULATION PROCEDURE

By the calculation procedure, we mean here, the algorithm or stepwise process for finding the solution to the clustering problem. The basic question is: how many clusters are in the data?

a. Input Quantities

The input data is a two-dimensional array of numbers as represented in the previous section by the array (matrix) symbol X. The columns of this array are dimensions of the measurement process—each number being the value of the reading on an "instrument" for measuring that dimension of the process. Thus if we have 10 instruments, we shall have 10 columns in the data matrix. The rows of the matrix represent different samples (or observations) of the process, usually in time sequence at different stages of the process. Each sample gives rise to one multivariate data point.

We have handled nonnumeric data in some applications, and also have considered "sparse" matrices with missing data entries, but these are complications of the input data format that we shall not be concerned with here.

Several such data matrices may be handled in succession, as we do for our cloud-tracking programs that cluster satellite pictures taken 25 minutes apart. Each picture is a separate data array, and the clouds over the earth are the clusters that the program finds. Our problem, in this meteorological application, is to find how far the clouds move during each picture interval, and in what precise directions, thus giving indications as to the global wind fields. These cloud motions are fed into numerical models of the atmosphere for prediction purposes. This type of data input gives rise to a series of clusterings that must be successively linked, and we have devised a new dynamic clustering approach for such problems [4]. However, we shall not discuss dynamic clustering in further detail here.

USER PARAMETERS, DEFAULT VALUES, AND ASSUMPTIONS

Provisions are made within the program design to allow the user to control many parameters and thus optimize the running of the program to his own particular purpose. However, this type of usage requires that the user understand the meaning and effects of these parameters. To serve the nonexpert user also, we have selected default values for these program parameters that correspond to typical-user assumptions as we interpret them. These user parameters, which are input quantities to the program, are described later in the contexts in which they naturally occur. A list of these parameters should be consulted before setting up a program run.

CATEGORY LABELS FOR PATTERN RECOGNITION

If the clustering is being used to verify or compare a previous classification of the data, it is advisable to include these previous category labels as input data because the program prints a useful comparison table showing categories compared to clusters. It is important to note that the program does not use these labels for any other purpose than arranging printout. These labels do not affect the clustering process, in contrast to a pattern-recognition process in which they would be used to bias the process toward a specified categorization based upon this prior labeling.

b. Order of Calculation

INITIAL CLUSTER CENTERS

The program may be started in four different ways: (a) continuation from a previous clustering output, (b) from some external knowledge of the location of trial cluster centers, (c) from a single cluster at the overall mean value, or (d) from several clusters at values determined by an "initial-cluster-generating" algorithm, requiring a user-given parameter called the sphere factor. In the latter two cases, the program does not expect any initial cluster center inputs.

Continuation from a Previous Clustering Result. In case (a), provision is made for continuing the clustering program from where it left off during a previous computer access. There is an option for punching out the final cluster centers onto cards at the end of a computer run, and these cards are in a suitable format to be accepted as input, if a continuation of the program is later required.

Starting from Prior Knowledge. In case (b), although previous clustering program results may not be available, there may be knowledge of where clusters should be searched for initially. The numerical values of these initial trial cluster centers may then be punched onto cards in the format acceptable for input. (Some versions of our programs provide the flexibility of run-time formats.) This prior knowledge may save con-

siderable computer time by eliminating many iterations. The success of this approach depends mainly on the accuracy and relevance of the prior knowledge to this clustering situation.

Single Cluster Starting from the Overall Mean. A starting method that is the least biased of all, is to assume initially that the data is one single cluster. In this case, the overall mean value for the data is used as the only initial cluster point. This method is the least biased because there are no inherent assumptions. It is not always used because it may take many iterations of ISO-DATA to split up the single initial cluster into many clusters. When a data analyst knows that he is looking for a fit in the 15- to 20-cluster region, he can save computer time by using the following sphere-factor algorithm to generate approximately this number of clusters without the lengthy computation involved in successive splittings starting from a single cluster.

Sphere-Factor Starting Algorithm. If it is desired to generate several clusters in a relatively unbiased manner, this algorithm provides a convenient method. This initial-cluster-generating algorithm starts by calculating the grand mean of all the data, which is then used as the first cluster center. The boundary of this first cluster is at the radius of a hypersphere calculated from the sphere factor. A value of 1.0 for the sphere factor is defined to be a distance equal to the average sample distance from the grand mean. The average distance is conveniently calculated when computing the grand mean. A large sphere factor produces a large initial sphere and hence fewer initial clusters. Points are then considered sequentially, and if they fall within this sphere, they become members of that cluster. The first point that does not fall within the sphere forms the center for a new sphere with the same radius, and successive points then will be allocated to one of the spheres already created, or be the center for yet another sphere, and so on.

THE INNER CORE OF THE PROGRAM

The "heart" of the program operates when the initial cluster generating phase has been completed. This inner core or iterative loop involves one complete pass through each data item, as follows:

1. Select the next data sample (observation) on the input data list.
2. Compute its distance to all existing cluster centers.
3. Allocate this sample to the closest cluster center.

After all the data on the list have been used,

4. Re-evaluate the cluster centers by recomputing their means.
5. If any mean values have changed because of a different allocation of data points to clusters, begin processing the list again, at step (1). If there is no change, the iteration has settled, and we know the final positions and statistics of the clusters for the specific number of clusters we are dealing with.

To explore a different number of clusters, we must either split (burst) existing clusters, or lump (un-burst) existing clusters. Throughout this whole clustering procedure, note that the input data is not changed or moved in any way. Only a re-labeling or re-allocating process takes place, giving rise to various interpretations of the structure or morphology of the data. No manipulation of the data is involved as far as changing its values is concerned.

THRESHOLD OF COMBINATION

There is a threshold value required by the clustering program analagous to a "level of detail" concept in cognitive processing. This value (called *THETAC* in the program) is a distance in the multivariate space below which combination of separate clusters can occur. Similarly, this same threshold is used for splitting clusters, as described below. In order to supply an appropriate value for the threshold of combination, it is necessary to run a few iterations of the program and inspect the printout for typical distance values and cluster spacings. This is easy to do in a conversational or on-line version of the program, but troublesome in batch versions.

CLUSTER-SPLITTING PROCEDURE

The algorithm for splitting is as follows: For each cluster, the maximum standard deviation and the dimension in which it occurs are found. The standard deviations for all clusters are sorted in decreasing order and a record is kept of which clusters the sorted values came from. Clusters are chosen for trial splitting in the highest order of their maximum standard deviations. That is, the clusters that are stretched out the farthest in some dimension are considered the most likely candidates for splitting. Clusters that contain only one point are never chosen for splitting. A trial splitting of each of the chosen clusters is performed using this rule: In a cluster to be tested for splitting, look up the number of the dimension of the cluster's maximum standard deviation. Suppose the dimension number is J. Then, each pattern in that cluster is assigned to one "subcluster" or the other, according to whether or not the pattern's Jth component is greater than the cluster center's Jth component. In other words, the cluster is "cut" in two by a hyperplane passing through the cluster center and orthogonal to the Jth dimension. After the cluster has been split, the averages (i.e., cluster centers) of the two subclusters are computed. If the Euclidean distance between these two averages is greater than or equal to $1.1 \times THETAC$, the two new averages replace the original cluster center. Otherwise, the original cluster center is retained.

CLUSTER-LUMPING PROCEDURE

If it is desired to reduce the number of clusters found, pairs of clusters may be lumped together. The intercluster distances are ranked, and only those closer than *THETAC* may be lumped. The closest pairs are lumped first and there is a user-specified limit to how many pairs may be lumped in any one iteration. This allows the user to control the amount of change that might occur from one iteration to the next.

Cluster-Ignoring Procedure

With some data sets, there may be several separated data points far removed from the bodies of the main clusters. These inconsistent points usually arise from measuring or keypunch errors, and in most cases the user wishes to ignore them as clusters, even though they are isolated and compact in the data space. Another reason to ignore these probably erroneous points, sometimes called "wild shots" or "outliers," is that they significantly increase the running time of the program if they become clusters. Therefore, there is provision in the program to ignore clusters with a small number of data points in them. The user specifies the least number of points that can be considered as a cluster. Thus, if there are fewer than this threshold number, *THETAN*, a cluster will not be formed. A typical value to use is *THETAN* = 3. If the user is interested in finding only large clusters, he can set the threshold *THETAN* to be fairly high.

The Sequence of Splitting, Lumping, and Ignoring Procedures

To summarize, we have described four basic procedures that can take place during an iteration:

1. Splitting—a process that divides one or more clusters into two parts.
2. Lumping—a process that joins together the patterns in two or more clusters.
3. Deleting—a process that ignores small groups of patterns and does not allow them to form a cluster.
4. Settling—during which process none of the first three processes above occurs, and only the average values are recomputed. Patterns can, however, change cluster membership, and this affects the new average value. The new average value affects the closeness relationships and so several cycles of settling may be necessary to achieve stable (converged) conditions.

During an iteration, lumping and splitting cannot occur together, but deleting of a cluster can occur during any iteration. The determining factors in whether lumping or splitting takes place are the lumping and splitting threshold parameter, *THETAC*, and the quantity *NRWDSD* (number of rows desired). *NRWDSD* is another parameter supplied by the user to bias the clustering towards the finding of either fewer or more clusters. (i.e., rows in the output array). If the number of clusters (*NROWS*) is less than half the number of clusters desired (*NRWDSD*), then splitting occurs. If the current number of clusters is more than twice the desired number of clusters, then lumping occurs.

c. Output Quantities

After every iteration through the data, the program computes various summary statistics about the iteration and prints these out. To summarize the details given below, this printout is the number of clusters and their locations, their deviations along each dimension, and the cluster-membership of each data point. Also, a table of intercluster distances is given. In more detail, the following information is listed:*

1. The iteration number.
2. The number, R, of clusters for this iteration.
3. The total number, N, of patterns currently being clustered.
4. The total number of patterns ignored as clusters.
5. The current value of the *SPLIT/ LUMP* parameters.
6. The number of patterns in each cluster (N_i patterns in the ith cluster)
7. The components of each cluster center. The jth component of the ith cluster center is:

$$C_{ij} = \frac{1}{N_i} \sum_{\substack{\text{Patterns} \\ \text{in } i\text{th} \\ \text{cluster}}} P_j$$

*An example printout is given later in Section 7 with the Sample Problem.

where P_j is the jth component of a pattern in the ith cluster.

8. The within-cluster standard deviations of the patterns in each cluster from their cluster centers. The standard deviation of the ith cluster in the jth dimension is:

$$\sigma_{ij} = \sqrt{\frac{1}{N_i} \sum_{\substack{\text{Patterns} \\ \text{in } i\text{th} \\ \text{cluster}}} (C_{ij} - P_j)^2}$$

9. The *RMS* average distance of patterns in a cluster to their cluster center. For the ith cluster this quantity is:

$$X_i = \sqrt{\frac{1}{N_i} \sum_{\substack{\text{Patterns} \\ \text{in } i\text{th} \\ \text{cluster}}} \sum_{j=1}^{M} (C_{ij} - P_j)^2}$$

where M is the number of dimensions.
Note. On the output page, N_i, X_i, C_{ij}, and σ_{ij} are arranged in the following format:

$$(N_i)$$
CLUSTER CENTER 3 WITH   45
PATTERNS AND *RMS* AVERAGE
$$(X_i)$$
PATTERN DISTANCE = .86285

6.69	3.01	5.64	2.05 (C_{ij})
.57	.30	.50	.27 (σ_{ij})

10. A table giving, for each cluster, the number of patterns from each category in the cluster. If no category information was read in, or if the patterns have the same category number, then the numbers in this table will just be the N_i (see Item 6).

11. The pattern cluster-membership table. The ith entry in this table, reading from left to right and from top to bottom, is the number of the cluster to which the ith pattern belongs. If the ith entry is zero, the ith pattern has been discarded and was not used in clustering.

12. The total squared error (i.e., the sum of the squared distances of the patterns

from their cluster centers) is:

T = Total squared error

$$= \sum_{i=1}^{R} \sum_{\substack{\text{Patterns} \\ \text{in } i\text{th} \\ \text{cluster}}} \sum_{j=1}^{M} (C_{ij} - P_j)^2$$

$$= \sum_{i=1}^{R} X_i^2 N_i$$

For a fixed number of clusters, ISODATA will tend to minimize T as the patterns are repartitioned.

13. The *RMS* average distance of all patterns from their cluster centers,

$$\sqrt{\frac{T}{N}}$$

14. For each cluster center, the average Euclidean distance from it to the other cluster centers. For the ith cluster center:

$$Y_i = \frac{1}{(R-1)} \sum_{j=1}^{R} D_{ij}$$

where D_{ij} is the Euclidean distance between the ith and jth cluster centers.

15. The average Euclidean distance between cluster centers.

16. For each cluster, the ratio of the average distance from all other cluster centers to the *RMS* average pattern distance within the cluster. For the ith cluster, this is:

$$\frac{Y_i}{X_i}$$

17. For each cluster center, the Euclidean distance to the nearest cluster center. For the ith cluster center this is:*

$$Z_i = MIN\; D_{ij}[\text{for } i \neq j \quad \text{and } j = 1(1)R]$$

18. For each cluster, the ratio of the distance from the nearest cluster center to the *RMS* average pattern distance within the cluster. For the ith cluster, this is:

$$\frac{Z_i}{X_i}$$

*By the notation $j = 1(1)R$ we mean FOR j: $= 1$ STEP 1 UNTIL R.

19. The overall standard deviation of patterns from their corresponding cluster center. The standard deviation in the jth dimension is:

$$= \sqrt{\frac{1}{N} \sum_{i=1}^{R} \sum_{\substack{\text{Patterns} \\ \text{in } i\text{th} \\ \text{cluster}}} (C_{ij} - P_j)^2}$$

$$= \sqrt{\frac{1}{N} \sum \sigma_{ij}^2 N_i}$$

20. The matrix of Euclidean distances between cluster centers. The i, jth element of this matrix is D_{ij}, the Euclidean distance between the ith and jth cluster centers.

When a cluster is split, the following information is also printed:

1. The iteration number.
2. The current value of θ_c.
3. The number of the cluster that was split.
4. The numbers of the two new clusters.
5. The value of the maximum within-cluster standard deviation of the original cluster.
6. The number of the dimension that had the maximum standard deviation.
7. The number of patterns in each of the two new clusters.
8. The components of the two new cluster centers.

d. Termination of the Program Run

Typically, the program is run several times with the same data set to explore it fully, yet checking the output of each run for intermediate results or adjusting user parameters in stages between the runs. Any one run is terminated by means of a user parameter giving the number of iterations for which the program must run. When this number of iterations is reached, the program run terminates. The final cluster centers can be written onto a convenient computer file for continuation during the next run.

4. FLOW CHARTS

The flow charts for ISODATA and several subroutines are given on pages 353–360.

5. DESCRIPTION OF FLOW CHART

a. Program ISODATA

The main program ISODATA reads in the input parameters of Type 1, allocates core to the various arrays and calls the main functional routine ISODAT.

Box 1: Input main parameters of Type 1. These parameters, which are invariant throughout the program are used to generate the core requirement for the problem. They also include input, output, and program termination options. A list of these parameters along with a brief description follows:

NCOLS	Number of variables, *excluding* pattern identifier field.
SPHRFC	Sphericity of initial clusters (typically set to 1.25).
NPARTS	Number of partitions per iteration.
NPATMX	Number of patterns (objects) in input data file.
NRWDSD	Number of clusters desired. (This parameter is also multiplied by 3 and then used to determine the maximum number of clusters allowed.)
NSCALE	1 = Scale factors provided (card 2.).
	2 = Variables scaled automatically to mean = 1, based on the grand mean.
	0 = No scale factors.
NWRITE	1 = Print listing of input data.
	0 = Omit listing of data.
ITER	Number of iterations.
IT	1 = input data file will *not* be rewound at start.
	0 = input data file *will* be rewound.
LOCID	0 = No pattern identifier fields are provided in data, pat-

Program ISODATA

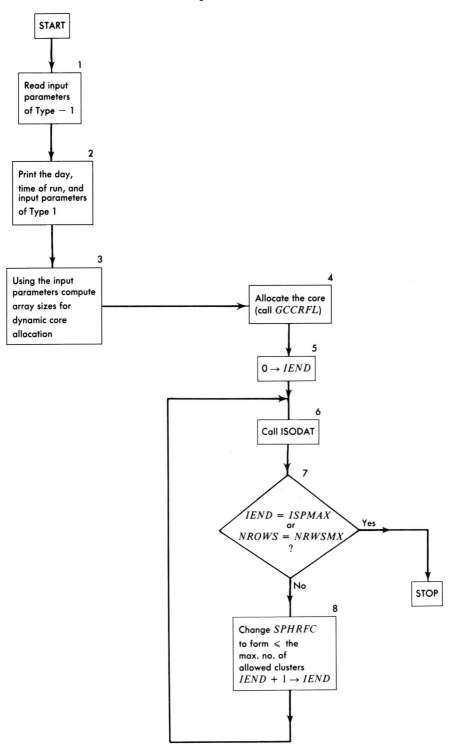

Subroutine ISODAT

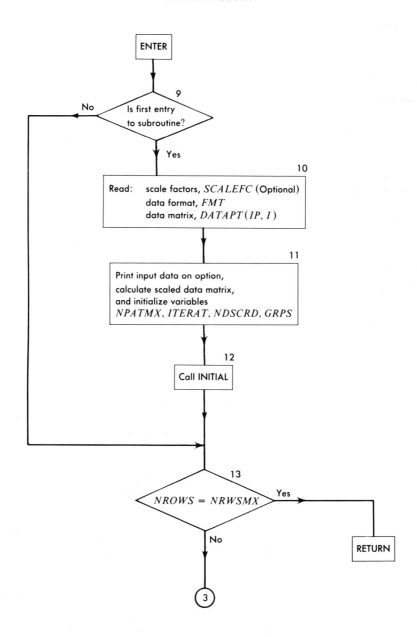

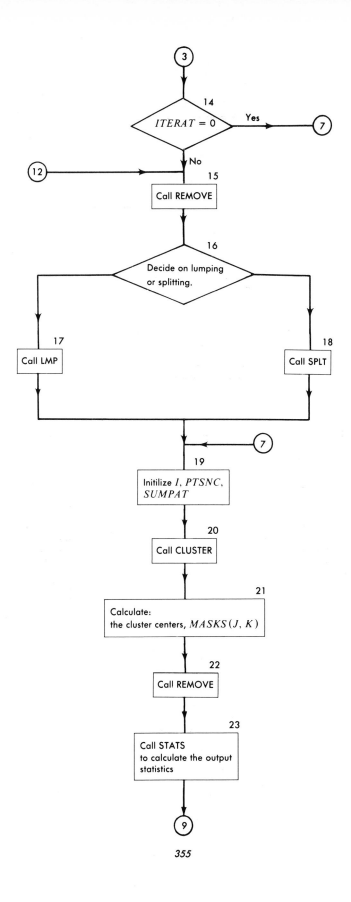

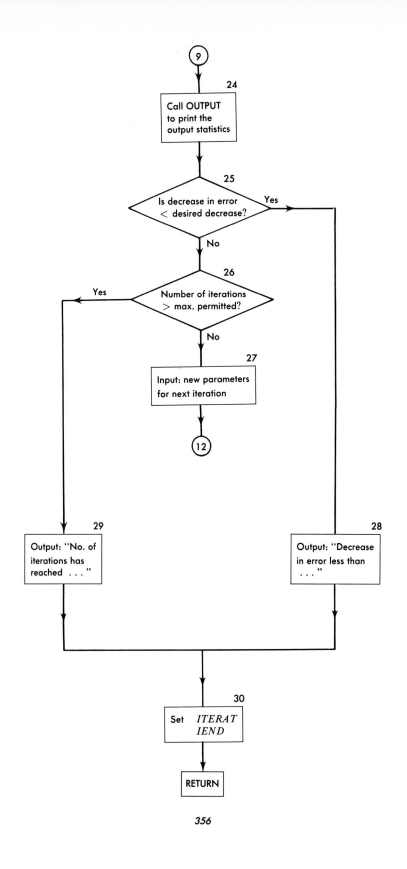

356

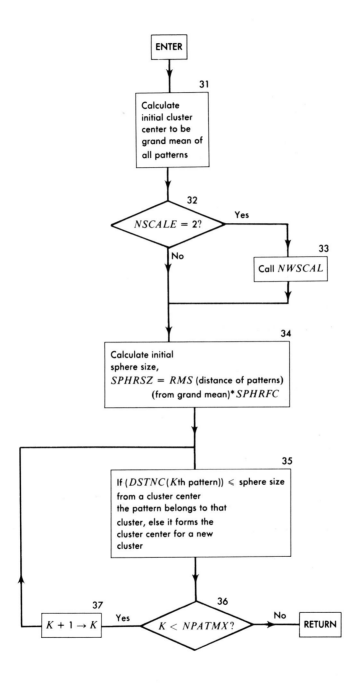

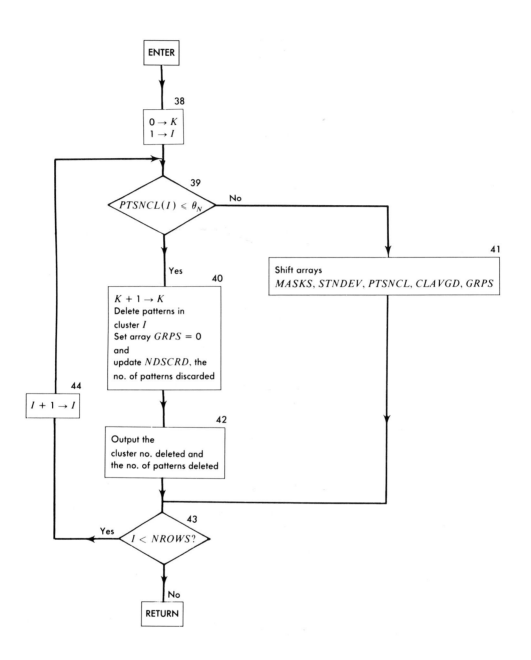

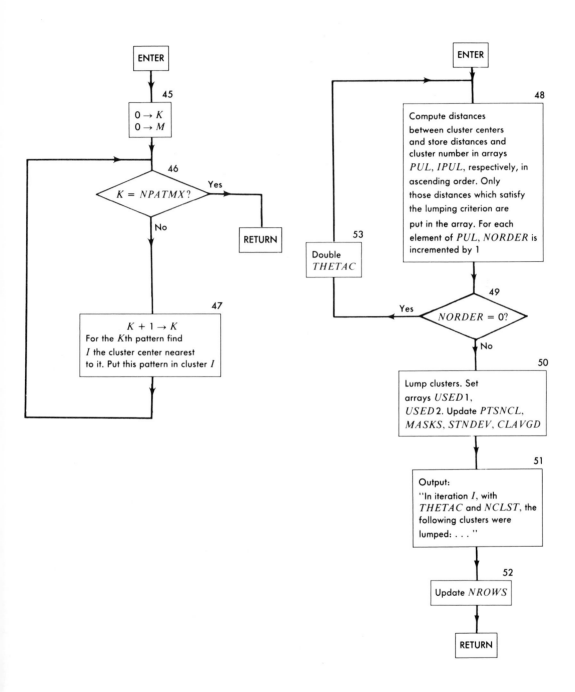

Subroutine SPLT

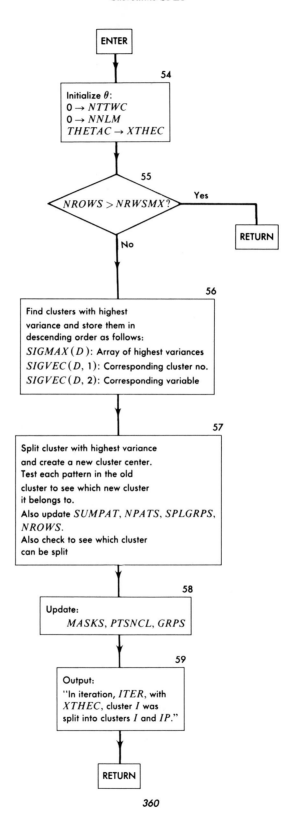

ENTER

54
Initialize θ:
$0 \rightarrow NTTWC$
$0 \rightarrow NNLM$
$THETAC \rightarrow XTHEC$

55
$NROWS > NRWSMX?$ — Yes → RETURN

No

56
Find clusters with highest
variance and store them in
descending order as follows:
$SIGMAX(D)$: Array of highest variances
$SIGVEC(D, 1)$: Corresponding cluster no.
$SIGVEC(D, 2)$: Corresponding variable

57
Split cluster with highest variance
and create a new cluster center.
Test each pattern in the old
cluster to see which new cluster
it belongs to.
Also update $SUMPAT, NPATS, SPLGRPS,$
$NROWS.$
Also check to see which cluster
can be split

58
Update:
$MASKS, PTSNCL, GRPS$

59
Output:
"In iteration, $ITER$, with
$XTHEC$, cluster I was
split into clusters I and IP."

RETURN

terns will be identified by their position in the input file.

Nonzero —The absolute value of this parameter identifies the pattern identifier field in the data input records, counting from one. If *LOCID* is positive, the identifier is an integer value, read under *I* format. If *LOCID* is negative, the identifier is alpha-numeric, read under *A* format. For example, -23 indicates that the 23rd field in each input record (pattern) contains an alphanumeric pattern identifier.

TSQLIM   Squared error criterion, minimum acceptable fractional change in the squared error term between iterations. If the fractional change is less than *TSQLIM*, the program will stop.

ISPMAX   Maximum number of times the sphericity can be changed for forming original clusters.

Box 2: Call routine DATIM to get the day and time of run as well as an echocheck of the main parameters.

Boxes 3, 4: GCCRFL called for actual core allocation.

Box 5: Initializes counter *IEND*.

Box 6: Call ISODAT, the actual functional routine.

Box 7: Test whether the number of times the sphericity has been changed is within limit or the number of clusters already created is equal to the maximum permitted. If so, the program stops.

Box 8: Increase the sphericity and call ISODAT again.

b. Subroutine ISODAT

ISODAT is the main functional routine; it reads in the data, performs scaling, reads in iteration-dependent data (Type 2) and organizes the calls to various routines.

Boxes 9, 10, 11: Test whether first entry to subroutine. If yes, read in scale factors, data format, and the data matrix. Print the input data (on option) and initialize the various pointers.

Box 12: Call the routine INITIAL, which calculates the intial cluster centers, *MASKS*, and the number of initial clusters, *NROWS*.

Box 13: Test whether $NROW = NRWSMX$, the maximum permissible number of clusters. If true, the control is returned to ISODATA, else proceed to Box 14.

Boxes 14, 15: Test whether on the 0th iteration. If so go to Box 19 else proceed to Box 15 and call routine REMOVE, to remove clusters with fewer than *THETAN* patterns.

Box 16: Decide on whether to lump or split on this iteration.

Box 17: Call routine LMP, which lumps those clusters to their nearest cluster depending on: (i) The clusters have less than *MINPAT*, the minimum number of patterns. (ii) They are closer than *THETAC*.

Box 18: Call routine SPLT, which splits a cluster on the basis of: (i) Cluster having greater than *MAXPAT* number of patterns. (ii) Cluster with the variable with the largest within cluster standard deviation.

Box 19: Initialize variables defining cluster statistics.

Box 20: Call routine CLUSTER, which shifts the patterns without creating new clusters or destroying existing ones. (See Section 3b, "settling")

Box 21: Calculate the cluster centers from the cluster-defining statistics.

Box 22: Call REMOVE.

Box 23: STATS calculates the statistics of each cluster.

Box 24: OUTPUT prints the above statistics.

Boxes 25, 26: Check program termination indices.

Box 27: Read in new parameters corresponding to the next iteration. These parameters, called Type 2, may change for each iteration. They are listed below:

NCLST   Maximum number of cluster pairs that may be lumped or split (1–9).

THETAC   Split/lump threshold (typically .25).

THETAN   Cluster deletion threshold (0–99). Clusters with fewer or equal to this number of patterns will be deleted.

LUMPST $LUMP$ = Lump desired on this iteration.
               $SPLIT$ = Split desired on this iteration.
               Blank if not specified.

NTTCBC   If "$LUMP$" or "$SPLIT$" is specified this variable will contain the number of times $THETAC$ can be changed to force lumping or splitting.

MAXPAT   Maximum number of patterns allowed in a cluster before a split must be made (optional).

MINPAT   Minimum number of patterns allowed in a cluster before lumping must take place (optional).

IPOCM   1 = Write cluster membership table on save file ($SAVE$).

IDARY   1 = Write Means, standard deviations, and RMS error on save file ($SAVE$).

IDPRIN   1 = Print listing of patterns in each cluster. Pattern identifier fields are used if provided.

IPRARY   1 = Print table of means and standard deviations of all variables for each cluster.

Boxes 28–30: Output suitable headings, set pointers $ITERAT$ and $IEND$ and return control to main program $ISODATA$.

c. Subroutine INITIAL

This routine calculates the initial cluster centers based on the externally specified parameter $SPHRFC$, the sphere factor, and the grand mean for the whole data set.

Box 31: Calculate the initial cluster center to be the grand mean of all the patterns.

Boxes 32, 33: On option transform the data such that its grand mean is unity.

Box 34: Calculate the initial sphere-size.

Boxes 35–37: Check each pattern to see if it falls within the initial sphere. The first pattern that doesn't do so becomes the next cluster center with the same sphere size. The subsequent patterns are allocated to the nearest cluster center.

d. Subroutine REMOVE

This routine discards patterns belonging to clusters with fewer than $THETAN$ patterns from further calculations. The parameter $THETAN$ is specified externally.

Box 38: Initialize pointers I and K.

Boxes 39, 43, 44: For each cluster, the number of patterns in that cluster are compared to $THETAN$, θ_n.

Box 40, 42: If the number of patterns are less than or equal to θ_n, that cluster is deleted and the array $GRPS$ is set accordingly. Also a brief statement to that effect is output.

Box 41: Shift arrays describing a cluster.

e. Subroutine CLUSTER

This routine allocates each pattern to its nearest cluster center as given by $MASKS$. The array $MASKS$ is calculated in the calling routine.

Box 45: Initialize pointers K and M.

Boxes 46, 47: Allocate each pattern to its nearest cluster center. Return control to the calling routine.

f. Subroutine LMP

This routine lumps two clusters nearest to each other and closer than $THETAC$ (θ_c), as specified externally. It will also change θ_c a specified number of times to try to lump two clusters.

Box 48: Calculate the intercluster distance matrix and store it in arrays *PUL* and *IPUL*. Only those distances that are less than θ_c are stored.

Boxes 49, 53: Change θ_c if necessary.

Box 50: Lump the two closest clusters and update the cluster defining arrays.

Boxes 51, 52: Output a brief statement listing the clusters lumped. Also update the number of clusters, *NROWS*.

g. Subroutine SPLT

This routine splits a cluster into two clusters. The splitting is monothetic and the cluster chosen is the one with a variable having the largest standard deviation and resulting in split clusters having distance between them greater than θ_c. θ_c is changed a preset number of times to force splitting.

Box 54: Initialize pointers.

Boxes 55–57: Find clusters with the highest variance and store them in descending order in arrays *SIGMAX* and *SIGVEC*. Split the cluster with highest variance (standard deviation) and check to see if the split is valid.

Box 58: Update the cluster-defining arrays.

Box 59: Output a brief statement to list the cluster split, and the variable on which the splitting occurred. Return control to the calling routine.

6. SAMPLE PROBLEM

We choose a simple two-dimensional representation of a three-dimensional problem to illustrate the way in which the program operates. (The usual limit on dimensions in the program is 50, but it is difficult to illustrate results simply in these highly multivariate cases.) Out of many possible examples that could be presented, we choose one from our recent meteorological research projects for tracking cloud motions by means of dynamic clustering [4]. The data

we present here were artificially generated using the data-generating clustering language discussed earlier. Figure 13.3 shows a line-printer plot of data to be clustered (i.e., described concisely). Each dot represents at least one data point (or cloud element) and the cluster centers found by the program are shown by **C**. As mentioned earlier when describing the function of ISODATA, if the data is elongated along some principal axis rather than being approximately spherical, several cluster centers may be needed alongside each other to adequately represent the elongation. The two clouds in the center of the picture are elongated and are thus each represented by three cluster centers. This illustrates that the clustering approach is inherently a circular (spherical, or point-like) model, in contrast to linear models such as the minimal spanning tree.

Figure 13.4 shows another artificially generated data set that represents similar clouds as in Fig. 13.3, but assumes that the clouds have been moved by realistic winds during the time elapsing between these two simulated satellite pictures. The central elongated clouds are at high altitude, and are subject to a wind moving them towards the top of the page. The other clouds in the corners are moved approximately diagonally, to the lower left corner, and are simulating low-level cumulus clouds. This configuration simulates a case in real satellite data that we have processed with the program. Note that although the general shapes of the clouds are similar in the two pictures, the dot patterns are quite different. This statistical similarity is achieved by using the same statistical parameters, but without resetting the random number generator to the same initial condition at the start of the data generation process for each picture.

These two examples illustrate two separate clusterings that each adequately describe the 760 data points by means of 10 cluster centers and the qualifiers for those centers.

Fig. 13.3. A printer plot for clouds of artificial data.

In the cloud-tracking applications, it is necessary to link corresponding clouds or cloud-elements to produce vectors representing their motion. Because the data is changing continuously as the clouds are blown by the winds, the clustering of these data must be dynamic, and the linking of corresponding clusters is performed by another program module called MOTION. We shall not discuss this program in detail here, but illustrate how it performs dynamic clustering in this simple example. The ISO-

DATA and MOTION programs are able to provide suitable vectors for this simple two-layer of clouds case. The output of the MOTION program is given in Fig. 13.5, which shows pairs of cluster centers labeled from *A* to *J*, and prefixed by a "1" or "2," denoting picture sequence. In interpreting these printer plots of motion vectors, note that each pair is labeled with a letter of the alphabet. If no single character label is given alongside the "1" or "2," this means that no pairing was made by the program.

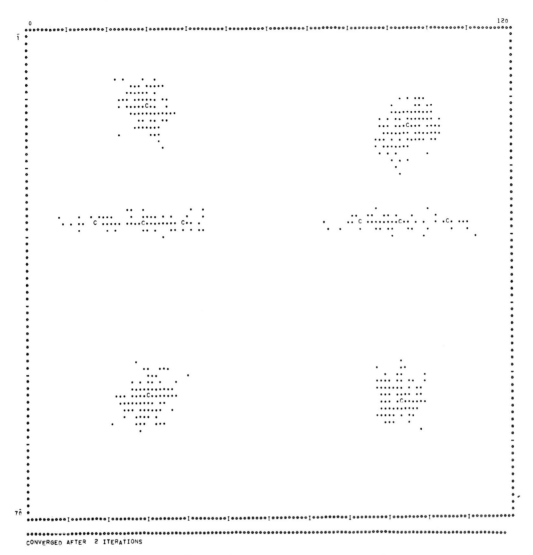

Fig. 13.4. Printer plot for successive picture of artificial data.

This would occur if a cloud dissipates completely, as frequently happens in practice. These vectors are the end product of our cloud-tracking system and are suitable input data for a numerical prediction model for the weather.

It is not feasible to illustrate some of our multivariate applications of clustering here. Even reams of computer printout may be inadequate to interpret complex multivariate data-generating processes such as are encountered in real applications. It was mainly for this reason that we developed the PROMENADE on-line system [6] using high performance interactive graphics. With this system, many graphic views of the raw data or clustering output could be obtained and the clustering process could be more intimately inspected and controlled [7].

7. ESTIMATION OF THE RUNNING TIME

The running time of the program is important because one is waiting (urgently or

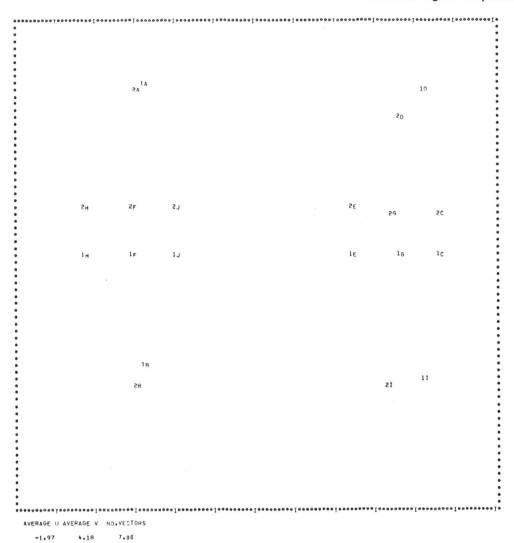

Fig. 13.5. Cloud motion vectors plotted on a line printer.

idly) for an answer, and because the running time is associated directly with the computer running cost. The computing time of this program is mostly spent in the inner-inner loop (or inner core, see Section 3b) that computes the distance of each point to each currently existing cluster center. The inner-inner loop is the basic distance computation carried out for each dimension of the data and involves accumulating the terms $(x_i - \bar{x})^2$. As an approximation, the

running time (T) of the program for one iteration is given by the equation

$$T = K \times NCOLS$$
$$\times NPATS \times NCLUST \; seconds,$$

where

NCOLS is the number of columns (dimensions) of the input data array

NPATS is the number of items in the input data array, each corresponding to one multivariate data point or pattern

NCLUST is the number of clusters used in this iteration

K is a constant factor that depends on the type of computer, its job mix, the optimization level of the compiler, etc.

For each computer installation, the system time clock should be programmed to print out the time after each iteration, and the factor *K* can be easily computed.

8. COMPUTER OUTPUT

What follows represents a typical (annotated) output from ISODATA on a small problem.

```
ISODATA — GCC VERSION OF 12/10/73

DATE = 06/21/74        TIME = 18.00.38.

   28  VARIABLES = M
  1.10 — SPHERICITY OF INITIAL CLUSTERS = SPHERE FACTOR
    1  PARTITIONS PER ITERATION
   89  PATTERNS (OBJECTS) = N
    2  CLUSTERS DESIRED
    2 — SCALE FACTOR OPTION — Program automatically scales the data on the grand mean.
   -0 — DATA LISTING OPTION
    5  ITERATIONS
   -0 — NO REWIND = 1
   -0 — PATTERN IDENTIFIER FIELD
 .010000 — SQUARED ERROR REDUCTION CRITERION (SERC)   (T_{k+1} − T_k)/T_k ≥ SERC

INPUT FORMAT -- (BLK)


     89 PATTERNS READ
```

$$\text{(SERC)}\quad \frac{T_{k+1} - T_k}{T_k} \geq SERC$$

```
ITERATION  0   CLUSTERS = 5   PATTERNS = 89   DISCARDS = 0  Initial clusters are generated using the spherefactor starting algorithm.
```
(R ↓ above 5, N ↓ above 89)

```
CLUSTER CENTER   1 WITH  66 PATTERNS AND RMS AVERAGE PATTERN DISTANCE = 587.31982 = X₁
```
$= X_1$

```
CLUSTER CENTER   2 WITH  11 PATTERNS AND RMS AVERAGE PATTERN DISTANCE = 690.97689 = X₂
```
$= X_2$

```
CLUSTER CENTER   3 WITH   2 PATTERNS AND RMS AVERAGE PATTERN DISTANCE = 320.60497 = X₃
```
$= X_3$

```
CLUSTER CENTER   4 WITH   5 PATTERNS AND RMS AVERAGE PATTERN DISTANCE = 518.47574 = X₄
```
$= X_4$

```
CLUSTER CENTER   5 WITH   5 PATTERNS AND RMS AVERAGE PATTERN DISTANCE = 493.96801 = X₅
```
$= X_5$

```
CLUSTER MEMBERSHIP TABLE..
 1 1 1 1 1 2 4 1 2 2 1 5 1 1 2 1 1 1 1 1 2 1 1 1 2 1 1 1 1 4 1 1 1 1 2 2
 1 1 4 1 1 1 2 1 1 5 1 1 2 1 1 1 1 1 1 1 1 1 1 2 5 1 1 1 1 1 1 1 4 4 2 5 1 5 1
 1 2 3 1 1 1 1 1
```

```
SQUARED ERROR = .30788DE+08 = T = Total squared error
```

$$T = \text{Total squared error} = \sum_{i=1}^{R} \sum_{\substack{\text{Patterns}\\ \text{in } i^{th}\\ \text{Cluster}}} \sum_{j=1}^{M} (c_{ij} - P_j)^2 = \sum_{i=1}^{R} X_i^2 N_i$$

```
RMS AVG DIST. OF PATTERNS FROM THEIR CENTERS = 588.15999
```
$= \sqrt{T/N}$

```
AVG. DIST. FROM EACH CLUSTER CENTER TO THE OTHER CLUSTER CENTERS
1700.493231306.880741473.790261867.588421901.39215
```
$(Y_i ; i = 1,5)$

```
AVG. DIST. BETWEEN CLUSTER CENTERS = 1650.02896
```
$\frac{1}{R}\sum_{i=1}^{R} Y_i$

```
FOR EACH CLUSTER,(AVG. DIST. TO OTHER CENTERS)/AVG.   PATTERN DIST. WITHIN CLUSTER)
2.89534   1.89135   4.59690   3.60207   3.84922
```
(Y_i/X_i)

```
FOR EACH CLUSTER,DIST. TO THE NEAREST CLUSTER CENTER.
862.68351  804.45088  804.450881051.29515  862.68351
```
Z_i

```
FOR EACH.CLUSTER,(DIST. TO NEAREST CENTER/(AVG. PATTERN DIST. WITHIN CLUSTER)
1.4E995   1.16422   2.50917   2.02767   1.74644
```
(Z_i/X_i)

```
OVERALL STANDARD DEVIATIONS =
50.00394 144.80262 110.49404  58.86421 112.38060  57.03848  51.14139  74.31815  26.01768  63.39678  36.55851  96.79755
172.26973 193.18613 111.96939 175.11445 113.92918  93.41272 145.61102  49.50745 114.00177  73.40758 143.66363  84.04603
104.33566  91.12095 158.78107 146.00844
```

$$= \sqrt{\frac{1}{N}\sum_{\text{For Patterns}}^{\text{all Patterns}}(c_{ij}-P_j)^2} = \sqrt{\frac{1}{N}\sum \sigma_{ij}^2 N_i}; \text{ where } \sigma_{ij} \text{ is the within cluster standard deviation of } i^{th} \text{ cluster in the } j^{th} \text{ dimension.}$$

```
EUCLIDEAN DISTANCES BETWEEN CLUSTER CENTERS
          1        2       3       4       5
 1      0.0   1521.4  1909.7  2508.1   862.7
 2   1521.4      0.0   804.5  1051.3  1850.3
 3   1909.7    804.5     0.0  1099.7  2081.3
 4   2508.1   1051.3  1099.7     0.0  2811.2
 5    862.7   1850.3  2081.3  2811.2     0.0
```
$\{D_{ij} ; i,j = 1,R\}$

```
ITERATION  1   CLUSTERS =   5   PATTERNS =  89   DISCARDS =  0

CLUSTER CENTER   1 WITH  56 PATTERNS AND RMS AVERAGE PATTERN DISTANCE = 519.25639


CLUSTER CENTER   2 WITH  12 PATTERNS AND RMS AVERAGE PATTERN DISTANCE = 658.79644


CLUSTER CENTER   3 WITH   3 PATTERNS AND RMS AVERAGE PATTERN DISTANCE = 390.95457


CLUSTER CENTER   4 WITH   6 PATTERNS AND RMS AVERAGE PATTERN DISTANCE = 554.03274


CLUSTER CENTER   5 WITH  12 PATTERNS AND RMS AVERAGE PATTERN DISTANCE = 568.02445


CLUSTER   1 CONTAINS THE FOLLOWING PATTERNS..
    2    3    4    5    6    9   12   14   15   18   19   20   22   24   25   26
   27   29   31   32   33   35   36   37   38   41   42   45   46   48   49   50
   52   53   55   56   57   58   59   60   61   62   63   66   67   69   70   72
   73   80   81   85   86   87   88   89

CLUSTER   2 CONTAINS THE FOLLOWING PATTERNS..
    7   11   16   23   28   30   39   47   54   76   78   82

CLUSTER   3 CONTAINS THE FOLLOWING PATTERNS..
   40   64   83

CLUSTER   4 CONTAINS THE FOLLOWING PATTERNS..
    8   10   34   43   74   75

CLUSTER   5 CONTAINS THE FOLLOWING PATTERNS..
    1   13   17   21   44   51   65   68   71   77   79   84

CLUSTER MEMBERSHIP TABLE..
  5 1 1 1 1 1 2 4 1 4 2 1 5 1 1 2 5 1 1 1 5 1 2 1 1 1 1 2 1 2 1 1 1 1 4 1 1 1 1 2 3
  1 1 4 5 1 1 2 1 1 5 1 1 2 1 1 1 1 1 1 1 1 1 1 3 5 1 1 5 1 1 5 1 1 4 4 2 5 2 5 1
  1 2 3 5 1 1 1 1 1

SQUARED ERROR =   .264793E+08

RMS AVG DIST. OF PATTERNS FROM THEIR CENTERS = 545.45463

AVG. DIST. FROM EACH CLUSTER CENTER TO THE OTHER CLUSTER CENTERS
1606.327361218.141271409.446011880.142761699.71515

AVG. DIST. BETWEEN CLUSTER CENTERS =1562.75451

FOR EACH CLUSTER,(AVG. DIST. TO OTHER CENTERS)/AVG.    PATTERN DIST. WITHIN CLUSTER)
  3.09351   1.84904   3.60514   3.39356   2.99233

FOR EACH CLUSTER,DIST. TO THE NEAREST CLUSTER CENTER.
  723.88240  763.86319  763.863191133.16147  723.88240

FOR EACH CLUSTER,(DIST. TO NEAREST CENTER/(AVG. PATTERN DIST. WITHIN CLUSTER)
  1.39408   1.15948   1.95384   2.04530   1.27439

OVERALL STANDARD DEVIATIONS
  49.41964 123.62011 105.94497  57.75614  99.92997  55.34749  48.04797  71.76227  25.77079  59.14590  36.73947  96.48492




 139.30422 183.75996 111.19832 150.92878 110.68590  87.76734 140.22452  49.02878 107.06785  73.92803 132.09696  80.20735
 103.77469  86.45419 148.89075 136.46230

EUCLIDEAN DISTANCES BETWEEN CLUSTER CENTERS
           1      2      3      4      5
  1      0.0 1363.1 1847.7 2490.6  723.9
  2   1363.1    0.0  763.9 1230.2 1515.3
  3   1847.7  763.9    0.0 1133.2 1893.0
  4   2490.6 1230.2 1133.2    0.0 2666.6
  5    723.9 1515.3 1893.0 2666.6    0.0
```

In iteration 1 some of the patterns have been moved from one cluster to another to reduce the squared error.

```
ITERATION  2   CLUSTERS =   5   PATTERNS =  89   DISCARDS =  0

CLUSTER CENTER   1 WITH  50 PATTERNS AND RMS AVERAGE PATTERN DISTANCE = 478.42222

CLUSTER CENTER   2 WITH  13 PATTERNS AND RMS AVERAGE PATTERN DISTANCE = 623.46645

CLUSTER CENTER   3 WITH   3 PATTERNS AND RMS AVERAGE PATTERN DISTANCE = 390.95457

CLUSTER CENTER   4 WITH   7 PATTERNS AND RMS AVERAGE PATTERN DISTANCE = 614.05779

CLUSTER CENTER   5 WITH  16 PATTERNS AND RMS AVERAGE PATTERN DISTANCE = 575.24017

CLUSTER   1 CONTAINS THE FOLLOWING PATTERNS..
    2    3    4    5    6    9   12   14   15   18   20   22   24   25   26   27
   29   31   32   33   36   37   38   42   45   46   48   49   50   52   53   57
   58   59   60   61   62   63   66   67   69   70   73   80   81   85   86   87
   88   89
CLUSTER   2 CONTAINS THE FOLLOWING PATTERNS..
    7   11   19   23   28   30   35   39   47   54   76   78   82
CLUSTER   3 CONTAINS THE FOLLOWING PATTERNS..
   40   64   83
CLUSTER   4 CONTAINS THE FOLLOWING PATTERNS..
    8   10   16   34   43   74   75
CLUSTER   5 CONTAINS THE FOLLOWING PATTERNS..
    1   13   17   21   41   44   51   55   56   65   68   71   72   77   79   84
CLUSTER MEMBERSHIP TABLE..
 5 1 1 1 1 2 4 1 4 2 1 5 1 1 4 5 1 2 1 5 1 2 1 1 1 2 1 2 1 1 1 4 2 1 1 1 2 3
 5 1 4 5 1 1 2 1 1 1 5 1 1 2 5 5 1 1 1 1 1 1 1 3 5 1 1 5 1 1 5 5 1 4 4 2 5 2 5 1
 1 2 3 5 1 1 1 1 1

SQUARED ERROR =     .248901E+08

RMS AVG DIST. OF PATTERNS FROM THEIR CENTERS = 528.83221

AVG. DIST. FROM EACH CLUSTER CENTER TO THE OTHER CLUSTER CENTERS
1575.973541191.114231417.148331832.090461610.17587

AVG. DIST. BETWEEN CLUSTER CENTERS =1525.30049

FOR EACH CLUSTER,(AVG. DIST. TO OTHER CENTERS)/AVG.    PATTERN DIST. WITHIN CLUSTER)
   3.29411   1.91047   3.62484   2.98358   2.79914

FOR EACH CLUSTER,DIST. TO THE NEAREST CLUSTER CENTER.
  713.08826 840.74583 840.745831077.40438 713.08826

   FOR EACH CLUSTER,(DIST. TO NEAREST CENTER)/(AVG. PATTERN DIST. WITHIN CLUSTER)
    1.49050   1.34850   2.15049   1.75457   1.23964

OVERALL STANDARD DEVIATIONS
   48.37938 119.43529  98.35963  56.40388  99.66455  50.78166  45.07174  65.41754  25.60554  55.16285  35.96847  94.78131


  143.75365 168.07002 109.07094 160.86301 101.17434  81.79205 127.63571  48.73513  99.53609  72.52824 132.33572  73.07398
  101.84379  78.77746 147.35167 137.16618

EUCLIDEAN DISTANCES BETWEEN CLUSTER CENTERS
        1      2      3      4      5
 1    0.0 1297.9 1883.7 2409.1  713.1
 2 1297.9    0.0  840.7 1303.3 1322.4
 3 1883.7  840.7    0.0 1077.4 1866.7
 4 2409.1 1303.3 1077.4    0.0 2538.5
 5  713.1 1322.4 1866.7 2538.5    0.0
```

In iteration 2 the program reallocates patterns to clusters such that T is reduced.

```
THETAC WAS CHANGED TO      .50 IN LUMP

THETAC WAS CHANGED TO     1.00 IN LUMP

THETAC WAS CHANGED TO     2.00 IN LUMP

THETAC WAS CHANGED TO     4.00 IN LUMP

THETAC WAS CHANGED TO     8.00 IN LUMP

THETAC WAS CHANGED TO    16.00 IN LUMP

THETAC WAS CHANGED TO    32.00 IN LUMP

THETAC WAS CHANGED TO    64.00 IN LUMP

THETAC WAS CHANGED TO   128.00 IN LUMP

THETAC WAS CHANGED TO   256.00 IN LUMP

THETAC WAS CHANGED TO   512.00 IN LUMP

THETAC WAS CHANGED TO  1024.00 IN LUMP
```

In iteration 3, lumping was desired (as specified on the iteration card). In order to accomplish lumping the program changed θ_c from 0.5 to 1024.

This means clusters will not be as 'tight' as before.

IN ITERATION 3 WITH THETAC=   1024.00 AND NCLIST= 1

CLUSTERS, 2 AND, 3 WERE LUMPED TOGETHER.

ITERATION 3   CLUSTERS =   4   PATTERNS = 89   DISCARDS = 0

CLUSTER CENTER   1 WITH 46 PATTERNS AND RMS AVERAGE PATTERN DISTANCE = 466.52027

CLUSTER CENTER   2 WITH 17 PATTERNS AND RMS AVERAGE PATTERN DISTANCE = 679.86294

CLUSTER CENTER   3 WITH   7 PATTERNS AND RMS AVERAGE PATTERN DISTANCE = 614.05779

CLUSTER CENTER   4 WITH 19 PATTERNS AND RMS AVERAGE PATTERN DISTANCE = 542.86865

CLUSTER   1 CONTAINS THE FOLLOWING PATTERNS..
     3   4   5   6   12   14   15   18   20   22   24   25   26   27   29   31
    32   33   36   37   38   42   45   46   48   49   50   53   58   59   60   61
    62   63   66   67   69   70   73   80   81   85   86   87   88   89

CLUSTER   2 CONTAINS THE FOLLOWING PATTERNS..
     7   11   19   21   23   28   30   35   39   40   47   54   64   76   78   82
    83

CLUSTER   3 CONTAINS THE FOLLOWING PATTERNS..
     8   10   16   34   43   74   75

CLUSTER   4 CONTAINS THE FOLLOWING PATTERNS..
     1   2   9   13   17   41   44   51   52   55   56   57   65   68   71   72
    77   79   84

CLUSTER MEMBERSHIP TABLE..
 4 4 1 1 1 1 2 3 4 3 2 1 4 1 1 3 4 1 2 1 2 1 2 1 1 1 1 2 1 2 1 1 1 3 2 1 1 1 2 2
 4 1 3 4 1 1 2 1 1 4 4 1 2 4 4 4 1 1 1 1 1 1 2 4 1 1 4 1 1 4 4 1 3 3 2 4 2 4 1
 1 2 2 4 1 1 1 1 1

SQUARED ERROR =   .261080E+08 *Note the increase in T from the previous iteration.*

RMS AVG DIST. OF PATTERNS FROM THEIR CENTERS = 541.61654

AVG. DIST. FROM EACH CLUSTER CENTER TO THE OTHER CLUSTER CENTERS
1497.751271329.556852065.936451510.82146

AVG. DIST. BETWEEN CLUSTER CENTERS =1601.01651

FOR EACH CLUSTER,(AVG. DIST. TO OTHER CENTERS)/AVG.   PATTERN DIST. WITHIN CLUSTER)
   3.21047   1.95562   3.36440   2.78303

FOR EACH CLUSTER,DIST. TO THE NEAREST CLUSTER CENTER.
677.656881258.037731258.03773 677.65688

FOR EACH CLUSTER,(DIST. TO NEAREST CENTER/(AVG. PATTERN DIST. WITHIN CLUSTER)
   1.45258   1.85043   2.04873   1.24829

OVERALL STANDARD DEVIATIONS
  50.31545 117.43328 100.91902 58.99269 101.46299 49.58290 44.56644 64.60421 25.20898 54.69084 36.24969 100.13670
 150.43746 172.14585 116.65108 171.87989 99.56089 81.36350 126.35143 47.98594 100.09539 73.24418 139.78718 72.42371
 108.26580 78.69115 142.00144 145.93120

EUCLIDEAN DISTANCES BETWEEN CLUSTER CENTERS
        1   2   3   4

1   0.0 1390.0 2425.6   677.7
2 1390.0   0.0 1258.0 1340.6
3 2425.6 1258.0   0.0 2514.2
4   677.7 1340.6 2514.2   0.0

ITERATION 4   CLUSTERS =   4   PATTERNS = 89   DISCARDS = .0

CLUSTER CENTER   1 WITH   45 PATTERNS AND RMS AVERAGE PATTERN DISTANCE = 465.99131

1	2	3	4	5	6	7	8	9	10
280.95	137.68	260.60	275.43	250.91	269.45	273.68	266.51	293.47	266.06
54.51	120.06	90.06	63.70	109.13	43.87	46.26	55.68	30.30	57.22
11	12	13	14	15	16	17	18	19	20
292.03	262.20	52.69	221.00	252.51	207.94	237.10	246.23	230.53	285.70
38.26	101.88	82.20	133.83	115.62	144.43	79.34	76.93	93.32	56.65
21	22	23	24	25	26	27	28		
231.91	282.59	122.98	247.31	257.29	241.72	117.62	120.10		
93.14	73.09	111.06	58.15	108.88	63.21	107.36	111.14		

The format here is variable index (j), c_{ij}, σ_{ij}

UNSCALED VALUES

1	2	3	4	5	6	7	8	9	10
113.52	20.44	58.84	82.59	24.27	77.16	8.51	668.28	83.94	10.29
22.02	17.83	20.33	19.10	10.56	12.56	1.44	139.63	9.67	2.21
11	12	13	14	15	16	17	18	19	20
59.41	133.72	7.36	38.75	71.86	7.00	61.11	.74	4660.96	71.21
7.78	51.96	11.48	23.47	32.90	4.86	20.45	.23	1886.71	14.12
21	22	23	24	25	26	27	28		
1.11	35.91	23.50	87.59	97.95	63.74	15.93	17.21		
.44	9.29	21.22	20.60	41.45	16.67	14.54	15.93		

CLUSTER CENTER   2 WITH   17 PATTERNS AND RMS AVERAGE PATTERN DISTANCE = 679.86294

1	2	3	4	5	6	7	8	9	10
333.74	653.24	342.79	341.17	324.21	348.85	325.01	336.10	315.33	328.35
52.40	123.64	100.76	62.53	100.92	70.72	49.94	66.05	14.38	60.56
11	12	13	14	15	16	17	18	19	20
319.43	365.36	697.91	371.09	380.11	320.25	403.07	345.59	364.87	327.05
44.61	112.89	243.84	185.38	138.45	186.07	152.16	99.53	144.24	29.48
21	22	23	24	25	26	27	28		
349.10	338.87	689.40	384.96	372.74	393.16	716.55	698.00		
119.58	99.62	192.82	104.99	125.08	113.43	205.91	209.25		

UNSCALED VALUES

1	2	3	4	5	6	7	8	9	10
134.85	97.00	77.39	102.30	31.36	99.89	10.10	842.78	90.20	12.69
21.17	18.36	22.75	18.75	9.76	20.25	1.55	165.63	4.11	2.34
11	12	13	14	15	16	17	18	19	20
64.99	186.33	97.46	65.07	108.17	10.79	103.89	1.04	7377.17	81.52
9.08	57.58	34.05	32.51	39.40	6.27	39.22	.30	2916.24	7.35
21	22	23	24	25	26	27	28		
1.67	43.06	131.72	136.35	141.90	103.68	97.06	100.01		
.57	12.66	36.84	37.19	47.62	29.91	27.89	29.98		

CLUSTER CENTER   3 WITH   7 PATTERNS AND RMS AVERAGE PATTERN DISTANCE = 614.05779

1	2	3	4	5	6	7	8	9	10
314.92	1029.41	251.70	316.70	169.85	301.28	270.58	288.73	290.38	254.18
44.00	89.74	94.69	51.93	70.11	53.55	47.53	94.44	23.51	49.29
11	12	13	14	15	16	17	18	19	20
304.53	323.70	1685.89	225.15	325.41	93.78	297.88	241.22	287.00	278.58
36.46	83.75	301.01	138.25	99.06	70.34	105.82	82.14	183.41	44.49
21	22	23	24	25	26	27	28		
209.92	306.44	1021.21	312.12	324.65	313.39	973.05	1017.22		
81.32	70.60	186.58	80.02	91.25	86.81	185.07	210.13		

UNSCALED VALUES

1	2	3	4	5	6	7	8	9	10
127.25	152.86	59.09	94.96	16.43	86.27	8.41	724.01	83.06	9.83
17.78	13.32	21.38	15.57	6.78	15.33	1.48	236.82	6.72	1.91
11	12	13	14	15	16	17	18	19	20
61.96	165.09	235.43	39.48	92.60	3.16	76.78	.73	5802.69	69.44
7.42	42.71	42.04	24.24	28.19	2.37	27.28	.25	3708.24	11.09
21	22	23	24	25	26	27	28		
1.00	38.94	195.12	110.55	123.59	82.64	131.81	145.75		
.39	8.97	35.65	28.34	34.74	22.89	25.07	30.11		

CLUSTER CENTER   4 WITH   20 PATTERNS AND RMS AVERAGE PATTERN DISTANCE = 539.14292

1	2	3	4	5	6	7	8	9	10
318.84	119.54	375.57	324.32	445.29	336.63	358.13	358.49	314.90	378.18
41.95	113.87	122.14	48.40	87.40	35.56	29.41	71.51	18.14	39.95
11	12	13	14	15	16	17	18	19	20
309.69	331.08	43.03	453.40	339.73	571.96	364.53	412.68	415.59	326.56
20.15	93.06	56.70	234.86	107.93	226.72	78.21	67.11	153.78	36.73
21	22	23	24	25	26	27	28		
452.86	313.75	124.75	351.96	335.51	357.12	130.60	125.32		
96.88	41.43	119.34	67.37	100.31	74.02	126.29	120.00		

UNSCALED VALUES

1	2	3	4	5	6	7	8	9	10
128.83	17.75	84.79	97.25	43.07	96.39	11.13	898.94	90.07	14.62
16.95	16.91	27.58	14.51	8.45	10.18	.91	179.32	5.19	1.54
11	12	13	14	15	16	17	18	19	20
63.01	168.85	6.01	79.51	96.68	19.26	93.96	1.25	8407.54	81.40
4.10	47.46	7.92	41.18	30.71	7.64	20.16	.20	3109.23	9.15
21	22	23	24	25	26	27	28		
2.16	39.87	23.84	124.66	127.72	94.17	17.69	17.96		
.46	5.26	22.80	23.86	38.19	19.52	17.11	17.19		

```
CLUSTER   1 CONTAINS THE FOLLOWING PATTERNS..
    3    4    5    6   12   14   15   18   20   22   24   25   27   29   31   32
   33   36   37   38   42   45   46   48   49   50   53   58   59   60   61   62
   63   66   67   69   70   73   80   81   85   86   87   88   89

CLUSTER   2 CONTAINS THE FOLLOWING PATTERNS..
    7   11   19   21   23   28   30   35   39   40   47   54   64   76   78   82
   83

CLUSTER   3 CONTAINS THE FOLLOWING PATTERNS..
    8   10   16   34   43   74   75

CLUSTER   4 CONTAINS THE FOLLOWING PATTERNS..
    1    2    9   13   17   26   41   44   51   52   55   56   57   65   68   71
   72   77   79   84

CLUSTER MEMBERSHIP TABLE..
    4  4  1  1  1  1  2  3  4  3  2  1  4  1  1  3  4  1  2  1  2  1  2  1  1  4  1  2  1  2  1  1  1  3  2  1  1  1  2  2
    4  1  3  4  1  1  2  1  1  4  4  1  2  4  4  4  1  1  1  1  1  1  2  4  1  1  4  1  1  4  4  1  3  3  2  4  2  4  1
    1  2  2  4  1  1  1  1  1

SQUARED ERROR =    .260823E+08

RMS AVG DIST. OF PATTERNS FROM THEIR CENTERS = 541.34931

AVG. DIST. FROM EACH CLUSTER CENTER TO THE OTHER CLUSTER CENTERS
1492.551871331.661272066.366401512.90940

AVG. DIST. BETWEEN CLUSTER CENTERS =1600.87224


FOR EACH CLUSTER,(AVG. DIST. TO OTHER CENTERS)/AVG.    PATTERN DIST. WITHIN CLUSTER)
  3.20296   1.95872   3.36510   2.80614

FOR EACH CLUSTER,DIST. TO THE NEAREST CLUSTER CENTER.
669.188141258.037731258.03773 669.18814

FOR EACH CLUSTER,(DIST. TO NEAREST CENTER/(AVG. PATTERN DIST. WITHIN CLUSTER)
  1.43605   1.85043   2.04873   1.24121

OVERALL STANDARD DEVIATIONS
  50.73919 117.28417 100.48862  59.47208 100.34790  49.37642  43.93929  65.20537  24.92249  53.90508  36.27825 100.89575
 150.40913 171.80803 117.51369 170.58575  99.30078  80.17036 127.81544  47.40737  98.72819  73.30901 138.83784  73.06662
 109.07387  79.38479 142.14182 146.00754

EUCLIDEAN DISTANCES BETWEEN CLUSTER CENTERS
           1        2        3        4
  1      0.0   1387.5   2421.0    669.2
  2   1387.5      0.0   1258.0   1349.5
  3   2421.0   1258.0      0.0   2520.1
  4    669.2   1349.5   2520.1      0.0

DECREASE IN SQUARED ERROR IS LESS THAN CRITERION VALUE, PROGRAM TERMINATED.
```

For this run, the above clusters are 'optimal'.

ACKNOWLEDGMENTS

DJH would like to acknowledge the fortunate situations under which he has been able to develop this work.

First, the clients who paid directly for the major part of this work are the following agencies of the U. S. Government:

1. Satellite Applications Department
   Environmental Prediction Research Facility
   Naval Postgraduate School
   Monterey, California 93940

2. Aerospace Research Laboratories
   Air Force Systems Command
   United States Air Force
   Wright-Patterson Air Force Base, Ohio 45433

3. The GARP Project Office, Code 901
   Goddard Space Flight Center
   Greenbelt, Maryland 20771

4. Head, Information Systems Branch
   Mathematical Sciences
   Office of Naval Research
   Washington, D. C. 20360

5. U. S. Department of Commerce
   Bureau of the Census
   Suitland, Maryland 20233

6. Rome Air Development Center
   Griffiss Air Force Base, New York 13440

Second, the management and scientific stimulation at SRI are much to be appreciated, even amidst the occasional frustrations of managerial edict and the rivalry for the ownership of scientific territory and facilities.

Finally, without sharing purposeful contact in meaningful personal relationships, this work would be empty. DJH is especially indebted to Daniel Wolf who has worked at his side so frequently, and to Mildred Kelley, a precise and understanding secretary. Many others at SRI deserve acknowledgment in this category, but are too numerous to mention in detail.

9. REFERENCES

1. Bela Julez, "Cluster Formation at Various Perceptual Levels," *International Conference on Methodologies of Pattern Recognition*, Satosi Watanabe (ed.), Honolulu, Hawaii, January 1968, Academic Press, New York, 1969.

2. D. J. Hall et al., *Development of New Pattern Recognition Methods*, AD 772614, National Technical Information Services, Springfield, Va. 22151, November 1973.

3. D. J. Hall, B. Tepping, and G. H. Ball, "Theoretical and Experimental Clustering Characteristics for Multivariate Random Structured Data," in *Applications of Cluster Analysis to Bureau of the Census Data*, Final Report, Contract Cco-9312, SRI Project 7600, Stanford Research Institute, Menlo Park, Calif., 1970.

4. D. J. Hall, F. K. Tomlin, and D. E. Wolf, *Objective Methods for Determining Cloud Motions from Satellite Data*, SRI Project 1005, Final Report, November 1973.

5. F. Perls, *Gestalt Therapy Verbation*, Real People Press, Lafayette, Calif., 1969.

6. D. J. Hall et al., "PROMENADE—An Interactive Graphics Pattern-Recognition System," *Proc. of the IFIP Congress 68*, pp. 951–956, August 1968. Also *IFIP Congress 68, Final Supplement*, Booklet J. pp. J46–J50, August 1968.

7. D. J. Hall, G. H. Ball, and D. E. Wolf, "Interactive Graphic Clustering Using the PROMENADE System," *Proc. of the 1969 Social Statistics Section*, American Statistical Association, pp. 65–73, 1969.

8. G. H. Ball and D. J. Hall, "ISODATA—A Self-Organizing Computer Program for the Design of Pattern Recognition Preprocessing," *Proc. IFIP Congress 65*, Vol. 2, pp. 329–330, May 1965.

PART **V** | TIME SERIES

The Fast Fourier Transform and its Application to Time Series Analysis

14

J. W. Cooley
IBM Thomas J. Watson Research Center

P. A. W. Lewis
U.S. Naval Postgraduate School (Monterey)

P. D. Welch
IBM Thomas J. Watson Research Center

1. FUNCTION

Let $x(j) : j = 0, 1, \ldots, N - 1$ be a finite sequence of complex numbers. We will discuss the fast Fourier transform (FFT) algorithm, a highly efficient method for calculating the discrete Fourier transform (DFT) of $x(j)$. Specifically the algorithm computes the transform

$$a(n) = \sum_{j=0}^{N-1} x(j)e^{-2\pi inj/N}$$

$$(n = 0, 1, \ldots, N - 1) \quad (1)$$

where $i = (-1)^{\frac{1}{2}}$, and the inverse transform

$$x(j) = \frac{1}{N} \sum_{n=0}^{N-1} a(n)e^{2\pi inj/N}$$

$$(j = 0, 1, \ldots, N - 1) \quad (2)$$

We will also discuss the application of this algorithm to the calculation of sample covariance and cross-covariance functions, to the estimation of variance spectra and cross-spectra, and, very briefly, to the implementation of moving average digital filters.

2. MATHEMATICAL DISCUSSION

a. Symbols Used

Table 1 lists symbols and their definitions. This is not a complete list. Those not included are defined and used in local regions of the text.

Table 1. SYMBOLS USED

Symbol	Explanation
$a(n), b(n), c(n)$	Sequences of complex numbers which are functions of a discrete frequency index
$a_e(n), b_e(n)$	The DFT's of time sequences $x_e(j)$ and $y_e(j)$, respectively, which time sequences have been extended by appending zeros
$\tilde{a}(n), \tilde{b}(n), \tilde{c}(n)$	Sequences of the complex conjugates of the corresponding sequences $a(n), b(n),$ and $c(n)$
DFT	Discrete Fourier transform
$E\{\ \}$	The expected value of the random variable within the brackets
FFT	Fast Fourier transform: the name of an efficient algorithm for computing the discrete Fourier transform
$\hat{\gamma}_{xx}(k), \hat{\hat{\gamma}}_{xx}(k), \bar{\gamma}_{xx}(k)$	Sample covariance functions corresponding to the estimators $\hat{\gamma}_{XX}(k), \hat{\hat{\gamma}}_{XX}(k),$ and $\bar{\gamma}_{XX}$, respectively
$\gamma_{XX}(k)$	The covariance function of a stationary stochastic sequence $X(j)$
$\hat{\gamma}_{XX}(k), \hat{\hat{\gamma}}_{XX}(k), \bar{\gamma}_{XX}(k)$	Estimators of the covariance function, $\gamma_{XX}(k)$. For fixed k, these are random variables.
$\hat{\gamma}_{xy}(k), \bar{\gamma}_{xy}(k)$	Sample cross-covariance functions corresponding to the estimators $\hat{\gamma}_{XY}(k)$ and $\bar{\gamma}_{XY}(k)$
$\gamma_{XY}(k)$	The cross-covariance function of two stationary stochastic sequences $X(j)$ and $Y(j)$
$\hat{\gamma}_{XY}(k), \bar{\gamma}_{XY}(k)$	Estimators of the cross-covariance function $\gamma_{XY}(k)$
$h(\omega)$	The spectral window associated with a spectral estimation procedure
$h_M(\omega)$	The basic periodogram spectral window
$h_M^*(\omega)$	The basic modified periodogram spectral window
i	$(-1)^{\frac{1}{2}}$
IDFT	Inverse discrete Fourier transform.
$I_{xx}(\omega)$	The sample periodogram corresponding to $I_{XX}(\omega)$
$I_{xx}^*(\omega)$	The sample modified periodogram corresponding to $I_{XX}^*(\omega)$
$I_{XX}(\omega)$	The periodogram of a stationary stochastic sequence $X(j)$. For fixed ω, this is a random variable.
$I_{XX}^*(\omega)$	The modified periodogram of a stationary stochastic sequence $X(j)$. For fixed ω, this is a random variable.
$I_{xy}(\omega)$	The sample cross-periodogram corresponding to $I_{XY}(\omega)$
$I_{xy}^*(\omega)$	The sample modified cross-periodogram corresponding to $I_{XY}^*(\omega)$

Table 1. SYMBOLS USED

Symbol	Explanation
$I_{XY}(\omega)$	The cross-periodogram of two stationary stochastic sequences, $X(j)$ and $Y(j)$. For fixed ω, this is a random variable.
$I_{XY}^*(\omega)$	The modified cross periodogram of two stationary stochastic sequences $X(j)$ and $Y(j)$. For fixed ω, this is a random variable.
j	The index of the "time" sequences $x(\ ), y(\ )$, and $z(\ )$
k	The index for the covariance and cross-covariance sequences
l	The index for the factors r_l, $(l = 1, 2, \ldots, m)$ of N
L	An integer denoting the length of a sequence
m	The number of factors of N, where N is the length of a sequence whose DFT or IDFT is to be computed.
M	An integer denoting the length of a sequence.
n	The index of the "frequency" sequences $a(\ )$, $b(\ )$, and $c(\ )$
N	An integer denoting the length of a sequence whose DFT or IDFT is to be computed
$p(\omega)$	The power spectrum associated with a stationary stochastic sequence
$\hat{p}(\omega)$	An estimator of the power spectrum, $p(\omega)$
$p_{XY}(\omega)$	The cross-power spectrum for two stationary stochastic sequences $X(j)$ and $Y(j)$
$\hat{p}_{XY}(\omega)$	An estimate of the cross-power spectrum $p_{XY}(\omega)$
r	The multiple factor of N when N is a power, i.e., $N = r^m$; the radix of the FFT algorithm
$r_1, \ldots, r_m$	The factors of N, i.e., $N = r_1 \ldots r_m$; the radices of the mixed radix FFT algorithm
$VAR\{\ \ \}$	The variance of the random variable within the brackets.
W_N	The principal Nth root of unity, i.e., $W_N = e^{2\pi i/N} = \exp(2\pi i/N)$
$x(j), y(j), z(j)$	Sequences of complex numbers which are functions of a discrete time index
$x_e(j), y_e(j), z_e(j)$	Extended sequences obtained by appending zeros to the original $x(j)$, $y(j)$, and $z(j)$ sequences, respectively
$X(j), Y(j), Z(j)$	Sequences of random variables
$\leftrightarrow$	The notation $x(j) \leftrightarrow a(n)$ for $n, j = 0, 1, \ldots, N - 1$ indicates that $a(n)$ is the N-point DFT of $x(j)$; i.e., that $x(j)$ and $a(n)$ are a DFT pair.

b. The Theory of the Discrete Fourier Transform

INTRODUCTION

In mathematical analysis and in scientific theory it is natural, or perhaps conventional, to think in terms of functions defined on variables taking values in a continuum. The continuum is usually infinite or doubly infinite in extent and the variable is often time. However, in numerical mathematics or data analysis, we usually deal with ordered sets of numbers—functions of a discrete variable—known as sequences. Moreover, these sets or sequences are finite in extent. The discreteness and finiteness are imposed by practical computing considerations, and by practical limitations on the duration and frequency of experimental observation.

Given that we have to operate on such sequences, say $x(j)$ for $j = 0, 1, \ldots, N - 1$, it is natural to develop a spectral theory for them, that is, to define a particular orthogonal transformation which takes the sequence $x(j)$ into another sequence of the same length, say $a(n)$, which describes the *frequency* structure of $x(j)$. This transformation, called the discrete (finite) Fourier transform or DFT and its properties are the subject of this section. Understanding of and facility with the DFT and its properties are essential for the proper application of Fourier theory to discrete sequences.

Specific references for the theory of the discrete Fourier transform do not appear to be available. This is probably because the theory can be subsumed, as we will discuss later, under the theory of Fourier series or Fourier–Stieltjes transforms. References on Fourier series are legion; see, for instance, Tolstov [37], Zygmund [45], and Jackson [20].

DEFINITION OF THE DISCRETE FOURIER TRANSFORM

Let $x(j)$, $j = 0, 1, \ldots, N - 1$, be a sequence of N complex numbers. The discrete Fourier transform or DFT of $x(j)$ is defined as

$$a(n) = \sum_{j=0}^{N-1} x(j) W_N^{-nj},$$

$$(n = 0, 1, \ldots, N - 1) \qquad (3)$$

where, here and in what follows, $W_N = \exp(2\pi i / N)$ with $i = \sqrt{-1}$. Similarly,

$$x(j) = \frac{1}{N} \sum_{n=0}^{N-1} a(n) W_N^{nj},$$

$$(j = 0, 1, \ldots, N - 1) \qquad (4)$$

The sequence $x(j)$ is called the inverse discrete Fourier transform (IDFT) of $a(n)$. That (3) and (4) are a transform pair, that is, that substituting $a(n)$ from (3) into (4) gives back $x(j)$, comes from the following orthogonality relationships of the exponential function W_N^{nj}:

$$\sum_{j=0}^{N-1} W_N^{nj} W_N^{-mj} = \begin{cases} N & \text{if } n \equiv m \pmod{N} \\ 0 & \text{otherwise} \end{cases} \qquad (5)$$

The exponential function W_N^{nj}, as a function of n and j, is periodic of period N; that is, $W_N^{nj} = W_N^{(n+N)j} = W_N^{n(j+N)}$. A direct consequence of this is that the sequences $a(n)$ and $x(j)$, as defined by their transforms, Eqs. (3) and (4), are periodic of period N. From here on we will consider $a(n)$ and $x(j)$ to be defined by (3) and (4) for all integers. Thus we have $x(j)$ $j = 0, \pm 1, \pm 2, \ldots$; $a(n)$ $n = 0, \pm 1, \pm 2, \ldots$ with

$$x(j) = x(kN + j), \quad k = 0, \pm 1, \pm 2, \ldots$$

$$a(n) = a(kN + n), \quad k = 0, \pm 1, \pm 2, \ldots$$

$$(6)$$

Another viewpoint is to consider $x(j)$ and $a(n)$ to be defined circularly on integer points of a circle with circumference N. However, the periodic extension (6) of the finite sequences to infinite sequences is more convenient. It simplifies the proofs of the properties of the discrete Fourier transform and makes the results easier to visualize. The finite sequences can always be recovered by considering the values of the infinite sequences at any N consecutive points, in particular the N points $0, 1, \ldots, N - 1$.

Following directly from (6) as special cases are two relationships we will use extensively, namely,

$$x(-j) = x(N - j)$$

$$a(-n) = a(N - n) \qquad (7)$$

The following convention will also be used extensively. By a double-headed arrow connecting two sequences, that is, by $x(j) \leftrightarrow a(n)$, we indicate that the two sequences are a discrete Fourier pair.

ELEMENTARY PROPERTIES OF THE DISCRETE FOURIER TRANSFORM

We now give, without proof, some elementary properties of the DFT. The proofs are simple and can be provided by the reader. A fundamental property of the DFT is that it is a linear operation. This is expressed by

THEOREM 1: The DFT is linear; that is, if

$$x_1(j) \leftrightarrow a_1(n)$$

and

$$x_2(j) \leftrightarrow a_2(n)$$

then for any complex constants c and d,

$$cx_1(j) + dx_2(j) \leftrightarrow ca_1(n) + da_2(n)$$

We next establish some results on the relationship between the DFT of the sequence and the DFT of another sequence obtained from the first by reversing the order of its elements.

THEOREM 2: If

$$x(j) \leftrightarrow a(n)$$

then

$$x(-j) \leftrightarrow a(-n)$$

A sequence $x(j)$ is said to be *even* if $x(j) = x(-j)$. A sequence $x(j)$ is said to be *odd* if $x(j) = -x(-j)$. These definitions form the basis for

COROLLARY 2.1: $x(j)$ is even if and only if $a(n)$ is even. $x(j)$ is odd if and only if $a(n)$ is odd.

The sequences $x(j)$ and $a(n)$ are periodic of period N. Now if $x(j)$ is even and periodic of period N, then $x(j) = x(-j) = x(N - j)$. If $x(j)$ is odd and periodic of period N, then $x(j) = -x(-j) = -x(N - j)$. Hence, over the interval $[0, N - 1]$ the evenness and oddness of sequences such as $x(n)$ and $a(n)$ show up in relationships of symmetries between the values of the sequences at j and $N - j$.

We now consider the relationship between the DFT of a sequence $x(j)$ and the DFT of its term-by-term complex conjugate. We denote by $\tilde{x}(j)$ the complex conjugate of $x(j)$.

THEOREM 3: If

$$x(j) \leftrightarrow a(n)$$

then

$$\tilde{x}(-j) \leftrightarrow \tilde{a}(n)$$

and

$$\tilde{x}(j) \leftrightarrow \tilde{a}(-n)$$

COROLLARY 3.1:
  (i) $x(j)$ is real if and only if $a(n) = \tilde{a}(-n)(= \tilde{a}(N - n))$.
  (ii) $a(n)$ is real if and only if $x(j) = \tilde{x}(-j)(= \tilde{x}(N - j))$.
  (iii) $x(j)$ is pure imaginary if and only if $a(n) = -\tilde{a}(-n)(= -\tilde{a}(N - n))$.
  (iv) $a(n)$ is pure imaginary if and only if $x(j) = -\tilde{x}(-j)(= -\tilde{x}(N - j))$.

The following theorem describes the behavior of the Fourier pair when one of the sequences is shifted along its j (time) axis or n (frequency) axis.

THEOREM 4: If

$$x(j) \leftrightarrow a(n)$$

then

$$x(j - k) \leftrightarrow W_N^{-nk}a(n) \qquad (8)$$

and

$$W_N^{mj}x(j) \leftrightarrow a(n - m) \qquad (9)$$

Note that shifting the sequence $x(j)$ along its time axis changes the phase but not the amplitudes of the components of the sequence $a(n)$.

We define the sequence $\delta(n)$ by

$$\begin{aligned} \delta(j) &= 1 \quad \text{if } j \equiv 0(\text{mod } N) \\ \delta(j) &= 0 \quad \text{otherwise} \end{aligned} \qquad (10)$$

Then we have

THEOREM 5:

$$\delta(j) \leftrightarrow 1$$

$$1 \leftrightarrow N\delta(n)$$

This theorem is very useful. For example, suppose we have the transform of $x(j)$ and wish the transform of $x(j) - b$; that is, we wish to move all the values of $x(j)$ up or down. Then if $x(j) \leftrightarrow a(n)$, $x(j) - b \leftrightarrow a(n) - bN \delta(n)$. Now $a(n) - bN \delta(n)$ is just $a(n)$ with $a(0)$ replaced by $a(0) - bN$. Hence, subtracting a constant from all the values of $x(j)$ is equivalent, in the frequency domain, to subtracting a modified constant from $a(0)$. (The physical interpretation is that adding a dc component to $x(j)$ affects only the zero frequency component of $a(n)$.)

Finally we have

THEOREM 6: If

$$x(j) \leftrightarrow a(n)$$

then

$$x(0) = \frac{1}{N} \sum_{n=0}^{N-1} a(n) \qquad (11)$$

and

$$a(0) = \sum_{j=0}^{N-1} x(j) \qquad (12)$$

This result is useful in statistical applications. If $x(j)$ is a set of observations of a random variable, then $a(0)/N$ is the sample mean.

CONVOLUTIONS AND TERM-BY-TERM PRODUCTS OF SEQUENCES

Next we will treat the subject of the transform of the term-by-term product of two sequences. Let $x_1(j)$ and $x_2(j)$ be two sequences with DFT's $a_1(n)$ and $a_2(n)$, respectively. The term-by-term product of the sequences $a_1(n)$ and $a_2(n)$ is the sequence whose nth term is $a_1(n)a_2(n)$. The inverse transform of this product sequence turns out to be a *convolution* of the sequences $x_1(j)$ and $x_2(j)$ as in the usual Fourier analysis; however, as we will see, the convolution is cyclic. Similarly, the transform of the product sequence $x_1(j)x_2(j)$ is the convolution of $a_1(n)$ and $a_2(n)$. To be explicit, we have

THEOREM 7: If

$$x_1(j) \leftrightarrow a_1(n)$$

and

$$x_2(j) \leftrightarrow a_2(n)$$

then

$$\sum_{k=0}^{N-1} x_1(k)x_2(j - k)$$

$$= \sum_{k=0}^{N-1} x_1(j - k)x_2(k) \leftrightarrow a_1(n)a_2(n) \qquad (13)$$

and

$$x_1(j)x_2(j) \leftrightarrow \frac{1}{N} \sum_{m=0}^{N-1} a_1(m)a_2(n - m)$$

$$= \frac{1}{N} \sum_{m=0}^{N-1} a_1(n - m)a_2(m) \qquad (14)$$

Proof: By direct substitution from (4)

$$\sum_{k=0}^{N-1} x_1(k)x_2(j-k)$$

$$= \sum_{k=0}^{N-1} \left\{ \frac{1}{N} \sum_{n=0}^{N-1} a_1(n) W_N^{nk} \right\}$$

$$\times \left\{ \frac{1}{N} \sum_{m=0}^{N-1} a_2(m) W_N^{m(j-k)} \right\}$$

$$= \frac{1}{N^2} \sum_{n=0}^{N-1} \sum_{m=0}^{N-1} a_1(n)a_2(m) W_N^{mj}$$

$$\times \left\{ \sum_{k=0}^{N-1} W_N^{k(n-m)} \right\}$$

Now using the orthogonality relationships (5), the sum in the brackets is nonzero, and equal to N if and only if $n = m$. Thus

$$\sum_{k=0}^{N-1} x_1(k)x_2(j-k) = \frac{1}{N} \sum_{n=0}^{N-1} a_1(n)a_2(n) W_N^{nj}$$

The other half of the theorem is proved similarly.   Q.E.D.

It is important to note that the convolutions defined in (13) and (14) are cyclic; that is, when the one sequence moves over the end of the other, it does not encounter zeros, but rather the periodic extension of the sequence. This is consistent with the periodic extension property of the discrete Fourier transform which was noted earlier. If viewed in terms of a sequence defined only for the values $0, 1, \ldots, N - 1$, the convolution is said to "wrap around."

Now consider the operation of forming the lagged product of two sequences. To get the lagged product of two sequences, we multiply one transform by the transform of the other with a negative argument. This is made explicit in the following:

COROLLARY 7.1: If

$$x_1(j) \leftrightarrow a_1(n)$$

and

$$x_2(j) \leftrightarrow a_2(n)$$

then

$$\sum_{k=0}^{N-1} x_1(k+j)x_2(k)$$

$$= \sum_{k=0}^{N-1} x_1(k)x_2(k-j) \leftrightarrow a_1(n)a_2(-n)$$

$$\tag{15}$$

$$\sum_{k=0}^{N-1} x_1(k)x_2(k+j)$$

$$= \sum_{k=0}^{N-1} x_1(k-j)x_2(k) \leftrightarrow a_1(-n)a_2(n)$$

$$\tag{16}$$

$$x_1(j)x_2(-j) \leftrightarrow \frac{1}{N} \sum_{m=0}^{N-1} a_1(m+n)a_2(m)$$

$$= \frac{1}{N} \sum_{m=0}^{N-1} a_1(m)a_2(m-n)$$

$$\tag{17}$$

and

$$x_1(-j)x_2(j) \leftrightarrow \sum_{m=0}^{N-1} a_1(m)a_2(m+n)$$

$$= \frac{1}{N} \sum_{m=0}^{N-1} a_1(m-n)a_2(m)$$

$$\tag{18}$$

Proof: The corollary follows directly from Theorems 7 and 2, since the lagged product of $x_1(j)$ and $x_2(j)$ is just the convolution of $x_1(j)$, and the reverse of $x_2(j)$, namely, $x_2(-j)$.   Q.E.D.

Although the proof of the corollary makes the relationship between the lagged product and convolution operations evident, there are essential differences. In particular, the lagged product operation is *not* commutative.

With regard to the application of Corollary 7.1, it should be kept in mind that, in general, $a(-n) = a(N - n)$, therefore values of $a(n)$ for negative n are directly available from values of $a(n)$ for $n = 0, 1, \ldots, N - 1$. Further if $x(j)$ is real, $a(-n) = a(N - n) = \tilde{a}(n)$.

The very important Parseval's theorem can be obtained from the preceding results.

COROLLARY 7.2 (Parseval's Theorem): If

$$x(j) \leftrightarrow a(n)$$

then

$$\sum_{j=0}^{N-1} |x(j)|^2 = \frac{1}{N} \sum_{n=0}^{N-1} |a(n)|^2 \quad (19)$$

Proof: Let

$$x_1(j) = x(j)$$
$$x_2(j) = \tilde{x}(j)$$

Then from Eq. (15) of Corollary 7.1, and the second part of Theorem 3, we have

$$\sum_{k=0}^{N-1} x(k + j)\tilde{x}(k) = \frac{1}{N} \sum_{n=0}^{N-1} a(n)\tilde{a}(n) W^{nj}$$

The corollary follows by setting $j = 0$. Q.E.D.

TRANSFORMS OF STRETCHED AND SAMPLED FUNCTIONS

We will now derive two theorems which we will use subsequently in an elementary derivation of the FFT algorithm. Given a sequence $x(j) : j = 0, 1, \ldots, N - 1$, we define the sequence $\text{Stretch}_K\{j : x\}$ for any positive integer K to be $x(j)$ stretched by a factor K with zeros filling in the gaps; that is

$$\text{Stretch}_K\{j : x\} = x(j/K) \text{ for } j = lK$$
$$l = 0, \ldots, N-1$$
$$= 0 \qquad \text{otherwise}$$

For $N = 3$ and $K = 2$, the definition is illustrated in Fig. 14.1. Note that $\text{Stretch}_K\{j : x\}$ is periodic with period NK.

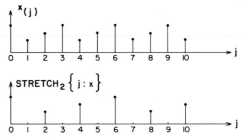

Fig. 14.1. The stretch function illustrated for $K = 2$ on a sequence $x(j)$ of length $N = 3$.

We now prove

THEOREM 8: If

$$x(j) \leftrightarrow a(n), \quad n = 0, 1, \ldots, N - 1;$$
$$j = 0, 1, \ldots, N - 1$$

then

$$\text{Stretch}_K\{j : x\} \leftrightarrow a(n),$$
$$n = 0, 1, \ldots, NK - 1 \quad (20)$$

and

$$x(j)/K \leftrightarrow \text{Stretch}_K\{n : a\},$$
$$j = 0, 1, \ldots, NK - 1 \quad (21)$$

Proof:

$$\sum_{j=0}^{KN-1} \text{Stretch}_K\{j : x\} W_{KN}^{-nj}$$

$$= \sum_{j'=0}^{N-1} x(j') W_{KN}^{-Kj'n}$$

where $j' = j/K$. Since $W_{KN}^K = W_N$ this becomes

$$\sum_{j'=0}^{N-1} x(j') W_N^{-nj'} = a(n)$$

The other half of the theorem is proved similarly.   Q.E.D.

Thus any sequence which is nonzero only at multiples of an integer K has a transform which is periodic with a period $1/K$ times the length of the sequence. Conversely, any sequence with a period N/K has a transform which has only N/K equally spaced nonzero values.

Given a sequence $x(j)$, $j = 0, 1, \ldots, N - 1$, and a positive integer K which divides N, we define the sequence

$$\text{Sample}_K\{j : x\} \quad j = 0,., \ldots, \frac{N}{K} - 1$$

by

$$\text{Sample}_K\{j : x\} = x(jK)$$

This sequence, $\text{Sample}_K\{j : x\}$, of period N/K, is initially defined for $j = 0, 1, \ldots, N/K - 1$, but extended to all integers in a periodic fashion.

THEOREM 9: If

$$x(j) \leftrightarrow a(n)$$

then

$$\text{Sample}_K\{j : x\} \leftrightarrow \frac{1}{K} \sum_{m=0}^{K-1} a\left(n + \frac{mN}{K}\right)$$

$$j, n = 0, 1, \ldots, \frac{N}{K} - 1 \quad (22)$$

and

$$\sum_{k=0}^{K-1} x\left(j + \frac{kN}{K}\right) \leftrightarrow \text{Sample}_K\{n : a\}$$

$$j, n = 0, 1, \ldots, \frac{N}{K} - 1 \quad (23)$$

Proof:

$$\text{Sample}_K\{j:x\} = x(jK) = \frac{1}{N} \sum_{n=0}^{N-1} a(n) W_N^{jnK}$$

$$= \frac{1}{N} \sum_{n=0}^{N-1} a(n) W_{N/K}^{nj}$$

However, $W_{N/K}^{nj}$ is periodic of period N/K;

hence, letting $n = n' + mN/K$,

$$\text{Sample}_k\{j : x\}$$

$$= \frac{K}{N} \sum_{n'=0}^{\frac{N}{K}-1} \left\{ \frac{1}{K} \sum_{m=0}^{K-1} a\left(n' + \frac{mN}{K}\right) \right\} W_{N/K}^{n'j}$$

The other half of the theorem is established similarly.   Q.E.D.

Note that Theorem 9 says that we can obtain the transform of a sampling of a sequence $x(j)$ at a sampling period which divides the period of $x(j)$ by simply overlapping and summing the transform of $x(j)$. This overlapped and summed version of $a(n)$ is called an "aliased" version of $a(n)$.

FOURIER THEORY AND THE DISCRETE FOURIER TRANSFORM

In our earlier development of the discrete Fourier transform we started with a finite sequence $x(j)$ and defined a Fourier relationship between it and another finite sequence $a(n)$. We will now show how this relationship is connected with and can be developed from the usual Fourier theory.

Suppose we have a periodic function $\alpha(f)$ with a period 1. Given certain conditions on the function $\alpha(f)$, it has a Fourier series expansion

$$\alpha(f) = \sum_{j=-\infty}^{\infty} x(j) e^{-2\pi i j f}, \quad 0 \leq f \leq 1$$

$$(24)$$

where the $x(j)$'s, the Fourier coefficients of $\alpha(f)$, are given by

$$x(j) = \int_0^1 \alpha(f) e^{2\pi i j f} \, df,$$

$$j = 0, \pm 1, \pm 2, \ldots \quad (25)$$

Conditions for the existence and convergence of such an expansion for a function $\alpha(f)$ are given in Tolstov [37] and in the many other texts on Fourier series. We do not give details here.

Now consider the following example. Let the $x(j)$ sequence be finite and complex valued, with value zero outside the range $j = 0, 1, \ldots, N - 1$. Then $\alpha(f)$ as defined by (24) is a continuous, periodic function of f. Moreover, Eq. (24) substituted back into (25) gives back the sequence $x(j)$, so that $x(j)$ and $\alpha(f)$ are a Fourier transform pair. It might be thought that "all" frequencies between 0 and 1 are needed to represent the "discontinuous" sequence $x(j)$, that is, the sequence that drops off abruptly to the constant value zero, although we will see later that $\alpha(f)$ is determined by any N of its values.

Suppose now that the sequence $x(j)$, instead of being zero outside of the range $j = 0, 1, \ldots, N - 1$, is repeated periodically outside of $j = 0, 1, \ldots, N - 1$. As we saw earlier, this is the situation induced by the definition of the discrete Fourier transform and the circular property of the exponential function W_N^{jn}. The periodic, infinite sequence $x(j)$ is neither absolutely summable (except in trivial cases), nor square summable, and it is not surprising that $\alpha(f)$ does not exist. Therefore, the Fourier theory of (24) and (25) does not encompass the theory given in this chapter.

However, consider a function $\mathcal{Q}(f)$ defined by the Stieltjes integral [14, p. 180], [42, p. 3]:

$$x(j) = \lim_{\Delta t \to 0} \int_{-\Delta t}^{1 - \Delta t} e^{-2\pi i j f} \, d\mathcal{Q}(f),$$

$$j = 0, \pm 1, \pm 2, \ldots \quad (26)$$

We call $\mathcal{Q}(f)$, if it exists, the finite Fourier–Stieltjes transform of the sequence $x(j)$. If $\mathcal{Q}(f)$ is differentiable with a derivative $\alpha(f)$, then (26) reduces to (25) and the inversion formula (24) holds. If, in (24) $f = f_n = n/N$ and $x(j)$, for $j < 0$ and $j \geq N$ are neglected, then (24) takes the form of the DFT

$$\alpha\left(\frac{n}{N}\right) = a(n) = \sum_{j=0}^{N-1} x(j) e^{-2\pi i j n/N} \quad (27)$$

If $\mathcal{Q}(f)$ is a jump function with step of height $a(n)/N$ at the points $f = f_n = n/N$, then the Stieltjes integral (26) reduces to

$$x(j) = \frac{1}{N} \sum_{j=0}^{N-1} a(n) e^{2\pi i j n/N} \quad (28)$$

The pair (27) and (28) is just the discrete Fourier transform pair (3) and (4), so that the DFT is in theory a special case of the finite Fourier–Stieltjes transform.

Finally, in certain contexts it is convenient to think of the sequence $a(n)$ in (1) as a sampling of a periodic function of the continuous variable f. By extension of the definition (1),

$$\alpha(f) = \sum_{j=0}^{N-1} x(j) e^{-2\pi i j f} \quad (29)$$

Then $\alpha(f)$ is periodic with period 1 and

$$a(n) = \alpha(f_n), \quad n = 0, 1, \ldots, N - 1$$

where $f_n = n/N$. As noted above, Eq. (24), the function $\alpha(f)$ is actually the finite continuous Fourier transform of the doubly infinite sequence with value $x(j)$ for $j = 0, 1, \ldots, N - 1$, and with value zero everywhere else.

The function, $\alpha(f)$, of the continuous variable f is a function of the N values $\alpha(f_n) = a(n)$. This function is obtained by substituting the expression for $x(j)$ given by (4) into the definition (29). This yields

$$\alpha(f) = \frac{1}{N} \sum_{n=0}^{N-1} a(n) \sum_{j=0}^{N-1} e^{2\pi i j (n/N - f)}$$

$$= \frac{1}{N} \sum_{n=0}^{N-1} a(n) \frac{1 - e^{2\pi i (n - Nf)}}{1 - e^{2\pi i (n/N - f)}} \quad (30)$$

c. The FFT Algorithm: Elementary Derivation and History

THE FAST FOURIER TRANSFORM ALGORITHM

The properties of the DFT developed in Section 2b will be used repeatedly in the remainder of this chapter. We use them now, however, to give an elementary derivation of the FFT algorithm. This elementary derivation reveals the essential idea behind the algorithm. A detailed derivation is given in the next section.

Suppose that we have a sequence $x(j)$ $j = 0, 1, \ldots, N - 1$, and that we wish to compute its DFT. A direct application of the formula

$$a(n) = \sum_{j=0}^{N-1} x(j) W_N^{-nj},$$

$$n = 0, 1, \ldots, N - 1 \quad (31)$$

would require N^2 operations where by an operation we mean a (complex) multiplication and addition. However, if N is the product of two integers r_1 and r_2, there is a circuitous way of calculating $a(n)$ which requires substantially fewer operations.

Let $x_k(j')$ for $k = 0, \ldots, r_1 - 1$ be the sequences r_2 units long defined by:

$$x_k(j') = x(j'r_1 + k) \quad j' = 0, \ldots, r_2 - 1$$
$$k = 0, \ldots, r_1 - 1$$
$$(32)$$

Note that if $x(j)$ is written in a left to right, top to bottom fashion as a two-dimensional array of r_2 rows and r_1 columns then $x_k(j')$ is the kth column. Now with this decomposition of $x(j)$ we have

$$a(n) = \sum_{j=0}^{N-1} x(j) W_N^{-jn}$$

$$= \sum_{k=0}^{r_1-1} \sum_{j'=0}^{r_2-1} x(j'r_1 + k) W_N^{-(j'r_1+k)n}$$

$$= \sum_{k=0}^{r_1-1} \sum_{j'=0}^{r_2-1} x(j'r_1 + k) W_N^{-j'r_1 n} W_N^{-kn}$$

$$= \sum_{k=0}^{r_1-1} \left\{ \sum_{j'=0}^{r_2-1} x(j'r_1 + k) W_{r_2}^{-j'n} \right\} W_N^{-kn}$$

$$= \sum_{k=0}^{r_1-1} a_k(n) W_N^{-kn} \quad (33)$$

where

$$a_k(n) = \sum_{j'=0}^{r_2-1} x(j'r_1 + k) W_{r_2}^{-j'n}$$

Now the sequence $a_k(n)$ $n = 0, 1, \ldots, N - 1$ is the DFT of the sequence $x_k(j')$, $j' = 0, 1, \ldots, r_2 - 1$ and hence is periodic of period r_2. Hence $a_k(n)$ only needs to be calculated for the r_2 values $n = 0, 1, \ldots, r_2 - 1$. Thus the calculation of each $a_k(n)$ requires r_2^2 operations and there are r_1 of them. Hence, altogether, the calculation of the $a_k(n)$ takes Nr_2 operations. The calculation of $a(n)$ from (33) for each of the N values of n takes r_1 operations, and therefore, for all n takes Nr_1 operations, yielding a total of $N(r_1 + r_2)$ operations in all. Finally, $N(r_1 + r_2) \leqslant N^2 = N(r_1 r_2)$ and we see that this circuitous method of calculating $a(n)$ is more economical. This procedure repeated on r_1 and r_2 until all factors are reached is the FFT algorithm. If $N = \prod_{l=1}^{m} r_l$ then the algorithm requires $N \left(\sum_{l=1}^{m} r_l \right)$ rather than $N^2 = N \left(\prod_{l=1}^{m} r_l \right)$ operations. If $N = 2^m$, the number of operations is Nm or $N \log_2 N$ and the savings are proportional to $N / \log_2 N$. The algorithm will be discussed in detail in the next section.

As a way of visualizing the decomposition that generates Eq. (33), if we define $x_k(j')$ as per Eq. (32) then we can write

$$x(j) = \sum_{k=0}^{r_1-1} \text{Stretch}_{r_1}(j - k; x_k) \quad (34)$$

This decomposition of $x(j)$ is illustrated in Fig. 14.2. Then since $a_k(n)$ is the discrete Fourier transform of $x_k(j)$ we get Eq. (33) by applying Theorems 1, 4, and 8 of Section 2b.

HISTORICAL REMARKS

The FFT algorithm has a fascinating history. When it was described by Cooley and Tukey [8] in 1965, it was regarded as new by

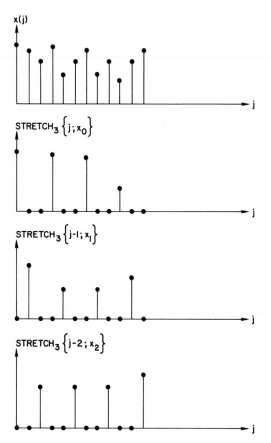

Fig. 14.2. The decomposition, for $N = 12$, $r_1 = 3$, and $r_2 = 4$, of $x(j)$ in subsequences for the application of the *FFT* algorithm.

the use of the method in X-ray scattering problems, an area where, for many years after 1942, the calculation of Fourier transforms presented a formidable bottleneck to researchers who were unaware of this efficient method. Danielson and Lanczos refer to Runge [29, 30] for the source of their method. These papers and the lecture notes of Runge and König [31] describe the procedure in terms of sine–cosine series. The greatest emphasis, however, is on the computational economy that could be derived from the symmetries of the sine and cosine functions. In a relatively short section of Runge and König [31], it is shown how one can use the periodicity of the sine–cosine functions to obtain a $2N$-point Fourier analysis from two N-point analyses with only slightly more than N operations. Going the other way, if the series to be transformed is of length N and N is a power of 2, the series can be split into $\log_2 N$ subseries and this doubling algorithm can be applied to compute the finite Fourier transform in $\log_2 N$ doublings. The number of computations in the resulting algorithm is, therefore, proportional to $N \log_2 N$ rather than N^2. The use of symmetries only reduces the proportionality factor while the successive doubling algorithm replaces N^2 by $N \log_2 N$. This distinction was not important for the values of N used at the time of the Runge and König publications. However, when the advent of computing machinery made calculations with large N possible, and the $N \log_2 N$ methods should have been thoroughly exploited, they were apparently overlooked, even though they had been published by well-read and well-referenced authors.

The fast Fourier transform algorithm of Cooley and Tukey [8] is more general than the Runge and König method in that it is applicable when N is composite and not necessarily a power of 2. Thus if two factors of N are used, so that $N = r_1 \times r_2$, the data is, in effect, put in an r_1-column, r_2-row rectangular array, and a two-dimensional

many knowledgeable people who believed Fourier analysis to be a process requiring something proportional to N^2 operations with a proportionality factor which could be reduced by using the symmetries of the trigonometric functions. Computer programs using the N^2 operation methods were, in fact, using up hundreds of hours of computing machine time. However, in response to the Cooley–Tukey paper, Rudnick [28], of Scripps Institution of Oceanography, La Jolla, California, described his computer program which also took a number of operations proportional to $N \log_2 N$ and was based on a method published by Danielson and Lanczos [11] in 1942. It is interesting that the Danielson–Lanczos paper described transform is performed with a phase-shifting operation intervening between the transformations in the two dimensions. This results, as was shown above, in $N(r_1 + r_2)$ operations instead of N^2. By selecting N to be highly composite, substantial savings result. For the very favorable situation when N is equal to a power of 2, the Cooley–Tukey method is essentially the successive doubling algorithm of Runge and König mentioned above and takes $N \log_2 N$ operations.

The 23-year hiatus in the use of the FFT algorithm seemed quite remarkable. Further inquiry revealed that L. H. Thomas had spent three months in 1948 doing calculations of Fourier series on a tabulating machine, using what he referred to as the "Stumpff method of subseries." The algorithm described by Thomas [36] was thought at first to be essentially the same as the fast Fourier transform algorithm of Cooley and Tukey [8] since it also achieved its economy by performing one-dimensional Fourier analysis by doing "multidimensional" Fourier analysis. However, the algorithms are different, and the genesis of the difference is as follows: Stumpff gave only a doubling and tripling algorithm and suggested [34, p. 442, line 11] that the reader generalize to obtain the method for factors of N other than 2 or 3. One generalization leads to the Cooley–Tukey algorithm. However, in making this generalization, Thomas made the further assumption that the factors of N must be mutually prime, and this led to his "prime factor" algorithm. The differences between the Thomas "prime factor" algorithm and the Cooley–Tukey (FFT) algorithm are that:

1. In the "prime factor" algorithm, the factors of N must be mutually prime.

2. In the Thomas algorithm, the calculation is precisely multidimensional Fourier analysis with no intervening phase shifts or "twiddle factors" as they have been called.

3. The correspondences between the one-dimensional index and the multidimensional indices when the data is put in the r_1-column, r_2-row array in the two algorithms are quite different.

The latter is the most striking difference between the two algorithms. The "prime factor" algorithm is described in detail and compared with the fast Fourier transform in [9].

There is additional history concerning the prime factor algorithm. Yates [44], in 1937, introduced a simple adding and subtracting algorithm for calculating the interactions of a 2^m factorial experiment. This has since become known as the fast Hadamard transform. It was generalized by Good [15] to an algorithm for a general $t_1 t_2 \cdots t_m$ factorial experiment and the transformation was shown to be expressible as a Kronecker product of relatively small matrices. He pointed out that the whole procedure could be used for streamlining multidimensional Fourier transforms. He then showed that an algorithm which he had previously given for expressing a one-dimensional Fourier transform as a multidimensional transform, and vice versa, enabled one to use his fast method for one-dimensional transforms with a composite N. In Good's algorithm, the factors of N had to be mutually prime. This was the full generalization of the Thomas prime factor algorithm.

d. The FFT Algorithm: Detailed Derivation and Discussion

THE GENERAL ALGORITHM

The derivation of the formula for factoring a Fourier series into a pair of subseries was given above. In this section, the general algorithm and formulas useful in programming are derived. We will be analyzing the DFT

$$a(n) = \sum_{j=0}^{N-1} x(j) W_N^{-jn} \qquad (35)$$

Since the IDFT, giving $x(j)$ in terms of $a(n)$, is a Fourier series of the same form as

(35), the algorithm can be used for computing the IDFT with minor alterations in the input and output arrays as described in Section 2e, Procedure 1.

Suppose $N = r_1 r_2 \ldots r_m$. We will first consider appropriate m-tuple representations of the indices j and n of (35). We define a correspondence between the m-tuple, $(n_1, n_2, \ldots, n_m)$ and the index n by the relation

$$n = n_1 + r_1 n_2 + r_1 r_2 n_3 + \cdots$$
$$+ r_1 r_2 \cdots r_{m-1} n_m \qquad (36)$$

where

$$n_l = 0, 1, \ldots, r_l - 1, \quad l = 1, \ldots, m$$

The correspondence between the m-tuple $(j_1, j_2, \ldots, j_m)$ and the index j is defined by

$$j = j_m + r_m j_{m-1} + r_m r_{m-1} j_{m-2} + \cdots$$
$$+ r_m \cdots r_2 j_1 \qquad (37)$$

where

$$j_l = 0, 1, \ldots, r_l - 1, \quad l = 1, \ldots, m$$

Let us refer to $j_1, \ldots, j_m$ and $n_1, \ldots, n_m$ as the "digits" of j and n, respectively. The indexing for j and n are similar with the difference being that the factors and the "digits" are taken in the opposite order. As an example, if $r_1 = 2$, $r_2 = 3$, $r_3 = 4$, then $N = 2 \cdot 3 \cdot 4 = 24$ and the correspondence between n and the triple (n_1, n_2, n_3) and between j and the triple (j_1, j_2, j_3) are as shown in Table 2.

Table 2. THE CORRESPONDENCE BETWEEN n AND THE TRIPLE (n_1, n_2, n_3) AND BETWEEN j AND THE TRIPLE (j_1, j_2, j_3) FOR $r_1 = 2$, $r_2 = 3$, $r_3 = 4$. (The last column gives the digit-reversal of j.)

$n = n_1 + 2n_2 + 6n_3$				$j = j_3 + 4j_2 + 12j_1$				$j' = j_1 + 2j_2 + 6j_3$
n	n_1	n_2	n_3	j	j_3	j_2	j_1	
0	0	0	0	0	0	0	0	0
1	1	0	0	1	1	0	0	6
2	0	1	0	2	2	0	0	12
3	1	1	0	3	3	0	0	18
4	0	2	0	4	0	1	0	2
5	1	2	0	5	1	1	0	8
6	0	0	1	6	2	1	0	14
7	1	0	1	7	3	1	0	20
8	0	1	1	8	0	2	0	4
9	1	1	1	9	1	2	0	10
10	0	2	1	10	2	2	0	16
11	1	2	1	11	3	2	0	22
12	0	0	2	12	0	0	1	1
13	1	0	2	13	1	0	1	7
14	0	1	2	14	2	0	1	13
15	1	1	2	15	3	0	1	19
16	0	2	2	16	0	1	1	3
17	1	2	2	17	1	1	1	9
18	0	0	3	18	2	1	1	15
19	1	0	3	19	3	1	1	21
20	0	1	3	20	0	2	1	5
21	1	1	3	21	1	2	1	11
22	0	2	3	22	2	2	1	17
23	1	2	3	23	3	2	1	23

We can now write

$$W_N^{-nj}$$

$$= W_N^{-n(j_1 r_2 \cdots r_m + j_2 r_3 \cdots r_m + \cdots + j_{m-1} r_m + j_m)} \tag{38}$$

Now if we substitute the expansion (36) for n in the factors $W_{r_1 \cdots r_l}^{-nj_l}$ then, since the exponent of $W_{r_1 \cdots r_l}$ is to be interpreted modulo $r_1 \ldots r_l$, terms of the n-series beyond the lth may be dropped. Therefore,

$$W_{r_1 \cdots r_l}^{-nj_l} = W_{r_1 \cdots r_l}^{-(n_1 + r_1 n_2 + \cdots + r_1 \cdots r_{l-1} n_l) j_l} \tag{39}$$

Hence the Fourier series (35) may be written as a sum over the indices $j_1, j_2, \ldots j_m$ instead of j. Substituting from (38) and summing first over j_1, then j_2, and so on, we can write (35) as nested sums of subseries,

$$a(n) = \sum_{j_m=0}^{r_m-1} \cdots \sum_{j_2=0}^{r_2-1} \sum_{j_1=0}^{r_1-1} x(j) W_{r_1}^{-nj_1} W_{r_1 r_2}^{-nj_2}$$

$$\cdots W_{r_1 \cdots r_m}^{-nj_m} \tag{40}$$

Equation (39) implies that $W_{r_1}^{nj_1}$ depends only upon n_1 and j_1. Hence the innermost sum is a function of the indices $n_1, j_2, \ldots, j_m$ and can therefore be stored in the same array as $x(j)$, over-writing $x(j)$ to save storage and indexing. The next sum over j_2, again from Eq. (39), depends only upon $n_1, n_2, j_3, \ldots, j_m$ and can over-write values of the first sum. Continuing in this manner, the FFT algorithm can be described by

$$a_0(j_1, \ldots, j_m) = x(j) \tag{41}$$

$$a_1(n_1, j_2, \ldots, j_m)$$

$$= \sum_{j_1=0}^{r_1-1} a_0(j_1, \ldots, j_m) W_{r_1}^{-nj_1} \tag{42}$$

$$a_2(n_1, n_2, j_3, \ldots, j_m)$$

$$= \sum_{j_2=0}^{r_2-1} a_1(n_1, j_2, \ldots, j_m) W_{r_1 r_2}^{-nj_2} \tag{43}$$

$$\vdots$$

$$a_l(n_1, \ldots, n_l, j_{l+1}, \ldots, j_m)$$

$$= \sum_{j_l=0}^{r_l-1} a_{l-1}(n_1, \ldots, n_{l-1}, j_l, \ldots, j_m)$$

$$\times W_{r_1, \ldots, r_l}^{-nj_l} \tag{44}$$

$$\vdots$$

$$a(n) = a_m(n_1, \ldots, n_m) \tag{45}$$

Here, and in what follows, the notation a, a_l, and x will refer to N-element arrays. Note that these will be written with one argument or with m arguments with the correspondence between the arguments being given by (36) or (37).

Let us examine the lth step in more detail. Since

$$W_{r_1 \cdots r_l}^{-r_1 \cdots r_{l-1} n j_l} = W_{r_l}^{-nj_l}$$

a_l can be written as

$$a_l(n_1, \ldots, n_l, j_{l+1}, \ldots, j_m)$$

$$= \sum_{j_l=0}^{r_l-1} a_{l-1}(n_1, \ldots, n_{l-1}, j_l, \ldots, j_m)$$

$$\times W_{r_1 \cdots r_l}^{-(n_1 + r_1 n_2 + r_1 r_2 n_3 + \cdots + r_1 \cdots r_{l-2} n_{l-1}) j_l}$$

$$\times W_{r_l}^{-n_l j_l} \tag{46}$$

This formula says that each element of the array a_{l-1} is multiplied by a phase factor and, with the resulting array, r_l-term Fourier series are computed with j_l being the index of the sum. Thus the FFT algorithm is really a nested sequence of Fourier series of subseries with intervening multiplications by phase factors. In actual computation, each term of (46) would take only one multiplication since the W-factors would be combined into a single factor.

Now consider the storage and indexing of the scheme. As the indices $n_1, \ldots, n_{l-1}$, $n_l, j_{l+1}, \ldots, j_m$ go through all of their values, the index of a_l, which can be written

$$n = n_1 + r_1 n_2 + \cdots + r_1 \cdots r_{l-1} n_l$$
$$+ r_1 \cdots r_l j_{l+1} \cdots + r_1 \cdots r_{m-1} j_m \quad (47)$$

goes through the values $n = 0, 1, \ldots,$ $N - 1$. The one-to-one mapping between the index n and the arguments of a_l is the same as the one given by (36) with $n_{l+1}, \ldots, n_m$ replaced by $j_{l+1}, \ldots, j_m$. If we let

$$N_1 = 0$$
$$N_l = n (\mathrm{mod}\ r_1 \cdots r_{l-1})$$
$$= n_1 + r_1 n_2 + \cdots + r_1 \cdots r_{l-2} n_{l-1}$$
$$l = 2, \ldots, m \quad (48)$$

and

$$J_l = j_{l+1} + r_{l+1} j_{l+2} + \cdots$$
$$+ r_{l+1} \cdots r_{m-1} j_m,$$
$$l = 1, \ldots, m - 1 \quad (49)$$
$$J_m = 0$$

the index n can be written

$$n = N_l + r_1 \cdots r_{l-1} n_l + r_1 \cdots r_l J_l \quad (50)$$

where $l = 1, 2, \ldots, m$ and, for each l,

$$N_l = 0, 1, \ldots, r_1 \cdots r_{l-1} - 1$$
$$n_l = 0, 1, \ldots, r_l - 1 \quad (51)$$
$$J_l = 0, 1, \ldots, r_{l+1} \cdots r_m - 1$$

If, for each l, we generate all values of $N_l, j_l,$ J_l in the ranges specified by (51) then n, as defined by (47), will go through its full range of values. Thus we can write (46) in

the form,

$$a_l (N_l + r_1 \cdots r_{l-1} n_l + r_1 \cdots r_l J_l)$$
$$= \sum_{j_l = 0}^{r_l - 1} a_{l-1} (N_l + r_1 \cdots r_{l-1} j_l$$
$$+ r_1 \cdots r_l J_l) W_{r_1 \cdots r_l}^{-N_l j_l} W_{r_l}^{-j_l n_l} \quad (52)$$

where the ranges of the indices are given by (51).

An important point to notice in the above procedure is that the definition (50) for the final array, with $l = m$, coincides with that for the index n of $a(n)$ given by (36). Hence the final array is $a_m(n) = a(n)$. However, for the initial array, we have

$$a_0(J_0) = x(j) \quad (53)$$

where, according to the definition (49), we have $J_0 = j'$, where j' is the digit-reversal of j defined by

$$j' = j_1 + r_1 j_2 + \cdots + r_1 \cdots r_{m-1} j_m$$
$$(54)$$

The digits of j are defined by (37). An example of a digit-reversal permutation is given in the last column of Table 2 above.

The above factorization of the Fourier series was given by Cooley and Tukey [8]. Almost simultaneously, and independently, Sande [13] worked out the algorithm which puts the multiplication by the phase factor, or "twiddle factor" as they called it, after each r_l-point Fourier transform. For this one uses, instead of (38),

$$W_N^{-jn} = W_{r_1 \cdots r_m}^{-j n_1} \cdots W_{r_{m-1} r_m}^{-j n_{m-1}} W_{r_m}^{-j n_m} \quad (55)$$

The lth factor

$$W_{r_l \cdots r_m}^{-(r_m \cdots r_{l+1} j_l + \cdots + r_m j_{m-1} + j_m) n_l} \quad (56)$$

is seen to be independent of $j_1, \ldots, j_{l-1}$. In

this case the general formula is

$$a_l(n_1, \ldots, n_l, j_{l+1}, \ldots, j_m)$$

$$= \sum_{j_l=0}^{r_l-1} a_{l-1}(n_1, \ldots, n_{l-1}, j_l, \ldots, j_m) W_{r_l \cdots r_m}^{-jn_l}$$

$$\tag{57}$$

which can be written

$$a_l(n_1, \ldots, n_l, j_{l+1}, \ldots, j_m)$$

$$= \sum_{j_l=0}^{r_l-1} a_{l-1}(n_1, \ldots, n_{l-1}, j_l, \ldots, j_m) W_{r_l}^{-j_l n_l}$$

$$\times W_{r_l \cdots r_m}^{-(r_m \cdots r_{l+2}j_{l+1} + \cdots + r_m j_{m-1} + j_m)n_l} \tag{58}$$

Here, the "twiddle factor" comes after each r_l-point Fourier transform. To obtain the exponent of W_N from the index of a_l, we define the index of a_l to be

$$j = j_m + r_m j_{m-1}$$

$$+ \cdots + r_m \cdots r_{l+2} j_{l+1}$$

$$+ r_m \cdots r_{l+1} n_l + \cdots + r_m \cdots r_2 n_1$$

$$\tag{59}$$

The Sande algorithm can be written as a programmable algorithm by letting

$$N_l = n_{l-1} + r_{l-1} n_{l-2} + \cdots + r_{l-1} \cdots r_2 n_1$$

$$\tag{60}$$

and

$$J_l = j(\mathrm{mod}\; r_m \cdots r_{l+1})$$

$$= j_m + r_m j_{m-1} + \cdots + r_m \cdots r_{l+2} j_{l+1}$$

$$\tag{61}$$

Then we can put (58) in the form

$$a_l(J_l + r_m \cdots r_{l+1} n_l + r_m \cdots r_l N_l)$$

$$= \sum_{j_l=0}^{r_l-1} a_{l-1}(J_l + r_m \cdots r_{l+1} j_l + r_m \cdots r_l N_l)$$

$$\times W_{r_l}^{-j_l n_l} W_{r_l \cdots r_m}^{-J_l n_l} \tag{62}$$

where

$$l = 1, 2, \ldots, m$$

$$N_l = 0, 1, \ldots, r_1 \cdots r_{l-1} - 1$$

$$j_l = 0, 1, \ldots, r_l - 1 \tag{63}$$

$$J_l = 0, 1, \ldots, r_{l+1} \cdots r_m - 1$$

The two programming forms of the general FFT algorithm, given above, are equivalent in speed and accuracy. If a program is to obtain powers of W_N from tables, the preference is based on whether one wishes to permute the array before or after the Fourier transformation.

CHOICE OF FACTORIZATION

The calculation of a discrete Fourier transform for a single value of n requires N operations where by "operation" we mean a complex multiplication and addition. Therefore, if the direct calculation were done for each of the N values of n, it would take N^2 operations. On the other hand, the lth step of the FFT algorithm described previously takes r_l^2 operations for each fixed set of values of $n_1, \ldots, n_{l-1}, j_{l+1}, \ldots, j_m$. There are $r_1 \cdots r_{l-1} \cdot r_{l+1} \cdots r_m$ values of these indices, meaning the lth step takes $r_l \cdot N$ operations. Hence, the total number of operations is

$$T_{op} = N \sum_{l=1}^{m} r_l \tag{64}$$

This is generally considerably less than N^2, the number of operations required by the direct method.

We now suppose some freedom in the selection of N and its factors, r_l, and determine choices to minimize T_{op} with respect to r_l, $l = 1, 2, \ldots, m$. If we consider a further factorization of any r_l, say using $r_l = s_l t_l$ we replace a term r_l by $s_l + t_l$ in (64). Since $s_l + t_l < s_l t_l$ unless $s_l = t_l = 2$, using as many factors as possible reduces T_{op} to a minimum but factors of 2 can be combined without loss.

If all of the factors of N are equal, that is, if $N = r^m$, so that $m = \log_r N$, then we have, from (64)

$$T_{op} = Nr \, m = Nr \log_r N \qquad (65)$$

In this case, we say that we have a radix r, or base r, algorithm. If the factors are not all equal, we say that we have a mixed radix algorithm. Equation (65) can be written

$$T_{op} = \left(\frac{r}{\log_2 r} \right) N \log_2 N \qquad (66)$$

Hence for a radix r algorithm T_{op} is proportional to $N \log_2 N$ with a proportionality factor $r/\log_2 r$, whose values are listed in Table 3.

Table 3

r	$r/\log_2 r$
2	2.00
3	1.33
4	2.00
5	2.15
6	2.32
7	2.49
8	2.67
11	3.18
16	4.00

Notice that the use of $r_l = 3$ is formally most efficient. However, the use of 2, 4, 8, and 16 has the advantage that some of the powers of W_N are simple numbers like ± 1, $\pm i$, $(1 \pm i)/\sqrt{2}$, and multiplications can be avoided.

Bergland [2] investigated in detail the number of additions and multiplications required for radices 2, 4, 8, and 16 if the program is written economically, omitting multiplications by simple powers of W_N and combining terms with common factors. His results show some economy in the use of radices 4, 8, and 16 but the savings for 8 and 16 are small compared to the increased complexity of the algorithm. Hence, the radix 2 and 4 algorithms are the ones most widely programmed and used.

However, mixed radix algorithms have been programmed and applied. One can see from Table 3 that the use of factors other than 2 and 4 does not increase the time of calculation substantially. For a detailed discussion of the programming of the mixed radix algorithm, see Singleton [33].

THE RADIX 2 ALGORITHM

Because of its simplicity in programming, the base 2 algorithm has been used extensively in subroutines and in hardware implementations. In mixed radix calculations, any subseries corresponding to a power of two can easily be calculated by such a subroutine. Particularly simple is the digit-reversal, consisting merely of a succession of pair-wise interchanges.

For the radix 2, the m-tuple $(n_1, \ldots, n_m)$ is the bit configuration in a binary representation of n and $(j_1, \ldots, j_m)$ is the same for j but with the bits in reverse order. We have $r_l = 2$, $W_{r_l}^{-n_l j_l} = (-1)^{n_l j_l}$, so that (52) can be written

$$a_l(i) = a_{l-1}(i) + a_{l-1}(k) \cdot W_{2^l}^{-N_l}$$

$$a_l(k) = a_{l-1}(i) - a_{l-1}(k) \cdot W_{2^l}^{-N_l} \qquad (67)$$

where

$$i = N_l + 2^l J_l$$

$$k = i + 2^{l-1}$$

The ranges of the indices are

$$l = 1, 2, \ldots, m$$

$$N_l = 0, 1, 2, \ldots, 2^{l-1} - 1 \qquad (68)$$

$$J_l = 0, 1, 2, \ldots, 2^{m-l} - 1$$

This is, essentially, the doubling algorithm described in the history of the FFT in Section 2c. The program and system flowgraph given in Section 4 below, describe in detail how this algorithm can be executed on a digital computer.

In the same way, the Sande–Tukey form of the FFT algorithm with radix 2 comes from (62) which can be written as

$$a_l(i) = a_{l-1}(i) + a_{l-1}(k)$$

$$a_l(k) = \left[a_{l-1}(i) - a_{l-1}(k) \right] W_{2^{m-l+1}}^{-J_l}$$

$$(69)$$

where

$$i = J_l + 2^{m-l+1} N_l$$

$$k = i + 2^{m-l}$$

and the ranges of the indices are

$$l = 1, 2, \ldots, m \qquad (70)$$

$$J_l = 0, 1, \ldots, 2^{m-l} - 1$$

$$N_l = 0, 1, \ldots, 2^{l-1} - 1$$

ROUNDOFF ERROR ANALYSIS

When programs for the FFT algorithm began to replace those using conventional methods, it was noticed very soon that not only was the speed improved by a factor proportional to $N/\log_2 N$, but, in general, the accuracy was much greater. A number of analyses of the effect of rounding errors have been published, all substantiating the empirical results. Gentleman and Sande [13] gave an upper bound on the root-mean square of the error using a direct application of Wilkinson's [43] floating point arithmetic rounding error analysis for matrix operations. Kaneko and Liu [22] performed a more detailed analysis giving bounds on the mean square error, the expected value of the error for each element of the DFT and expected values of the mean square error for various types of data. Kaneko and Liu also treated the case of truncation as well as rounding of the excess digits. In the case of white noise data and rounding arithmetic, their result has been obtained by Weinstein [39]. Welch [41] has done a statistical analysis of the error when using fixed-point arithmetic. A very good overview has been written by Oppenheim and Weinstein [24].

A coarse summary of these studies is as follows. For a radix r program, that is, when $N = r^m$, the ratio of the mean square error to the mean square signal increases asymptotically as $m = \log_r N$ for rounding and as $m^2 = (\log_r N)^2$ for truncation. These results have been confirmed experimentally.

e. Basic DFT Computational Procedures

INTRODUCTION

We will now describe a set of five procedures which permit one to use the complex FFT algorithm efficiently for special types of input. All of these are written so that one can execute them by using a complex DFT subroutine with some pre- or post-processing of the data. The DFT subroutine will be assumed to accept as input, an integer N and a sequence of complex numbers $x(j)$, $j = 0, 1, \ldots, N-1$, and to yield, as output, the DFT sequence

$$a(n) = \sum_{j=0}^{N-1} x(j) W_N^{-nj} \qquad (71)$$

The inverse relationship to (71) is

$$x(j) = \frac{1}{N} \sum_{n=0}^{N-1} a(n) W_N^{nj} \qquad (72)$$

where $x(j)$ is referred to as the IDFT of $a(n)$. This pair of relationships is written in functional notation,

$$a = \mathrm{DFT}(x)$$

$$x = \mathrm{IDFT}(a) \qquad (73)$$

PROCEDURE 1: THE INVERSION ALGORITHM

Taking complex conjugates of both sides of (72) puts it in the form of (71) so that

$$\tilde{x} = \mathrm{DFT}\left(\frac{\tilde{a}}{N} \right) \qquad (74)$$

Therefore, a computer subroutine, written to compute the DFT (71) can be used to compute the IDFT defined by (72) by using the following procedure:

1. Let the input to the DFT subroutine be $\tilde{a}(n)/N$.

2. Take the complex conjugate of the output of the DFT subroutine. The result is x, the IDFT of a as defined by (72).

Similarly, taking complex conjugates of both sides of (71) and dividing by N puts it in the form of (72) so that in functional notation, $\tilde{a} = \text{IDFT}(N\tilde{x})$. Therefore, a subroutine for computing the IDFT can be used to compute the DFT by the following procedure:

PROCEDURE 1′: INVERSION OF AN IDFT ALGORITHM.

1. Let the input to the IDFT subroutine be $\tilde{x}(j)$.

2. Divide the complex conjugate of the output sequence by N to obtain $a(n)$.

The procedures described next are all designed to take advantage of some special properties of the input data to effect some economy of computation. Each procedure is described in terms of an input data sequence $x(j)$ with its DFT, $a(n)$, as the output sequence. This is followed by a primed form of the procedure which computes the inverse, that is, given $a(n)$, it computes its IDFT $x(j)$. In each case, some special property is assumed for the input and results in some special property of the output. For example, if the data $x(j)$ is real, its DFT $a(n)$ is conjugate even. In some cases, one may wish to compute an IDFT of a given sequence $a(n)$ when $\tilde{a}(n)$ has the properties of the input to a DFT algorithm described by one of the procedures. This can be done by using Procedure 1 above with the DFT in step (1) being computed by the appropriate special algorithm. The same idea may be applied in the reverse direction when one wishes to compute the DFT of a sequence $x(j)$ when $\tilde{x}(j)$ has a special property assumed for $a(n)$ in some IDFT algorithm.

PROCEDURE 2: THE DOUBLING ALGORITHM

Suppose N is even and we have an N-point sequence, $x(j)$, which is too long to compute in one application of the DFT algorithm while a sequence of $N/2$ points can be accommodated. We define the two $N/2$ point sequences and their transforms

$$x_1(j) = x(2j) \leftrightarrow a_1(n) \qquad (75)$$

$$x_2(j) = x(2j + 1) \leftrightarrow a_2(n)$$

Separating the odd- and even-indexed terms of the series for $a(n)$ gives

$$a(n) = \sum_{j=0}^{N/2-1} x(2j) W_N^{-2jn}$$

$$+ \sum_{j=0}^{N/2-1} x(2j + 1) W_N^{-(2j+1)n}$$

$$a(n) = \sum_{j=0}^{N/2-1} x(2j) W_{N/2}^{-jn}$$

$$+ \left\{ \sum_{j=0}^{N/2-1} x(2j + 1) W_{N/2}^{-jn} \right\} W_N^{-n}$$

$$(76)$$

The two sums are the $N/2$-point DFT's of $x_1(j)$ and $x_2(j)$, so

$$a(n) = a_1(n) + a_2(n) W_N^{-n} \qquad (77)$$

Substituting $n + N/2$ for n and using the fact that $a_1(n)$ and $a_2(n)$ are periodic with period $N/2$, $W_N^{N/2} = -1$, we get

$$a\left(n + \frac{N}{2}\right) = a_1(n) - a_2(n) W_N^{-n} \qquad (78)$$

Therefore, to obtain the DFT of $x(j)$, the procedure is as follows:

1. Form the two sequences

$$x_1(j) = x(2j) \quad \text{and} \quad x_2(j) = x(2j + 1),$$

$$j = 0, 1, 2, \ldots, \frac{N}{2} - 1$$

2. Compute the two $N/2$-point DFT's $a_1(n)$, $a_2(n)$.

3. Use (77) and (78) with $n = 0, 1, \ldots, N/2 - 1$ to compute the DFT $a(n)$.

PROCEDURE 2'. The IDFT form of this procedure enables one to obtain the data sequence $x(j)$ from $a(n)$ with two $N/2$-point IDFT's. One obtains the procedure by solving (77) and (78) for $a_1(n)$ and $a_2(n)$. In particular,

1. Given $a(n)$, compute

$$a_1(n) = \frac{1}{2}\left[a(n) + a\left(n + \frac{N}{2}\right)\right] \quad (79)$$

$$a_2(n) = \frac{1}{2}\left[a(n) - a\left(n + \frac{N}{2}\right)\right]W_N^n,$$

$$n = 0, 1, \ldots, \frac{N}{2} - 1 \quad (80)$$

2. Compute the two IDFT's of $a_1(n)$ and $a_2(n)$.

3. Form the composite sequence $x(j)$, $j = 0, 1, \ldots, N - 1$ as follows:

$$x(2j) = x_1(j), x(2j + 1) = x_2(j),$$

$$j = 0, 1, \ldots, \frac{N}{2} - 1$$

PROCEDURE 3: TWO-AT-A-TIME ALGORITHM FOR REAL SEQUENCES

If two data sequences $x_1(j)$ and $x_2(j)$ are real, and if we form a single complex sequence

$$x(j) = x_1(j) + ix_2(j),$$

$$j = 0, 1, \ldots, N - 1 \quad (81)$$

then letting

$$x(j) \leftrightarrow a(n)$$

$$x_1(j) \leftrightarrow a_1(n)$$

$$x_2(j) \leftrightarrow a_2(n)$$

it follows that

$$a(n) = a_1(n) + ia_2(n),$$

$$n = 0, 1, \ldots, N - 1 \quad (82)$$

where $a_1(n)$ and $a_2(n)$ are conjugate even, (i.e., $a_k(n) = \tilde{a}_k(N - n)$, $k = 1, 2$). Taking the complex conjugate of the right-hand side of (82) and replacing n by $N - n$, we have,

$$\tilde{a}(N - n) = a_1(n) - ia_2(n) \quad (83)$$

Solving (82) and (83) for $a_1(n)$ and $a_2(n)$, we obtain,

$$a_1(n) = \frac{1}{2}(\tilde{a}(N - n) + a(n)) \quad (84)$$

$$a_2(n) = \frac{i}{2}(\tilde{a}(N - n) - a(n)),$$

$$n = 0, 1, \ldots, \frac{N}{2} \quad (85)$$

Therefore, the procedure is:

1. Given the two real sequences, $x_1(j)$, $x_2(j)$, form

$$x(j) = x_1(j) + ix_2(j)$$

2. Compute the complex N-point DFT $a(n)$ of $x(j)$.

3. Use (84) and (85) for $n = 0, 1, \ldots, N/2$ to obtain the $a_1(n)$ and $a_2(n)$.

Values of $a_1(n)$, $a_2(n)$ for $n > N/2$ need not be computed since $a_1(n)$ and $a_2(n)$ are conjugate even.

PROCEDURE 3': TWO-AT-A-TIME ALGORITHM FOR CONJUGATE EVEN SEQUENCES.

1. Given two conjugate even DFTs $a_1(n)$ and $a_2(n)$, $n = 0, 1, \ldots, N - 1$, where only $N/2 + 1$ values of each sequence need be actually given, form $a(n)$ using (82) for $n = 0, 1, \ldots, N/2 - 1$ and (83) for $n = 1, \ldots, N/2$.

2. Compute the IDFT of $a(n)$.

3. One then has $x_1(j)$ and $x_2(j)$ in the real and imaginary parts, respectively, of $x(j)$.

PROCEDURE 4: THE DFT OF A REAL
SEQUENCE

If $x(j)$, $j = 0, 1, \ldots, N - 1$ is a real sequence and N is even we can use the following procedure to halve the computation time. Since $x(j)$ is real, it has a conjugate even DFT, $a(n)$, $n = 0, 1, \ldots, N - 1$. We define the $N/2$ point sequence

$$y(j) = x(2j) + ix(2j + 1),$$

$$j = 0, 1, \ldots, \frac{N}{2} - 1 \quad (86)$$

and the $N/2$ point DFT pairs

$x(2j) \longleftrightarrow a_1(n)$
$x(2j + 1) \longleftrightarrow a_2(n)$

$$y(j) \longleftrightarrow c(n), \quad j, n = 0, 1, \ldots, \frac{N}{2} - 1$$

The DFT of $x(j)$ can be computed by the doubling algorithm, from the DFT's $a_1(n)$ and $a_2(n)$ of the real sequences $x(2j)$ and $x(2j + 1)$, $j = 0, 1, \ldots, N/2 - 1$. The latter can be computed by computing the DFT, $c(n)$ of $y(j)$ and using the two-at-a-time algorithm for real sequences. Thus the procedure is:

1. Given the real sequence $x(j)$, $j = 0, 1, \ldots, N - 1$, form the $N/2$ point complex sequence $y(j)$ according to (86).
2. Compute $c(n)$, the complex $N/2$ point DFT of $y(j)$.
3. Compute, using Eqs. (84) and (85) from the two-at-a-time algorithm for real sequences

$$a_1(n) = \frac{1}{2}\left(\tilde{c}\left(\frac{N}{2} - n\right) + c(n)\right) \quad (87)$$

$$a_2(n) = \frac{i}{2}\left(\tilde{c}\left(\frac{N}{2} - n\right) - c(n)\right),$$

$$n = 0, 1, \ldots, \frac{N}{4} \quad (88)$$

4. With Eq. (77) of the doubling algorithm expressed separately for n and $N/2 - n$ and using the fact that $a_1(n)$ and $a_2(n)$ are

$N/2$-point conjugate even sequences, one can compute

$$a(n) = a_1(n) + a_2(n)W_N^{-n},$$

$$n = 0, 1, \ldots, \frac{N}{4} \quad (89)$$

$$\tilde{a}\left(\frac{N}{2} - n\right) = a_1(n) - a_2(n)W_N^{-n},$$

$$n = 0, 1, \ldots, \frac{N}{4} - 1 \quad (90)$$

to obtain $a(n)$ for $n = 0, 1, \ldots, N/2$. Values of $a(n)$ for $n > N/2$ are not needed since $a(n)$ is conjugate even.

PROCEDURE 4': THE IDFT OF A CONJUGATE EVEN SEQUENCE. The previous procedure led from a real data sequence $x(j)$ to a conjugate even sequence $a(n)$. Solving (87)–(90) for right-hand side quantities in terms of left-hand side quantities permits one to compute the real sequence $x(j)$, $j = 0, 1, \ldots, N - 1$ from the conjugate even sequence $a(n)$, $n = 0, 1, \ldots, N - 1$.

1. Given $a(n)$, $n = 0, 1, \ldots, N/2$, compute

$$a_1(n) = \frac{1}{2}\left[a(n) + \tilde{a}\left(\frac{N}{2} - n\right)\right] \quad (91)$$

$$a_2(n) = \frac{1}{2}\left[a(n) - \tilde{a}\left(\frac{N}{2} - n\right)\right]W_N^n,$$

$$n = 0, 1, \ldots, \frac{N}{4} \quad (92)$$

2. Let

$$c(n) = a_1(n) + ia_2(n) \quad (93)$$

$$\tilde{c}\left(\frac{N}{2} - n\right) = a_1(n) - ia_2(n),$$

$$n = 0, 1, \ldots, \frac{N}{4} \quad (94)$$

3. Compute the $N/2$-point IDFT of $c(n)$, to obtain $y(j)$. Use (86) to obtain $x(j)$ from $y(j)$.

PROCEDURE 5: THE DFT OF A REAL EVEN
SEQUENCE; THE COSINE TRANSFORM

The DFT of the real even sequence $x(j)$,
$j = 0, 1, \ldots, N - 1$, where N is an even
integer, is equivalent to the cosine transform
of the real sequence $x(j)$, $j = 0,
1, \ldots, N/2$. The DFT is also real and even
and can be related to the coefficients of the
cosine series

$$x(j) = \sum_{n=0}^{N/2} \alpha(n)\cos\left(2\frac{\pi nj}{N}\right) \quad (95)$$

by the formulas

$$\alpha(n) = \frac{a(n)}{N}, \quad n = 0, \frac{N}{2}$$

$$\alpha(n) = \frac{2a(n)}{N}, \quad n = 1, 2, \ldots, \frac{N}{2} - 1 \quad (96)$$

To derive the procedure, consider the
$N/2$-point conjugate even sequence

$$y(j) = x(2j) + i[x(2j + 1) - x(2j - 1)],$$

$$j = 0, 1, \ldots, \frac{N}{2} - 1 \quad (97)$$

We may use the inverted form of Procedure
4′, to compute the real transform, $c(n)$ of
$y(j)$. We define the transform pairs,

$$x(j) \longleftrightarrow a(n), \quad j, n = 0, 1, \ldots, N - 1$$
$$x(2j) \longleftrightarrow a_1(n)$$
$$x(2j + 1) \leftrightarrow a_2(n)$$

$$x'(2j) = x(2j + 1) - x(2j - 1) \leftrightarrow a_2'(n),$$

$$n, j = 0, 1, \ldots, \frac{N}{2} - 1 \quad (98)$$

From Procedure 3, $a_1(n)$ and $a_2'(n)$ can be
obtained from the two-at-a-time algorithm

$$a_1(n) = \frac{1}{2}\left[c(n) + c\left(\frac{N}{2} - n\right)\right] \quad (99)$$

$$a_2'(n) = \frac{1}{2i}\left[c(n) - c\left(\frac{N}{2} - n\right)\right],$$

$$n = 0, 1, \ldots, \frac{N}{4} \quad (100)$$

where, it is to be remembered that $c(n)$ is
real. From Theorem 4, Section 2b,

$$x(2j - 1) \leftrightarrow W_{N/2}^{-n}a_2(n),$$

$$j, n = 0, 1, \ldots, \frac{N}{4} - 1 \quad (101)$$

and, therefore,

$$a_2'(n) = a_2(n) - W_{N/2}^{-n}a_2(n) \quad (102)$$

giving

$$a_2(n) = \frac{a_2'(n)}{(1 - W_{N/2}^{-n})} \quad (103)$$

A special calculation must be made for
$n = 0$ and $n = N/2$. For this we must compute

$$a_2(0) = \sum_{j=0}^{N/2-1} x(2j + 1) \quad (104)$$

Finally, substituting the formulas for $a_1(n)$
and $a_2(n)$ in the doubling algorithm (77) and
using the fact that $W_N^{-n}/\{(1 - W_{N/2}^{-n})i\} =
1/\{2\sin(2\pi n/N)\}$, Procedure 2 gives

$$a(n) = \frac{1}{2}\left\{\left[c(n) + c\left(\frac{N}{2} - n\right)\right]\right.$$

$$\left. + \left[c(n) - c\left(\frac{N}{2} - n\right)\right]\Big/\left[2\sin\frac{2\pi n}{N}\right]\right\}$$

and

$$a\left(\frac{N}{2} - n\right) = \frac{1}{2}\left\{\left[c(n) + c\left(\frac{N}{2} - n\right)\right]\right.$$

$$\left. - \left[c(n) - c\left(\frac{N}{2} - n\right)\right]\Big/\left[2\sin\frac{2\pi n}{N}\right]\right\}$$

$$(105)$$

for $n = 1, 2, \ldots, N/4$. One uses the special
formulas for $n = 0, N/2$,

$$a(0) = \frac{1}{2}\{a_1(0) + a_2(0)\}$$

$$a\left(\frac{N}{2}\right) = \frac{1}{2}\{a_1(0) - a_2(0)\} \quad (106)$$

Summarizing, the procedure is

1. Given the real even sequence $x(j), j = 0, 1, \ldots, N - 1$, form $y(j)$ according to (97).

2. Letting $\tilde{y}(j)/N$ be the input sequence to Procedure 4′, one obtains the real sequence $c(n)$, $n = 0, 1, \ldots, N/2 - 1$ as output.

3. Compute $a(n)$ using (105) for $n = 1, 2, \ldots, N/4$.

4. For $n = 0$ and $N/2$, let $a_1(0) = c(0)$, compute $a_2(0)$ from (104) and use (106) to compute $a(0)$ and $a(N/2)$.

f. The Application of the FFT Algorithm to the Calculation of Sample Covariance Functions

Let $x(j), j = 0, \ldots, M - 1$, be a sample sequence from a second-order, stationary stochastic sequence $\{X(j)\}$. Further suppose that $E\{X_j\} = 0$. Then the sample covariance function is given by

$$\hat{\gamma}_{xx}(k) = C(M, k) \sum_{j=0}^{M-k-1} x(j)x(j + k),$$

$$k \geqslant 0 \qquad (107)$$

where generally

$$C(M, k) = \frac{1}{M} \text{ or } \frac{1}{(M - k)}$$

Note that $\hat{\gamma}_{xx}(k)$ is even, hence for $k < 0$, $\hat{\gamma}_{xx}(k) = \hat{\gamma}_{xx}(-k)$. This sample covariance function is an estimate of the covariance function, (sometimes called the auto-covariance function)

$$\gamma_{XX}(k) = E\{X(j)X(j + k)\} \quad (108)$$

It can be calculated either directly from (107) or indirectly by taking discrete Fourier transforms and using Corollary 7.1 of Section 2b. The fact that this latter indirect, circuitous route via the frequency domain is, under certain conditions, computationally more efficient than the direct application of

(107) is one of the remarkable consequences of the FFT algorithm.

In applying Corollary 7.1 we must append zeros to the sequence $x(j)$ to avoid the wrap-around of terms caused by the circular property of the DFT convolution. The details of this plus problems of compensating for a nonzero mean and the comparison of computing times for the two alternatives are discussed in Section 3a.

If $y(j) : j = 0, \ldots, M - 1$ is a sample from another, second-order, stationary, stochastic sequence $\{Y(j)\}$ with $E\{Y(j)\} = 0$, then the sample cross-covariance function of $x(j)$ leading $y(j)$ is

$$\hat{\gamma}_{xy}(k) = C(M, k) \sum_{j=-k}^{M-1} x(j + k)y(j),$$

$$k < 0$$

$$= C(M, k) \sum_{j=0}^{M-k-1} x(j + k)y(j),$$

$$k \geqslant 0 \qquad (109)$$

This sample cross-covariance function is an estimate of the cross-covariance function

$$\gamma_{XY}(k) = E\{X(j + k)Y(j)\} \quad (110)$$

The sample cross-covariance function of $y(j)$ leading $x(j)$, $\hat{\gamma}_{yx}(k)$, is defined in an obvious fashion and $\hat{\gamma}_{xy}(k) = \hat{\gamma}_{yx}(-k)$.

Again, as with the sample covariance function, the sample cross-covariance function can be calculated either directly using (109) or indirectly using Corollary 7.1. As before, under certain circumstances, the indirect calculation via the FFT is more efficient. The details of this indirect computational procedure, the compensation for nonzero means and the comparison of the two methods are given in Section 3a.

The relationship between the covariance function and the problem of spectral estimation is discussed in the next section.

g. The Application of the FFT to the Estimation of Spectra

THE POWER SPECTRUM AND THE PERIODOGRAM

Let $X(j) : j = 0, \pm 1, \pm 2, \ldots$ be a second-order, stationary, stochastic sequence. For simplicity we will assume that the expected value of $X(j)$ is zero, i.e., $E\{X(j)\} = 0$. The covariance function, $\gamma_{XX}(k)$, is given by

$$\gamma_{XX}(k) = E\{X(j)X(j+k)\} \quad (111)$$

Again for simplicity we assume that the process has a spectral density, $p(\omega) : -\pi \leqslant \omega \leqslant \pi$. Then, as is well known, $p(\omega)$ is the Fourier transform of $\gamma_{XX}(k)$; that is,

$$p(\omega) = \frac{1}{2\pi} \sum_{k=-\infty}^{\infty} \gamma_{XX}(k)\cos \omega k \quad (112)$$

We will now consider a finite sequence of random variables $X(j) : j = 0, \ldots, M-1$ and a sample sequence $x(j) : j = 0, \ldots, M-1$. We will be considering functions of these finite sequences and as before will use subscript Xs when referring to random variables and subscript x's when referring to sample functions.

One common estimator of $\gamma_{XX}(k)$ is

$$\bar{\gamma}_{XX}(k) = \frac{1}{M} \sum_{j=0}^{M-k-1} X(j)X(j+k),$$

$$k \geqslant 0 \quad (113)$$

Note that $\bar{\gamma}_{XX}(k)$ is even, hence, for $k < 0$, $\bar{\gamma}_{XX}(k) = \bar{\gamma}_{XX}(-k)$. The sample covariance function for this estimator is obtained by substituting $C(M, k) = 1/M$ in Eq. (107). This estimator is biased since

$$E\{\bar{\gamma}_{XX}(k)\} = \frac{M - |k|}{M} \gamma_{XX}(k)$$

$$= \left(1 - \frac{|k|}{M}\right)\gamma_{XX}(k) \quad (114)$$

It is for this reason that the multiplier $1/$ $(M - |k|)$ rather than $1/M$ is sometimes used.

The periodogram $I_{XX}(\omega)$ $(-\pi \leqslant \omega \leqslant \pi)$ of $X(j)$ is proportional to the Fourier cosine transform of $\bar{\gamma}_{XX}(k)$; that is,

$$I_{XX}(\omega) = \frac{1}{(2\pi)} \sum_{k=-(M-1)}^{M-1} \bar{\gamma}_{XX}(k)\cos \omega k$$

$$(115)$$

The periodogram dates back to Schuster and work on the problem of hidden periodicities (mixed spectra) at the turn of the century. One can see from a comparison of Eqs. (112) and (115) that it is a sample analog of the spectral density. One consequence of the fast Fourier transform has been to return the periodogram to a position of prominence in time series analysis. The reasons for this will become clear below.

Next consider the expected value of the periodogram.

$$E\{I_{XX}(\omega)\} = E\left\{\frac{1}{(2\pi)} \sum_{k=-(M-1)}^{M-1} \bar{\gamma}_{XX}(k)\cos \omega k\right\}$$

$$= \frac{1}{(2\pi)} \sum_{k=-(M-1)}^{M-1} E\{\bar{\gamma}_{XX}(k)\}\cos \omega k$$

$$= \frac{1}{(2\pi)} \sum_{k=-(M-1)}^{M-1} \left(1 - \frac{|k|}{M}\right)\gamma_{XX}(k)\cos \omega k$$

$$(116)$$

Notice that $E\{I_{XX}(\omega)\}$ is the Fourier transform of the product of the covariance function $\gamma_{XX}(k)$ and the function

$$f_M(k) = 1 - \frac{|k|}{M} \qquad |k| \leqslant M - 1$$

$$= 0 \qquad \text{otherwise}$$

Hence, it is also equal to the convolution of the continuous transforms of $\gamma_{XX}(k)$ and

$f_M(k)$; and we have

$$E\{I_{XX}(\omega)\} = \int_{-\pi}^{\pi} h_M(\sigma)p(\omega - \sigma)\,d\sigma$$

(117)

where

$$h_M(\omega) = \frac{1}{2\pi}\sum_{k=-(M-1)}^{M-1}\left(1 - \frac{|k|}{M}\right)\cos(\omega k)$$

$$= \frac{1}{2\pi M}\frac{\sin^2(M\omega/2)}{\sin^2(\omega/2)}$$

(118)

and

$$\int_{-\pi}^{\pi} h_M(\omega)\,d\omega = 1$$

(119)

From Eq. (117) we see that there is a *spectral window* $h_M(\omega)$ associated with the periodogram. By this we mean that the expected value of the periodogram may be considered to be the actual spectrum filtered through (or seen through) the window $h_M(\omega)$. We will call this the *basic periodogram window*. The great utility of the idea of a spectral window is that it allows us to assess the effect of the finite sample size as a weighted average of the spectrum at different frequencies. It has similar utility in assessing the variance of and correlation between spectral estimates at different frequencies.

The basic spectral window is the Fourier transform of the triangular function $f_M(k)$. For small ω/M we have

$$h_M(\omega) \approx \left(\frac{M}{2\pi}\right)\frac{\sin^2(M\omega/2)}{(M\omega/2)^2}$$

(120)

This window, therefore, has a $\sin^2 x/x^2$ shape. The approximation of Eq. (120) is plotted in Fig. 14.3.

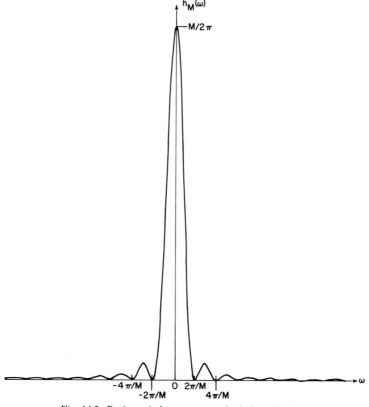

Fig. 14.3. Basic periodogram spectral window: $h_M(\omega)$.

The DFT, $a(n)$, of the M point sample sequence, $x(j)$, can be related to the periodogram by Corollary 7.1, Eq. (15). Corollary 7.1 yields

$$|a(n)|^2 = \sum_{k=0}^{M-1} R_{xx}(k)W_M^{-nk},$$

$$n = 0, 1, \ldots, M - 1 \quad (121)$$

where $R_{xx}(k)$ is the *cyclic* lagged product

$$R_{xx}(k) = \sum_{j=0}^{M-1} x(j+k)x(j) \quad (122)$$

With some algebraic manipulation, we get from (122) and (113) that $R_{xx}(k)$ and $\bar{\gamma}_{xx}(k)$ are related by

$$\frac{1}{M} R_{xx}(0) = \bar{\gamma}_{xx}(0)$$

$$\frac{1}{M} R_{xx}(k) = \bar{\gamma}_{xx}(k) + \bar{\gamma}_{xx}(M-k),$$

$$k = 1, 2, \ldots, M - 1 \quad (123)$$

Therefore, dividing both sides of (121) by M and noting that $R_{xx}(k)$ is even, we have

$$\frac{1}{M} |a(n)|^2 = \sum_{k=-M+1}^{k=M-1} \bar{\gamma}_{xx}(k)\cos\left(\frac{2\pi nk}{M}\right)$$

$$(124)$$

Hence,

$$I_{xx}(\omega_n) = \frac{1}{2\pi M} |a(n)|^2 \quad (125)$$

where

$$\omega_n = \frac{2\pi n}{M}, \quad n = 0, 1, 2, \ldots, M - 1$$

SIMPLE SMOOTHING OF THE PERIODOGRAM

In what follows, we will let arrows to the right indicate a DFT and arrows to the left, an IDFT. Downward arrows indicate other operations such as multiplication and addition. With this convention if $x(j) : j =$

$0, \ldots, M - 1$ is a finite sample of length M from a stochastic sequence and $I_{xx}(\omega)$ is the sample periodogram, we have from Eq. (125) that

$$x(j) \rightarrow a(n)$$
$$\downarrow$$
$$\frac{|a(n)|^2}{2\pi M} = I_{xx}(\omega_n)$$

$$(126)$$

where

$$\omega_n = \frac{2\pi n}{M}, \quad n = 0, \ldots, M - 1$$

Thus the modulus squared of the DFT, properly normalized, gives M equally spaced values of the sample periodogram. Note, however, that since $I(\omega_n)$ is an even function, only $[M/2] + 1$ values are distinct. Here $[M/2]$ denotes the integer part of $M/2$.

Now, as is well known, the periodogram itself is not a good estimate of the spectrum, $p(\omega)$. In the first place, it is not a consistent estimate in the sense of mean square convergence; its variance does not go to zero as M increases. In fact, if $X(j)$ is a moving average of independent random variables (this includes Gaussian processes which have a spectral density), then in the limit as M increases, $I_{XX}(\omega_n)$ converges in distribution to a χ^2 random variable with 2 degrees of freedom. (Results on this and other properties of $I_{XX}(\omega_n)$ are given by Olshen [23]). To get a good estimate of $p(\omega)$, we must "smooth" the periodogram; that is, we must take a weighted sum of adjacent values. Let $H(k) : |k| \leqslant K$ be a set of nonnegative weights which sum to unity. Then the estimators of $p(\omega)$ are of the form

$$\hat{p}(\omega_n) = \sum_{k=-K}^{K} H(k)I_{XX}(\omega_{n-k}) \quad (127)$$

Here we have assumed for simplicity that $H(k)$ is independent of ω_n. This is not necessary, and a more general scheme includes this case.

With an estimate of the form given by Eq. (127) we have

$$E\left\{\hat{p}\left(\omega_n\right)\right\} = \int_{-\pi}^{\pi} h(\sigma)\, p(\omega_n - \sigma)\, d\sigma \quad (128)$$

where

$$h(\omega) = \sum_{k=-K}^{K} H(k)\, h_M(\omega - \omega_k) \quad (129)$$

Hence the spectral window, $h(\omega)$, associated with $\hat{p}(\omega_n)$ is a weighted linear combination of shifted, equally spaced, basic spectral windows. Moreover, from Eqs. (129) and (119), if

$$\sum_{k=-K}^{K} H(k) = 1$$

then

$$\int_{-\pi}^{\pi} h(\omega)\, d\omega = 1$$

The simplest way of smoothing the periodogram is with a set of equal weights or by taking a "moving average." In this case

$$\hat{p}\left(\omega_n\right) = \frac{1}{2K+1} \sum_{k=-K}^{K} I_{XX}\left(\omega_{n-k}\right) \quad (130)$$

This was first suggested by Daniell in 1946. The window for this type of smoothing and for $K = 7$ is shown in Fig. 14.4. It is a symmetrical function so that only the right half is shown. It is normalized to have unity half power width. Figure 14.5 contains this window on a db scale; that is, it is a plot of $10 \log_{10} h(\omega)$. This window, for $K = 7$, is typical of the windows for all values of K. They are roughly rectangular in shape and there is strong ripple in the pass and reject bands. They fall off at the rate of 6 db per octave in the tails. The initial falloff is a function of K.

SMOOTHING A FINER GRID OF PERIODOGRAM VALUES

We saw in Section 2d that the efficiency of the fast Fourier transform algorithm depends upon N having a highly composite

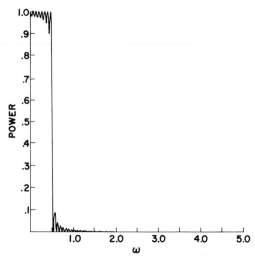

Fig. 14.4. Spectral window (Power). Rectangular smoothing, $K = 7$. Frequency in units of window width at half power points.

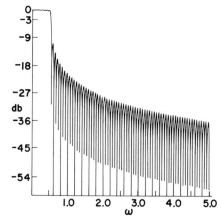

Fig. 14.5. Spectral window (db). Rectangular smoothing, $K = 7$. Frequency in units of window width at half power points.

number of terms. In fact, most of the available programs and special hardware devices are equipped for sequences of length $N = 2^m$. Mixed radix programs are usually written to handle only a few radices and, in any case, run faster if one limits usage to highly composite values of N. Often, however, the length of the sample $x(j) : j = 0, \ldots, M - 1$ is not such a number. The simplest way to handle this is to extend $x(j)$ with zeros to length $M + L = N$, where N is highly composite or a power of 2. This extension yields a more finely spaced grid of periodogram values, as we will see below. Let

$$x_e(j) = x(j), \quad j = 0, \ldots, M - 1$$
$$x_e(j) = 0, \quad j = M, \ldots, M + L - 1$$
$$= N - 1 \qquad (131)$$

Then one proceeds as follows:

$$x_e(j) \rightarrow a_e(n)$$
$$\downarrow$$
$$\frac{|a_e(n)|^2}{2\pi M} = I_{xx}(\omega_n^*)$$

$$(132)$$

where $\omega_n^* = 2\pi n / N$ and $n = 0, \ldots, N/2$. Hence the appending of zeros to the sequence $x(j)$ to get a more efficient transform gives us a more finely spaced set of periodogram values.

Again, in general, $I(\omega_n^*)$ must be smoothed to yield reasonable estimates of the spectrum. Thus spectral estimates would take the form

$$\hat{p}(\omega_n^*) = \sum_{k=-K}^{K} H(k) I(\omega_{n-k}^*) \quad (133)$$

As before

$$E\{\hat{p}(\omega_n^*)\} = \int_{-\pi}^{\pi} h(\sigma) p(\omega_n^* - \sigma) \, d\sigma \quad (134)$$

where

$$h(\omega) = \sum_{k=-K}^{K} H(k) h_M(\omega - \omega_k^*) \quad (135)$$

Hence the resulting spectral window is again a linear combination of shifted basic spectral windows. However, the finer spacing has some helpful effects on the characteristics of the spectral window. The basic spectral windows are no longer in phase so there is less ripple and the initial falloff is slightly greater. The falloff in the tail remains 6 db/octave. In Fig. 14.6 we have

plotted the window, $h(\omega)$, of Eq. (135) for rectangular weights with $K = 7$ and the addition of 25% zeros to $x(j)$. In Fig. 14.7 the db window, $10 \log_{10} h(\omega)$, is plotted. These figures should be compared to Figs. 14.4 and 14.5 where the comparable

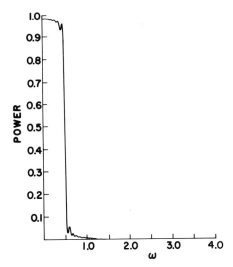

Fig. 14.6. Spectral window (power). 25% additional zeros. Rectangular smoothing, $K = 7$. Frequency in units of window width at half power points.

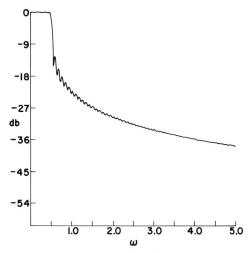

Fig. 14.7. Spectral window (db). 25% additional zeros. Rectangular smoothing, $K = 7$. Frequency in units of window width at half power points.

windows obtained without appending zeros are given.

Note that the appending of zeros to the sequence may not be convenient if it is required to use the periodogram in testing for white noise or for harmonic components in the time series [10, 12]. In this case, if M is prime or not highly composite, a method of Bluestein [5] may be used to obtain efficiently the transform of $x(j)$.

USE OF OTHER THAN RECTANGULAR WEIGHTING

Although the examples we have given concern smoothing with equal weights any weighting scheme could be used. A set of triangular weights or truncated triangular weights, for example, would be good in the estimation of spectra which have sharp peaks. A very sharp peak traces out the window $h(\omega)$. For other windows developed for direct smoothing of the periodogram see [38]. Windows of rather large K/M value derive from the traditional approach to periodogram estimation which is discussed next.

THE TRADITIONAL APPROACH: SMOOTHING THE PERIODOGRAM THROUGH THE ESTIMATED COVARIANCE FUNCTION

As we saw in Section 2e the FFT algorithm can be used as an alternative method of calculating the sample covariance function. The estimate of the spectrum can then be obtained in the traditional way. This is equivalent to smoothing the periodogram with a long weighting function in the same fashion we have discussed above.

Let $x(j) : j = 0, \ldots, M - 1$ be the sample sequence. Let $x(j)$ be extended with L zeros producing $x_e(j)$. Then if $a_e(n)$ is the DFT of $x_e(j)$ and if we form $|a_e(n)|^2 / M$ and take its IDFT, we get a function $g(j)$ such that $g(j) = \bar{\gamma}_{xx}(j) : j = 0, \ldots, L$. The estimates $\bar{\gamma}_{xx}(j)$ can then be multiplied by a lag window, $\lambda(j)$, and another discrete Fourier transform taken obtaining $\hat{p}(\omega)$. This

process is depicted as follows.

$$
\begin{array}{l}
x(j) \\
\quad\downarrow \\
x_e(j) \longrightarrow a_e(n) \\
\qquad\qquad\qquad\downarrow \\
\bar{\gamma}_{xx}(j) \longleftarrow \dfrac{1}{M}\,|a_e(n)|^2 = 2\pi I_{xx}(\omega_n^*) \\
\quad\downarrow \qquad\qquad\quad\vdots \\
\dfrac{1}{2\pi}\,\bar{\gamma}_{xx}(j)\lambda(j) \to \hat{p}(\omega)
\end{array}
$$

$$(136)$$

Notice that the procedure of using a lag window is equivalent to the direct smoothing of the periodogram described above. Instead of smoothing by convolution in the frequency domain, the smoothing is done by multiplication in the time domain. If the lag weighting function, $\lambda(j)$, is short compared to M, the equivalent frequency domain function $H(k)$ will be very long. Thus the traditional approach to spectral estimation can be thought of as an efficient way of applying a long smoothing function to the periodogram. In fact, an interesting property of the fast Fourier transform is that it is cheaper computationally to go back and obtain the $\bar{\gamma}_{xx}(j)$'s rather than proceeding by way of the broken arrow in (136).

GENERAL VARIANCE RESULTS AND A COMPARISON OF METHODS

The alternative procedures discussed above yield estimates that involve smoothing the periodogram and the usual asymptotic variance results apply to both. Suppose we have a spectral window $h(\omega)$; that is,

$$ E\{\hat{p}(\omega)\} = \int_{-\pi}^{\pi} h(\sigma) p(\omega - \sigma) d\sigma \quad (137) $$

Then for a stationary sequence and a window $h(\omega)$ whose bandwidth $B(M) \to 0$ as $M \to \infty$, but for which $MB(M) \to \infty$ as $M \to \infty$ we have (see for example, [7])

$$ E\{\hat{p}(\omega)\} \approx p(\omega)\int_{-\pi}^{\pi} h(\omega)d\omega = p(\omega) \quad (138) $$

and

$$\mathrm{Var}\{\hat{p}(\omega)\} \approx \frac{2\pi}{M} p^2(\omega) \int_{-\pi}^{\pi} h^2(\omega) d\omega$$

$$(139)$$

The equivalent number of degrees of freedom (*EDF*) of the approximate χ^2 distribution of $\hat{p}(\omega)$ is given by

$$EDF = M \left[2\pi \int_{-\pi}^{\pi} h^2(\omega) d\omega \right]^{-1} \quad (140)$$

(Some studies on the adequacy of this χ^2 approximation to the distribution of $\hat{p}(\omega)$ for small M have been given recently by Granger and Hughes [17].)

The question of which procedure, the direct or indirect smoothing of the periodogram, is preferable depends on the experimentor's needs and the importance of computational economy to him. If he is interested in the sample covariance function, he would likely use the traditional approach and hence use the FFT algorithm as an efficient procedure for calculating the sample covariance function. If computational considerations are important, if rectangular or triangular windows are adequate, and if there is no interest in the sample covariance function, then he would likely choose the direct smoothing of the periodogram. Rectangular and triangular smoothing can be achieved very efficiently by recursive means. More details on computational aspects are given in Section 3b.

The Application of Regression Analysis to the Periodogram

As we have seen, with the advent of the FFT the natural way to view spectral estimation is as a smoothing of the periodogram. This leads to viewing the periodogram as a "time series" and to serious consideration of the general application of time series methods to its "smoothing."

As was mentioned previously, for moving average processes (and in particular Gaussian processes) and under fairly general conditions, $I_{XX}(\omega_n)$ is approximately proportional to a χ_2^2 random variable with

$$E\{I_{XX}(\omega_n)\} = p(\omega_n)$$

and

$$\mathrm{Var}\{I_{XX}(\omega_n)\} = p^2(\omega_n) \quad (141)$$

Further the $I_{XX}(\omega_n)$ are approximately uncorrelated. Thus we have a natural setting for the application of least-squares techniques except that the variance is not constant and the χ_2^2 random variable has a distribution which is quite skewed.

However, if we make a logarithmic transformation then $\log I_{XX}(\omega_n)$ is approximately proportional to a $\log \chi_2^2$ random variable and

$$E\{\log I_{XX}(\omega_n)\} = \psi(2) + \log p(\omega_n)$$

$$\mathrm{Var}\{\log I_{XX}(\omega_n)\} = \psi'(2)$$

where

$$\psi(x) = \frac{d \log \Gamma(x)}{dx}, \quad \psi'(x) = \frac{d\psi(x)}{dx}$$

$$(142)$$

and $\Gamma(x)$ is the gamma function. Hence the variance of $\log I_{XX}(\omega_n)$ is known and is independent of $E\{p(\omega_n)\}$. Further the $\log \chi_2^2$ distribution is more nearly normal than the χ_2^2 distribution.

Hence it is reasonable to apply regression or least-squares techniques to the sequence $\log I_{xx}(\omega_n)$. This could be done in two ways. A function could be fitted to the $\log I_{xx}(\omega_n)$'s over the entire range $n = 0, \ldots, M/2$ or functions could be fit locally giving, say, the best polynomial fit about a point. For details of these procedures in the general context of the regression analysis of χ^2 random variables, see

[10]. Theoretical reasons are given there for applying a uniform weighting scheme before doing the regression analysis, with the weighting being done over at least four points $I(\omega_n)$. In that case $\psi(2)$ and $\psi'(2)$ in (142) are replaced by $\psi(8)$ and $\psi'(8)$, respectively.

Other methods of direct regression analysis of $I(\omega_n)$ are given by Watson [38].

THE MODIFIED PERIODOGRAM

A basic periodogram spectral window with better side lobe rejection than that of (120) can be obtained by modifying the periodogram. This is accomplished [3] by applying a data window prior to taking the initial transform. Consider the procedure diagrammed below.

$$x(j)$$
$$\downarrow$$
$$x(j) \cdot w_M(j) \longrightarrow b(n)$$
$$\downarrow$$
$$\frac{1}{2\pi UM} |b(n)|^2 = I_{xx}^*(\omega_n)$$

$$\text{(143)}$$

where

$$U = \frac{1}{M} \sum_{j=0}^{M-1} w_M^2(j)$$

Here $I_{xx}^*(\omega_n)$ is what is called the modified periodogram. The ordinary periodogram comes from the data window $w_M(j) = 1$, $j = 0, \ldots, M - 1$ and $w_M = 0$ otherwise.

Using an argument parallel to that leading to Eq. (134) we obtain

$$E\{I_{XX}^*(\omega_n)\} = \int_{-\pi}^{\pi} h_M^*(\sigma) p(\omega_n - \sigma) d\sigma$$

$$\text{(144)}$$

where

$$h_M^*(\omega) = \frac{1}{2\pi MU} \left| \sum_{j=0}^{M-1} w_M(j) e^{i\omega j} \right|^2 \quad \text{(145)}$$

and

$$\int_{-\pi}^{\pi} h_M^*(\omega) d\omega = 1$$

Thus $I_{XX}^*(\omega_n)$ has a basic spectral window that is proportional to the modulus squared of the transform of the data window $w_M(j)$. For $w_M(j) = 1, j = 0, 1, \ldots, M - 1, h_M^*(\omega)$ is given by (118).

The major application for the modified periodogram is in signal analysis where there is interest in the phase as well as the amplitude of the Fourier transform of $x(j)$. The sharp window obtained operates on phase estimates. An identical window can be obtained by applying the convolution of $w_M(j)$ with itself as a lag window to the sample covariance function. Such a window, however, does not apply to the phase.

The modified periodogram values for a Gaussian process again are approximately proportional to a χ_2^2 random variable. Hence it also must be smoothed to yield reasonable estimates of the spectrum. Equations (127)–(129) continue to hold with $I_{XX}^*(\omega_n)$ and $h_M^*(\omega)$ replacing $I_{XX}(\omega_n)$ and $h_M(\omega)$, respectively. It must be pointed out, however, that the variance results given above do not apply. The $I_{XX}^*(\omega_n)$ are correlated and there is consequently an increase in the variance or loss of statistical accuracy in spectral estimation from applying a data window.

Bingham, Godfrey, and Tukey [3] suggest a data window which is flat over 80% of its range with a 10% cosine arch roll off at each end. With this data window, there is a modest increase in the variance, but there is also only a slight improvement in the side lobe rejection.

TIME AVERAGING OVER SHORT MODIFIED PERIODOGRAMS

Another method for the estimation of spectra is the time averaging over short, possibly overlapping, modified periodograms. It is simple and of particular interest when one has a machine with small core storage or when one is interested in investigating possible nonstationarity in the data. It also has computational advantages in certain circumstances independent of the size of core storage.

In this approach, the sample sequence $x(j)$ is divided into possibly overlapping sections $x_1(j), \ldots, x_K(j)$ of length L as indicated in Fig. 14.8. Modified periodograms of these sections are taken and the time average of these modified periodograms is the spectral estimate. Here the statistical stability is obtained by time rather than frequency averaging. The procedure is diagrammed below.

$$x(j)$$
$$\downarrow$$
$$x_k(j) \qquad \{k = 1, \ldots, K\}$$
$$\downarrow$$
$$w(j)x_k(j) \longrightarrow c_k(n)$$
$$\downarrow$$
$$I_k^*(\omega_n) = \frac{|c_k(n)|^2}{2\pi UL}$$
$$\downarrow$$
$$\hat{p}(\omega_n) = \left(\frac{1}{K}\right) \sum_{k=1}^{K} I_k^*(\omega_n)$$

$$(146)$$

where $\omega_n = n/2\pi L$.

The spectral window is the basic spectral window of the modified periodograms. The variance of the estimate is given in [40]; this reference also contains a detailed discussion of the procedure. Without the overlapping and modification, the method is that proposed by Bartlett [1] in 1948. It is also closely related to the method of complex demodulation [3].

ESTIMATION OF CROSS-SPECTRA

Let $X(j)$, $Y(j) : j = 0, \pm 1, \pm 2, \ldots$ be two second-order, stochastic sequences. For simplicity we will assume that

$$E\{X(j)\} = E\{Y(j)\} = 0 \quad (147)$$

Their cross-covariance function $\gamma_{XY}(k)$ is defined by

$$\gamma_{XY}(k) = E\{X(j + k)Y(j)\} \quad (148)$$

Again for simplicity we will assume that the processes have a cross-spectral density $p_{XY}(\omega)$. Then, as is well known, $p_{XY}(\omega)$ is the Fourier transform of $\gamma_{XY}(k)$; that is,

$$p_{XY}(\omega) = \frac{1}{2\pi} \sum_{k=-\infty}^{\infty} \gamma_{XY}(k)e^{-i\omega k} \quad (149)$$

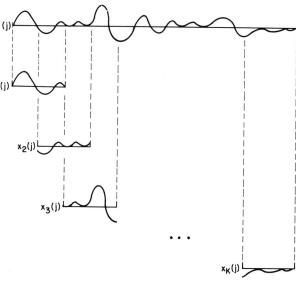

Fig. 14.8. Sectioning of $x(j)$ into sections $x_k(j)$: $k = 1, \ldots, K$.

Now suppose we have two finite samples $x(j)$ and $y(j)$ from $X(j)$ and $Y(j)$, respectively. For simplicity, we assume that the samples are both over the same time period; that is, $j = 0, \ldots, M - 1$. Then a commonly used estimate of $\gamma_{XY}(k)$ is

$$\bar{\gamma}_{xy}(k) = \frac{1}{M} \sum_{j=0}^{M-k-1} x(j+k)y(j),$$

$$0 \leqslant k < M \qquad (150)$$

$$\bar{\gamma}_{xy}(k) = \frac{1}{M} \sum_{j=-k}^{M-1} x(j+k)y(j),$$

$$-M < k < 0$$

The cross-periodogram $I_{xy}(\omega)$ is defined by

$$I_{xy}(\omega) = \left(\frac{1}{2\pi} \right) \sum_{k=-(M-1)}^{M-1} \bar{\gamma}_{xy}(k)e^{-i\omega k},$$

$$-\pi \leqslant \omega \leqslant \pi \qquad (151)$$

As with the periodogram, comparison of Eqs. (149) and (151) shows the cross-periodogram to be a sample analog of the cross-spectrum.

The cross-periodogram at points $\omega_n = 2\pi n/M$ is easily obtained using the fast Fourier transform as diagrammed as follows:

$$x(j) \rightarrow a_x(n)$$
$$y(j) \rightarrow a_y(n)$$
$$\downarrow$$
$$\frac{1}{2\pi M} a_x(n)\tilde{a}_y(n) = I_{xy}(\omega_n)$$

$$(152)$$

where

$$\omega_n = \frac{2\pi n}{M}, \quad n = 0, \ldots, M - 1$$

Here $\tilde{a}_y(n)$ is the complex conjugate of $a_y(n)$. Thus as with the periodogram, we obtain a set of equally spaced samples. Notice that the samples run from 0 to 2π rather than from 0 to π. This is because the cross-spectrum is not an even function. However, $I_{xy}(\omega)$ and $p_{XY}(\omega)$ are periodic of period 2π. The values from $-\pi$ to 0 are the same as those from π to 2π.

Procedures for estimating the cross-spectrum from the cross-periodogram are parallel to those given for the periodogram. The cross-periodogram has the same basic spectral window as the periodogram. It also must be smoothed to obtain reasonable estimates. The same alternatives described in the preceding sections for the periodogram are available.

Concluding Remarks

This discussion of spectral analysis is very brief and should be considered more an outline than an exposition. For more details, see [3, 4, 18, 25, 35].

h. Application of the FFT to Moving Average Digital Filtering

Frequently, there is interest in "filtering" a sequence $x(j)$ by convolving it with the weighting function $w(j)$ of a digital filter; that is, there is interest in the function $y(j)$ given by

$$y(j) = \sum_k x(j-k)w(k) \qquad (153)$$

An example is the smoothed periodogram (127).

If such a filter is implemented by a convolution, we call it a nonrecursive or moving average digital filter. Such a nonrecursive filter can be implemented either directly using (153) or indirectly, in the frequency domain, using Theorem 7 of Section 2b. In the latter case, care must be taken, usually through the addition of zeros, to avoid the wrap-around effect of the cyclic convolution.

The subject of digital filtering is a vast one and will not be discussed here. Rader and Gold [15] is a good, general reference and contains a chapter by Stockham on the FFT implementation of nonrecursive filters. Important material on the use of mathematical programming techniques in the design of nonrecursive filters is contained in [19] and [27].

3. SUMMARY OF TIME SERIES CALCULATION PROCEDURES

a. Calculation of Sample Covariance and Cross-Covariance Functions

INTRODUCTION

We will now discuss the practical details of the calculation of sample covariance functions indirectly via DFT's and the FFT algorithm. As in Section 2e we let $x(j)$ and $y(j)$, $j = 0, \ldots, M - 1$ be sample sequences from two real stochastic sequences $\{X(j)\}$ and $\{Y(j)\}$ with $E(X) = E(Y) = 0$. We are interested in the calculation of the sample covariance function

$$\hat{\gamma}_{xx}(k) = C(M, k) \sum_{j=0}^{M-k-1} x(j)x(j + k),$$

$$0 \leqslant k \leqslant L \qquad (154)$$

and the sample cross-covariance function

$$\hat{\gamma}_{xy}(k) = C(M, k) \sum_{j=0}^{M-k-1} x(j + k)y(j),$$

$$0 \leqslant k \leqslant L \qquad (155)$$

$$\hat{\gamma}_{xy}(k) = C(M, k) \sum_{j=-k}^{M-1} x(j + k)y(j),$$

$$-L \leqslant k \leqslant 0$$

where generally either $C(M, k) = 1/M$ or $C(M, k) = 1/(M - k)$

THE GENERAL CASE

We first consider the calculation of $\hat{\gamma}_{xx}(k)$ for $0 \leqslant k \leqslant L$. It is apparent that $\hat{\gamma}_{xx}(-k) = \hat{\gamma}_{xx}(k)$ so that this calculation yields the function for $-L \leqslant k \leqslant L$. We will be using Corollary 7.1 of Section 2. This corollary relates cyclic lagged products in the time domain with term by term functional products in the frequency domain. By appending zeros to the sequence $x(j)$ before transformation, values of noncyclic lagged products of the type given by Eqs. (154) and (155) can be obtained.

Specifically let

$$N \geqslant M - 1 + L$$

and let

$$x_e(j) = x(j), \quad 0 \leqslant j \leqslant M - 1 \quad (156)$$

$$x_e(j) = 0, \quad M \leqslant j \leqslant N$$

Further, as in Section 2g, let arrows to the right indicate a DFT, arrows to the left indicate an IDFT and downward arrows indicate the particular arithmetic operations shown. With these conventions and the application of Corollary 7.1 we have the following indirect computation scheme for $\hat{\gamma}_{xx}(k)$. $\tilde{a}_e(n)$ is the complex conjugate of $a_e(n)$ and, since $x(j)$ is real, equals $a_e(-n)$.

$$x_e(j) \to a_e(n)$$
$$\downarrow$$
$$z_{xx}(k) \leftarrow a_e(n)\tilde{a}_e(n)$$
$$\downarrow$$
$$\hat{\gamma}_{xx}(k) = C(M, k)z_{xx}(k) \quad 0 \leqslant k \leqslant L$$

$$(157)$$

Because of the addition of zeros, the first L values (actually the first $N - M + 1 \geqslant L$ values) of $z_{xx}(k)$ are uncorrupted by "wraparound" and yield the sample covariance function. Usually a radix 2 program is used and N is chosen as the smallest appropriate power of 2.

If $E\{X\} \neq 0$, then corrections for the nonzero mean can be made in alternative ways. Suppose that $E\{X\} = c$ and is known. As a first alternative we can create a new sequence $x(j) - c$ and follow the above set of steps with the new sequence. Equivalently, instead of appending zeros to obtain $x_e(j)$, we append c's. Then, using Theorem 5 of Section 2b, we take the transform of $x_e(j)$, replace $a_e(0)$ by $a_e(0) - Nc$ and proceed. Either of these will yield

$$\hat{\gamma}_{xx}(k) = C(M, k) \sum_{j=0}^{M-1-k} \{(x(j + k) - c)$$

$$\times (x(j) - c)\} \qquad (158)$$

Alternatively the covariance estimates can be corrected by reducing them by c^2. This last alternative is not functionally equivalent to the first two, but yields

$$\hat{\gamma}'_{xx}(k) = C(M, k) \left[\sum_{j=0}^{M-1-k} \{x(j)x(j + k)\} \right]$$

$$- c^2 \qquad (159)$$

Similarly if $E\{X\}$ is unknown then $\bar{x} = (1/M) \sum_{j=0}^{M-1} x(j)$ can be subtracted from the samples in the same way as the known mean was subtracted in the first two procedures. Also, the covariance estimate can be corrected by subtracting $(\bar{x})^2$. In this case $\bar{x}$ can be obtained from $\bar{x} = a_e(0)/M$. As before the two procedures are not quite equivalent in the estimates they produce.

Since $x(j)$ is real, Procedure 4 of Section 2e can be used to obtain the DFT, $a_e(n)$. Further since $a_e(n)\tilde{a}_e(n)$ is real and even, Procedure 5 can be used to obtain the IDFT. The use of these special procedures will result in substantial computational savings over direct application of a general DFT program.

The sample cross-covariance function can be obtained similarly as indicated below.

We define L and N and the extended sequences, $x_e(j)$ and $y_e(j)$, as before.

$$x_e(j) \rightarrow a_e(n)$$
$$y_e(j) \rightarrow b_e(n)$$
$$\downarrow$$
$$z_{xy}(k) \leftarrow a_e(n)\tilde{b}_e(n)$$
$$\downarrow$$
$$\hat{\gamma}_{xy}(k) = C(M, k)z_{xy}(k) \qquad 0 \leqslant k \leqslant L$$
$$\hat{\gamma}_{xy}(k) = C(M, k)z_{xy}(N + k), -L \leqslant k < 0$$

$$(160)$$

Considering $z_{xy}(k)$ for $k = 0, \ldots, N - 1$, the first $L + 1$ values yield $\hat{\gamma}_{xy}(k)$ for $k = 0, \ldots, L$ and the last L values yield $\hat{\gamma}_{xy}(k)$ for $k = -1, \ldots, -L$. Corrections for non-zero means can be made following the same alternatives available for straight covariance functions.

Again since $x(j)$ and $y(j)$ are real, Procedure 4 of Section 2e can be used to obtain $a_e(n)$ and $b_e(n)$. Similarly, since $a_e(n)\tilde{b}_e(n)$ is conjugate even, Procedure 4' can be used to obtain $z_{xy}(k)$.

RECORD SECTIONING PROCEDURES

The calculation of covariance and cross-covariance functions can be done indirectly in a piecemeal fashion by operating on DFT's of sections of the record. This is sometimes convenient because of memory constraints, and usually results in little loss and sometimes yields a gain in computation speed.

We will examine the case $L \ll M$, a case of considerable practical interest. We will also consider only the sample covariance function. The calculation of the sample cross-covariance function proceeds in a parallel manner.

Let $x(j) : j = 0, \ldots, M - 1$ be defined as before. Also assume we wish to calculate the sample covariance function $\hat{\gamma}_{xx}(k)$ for $k = 0, 1, \ldots, L$. Let $x(j)$ be partitioned into nonoverlapping sections, $x_h(j)$, of length S as follows:

$$x_1(j) = x(j) \qquad\qquad j = 0, \ldots, S - 1$$
$$x_2(j) = x(j + S) \qquad j = 0, \ldots, S - 1$$
$$\vdots$$
$$x_H(j) = x(j + (H - 1)S) \quad j = 0, \ldots, S - 1$$

$$(161)$$

We assume $M = HS$. If this is not the case the last section can be handled individually in an obvious way. Let $x_1(j), x_2(j), \ldots, x_H(j)$ be extended to length $T = S + L$ by appending L zeros. Call these extended functions $x'_h(j) : h = 1, \ldots, H$. Now an estimate $\hat{\hat{\gamma}}_{xx}(k)$ can be obtained from the $x'_h(j)$ by simply averaging over section estimates obtained as in (157). Let $a'_h(n)$ be the DFT of $x'_h(j)$ then $\hat{\hat{\gamma}}_{xx}(k)$ is obtained as indicated below:

$$
\begin{array}{c}
x'_h(j) \longrightarrow a'_h(n) \\
h = 1, 2, \ldots, H \\
\big\downarrow \\
v_{xx}(k) \longleftarrow \sum_h a'_h(n)\tilde{a}'_h(n) \\
\big\downarrow
\end{array}
$$

$$(162)$$

$$\hat{\hat{\gamma}}_{xx}(k) = \frac{C(S, k)}{H} v_{xx}(k), \quad k = 0, \ldots, L$$

$$= \frac{C(S, k)}{H} \sum_{h=1}^{H} \left\{ \sum_{j=0}^{M-k-1} x_h(j + k)x_h(j) \right\}$$

The summation is done in the frequency domain to save on the number of transforms. This way, using the linearity property of the *DFT*, only one, rather than H, IDFTs have to be taken to obtain $v_{xx}(k)$.

The estimate $\hat{\hat{\gamma}}_{xx}(k)$ is a valid estimate of $\gamma_{xx}(k)$ but it is not statistically as accurate as $\hat{\gamma}_{xx}(k)$ because information between sections is lost. If one has sufficient data this loss could be unimportant and $\hat{\hat{\gamma}}_{xx}(k)$ could

be an attractive estimate. To obtain the estimate $\hat{\gamma}_{xx}(k)$ the following additional functions are defined:

$$f_h(j) = x_h(S - L + j), \quad j = 0, \ldots, L - 1$$
$$g_h(j) = x_{h+1}(j), \qquad\qquad h = 0, \ldots, H - 1$$

Further let $f_1(j), f_2(j) \cdots f_{H-1}(j)$ be extended to length $2L$ by *appending* L zeros and let $g_1(j), g_2(j), \ldots, g_{H-1}$ be extended to length $2L$ by *prefixing* L zeros. Call these extended functions $f'_h(j)$ and $g'_h(j)$ and call their *DFT*'s $c'_h(n)$ and $d'_h(n)$, respectively. The sectioning of $x(j)$ into $x_h(j)$, $f_h(j)$ and $g_h(j)$ is illustrated in Fig. 14.9. Then $\hat{\gamma}_{xx}(k)$ can be obtained from the $x'_h(j)$, $f'_h(j)$ and $g'_h(j)$ as indicated below.

$$
\begin{array}{c}
x'_h(j) \longrightarrow a'_h(n) \\
f'_h(j), g'_h(j) \longrightarrow c'_h(n), d'_h(n) \\
\big\downarrow \\
v_{xx}(k) \longleftarrow \sum_{h=1}^{H} \tilde{a}'_h(n)a'_h(n) \\
w_{xx}(k) \longleftarrow \sum_{h=1}^{H-1} \tilde{c}'_h(n)d'_h(n) \\
\big\downarrow
\end{array}
$$

$$(163)$$

$$\hat{\gamma}_{xx}(k) = C(M, k)(v_{xx}(k) + w_{xx}(k)),$$
$$k = 0, 1, \ldots, L$$

The function $w_{xx}(k)$ gives the sum of lagged products over the ends of the sections $x_h(j)$.

Comparison of Computing Times for the Direct and Indirect Methods

In the discussion that follows we will assume that the radix 2 algorithm is used in all the indirect calculations, We will use the approximation developed in Section 6 that the time required for an N-point DFT or IDFT is $k_1 N \log_2 N$ where k_1 depends on the machine and the program. We will also use the approximation, discussed in Section 6 that the time required for N-point real

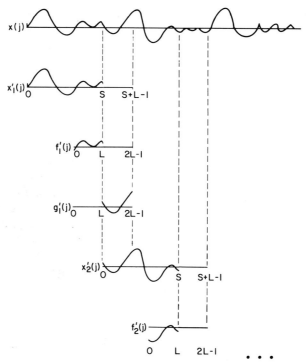

Fig. 14.9. Sectioning of $x(j)$ into extended sections $x'_k(j)$, $f'_h(j)$, and $g'_h(j)$.

transforms and N-point real even transforms are $k_1(N/2)\log_2 N$ and $k_1(N/4)$ $\log_2 N$, respectively. Finally, we will use the approximation, again discussed in Section 6, that the time required for the direct calculation of $\hat\gamma_{xx}(k)$ and $\hat\gamma_{xy}(k)$ for $|k| \leqslant L$ is proportional to the number of multiply–adds or $k_2(M - L/2)(L + 1)$ and $k_2(M - L/2)(2L + 1)$, respectively. Here again, k_2 is a function of the program and machine. Obviously the ratio k_1/k_2 is key to a comparison of computing times. In Section 6d we show that $k_1/k_2 \approx 7/3$.

We first consider the case of the calculation of a single covariance function. In this case, for the indirect calculation we require one real DFT and one real even IDFT or a time of

$$k_1\left(\frac{3N}{4}\right)\log_2 N$$

$$\approx k_1\left(3\frac{(M + L)}{4}\right)\log_2(M + L)$$

The latter approximation is fairly coarse but off by at most a factor of two (when $M + L$ is just greater than a power of two). For the direct calculation, that is the application of formula (154), we have

$$k_2\left(M - \frac{L}{2}\right)(L + 1)$$

It is clear that for M and L sufficiently large the indirect method is substantially faster than the direct. For example if $M = 1500$ and $L = 300$ then $N = 2048$ and the indirect time would be

$$k_1(1536)(11) = 16896k_1 \approx 40{,}000\, k_2$$

while the direct time would be

$$k_2(1350)(301) = 406350\, k_2$$

Thus the indirect calculation would be about 10 times as fast as the direct.

Next consider the calculation of a single cross-covariance function. In this case for the indirect calculation we have two real DFT's and one real IDFT or a time of

$$k_1 \left(3 \frac{N}{2} \right) \log_2 N$$

$$\underset{(\geqslant)}{\approx} k_1 \left(3 \frac{(M+L)}{2} \right) \log_2(M+L)$$

For the direct calculation we have

$$k_2 \left(M - \frac{L}{2} \right)(2L + 1)$$

Hence both the indirect and direct times are doubled.

If we have two sample sequences $x(j), y(j)$ and calculate indirectly both sample covariance functions and the sample cross-covariance function we require two real DFT's, one real IDFT and two real even IDFT's or a time of

$$k_1(2N)\log_2 N \underset{(\geqslant)}{\approx} 2k_1(M+L)\log_2(M+L)$$

There is a saving over the time required to do them separately. If we calculate them directly we require a time of

$$2k_2 \left(M - \frac{L}{2} \right)(L+1) + k_2 \left(M - \frac{L}{2} \right)$$

$$(2L + 1) = k_2 \left(M - \frac{L}{2} \right)(4L + 3)$$

Thus in this case there is additional advantage to the indirect calculation. For the case $M = 1500$, $L = 300$ the indirect calculation would now be about 15 times as fast as the direct.

b. Calculation of Spectral Estimates

Direct Calculation and Smoothing of the Sample Periodogram and Cross-Periodogram

We let $x(j)$ and $y(j)$ $j = 0, \ldots, M - 1$ be sample sequences as defined in Sections 2 and 3a. Further, as earlier, we let $x_e(j)$ and $y_e(j)$ be the sequences extended to

length $N = M + L$ by the addition of L zeros. L may be zero. Then the sample periodogram is calculated as follows:

$$x_e(j) \longrightarrow a_e(n)$$
$$\downarrow$$
$$I_{xx}(\omega_n) = \frac{1}{2\pi M} |a_e(n)|^2$$

$$(164)$$

for

$$\omega_n = \frac{2\pi n}{N}, \quad n = 0, 1, \ldots, \left[\frac{N}{2} \right]$$

where $[N/2]$ denotes the integer part of $N/2$.

Similarly the sample cross-periodogram is obtained as shown below.

$$x_e(j) \longrightarrow a_e(n)$$

$$y_e(j) \longrightarrow b_e(n)$$
$$\downarrow$$
$$I_{xy}(\omega_n) = \frac{1}{2\pi M} a_e(n)\tilde{b}_e(n)$$

$$(165)$$

for

$$\omega_n = \frac{2\pi n}{N}, \quad n = 0, 1, \ldots, N - 1$$

The sample periodogram and cross-periodogram can be smoothed as discussed in Section 2g to yield estimates of the spectrum. Section 2g also contains a discussion of the resultant spectral windows and statistical accuracy.

Calculation of Spectral Estimates Through the Sample Covariance and Cross-Covariance Functions

The calculation of the sample covariance function $\hat{\gamma}_{xx}(k)$ is discussed in detail above and in Section 3a. Given the sample covariance function for $k = 0, 1, \ldots, L$ spectral estimates are given by

$$\hat{p}_{xx}(\omega) = \frac{1}{2\pi} \sum_{k=-L}^{L} \lambda(k)\hat{\gamma}_{xx}(k)\cos \omega k$$

$$(166)$$

where $\lambda(k)$ is the lag function. The choice of lag function and choice of spacing for the computed values of ω are discussed in detail in [4, 21]. Calculation of (166) can be done in a straightforward fashion using the FFT algorithm. This calculation is however usually minor compared to that required for $\hat{\gamma}_{xx}(k)$.

Similarly, given the sample cross-covariance function $\hat{\gamma}_{xy}(k)$ whose calculation is discussed above and in Section 3a, estimates of the cross-spectra are given by

$$\hat{p}_{xy}(\omega) = \frac{1}{2\pi} \sum_{k=-L}^{L} \lambda(k)\hat{\gamma}_{xy}(k)e^{-i\omega k} \quad (167)$$

where $\lambda(k)$ is the lag function. Again (167) can be calculated in a straightforward fashion using the FFT algorithm.

OBTAINING SPECTRAL ESTIMATES BY TIME AVERAGING OVER SHORT MODIFIED PERIODOGRAMS

This method of time averaging over short modified periodograms is discussed in Section 2g and reference [40]. The sequence $x(j)$ is divided into K overlapping segments $x_k(j)$ each of length L. Each segment is multiplied by a data window $w(j)$ yielding the weighted sequences $w(j)x_k(j) : k = 1, \ldots, K$. These weighted sequences are handled as described below to obtain spectral estimates.

$$w(j)x_k(j) \longrightarrow c_k(n)$$
$$k = 1, \ldots, K \quad k = 1, \ldots, K$$
$$\downarrow$$
$$\hat{p}(\omega_n) = (1/K)(1/2\pi UL) \sum_{k=1}^{K} |c_k(n)|^2$$
$$\omega_n = \frac{n}{2\pi L}, \quad \text{for } n = 0, 1, \ldots, L-1,$$

where $U = (1/L) \sum_{j=0}^{L-1} w^2(j)$. Cross-spectral estimates are obtained in a similar fashion. In actual applications, since the $w(j)x_k(j)$ are real, Procedure 4 of Section 2e can be used to obtain the $c_k(n)$. This will halve the computing time.

c. Calculation of Moving Average Filter Outputs

Practical details on the calculation of moving average filtered outputs of the form

$$y(j) = \sum_k w(k)x(j-k) \quad (168)$$

via the FFT algorithm are given in [15]. Generally speaking, if the weighting function $w(k)$ of the filter is of length greater than 30, the convolution can be performed more rapidly on a general-purpose computer indirectly via the FFT than directly via Eq. (168).

4. PROGRAMMING THE RADIX 2 FFT ALGORITHM

a. Discussion

Equation (52) describes the general FFT algorithm while Eq. (67) describes the base 2 algorithm. There is an enormous variety of ways in which the sequence of operations can be scheduled to suit various programming languages, storage allocation schemes, and special hardware. Special procedures have been designed for computers with hierarchical storage, that is, high-speed core storage with tape and disk auxiliary storage. (See, for example, [6] and [32].) Other variations are used for parallel processors [26]. We will confine our discussion below to the radix 2 algorithm.

The basis for the programming of the radix 2 algorithm is Eq. (67), repeated here,

$$a_l(i) = a_{l-1}(i) + a_{l-1}(k)W_{2^l}^{-N_l}$$
$$a_l(k) = a_{l-1}(i) - a_{l-1}(k)W_{2^l}^{-N_l} \quad (169)$$

where

$$l = 1, 2, \ldots, m$$
$$N_l = 0, 1, \ldots, 2^{l-1} - 1$$
$$J_l = 0, 1, \ldots, 2^{m-l} - 1 \quad (170)$$
$$i = N_l + 2^l J_l$$
$$k = i + 2^{l-1}$$

The outermost loop for the program is the one indexed by l. In the next loop, indexed by N_l, one must compute or obtain from tables, values of $W_{2^l}^{-N_l}$. Since this is independent of J_l, the innermost loop is indexed by J_l.

The bit-reversal algorithm used below accomplishes its task by simultaneously generating the index $I = 1, 2, \ldots, N$ and J, such that $J - 1$ is the bit-reversal of $I - 1$. The index J is generated by a programmed counter in which the units position is the 2^{m-1} bit position and carries are performed to the right instead of the left. Thus at each increase of I by 1, the program adds 2^{m-1} to J after a test to see if the 2^{m-1} bit position is zero. If not, that position is made zero and a carry to the right is performed by following the same procedure for the 2^{m-2} bit position. This is repeated for successive bit positions, going from left to right, until a zero is found. The program is written to over-write data with computed values. Therefore, interchanging the contents of locations I and J yields both $a_0(I)$ and $a_0(J)$, placing them in the locations previously occupied by $x(J)$ and $x(I)$, respectively. Obviously it suffices to do this only for $I < J$. For each execution of (169) only two indices i and k need be generated and the two computed values of a_l can replace, or over-write the two values a_{l-1} with the same indices.

b. System Flow Graphs

The system flow graph is particularly useful for describing the algorithm since it describes the operations in terms of precedence rather than prescribing the order of execution of each step. The operation of the radix 2 algorithm, see Eq. (169), for a single set of indices is described by the system flow graph in Fig. 14.10. The appeerence of the flow graph has resulted in the name "butterfly." Each node represents a variable and the arrows terminating at that node originate at the nodes whose variables contribute to the value of the variable at that node. The contributions are additive and

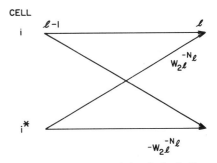

Fig. 14.10. System flow graph for the basic "butterfly" operation for *FFT*, radix 2.

the weight of each contribution, if other than unity, is indicated by the constant written close to the arrowhead of the contribution. The full system flow graph for the radix 2 FFT with $N = 8$ is shown in Fig. 14.11. Variables at nodes in row n replace each other as they are computed and are stored in the cell with index n. All node variables in column l are computed in iteration l.

c. Flow Charts

The following description of the flow charts in Figs. 14.12 and 14.13 is given in terms of the quantities in (169) and (170) except that the calculation is given in terms of the elements of the array A. Initially, A contains the given data x, during the calculation it contains a_l, and at the end, it contains the final result, a. The variables of the flow chart are related to those in (169) and (170) as follows:

$$
\begin{aligned}
&J \text{ is } N_l + 1 \\
&I \text{ is } i + 1 \\
&K \text{ is } k + 1 \\
&U \text{ is } W_{2^l}^{-N_l} \\
&W \text{ is } W_{2^l}^{-1}
\end{aligned}
\tag{171}
$$

Box 1: The integer $m = \log_2 N$ and the data $x(0), x(1), \ldots, x(N - 1)$, are supplied to the program with the x's stored in the array A so that $A(J) = x(J - 1)$.

Box 2: Calculate $N = 2^m$ and set I and J to their initial values.

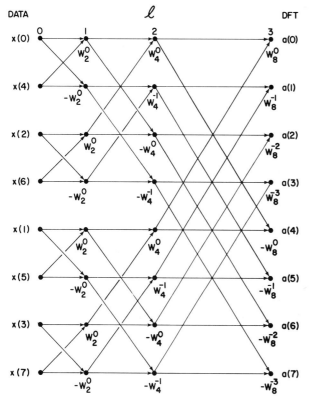

Fig. 14.11. System flow graph for computation of the *DFT*, radix 2, with $N = 8$ and with initial data in bit-reversed order.

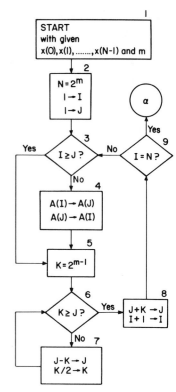

Fig. 14.12. Flow chart for bit reversal.

Box 3: Test for $I \geq J$ and if true, skip the interchange of $A(I)$ and $A(J)$.

Box 4: Perform the interchange.

Box 5: Set K equal to the test-bit, that is, a word with a 1 in the units position of the J-register and zeros elsewhere.

Box 6: Test to see if there is already a 1 in that position.

Box 7: If "No" in Box 6, the 1 in the position of the J-register being tested is replaced by zero and the test-bit is shifted to the right one position. Control returns to Box 6 where the test is repeated.

Box 8: If the bit in the J-register being tested is zero it is replaced by 1, effectively increasing the bit-reversed J-register by 1. The index I is also increased by 1.

Box 9: I is tested against N to see if the entire bit-reversal is finished. If $I < N$, it

goes to Box 3 and repeats the procedure. If $I = N$ control passes to the FFT algorithm starting at Box 10 in Fig. 14.13.

Box 10: Set l to 1.

Box 11: Set U to 1 and W to $W_{2^l}^{-1}$.

Box 12: Set J to 1.

Box 13: Set I to J.

Box 14: Set K to $I + 2^{l-1}$.

Box 15: The calculation in (169) is carried out. The As on the left-hand sides in Box 15 are a_{l-1}s while the As on the right-hand sides are a_l's.

Box 16: I is increased by 2^l, which is equivalent to increasing J_l in (170) by 1.

Box 17: Test for the end of the I-loop.

Box 18: J is increased by 1, which is equivalent to increasing N_l by 1. Multiplication of $U = W_{2^l}^{-N_l}$ yields U for the new N_l.

Box 19: Test for the end of the J-loop.

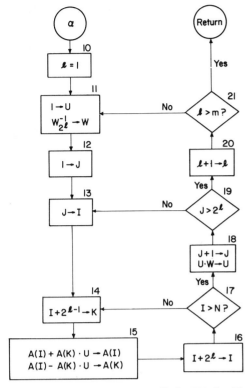

Fig. 14.13. Flow chart for the radix 2 *FFT* algorithm.

```
SUBROUTINE FFT (A,M)
COMPLEX A (1) ,U, W, T
N=2**M
NV2=N/2
NM 1=N-1
J=1
DO 7 I=1, NM 1
IF (I.GE.J) GO TO 5
T=A (J)
A (J)=A (I)
A (I)=T
5 K=NV2
6 IF (K.GE.J) GO TO 7
J=J-K
K=K/2
GO TO 6
7 J=J+K
DO 20 L=1,M
LE=2**L
LE1=LE/2
U= (1.,0.)
ANG=3.14159265358979/LE1
W=CMPLX (COS (ANG) ,-SIN (ANG))
DO 20 J=1,LE1
DO 10 I=J,N,LE
IP=I+LE1
T=A (IP) *U
A (IP) =A (I) - T
10 A (I)=A (I) + T
20 U=U*W
RETURN
END
```

Fig. 14.14. Radix 2 Fortran program for computing the *DFT* by the *FFT* Method.

Box 20: Increase *l* by 1.
Box 21: Test for the end of the *l*-loop.

d. Program

In the Fortran program listed Fig. 14.14, the "DO 7" loop does the bit-reversal described by the flow chart in Fig. 14.12 and the "DO 20" loop executes the FFT algorithm according to the flow charts in Fig. 14.13. The Fortran variables are defined in the flow chart description in Section 4c and in Eqs. (171) and by the following:

$$
\begin{aligned}
&L \text{ is } l\\
&LE1 \text{ is } 2^{l-1}\\
&LE \text{ is } 2^{l}\\
&ANG \text{ is } 2\pi/2^{l-1}
\end{aligned}
\tag{172}
$$

5. SAMPLE CALCULATION

As an example we consider the calculation via the FFT algorithm of the lagged product of the sequence $x(j)$ with itself, where

$$x(j) = 1, \quad j = 0, \ldots, 3$$

That is, we will calculate

$$y(k) = \sum_{j=0}^{3-k} x(j)x(j + k)$$

for $k = 0, \ldots, 3$. By observation the correct answer is

$$y(0) = 4, y(1) = 3, y(2) = 2, \quad y(3) = 1$$

Following the methods of Section 3a, we append 4 zeros forming the function

$$
\begin{aligned}
x_e(j) &= x(j) & j &= 0, \ldots, 3\\
x_e(j) &= 0 & j &= 4, \ldots, 7
\end{aligned}
$$

We compute its DFT, $a(n)$, then $|a_e(n)|^2$, and finally the IDFT of $|a_e(n)|^2$. The results of a machine calculation are given in Table 4. Note the wrap-around effect in the values of $y(k)$ for $k = 5$, 6, and 7. These are $y(-3), y(-2)$, and $y(-1)$, respectively.

Table 4. SAMPLE CALCULATION OF LAGGED PRODUCTS VIA THE FFT ALGORITHM

j	$x_e(j)$	$a_e(n)$	$|a_e(n)|^2$	$y(j)$
0	1	.5	.25	3.9999976
1	1	$.125 - .3017766i$	.1066941	2.9999992
2	1	.0	.0	2.0000000
3	1	$.125 - .0517767i$	.0183058	1.0000008
4	0	.0	.0	0.0000024
5	0	$.125 - .0517767i$	.0183058	1.0000008
6	0	.0	.0	2.0000000
7	0	$.125 - .301777i$	.1066941	2.9999992

6. ESTIMATION OF RUNNING TIME

a. The FFT algorithm

The basic "butterfly" operation described by Eq. (169) must be performed $\frac{1}{2}Nm$ times in the FFT calculation where $m = \log_2 N$. Except for special cases, two complex additions and one complex multiplication are required for each butterfly. Letting η and μ represent the time required for real addition and multiplication, respectively, the time for the complex multiplication is

$$T_m = 2\eta + 4\mu \qquad (173)$$

Four real additions are needed for the two complex additions giving a total computing time of

$$T_b = 6\eta + 4\mu \qquad (174)$$

for the arithmetic in each butterfly.

For butterflies with $N_l = 0$, (see Eq. (169)) we have $W_N^{-N_l} = 1$ so the multiplication is not necessary. The number of butterflies for which this occurs is

$$\sum_{l=1}^{m} \sum_{K=0}^{2^{m-L}-1} 1 = \sum_{l=1}^{m} 2^{m-1} \approx N \quad (175)$$

Therefore, the total arithmetic time is

$$T_{\text{FFT}}(N) = \left(\tfrac{1}{2}mT_b - T_m\right)N$$

$$= \left[m(3\eta + 2\mu) - (2\eta + 4\mu)\right]N \quad (176)$$

Further savings, proportional to N, can be made by avoiding multiplication in Eq. (169) whenever $W_N^{-N_l} = i$ or $\sqrt{i}$ but these will not be included here.

The other operations required for the execution of a "butterfly" are referred to as "bookkeeping" and consist of address formation, load, store, and test operations. Our experience shows that the bookkeeping time is roughly 75% of the arithmetic time. Hence from Eq. (173) the total computing time is given approximately by an equation of the form

$$T_{\text{FFT}}^*(N) \approx k_1 Nm - cN \qquad (177)$$

where

$$k_1 \approx \frac{7}{4} \frac{T_b}{2} = \frac{7}{4}(3\eta + 2\mu) \quad (178)$$

$$c \approx \frac{7}{4} T_m = \frac{7}{4}(2\eta + 4\mu) \quad (179)$$

or

$$T_{\text{FFT}}^*(N) \approx \frac{7}{4} N\left[(3\eta + 2\mu)m - (2\eta + 4\mu)\right]$$

$$(180)$$

b. The FFT Algorithm for Real Data

If Procedure 2 of Section 2e is used to calculate the DFT of two real N-point sequences simultaneously, then one must compute an N-point DFT followed by the $2N$ real additions in (84) and (85). Therefore, the total arithmetic time for each DFT is

$$T_{\text{RFFT}}(N) = \frac{T_{\text{FFT}}(N)}{2} + N\eta$$

$$= \frac{[m(3\eta + 2\mu) - 4\mu]N}{2} \quad (181)$$

The extra operations outside the FFT algorithm, are similar enough to the butterfly computation to permit the same scaling for bookkeeping as was done for the FFT itself.

On the other hand, if Procedure 4 of Section 2e is used to compute the DFT of a single N-point real sequence, one computes a DFT of an $N/2$-point complex sequence followed by N real additions (87) and (88) and $N/4$ butterflies (89) and (90). In all, the total arithmetic time is

$$T_{\text{FFT}}\left(\frac{N}{2}\right) + N\eta + \frac{NT_b}{4}$$

$$= \left[\tfrac{1}{2}(m-1)T_b - T_m\right]\frac{N}{2} + N\eta + \frac{NT_b}{4}$$

$$= \left[\tfrac{1}{2}mT_b - T_m\right]\frac{N}{2} + N\eta$$

$$= T_{\text{FFT}}\frac{(N)}{2} + N\eta$$

This is seen to be identical to (181). Hence there is no advantage in doing two real transforms at a time. However, the use of either Procedure 2 or 4 results in a saving of approximately one-half for the transform of real data. The same timing estimates apply to the inverse transformation except that one has the extra division by N.

c. The Cosine Transform (Real Even Sequences)

The cosine transform of $N/2$ data points (95) is actually a DFT of a real even N-point sequence. Following Procedure 5 of Section 2e, we calculate the real DFT of the $N/2$-point sequence $y(j)$, defined by (97) and then calculate $a(n)$ according to (105).

The latter takes N additions and $N/2$ multiplications. Hence neglecting terms not containing N, the total amount of arithmetic is

$$T_{\cos}(N) = T_{\text{RFFT}}\left(\frac{N}{2}\right) + N\left(\eta + \frac{1}{2}\mu\right)$$

or

$$T_{\cos}(N) = \frac{1}{2}T_{\text{FFT}}\left(\frac{N}{2}\right) + N\left(\frac{3}{2}\eta + \frac{1}{2}\mu\right)$$

$$= \left[m(3\eta + 2\mu) + \eta - 4\mu\right]\frac{N}{4} \quad (182)$$

If $\mu = 2\eta$

$$T_{\cos}(N) = 7[m-1]\frac{N\eta}{4} \quad (183)$$

Thus the fourfold redundancy of the real even data can be used to permit the DFT to be computed with $\frac{1}{4}$ the computing effort required for general complex data.

d. Comparison of the Direct and Indirect Methods of Calculating Sample Covariance Functions

In Section 3a we discuss the comparison of direct and indirect methods of calculating sample covariance functions. If one calculates sample covariance functions directly, one computes sums of products of the form

$$\hat{\gamma}(k) = C(M, k) \sum_{j=0}^{N-k} x(j)x(k+j)$$

Now if $x(j)$ is real this requires approximately $N - k + 1$ real multiple-adds. Experience shows the overhead for lagged products to take roughly 75% additional time and hence that the total time for one value of k is

$$k_2(N - k + 1)$$

where

$$k_2 \approx 1.75(\eta + \mu) \quad (184)$$

The comparison of the direct and indirect

methods asymptotically involves the ratio k_1/k_2 where k_1 and k_2 are given by (178) and (184), respectively. Substituting from these equations we obtain

$$\frac{k_1}{k_2} \approx \frac{7/4(3\eta + 2\mu)}{7/4(\eta + \mu)} \qquad (185)$$

and using the additional approximation $\mu = 2\eta$ we obtain

$$\frac{k_1}{k_2} \approx \frac{7\mu}{3\mu} = \frac{7}{3} \qquad (186)$$

This is the figure used in Section 3a. It must be understood that this is an approximation and that depending upon the programs and machines this ratio could easily vary by 50% in either direction.

7. CONCLUSION

The FFT algorithm makes a remarkable improvement in the ease and practicality with which one can apply Fourier methods in numerical calculation. Its introduction revised the economies of the use of the discrete Fourier transform and consequently the economy of covariance function calculation, spectral estimation, and moving average filtering. In this chapter we have discussed the algorithm in detail and provided guidelines for its economic application, *vis à vis* earlier methods, in the above areas.

8. REFERENCES

1. M. S. Bartlett, "Smoothing Periodograms from Time-Series with Continuous Spectra," *Nature*, **161**, 686–687 (1948).

2. G. D. Bergland, "A Fast Fourier Transform Algorithm Using Base Eight Iterations," *Math. Computation*, **22**, 275–279, (April 1968).

3. C. Bingham, M. D. Godfrey, and J. W. Tukey, "Modern Techniques of Power Spectral Estimation," *IEEE Trans. Audio and Electroacoustics*, **AU-15**, 56–66 (June 1967).

4. R. B. Blackman and J. W. Tukey, *The Measurement of Power Spectra*, Dover, New York, 1959.

5. L. I. Bluestein, "A Linear Filter Approach to the Computation of the Discrete Fourier Transform," *Nerem Rec.*, **1968**, 218–219.

6. N. M. Brenner, "Fast Fourier Transform of Externally Stored Data," *IEEE Trans. Audio and Electroacoustics*, **AU-17**, 128–132 (June 1969).

7. D. R. Brillinger and M. Rosenblatt, "Asymptotic Theory of Estimates of Kth Order Spectra," *Advanced Seminar on Spectral Analysis of Time Series*, B. Hannes ed., Wiley, New York, 1967.

8. J. W. Cooley and J. W. Tukey, "An Algorithm for Machine Calculation of Complex Fourier Series," *Math. Computation*, **19**, 297–301 (April 1965).

9. J. W. Cooley, P. A. W. Lewis, and P. D. Welch, "Historical Notes on the Fast Fourier Transform," *IEEE Trans. Audio and Electroacoustics*, **AU-15**, No. 2, 76–79 (June 1967).

10. D. R. Cox and P. A. W. Lewis, *The Statistical Analysis of Series of Events*, Barnes and Noble, London, Methuen, New York, 1966.

11. G. C. Danielson and C. Lanczos, "Some Improvements in Practical Fourier Analysis and Their Application to X-ray Scattering from Liquids," *J. Franklin Inst.*, **233**, 365–380; 435–452 (1942).

12. J. Durbin, "Tests of Serial Independence Based on the Cumulated Periodogram," *Bull. I.S.I.*, **42**, 1039–1049 (1969).

13. W. M. Gentleman and G. Sande, "Fast Fourier Transforms—for Fun and Profit," 1966 *Fall Joint Computer Conf.*, AFIPS *Proc.*, Vol. 29, Washington, D. C.: Spartan, pp. 563–578 (1969).

14. B. V. Gnedenko, *The Theory of Probability*, 2nd edit., New York, Chelsea, 1962.

15. B. Gold and C. M. Rader, *Digital Processing of Signals*, McGraw-Hill, New York, 1969.

16. I. J. Good, "The Interaction Algorithm and Practical Fourier Series," *J. Roy. Static. Soc.*, Ser. B, **20**, 361–372 (1958); Addendum, **22**, 372–375 (1960).

17. C. W. J. Granger and A. O. Hughes, "Spectral Analysis of Short-Series Simulation Study," *J. Roy. Statist. Soc.*, Ser. A., **131**, 83–99 (1968).

18. E. J. Hannan, *Multiple Time Series*, Wiley, New York, 1970.

19. H. Helms, "Digital Filters with Equiripple or Minimax Responses," *IEEE Trans. Audio and Electroacoustics*, **AU-19**, 87–93 (March 1971).

20. D. Jackson, *Fourier Series and Orthogonal Polynomials*, Math. Assoc. of America, 1941.

21. G. M. Jenkins and D. G. Watts, *Spectral Analysis and Its Applications*. Holden-Day, San Francisco, 1968.

22. T. Kaneko and B. Liu, "Accumulation of Round-

off Error in Fast Fourier Transforms," *J. Assoc. Comput. Mach.*, **17**, 637–654 (Oct. 1970).

23. R. A. Olshen, "Asymptotic Properties of the Periodogram of a Discrete Stationary Process," *J. Appl. Prob.*, **4**, 508–528 (1967).

24. A. V. Oppenheim and C. Weinstein, "Effects of Finite Register Length in Digital Filtering and the Fast Fourier Transform," *Proc. IEEE*, **60** (8), 957–976 (August 1972).

25. E. Parzen, "Statistical Spectral Analysis (Single Channel Case) in 1968," Stanford University, Dept. of Statistics, Stanford, Calif., *Tech. Rept. 11, ONR Contract Nonr-225 (80) (NR-042/234)*, June 10, 1968.

26. M. C. Pease, "An Adaptation of the Fast Fourier Transform for Parallel Processing," *J. ACM*, **15**, 252–264 (April 1968).

27. L. R. Rabiner, "The Design of Finite Impulse Response Digital Filters Using Linear Programming Techniques," *BSTJ*, **51** (6), 1177–1198 (July–August 1972).

28. P. Rudnick, "Note on the Calculation of Fourier Series," *Math. Computation*, **20**, 429–430 (July 1966).

29. C. Runge, *Zeit. Math. Physik*, **48**, 443 (1903).

30. C. Runge, *Zeit Math. Physik*, **53**, 117 (1905).

31. C. Runge and König, "Die Grundlehren der Mathematischen Wissenschaften," in *Vorlesunge über Numerisches Rechnen*, **11**, Springer, Berlin, 1924.

32. R. C. Singleton, "A Method for Computing the Fast Fourier Transform with Auxiliary Memory and Limited High-speed Storage," *IEEE Trans. Audio and Electroacoustics*, **AU-15**, 91–98 (June 1967).

33. R. C. Singleton, "An Algorithm for Computing the Mixed Radix Fast Fourier Transform," *IEEE Trans. Audio and Electroacoustics*, **AU-17**, No. 2, 93–103 (June 1969).

34. K. Stumpff, *Tafeln und Aufgaben zur Harmonischen Analyse und Periodogrammrechnung*, Springer, Berlin, 1939.

35. *Technometrics*, **3** (2), (May 1961), (This entire issue is devoted to spectral estimation).

36. L. H. Thomas, "Using a Computer to Solve Problems in Physics," in *Application of Digital Computers*. Ginn, Boston, Mass., 1963.

37. G. P. Tolstov, *Fourier Series*, Prentice-Hall, Englewood Cliffs, N. J., 1962.

38. G. S. Watson, "Smooth Regression Analysis," *Sankya*, **1964**, 359–372, 1964.

39. C. J. Weinstein, "Roundoff Noise in Floating Point Fast Fourier Transform Computation," *IEEE Trans. Audio Electroacoustics*, **AU-17**, 209–215 (Sept. 1969).

40. P. D. Welch, "The Use of Fast Fourier Transform for the Estimation of Power Spectra: A Method Based on Time Averaging over Short Modified Periodograms," *IEEE Trans. Audio and Electroacoustics*, **AU-15**, 70–73 (June 1967).

41. P. D. Welch, "A Fixed-Point Fast Fourier Transform Error Analysis," *IEEE Trans. Audio Electroacoustics*, **AU-17**, 153–157 (June 1969).

42. D. V. Widder, *The Laplace Transform*, Princeton Univ. Press, 1941.

43. J. H. Wilkinson, *Rounding Errors in Algebraic Processes*, Prentice-Hall, Englewood Cliffs, N.J., 1963.

44. F. Yates, *The Design and Analysis of Factorial Experiments*, Imperial Bureau of Soil Science, Harpenden, 1937.

45. A. Zygmund, "*Trigonometric Series*," Cambridge Univ. Press, 1959.

Time Series Forecasting

15

David W. Bacon and Louis H. Broekhoven
Queen's University
Kingston, Ontario, Canada

1. FUNCTION

In this chapter a method of forecasting the future performance of a time series is discussed. The forecast model is developed from a linear stochastic model that adequately represents the available data record for the series. Forecasts of series values within the data record can be calculated as a means of evaluating the proposed forecasting model. Forecasts of series values beyond the data record can also be calculated to estimate the future behavior of the series.

The only reliable basis for forecasting future performance of a time-dependent variable is a mathematical model that incorporates both the deterministic and the stochastic components of its recent behavior. The deterministic component is necessarily peculiar to the particular phenomenon under study. Considerable success has been achieved in representing the stochastic behavior of a number of time series from a variety of fields of application using linear stochastic models. Box and Jenkins [1] have published an extremely useful account of a general class of linear stochastic models that includes traditional autoregressive and moving average models but also accommodates seasonal and nonstationary forms of behavior. They have demonstrated the development of appropriate stochastic model forms for particular time series and the use of these models for forecasting future series performance.

An important guideline in time series analysis is the selection of a model form involving as few parameters as possible. An iterative three-stage procedure has been proposed by Box and Jenkins for determining a suitable model for a time series:

1. identification
2. fitting
3. diagnostic checking

In the identification stage the estimated autocorrelation function, described in the previous chapter, and other appropriate statistics for the time series are used to select a tentative model form. The fitting stage is concerned with efficient estimation of the unknown parameters. The next stage involves subjecting the fitted model to rigorous diagnostic tests to determine its adequacy for the series it represents. If the fitted model is found to be inadequate it is modified in a manner prescribed by the results of the diagnostic tests and stages 1–3 are repeated. Only a confirmed adequate fitted model should be used to forecast future values of the time series.

This chapter describes a computer program that computes forecasts for a given time series using any model form from the general linear class described by Box and Jenkins. It is assumed that the proposed model has been developed by the foregoing three-stage procedure and in particular that it does adequately represent the behavior of the time series. Base points and lead times for the forecasts are specified by the user. Probability error limits for each forecast are also calculated and provision is made for documenting the agreement of forecast values with corresponding observed data that become available subsequently.

2. MATHEMATICAL DISCUSSION

a. Symbols Used

$A(x)$ A polynomial in x

$\{\mathbf{a}\}$ The set of random errors for a time series

a_j The coefficient of x^j in $A(x)$

a_t The random error at time t

B The backward shift operator

B^{-1} The forward shift operator

$B(x)$ A polynomial in x

b_j The coefficient of x^j in $B(x)$

$C(x)$ A polynomial in x

c_j The coefficient of x^j in $C(x)$

D_1 The degree of the differencing operator for period s_1

D_2 The degree of the differencing operator for period s_2

D_3 The degree of the differencing operator for period s_3

$D(x)$ A polynomial in x

d_1 The degree of the differencing operator for period 1

d_j The coefficient of x^j in $D(x)$

E The unconditional expectation

E_t The conditional expectation given all information up to and including time t

i A general index

j A general index

k A general index

l The forecast lead time

m The degree of $A(x)$

N The number of values in the data record

n The degree of $B(x)$

P_1 The degree of $\Phi_1(B)$

p The degree of $\phi(B)$

p_1 The degree of $\phi_1(B)$

Q_1 The degree of $\Theta_1(B)$

q The degree of $\theta(B)$

q_1 The degree of $\theta_1(B)$

s_1 The period of a seasonal fluctuation

s_2 The period of a seasonal fluctuation

s_3 The period of a seasonal fluctuation

s_a^2 An estimate of σ_a^2

t A subscript denoting time t

$V(l)$ The variance of $\hat{y}_t(l)$

$\{\mathbf{w}\}$ A stationary time series obtained by differencing $\{\mathbf{y}\}$

w_t The value of the series $\{\mathbf{w}\}$ at time t

x A general variable

$\{\mathbf{y}\}$ A time series

y_t The value of the series $\{\mathbf{y}\}$ at time t

$\hat{y}_m$ An estimate of y_m

$\hat{y}_t(l)$ The minimum variance forward forecast of y_{y+l} from base point t

$\breve{y}_t(1)$ The minimum variance backward forecast of y_{t-1} from base point t

$\alpha(x)$ A polynomial in x

α_j The coefficient of x^j in $\alpha(x)$

$\beta(x)$ A polynomial in x

β_j The coefficient of x^j in $\beta(x)$

$\{\boldsymbol{\varepsilon}\}$ The set of random errors in a time series described by a reverse model

ε_t The backward random error at time t

$\Theta_1(B)$ The moving average polynomial operator for period s_1

$\Theta_2(B)$ The moving average polynomial operator for period s_2

$\Theta_3(B)$ The moving average polynomial operator for period s_3

Θ_{1k} The coefficient of B^{ks_1} in $\theta_1(B)$

$\theta(B)$ The combined moving average polynomial operator

$\theta_1(B)$ The moving average polynomial operator for period 1

θ_k The coefficient of B^k in $\theta(B)$

θ_{1k} The coefficient of B^k in $\theta_1(B)$

π_k The coefficient of y_{t-k} in Eq. (28)

σ_a^2 The variance of a_t for all t

σ_ε^2 The variance of ε_t for all t

$\Phi_1(B)$ The autoregressive polynomial operator for period s_1

$\Phi_2(B)$ The autoregressive polynomial operator for period s_2

$\Phi_3(B)$ The autoregressive polynomial operator for period s_3

Φ_{1k} The coefficient of B^{ks_1} in $\Phi_1(B)$

$\phi(B)$ The combined autoregressive polynomial operator

$\phi^{-1}(B)$ The inverse of $\phi(B)$

$\phi_1(B)$ The autoregressive polynomial operator for period 1

ϕ_j The coefficient of B^j in $\phi(B)$

ϕ_{1j} The coefficient of B^j in $\phi_1(B)$

ψ_k The coefficient of $-a_{t-k}$ in Eq. (28)

b. Introduction

In the following discussion the term "time series" signifies a sequence of observations taken at discrete and equally spaced intervals of time. Each interval is assumed to have unit length. A subscript t identifies the observation at point t in time so that the series can be written as

$$\cdots y_{t-1}, y_t, y_{t+1}, \cdots$$

or as $\{\mathbf{y}\}$. Conceptually, such a series may be imagined to extend indefinitely into the past and into the future although of course in practice only a sample of finite length is available for analysis.

c. Smoothing and Forecasting

Like other types of data, time-dependent data can be analyzed in a variety of ways, depending upon the final objective of the analysis. Two common operations are *smoothing* and *forecasting*. Unfortunately in classical analysis of time series considerable confusion has arisen because the distinction between these two operations has not always been stated precisely. Smoothing generally implies some form of empirical representation of the local behavior of a time series about a point within the available data record. Forecasting is the estimation of future series values beyond the available data record.

Traditional approaches to time series analysis have usually considered a series to consist of three components: trend, oscillatory behavior, and random fluctuation. These terms are necessarily vague, it being never possible to decide in practice where one component ends and another begins.

Early methods for obtaining smoothed values of the level and trend at a particular position in a time series that did not exhibit periodic behavior involved a "sliding polynomial" of low degree applied at the position of interest. Several moving average formulas resulting from this approach have been proposed to achieve a form of local representation of the series behavior [2, 3]. Periodic series were dealt with by "removal" of cyclic components using some form of harmonic function or another form of moving average prior to calculating smoothed values of the level and trend.

The arbitrary nature of these types of smoothing operations often creates significant difficulties in interpretation of the behavior of the original time series under study [4, 5]. The smoothed series will exhibit certain characteristics that the original series does not, such characteristics having been induced by the smoothing operation. Consequently one cannot consider either the smoothed series or, alternatively, the deviations from the smoothed series as if the operation has never been performed.

A much more reliable and systematic approach to time series analysis was proposed by Wold [6]. He advocated the use of a general class of linear stochastic models and suggested useful techniques for identifying appropriate model forms from the observed data. His work has served as a basis for many recent developments in the field. The forecasting procedure described in this chapter is clearly in the spirit of Wold's proposals.

d. A Basis for Forecasting

Although some degree of arbitrariness is to be expected in the choice of smoothing procedure, any procedure for forecasting future values of a time series should depend upon the deterministic and stochastic nature of the available series record. It is unreasonable to expect a smoothing function, designed to describe local behavior of a series, to serve equally well as a forecasting function. A mathematical model fitted to the entire available data record should be used as a basis for forecasting. The development of such models will not be discussed here. An excellent account of this important phase of time series analysis is provided by Box and Jenkins [1].

The forecasting operations discussed in this chapter will be further restricted to the stochastic portion of the series behavior. That is, it will be assumed that the series being forecast is the original time series *minus* any deterministic function values. In many situations it may not be feasible to formulate a deterministic model. In such cases the procedures to be discussed would then provide forecasts for the original series. It will be further assumed that an adequate form of stochastic model is being employed and that the values of the coefficients in this

model are known. Box and Jenkins have shown that the effect of this latter assumption is to increase the variance of a forecast by a factor of the order of $(1 + 1/N)$ where N is the number of values in the available data record used to fit the stochastic model.

Both the general class of stochastic models and the method of computing forecasts used in this chapter are those described by Box and Jenkins.

e. A General Class of Stochastic Models

A reasonable form of model to represent many univariate time series is one that expresses the current observed series value, y_t, as a linear function of previous observed series values, $y_{t-1}, y_{t-2}, \ldots \ldots$ and current and previous random errors $a_t, a_{t-1}, a_{t-2}, \ldots$. One class of linear models that is parsimonious in its use of parameters is

$$y_t = \phi_{11} y_{t-1} + \phi_{12} y_{t-2} + \cdots + \phi_{1p_1} y_{t-p_1}$$
$$+ a_t - \theta_{11} a_{t-1} - \theta_{12} a_{t-2} - \cdots$$
$$- \theta_{1q_1} a_{t-q_1} \qquad (1)$$

It is assumed that for all t values $E(a_t) = 0$

$$\text{and } E(a_t a_{t-j}) = \begin{pmatrix} \sigma_a^2 & \text{for } j = 0 \\ 0 & \text{for } j \neq 0 \end{pmatrix} \qquad (2)$$

Using the backward shift operator B, where

$$B^j y_t = y_{t-j} \qquad (3)$$

model (1) can be written more compactly as

$$\phi_1(B) y_t = \theta_1(B) a_t \qquad (4)$$

where $\phi_1(B) = \left(1 - \phi_{11} B - \phi_{12} B^2 - \cdots\right.$
$$\left. - \phi_{1p_1} B^{p_1}\right) \qquad (5)$$

is called an autoregressive operator in B

$$\text{and } \theta_1(B) = \left(1 - \theta_{11} B - \theta_{12} B^2\right.$$
$$\left. - \cdots - \theta_{1q_1} B^{q_1}\right) \qquad (6)$$

is called a moving average operator in B.

A process $\{y\}$ whose joint probability distribution remains unchanged through time is called a *stationary* process. Model (4) can be written as

$$y_t = \phi_1^{-1}(B)\theta_1(B)a_t \qquad (7)$$

so that the current observed series value is a linear function of only current and past random errors. The expression on the right-hand side of (7) will only have a finite variance if all of the roots of the polynomial $\phi_1(B)$ lie outside the unit circle. Consequently, the stochastic process represented by model (4) will be stationary only if all the roots of $\phi_1(B)$ lie outside the unit circle.

The majority of time series encountered in practice are nonstationary. For many such series nonstationarity exists because one or more of the roots of $\phi_1(B)$ are equal to 1 but no roots lie inside the unit circle. Box and Jenkins refer to such processes as *homogeneously nonstationary* processes. A time series $\{y\}$ that behaves in this fashion can be transformed into a stationary series $\{w\}$ by differencing it a number of times equal to the number of roots d_1 lying on the unit circle. Model (4) can then be extended to accommodate both stationary and homogeneously nonstationary behavior using the more general form

$$\phi_1(B)(1 - B)^{d_1}y_t = \theta_1(B)a_t \qquad (8)$$

or, equivalently,

$$\phi_1(B)w_t = \theta_1(B)a_t \qquad (9)$$

where

$$w_t = (1 - B)^{d_1}y_t \qquad (10)$$

The model

$$(1 - B)y_t = (1 - \theta_{11}B)a_t \qquad (11)$$

is a commonly occurring special case of the general form (8). As shown by Muth [7], minimum variance forecasts derived from this model are exactly the first-order ex-

ponential smoothing estimates proposed by Holt [8], Brown and Meyer [9], and others.

Time series exhibiting periodic behavior, hereafter referred to as *seasonal* time series, can be accommodated within this general class of models by a further extension. For example, if a periodicity of s_1 intervals exists within a series, then the model

$$\phi_1(B)\Phi_1(B)(1 - B)^{d_1}(1 - B^{s_1})^{D_1}y_t$$
$$= \theta_1(B)\Theta_1(B)a_t \qquad (12)$$

would be appropriate where

$$\Phi_1(B) = \Big(1 - \Phi_{11}B^{s_1} - \Phi_{12}B^{2s_1} - \cdots$$
$$- \Phi_{1,P_1}B^{P_1s_1}\Big) \qquad (13)$$

$$\Theta_1(B) = \Big(1 - \Theta_{11}B^{s_1} - \Theta_{12}B^{2s_1} - \cdots$$
$$- \Theta_{1,Q_1}B^{Q_1s_1}\Big) \qquad (14)$$

and D_1 is the degree of differencing by period s_1 that is required, in combination with differencing d_1 times by period 1, to reduce the series $\{y\}$ to a stationary series.

The appropriate values of d_1 and D_1 for a particular time series are determined in the identification stage (1) by examination of the estimated autocorrelation functions of various combinations of differences of the original series record. The values of d_1 and D_1 selected are the smallest values that yield a stationary series.

It is not uncommon to encounter time series, such as the one used as an example later in this chapter, in which more than one periodicity occurs. For example, a linear stochastic model that accommodates three types of seasonal behavior is

$$\phi_1(B)\Phi_1(B)\Phi_2(B)\Phi_3(B)(1 - B)^{d_1}$$
$$\times (1 - B^{s_1})^{D_1}(1 - B^{s_2})^{D_2}(1 - B^{s_3})^{D_3}y_t$$
$$= \theta_1(B)\Theta_1(B)\Theta_2(B)\Theta_3(B)a_t \qquad (15)$$

where $\Phi_2(B)$, $\Phi_3(B)$, $\Theta_2(B)$, $\Theta_3(B)$, D_2, and

D_3 are defined in analogous fashion to $\Phi_1(B)$, $\Theta_1(B)$, and D_1, respectively. Formidable as the model form (15) may appear, it should be recognized that by suitable multiplication of the operators this model can be reduced to the simpler general form

$$\phi(B)y_t = \theta(B)a_t \qquad (16)$$

where

$$\phi(B) = \phi_1(B)\Phi_1(B)\Phi_2(B)\Phi_3(B)$$

$$\times(1 - B)^{d_1}(1 - B^{s_1})^{D_1}$$

$$\times(1 - B^{s_2})^{D_2}(1 - B^{s_3})^{D_3}$$

$$= \left(1 - \phi_1 B - \phi_2 B^2 - \cdots - \phi_p B^p\right)$$

$$\qquad (17)$$

$$\theta(B) = \theta_1(B)\Theta_1(B)\Theta_2(B)\Theta_3(B)$$

$$= \left(1 - \theta_1 B - \theta_2 B^2 - \cdots - \theta_q B^q\right)$$

$$\qquad (18)$$

f. Forecasting with a Linear Stochastic Model

Using model form (16) a forecast made at time t of the series value at time $t + l$ can be developed as follows. It has been shown by Whittle [10] that at time t the minimum mean square error forecast (which is also the minimum variance forecast under our assumptions) of y_{t+l} is $E_t(y_{t+l})$ where E_t denotes the conditional expectation given all information up to and including time t. Now from model (16)

$$y_{t+l} = \phi_1 y_{t+l-1} + \phi_2 y_{t+l-2} + \cdots$$

$$+ \phi_p y_{t+l-p}$$

$$+ a_{t+l} - \theta_1 a_{t+l-1} - \theta_2 a_{t+l-2} - \cdots$$

$$- \theta_q a_{t+l-q} \qquad (19)$$

Then $E_t(y_{t+l})$, which is also denoted by

$\hat{y}_t(l)$ for $l > 0$, can be expressed as

$$E_t(y_{t+l})$$

$$= \phi_1 E_t(y_{t+l-1}) + \phi_2 E_t(y_{t+l-2})$$

$$+ \cdots + \phi_p E_t(y_{t+l-p})$$

$$+ E_t(a_{t+l}) - \theta_1 E_t(a_{t+l-1}) - \theta_2 E_t(a_{t+l-2})$$

$$- \cdots - \theta_q E_t(a_{t+l-q}) \qquad (20)$$

where

$$E_t(y_{t+j}) = \begin{pmatrix} y_{t+j} & \text{for } j \leqslant 0 \\ \hat{y}_t(j) & \text{for } j > 0 \end{pmatrix} \qquad (21)$$

and

$$E_t(a_{t+j}) = \begin{pmatrix} a_{t+j} & \text{for } j \leqslant 0 \\ 0 & \text{for } j > 0 \end{pmatrix} \qquad (22)$$

Furthermore, the one step ahead forecast error is

$$y_{t+1} - \hat{y}_t(1) = a_{t+1} \qquad (23)$$

which can be verified by substracting (20) from (19) with $l = 1$. This approach, using expression (20), provides an easy method for obtaining minimum variance forecasts. It incorporates a natural adaptive feature in that forecasts made at any time are always based on the most current information. A forecast made at time t uses observed y's up to time t and expected values of y's beyond time t as well as known errors $a_1, a_2, \ldots, a_t$ up to time t and zeros (their expected values) for a's beyond time t.

In this way it is a straightforward operation to compute several forecasts from a given base point t, beginning with lead time $l = 1$ and continuing with lead times $l = 2$, $l = 3$, and so on as far as desired. It will be noted that the method is of a "bootstrap" nature in that $\hat{y}_t(l)$, the forecast at base point t for lead time l, uses all of the "prior" forecasts from that base point,

$$\hat{y}_t(l-1), \hat{y}_t(l-2), \ldots, \hat{y}_t(1)$$

In practice the difficulty arises of getting these recursive forecast calculations started. In forecasting low order nonseasonal time series such as might be described by model (8) it is often sufficiently precise to consider the one step ahead forecast errors for the first $p_1 + d_1$ series values to be zero. For many seasonal series this simple approach would not be acceptable because of the large number of initial series values that might be involved.

A more precise method is as follows. As shown by Box and Jenkins [1], any time series $\{y\}$ that can be described by the general model (16)

$$\phi(B)y_t = \theta(B)a_t \qquad (24)$$

can also be described by the *reverse model*

$$\phi(B^{-1})y_t = \theta(B^{-1})\varepsilon_t \qquad (25)$$

where ε_t is also a random error term

for which $E(\varepsilon_t) = 0$ \qquad (26)

and $E(\varepsilon_t\varepsilon_{t-j}) = \begin{pmatrix} \sigma_\varepsilon^2 & \text{for } j = 0 \\ 0 & \text{for } j \neq 0 \end{pmatrix}$ for all t

$$(27)$$

and $B^{-1}y_t = y_{t+1}$.

Derivations of the relationships between the sequences $\{a\}$ and $\{\varepsilon\}$ are also shown in [1].

To compute the one step ahead forecast of y_1, the first series value in the data record, using the general model (16), p "prior" series values, $y_0, y_{-1}, \ldots, y_{1-p}$, are required. These can be estimated by forecasting *backwards* one step at a time, beginning with the backward forecast of y_{N-p} so that all necessary starting values are available. Initial backward forecast errors are assumed to be zero. In practice any transient effect introduced by this approximation will have vanished by the time the backward forecast of y_1 is computed. Now backward forecasts of $y_0, y_{-1}, \ldots, y_{1-p}$ can be made, using zero for the associated backward forecast

errors for these p required starting values. The estimates $\hat{y}_0, \hat{y}_{-1}, \ldots, \hat{y}_{1-p}$ obtained in this manner will be maximum-likelihood estimates given the choice of model and the parameter values in that model. Forward forecasts of $y_1, y_2, \ldots, y_N$ can now be computed as described earlier. In Section 3 this procedure is described, step by step, for the sample problem.

Variance of a Forecast

The model (16) can be expressed equivalently as

$$y_t = \pi_t y_0 + \pi_{t+1} y_{-1} + \cdots + \pi_{t+p-1} y_{1-p}$$
$$+ a_t - \psi_1 a_{t-1} - \cdots - \psi_{t+q-1} a_{1-q} \qquad (28)$$

where the π weights and the ψ weights can be determined by successive substitution for $y_{t-1}, y_{t-2}, \ldots$ in terms of prior y's and a's. Now for $l > 0$

$$y_{t+l} = \pi_{t+l} y_0 + \pi_{t+l+1} y_{-1}$$
$$+ \cdots + \pi_{t+l+p-1} y_{1-p}$$
$$+ a_{t+l} - \psi_1 a_{t+l-1}$$
$$- \cdots - \psi_{t+l+q-1} a_{1-q} \qquad (29)$$

and for $t > 0$

$$E_t(y_{t+l}) = \hat{y}_t(l)$$
$$= \pi_{t+l} y_0 + \pi_{t+l+1} y_{-1}$$
$$+ \cdots + \pi_{t+l+p-1} y_{1-p}$$
$$- \psi_l a_t - \psi_{l+1} a_{t-1}$$
$$- \cdots - \psi_{t+l+q-1} a_{1-q} \qquad (30)$$

The variance of the forecast $\hat{y}_t(l)$ is then

$$V(l)$$
$$= E_t\left(\left[y_{t+l} - \hat{y}_t(l)\right]^2\right)$$
$$= E_t\left(\left[a_{t+l} - \psi_1 a_{t+l-1} - \cdots - \psi_{l-1} a_{t+1}\right]^2\right)$$
$$= \left[1 + \sum_{j=1}^{l-1} \psi_j^2\right] \sigma_a^2 \qquad (31)$$

Because the selected stochastic model has been assumed to provide an adequate representation of the series, σ_a^2 can be estimated by

$$s_a^2 =$$

$$\frac{\sum_{t=1}^{N} \left[y_t - \hat{y}_{t-1}(1) \right]^2}{\left[N - p - \text{number of estimated parameters in the model form} \right]} \quad (32)$$

where N = number of observations in the data record and p = degrees of the expanded autoregressive operator in model form (16). If it can be assumed that the random errors $\{a\}$ follow a normal distribution then approximate 95% probability error limits for $\hat{y}_t(l)$ are given by

$$\hat{y}_t(l) \pm 1.96 \left[V(l) \right]^{\frac{1}{2}} \quad (33)$$

3. SUMMARY OF CALCULATIONS

a. Input Information

The program which this chapter describes requires the following information:
Number of data values
Number of Forecast Option Cards
Title
Format of data record cards
Series data record
Number of autoregressive operators
Period, order and coefficients of each autoregressive operator.
Number of moving average operators
Period, order and coefficients of each moving average operator.
Forecast option cards specifying which forecasts are to be made.
An example of input cards for the sample problem is shown in Section 6.

b. Model Expansion

From the input information about the individual autoregressive operators (for purposes of this program each difference operator such as $(1 - B)$ is also considered as an autoregressive operator with a coefficient of unity) and the individual moving average operators an expanded model of the form (16) is created.

For example, given the coefficients of the two polynomials

$$A(x) = a_0 + a_1 x + a_2 x^2 + \cdots + a_m x^m \quad (34)$$

and

$$B(x) = b_0 + b_1 x + b_2 x^2 + \cdots + b_n x^n \quad (35)$$

The coefficients of the product polynomial

$$C(x) = A(x) \cdot B(x)$$
$$= c_0 + c_1 x + c_2 x^2 + \cdots + c_{m+n} x^{m+n} \quad (36)$$

are calculated as

$$c_i = \sum_{k=0}^{m} a_k b_{i-k}, \quad i = 0, 1, \ldots, m + n \quad (37)$$

where b_j is defined as zero for $j < 0$.

c. Backward One-Step Forecasts

Now backward one-step forecasts are calculated in order to provide estimates of the p starting values $y_0, y_{-1}, \ldots, y_{1-p}$ that are required to calculate the forward one-step forecast of y_1 and subsequent forward forecasts. This backward forecasting procedure can be illustrated using the sample problem described in Section 6. A data record of $N = 183$ values was provided and the proposed model was

$$(1 - .389B - .105B^2)(1 - .305B^3 - .079B^6)$$
$$\times (1 - B^{21})y_t = (1 - .776B^{21})a_t \quad (38)$$

which can be expressed in the equivalent form

$$y_t = .389y_{t-1} + .105y_{t-2} + .305y_{t-3}$$
$$- .119y_{t-4} - .032y_{t-5} + .079y_{t-6}$$
$$- .031y_{t-7} - .008y_{t-8} + y_{t-21}$$
$$- .389y_{t-22} - .105y_{t-23} - .305y_{t-24}$$
$$+ .119y_{t-25} + .032y_{t-26} - .079y_{t-27}$$
$$+ .031y_{t-28} + .008y_{t-29} + a_t - .776a_{t-21}. \quad (39)$$

Because $p = 29$ "prior" values of the series are required to calculate any forecast the backward forecasting procedure is started at base point $t = N + 1 - p = 155$. The backward one-step forecast for y_{154}, denoted by $\breve{y}_{155}(1)$, is calculated using equation (20) in a *reverse* direction with a "lead time" of one.

$$\breve{y}_{155}(1) = .389y_{155} + .105y_{156} + .305y_{157}$$
$$- .119y_{158} - .032y_{159} + .079y_{160}$$
$$- .031y_{161} - .008y_{162} + y_{175}$$
$$- .389y_{176} - .105y_{177} - .305y_{178}$$
$$+ .119y_{179} + .032y_{180} - .079y_{181}$$
$$+ .031y_{182} + .008y_{183} \qquad (40)$$

The backward forecast error associated with $\breve{y}_{155}(1)$, denoted by ε_{154}, can now be evaluated as

$$\varepsilon_{154} = y_{154} - \breve{y}_{155}(1) \qquad (41)$$

Now $\breve{y}_{154}(1)$ can be evaluated and this process is continued back to the forecast for y_1,

$$\breve{y}_2(1) = .389y_2 + .105y_3 + .305y_4 - .119y_5$$
$$- .032y_6 + .079y_7 - .031y_8$$
$$- .008y_9 + y_{22} - .389y_{23} - .105y_{24}$$
$$- .305y_{25} + .119y_{26} + .032y_{27}$$
$$- .079y_{28} + .031y_{29} + .008y_{30}$$
$$- .776\varepsilon_{22} \qquad (42)$$

Having arrived at y_1, backward forecasts of $y_0, y_{-1}, \ldots, y_{-28}$ can be calculated.

$$\breve{y}_1(1) = .389y_1 + .105y_2 + .305y_3 - .119y_4$$
$$- .032y_5 + .079y_6 - .031y_7 - .008y_8$$
$$+ y_{21} - .389y_{22} - .105y_{23} - .305y_{24}$$
$$+ .119y_{25} + .032y_{26} - .079y_{27}$$
$$+ .031y_{28} + .008y_{29} - .776\varepsilon_{21}$$
$$\qquad (43)$$

$$\breve{y}_0(1) = .389\breve{y}_1(1) + .105y_1 + .305y_2 - .119y_3$$
$$- .032y_4 + .079y_5 - .031y_6 - .008y_7$$
$$+ y_{20} - .389y_{21} - .105y_{22} - .305y_{23}$$
$$+ .119y_{24} + .032y_{25} - .079y_{26}$$
$$+ .031y_{27} + .008y_{28} - .776\varepsilon_{20} \qquad (44)$$
$$\vdots$$
$$\breve{y}_{-27}(1) = .389\breve{y}_{-26}(1) + .105\breve{y}_{-25}(1)$$
$$+ .305\breve{y}_{-24}(1) - .119\breve{y}_{-23}(1)$$
$$- .032\breve{y}_{-22}(1) + .079\breve{y}_{-21}(1)$$
$$- .031\breve{y}_{-20}(1) - .008\breve{y}_{-19}(1)$$
$$+ \breve{y}_{-6}(1) - .389\breve{y}_{-5}(1)$$
$$- .105\breve{y}_{-4}(1) - .305\breve{y}_{-3}(1)$$
$$+ .119\breve{y}_{-2}(1) + .032\breve{y}_{-1}(1)$$
$$- .079\breve{y}_0(1) + .031\breve{y}_1(1) + .008y_1$$
$$\qquad (45)$$

d. Forward One-Step Forecasts

Using $\breve{y}_{-27}(1), \breve{y}_{-26}(1), \ldots, \breve{y}_1(1)$ as estimates of the necessary starting values, $y_{-28}, y_{-27}, \ldots, y_0$, the forward one-step forecasts, denoted by $\hat{y}_t(1)$, and the associated forward forecast errors, denoted by a_t, are now calculated beginning with the forecast of y_1 from base point $t = 0$ and continuing up to the forecast of y_N from base point $t = N - 1$.

$$\hat{y}_0(1) = .389\breve{y}_1(1) + .105\breve{y}_0(1) + .305\breve{y}_{-1}(1)$$
$$- .119\breve{y}_{-2}(1) - .032\breve{y}_{-3}(1)$$
$$+ .079\breve{y}_{-4}(1) - .031\breve{y}_{-5}(1)$$
$$- .008\breve{y}_{-6}(1) + \breve{y}_{-19}(1)$$
$$- .389\breve{y}_{-20}(1)$$
$$- .105\breve{y}_{-21}(1) - .305\breve{y}_{-22}(1)$$
$$+ .119\breve{y}_{-23}(1) + .032\breve{y}_{-24}(1)$$
$$- .079\breve{y}_{-25}(1) + .031\breve{y}_{-26}(1)$$
$$+ .008\breve{y}_{-27}(1) \qquad (46)$$

$$a_1 = y_1 - \hat{y}_0(1) \qquad (47)$$

$$\hat{y}_1(1) = .389y_1 + .105\ddot{y}_1(1) + .305\ddot{y}_0(1)$$

$$- .119\ddot{y}_{-1}(1) - .032\ddot{y}_{-2}(1)$$

$$+ .079\ddot{y}_{-3}(1) - .031\ddot{y}_{-4}(1)$$

$$- .008\ddot{y}_{-5}(1) + \ddot{y}_{-18}(1)$$

$$- .389\ddot{y}_{-19}(1) - .105\ddot{y}_{-20}(1)$$

$$- .305\ddot{y}_{-21}(1) + .119\ddot{y}_{-22}(1)$$

$$+ .032\ddot{y}_{-23}(1) - .079\ddot{y}_{-24}(1)$$

$$+ .031\ddot{y}_{-25}(1) + .008\ddot{y}_{-26}(1) \qquad (48)$$

$$a_2 = y_2 - \hat{y}_1(1) \qquad (49)$$

$$\vdots$$

$$\hat{y}_{182}(1) = .389y_{182} + .105y_{181} + .305y_{180}$$

$$- .119y_{179} - .032y_{178} + .079y_{177}$$

$$- .031y_{176} - .008y_{175} + y_{162}$$

$$- .389y_{161} - .105y_{160} - .305y_{159}$$

$$+ .119y_{158} + .032y_{157} - .079y_{156}$$

$$+ .031y_{155} + .008y_{154} - .776a_{162}$$

$$(50)$$

$$a_{183} = y_{183} - \hat{y}_{182}(1) \qquad (51)$$

e. Error Variance Estimate

The estimated variance of the random errors $\{a\}$ is now calculated using Eq. (33).

f. Printout and Plot of Forward One-Step Forecasts

A forecast option card is read indicating whether one step forecasts and/or forecasts with lead times greater than 1 are required. If one step forecasts are requested they are printed beginning with the forecast from the specified base point and continuing up to the end point specified. Approximate 95% probability error limits for each step forecast are calculated, using Eqs. (31) and (33) as

$$\hat{y}_t(l) \pm 1.96s_a \qquad (52)$$

A printer plot of the requested one-step forecasts and the associated data record values is then produced.

g. Forecasts with Lead Times Greater than 1

On the same forecast option card discussed in Section 3f the number of forecasts with lead times greater than 1 is specified. Using Eq. (20) all of the requested forecasts are calculated from a common base point, specified on this forecast option card, beginning with a lead time of 1 and extending up to the specified maximum lead time.

Using the sample problem of Section 7 as an example, forecasts of series values from the base point $t = 183$ for lead times 1 through 21 would be as follows.

$$E_{183}(y_{184}) = \hat{y}_{183}(1)$$

$$= .389y_{183} + .105y_{182} + .305y_{181}$$

$$- .119y_{180} - .032y_{179} + .079y_{178}$$

$$- .031y_{177} - .008y_{176} + y_{163}$$

$$- .389y_{162} - .105y_{161} - .305y_{160}$$

$$+ .119y_{159} + .032y_{158} - .079y_{157}$$

$$+ .031y_{156} + .008y_{155} - .776a_{163}$$

$$(53)$$

$$E_{183}(y_{185}) = \hat{y}_{183}(2)$$

$$= .389\hat{y}_{183}(1) + .105y_{183} + .305y_{182}$$

$$- .119y_{181} - .032y_{180} + .079y_{179}$$

$$- .031y_{178} - .008y_{177} + y_{164}$$

$$- .389y_{163} - .105y_{162} - .305y_{161}$$

$$+ .119y_{160} + .032y_{159} - .079y_{158}$$

$$+ .031y_{157} + .008y_{156} - .776a_{164}$$

$$(54)$$

$$E_{183}(y_{204}) = \hat{y}_{183}(21)$$

$$\begin{aligned}
= &.389\hat{y}_{183}(20) + .105\hat{y}_{183}(19) \\
&+ .305\hat{y}_{183}(18) - .119\hat{y}_{183}(17) \\
&- .032\hat{y}_{183}(16) + .079\hat{y}_{183}(15) \\
&- .031\hat{y}_{183}(14) - .008\hat{y}_{183}(13) \\
&+ y_{183} - .389y_{182} \\
&- .105y_{181} - .305y_{180} \\
&+ .119y_{179} + .032y_{178} \\
&- .079y_{177} + .031y_{176} \\
&+ .008y_{175} - .776a_{183}
\end{aligned}$$

$$(55)$$

Preparatory calculations for the variances of these forecasts are now carried out. As indicated in Eqs. (32) and (30) the polynomial product of the inverse operator $\phi^{-1}(B)$ and the operator $\theta(B)$ is required. The combined operation is accomplished using the subroutine INVERT.

Given the coefficients of the two polynomials

$$A(x) = a_0 + a_1 x + a_2 x^2 + \cdots + a_m x^m$$

$$(56)$$

and

$$B(x) = b_0 + b_1 x + b_2 x^2 + \cdots + b_n x^n$$

$$(57)$$

the program computes as many coefficients of the ratio

$$D(x) = \frac{A(x)}{B(x)}$$

$$= d_0 + d_1 x + d_2 x^2 + \cdots \quad (58)$$

as may be required. If $B(x)$ is of degree greater than zero then $D(x)$ will be an infinite series in x. Calculation of the coefficients of $D(x)$ is carried out as

follows.

$$A(x) = B(x) \cdot D(x) \quad (59)$$

implies that

$$a_i = \sum_{j=1}^{i} d_{i-j}b_j + d_i b_0, \quad i = 0, 1, \ldots, m$$

$$(60)$$

and so

$$d_i = \frac{1}{b_0}\left\{ a_i - \sum_{j=1}^{i} d_{i-j}b_j \right\},$$

$$i = 0, 1, \ldots, m \quad (61)$$

This is a recurrence formula from which the d_i's may be computed successively starting with

$$d_0 = \frac{a_0}{b_0} \quad (62)$$

The number of coefficients from the infinite series

$$1 - \psi_1 B - \psi_2 B^2 - \cdots \quad (63)$$

is one less than the specified maximum lead time (see Eq. (31)).

The variance and approximate 95% probability error limits for each forecast are now calculated according to Eqs. (31) and (33), respectively. The forecasts and their respective error limits are printed and plotted.

4. FLOW CHART

The flow chart appears on pages 435 and 436.

5. DESCRIPTION OF THE FLOW CHART

Box 1: The series record, arranged in a format specified by the user, and a descriptive title are read. The number of forecast option cards which are to be read subsequently is read as well. Also read are the number of autoregressive and moving average operators and the period, order, and coefficient values for each operator. Any input card having an incorrect type number causes the run to be terminated and an error message printed, indicating the incorrect card type number.

Box 2: Appropriate operators are multiplied together to produce the model in its expanded form described by Eq. (16).

Box 3: As described in Section 3, backward one-step forecasts of the series values are made, beginning with the backward forecast of y_{N-p} so that all necessary starting values are available. Backward forecasts of $y_0, y_{-1}, \ldots, y_{1-p}$ from the base point $t = 1$ will be used as starting values for the forward forecasting operation.

Box 4: Again as described in Section 3, forward one-step forecasts of $y_1, y_2, \ldots, y_N$ are calculated along with the associated forward one-step forecast errors, $a_1, a_2, \ldots, a_N$.

Box 5: The error variance σ_a^2 is estimated using Eq. (32).

Box 6: If all desired forecasts have been calculated the program stops; otherwise it continues to Box 7.

Box 7: A forecast option card is read indicating

    (i) an initial base point within the data record and a desired number of successive forward one-step forecasts of series values within the data record.

    (ii) a base point within the data record and the maximum lead time for desired forward forecasts from that base point.

    Error limits for these forecasts are computed in Box 9.

Box 8: If forward one-step forecasts within the data record are required, the program proceeds to Box 9; otherwise it branches to Box 11.

Box 9: Since forward one-step forecasts for the entire data record have been calculated in Box 4, the particular set required by Box 7 can be printed directly. 95% probability error limits for each forecast are calculated and printed, using expression (33).

Box 10: A printer plot of the forecasts in Box 9 along within the corresponding values from the data record is provided.

Box 11: If forecasts with lead times greater than one from a base point within the data record are required, the program proceeds to Box 12; otherwise it returns to Box 6.

Box 12: The desired future forecasts are calculated as described in Section 3. These

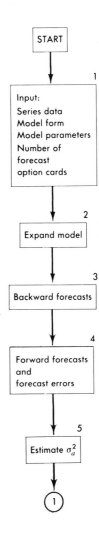

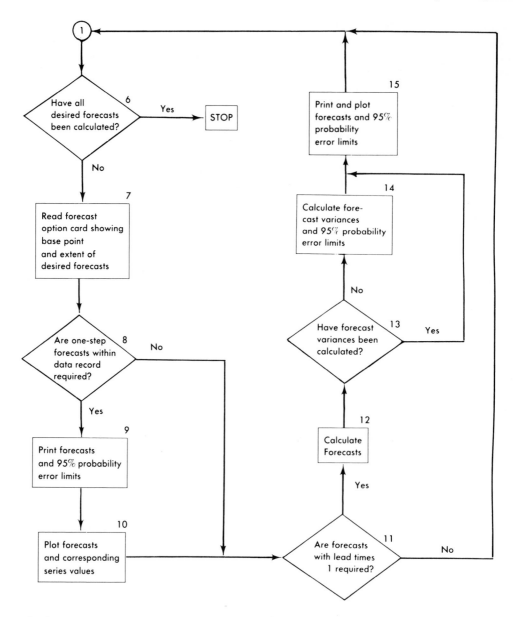

may be forecasts of series values beyond the data record.

Box 13: If the variances of the forecasts calculated in Box 12 have been calculated previously, the program banches to Box 15; otherwise it continues to Box 14.

Box 14: The variance of each forecast *outside the data record* calculated in Box 12 is calculated using equation (31). The program converts the expanded model from the

form described in Eq. (16) to the form described in Eq. (28), truncating the latter form at a point such that all required forecast variances can be calculated. 95% probability error limits for each forecast are then calculated.

Box 15: The forecasts calculated in Box 12 along with their 95% probability error limits are printed and plotted. The program then returns to Box 6.

6. SAMPLE PROBLEM

The data record shown in Fig. 15.1 is the square-root of the number of meals served at each sitting of the men's mess at Canadian Forces Base at Kingston, Ontario during a 61-day interval. Square-roots of the number of meals were used to stabilize the variance of the data in developing an ap-

propriate stochastic model. The fitted model

$$(1 - .3888B - .1049B^2)$$

$$\times (1 - .3046B^3 - .0787B^6)(1 - B^{21})y_t$$

$$= (1 - .7758B^{21})a_t$$

where y_t = number of meals served at sit-

Input Cards for Sample Problem

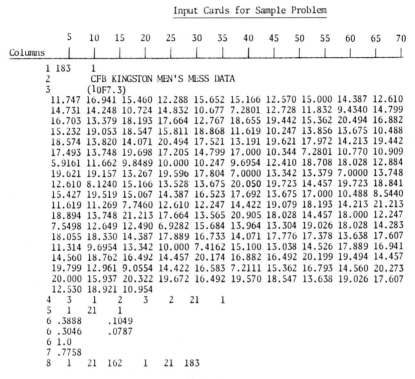

Fig. 15.1.

ting t, was found to provide a very good fit to the 183 data. It is not surprising to find three different periodicities occurring in this model, one from meal to meal, one from day to day, and the third from week to week.

For demonstration purposes the program has been used to examine the performance of the one-step forward forecasts during the final week of the data record (i.e., the final 21 values) and also to calculate forecasts for

lead times of 1 to 21 using the final point of the data record, $t = 183$, as a base point.

The input cards for this problem are shown in Fig. 15.1. It will be noted that three autoregressive operators are identified, the difference operator $(1 - B^{21})$ being included as explained in Section 3. Only one forecast option card is required to obtain the requested information.

The output for this problem is shown in Fig. 15.2.

CFB KINGSTON MEN'S MESS DATA

11.747	16.961	15.460	12.288	15.652	15.166	12.570	15.000	14.387	12.610
14.731	14.248	10.724	14.832	10.677	7.2801	12.728	11.832	9.4340	14.799
16.703	13.379	18.193	17.663	12.767	18.655	19.442	15.362	20.494	16.882
15.232	19.053	18.547	15.811	18.868	11.619	10.247	13.856	13.675	10.488
18.574	13.820	14.071	20.494	17.521	13.191	19.621	17.972	14.213	19.442
17.493	13.748	19.698	17.205	14.799	17.000	10.344	7.2801	10.770	10.909
5.9161	11.662	9.8489	10.000	10.247	9.6954	12.410	18.708	18.028	12.884
19.621	19.157	13.266	19.596	17.804	7.0000	13.342	13.379	7.0000	13.748
12.610	8.1240	15.166	13.528	13.675	20.050	19.723	14.457	19.723	18.841
15.427	19.519	15.067	14.387	16.523	17.692	13.675	17.000	10.488	8.5440
11.619	11.269	7.7460	12.610	12.247	14.422	19.079	18.193	14.213	21.213
18.894	13.748	21.213	17.663	13.565	20.905	18.028	14.457	18.000	12.247
7.5498	12.649	12.490	6.9282	15.684	13.964	13.304	19.026	18.028	14.283
18.055	18.330	14.387	17.889	16.733	14.071	17.775	17.378	13.638	17.607
11.314	9.6954	13.342	10.000	7.4162	15.100	13.038	14.526	17.889	16.941
14.560	18.762	16.492	14.457	20.174	16.882	16.492	20.199	19.494	14.457
19.799	12.961	9.0554	14.422	16.583	7.2111	15.362	16.793	14.560	20.273
20.000	15.937	20.322	19.672	16.492	19.570	18.547	13.638	19.026	17.607
12.530	18.921	10.954							

AUTOREGRESSIVE OPERATORS

PERIOD	COEFFICIENTS	
1	0.7888	0.1049
3	0.3046	0.0787
21	1.0000	

MOVING AVERAGE OPERATORS

PERIOD	COEFFICIENTS
21	0.7758

CALCULATED ERROR VARIANCE 2.6541

CALCULATIONS WILL BE MADE AS FOLLOWS

ONE STEP AHEAD FORECASTS FOR TIMES 163 TO 183

21 FORECASTS INTO THE FUTURE WITH BASE POINT 183

ONE STEP AHEAD FORECASTS STARTING AT TIME 163

9.5073	13.844	12.551	9.7251	15.547	14.646	14.115	18.994	19.345	14.980
20.560	19.486	15.280	20.634	17.630	15.654	18.472	18.385	12.896	17.225
12.289									

95% NORMAL PROBABILITY LIMITS FOR THESE FORECASTS 3.1931

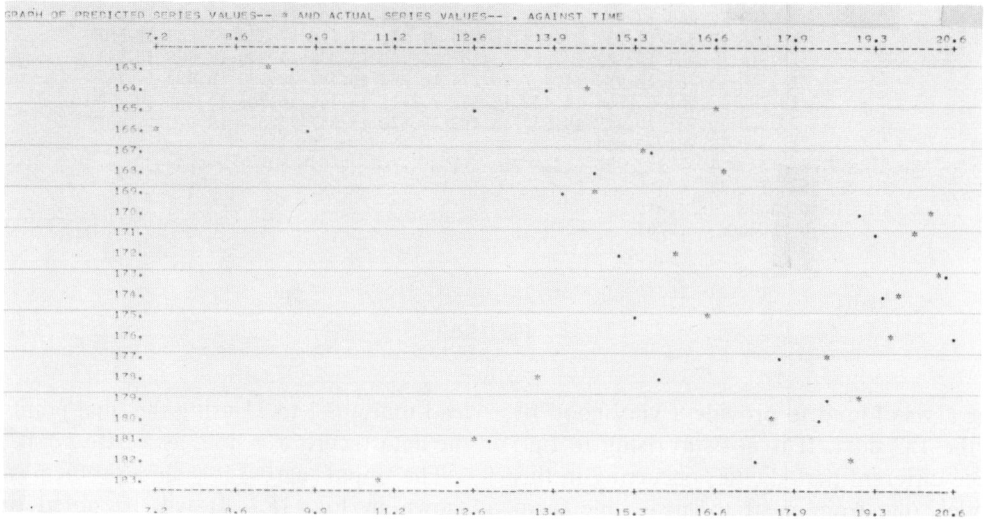

7. ESTIMATION OF RUNNING TIME

The running time for this program depends upon the length of the data record, the complexity of the model and the size of the lead times for the forecasts requested.

The actual calculation operations require an execution time of approximately

$$\left[2N(p+q) + \left(l_{\max}^3 - l_{\max}\right) + l_{\max}(p+q)\right](\alpha + \beta)$$

where α and β are the add and multiply

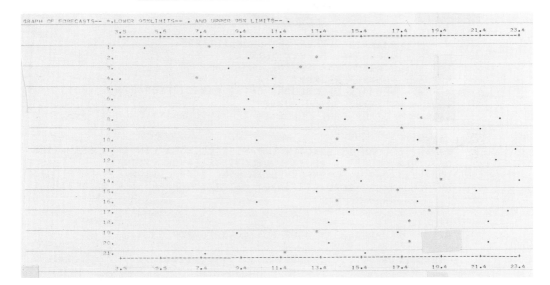

times, respectively, for the particular computer being used. For the sample problem the execution time on an IBM 360/50 under Fortran H was 10 seconds.

ACKNOWLEDGMENT

We are grateful to Professor H. S. Wilf for suggesting the efficient calculation method of equation (61).

9. REFERENCES

1. G. E. P. Box and G. M. Jenkins, *Time Series Analysis, Forecasting and Control*, Holden-Day, San Francisco, Calif., 1970.

2. E. T. Whittaker and G. Robinson, *The Calculus of Observations*, 4th edit., Blackie and Sons, London and Glasgow, 1944.

3. M. Sasuly, *Trend Analysis of Statistics*, Brookings Institution, Washington, D.C., 1934.

4. E. Slutzky, "The Summation of Random Causes as the Source of Cyclic Processes," *Econometrica*, **5**, 105–146 (1937).

5. M. G. Kendall, "The Effect of the Elimination of Trend on Oscillations in Time-Series," *J. Roy. Statist. Soc.* **104**, 43–52 (1941).

6. H. O. Wold, *A Study in the Analysis of Stationary Time Series*, Almquist and Wicksell, Uppsala, 1938.

7. J. F. Muth, "Optimal Properties of Exponentially Weighted Forecasts of Time Series with Permanent and Transitory Components," *J. Amer. Statist. Assoc.*, **55**, 299–306 (1960).

8. C. C. Holt, "Forecasting Trends and Seasonals by Exponentially Weighted Moving Averages," *O.N.R. Memorandum No.* 52, Carnegie Institute of Technology, 1957.

9. R. G. Brown and R. F. Meyer, "The Fundamental Theorem of Exponential Smoothing," *Operations Research*, **9**, 673–685 (1961).

10. P. Whittle, *Prediction and Regulation by Linear Least-Squares Methods*, English Universities Press, London, 1963.

APPENDIX

```
      SUBROUTINE ORT(A,D,T,M,N,IOUT,IERR)
C
C     .................................................................
C
C        SUBROUTINE ORT
C
C        PURPOSE
C           ORTHONORMALIZE AN M X N MATRIX BY COLUMNS, USING A MODIFIED
C           GRAM-SCHMIDT TECHNIQUE (BJORK, 1967)
C
C        PARAMETERS
C           A - - - -MATRIX TO  BE ORTHONORMALIZED
C           D - - - -DIAGONAL MATRIX METRIX
C           T - - - -TRIANGULAR FACTOR
C           M - - - -NUMBER OF ROWS OF A
C           N - - - -NUMBER OF COLUMNS OF A. CANNOT EXCEED M
C           IOUT - - SYSTEM OUTPUT UNIT
C           IERR - - ERROR CODE FOR EXIT IF SINGULARITY ENCOUNTERED
C
C        REMARKS
C           IF ANY COLUMN IS EXACTLY EXPRESSABLE AS A LINEAR COMBINATION
C           OF OTHER COLUMNS, ROUTINE WILL TAKE ERROR EXIT.
C           COMPUTATIONS ARE PERFORMED IN DOUBLE PRECISION
C           ORTHONORMAL A REPLACES INPUT MATRIX.  UPPER HALF OF TRIANGLE
C              IGNORED
C
C        SUBPROGRAMS REQUIRED
C           ERROR  (SUPPLIED BY USER FOR CLEAN ERROR EXIT)
C
C     .................................................................
C
C
      DIMENSION A(M,N), D(M), T(N,N)
      DOUBLE PRECISION X,Y,Z,B
      DO 7 I=1,N
      X=0.0D0
      DO 2 J=1,M
      Y=A(J,I)
    2 X = X + Y*Y*D(J)
      IF(X.LE..000001D0)CALL ERROR(IERR,IOUT)
      B = DSQRT(X)
      IF(I.EQ.N)GO TO 3
      I1=I+1
      DO 6 K=I1,N
      Y=0.0D0
      DO 5 J=1,M
      Z=A(J,I)
    5 Y = Y + Z*A(J,K)*D(J)
      Z=Y/X
      T(K,I) = Y/B
      DO 6 J=1,M
      Y=A(J,K)
    6 A(J,K) = Y - Z*A(J,I)
    3 T(I,I) = B
      DO 7 J=1,M
    7 A(J,I) = A(J,I)/B
      RETURN
      END
```

```
      SUBROUTINE INV(A,N,IN,IOUTT,PIVOT,IPIVOT,IERR,IOUT)
C
C.................................................................
C
C         SUBROUTINE INV
C
C         METHOD
C            CHOLESKY OR SQUARE ROOT METHOD IS USED FOR COMPUTING
C            INVERSE OF A SYMMETRIC POSITIVE DEFINITE MATRIX.
C
C         PURPOSE
C            SEE DETAILS LISTED UNDER DESCRIPTION OF PARAMETERS
C
C         USAGE
C            CALL INV(A,N,IN,IOUTT,PIVOT,IPIVOT,IERR,IOUT)
C
C         DESCRIPTION OF PARAMETERS
C            A - - - MATRIX TO BE INVERTED(PACKED SYMMETRIC).
C                    SIZE  N*(N+1)/2
C            N - - - NUMBER OF COLUMNS IN A
C            IN- - - ONE DIGIT INPUT CODE
C            IOUTT - ONE DIGIT OUTPUT CODE
C                                                         *  IN    IOUTT
C                                                         *
C                    UPPER TRIANGALIZE A PACKED SYMMETRIC *  1       1
C                    MATRIX A IN PLACE                    *
C                    ***********************************************************
C                    INVERT A PACKED UPPER TRIANGULAR     *  2       2
C                    MATRIX IN PLACE                      *
C                    ***********************************************************
C                    MULTIPLY A PACKED UPPER TRIANGULAR   *  3       3
C                    MATRIX TIMES ITS TRANSPOSE. PRODUCT  *
C                    WILL BE A PACKED SYMMETRIC MATRIX    *
C                    STORED IN PLACE.                     *
C                    ***********************************************************
C            PIVOT - PIVOTAL ELEMENTS OF THE INVERSION RETURNED HERE
C                    IF IPIVOT = 1.   OTHERWISE NOT USED. SIZE N
C                    (THESE ARE SQUARES OF THE DIAGONAL ELEMENTS OF THE
C                    CHOLESKY FACTOR).
C            IPIVOT- IF IPIVOT = 1 THE N PIVOTAL ELEMENTS OF THE
C                    INVERSION WILL BE STORED IN PIVOT.
C            IERR- - INPUT ERROR CODE
C            IOUT- - SYSTEM OUTPUT TAPE
C
C         SUBROUTINES AND FUNCTION SUBPROGRAMS REQUIRED
C            ERROR  (SUPPLIED BY USER FOR CLEAN ERROR EXIT).
C
C         REMARKS
C            DOULBE PRECISION IS USED FOR ALL CALCULATIONS
C            A AND T ARE ALWAYS IN PACKED FORM BY ROWS, I.E.
C                    A(1,1),A(2,1),A(2,2),A(3,1),A(3,2),A(3,3),A(4,1)ETC
C            IF IN = 1, A IS REPLACED BY
C                        CHOLESKY FACTORS IF IOUTT = 1
C                        INVERSE OF CHOLESKY FACTORS IF IOUTT = 2
C                        A INVERSE IF IOUTT = 3
C            ****** IOUTT MUST BE .GE. IN ******
C
C.................................................................
C
      DIMENSION A(1),PIVOT(1)
      DOUBLE PRECISION X,Y,Z,U
      GO TO (111,222,333), IN
C
C  TRANSFORM MATRIX A TO AN UPPER-RIGHT TRIANGULAR MATRIX
```

```
C
  111 IF(IPIVOT .EQ. 1)  PIVOT(1) = A(1)
      I=1
      X = A(1)
      IF(X .LE. .00001D0)  GO TO 1134
      X = DSQRT(X)
      A(1) = X
      IF(N .EQ. 1)  GO TO 2222
      IJ = 1
      NN = N - 1
      DO 3 I=1,NN
      IJ = IJ + I
    3 A(IJ) = A(IJ)/X
      II = 1
      IRIS = 2
      DO 7 I=2,N
      II = II + I
      IRJ = II + 1
      IM1 = II - 1
      X = 0.0D0
      DO 4 IRI=IRIS,IM1
      Y = A(IRI)
    4 X = X + Y**2
      X = A(II) - X
      IF(X/A(II) .LE. .00001)  GO TO 1134
      IF(IPIVOT .EQ. 1)  PIVOT(I) = X
      A(II) = DSQRT(X)
      IF(I .EQ. N)  GO TO 2222
      IM2 = I - 2
      IJ = II
      DO 6 K=2,NN
      IJ = IJ + K + IM2
      X = 0.0D0
      DO 5 IRI=IRIS,IM1
      Y = A(IRI)
      Z = A(IRJ)
      X = X + Y*Z
    5 IRJ = IRJ + 1
      A(IJ) = (A(IJ) - X)/A(II)
    6 IRJ = IRJ + K
      NN = NN - 1
    7 IRIS = II + 1
 2222 IF(IOUTT .EQ. 1)  RETURN
C
C   INVERT A PACKED TRUE UPPER TRIANGULAR N BY N MATRIX A IN PLACE
C
  222 II = 0
      I = 1
  120 IF(I .GT. N)  GO TO 333
      II = II + I
      X' = A(II)
      IF(X .LE. .00001 D0)  GO TO 1134
      A(II) = 1.0D0/X
   20 IRI = II
      K = 1
   90 IF(K .GE. I)  GO TO 50
      IRI = IRI - 1
      Y = A(IRI)
      Y = -Y/X
      A(IRI) = Y
      IRJ = II
      IJ = IRI
      J = I
   80 IF(J .GE. N)  GO TO 70
```

```
      IRJ = IRJ + J
      IJ = IJ + J
      Z = A(IJ)
      U = A(IRJ)
      A(IJ) = Z + Y*U
      J = J + 1
      GO TO 80
   70 K = K + 1
      GO TO 90
   50 IRJ = II
      J = I
   30 IF(J .GE. N)  GO TO 200
      IRJ = IRJ + J
      Y = A(IRJ)
      A(IRJ) = Y/X
      J = J + 1
      GO TO 30
  200 I = I + 1
      GO TO 120
C
 1134 IF(IERR.EQ.40)GO TO 200
      WRITE(IOUT,1000) I
 1000 FORMAT(1H0,20HVARIABLE IN POSITION I3,
     *41H IS A FUNCTION OF THE PRECEDING VARIABLES)
      CALL ERROR(IERR,IOUT)
C
C   MULTIPLY A PACKED UPPER TRIANGULAR MATRIX TIMES ITS TRANSPOSE
C   PRODUCT WILL BE A PACKED SYMMETRIC MATRIX
C
  333 IF(IOUTT .EQ. 2)  RETURN
      IJ = 1
      NN = 0
      DO 990 K=1,N
      NN = NN + K
      DO 990 J=1,K
      X = 0.0D0
      II = NN
      JJ = IJ
      DO 85 I=K,N
      Y = A(II)
      Z = A(JJ)
      X = X + Y*Z
      II = II + I
   85 JJ = JJ + I
      A(IJ) = X
  990 IJ = IJ + 1
      RETURN
      END
```

AUTHOR INDEX

Allen, D. M., 41, 57
Anderson, T. W., 95, 120, 153, 264
Arvesen, J., 8, 15

Bacon, D. W., 424
Balcar, K. R., 201
Ball, G. H., 373
Bargmann, R. E., 201, 264
Barlow, 335
Bartholomew, 335
Bartlett, M. S., 422
Beale, E. M. L., 40, 57
Beaton, A. E., 75
Bellman, R., 153
Bendat, J. S., 15
Bergland, G. D., 394, 422
Bingham, C., 408, 422
Björk, A., 264
Black, P., 327
Blackman, R. B., 422
Block, H. D., 15
Bluestein, L. I., 422
Bock, R. D., 9, 15, 212, 225, 264
Bolz, C. R., 168, 201
Bosinoff, I., 29, 33
Boulton, D. M., 278, 282, 294, 295
Box, G. E. P., 33, 120, 424, 427, 430, 439
Bremner, 335
Brenner, N. M., 422
Brillinger, D. R., 422
Broekhoven, L. H., 424
Brown, R. G., 428, 439
Brunk, 335
Burr, E. J., 279, 285, 294

Burt, C. L., 168, 171, 201
Butler, E. L., 18

Carroll, J. B., 201
Carroll, J. D., 308, 355
Cattell, A. K. S., 201
Cattell, M. D., 202
Cattell, R. B., 166, 168, 201, 202
Chambers, J. M., 335
Chang, J. J., 335
Clifford, H. T., 295
Clyde, D., 10, 15
Cochran, W., 25, 33
Cole, A. J., 269, 294
Cooley, J. W., 377, 387, 388, 392, 422
Cormack, R. M., 269, 294
Coulter, M. A., 168, 201
Cox, D. R., 422
Cramer, E. M., 218, 264

Dale, M. B., 270, 278, 281, 290, 294, 295
Daniel, C., 40, 57
Danielson, G. C., 388, 422
De Leeuw, J., 307, 335
Dempster, A. P., 75
Dickman, K. W., 202
Dixon, W. J., 15, 75, 95
Draper, N. R., 41, 46, 57, 75, 264
Durbin, J., 422

Eber, H. W., 202
Eckart, C., 154, 165
Efroymson, M. A., 9, 15, 37, 60, 75

Enslein, K., 3, 9, 15
Eysenck, H. J., 168, 171, 202

Feinberg, S., 39, 57
Feiveson, A. H., 22, 34
Feller, W., 120
Fieller, E. C., 22, 33, 34
Finn, J. D., 10, 203, 264
Fisher, R. A., 15, 76, 95, 99, 100, 120
Foster, M. J., 202
Fox, L., 264
Fukuda, Y., 157, 165
Furnival, G. M., 39, 46, 57

Garside, M. J., 39, 57
Gates, C. E., 18
Gentleman, W. M., 392, 395, 422
Gnedenko, B. V., 422
Godfrey, M. D., 408, 422
Gold, B., 410, 422, 423
Goldberger, A. S., 153
Golub, G. H., 264
Good, I. J., 389, 422
Gorman, J. W., 40, 50, 57
Gower, J. C., 276, 294
Granger, C. W. J., 407, 422
Gray, D., 8, 15
Graybill, F. A., 153, 264
Greenstadt, J., 153
Guttman, L., 335

Hall, D. J., 340, 373
Hammersley, J. M., 34
Hannan, E. J., 422
Harman, H. H., 7, 15, 153, 154, 156, 157, 165, 202
Harris, D., 21, 34
Harter, H. L., 34
Hartigan, J. A., 314, 335
Hartley, H. O., 16, 20, 21, 22, 26, 33, 34
Hastings, S. C., 34
Hayward, T., Jr., 34
Heck, D. L., 264
Helms, H., 422
Hendrickson, A. E., 202
Hilferty, M. M., 34
Hocking, R. R., 22, 34, 37, 39, 40, 46, 56, 57
Hoel, P., 120
Hoerl, A. E., 15, 37, 40, 57
Holt, C. C., 428, 439
Horn, J. L., 201
Hotelling, H., 9, 15, 335
Householder, A. S., 220, 264
Hurley, J. R., 202

Jackson, D., 390, 422
Jacobs, R., 29, 33
Jardine, N., 269, 295
Jaspers, J., 202

Jenkins, G. M., 422, 424, 427, 430, 439
Jennrich, R. I., 9, 37, 58, 76
Johnson, R., 335
Jones, H. H., 154, 156, 165
Jöreskog, K. G., 125, 153
Julez, B., 373

Kaiser, H. F., 202
Kahn, H., 16, 34
Kaneko, T., 395, 422
Kendall, M. G., 40, 57, 439
Kendrick, W. B., 271, 295
Kennard, R. W., 37, 40, 57
Kernighan, B. W., 314, 335
Khanna, D., 166, 340
Krishnaiah, P. R., 120
Kruskal, J. B., 296, 307, 308, 335
Kurkjian, B., 213, 264

Lamotte, L. R., 46, 57
Lance, G. N., 10, 11, 269, 274, 277, 278, 290, 295
Lanczos, C., 388, 422
Landahl, H. D., 180, 202
Lawley, D. N., 153, 202
Leslie, R. N., 40, 42, 46, 57
Lewis, C., 137, 153
Lewis, P. A. W., 377, 422
Lin, S., 314, 335
Lingoes, J., 335
Liu, B., 395, 422
Lurie, D., 20, 21, 34

McDonald, G. C., 56, 57
Mackay, D. M., 295
MacNaughton-Smith, P., 269, 283, 290, 295
McNeill, J., 271, 295
Mallows, C. L., 40, 57
Mann, D. W., 40, 57
Mantel, N., 15, 37
Marshall, A. W., 34
Massey, F. J., 34
Maxwell, A. E., 153
Mendenhall, W., 264
Meyer, H., 16, 23, 34
Meyer, R. F., 428, 439
Minsky, M., 15
Morrison, D. F., 75, 95, 120
Morton, K. W., 34
Mosteller, F., 8, 15
Muerle, J. L., 202
Muller, M. E., 33
Muth, J. F., 428, 439

Nesselrode, J. R., 201
Neuhaus, J. O., 179, 202
Nunally, J. C., 202

Odell, P. L., 22, 34

Olshen, R. A., 423
Oppenheim, A. V., 395, 423
Ortega, J. M., 220, 264

Papert, S., 15
Parzen, E., 423
Pearson, E. S., 34
Pease, M. C., 423
Perls, F., 373
Piersol, A. G., 15
Pillai, K. C. S., 264
Pinzca, C., 202
Pothoff, R. F., 264
Press, S. J., 264

Rabiner, L. R., 423
Rader, C. M., 410, 422, 423
Rao, C. R., 3, 15, 95, 210, 264
Richardson, M. W., 310, 335
Rippe, D. D., 159, 165
Robinson, G., 439
Rosenblatt, F., 15
Roskam, E. E., 15, 335
Ross, J. A., 167, 202
Roy, J., 264
Roy, S. N., 75, 264
Rudnick, P., 388, 423
Runge, C., 388, 423

Salsburg, D., 8, 15
Sande, G., 295, 392, 422
Sasuly, M., 439
Saunders, D. R., 202
Schatzoff, M., 39, 57
Schonemann, P. H., 170, 202, 314, 335
Schucany, W. R., 8, 15
Schwing, R. C., 56, 57
Searle, S. R., 264
Shepard, R., 298, 307, 313, 335, 336
Shocker, A. D., 335
Sibson, R., 269, 295
Simon, F. H., 295
Singleton, R. C., 423
Slutzky, E., 439
Smith, N., 41, 46, 57, 75, 264
Smith, W. B., 22, 34
Sneath, R. H. A., 10, 15, 269, 295
Sokal, R. R., 10, 15, 176, 202, 269, 295
Sonquist, J. A., 15
Srinivasan, V., 335
Stephenson, W., 202

Stumpff, K., 423
Styan, G. P. H., 264

Tausworthe, R. C., 18, 34
Taylor, L. R., 275, 295
Tepping, B., 373
Thomas, L. H., 389, 423
Thurstone, L. L., 152–154, 165, 167, 170, 171, 202
Tolstov, G. P., 380, 385, 423
Toman, R. J., 40, 50, 57
Tomlin, F. K., 373
Torgerson, W., 298, 310, 335
Tremeling, R. N., 34
Trotter, H. F., 34
Tsao, R., 39, 57
Tsujioka, B., 168, 201
Tucker, L. R., 137, 153, 168, 176, 202
Tukey, J. W., 34, 387, 388, 392, 408, 422

Wagner, A., 202
Wall, F. J., 264
Wallace, C. S., 278, 282, 294, 295
Watson, G. S., 423
Watts, D. G., 422
Weinstein, C. J., 395, 423
Welch, P. D., 377, 395, 422, 423
Westlake, W. J., 18, 34
White, P. O., 202
Whittaker, E. T., 439
Whittle, P., 429, 439
Widder, D. V., 423
Wilf, H. S., 96
Wilkinson, J. H., 153, 220, 264, 395, 423
Williams, W. T., 10, 11, 269, 270, 271, 274, 277, 278, 290, 292, 295
Wilson, E. B., 34
Wold, H. O., 427, 439
Wolf, D. E., 373
Wolfe, J. H., 11, 15
Wong, J. P., Jr., 34
Wood, F. S., 40, 57
Wrigley, C., 179, 202

Yates, F., 389, 423
Young, F. W., 335
Young, G., 154, 165
Youngs, E. A., 218, 264

Zelen, M., 213, 264
Zygmund, A., 380, 423

SUBJECT INDEX

Note: Subjects in CAPITALS are program, subprogram or function names.

AID, 11
Alienation, coefficient of, Guttman, 307
Allocation, optimum, 25
  proportional, 24, 26
Analysis, canonical, 204
  discriminant, 6–8, 11, 76, 96, 98
    multigroup, 76
    plots of, 81
    stepwise, 4, 9, 76, 77
    see also Coalitions, method of; Convex hull
      method
  multivariate, 3
  time series, 377
Ancova, 21, 26, 203ff
Anova, 7, 21, 203, 205
  column basis, 207, 212
  designs, complete, 204
    bases, construction of, 212
    crossed, 206
    incomplete, 204
    nested, 206
    two-way fixed effects, 205
  means, 208
  normal equations, 207
  orthogonal estimates, 209
  reparametrization, 207
  residuals, means, 208
ASSOPRED, 290
Attributes, linked, 271
  missing, 270
  serially dependent, 271
Autocorrelation, 12

Autoregression model, forecasting, 424
AVG, 115

Bargmann's criterion, 183
Bartlett's statistic, 26, 28, 33, 210
BINORMAMIN, 178
Biometrika tables, 26
BIQUARTIMIN, 178
Bit-reversal algorithm, 417
BMD, 9, 13, 14, 58, 65, 76, 84
BMDO2R, 9, 65, 71
BMDO7M, 9, 84, 91, 95
BMDPO2R, 9
Branch and bound algorithm, subset selection, 40

CANDECOMP, 297, 309, 334
Canonical analysis, 204
  form, 164
  sequence, 76, 77, 80
Cattell-Dickman ball problem, 177, 180
Central limit theorem, 98, 341
CHISQ, 115
Chi-square statistic, 17
Cholesky factorization, 84, 209, 211
CLASS, 269ff
Classification, 6, 7, 76, 79
  agglomerative, 272
  divisive, 272
  exclusive, 271
  extrinsic, 271
  function, constant in, 83
    group, 77, 79, 83, 95

hierarchical, 5, 11, 267, 272
intrinsic, 271
matrix, 84
minimum variance, 270
monothetic, 272
nonexclusive, 271
nonhierarchical, 272
polythetic, 272
types of, 271
variables, 77
Cluster, 362
analysis, 6, 10, 269, 340
centers, initial, 348
correlation, 174
factor, 168
membership in, 343
number of, 342
Clustering, 7, 10, 269, 340
agglomerative, 278, 349
centroid, 280
combinatorial solutions, 279
dendrogram, 279
flexible, 280
furthest neighbor, 280
group average, 280
incremental sum of squares, 280
nearest neighbor, 280
programs, 287
space distortion, 279
divisive, 280, 349
association analysis, 282
dichotomizing, 281
information analysis, 282
POLYDIV, 282, 287
predictive attribute analysis, 283
dynamic, 347
hierarchical, 267
see also Classification
Coalitions, maximal, 101
method of, 4, 96, 100
Coefficient, reliability, 137
Communalities, 156, 176
Component analysis, 166
Computation, reduction of, 44, 53
speed, 4, 5
Confirmatory solution, 155
Congruence coefficient, 182
Content addressing, 20
Contrasts, Anova and Manova, arbitrary, 213
deviation, 213
Helmert, 212
Matrix, 212
Orthogonal polynomials, 212
simple, 212
Convergence criterion, rotation, 160, 163
speed, 134
Convex hull method, discriminant analysis, 98

Convolution, 382
Correlation, canonical, 215
coefficient, 21, 22, 308
partial, 65, 69, 125
matrix, 37, 50
multiple, R^2, 40, 59, 65, 215
residual, 154, 156, 157
simple, 21, 76, 215
COSCHK, 195
Cost of computation, 4, 5, 12
misclassification, 99
COVAR, 115
Covariance, analysis of, generalized, 9
multivariate, 10, 203
Covariates, 6, 7, 204
COVARMIN, 178
C_p, 40, 55
Cross-spectral estimation, 409
Cumulative probability distribution, 22

Data analysis, choosing method for, 297
checking, 283
points, unusual, 98
see also Outliers
Deletion, variable, 42
Dendrograms, 10, 269
Description, parsimonious, 6, 7
DETE, 164
Discriminant analysis, 6–8, 11, 76, 96, 98
Discriminant function, canonical, 79, 84
coefficients, 210
development of, 83
Fisher's linear, 102
Dissimilarity, measures of, 273
Bray-Curtis, 276
Canberra metric, 276
correlation coefficient, 273
Euclidean metric, 274
Gower metric, 276
information statistic, 276
LINKED algorithm, 276, 290
Manhattan metric, 275
Minkowski order, **1**, 275
Minkowski order, **2**, 275
Distance, Euclidean, 10, 81, 274, 344
Mahalabonis, 10, 76ff
Distribution density functions, 16
exponential, 18
frequency, 16
normal, 98
DIVINF, 287
Double-centering, 309

Eigenvalue method, Householder-Wilkinson, 136
Jacobi, 136
problem, generalized, 80
Empirical frequency distribution, 16

EQCOV, 115
Error, truncation, 25
    round-off, 395
Euler-McLaurin formula, 17
Exchange operator, 60

Factor analysis, 4, 6, 7, 9, 123, 125, 154, 166
    canonical, 167
    hypothesis-creating, 169
    hypothesis-testing, 169
    least-squares, 154
    maximum likelihood, 154
    model, 126
    nonlinear, 7, 296
    programs, analytical, 174, 176
        topological, 174, 176
Factorization, completeness of, 159
    FFT, choice, 393
    Gram-Schmidt, 209, 219
    Householder, 219
    square-root, 134
Factors, common, 156
    least-squares fit, 169
    loadings, 157
        standard error of, 176
    number of, 176
        tests, 159
            significance, 159
            maximum likelihood, 176
            scree, 176
            Sokal, 176
            Tucker's, 176
    scores, 167
    specific, 126
    underlying, 125
Fast Fourier transform, 5, 12, 377. *See also* FFT
        algorithms
FCTGR, 150
F function, 164
FFT algorithms, 386
    application to, digital filtering, 410
        sample covariance, 400
        spectral estimation, 401
    calculation, 411ff
    computing time, 413
    DFT, 398
        cosine transform, 399
    doubling, 396
    history, 387
    inversion, 395
    radix, 2, 394
    record sectioning, 412
    round-off error, 395
    two-at-a-time, 397
Fisher Iris problem, 94, 367
Fisher's method, discriminant analysis, 100
Fisher's ratio, 77

Fission strategy, *see* Clustering, divisive
Forecast, variance of, 430
Forecasting, 5, 12, 424
    backwards, 430
    time series, 424, 426
Fourier-Stieltjes transform, 380
Fourier transform, discrete, 12, 380
F-statistic, 77
F-to-enter, 59, 60, 63, 65, 69, 70, 77, 79, 83, 94
F-to-remove, 59, 60, 63, 64, 69, 70, 77, 79, 83, 94
Function, canonical, 80, 95
    classification, group, 77, 79, 83, 95
    density, normal probability, 98, 99
    discriminant, linear, 76, 96, 98, 100
    separation, group, 77
Fusion strategy, *see* Clustering, agglomerative

G, reduction of, 129
Gain, precision, 25
Gauss-Seidel, 157, 161, 163
GENPRED, 290
GLS, 127
GRAPHL, 433
GROUPER, 287
Guttman-Lingoes, SSA-1, 313
    two-phase method, 337

Hadamard transform, 389
Harris-Kaiser rotation, factor analysis, 178, 180, 183.
        See also Varimax
Heterogeneity, variance, 26
Heywood case, factor analysis, 123, 124, 156, 157, 161
Householder transformation, 134
    factorization, 219
HYPCC, 194
Hyperplane, 77, 80, 173
    count, 176

IBM SSP subroutines, 115
Incomplete gamma function, 17
INCPSI, 151
Individual differences scaling, 276, 311. *See also*
        INDSCAL
INDSCAL, 297, 298, 311, 334
INITIAL, 362
Intervention analysis, 12
Inverse, generalized, 207
    product form, 46
Inversion, Cholesky, 219
INVERT, 434
ISODAT, 361
Isodata, 5, 9–11, 267, 340
    function of, 343
ISOGEN, *see* Isodata

Jackknife, 8

Kolmogornov-Smirnov, 22
Kronecker delta, 80
KYST, 297, 298, 304ff, 325, 334

Lagrange multiplier, 159
Lambda, F-approximation to, 82
  Wilk's, 77, 83, 95
Learning without a teacher, 10
Least squares, generalized, 127
  unweighted, 127
LEQN, 164
Limitations of techniques, 12
Linear model, 39, 45
  general, multivariate, 203
LMP, 362

M, reduction of, 130
MANCOVA, 5, 6, 203
MANOVA, 6, 7, 203
MATCAL, 225
Matrix, classification, 84
  correlation, 126, 156
    partial, 217
    residual, 137
  covariance, 99, 126
    residual, 217
    sample, 62
  cross-products, 62, 63
  diagonal, 156
  orthogonal, unrotated, 167
    transformation, 166
  partitioned, 61, 78
  status, 63, 64, 70, 78, 83
  symmetric, 60
  variance-covariance, 215
Maximum likelihood, factor analysis, 125, 127
MAXPLANE, 178ff
  PRESCRIBED, 178
M-D-SCAL, 297ff, 334
Means, predicted, 218
  provisional, method of, 63, 69, 82
  treatment, adjusted, 218
Mean-square, between strata, 25
  residual, 40, 55
Measure theory, 16
Memory, core, 4, 5
Methods, nonparametric, discriminant analysis, 97
Minimum spanning tree, 280
MINISSA, 297, 334, 338
MINITRI, 297, 305, 334
MINRES, 4, 127, 154
MINV, 115
Model building, 6, 7
MONANOVA, 309, 313, 334
Monte-Carlo methods, 16ff
  simulation, 30
  stratified, 16, 23, 25, 27, 31

Moving average model, forecasting, 424, 426
MULASS, 287
MULTBET, 287
MULTCLAS, 287
MULTDIV, 287
Multidimensional scaling, 296
  history of, 298
  models for, 304, 305
  unfolding, 297
MUMP, 313, 314, 334
MXCYCL, 194
MXROTN, 194
MXZERO, 194

Neighbor, furthest, 10, 280
  nearest, 10, 280
Nicety, 309
Nonstationarity, 424
  homogeneous, 428
Normal deviate, 19
Normal range, 18
NWTRAP, 136, 150, 151

OBLIMAX, 178, 180, 183
OBLIMIN, 178, 183
Observations, missing, 9
OMNITAB, 13, 14
Optimality principle, subset selection, 41, 42
Optimization, nonlinear, 8
  nonsystematic, 31
  numerical procedures, 314
  systematic, 306, 312
Order-statistics, 20
Orthogonal decomposition, 81
Orthogonalization, variable, 37
Orthonormalization, 218
O. T. Us., 270
Outliers, 11
Overdetermined case, 37

PARAFAC, 297, 309, 311, 334
PARSCL, 297, 305, 335
Parseval's theorem, 384
Pattern recognition, 10, 347
Perceptron, 10
Performance measures, 28
Periodogram, regression analysis and, 407
  modified, 408
Plasmode, 176, 180
Poisson series, 17
POLYCON, 335
Power residue method, 18
Precision, 23, 25, 395
Principal components, 9, 123, 306
Principal factor solution, 127, 164
Probability, classification, a priori, 99
  posterior, 80, 83, 95

integral of range, 17
Problem-solving, 3
PROCRUSTES, 169, 178
Program availability, 15
Programming, convex, 26
PROMAX, 178, 180, 183
PROMENADE, 365
PRTA, 164
PRTR, 164
Pseudodistances, 307
P-STAT, 14

Q-Analysis, 167, 168
Quadratic forms, 100
QUARTIMAX, 178, 179
QUARTIMIN, 178

R-Analysis, 167, 168
Random numbers, 18
  generator, Tausworthe, 18, 19
    Westlake, 19
Rao's test statistic, 210
Reference basis, 164
  structure vector, 167, 173
Regression, application to periodogram, 407
  coefficient, 21, 58, 63, 65, 69
    partial, 214
  damped, 8
  function, 58, 62, 69
    development of, 64
  isotone, 307
  linear, 6, 8, 58, 203
  monotone, 307
  multiple, 9, 39, 58
  multivariate, 214
  optimum, 37
  residuals, 58
  ridge, 8, 9, 37, 40
  stepwise, 4, 41, 58, 62, 77
    backward, 59
    down, 37
    forward, 59
    steering of, 63
    up, 37
  subset, 39
    constant term, 45, 47, 50
    forcing variables into, 45
    intercept, 65, 69
    selection, LaMotte-Hocking, 43
  sum of products for, 215
Reliability, systems, physical, 28
REMOVE, 362
REMUL, 287
Repeated measures data, 204
Residuals, Anova, 206
  minimum, 154
Reverse model, forecasting, 430

RIDGE, 9
Ridge trace, 37
RIEMANN, 16
Robustness, 8
Rotation, axes, 167
  confactor, 168, 171, 172
  criterion, 167
  formulae, basic, 170
  methods of, 9
  oblique, 9, 123
  optimum, 9
  programs, survey of, 176
  promax, 137
  unique, 5, 166
  Varimax, 137, 152
ROTOPLOT, 178, 180ff
Roy's test criterion, 224

Sampling, conditional, 23
  correction, 23
  importance of, 23
  multistage, 23
  ordered, 20
  random, 18
  stratified, 23
Scaling, ultidimensional, 5–7, 96ff, 112
    classical, 309
    polynomial, 304
Search, systematic, 183
SELECT, 9, 46, 56
SELVAR, 70, 91
Sequential hypotheses, testing of, 211
Sequential procedure, 127
Shepard, R., iterative procedure, 336
Similarity, 10
  coefficient, pattern, 168
  definition of, 341
  index, salient variable, 182
  measures, 273
  perception of, 340
Simple structure solution, factor analysis, 155, 168,
    172, 178
Smoothing, 426
  periodogram, 403
Sorting by coordinates, 98
Space, minimal complete, 81
Spearman rank correlation, 22
Special effects error term, Anova, 210
SPLT, 363
SPSS, 13, 14
SSA, 298, 313, 335
Stationarity, 428
STDEV, 115
Step-down analysis, Roy-Bargmann, 211
Stepping, backward, 83
  algorithm, override, 94
  forward, 83

process, 78
STEPREG, 9
Stieltjes integral, 386
Storage allocation, 65
    conservation, 218
STPCRS, 70
Stress, fit measure, 306
Structure, discovering, 296
    simple, 155, 168, 172, 178
    underlying, 6, 7
Subset selection, 4, 6, 9, 37, 39ff
    variables, predictors, 7, 58
Summarization, 6, 7
Sum of squares, precision, 40
    regression, 65
    residual, 39, 55, 59, 60, 65, 69
        minimum, 42
Sweep, forward, 69
    inverse, 60, 83
    operator, 60ff, 78, 83
SWP, 71

Tausworthe, random number generator, 18, 19
Taxonome program, 168
Taxonomy, numerical, 10, 269. *See also* Classification; Clustering
Techniques, characteristics of, 12
Time series analysis, 377
    forecasting, 424
Tolerance, 59, 65ff, 83, 94
    within group, 79
TORSCA, 297ff, 335
Transfer functions, 29

Transformation, data, 65
Transient analysis, 12
TRANSMAT, 290
Tucker synthesis method, 168

U, reduction of, 128
ULS, 127, 155
Underlying structure, finding, 6, 7
U-statistic, 210. *See also* LAMBDA, F-approximation to

Variables, antithetic, 23
    control, 23
    selection of, stepdown, 8, 78
        stepup, 8, 78
Variance, analysis of, generalized, 9
    multivariate, 10, 203ff
    reduction, 26
    residual, 126
    sample, generation of, 21
    unique, 126
Varimax, 9, 171ff, 183. *See also* Rotation, Varimax; Harris-Kaiser rotation
VARISIM, 178

Westlake random number generator, 19
Wilk's lambda, 210
Wilson-Hilferty formula, 21
Window, periodogram, basic, 402
    spectral, 402
Wishart matrices, random, 22
Word size, 4, 5